VERDI'S *AIDA*
THE HISTORY OF AN OPERA
IN LETTERS
AND
DOCUMENTS

OVERLEAF

Photograph of the bust of Verdi sculpted in 1873 by Vincenzo Gemito (1852–1929), courtesy of G. Ricordi & Co., Milan. Verdi had paid the artist for terra-cotta sculptures of himself and his wife, and was surprised to find this bust in bronze. In a letter to Verdi of 8 December 1873 (Autograph: St. Agata) Cesare De Sanctis explained, quoting Gemito: "I had done what I could to make the bust work out in clay, but I remained dissatisfied. . . . I couldn't make another one, because the Maestro wasn't around. . . . Then I had an idea: fire and clay would betray me and ruin my work; even if it were successful, it could not withstand the open air. Therefore, another material — bronze! . . . Thus nothing would destroy my work . . . for which the Maestro so generously compensated me. Now he will even be able to put his bust in the garden. Wind, water, and sun cannot harm it. . . . I made the bust of the Maestro in bronze, because it must be eternal like him."

VERDI'S
AIDA

THE HISTORY OF AN OPERA
IN LETTERS
AND
DOCUMENTS

Collected and translated by

HANS BUSCH

University of Minnesota Press,
Minneapolis

Published by the University of Minnesota Press, 2037 University
Avenue Southeast, Minneapolis, Minnesota 55455, and
published in Canada by Burns & MacEachern Limited,
Don Mills, Ontario

Library of Congress Catalog Card Number 76-11495

ISBN 0-8166-0800-8

In the translations of the letters and documents I have been assisted by Dr.
Lawrence Baldassaro, who has contributed to the translation of approxi-
mately 400 letters by Giuseppe Verdi. Thomas Holliday and Dr. Michael
Pisoni helped me with editing, research, and most other translations.

H. B.

In memoriam

FRITZ BUSCH

and to my students

L'arte non ha confine che pei mediocri.

Verdi

CONTENTS

Preface   ix

Permissions and Acknowledgments   xxi

Editorial Notes   xxiii

Abbreviations   xxvii

List of the Letters   xxxi

Introduction   li

LETTERS   3

DOCUMENTS   431

Biographical Notes   627

A Brief Chronology of Verdi's Life and Works   659

A Selected Bibliography   665

Index to the Letters   675

Addenda and Errata   686

PREFACE

Your letters are works of art; why can't they be
published? All prejudices and errors would
vanish before your powerful words.

Cesare De Sanctis to Giuseppe Verdi
3 May 1872 (Luzio, *Carteggi Verdiani*,
vol. I, p. 152).

This is a book by Verdi, his friends, and his collaborators. It is not a book about
Verdi. In order to present facts instead of opinions, I have attempted to
assemble all available source material concerning one of his greatest works,
Aida. The letters and documents in this collection, presented chronologically,
span a period of twenty-three years and pertain to the genesis, the development,
and the first productions of this opera, as well as to significant historical events
that affected its fate. The few letters not dealing directly with *Aida* reflect
Verdi's wide range of interests, everyday activities, and thoughts and moods
during this time. Choosing these letters from the many that exist was no easy
task. But I hope they will link the past to the future and deepen the perspectives
of the collection.

   This book is a result of a lifelong and ever-growing admiration for Giuseppe
Verdi, the man and his work. Actually my enthusiasm began some fifty years
ago, when *Giuseppe Verdi Briefe*, edited by Franz Werfel and translated into
German by Paul Stefan, added depth and dimension to my youthful enjoyment
of the Verdi operas my father conducted in Dresden. And then, in 1941,
personal conversations with the dedicated and erudite Werfel provided further
insights into the composer's life and work. We had met on the occasion of the
first American performance in this century of Verdi's *Macbeth*, which I staged
at the Forty-fourth Street Theatre in New York with a company of then
unknown youngsters under my father's direction. (This was also the first
American performance of Verdi's 1865 revision of *Macbeth*. The original 1847
version of the opera was first performed in the United States at New York's

Niblo's Garden in 1851). The production was declared a "smash hit," but in its wake the first volume of Verdi letters in English translation, appearing a few months later, was not. The young firm of L. B. Fischer, which, in exile, continued some activities of the distinguished German publisher S. Fischer, had decided that Franz Werfel's selection of Verdi letters, translated by Edward Downes, would be its first publication. Arturo Toscanini gave a hundred copies of the book to the members of his NBC Symphony Orchestra, but not many others were sold. For years this important publication was out of print, and various efforts to have it reprinted were futile. When, in 1969, a student of mine suggested a new edition to some two dozen American publishers, the few who replied stated that "there is no market for Verdi letters in this country."

A number of people who have made this publication possible think differently and share my belief that Verdi letters enlighten professionals and laymen alike — not only about his own compositions, but also about the creation and production of any opera. In spite of its shortcomings, Charles Osborne's *Letters of Giuseppe Verdi*, mainly based on Werfel's edition, yet claiming to be "the first book in the English language to be devoted to Verdi's letters," enjoyed much success. In a review of this book Philip Gossett describes the lamentable state of Verdi research:

The enormous number of errors in translation and commentary is itself distressing, but worse is the very conception of the edition and the attitude it assumes towards the problems surrounding the Verdi correspondence.

Because so many of them intimately relate to the creation of his operas, Verdi's letters hold a special fascination. In correspondence with his librettists, his publishers, critics, and artists, Verdi struggles with the preparation of librettos, compositional problems, aesthetic attitudes, details of production and costumes, in short, all stages in the making of an opera. His extensive personal correspondence . . . documents most aspects of Italian life from 1840 through 1900. In both his business and personal correspondence, Verdi emerges as perhaps the most appealing human being among major composers of the nineteenth century: fiercely independent, a true patriot, full of shrewdness and common sense.

In the absence of a complete edition of his correspondence, we must turn to hundreds of separate publications, often in obscure, regional periodicals or newspapers. Many important letters remain unpublished. Even restricting our inquiries to major editions, difficulties abound. A fundamental source, *I Copialettere*, published by Gaetano Cesari and Alessandro Luzio in 1913, has two parts. The first is a transcription of five notebooks containing Verdi's drafts for some of his business correspondence, contract negotiations, and dealings with impresarios, to which he also attached some letters received. Running from 1844 through 1901, these letters represent a minute (and often dry) portion of Verdi's letters. There are furthermore large lacunae, no letters being entered (or at least edited here) from May 22, 1858, to September 20, 1867, or from February 9, 1875, to January 1877. The editors assert they will omit "writings absolutely superfluous for illustrating the personality of the Maestro or the world with which he was in contact'' (page xix). With some twenty of eighty written pages unaccounted for in the first book and some fifty of 127 in the second, we might wonder whether we would share their view of what is superfluous. . . . In any event, we must remember these are drafts, not letters sent. Though they may sometimes be identical to the actual letters, often there are divergencies.

The second part of *I Copialettere* poses more serious problems. Luzio and Cesari offer here selected letters to illustrate specific aspects of Verdi's life, works, and character. Though these are more intimate documents, they are casually presented. The editors have felt free to quote only portions of a letter, to divide the same letter into various parts and print these in different sections of the volume, and to suppress information (particularly surrounding the letters to Opprandino Arrivabene). Thus the documents in this part must be used with extreme caution.

. . . With few exceptions, scholars have failed to probe the Verdi correspondence. Those communications which seem of greatest interest, letters between Verdi and his librettists, have gone largely unread. The letters of Verdi to Antonio Ghislanzoni, the librettist of *Aida*, have been available since their publication in *I Copialettere* in 1913, and have been cited again and again by, among others, Edgar Istel, Franco Abbiati, and Saleh Abdoun. But no commentator has mentioned that their published order (many are dated only with days of the week) is largely wrong. Yet if one *reads* the letters and seeks to understand them, their correct order is perfectly apparent. If letters dealing with the creation of *Aida* have been misunderstood, what can we hope for the rest? (*The Musical Quarterly*, 1973, 59, no. 4, pp. 633–39)

In view of the popularity of Verdi's operas and the vast amount of literature about him, the scarcity of published and translated correspondence as well as related documents is surprising. Not only do his own words answer questions that arise concerning the performance of his works, but they also sharpen the image of his life, his art, and his reactions to his own time. He expressed his ideas very clearly, but they are still very little known. Too much has been said about Verdi and too little by Verdi himself, although he was as prolific a correspondent as he was a composer. His letters offer infinitely more authentic and revealing insight into his creations, his character, and his intentions than does any biography. For it is inevitable that even the most thoughtful and objective writers are influenced by their own tastes and opinions. Reacting to irresponsible reporting. Verdi himself remarked: ''Such writing cannot be but a bundle of errors, even when one is inspired by the *protagonist*, because there is always an *amour propre* involved, or at least a vainglory, which hides what is bad and enlarges what is good. There are so few honest men, so few high-minded men. And, as a result, those writers copy what others have said on the same subject; and what they don't know, they invent.'' (Verdi to Opprandino Arrivabene, 8 February 1878.) Unfortunately we have too many Verdi biographies of this kind, marred by scholarly vanity and presumption, as well as by arbitrary, undated, and inaccurate excerpts from his letters — *coglionerie* (bullshit), as Verdi himself called such stories by *i nostri riparatori* (our repairmen).

Judging fact to be more interesting, poetic, and dramatic than much fiction, and inspired by the correspondence of great personalities from different times and backgrounds, I determined to study as many Verdi letters and documents as I could. This led to six stimulating and adventurous years of research and discovery that were not without trial and error and the constant reminder that the more we learn the more we realize how little we know.

In 1970 I spent part of a sabbatical leave from Indiana University at the Istituto di Studi Verdiani in Parma. The wealth of documents, scores, and reference books contained in the spacious rooms of the Palazzo Marchi, the seat of the institute, was impressive. Since its founding in 1959 this organization had collected some four thousand photocopies of published and unpublished Verdi letters, acquired from individuals and institutions in Europe, Egypt, and the Americas. But this large collection represents only a relatively small portion of the many thousands of letters he wrote during his long life, which are now scattered all over the world. Impressed by the amount of authentic documentation, I was, however, shocked by the many inaccuracies in published transcriptions. As I began to decipher Verdi's handwriting, it became apparent that quite a number of publications do not adhere to the original text and that the only reliable source is the autograph. This is not an unusual experience. Jacques Barzun has aptly recorded the same problems in his introduction to *New Letters of Berlioz 1830–1868*, pp. xv–xvi.

For a short while I entertained the naïve idea of trying to collect all the letters that Verdi had ever written. But I concluded that even a trained musicologist could not begin such a complex task at my age and expect to finish it. Others must eventually discover, transcribe, and publish a good deal of Verdi's correspondence in an accurate and responsible manner. "Your feelings about the art, to which you are giving so much splendor, are so right and deep," Giuseppina Strepponi wrote to her future husband on 5 July 1854, "and you express them with such truthfulness that your letters, written with a golden pen, should really be published if this were the moment for it. In time, this moment will come" (Luzio, *Carteggi*, vol. IV, p. 184). Verdi in a letter to the Director of Deutsche Verlags-Anstalt in Stuttgart dated 21 June 1895 (Cesari and Luzio, *I Copialettere*, p. 403) wholeheartedly disagreed: "It's quite enough that the musical world has tolerated my music so long! Never shall I condemn it to read my prose!" And in a letter to Opprandino Arrivabene dated 18 October 1880: "What need is there to go and drag into the open a composer's letters? They are always written in haste, without care, without attaching any importance to them, because the composer knows that he has no reputation to sustain as a writer. Isn't it enough that they boo him for his music? No, sir! The letters too!

Oh, fame is a great nuisance! The poor little great famous men pay dearly for popularity! Never an hour of peace for them, neither in life nor in death!'' (Alberti, *Verdi intimo*, pp. 260–61).

For obvious reasons posterity begs to differ with Verdi's condemnation of such publications, if sensationalism is avoided. This would not add an iota to our understanding and appreciation of Verdi's healthy and genuine art. Therefore rather than speculate about his intimate personal life, I chose to collect and translate material concerning specific works and to start with *Aida*. Initially conceived as a book in which Verdi through his letters would speak as his own interpreter, the manuscript grew in scope. Unexpected discoveries of unpublished letters and documents kept postponing publication, while my research in all its phases took place under a lucky star.

Since 1970 various grants and fellowships, gratefully received from Indiana University, The American Council of Learned Societies, and The American Philosophical Society, allowed me to work in Europe, mainly in Italy, for five to six weeks every year. While performing my duties at Indiana University, I organized, evaluated, and translated the photocopies of autographs and other papers I was privileged to bring home. Dr. Lawrence Baldassaro helped with the first translations of Verdi's letters. These letters steadily accumulated after his departure from Indiana University and Thomas Holliday, a student of mine, became an intelligent and efficient assistant. When he too left the campus, this book was greatly enhanced by the dedicated collaboration of Dr. Michael Pisoni, whose idealistic commitment and faithful perseverance were priceless.

Dr. Gabriella Carrara Verdi, whose family inherited Verdi's estate and archives at St. Agata, agreed with my plan to transcribe and translate significant letters and related documents. Thanks to her trust and generous cooperation, previously unpublished letters and documents of particular interest can be included in this collection. In Milan, Dr. Giampiero Tintori, director of the Museo Teatrale alla Scala, and the well-known musicologist Dr. Guglielmo Barblan of the Conservatory provided useful information. Visits to the Nationalbibliothek in Vienna and the Bibliothèque Nationale in Paris were less rewarding but were informative and inspiring.

In 1971 I happened to meet Lucien Goldschmidt, a New York autograph dealer, who recognized me after we had served together in the U.S. Army in World War II. He referred me to Herbert Cahoon of the Pierpont Morgan Library in New York, who graciously sent me photocopies of the autographs of the twenty-five letters from Verdi to Antonio Ghislanzoni, which The Mary Flagler Cary Music Collection of the Pierpont Morgan Library had acquired in 1968 from a dealer in England. The major "find" of this year, however, was in Milan, where a dear, old friend, attorney and music enthusiast Alfredo Amman, president of the Società del Quartetto, introduced me to Signora

Luciana Pestalozza of the House of Ricordi, who authorized Maestro Fausto Broussard, an archivist and editor of the firm, to open a vault which contained, among other treasures, 1,471 letters written by Verdi to his publishers between 1845 and 1900, as well as most of his autograph scores. The House of Ricordi photocopied for me hundreds of letters from Verdi and other correspondents concerning *Aida*. Only a small portion of these letters had been published — in most instances only partially and often incorrectly — by Franco Abbiati in his biography of Giuseppe Verdi.

The Verdi Institute in Parma has photocopies of the entire *Aida* correspondence that was kept in the archives of the Cairo theatre, where *Aida* was premiered on 24 December 1871. Soon after these photocopies were made, the original documents were destroyed in a disastrous fire on 28 October 1971. Most of these letters were published in the *Quaderno 4 dell' Istituto di Studi Verdiani con documentazione inedita sulla genesi dell' "Aida" a cura di Saleh Abdoun* and, with a few exceptions, are translated here.

In 1972, when I was seeking information about Verdi's correspondents, I spent time in Hamburg with the German Egyptologist Professor Dr. Wolfgang Helck, as well as at the Biblioteca della Cassa di Risparmio e Monte di Credito su Pegno in Busseto, the Biblioteca del Senato, the publishing firm of Treccani, and the German Historical Institute in Rome. Professor Giuseppina Allegri Tassoni in Parma furnished important data on the scenic designer Girolamo Magnani, but my efforts to obtain authentic production records of the first *Aida* performances at La Scala in Milan, in Parma, and in Naples were unsuccessful. However, I did acquire from the Ricordi Archives additional correspondence between Verdi's collaborators and his publishers. Useful material was also obtained from the Museo Teatrale alla Scala in Milan, where the Third International Verdi Congress took place. In London, Frankfurt, and Rome, meetings with the well-known autograph dealers Hermann Baron and Hans Schneider acquainted me with the locations of significant documents. In Zurich the distinguished musicologist Professor Dr. Erwin R. Jacobi offered generous hospitality and advice. In Rome I was introduced to Countess Elena Carandini Albertini, a granddaughter of Puccini's librettist and Arrigo Boito's friend Giuseppe Giacosa, who invited me to consult all of Verdi's letters to Boito. The Countess asked me to suggest an Italian institution to which she might donate these treasures. I suggested the Verdi Institute in Parma and now 141 formerly inaccessible autographs of Verdi's letters to his librettist for *Otello* and *Falstaff*, as well as of his letter to Vincenzo Luccardi of 5 June 1872, are in the care of the Institute.

Many previous attempts to obtain biographical data on Draneht Bey, the Khedive's intendant in Cairo at the time of the *Aida* premiere, had been fruitless. In 1973, however, the crescendo of good fortune continued when my former colleague Professor Andreas Nomikos suggested I contact his friend, Draneht's grandson, Peter Emmanuel Zervudachi in Vevey, Switzerland. M. Zervudachi provided the answers to my biographical inquiries and also the extraordinary bonus to study, translate, and publish Draneht's hitherto unpublished correspondence, for which I am deeply obliged.

In Tutzing near Munich, Hans Schneider showed me 277 letters from Verdi to Giulio Ricordi — letters that once were part of the collection in the Ricordi Archives in Milan. How they found their way to Germany was a mystery their present owner could not explain. He speculated that in the early years of this century Giulio Ricordi's son Tito II might have been responsible for selling them. To prevent the further commercial exploitation and possible disappearance of these precious autographs and to make them available for publication, I tried, unsuccessfully, to interest several individuals and institutions in the United States and abroad in purchasing them from Hans Schneider. Plans by the Italian government to acquire Herr Schneider's Verdi letters for the Institute did not materialize. However, additional discoveries in the Ricordi Archives, at St. Agata, and elsewhere helped to compensate for this disappointment. In Busseto Professor Corrado Mingardi, librarian of the Biblioteca della Cassa di Risparmio e Monte di Credito su Pegno, showed me 333 letters from Emanuele Muzio, Verdi's student and lifelong friend, many of them written from America. Photocopies of these letters were made for the collection of the Institute of Verdi Studies in Parma as well as for mine. A visit with Dr. Rodney Dennis, curator of manuscripts at the Houghton Library of Harvard University, led to the addition of the photocopies of eighteen letters from Verdi to Edoardo Mascheroni, the first conductor of *Falstaff*, to my collection.

In 1974 I found letters and documents, particularly in Vevey and St. Agata, that answered many questions and closed many gaps in the *Aida* correspondence I had collected and translated to this point. In Vevey M. Zervudachi entrusted me with Draneht's entire *Aida* correspondence, which I deciphered, transcribed, and translated. The work I was permitted to do in Verdi's own library at St. Agata was especially rewarding, and Dr. Gabriella Carrara Verdi was extremely helpful. Continued biographical research at municipal offices and state archives in Milan and Rome led to more information. In Naples, however, my efforts to track down material were thwarted. The Teatro San Carlo has no archive and the organization of the Lucchesi Palli library requires more time than I could afford. At the Conservatory in Bologna, however, photocopies of ninety-four autograph letters from Verdi and his wife to Maria Waldmann became available within a few hours.

In 1975 Dr. Michael Pisoni again was of great assistance in the completion of notes and translations. My sister and her French husband, Martial Singher, helped to transcribe and translate Camille Du Locle's Scenario (Document III), and also to solve other riddles. From the Library of Congress in Washington, D.C., my investigations led to the State Department and the National Archives. At the Library of Congress I had the good fortune of meeting Charles Jahant, a visitor to the Library, who answered at least a dozen questions concerning even secondary artists in the nineteenth century. In writing he later generously gave me much information unavailable elsewhere. The hospitality of the German Historical Institute in Rome under the direction of Professor Dr. Reinhard Elze, and its Music Division headed by Dr. Friedrich Lippmann, provided ideal conditions for extended studies. The director of the Théatre National de l'Opéra in Paris, Professor Rolf Liebermann's introduction to Mlle. Martine Kahane, the curator of the Bibliothèque-Musée de l'Opéra, augmented my collection and helped to answer several queries. In Busseto Dr. Gabriella Carrara Verdi photocopied some thirty additional unpublished letters from Giulio Ricordi to Verdi and his wife for which I am especially grateful to her; and in August 1976 she informed me of a sudden discovery in Paris, closing a lacuna that has disturbed Verdi scholars for years (See Documents I and II).

Most of the autographs I transcribed and translated have been fairly well preserved and are not too difficult to read if one has a good knowledge of Italian and French. Paul Draneht's letters in M. Zervudachi's possession are copies of the original letters Draneht wrote or dictated. The document, written by hand in copying ink, was pressed through rollers onto very thin, absorbent paper. Such copies of Draneht's letters exist on hundreds of brittle and disintegrating pages in Vevey. Verdi, on the other hand, drafted many of his letters in simple notebooks approximately seven inches wide and nine and one-half inches long. His wife did the same. These copybooks, which are kept at St. Agata, were the basis for Gaetano Cesari and Alessandro Luzio's *I Copialettere di Giuseppe Verdi*, and Alessandro Luzio's *Carteggi Verdiani* now out of print. Unfortunately Cesari and Luzio's many errors of transcription were repeated in the editions of Werfel, Abbiati, and others. Abbiati not only perpetuated the errors of his predecessors, but — with all his apparent dedication to his subject and access to many of Verdi's autographs — added many of his own. In Verdi's letter to Giulio Ricordi of 7 October 1870, for example, Abbiati (vol. III, p. 401) misread *quart'atto* as *quartetto*. There is no quartet in *Aida*, as we know it, and never was. Abbiati's pronouncement that "nothing more was said about an *Aida* in Vienna; the time was lacking for adequate preparation" (see note 1, Verdi to Maria Waldmann of 5 June 1875) is one of many false and misleading bits of information. In Jacques-Gabriel Prod'homme's transcription of Verdi's letter to Du Locle of 26 May 1870 even the scarcely infallible Luzio (vol. IV, p. 9n) noted this amusing misreading: "Now let us consider the general feminine situation in Egypt, and then we shall decide." Verdi, who was interested in the Khedive's money rather than his harem, wrote *le condizioni pecuniarie*. The same Prod'homme said Du Locle died ten years before he actually did and declared that "Madame Verdi had created *La Traviata* and died three years later than the maestro" (*The Musical Quarterly*, 1921, 7, no. 4, p. 76). To point out the many errors committed in the *Aida* literature alone would fill another book. Verdi research needs unbiased and accurate presentations of fact without emotional interpretation and superfluous comment.

Most of the letters I have collected, selected, and translated will be self-explanatory and will enable the reader to draw his or her own conclusions. Since so many published transcriptions and the resulting translations are inaccurate, all translations in this book are based, whenever possible, on the autographs or photocopies of them. When autographs of Verdi's draft and the actual letter were available, the final text of the letter was used. In the translation of Verdi's letters I have tried to maintain his distinctive, very simple, and straightforward style, which contrasts strikingly with the Victorian flavor of some of his contemporaries' correspondence. The speech of a man who was proud to remain a peasant to the end of his days must not be edited or romanticized. By the same token, neither Muzio's clumsy style nor Teresa Stolz's unsophisticated writing has been improved.

To the best of my knowledge this is the first English translation of the fourteen documents in this collection. Eight are published for the first time.

Brief as they are, the biographical notes on the correspondents provide some hitherto unknown details. Discrepancies in dates and conjectural dates given by various biographies and dictionaries caused problems and I was amazed to learn how little is known about even such prominent personalities as Count Opprandino Arrivabene, Draneht Bey, and Giuseppe Piroli, who deserve to be remembered.

The word "missing," which occurs with unfortunate frequency in my notes, indicates that a letter or document is, to the best of my knowledge, unavailable at this time. Many of these letters and documents may one day be discovered. The absence of the many letters Ghislanzoni wrote to Verdi during their collaboration and the severe gaps in the Ricordi letters to Verdi are particularly disturbing. But I am confident they are not lost. Dr. Gabriella Carrara Verdi assures me that Verdi destroyed all the musical sketches he jotted down for *Aida* like any others. It seems incredible, however, that none of the scenic designs for the first Italian productions of *Aida* are extant, and I would welcome learning the location of such and any other material not included here. This volume is as complete as I have been able to make it at this time; but it is by no means exhaustive and it invites further research.

The purpose of this project hardly needs to be stressed. Glimpses that letters and documents such as these afford into the minds and workshops of the masters deepen our understanding of their creations. But unfortunately there is little concern and respect for the specific wishes of the authors. It is difficult, if not impossible, to destroy the power of operas like *Carmen*, *Tosca*, and *Aida*, even in the most mediocre or misguided performances. The popularity of such works is their greatest enemy. In 1969, for instance, when I staged *Aida* at the Teatro San Carlo in Naples and asked for the Chorus of Ethiopian Prisoners that is clearly marked in the score, I was informed they had always been eliminated and substituted with supers — *si è sempre fatto così*. The late Wieland Wagner, one of the most gifted and controversial stage directors of our age, decided that the triumphal scene in *Aida* should take place at night (1961 Deutsche Oper Berlin program and Goléa, *Gespräche mit Wieland Wagner*, pp. 57–63). Had Verdi been alive, he might have taken Wieland Wagner to court. Those who consider Verdi bullheaded or old-fashioned because he fought for integrity in the performance of his works and forbade the eccentricities to which they and others are subjected today should be reminded of some of Hofmannsthal's letters to Strauss (Strauss and Schuh, eds.), of Pfitzner's *Werk und Wiedergabe*, or, more recently, of Stravinsky's writings. I had the honor to be associated with Stravinsky and remember his outburst "I h-h-ate interpretation!" (Horgan, *Encounters with Stravinsky*, p. 116). Toscanini and my family were admired for their research and *Werktreue*, which, far from being conventional or pedantic, resulted in surprising musical and dramatic effects. Yet although we wish we could hear *Aida* as it sounded under Verdi's baton, few of us would care for the melodramatic style in which the opera was visually produced at that time. Giulio Ricordi's exhaustive production book may therefore be of relatively little value to us, since many of his stage directions are now taken as much for granted as Felix Mottl's annotations in Wagner's scores. Nevertheless Ricordi's *disposizioni sceniche* for *Aida* — as well as for *Otello* — remain professional documents with which every conscientious artist should be acquainted.

In the pages that follow it is Verdi who consistently holds the reader's attention. I do not indulge in hero worship of him at the expense of Mariette and Du Locle, whose vital roles in the creation of *Aida* come to life in these letters and documents. But I feel today, as Franz Werfel (Werfel and Stefan, *Verdi: The Man in His Letters*, p. 79) felt fifty years ago, that "at such a moment as this," in which "vulgar disbelief in all higher levels of existence is rising in a torrent, a life full of truth and without illusions, like that of the poet and farmer Giuseppe Verdi, seems a very star in the murk. Especially the young artist, the musician, writer, singer, actor, who is at the beginning of his career, can find in Verdi's letters, if he knows how to read them aright, mysterious sources of strength like those of a radium bath.''

Indiana University, 1976   Hans Busch

PERMISSIONS AND ACKNOWLEDGMENTS

The story of my struggle to obtain permission for the publication of previously published as well as unpublished materials from all over the world could constitute a book. Although many individuals and institutions seemed to consider them an unnecessary formality or a simple matter of scholarly courtesy, questions arose in some cases, causing legal consultations, tedious world-wide correspondence, and delays.

When publication of some of the more interesting pages in this volume was threatened, the former Dean of Faculties at Indiana University, Vice Chancellor Henry H. H. Remak, arranged a meeting with Professors Arghyrios A. Fatouros and Maurice J. Holland of our Law School, whose solid information and advice solved the problem. Indiana University Chancellor Herman B Wells's personal introduction to His Excellency Dr. Ashraf Ghorbal, the Ambassador of the United Arab Republic of Egypt in Washington, D.C., was also deeply appreciated at that moment of crisis.

Indiana University's Vice President Robert M. O'Neil, an authority on copyright law, offered exceptionally careful and cautious advice. Dr. David Fenske, the head of our Music Library, gave much of his time in helping me to understand and follow it. Caught within the intricacies of complex international copyright situations, I once again appealed to my great, old friend Avv. Alfredo Amman in Milan. His colleague, Avv. Giorgio Jarach, a specialist in Italian copyright law, provided clear and definite answers which were confirmed by the appropriate Italian agency, the Società Italiana degli Autori ed Editori in Rome.

The three major owners of thus far unpublished autographs — Dr. Alberto Carrara Verdi and family at St. Agata, G. Ricordi & C. in Milan, and M. Peter Emmanuel Zervudachi in Vevey — authorized publication of the autographs in my translation, as have the other owners. All sources are identified in the List of the Letters and the Key to the Abbreviations. All quotations in notes and footnotes were authorized by the authors and/or their respective publishers.

I thank all those, dead or alive, named or unnamed, who have promoted my labors. In addition to the friends, colleagues, and institutions already mentioned, I received advice and assistance in varying degrees from Hans Apel, Willi Apel, Barbara Baugh, Claudette Beaulieu, Teresita Beretta, Sir Rudolf Bing, Beverly M. Brooks, Susanne Burbach, Carroll Frederick Busch, Giuliana Busch, John A. Busch, Cecil K. Byrd, William R. Cagle, William B. Christ, Carlo Clausetti, Marcello Conati, Adriana Corbella, Mario Cristini, Ralph T. Daniel, Bertrand and Shehira Davezac, Harry Day, Dominique René de Lerma, Maria Di Gregorio Casati, John Eaton, Battista Figoni, Lia Frey, Hans Gál, Thomas Glastras, Philip Gossett, Ursula Günther, Paul Horgan, Jean Humbert, François Lesure, Fritz Magg, Mary Jane Matz, Martha Mosier, Jean-Michel Nectoux, Juan and Juan Felipe Orrego-Salas, Franco and Pia Passigli, Lina Re Ferretti, Walter Robert, Max Röthlisberger, Baroness Marianne Goldschmidt-Rothschild, Guido Ruzzier, Bambi Sahu, Harrison Shull, Lorenzo Siliotto, George Springer, David Terry, J. Rigbie Turner, Richard Turner, Abdul Wahab, and Helmut Wiens.

The unusually hard work of editor Beverly Kaemmer was of immeasurable help. Walter Kaufmann, Tibor Kozma, and Oskar Seidlin, three friends and distinguished colleagues at Indiana University, contributed essential suggestions, and I am particularly grateful to Walter Kaufmann for photographing the music examples and diagrams in Verdi's and Giulio Ricordi's letters. Close ties of friendship to J. Hellmut Freund of the S. Fischer Verlag in Frankfurt inspired this project from its inception. As a frequent collaborator and honest critic my wife has stood by me in this endeavor beyond words of gratitude.

Last, but not least, I want to thank Alexander Graham Bell for having sufficiently delayed his invention of the telephone to enrich us with the gift of this correspondence. The inventors of the Xerox machine, however, seriously merit my appreciation, for without their revolutionary product this volume could not have materialized.

EDITORIAL NOTES

Since this volume focuses on the opera *Aida*, it seemed advisable to make some editorial omissions in the letters and documents. But the meaning is not distorted by any of these omissions, which are indicated by bracketed ellipses [. . .].

Letterheads indicating the positions and addresses of the senders — such as Camille Du Locle's Théâtre Impérial de l'Opéra-Comique, Cabinet du Directeur — are excluded, and dates and salutations of the letters are given in a uniform style. A comma follows all salutations, and Verdi's frequent abbreviations, such as C. for *Caro* or G. for Giulio, do not appear in the translations. The typically formal closings of all the letters are almost always omitted. (Verdi frequently ended his letters with *addio, addio*, and without exception, even when writing to his most intimate friends, signed himself G. Verdi.)

Dates within editorial brackets do not appear on the autograph but were indicated either by a postmark on the envelope or by other circumstances. Undated letters — some spuriously dated by Luzio and others — are placed where they seem logically to belong. In formal letters, or when addressing strangers, Verdi sometimes dated his letters at nearby Busseto rather than at St. Agata. During the years of the *Aida* correspondence, Verdi's homes were at St. Agata and in Genoa. We may assume, therefore, that any letter he addressed from Busseto during that period was actually written at St. Agata.

After careful consideration I decided against a strict adherence to the haphazard and inconsistent original punctuation, particularly in Verdi's letters and in his quotations from Italian texts. Whenever authentic paragraphing could be reliably established from the autographs, or assumed from the transcriptions, it was maintained in translation. In a few instances one or several dashes after a period in an Italian letter suggested the beginning of a new paragraph in the English text.

None of the poetry quoted by Verdi, Ghislanzoni, and others is translated. For the sake of clarity and consistency the names of the characters in *Aida*, though often abbreviated in the original letters and documents, are spelled out and capitalized in the translation of the letters.

In the autographs (of Verdi's letters in particular) underlining was used for emphasis, for foreign words, and for quotations. In this translation, most foreign words are italicized and underlining indicates emphasis. In a few instances when a foreign word seemed to have been underlined for emphasis, the word is italicized and underlined. Exceptions to the italicizing of foreign words are words that are frequently used in English, such as libretto or cello (plurals are anglicized as librettos and cellos) which appear in roman. Some French words underlined in the Italian letters are translated and, therefore, not underlined. An exception is the French term *mise-en-scène*, which refers to all but the musical elements of theatrical production. Since an equivalent term does not exist in English — "stage direction" does not denote all the visual and technical components implied by *mise-en-scène* — I use the French term. Verdi used it in his letters rather than the Italian *messa in scena*.

Frequent and sometimes consistent misspelling of names, such as Verdi's misspelling of Draneht as Draneth or of Waldmann as Waldman, Valdman, or Waldaman, of Mendelssohn, Schumann, and Wagner, are corrected except in a few instances, where *sic* is used. In the creative development of *Aida*, the spelling of the names of some characters underwent a few changes — from Rhadamés or Radamés to Radames, Ramphis or Rhamphis to Ramfis, and Amounasro or Amunasro to Amonasro. The various spellings appear in the translated documents but are eliminated in the letters.

To avoid confusion caused by the fact that at the time of their association with *Aida* both Auguste Mariette and Paul Draneht had the Turkish title Bey, I have, with all due respect, stripped them of this honor. All female singers are consistently referred to as *la* Stolz, *la* Waldmann, etc., as they are in most of the Italian correspondence. Similarly the Scala Opera House or Teatro alla Scala in Milan is referred to as La Scala. In keeping with the original correspondence, the French and Italian names of opera houses, such as Opéra-Comique, Théâtre-Lyrique, Teatro Fenice, Teatro San Carlo, are not translated; but the Théâtre Italien or Théâtre des Italiens in Paris, called Teatro Italiano by Verdi, is referred to as the Italian Theatre in the translation. I follow Verdi's spellings of St. Agata and St. Donnino.

Biographical notes are provided for all major correspondents. When the years of birth and death of other persons mentioned in the letters could be credibly ascertained, they are given in parentheses in the notes. In a few instances, however, such dates could not be obtained.

Since the Franco-Prussian War was actually a war in which all the German states were allied with Prussia, the Germans rather than the Prussians are mentioned in the notes pertaining to that war.

In the lists of the letters and documents, asterisks indicate, to the best of my knowledge, first publications. The language and location of the autographs I translated are given in the List of the Letters. Whenever autographs were unavailable, I translated from the Italian and French publications, which are referred to in parentheses. I also cite the English translations of Verdi letters that appear in the Werfel-Stefan and Charles Osborne books, in *The Musical Quarterly*, and in *Opera News*.

ABBREVIATIONS

Autographs

RI   Archivio Ricordi, Milano

SA   Collezione Carrara Verdi, St. Agata

SC   Museo Teatrale alla Scala, Milano

SU   Staedtische- und Universitaetsbibliothek, Frankfurt am Main

VE   Collection Peter Emmanuel Zervudachi, Vevey

Published Letters (not available as autographs)

(A)   Cesari, Gateano, and Alessandro Luzio, eds. *I Copialettere di Giuseppe Verdi*. Milano: Comune di Milano, 1913.

(B)   Luzio, Alessandro, ed. *Carteggi Verdiani*. 2 vols. Roma: Reale Accademia d'Italia, 1935.
————, ed. *Carteggi Verdiani*. 2 vols. Roma: Accademia Nazionale dei Lincei, 1947.

(C)   Alberti, Annibale, ed. *Verdi intimo: Carteggio di Giuseppe Verdi con il Conte Opprandino Arrivabene*. Milano: A. Mondadori, 1931.

(F)   Cassi, Paolo. "Gerolamo Magnani e il suo carteggio con Verdi." *Vecchie Cronache di Fidenza*. Milano: Stabilimento Tipografico Gazzetta dello Sport, 1941, 129–35.

(G)   Gatti, Carlo, *Verdi*. 2 vols. Milano: Alpes, 1931.

(M)   Mariette, Edouard. *Mariette Pacha: Lettres et souvenirs personnels*. Paris: H. Jouve, 1904.

(P)   Pougin, Arthur. *Verdi: Histoire anecdotique de sa vie et ses oeuvres*. Paris: Calman Lévy, 1886.

(R)   De Rensis, Rafaello, ed. *Franco Faccio e Verdi: Carteggi e documenti inediti*. Milano: Fratelli Treves, 1934.

(S)   Stefani, Giuseppe. *Verdi e Trieste*. Trieste: Comune di Trieste, 1951.

(X)   Abbiati, Franco. *Giuseppe Verdi*. 4 vols. Milano: G. Ricordi, 1959.

(Y)   *La Gazzetta Musicale di Milano*.

(Z)   Günther, Ursula. "Documents inconnus concernant les relations de Verdi avec l'Opéra de Paris." *Atti del III⁰ Congresso Internazionale di Studi Verdiani*. Parma: Istituto di Studi Verdiani, 1974, 564–83.

Other English Translations of Verdi Letters

MQB   Prod'homme, Jacques-Gabriel, ed. "Unpublished letters from Verdi to Du Locle (1866–1876)," trans. by Theodore Baker. *The Musical Quarterly*, 1921, 7, no. 4, 73–103.

MQK   Istel, Edgar. "A genetic study of the Aida libretto," trans. by Otto Kinkeldey. *The Musical Quarterly*, 1917, 3, no. 1, 34–52.

ON   Busch, Hans, ed. and trans. "(signed) G. Verdi." *Opera News*, 1972, 36, no. 19, 8–11.

OS   Osborne, Charles, ed. and trans. *Letters of Giuseppe Verdi*. New York: Holt, Rinehart and Winston, 1971.

WE   Werfel, Franz, and Paul Stefan, eds. *Verdi: The Man in His Letters*, trans. by Edward Downes. New York: L. B. Fischer, 1942. 2d ed., New York: Vienna House, 1970.

LIST OF THE LETTERS

When two locations of an autograph are given, the first refers to the location of a draft or a copy. Asterisks indicate first publications.

From	To	Date	Autograph	English Publication
Verdi	Du Locle	19 Feb. 68	It. OP	MQB
Verdi	Draneht	9 Aug. 69	Fr. CA	
Verdi	Du Locle	8 Dec. 69	It. SA-OP	MQB-WE-OS
*Muzio	G. Ricordi	7 Jan. 70	It. RI	
Verdi	Du Locle	23 Jan. 70	It. OP	MQB
Verdi	G. Ricordi	3 Feb. 70	It. RI	
*G. Ricordi	Giuseppina Verdi	10 Feb. 70	It. SA	
Verdi	G. Ricordi	14 Feb. 70	It. RI	
Verdi	Du Locle	18 Feb. 70	It. OP	MQB
*Muzio	G. Ricordi	5 Mar. 70	It. RI	
*G. Ricordi	Verdi	11 Mar. 70	It. SA	
Verdi	Du Locle	26 Mar. 70	It. OP	MQB
*Muzio	G. Ricordi	15 Apr. 70	It. RI	
Verdi	Du Locle	23 Apr. 70	It. OP	MQB
Verdi	Du Locle	25 Apr. 70	It. OP	MQB
Mariette	Du Locle	27 Apr. 70	Fr. OP	
Mariette	Du Locle	28 Apr. 70	Fr. SA	
Verdi	Maffei	30 Apr. 70	It. CH	
Du Locle	Verdi	3 May 70	Fr. SA	
Du Locle	Verdi	7 May 70	Fr. SA	
Du Locle	Verdi	10 May 70	Fr. SA	
Du Locle	Verdi	14 May 70	Fr. SA	
Mariette	Du Locle	19 May 70	Fr. OP	
Du Locle	Verdi	26 May 70	Fr. SA	
Verdi	Du Locle	26 May 70	It. OP	MQB

From	To	Date	Autograph	English Publication
Du Locle	Verdi	29 May 70	Fr. SA	
Mariette	Du Locle	29 May 70	Fr. OP	
Du Locle	Verdi	31 May 70	Fr. SA	
Verdi	Du Locle	2 June 70	It. SA-OP	MQB-WE-OS
Verdi	G. Ricordi	2 June 70	It. RI	
Mariette	Du Locle	4 June 70	Fr. OP	
G. Ricordi	Verdi	4 June 70	It. SA	
*G. Ricordi	Giuseppina Verdi	4 June 70	It. SA	
Verdi	G. Ricordi	5 June 70	It. RI	
Du Locle	Verdi	6 June 70	Fr. SA	
Verdi	Du Locle	9 June 70	It. OP	MQB
Mariette	Du Locle (Telegram)	10 June 70	Fr. OP	
Du Locle	Verdi (Telegram)	10 June 70	Fr. SA	MQB
Muzio	Verdi (Telegram)	10 June 70	It. SA	
Verdi	Du Locle (Telegram)	12 June 70	It. OP	
Verdi	Du Locle	12 June 70	It. OP	
Du Locle	Verdi	13 June 70	Fr. SA	
Verdi	Du Locle	18 June 70	It. OP	MQB-WE
Verdi	Muzio	20 June 70	It. SA	
Mariette	Du Locle	21 June 70	Fr. OP	
Mariette	E. Mariette	21 June 70	Fr. ? (M)	
*T. Ricordi	Verdi	21 June 70	It. SA	
Verdi	G. Ricordi	25 June 70	It. RI	WE-OS
*G. Ricordi	Verdi	1 July 70	It. SA	
Du Locle	Verdi	2 July 70	Fr. SA	
G. Ricordi	Verdi	3 July 70	It. SA	
Verdi	G. Ricordi	4 July 70	It. RI	
Giuseppina Verdi	Maffei	6 July 70	It. CH	
G. Ricordi	Verdi	8 July 70	It. SA	
Du Locle	Verdi	9 July 70	Fr. SA	
Verdi	G. Ricordi	10 July 70	It. RI	ON
G. Ricordi	Verdi	14 July 70	It. SA	
Verdi	Du Locle	15 July 70	It. OP	MQB
*Ghislanzoni	Tornaghi	15 July 70	It. RI	
Mariette	Draneht	15 July 70	Fr. CA	
Verdi	Piroli	16 July 70	It. AC	
Mariette	Draneht	19 July 70	Fr. CA	
Mariette	Draneht	21 July 70	Fr. CA	
G. Ricordi	Verdi	21 July 70	It. SA	

From	To	Date	Autograph	English Publication
Verdi	Du Locle	23 July 70	It. OP	MQB
Du Locle	Verdi	26 July 70	Fr. SA	
*Ghislanzoni	Verdi	26 July 70	It. SA	
Galletti Gianoli	Draneht	28 July 70	It. CA	
*Draneht	Riaz Pasha	29 July 70	Fr. VE	
Verdi	G. Ricordi	31 July 70	It. RI	
Draneht	Mariette	4 Aug. 70	Fr. CA	
*Draneht	Barrot	5 Aug. 70	Fr. VE	
Vitali	Draneht	6 Aug. 70	It. CA	
*G. Ricordi	Verdi	8 Aug. 70	It. SA	
Mariette	Draneht	8 Aug. 70	Fr. CA	
Verdi	De Sanctis	10 Aug. 70	It. AC	
Verdi	Ghislanzoni	12 Aug. 70	It. PM	MQK-OS
Verdi	G. Ricordi	12 Aug. 70	It. RI	
*Draneht	Riaz Pasha	12 Aug. 70	Fr. VE	
*Draneht	Barrot	12 Aug. 70	Fr. VE	
Lampugnani	Draneht	13 Aug. 70	It. CA	
Verdi	Ghislanzoni	14 Aug. 70	It. PM	MQK-OS
Verdi	Ghislanzoni	16 Aug. 70	It. PM	MQK-OS
*G. Ricordi	Verdi	16 Aug. 70	It. SA	
Verdi	Ghislanzoni	17 Aug. 70	It. LA	MQK-OS
Draneht	Galletti Gianoli	17 Aug. 70	Fr. & It. CA	
Draneht	Verdi	18 Aug. 70	Fr. CA-SA	
Draneht	Lampugnani	18 Aug. 70	Fr. & It. CA	
Draneht	Monplaisir	18 Aug. 70	Fr. CA	
*Draneht	Riaz Pasha	19 Aug. 70	Fr. VE	
Galletti Gianoli	Draneht	20 Aug. 70	It. CA	
Vitali	Draneht	21 Aug. 70	It. CA	
Lampugnani	Draneht	21 Aug. 70	Fr. CA	
*Du Locle	Verdi	21 Aug. 70	Fr. SA	
Verdi	Du Locle	22 Aug. 70	It. OP	MQB
Verdi	Ghislanzoni	22 Aug. 70	It. PM	MQK-WE-OS
Draneht	Monplaisir	23 Aug. 70	Fr. CA	
Verdi	Ghislanzoni	25 Aug. 70	It. PM	
Verdi	Du Locle	26 Aug. 70	It. & Fr. SA-OP	MQB-WE
Du Locle	Verdi	26 Aug. 70	Fr. SA	
*Draneht	Barrot	28 Aug. 70	Fr. VE	
Du Locle	Verdi	28 Aug. 70	Fr. SA	
Mariette	Draneht	1 Sep. 70	Fr. OP	
Du Locle	Verdi	1 Sep. 70	Fr. SA	
Du Locle	Verdi	2 Sep. 70	Fr. SA	

From	To	Date	Autograph	English Publication
*Tornaghi	Verdi	5 Sep. 70	It. SA	
*Draneht	Mariette	7 Sep. 70	Fr. CA	
Verdi	Ghislanzoni	8 Sep. 70	It. PM	MQK-WE
Ghislanzoni	Verdi	11 Sep. 70	It. SA	
Verdi	Ghislanzoni	12 Sep. 70	It. PM	
*Ghislanzoni	Verdi	12 Sep. 70	It. SA	
Verdi	Ghislanzoni	13 Sep. 70	It. PM	MQK
*Mariette	Draneht	13 Sep. 70	Fr. CA	
Draneht	Mariette	21 Sep. 70	Fr. CA	
Verdi	Ghislanzoni	27 Sep. 70	It. PM	
Verdi	Ghislanzoni	28 Sep. 70	It. ? (A)	MQK
Verdi	Ghislanzoni	30 Sep. 70	It. LA	MQK
Verdi	Maffei	30 Sep. 70	It. BN	WE-OS
*Ghislanzoni	Tornaghi	1 Oct. 70	It. RI	
Verdi	Ghislanzoni	7 Oct. 70	It. ? (A)	
Verdi	G. Ricordi	7 Oct. 70	It. RI	
Verdi	Ghislanzoni	8 Oct. 70	It. ? (A)	MQK-WE-OS
Verdi	Ghislanzoni	9 Oct. 70	It. LA	
Verdi	Ghislanzoni	16 Oct. 70	It. ? (A)	MQK
Verdi	Ghislanzoni	17 Oct. 70	It. PM	WE
*Verdi	T. Ricordi	18 Oct. 70	It. RI	
Verdi	Ghislanzoni	18 Oct. 70	It. PM	
Verdi	Ghislanzoni	22 Oct. 70	It. PM	
Verdi	Du Locle	24 Oct. 70	Fr. OP	
*Ghislanzoni	Tornaghi	24 Oct. 70	It. RI	
Verdi	Ghislanzoni	25 Oct. 70	It. PM	MQK
Verdi	Ghislanzoni	26 Oct. 70	It. PM	MQK
Verdi	Luccardi	26 Oct. 70	It. ? (A)	
Verdi	Ghislanzoni	27 Oct. 70	It. PM	
*Ghislanzoni	Verdi	31 Oct. 70	It. SA	
Muzio	Du Locle	1 Nov. 70	Fr. OP	
*Ghislanzoni	Tornaghi	2 Nov. 70	It. RI	
Verdi	Ghislanzoni	2 Nov. 70	It. PM	MQK
*G. Ricordi	Verdi	2 Nov. 70	It. SA	
*T. Ricordi	Verdi	3 Nov. 70	It. SA	
Verdi	Ghislanzoni	4 Nov. 70	It. LA	
Verdi	Ghislanzoni	5 Nov. 70	It. PM	
*G. Ricordi	Verdi	5 Nov. 70	It. SA	
*G. Ricordi	Verdi	7 Nov. 70	It. SA	
Verdi	G. Ricordi	7 Nov. 70	It. RI	
Verdi	G. Ricordi	8 Nov. 70	It. RI	
Verdi	Ghislanzoni	9 Nov. 70	It. PM	

From	To	Date	Autograph	English Publication
*G. Ricordi	Verdi	12 Nov. 70	It. SA	
Verdi	Piroli	12 Nov. 70	It. AC	
Verdi	Mariette	12 Nov. 70	Fr. CA	
Verdi	Ghislanzoni	12 Nov. 70	It. LA	MQK-WE-OS
Verdi	Ghislanzoni	13 Nov. 70	It. PM	MQK
*G. Ricordi	Verdi	13 Nov. 70	It. SA	
Verdi	G. Ricordi	15 Nov. 70	It. RI	
Verdi	Ghislanzoni	Undated	It. PM	WE-OS
*Ghislanzoni	G. Ricordi	28 Nov. 70	It. RI	
Verdi	G. Ricordi	30 Nov. 70	It. RI	
*G. Ricordi	Verdi	4 Dec. 70	It. SA	
Verdi	Piroli	5 Dec. 70	It. AC	
Verdi	Du Locle	5 Dec. 70	Fr. OP	
Muzio	Draneht	5 Dec. 70	It. CA	
Verdi	G. Ricordi	9 Dec. 70	It. RI	
Barrot	Draneht	10 Dec. 70	Fr. CA	
*G. Ricordi	Verdi	12 Dec. 70	It. SA	
Verdi	Piroli	13 Dec. 70	It. AC	
Draneht	Verdi	16 Dec. 70	Fr. CA-SA	
*G. Ricordi	Verdi	Undated	It. SA	
Verdi	G. Ricordi	17 Dec. 70	It. RI	
Verdi	G. Ricordi	Undated	It. RI	
Verdi	Ghislanzoni	21 Dec. 70	It. PM	MQK
Verdi	Piroli	21 Dec. 70	It. AC	
Draneht	Verdi	22 Dec. 70	Fr. CA-SA	
*Draneht	Muzio	22 Dec. 70	Fr. SA	
*G. Ricordi	Verdi	22 Dec. 70	It. SA	
Verdi	T. Ricordi	28 Dec. 70	It. RI	
Verdi	Ghislanzoni	28 Dec. 70	It. PM	
Verdi	Piroli	29 Dec. 70	It. AC	
*G. Ricordi	Verdi	29 Dec. 70	It. SA	
Verdi	Luccardi	30 Dec. 70	It. ? (A)	OS
Verdi	G. Ricordi	30 Dec. 70	It. RI	
G. Ricordi	Verdi	31 Dec. 70	It. SA	
Ghislanzoni	Verdi	31 Dec. 70	It. ? (B)	
Verdi	De Sanctis	1 Jan. 71	It. AC	
Verdi	G. Ricordi	1 Jan. 71	It. RI	
Verdi	G. Ricordi	3 Jan. 71	It. RI	
Muzio	Draneht	4 Jan. 71	It. CA	
G. Ricordi	Verdi	4 Jan. 71	It. SA	
Verdi	G. Ricordi	5 Jan. 71	It. RI	
Verdi	Draneht	5 Jan. 71	Fr. SA-CA	WE-OS

From	To	Date	Autograph	English Publication
Verdi	De Giosa	5 Jan. 71	It. ? (A)	WE-OS
*G. Ricordi	Verdi	6 Jan. 71	It. SA	
Verdi	Ghislanzoni	7 Jan. 71	It. PM	MQK
Verdi	G. Ricordi	7 Jan. 71	It. RI	
G. Ricordi	Verdi	7 Jan. 71	It. SA	
Stolz	G. Ricordi	6 Jan. 71	It. ? (B)	
G. Ricordi	Stolz	7 Jan. 71	It. ? (B)	
Verdi	G. Ricordi	8 Jan. 71	It. RI	
*G. Ricordi	Verdi	8 Jan. 71	It. SA	
Verdi	G. Ricordi	11 Jan. 71	It. RI	
Verdi	Ghislanzoni	13 Jan. 71	It. PM	
*Verdi	T. Ricordi	13 Jan. 71	It. RI	
*G. Ricordi	Verdi	15 Jan. 71	It. SA	
Verdi	G. Ricordi	16 Jan. 71	It. RI	
Draneht	Verdi	19 Jan. 71	Fr. CA-SA	
Draneht	Verdi	20 Jan. 71	Fr. CA-SA	
*Draneht	Verdi	2 Feb. 71	Fr. SA	
Verdi	Draneht	4 Feb. 71	Fr. SA-CA	
Verdi	Du Locle	4 Feb. 71	Fr. OP	MQB
Verdi	G. Ricordi	5 Feb. 71	It. RI	
Draneht	Verdi	11 Feb. 71	Fr. CA-SA	
*Verdi	Du Locle	14 Feb. 71	It. OP	
*Verdi	Du Locle	14 Feb. 71	Fr. OP	
Verdi	Piroli	20 Feb. 71	It. ? (B)	WE-OS
*Verdi	G. Ricordi	23 Feb. 71	It. RI	
Stolz	Lampugnani	25 Feb. 71	It. CA	
*G. Ricordi	Verdi (*Telegram*)	28 Feb. 71	It. SA	
*Verdi	G. Ricordi (*Telegram*)	Undated	It. SA	
Verdi	Draneht	1 Mar. 71	It. SA-CA	OS
*G. Ricordi	Verdi	7 Mar. 71	It. SA	
Verdi	G. Ricordi	10 Mar. 71	It. RI	
Lampugnani	Draneht	12 Mar. 71	Fr. CA	
Lampugnani	Draneht	12 Mar. 71	Fr. CA	
*Draneht	Verdi	13 Mar. 71	Fr. VE	
Verdi	G. Ricordi	13 Mar. 71	It. RI	
*Draneht	Lampugnani (*Telegram*)	16 Mar. 71	Fr. VE	
Somigli	Draneht	19 Mar. 71	It. CA	
*Draneht	Gazzetta dei Teatri (*Telegram*)	20 Mar. 71	Fr. VE	
Verdi	Draneht	23 Mar. 71	Fr. CA	

From	To	Date	Autograph	English Publication
Draneht	Verdi	24 Mar. 71	Fr. CA-SA	
*Verdi	T. Ricordi	28 Mar. 71	It. RI	
*G. Ricordi	Verdi	30 Mar. 71	It. SA	
Verdi	Draneht	30 Mar. 71	Fr. SA-CA	OS
Draneht	Verdi	3 Apr. 71	Fr. CA	
Stolz	Lampugnani (*Telegram*)	7 Apr. 71	It. CA	
A. Mariani	Lampugnani (*Telegram*)	7 Apr. 71	It. CA	
Lampugnani	Draneht	9 Apr. 71	It. CA	
Verdi	G. Ricordi	11 Apr. 71	It. SA-RI	WE
*Draneht	Bottesini	12 Apr. 71	Fr. VE	
Draneht	Verdi	13 Apr. 71	Fr. CA-SA	
Verdi	Draneht	14 Apr. 71	Fr. SA-CA	OS
Lampugnani	Draneht	16 Apr. 71	Fr. CA	
*Draneht	Verdi	24 Apr. 71	Fr. VE	
*Draneht	Mariette	28 Apr. 71	Fr. VE	
Draneht	Marini	28 Apr. 71	Fr. CA	
Verdi	Draneht	28 Apr. 71	Fr. SA-CA	OS
Verdi	Lampugnani	1 May 71	It. CA	
Lampugnani	Draneht	4 May 71	It. & Fr. CA	
Verdi	Lampugnani	4 May 71	It. CA	
Verdi	Lampugnani	9 May 71	It. CA	
*Draneht	Verdi	12 May 71	Fr. VE	
Verdi	Draneht	15 May 71	Fr. CA	
*Draneht	Verdi	17 May 71	Fr. VE	
*T. Ricordi	Verdi	19 May 71	It. SA	
Mariette	Draneht	19 May 71	Fr. CA	
*Draneht	Barrot	20 May 71	Fr. VE	
Verdi	T. Ricordi	22 May 71	It. SA-RI	
*G. Ricordi	Verdi	23 May 71	It. SA	
*G. Ricordi	Verdi	24 May 71	It. SA	
Verdi	G. Ricordi	24 May 71	It. RI	
Verdi	G. Ricordi	25 May 71	It. RI	
Verdi	Magnani	25 May 71	It. ? (F)	
*G. Ricordi	Verdi	27 May 71	It. SA	
*G. Ricordi	Verdi	31 May 71	It. SA	
Verdi	G. Ricordi	1 June 71	It. RI	
*Draneht	Verdi	3 June 71	Fr. VE	
Verdi	Du Locle	6 June 71	It. OP	MQB
*G. Ricordi	Verdi	7 June 71	It. SA	
Verdi	G. Ricordi	8 June 71	It. RI	

From	To	Date	Autograph	English Publication
Verdi	Draneht	8 June 71	It. CA	
*Draneht	Verdi	9/10 June 71	It. VE	
*Draneht	Mariette	10 June 71	Fr. VE	
Verdi	Draneht	12 June 71	It. SA-CA	
*G. Ricordi	Verdi	14 June 71	It. SA	
Verdi	T. Ricordi	15 June 71	It. RI	
*Verdi	Mayor of Milan	17 June 71	It. SC	
Verdi	Du Locle	17 June 71	It. OP	MQB
*Draneht	Mariette	17 June 71	Fr. VE	
Verdi	Lampugnani	20 June 71	It. CA	
*Waldmann	Tornaghi	20 June 71	It. RI	
*Tornaghi	Verdi	21 June 71	It. SA	
Lampugnani	Draneht	22 June 71	It. CA	
*Draneht	Verdi	26 June 71	Fr. VE	
*Draneht	Grossi	26 June 71	Fr. VE	
Draneht	Verdi	4 July 71	It. CA-SA	
*T. Ricordi	Verdi	5 July 71	It. SA	
*G. Ricordi	Verdi	7 July 71	It. SA	
Mariette	Draneht	7 July 71	Fr. CA	
*G. Ricordi	Verdi	8 July 71	It. SA	
Barrot	Draneht	9 July 71	Fr. CA	
Verdi	G. Ricordi	9 July 71	It. RI	
Verdi	G. Ricordi	10 July 71	It. RI	WE-OS-ON
*Tornaghi	Verdi	14 July 71	It. SA	
*G. Ricordi	Verdi	16 July 71	It. SA	
*Draneht	Verdi	17 July 71	It. VE	
*Draneht	Mariette	18 July 71	Fr. VE	
Mariette	Draneht	19 July 71	Fr. CA	
Verdi	Du Locle	20 July 71	It. SA-OP	MQB
Verdi	Draneht	20 July 71	It. SA-CA	OS
*Draneht	Barrot	21 July 71	Fr. VE	
*Draneht	Verdi	21 July 71	It. VE	
Verdi	Draneht	22 July 71	It. SA-CA	
*Draneht	Barrot	24 July 71	Fr. VE	
*Draneht	Mariette	24 July 71	Fr. VE	
*Draneht	Verdi	24 July 71	It. VE	
*Draneht	Verdi	25 July 71	It. VE	
Verdi	T. Ricordi	25 July 71	It. RI	
*Verdi	Du Locle	26 July 71	It. OP	
D. Baron	Draneht	30 July 71	Fr. CA	
Verdi	T. Ricordi	31 July 71	It. RI	
*Tornaghi	Verdi	1 Aug. 71	It. SA	

From	To	Date	Autograph	English Publication
*Draneht	Mariette	1 Aug. 71	Fr. VE	
Verdi	Draneht	2 Aug. 71	It. SA-CA	WE-OS
Verdi	T. Ricordi	4 Aug. 71	It. RI	
*Tornaghi	Verdi	5 Aug. 71	It. SA	
*Draneht	Verdi	5 Aug. 71	It. VE	
*Draneht	Barrot	5 Aug. 71	Fr. VE	
*Verdi	T. Ricordi	5 Aug. 71	It. RI	
Verdi	Ghislanzoni	5 Aug. 71	It. PM	MQK
*Verdi	T. Ricordi	6 Aug. 71	It. RI	
*Verdi	G. Ricordi	6 Aug. 71	It. RI	
Verdi	Ghislanzoni	6 Aug. 71	It. ? (S)	
*G. Ricordi	Verdi	7 Aug. 71	It. SA	
*Verdi	G. Ricordi	10 Aug. 71	It. RI	
*Verdi	G. Ricordi	11 Aug. 71	It. RI	
Verdi	De Sanctis	11 Aug. 71	It. AC	
Verdi	Du Locle	12 Aug. 71	It. SA-OP	
Verdi	Draneht	12 Aug. 71	It. SA-CA	
Verdi	G. Ricordi	12 Aug. 71	It. RI	MQK-WE-OS
*Verdi	G. Ricordi	14 Aug. 71	It. RI	
*Tornaghi	Verdi	16 Aug. 71	It. SA	
Barrot	Draneht	18 Aug. 71	Fr. CA	
*Draneht	Sass	22 Aug. 71	Fr. VE	
*T. Ricordi	Verdi	23 Aug. 71	It. SA	
Verdi	T. Ricordi	26 Aug. 71	It. RI	
*Verdi	T. Ricordi	27 Aug. 71	It. RI	
*Verdi	T. Ricordi	28 Aug. 71	It. RI	
*Faccio	Tornaghi	28 Aug. 71	It. RI	
Verdi	Draneht	29 Aug. 71	It. CA	
Verdi	Du Locle	29 Aug. 71	It. OP	
*Draneht	Verdi	29 Aug. 71	It. VE	
Mariette	Draneht	30 Aug. 71	Fr. CA	
*G. Ricordi	Verdi	31 Aug. 71	It. SA	
Verdi	Draneht	1 Sep. 71	It. SA-CA	
Verdi	T. Ricordi	1 Sep. 71	It. RI	
Verdi	Arrivabene	2 Sep. 71	It. ? (A)	WE-OS
Verdi	G. Ricordi	2 Sep. 71	It. RI	
*G. Ricordi	Verdi	2 Sep. 71	It. SA	
*G. Ricordi	Verdi	3 Sep. 71	. SA	
*G. Ricordi	Verdi	4 Sep. 71	It. SA	
*Verdi	G. Ricordi	4 Sep. 71	It. RI	
*Faccio	G. Ricordi	4 Sep. 71	It. RI	
Verdi	G. Ricordi	5 Sep. 71	It. RI	

From	To	Date	Autograph	English Publication
*Draneht	Verdi	5 Sep. 71	It. VE	
*Draneht	Ghislanzoni	5 Sep. 71	It. VE	
*Draneht	Mariette	6 Sep. 71	Fr. VE	
*G. Ricordi	Verdi	6 Sep. 71	It. SA	
Verdi	G. Ricordi	7 Sep. 71	It. RI	
Verdi	Faccio	10 Sep. 71	It. CM	
*Verdi	Du Locle	10 Sep. 71	It. OP	
Verdi	Draneht	10 Sep. 71	It. CA	
*G. Ricordi	Verdi	12 Sep. 71	It. SA	
*Verdi	G. Ricordi	16 Sep. 71	It. RI	
*Draneht	Barrot	16 Sep. 71	Fr. VE	
*Draneht	Mariette	18 Sep. 71	Fr. VE	
Verdi	Draneht	20 Sep. 71	It. CA	
Verdi	Draneht	20 Sep. 71	It. CA	
Verdi	Draneht	21 Sep. 71	It. CA	
*Ghislanzoni	G. Ricordi	21 Sep. 71	It. RI	
Verdi	Du Locle	23 Sep. 71	It. SU	
Verdi	G. Ricordi	Sep. 71	It. RI	
Mariette	Draneht	28 Sep. 71	Fr. CA	
*Verdi	G. Ricordi	Sep. 71	It. SC	
*Verdi	G. Ricordi	Sep. 71	It. RI	
*G. Ricordi	Verdi	4 Oct. 71	It. SA	
*Verdi	G. Ricordi	5/6 Oct. 71	It. HS	
Mariette	Draneht	6 Oct. 71	Fr. CA	
*Ghislanzoni	G. Ricordi	6 Oct. 71	It. RI	
Verdi	G. Ricordi	10 Oct. 71	It. RI	
Verdi	Escudier	11 Oct. 71	It. SA-OP	OS
Draneht	Mariette	12 Oct. 71	Fr. CA	
*G. Ricordi	Verdi	13 Oct. 71	It. SA	
Verdi	Mayor of Milan	13 Oct. 71	It. SC	WE-OS
*Verdi	G. Ricordi	13 Oct. 71	It. RI	
Verdi	G. Ricordi	14 Oct. 71	It. RI	
D. Baron	Draneht	14 Oct. 71	Fr. CA	
*G. Ricordi	Verdi	15 Oct. 71	It. SA	
Verdi	G. Ricordi	15 Oct. 71	It. RI	
Draneht	Bottesini	17 Oct. 71	It. CA	
*Verdi	Du Locle	20 Oct. 71	It. OP	
*G. Ricordi	Verdi	24 Oct. 71	It. SA	
Verdi	G. Ricordi	26 Oct. 71	It. RI	
*G. Ricordi	Verdi	28 Oct. 71	It. SA	
Verdi	G. Ricordi	31 Oct. 71	It. RI	
Draneht	Lampugnani	3 Nov. 71	Fr. CA	

From	To	Date	Autograph	English Publication
D. Baron	Draneht	4 Nov. 71	Fr. CA	
Draneht	D. Baron	6 Nov. 71	Fr. CA	
*Verdi	Du Locle	7 Nov. 71	It. OP	
Verdi	G. Ricordi	7 Nov. 71	It. RI	
*G. Ricordi	Verdi	8 Nov. 71	It. SA	
Verdi	G. Ricordi	10 Nov. 71	It. RI	
*G. Ricordi	Verdi	12 Nov. 71	It. SA	
Verdi	G. Ricordi	13 Nov. 71	It. RI	
*Verdi	G. Ricordi	15 Nov. 71	It. RI	
Verdi	G. Ricordi	Undated	It. RI	
Verdi	G. Ricordi	17 Nov. 71	It. RI	
Verdi	G. Ricordi	19 Nov. 71	It. RI	
Verdi	G. Ricordi	21 Nov. 71	It. SA-RI	
*Verdi	Du Locle	21 Nov. 71	It. OP	
Verdi	G. Ricordi	22 Nov. 71	It. RI	
Verdi	G. Ricordi	23 Nov. 71	It. RI	
Draneht	Barrot	24 Nov. 71	Fr. CA	
Verdi	G. Ricordi	26 Nov. 71	It. RI	
Verdi	Faccio	26 Nov. 71	It. CM	
*Verdi	Du Locle	28 Nov. 71	It. OP	
Verdi	G. Ricordi	28 Nov. 71	It. RI	
Verdi	G. Ricordi	29 Nov. 71	It. RI	
*Verdi	Du Locle	29 Nov. 71	It. OP	
Verdi	G. Ricordi	2 Dec. 71	It. RI	
Draneht	Grand	3 Dec. 71	Fr. CA	
Draneht	D. Baron	4 Dec. 71	Fr. CA	
Verdi	G. Ricordi	6 Dec. 71	It. RI	
Verdi	Bottesini	7 Dec. 71	It. CO	MQK
Draneht	Magnier	8 Dec. 71	Fr. CA	
Verdi	G. Ricordi	9 Dec. 71	It. SA-RI	ON
Filippi	Verdi	8 Dec. 71	It. SA-RI	ON
Verdi	Filippi	9 Dec. 71	It. SA-RI	WE-OS-ON
Verdi	G. Ricordi	10 Dec. 71	It. RI	
Verdi	Bottesini	10 Dec. 71	It. CO	MQK
Verdi	Maffei	11 Dec. 71	It. BN	WE-OS
*Verdi	G. Ricordi	13 Dec. 71	It. RI	
*Verdi	Du Locle	14 Dec. 71	It. OP	
Verdi	G. Ricordi	18 Dec. 71	It. RI	
Draneht	Rassik Effendi	20 Dec. 71	Fr. CA	
Draneht	Magnier	23 Dec. 71	Fr. CA	
Verdi	G. Ricordi	24 Dec. 71	It. RI	
Verdi	Du Locle	25 Dec. 71	It. OP	MQB

From	To	Date	Autograph	English Publication
Verdi	G. Ricordi	25 Dec. 71	It. RI	
Verdi	G. Ricordi	26 Dec. 71	It. RI	
Verdi	Bottesini	27 Dec. 71	It. CO	
Verdi	Draneht	27 Dec. 71	Fr. CA	
Verdi	G. Ricordi	28 Dec. 71	It. RI	
Verdi	Du Locle	29 Dec. 71	It. OP	MQB
Draneht	Tinti	29 Dec. 71	Fr. CA	
Verdi	G. Ricordi	31 Dec. 71	It. RI	
Verdi	Escudier	1 Jan. 72	It. OP	
Giuseppina Verdi	De Sanctis	3 Jan. 72	It. AC	
Draneht	D. Baron	4 Jan. 72	Fr. CA	
*Verdi	Du Locle	7 Jan. 72	It. OP	
*Verdi	Luccardi	9 Jan. 72	It. AM	
Ghislanzoni	G. Ricordi	9 Jan. 72	It. RI	
Ghislanzoni	G. Ricordi	Jan. 72	It. RI	
Verdi	Du Locle	11 Jan. 72	It. OP	
Verdi	Arrivabene	13 Jan. 72	It. ? (C)	
Verdi	Bottesini	13 Jan. 72	It. CO	OS
Mariette	Draneht	17 Jan. 72	Fr. CA	
*Verdi	Du Locle	18 Jan. 72	It. OP	
Giuseppina Verdi	De Sanctis	21 Jan. 72	It. AC	
Verdi	Du Locle	26 Jan. 72	It. OP	MQB
Giuseppina Verdi	De Sanctis	30 Jan. 72	It. AC	
Verdi	Torelli	30/31 Jan. 72	It. LP	
Verdi	Piroli	5 Feb. 72	It. AC	
Verdi	Arrivabene	9 Feb. 72	It. ? (C)	WE
Draneht	Verdi	18 Feb. 72	It. CA	
Verdi	G. Ricordi	21 Feb. 72	It. RI	
*Verdi	Du Locle	21 Feb. 72	It. OP	
*Verdi	Escudier	21 Feb. 72	It. OP	
Verdi	Luccardi	21 Feb. 72	It. ?	
Verdi	Piroli	22 Feb. 72	It. AC	
Verdi	De Sanctis	22 Feb. 72	It. AC	
Verdi	De Sanctis	25 Feb. 72	It. SA-AC	
*Verdi	G. Ricordi	28 Feb. 72	It. RI	
Verdi	Mazzucato	29 Feb. 72	It. SC	
*Ghislanzoni	G. Ricordi	2 Mar. 72	It. RI	
Verdi	Mayor of Parma	2 Mar. 72	It. AS	
Verdi	G. Ricordi	9 Mar. 72	It. RI	

From	To	Date	Autograph	English Publication
*Verdi	G. Ricordi	9 Mar. 72	It. RI	
Verdi	Torelli	10 Mar. 72	It. LP	
*Verdi	G. Ricordi	12 Mar. 72	It. RI	
*Verdi	Torelli	13 Mar. 72	It. LP	
Verdi	Draneht	22 Mar. 72	It. CA	
Verdi	G. Ricordi	28 Mar. 72	It. RI	
Verdi	De Sanctis	29 Mar. 72	It. AC	
Verdi	Escudier	30 Mar. 72	It. OP	
*Verdi	G. Ricordi	30 Mar. 72	It. RI	
Verdi	G. Ricordi	31 Mar. 72	It. SA-RI	WE-OS
*T. Ricordi	Verdi	6 Apr. 72	It. SA	
*Verdi	G. Ricordi	6 Apr. 72	It. RI	
*G. Ricordi	Verdi	7 Apr. 72	It. Sa	
Verdi	Escudier	15 Apr. 72	It. OP	
*Verdi	G. Ricordi	15 Apr. 72	It. RI	
Verdi	De Sanctis	17 Apr. 72	It. AC	
Verdi	Du Locle	17 Apr. 72	It. OP	MQB
*Verdi	De Sanctis	21 Apr. 72	It. LP	
*Giuseppina Verdi	Faccio	23 Apr. 72	It. CM	
Du Locle	Verdi	26 Apr. 72	Fr. SA	
Verdi	De Sanctis	26 Apr. 72	It. AC	WE-ON
Verdi	Arrivabene	27 Apr. 72	It. ? (C)	
Verdi	Piroli	27 Apr. 72	It. AC	
*Ghislanzoni	G. Ricordi	30 Apr. 72	It. RI	
*G. Ricordi	Verdi	1 May 72	It. SA	
Verdi	G. Ricordi	2 May 72	It. RI	
Verdi	G. Ricordi	3 May 72	It. RI	
Verdi	G. Ricordi	10 May 72	It. RI	WE
Bertani	Verdi	7 May 72	It. ? (Y)	WE
G. Ricordi	Verdi	16 May 72	It. SA	
Bertani	Verdi	15 May 72	It ? (Y)	WE
Verdi	Mayor of Padua	18 May 72	It. MC	
Du Locle	Verdi	21 May 72	Fr. SA	
*G. Ricordi	Verdi	21 May 72	It. SA	
Verdi	Piroli	5 June 72	It. AC	
Verdi	Luccardi	5 June 72	It. IS	
*G. Ricordi	Verdi	7 June 72	It. SA	
Verdi	G. Ricordi	11 June 72	It. RI	
*G. Ricordi	Giuseppina Verdi	11 June 72	It. SA	
Verdi	G. Ricordi	12 June 72	It. RI	
*Faccio	G. Ricordi	13 June 72	It. RI	

From	To	Date	Autograph	English Publication
*Faccio	G. Ricordi	16 June 72	It. RI	
Verdi	G. Ricordi	19 June 72	It. RI	
Faccio	Verdi	21 June 72	It. ? (R)	
*G. Ricordi	Verdi	22 June 72	It. SA	
Verdi	Du Locle	22 June 72	It. OP	MQB
Verdi	Escudier	23 June 72	It. OP	
*Faccio	G. Ricordi	23 June 72	It. RI	
Verdi	Faccio	25 June 72	It. CM	ON
*Faccio	G. Ricordi	27 June 72	It. RI	
*G. Ricordi	Verdi	27 June 72	It. SA	
Verdi	G. Ricordi	28 June 72	It. RI	
*G. Ricordi	Verdi	8 July 72	It. SA	
Verdi	G. Ricordi	8 July 72	It. RI	
*Tornaghi	Verdi	11 July 72	It. SA	
Verdi	Piroli	16 July 72	It. AC	
*Faccio	G. Ricordi	22 July 72	It. RI	
Giuseppina Verdi	G. Ricordi	22 July 72	It. HS	
Verdi	G. Ricordi	27 July 72	It. RI	
*Verdi	Escudier	7 Aug. 72	It. OP	
Verdi	Torelli	22 Aug. 72	It. LP	MQK
*Tornaghi	Verdi	24 Aug. 72	It. SA	
Verdi	Halanzier-Dufrenoy	24 Aug. 72	?? (P)	
Verdi	G. Ricordi	26/28 Aug. 72	It. RI	
*Verdi	T. Ricordi	28 Aug. 72	It. RI	
Verdi	Arrivabene	29 Aug. 72	It. ? (C)	WE-OS
Verdi	Magnani	2 Sep. 72	It. ? (F)	
Verdi	Torelli	13 Sep. 72	It. LP	
*Verdi	Torelli	19 Sep. 72	It. LP	
Verdi	T. Ricordi	4 Oct. 72	It. RI	
Verdi	T. Ricordi	7 Oct. 72	It. RI	
Verdi	De Sanctis	7 Oct. 72	It. ? (B)	
*Verdi	Torelli	18 Oct. 72	It. LP	
*Verdi	T. Ricordi	24 Oct. 72	It. RI	
*G. Ricordi	Giuseppina Verdi	1 Nov. 72	It. SA	
Verdi	Piroli	23 Nov. 72	It. AC	
*Faccio	G. Ricordi	26 Nov. 72	It. RI	
Verdi	Faccio	8 Dec. 72	It. ? (R)	
Verdi	G. Ricordi	12 Dec. 72	It. RI	
Verdi	Escudier	20 Dec. 72	It. OP	
*G. Ricordi	Giuseppina Verdi	25 Dec. 72	It. SA	

From	To	Date	Autograph	English Publication
*G. Ricordi	Verdi	25 Dec. 72	It. SA	
*Verdi	G. Ricordi	26 Dec. 72	It. RI	
Verdi	G. Ricordi	26 Dec. 72	It. RI	
Verdi	Arrivabene	29 Dec. 72	It. ? (C)	
Verdi	Maffei	29 Dec. 72	It. CH	WE-OS
Verdi	Du Locle	2 Jan. 73	It. OP	MQB
Verdi	T. Ricordi	3 Jan. 73	It. RI	WE
Verdi	G. Ricordi	14 Jan. 73	It. RI	
*Verdi	Escudier	18 Jan. 73	It. OP	
Verdi	Escudier	25 Jan. 73	It. OP	
Verdi	Baron ?	6 Feb. 73	It. PM	
*Verdi	G. Ricordi	16 Feb. 73	It. RI	
*Verdi	G. Ricordi	25 Feb. 73	It. RI	
Verdi	Du Locle	27 Feb. 73	It. OP	
*Verdi	G. Ricordi	8 Mar. 73	It. RI	
*Verdi	Du Locle	12 Mar. 73	It. OP	
Verdi	Escudier	20 Mar. 73	It. OP	
Verdi	Arrivabene	22 Mar. 73	It. ? (C)	
*Verdi	Piroli	30 Mar. 73	It. AC	
Verdi	Maffei	9 Apr. 73	It. BN	WE-OS
Verdi	Mayor of Naples	9 Apr. 73	It. ? (A)	
*Verdi	G. Ricordi	12 Apr. 73	It. RI	
Verdi	Arrivabene	16 Apr. 73	It. ? (C)	
*G. Ricordi	Verdi	30 Apr. 73	It. SA	
Verdi	G. Ricordi	2 May 73	It. RI	
Verdi	G. Ricordi	5 May 73	It. RI	
Verdi	G. Ricordi	23 May 73	It. SA	
Verdi	Cencetti	June 73	It. ? (P)	
Verdi	Du Locle	24 June 73	It. OP	MQB
Verdi	G. Ricordi	24 Aug. 73	It. RI	
*G. Ricordi	Verdi	27 Aug. 73	It. SA	
Verdi	G. Ricordi	31 Aug. 73	It. RI	
*G. Ricordi	Verdi	4 Sep. 73	It. SA	
Verdi	G. Ricordi	6 Sep. 73	It. RI	
Verdi	President in Trieste	6 Sep. 73	It. CM	WE-OS
Verdi	Du Locle	13 Sep. 73	It. OP	MQB
*Verdi	G. Ricordi	22 Sep. 73	It. RI	
*G. Ricordi	Verdi	25 Sep. 73	It. SA	
*Verdi	G. Ricordi	29 Sep. 73	It. RI	
*G. Ricordi	Verdi	2 Oct. 73	It. SA	
*Faccio	G. Ricordi	6 Oct. 73	It. RI	

From	To	Date	Autograph	English Publication
*Tornaghi	Verdi	24 Oct. 73	It. SA	
*Verdi	Tornaghi	25 Oct. 73	It. RI	
Verdi	Tornaghi	3 Nov. 73	It. RI	
*Muzio	Verdi	8 Nov. 73	It. SA	
*Verdi	G. Ricordi	9 Nov. 73	It. RI	
*Verdi	G. Ricordi	19 Nov. 73	It. RI	
*G. Ricordi	Verdi	20 Nov. 73	It. SA	
*Faccio	Tornaghi	20 Nov. 73	It. RI	
Verdi	G. Ricordi	21 Nov. 73	It. RI	
*Muzio	Verdi	22 Nov. 73*	It. SA	
*Faccio	Tornaghi	24 Nov. 73	It. RI	
*Muzio	Verdi	27 Nov. 73	It. SA	
Verdi	Faccio	29 Nov. 73	It. ? (R)	
Stolz	Verdi	5 Dec. 73	It. ? (B)	
Verdi	G. Ricordi	16 Dec. 73	It. RI	
Verdi	G. Ricordi	19 Dec. 73	It. RI	
*G. Ricordi	Verdi	21 Dec. 73	It. SA	
Verdi	G. Ricordi	23 Dec. 73	It. RI	
Verdi	G. Ricordi	26 Dec. 73	It. RI	
Verdi	G. Ricordi	28 Dec. 73	It. RI	
Verdi	G. Ricordi	23 Jan. 74	It. RI	
Verdi	De Sanctis (Telegram)	17 Feb. 74	It. AC	
Verdi	Terziani	Feb. 74	It. ? (X)	
Verdi	G. Ricordi	25 Feb. 74	It. RI	
Verdi	Waldmann	27 Feb. 74	It. GB	
Stolz	Verdi	28 Feb. 74	It. ? (B)	
Verdi	De Sanctis (Telegram)	1 Mar. 74	It. AC	
Verdi	T. Ricordi	1 Mar. 74	It. RI	WE-OS
Verdi	G. Ricordi	1 Mar. 74	It. RI	
Verdi	T. Ricordi	4 Mar. 74	It. RI	
Verdi	T. Ricordi	6 Mar. 74	It. RI	
*T. Ricordi	Verdi	7 Mar. 74	It. SA	
Verdi	Escudier	7 Mar. 74	It. OP	OS
Verdi	T. Ricordi	8 Mar. 74	It. RI	
Verdi	T. Ricordi	11 Mar. 74	It. RI	WE-OS
*Tornaghi	Verdi	13 Mar. 74	It. SA	
Verdi	T. Ricordi	Mar. 74	It. ? (X)	
Verdi	Waldmann	14 Mar. 74	It. GB	
Verdi	Piroli	16 Apr. 74	It. AC	
Verdi	G. Ricordi	16 Apr. 74	It. RI	

From	To	Date	Autograph	English Publication
Giuseppina Verdi	De Sanctis	6 May 74	It. ? (B)	
Verdi	G. Ricordi	1 July 74	It. RI	
Verdi	Arrivabene	21 July 74	It. ? (C)	WE
Verdi	Arrivabene	15 Aug. 74	It. ? (C)	
Verdi	Luccardi	18 Aug. 74	It. IA	
Verdi	Escudier	30 Sep. 74	It. OP	
Verdi	Tornaghi	10 Oct. 74	It. RI	
Verdi	G. Ricordi	20 Oct. 74	It. RI	
Verdi	G. Ricordi	18 Nov. 74	It. RI	
Verdi	Piroli	21 Nov. 74	It. AC	
Verdi	G. Ricordi	16 Dec. 74	It. RI	
*Verdi	G. Ricordi	20 Dec. 74	It. RI	
Verdi	Waldmann	26 Dec. 74	It. GB	
Verdi	Pedrotti	1 Jan. 75	It. ? (A)	
Verdi	G. Ricordi	2 Jan. 75	It. RI	
Verdi	G. Ricordi	3 Jan. 75	It. RI	
Verdi	G. Ricordi	4 Jan. 75	It. RI	
Verdi	Waldmann	9 Jan. 75	It. GB	
Verdi	T. Ricordi	25 Jan. 75	It. RI	
Verdi	Usiglio	26 Jan. 75	It. ? (B)	
Verdi	G. Ricordi	26 Jan. 75	It. RI	
*Verdi	G. Ricordi	13 Feb. 75	It. RI	
Verdi	Piroli	24 Feb. 75	It. AC	
Verdi	G. Ricordi	27 Feb. 75	It. RI	
Verdi	Waldmann	27 Feb. 75	It. GB	
Verdi	G. Ricordi	3 Mar. 75	It. RI	
Verdi	G. Ricordi	21 Mar. 75	It. RI	
*Verdi	Luccardi	21 Mar. 75	It. AC	
*Verdi	Ghislanzoni	24 Mar. 75	It. IA	
Verdi	G. Ricordi	25 Mar. 75	It. RI	WE-ON
*Verdi	G. Ricordi	26 Mar. 75	It. RI	
Verdi	G. Ricordi	30 Mar. 75	It. RI	
Verdi	G. Ricordi	4 Apr. 75	It. RI	WE
Verdi	Piroli	6 May 75	It. AC	
Verdi	G. Ricordi	25 May 75	It. RI	
Verdi	Waldmann	5 June 75	It. GB	
Verdi	Arrivabene	16 July 75	It. ? (C)	WE-OS
*Faccio	Tornaghi	28 Sep. 75	It. RI	
*Faccio	Tornaghi	6 Oct. 75	It. RI	
Verdi	Escudier	28 Dec. 75	It. OP	
*Verdi	Escudier	20 Jan. 76	It. OP	

From	To	Date	Autograph	English Publication
Verdi	Maffei	30 Jan. 76	It. BN	WE-OS
Verdi	Arrivabene	5 Feb. 76	It. ? (C)	WE-OS
*Verdi	G. Ricordi	12 Feb. 76	It. RI	
*Verdi	G. Ricordi	29 Feb. 76	It. RI	
Verdi	Escudier	12 Mar. 76	It. OP	
Verdi	Arrivabene	15 Mar. 76	It. ? (C)	
Verdi	Perrin	23 Mar. 76	It. ? (X)	
Giuseppina Verdi	De Sanctis	4 Apr. 76	It. AC	
Verdi	Escudier	16 Apr. 76	It. ? (B)	
Verdi	Escudier	16 Apr. 76	It. OP	
Giuseppina Verdi	G. Ricordi	22 Apr. 76	It. RI	
*Giuseppina Verdi	Corticelli	22 Apr. 76	It. SC	
*Muzio	Evers	26 Apr. 76	It. CR	
Verdi	Piroli	28 Apr. 76	It. AC	
Verdi	T. and G. Ricordi	28 Apr. 76	It. RI	
Verdi	T. Ricordi	17 May 76	It. ? (X)	
Verdi	Escudier	19 May 76	It. OP	
Verdi	T. Ricordi	20 May 76	It. RI	
Verdi	T. Ricordi	24 May 76	It. RI	
Verdi	T. Ricordi	30 May 76	It. RI	
Verdi	T. Ricordi	3 June 76	It. RI	
*Muzio	Evers	8 June 76	It. CR	
Verdi	Escudier	20 June 76	It. OP	
Verdi	Maffei	1 July 76	It. BN	
Verdi	Waldmann	10 July 76	It. GB	
Verdi	Escudier	10 July 76	It. OP	
*Verdi	Ghislanzoni	3 Aug. 76	It. IA	
Verdi	Escudier	21 Jan. 77	It. OP	WE
Verdi	Waldmann	9 Mar. 77	It. GB	
Verdi	Waldmann	10 Mar. 77	It. GB	
Verdi	T. Ricordi	10 Mar. 77	It. RI	OS
Verdi	Waldmann	14 Apr. 77	It. GB	
Verdi	G. Ricordi	5 Oct. 77	It. RI	WE
*Verdi	Monaldi	5 Dec. 77	It. IA	
Verdi	Arrivabene	8 Feb. 78	It. ? (C)	
Verdi	G. Ricordi	12 Mar. 78	It. RI	
Stolz	Verdi and Giuseppina V.	18 Mar. 78	It. ? (B)	
Verdi	Maffei	19 Mar. 78	It. ? (G)	

From	To	Date	Autograph	English Publication
Verdi	Dennery	19 June 78	Fr. OP	
*Verdi	Dennery	9 July 78	Fr. OP	
*Verdi	Dennery	23 July 78	Fr. OP	
*Verdi	Ghislanzoni	26 Dec. 78	It. IA	
Verdi	Maffei	21 Feb. 79	It. CH	WE-OS
Verdi	Orchestral Society	4 Apr. 79	It. ? (A)	WE-OS
Verdi	G. Ricordi	2 May 79	It. RI	
Verdi	Maffei	2 May 79	It. CH	
Verdi	Muzio	7 Oct. 79	It. ? (A)	WE-OS
Verdi	Hiller	Oct. 79	It. ? (X)	
Verdi	Piroli	8 Nov. 79	It. AC	
Verdi	Hiller	11 Nov. 79	It. HA	
Vaucorbeil	Verdi	18 Nov. 79	·Fr. ? (Z)	
Verdi	Vaucorbeil	24 Nov. 79	Fr. ? (Z)	
Verdi	Vaucorbeil	4 Jan. 80	Fr. ? (Z)	
Verdi	Hiller	7 Jan. 80	It. HA	
*Verdi	Ghislanzoni	13 Jan. 80	It. IA	
Verdi	Vaucorbeil	31 Jan. 80	Fr. ? (Z)	
Verdi	Piroli	10 Feb. 80	It. AC	
Verdi	Maffei	7 Mar. 80	It. BN	
*Stolz	Evers	13 Mar. 80	It. SC	
Verdi	Waldmann	20 Mar. 80	It. GB	
Verdi	Maffei	24 Mar. 80	It. BN	
*Stolz	Evers	25 Mar. 80	It. SC	
Verdi	Piroli	26 Mar. 80	It. AC	
Verdi	Hiller	27 Mar. 80	It. GK	
Du Locle	Editor of *L'Italie*	28 Mar. 80	Fr. (B)	
Du Locle	Marie Du Locle	Undated	Fr. OP	
*Verdi	G. Ricordi	9 Apr. 80	It. RI	
*Verdi	Tornaghi	13 Jan. 81	It. RI	
Verdi	G. Ricordi	21 Feb. 81	It. RI	
Nuitter	Verdi	13 May 82	Fr. ? (A)	
Verdi	Bottesini	4 Mar. 83	It. CM	
Verdi	G. Ricordi	26 Dec. 83	It. RI	WE
Verdi	Arrivabene	10 June 84	It. ? (C)	WE-OS
Verdi	Ritt	24 Mar. 87	Fr. ? (Z)	
Verdi	G. Ricordi	9 Jan. 89	It. RI	
Du Locle	Verdi	3 Dec. 91	Fr. ? (A)	
Verdi	Du Locle	9 Dec. 91	It. ? (A)	

INTRODUCTION

The artist who represents his country and his
time becomes necessarily universal in the
present and in the future.

Giuseppe Verdi to Domenico Morelli[1]

"This opera is certainly not one of my worst," Verdi wrote[2] with admirable
modesty following the European premiere of *Aida* at La Scala in 1872. A
hundred years later this noble work is still one of Verdi's greatest gifts to all
whose lives are enriched by his art.

Thomas Mann observed that some humans have an instinctive sense of their
own longevity and, therefore, take more time for their achievements than their
less fortunate fellows. Certainly Verdi took a remarkably long time to achieve
artistic maturity. His early works are permeated with the characteristics of the
so-called bel canto opera — in which Rossini, Bellini, and Donizetti all too
often did not care to remember Mozart's rich orchestration, reduced the libretto to providing a pretext for beautiful melodies, and the singer to a laryngal
athlete. From these restricted beginnings, Verdi — aware of the dramatic
potential of opera and the growth of orchestral polyphony in his time —
gradually developed his distinctive style. *Aida* represents this fulfillment and
the first step toward the solitary heights of *Otello* and *Falstaff*.

The correspondence concerning *Aida* extends from 1868 to 1891. In its
early stages it kept the mails and wires — which functioned with enviable
speed and dependability in those days — very busy between St. Agata or
Genoa, and Paris, Cairo, Milan, or a little village above Lake Como. After the
initial productions of *Aida* in Cairo, Milan, Parma, Padua, and Naples, the
letters pertaining to the opera were not as frequent, since Verdi was then
occupied with the *Requiem* and, later with *Otello* and *Falstaff*. None of his
works, however, evoked as much correspondence over as many years.

A drama unfolds in the following pages which at times seems like a very
human comedy fraught with emotions and errors. Set against a background of

politics and backstage intrigues of every conceivable kind, a large cast of characters revolves around Verdi, who stands fast, neither proud nor humble, as he had said of himself.[3] Yet even he, in rare instances, gives in to compromise and has no other choice but to join the *risata final* of his own *Falstaff*.

Five major personalities, in addition to Verdi, emerge as the principals and dominate the action of the drama at various times: Auguste Mariette, Camille Du Locle, Antonio Ghislanzoni, Paul Draneht, and Giulio Ricordi. They enter and leave the stage at given times, but the presence of Giulio Ricordi is always felt. Several no less prominent *dramatis personae* — particularly Verdi's wife, Giuseppina, the conductor Franco Faccio, and the singers Teresa Stolz and Maria Waldmann — play active roles in certain scenes; and some of Verdi's closest friends, although not always directly involved with the action, receive his meditations on the pathos of life and death and on the events of his times. The rest of the cast is made up of a variety of individuals, most in pursuit of selfish interests and ambitions. The remarkable series of events begins in Egypt in 1868 and reaches a climax with the European premiere of *Aida* in Milan in 1872, a glorious summit with Verdi's final victory at the Paris Opéra in 1880, and a tranquil end in his winter quarters at Genoa in 1891.

In a letter to the conductor Michael Costa dated 6 July 1867 [4], Verdi revealed his state of mind at a critical time in his life: "I had planned to write you sooner, in order to thank you for the great care given the production of *Don Carlos* in London, but tragic family circumstances[5] prevented me from doing so. You will probably be surprised that I am writing you a letter, for the first time in so many years, when I should have written you several times for my other productions. But at that time, in the midst of my career, I refrained from doing so because I feared a letter of sincere admiration for you might be confused with the kind that many others usually write, scattering incense to obtain assistance and protection. Now that this career has ended, or almost, such doubts melt away, and this perhaps mistaken pride of mine is gone. You, whom I know to be as great an artist as a man of upstanding character, will understand this pride and will not be shocked by it."

"Now that this career has ended, or almost . . ." How amazing that Giuseppe Verdi could write such words three summers before he embarked on *Aida* and twenty-five years before he finished *Falstaff*! When he wrote that letter to Costa, four months after the ill-fated premiere of *Don Carlos* in Paris, Verdi was fifty-four years old. The objections of the Catholic Church, as represented by the Spanish-born Empress Eugénie, and other circumstances contributed to the unfavorable reception at the Opéra, and Verdi was even accused of imitating Richard Wagner. He never wrote for the Opéra in Paris again. And he had ample reason to despise the theatre per se, where he had known more than his share of frustrations and humiliations. His "years on the galleys," when he had to compose for a living, were past. Despite the bitter experience of *Don Carlos* in Paris, Verdi stood at the height of a firmly established career, a wealthy and independent man, reluctant to involve himself in the theatre any longer, and ready to retire to his farm for the rest of his days. He had earned his privacy. His pride and his humility — to which he himself would not admit — made him prefer talking to his trees at St. Agata to showing himself in public. At work in his fields he could even forget the *maledetta musica* — a curse he had uttered in a letter to Léon Escudier on 8 February 1856.[6] What made him return to the stage?

La Forza del Destino, it seems, played a decisive role in the composer's destiny. After the debacle of *Don Carlos* at the Opéra, Verdi appeared to be determined to settle a score and set out to prove his point by personally supervising every phase and detail in the preparation of his revision of *La Forza* at La Scala. The success of this production, which opened on 27 February 1869, must have restored his faith in the ultimate victory of his unflinching battle for integrity and perfection in all elements of the musical drama. The Leonora of this performance, Teresa Stolz, a thirty-five-year-old soprano from Bohemia, would be Verdi's first Aida in the same opera house and an intimate friend until his death. Formerly she had lived with Verdi's close friend, the conductor Angelo Mariani, to whom she was engaged to be married. In *The Man Verdi* Frank Walker — more thoroughly and impartially than any other biographer — investigates the sad and complicated story of Verdi's break with Mariani, his later infatuation with Teresa Stolz, and his wife's reactions to this relationship.

Also complicated and confusing were Italy's manifold political struggles — from the country's Risorgimento to the end of the Church State on 20 September 1870 and the proclamation of Rome as the capital of the finally united kingdom under Victor Emanuel II. On the European scene of the time the destinies of Italy and France were largely interdependent. When the Second Empire collapsed after France's defeat at Sedan in 1870 and more bloodshed followed in a civil war, no one could have been more keenly and more passionately afflicted than Giuseppe Verdi, who rose from Italian patriot to citizen of the world. A thoroughly practical and modern man, rather than the stereotype of a romantic genius, he was fully aware of scientific and technical progress, which he applied to his farm.

The war in France was to postpone the world premiere of *Aida* in Cairo and, consequently, the European premiere at La Scala. For *Aida*, however, this tragedy turned out to be a blessing, because it enabled Verdi to make improvements in the score, to orchestrate it with leisure, and to plan its production with care. In the midst of these delays he was urged to succeed Saverio

Mercadante as the director of the conservatory in Naples, the most reputable in Italy. Realizing that theory and academic life were not for him, he refused. But later he reluctantly agreed to preside over a government commission established for the reform of the conservatories and professional orchestras.

Verdi did not like to leave his farm at St. Agata, although he was attracted to the circle of congenial friends and other charms that a city like Naples had to offer. He was a peasant of the North. And if he left his native soil of the Po Valley in the cold and foggy winter for a comfortable apartment in Genoa, he did so mainly, if not solely, for the sake of his wife. Except for occasional vacations in Paris, Cauterets (a spa in the Pyrenees), Tabiano (a spa in the Appenine hills not far from St. Agata), and, later, in Montecatini, most of his travels were dictated by professional considerations and were limited to cities in Italy and to Paris, London, St. Petersburg, Madrid, Vienna, and Cologne.

A positive aspect of the *Don Carlos* premiere in Paris was Verdi's friendship with Camille Du Locle who collaborated on the French libretto for the opera. About to become co-director of the Opéra-Comique in July 1870, Du Locle tried to persuade Verdi to write for his theatre. It was not meant to be, but *Aida* was born in the meantime. Some phases of the opera's genesis are still shrouded in mystery. The correspondence proves, however, that Du Locle was instrumental in the realization of unusual ideas and actions by two other key figures: Ismail Pasha, the Khedive and Viceroy of Egypt, who remained remote and lofty behind the walls of his exotic palace in Cairo or on the Nile with his harem; and the eminent French Egyptologist, Auguste Mariette, who created the original plot, sets, and costumes. Like his friend Du Locle, Mariette was a dreamer, and he was easily pushed aside by the powerful intendant Paul Draneht, who bought prima donnas and milk cows for the Khedive in Europe. Their letters tell much of the story. But two recent publications[7] inform us of all that is known about the sad circumstances that, in 1876, caused Verdi to initiate legal procedures against Du Locle to secure repayment of a substantial loan.

For the Khedive's Italian opera house in Cairo, built by Italian architects and inaugurated in 1869 by an Italian company, Verdi wanted to write an Italian opera. For this reason he asked Antonio Ghislanzoni to furnish Italian lyrics based on Mariette's original French outline and Du Locle's scenario. As Verdi's letters to Ghislanzoni reveal, a great deal more had to be done in the four months of their collaboration.

The letters and documents telling the story of this masterwork should not only set some records straight but also open a few new vistas. The correspondence begins with a few lines from Verdi to Du Locle at a time when the veteran composer could not have imagined the consequences of his friend's voyage to Egypt with Auguste Mariette as his guide.

NOTES

1. A Neapolitan painter (1826–1901) to whom Verdi wrote these lines in a letter of 27 February 1871 (Photocopy of autograph: Istituto di Studi Verdiani, Parma).

2. In his letter to Opprandino Arrivabene of 9 February 1872.

3. In his letter to Cesare De Sanctis of 29 April 1855 (Luzio, *Carteggi*, vol. I, pp. 31–32, and vol. IV, p. 94).

4. Photocopy of autograph: Istituto di Studi Verdiana, Parma.

5. After Carlo Verdi, the composer's father, had died at Vidalenzo near Busseto on 14 January 1867, Antonio Barezzi, Giuseppe Verdi's benefactor and first wife's father, was, after a prolonged illness, near death.

6. Photocopy of autograph: Istituto di Studi Verdiana, Parma.

7. Ursula Günther, "Zur Entstehung von Verdi's *Aida*," and "Der Briefwechsel Verdi-Nuitter-Du Locle zur Revision des *Don Carlos*," Gabriella Carrara Verdi and Ursula Günther, eds.

VERDI'S *AIDA*
THE HISTORY OF AN OPERA
IN LETTERS
AND
DOCUMENTS

LETTERS

Verdi to Camille Du Locle [1]

Genoa, 19 February 1868

Dear Du Locle,

I am very glad to have just received your letter from Thebes and to know that you are safe and sound and pleased with your voyage. I am writing to you immediately in Paris so that if you arrive on the <u>20th</u>, as you say you will, this letter of mine may be among the first to reach you; let me cordially take your hand and tell you <u>welcome home</u>. When we see each other, you must describe all the events of your voyage, the wonders you have seen, and the beauty and ugliness of a country which once had a greatness and a civilization I have never been able to admire. [. . .]

1. Auguste Mariette had collected material for a short story — *La Fiancée du Nil* — during an archaeological trip through Upper Egypt in 1866. Quite possibly during Mariette's visit to Paris for the Exposition in 1867 and during Camille Du Locle's voyage to Egypt in 1868, the two discussed this plot for the operatic stage. See Verdi's letter to Giulio Ricordi of 25 June 1870, Document I, and Ursula Günther, "Zur Entstehung von Verdis *Aida*," *Studi Musicali* (Firenze: Leo S. Olschki Editore, 1973), Anno II, n. 1 pp. 15–71.

Verdi to Paul Draneht [1]

Genoa, 9 August 1869

Monsieur le Bey,

I am aware that a new theatre will be opened in Cairo on the solemn occasion which will celebrate the cut through the Isthmus of Suez.

Although I deeply appreciate that you, Monsieur le Bey, wanted to give me the honor of writing a hymn to mark the date of the opening, I regret that I must decline this honor, because of the number of my current activities and because it is not my custom to compose <u>occasional</u> pieces. [. . .]

1. Paul Draneht, general manager of the Cairo Opera, whose original letter to Verdi is missing. This response was drafted in French by Verdi's wife, Giuseppina.

Verdi to Camille Du Locle [1]

Genoa, 8 December 1869

[. . .] *Hélas*, it is neither the labor of writing an opera nor the judgment of the Parisian public that holds me back but rather the certainty of not being able to have my music performed in Paris the way I want it. It is quite singular that an author must always see his ideas frustrated and his conceptions distorted! In your opera houses — I say this without the slightest sarcasm — there are too many know-it-alls! Everyone wants to judge according to their own ideas, their own tastes, and, what is worse, according to a system, without taking into account the character and individuality of the author. Everyone wants to express an opinion, to voice a doubt; and the author who lives in that atmosphere of doubt for any length of time cannot help but be somewhat shaken in his convictions and end up revising, adjusting, or, to put it more precisely, ruining his work. In this way one ultimately finds in one's hands not a unified opera but a mosaic; and beautiful as it may be, it is still a mosaic. You will argue that the Opéra has produced a string of masterpieces in this manner. You may call them masterpieces all you want, but permit me to say that they would be much more perfect if the patchwork and the adjustments were not felt all the time. Certainly no one will deny genius to Rossini. Nevertheless, in spite of all his genius, in *Guillaume Tell* one detects this fatal atmosphere of the Opéra; and several times, although less frequently than with other authors, one feels that there is too much here, too little there, and that the musical flow is not as free and secure as in the *Barbiere*. By this I don't mean to disapprove of what you people do; I only mean to tell you that it is absolutely impossible for me to subject myself again to the Caudine Yokes [2] of your theatres, when I know that a true success is not possible for me unless I write as I feel, free from any influence and without considering that I am writing for Paris rather than for the world of the moon. Furthermore, the artists would have to sing not in their fashion but in mine; the entire company, "which also in Paris has a great deal of ability," [3] should have just as much good will; everything should depend on me, after all, and only one will should dominate everything: my own. This may seem somewhat tyrannical; perhaps it is. But if the work is unified, the idea is ONE, and everything must converge to form this ONE. Perhaps you will say that nothing bars the way to obtaining all this in Paris. No. In Italy one can have it, at least I always can; in France, no. If, for example, I present myself in the foyer of an Italian theatre with a new opera, no one dares express an opinion of it, or a judgment, before having understood it well; and no one ever ventures ridiculous questions. They respect the work and the author, and they let the public decide. In the foyer of the Opéra, on the contrary, after four chords they whisper all over the place: *"Olà, ce n'est pas bon . . . c'est commun . . . c'est n'est pas de bon goût . . . ça n'ira pas à Paris!"* What do such poor words as *commun . . . bon goût . . . Paris* mean, if you are dealing with a work of art that must be universal!

The conclusion of all this is that I am not a composer for Paris. I do not know if I have the talent, but I do know that my ideas in matters of art are quite different from yours. I believe in <u>inspiration,</u> you in <u>workmanship.</u> I am willing to discuss your criterion, but I need the <u>enthusiasm</u> you lack in feeling and in judging.

I want <u>art</u> in any of its manifestations, not the <u>arrangement,</u> the <u>artifice,</u> and the <u>system</u> that you prefer. Am I wrong? Am I right? However it may be, I am right in saying that my ideas are quite different from yours; and I add that my backbone isn't as flexible as those of many others, so that I shall not yield and deny my convictions, which are most profound and deeply rooted. Also, I would very much regret writing an opera for you, my dear Du Locle, which you would perhaps have to put aside after one or two dozen performances, as Perrin[4] did with *Don Carlos.* If I were some twenty years younger, I would tell you: "Let's see if, later, your theatrical affairs take a turn and conform more with my ideas." But time is passing rapidly, and for now it's impossible to understand each other, unless something unforeseen happens, which I cannot imagine. If you should come here, as you have caused my wife to hope, we shall speak further of this and at length;[5] if you don't come, it's probable that I'll make my way to Paris at the end of February.[6]

If you should come to Genoa, we could no longer offer you <u>ravioli</u> because we no longer have our Genoese cook; but at any rate, you won't die of hunger, and — this much is certain — you will find two friends who are very fond of you and to whom your presence will be the greatest gift. [. . .]

1. On 1 November 1869, before the opening of the Suez Canal on 17 November 1869, the theatre in Cairo was inaugurated with a performance of Verdi's *Rigoletto*, conducted by Emanuele Muzio, the composer's former student and close friend. At the same time Du Locle was pleading with Verdi to write another opera for Paris. At the Opéra, Verdi's *Jérusalem* (a revision of *I Lombardi alla Prima Crociata*) had been premiered in 1847, *Les Vêpres Siciliennes* in 1855, and *Don Carlos* in 1867. At the Théâtre-Lyrique Verdi's second version of *Macbeth* had been produced in 1865

2. At the Caudine Forks, two narrow passes in the southern Apennines, the Roman army was defeated by the Samnites in 321 B.C. and suffered the humiliation of having to file below a yoke.

3. Verdi seems to quote from a missing letter Du Locle had written him.

4. Emile Perrin, Director of the Opéra.

5. On Christmas Eve 1869, Verdi wrote to Du Locle: "You will find me at the port of Genoa, where I shall receive you with open arms." (Autograph: Bibliothèque de l'Opéra, Paris) Thus we may assume that Du Locle arrived in Genoa (via Marseilles or Nice) before the end of the year 1869. During this visit Du Locle, quite possibly, brought Verdi an invitation to write an opera for Egypt. See Verdi's letter to Giulio Ricordi of 25 June 1870 and Günther, p. 24.

6. In spite of Du Locle's visit in Genoa, Verdi and his wife went to Paris, but not until 26 March 1870. See Verdi's letter to Du Locle on the same date.

Emanuele Muzio to Giulio Ricordi[1]

Cairo, 7 January 1870

Dearest friend,

    [. . .] Here they change their minds from one moment to the next. [. . .]

    The season proceeds very well, but since H.H.[2] has left for Upper Egypt, taking his harem along, the theatre is not very much frequented; he will be back in eight days, and so we shall see the theatre repopulated. On New Year's Eve we had a fire in the theatre, right in the clock,[3] which was suddenly all aflame. The firemen, pumps, and water arrived at once; otherwise the fire would have spread to the roof and destroyed the whole theatre.[4] The fright of the audience, artists, choristers, and ballet is not easily described. Scared wives and husbands rushed to the stage; but about an hour later the performance was resumed, and it ended before empty seats because there was no audience left.

1. Verdi's music publisher in Milan.
2. Abbreviation for His Highness, the Viceroy of Egypt. Mariette's reference in French is S.A. for Son Altesse. At this time the Viceroy was Ismail Pasha, who was born in Cairo on 31 December 1830 and on whom the Sultan of Turkey bestowed the title Khedive, i.e., August, in 1869. The son of Ibrahim Pasha (an adventurous Turkish potentate, warrior, and statesman) and the nephew of Said Pasha (who ruled Egypt from 1843 to 1863), Ismail was educated in Paris. On his return to Egypt in 1849 he was entrusted by his uncle with important missions to the Pope, to Napoleon III, and to the Sultan of Turkey. In 1861 he led an army of 14,000 men to suppress an insurgence of slaves in the Sudan. This recurring hostility with the Ethiopians may have contributed to his decision to have the story of *Aida* made into an opera.
    At the death of Said Pasha on 18 January 1863 Ismail Pasha became his uncle's successor as Viceroy, with fourteen wives and countless concubines. As an autocrat with extravagant ideas and ambitious plans for the progress of his country, he modernized and enlarged commerce and industry, reformed and augmented Egypt's political administration, its courts, schools, and universities, and brought his country to the attention of the world with the inauguration of the Suez Canal. He assisted the eminent Egyptologist Auguste Mariette in founding and directing a museum for the preservation of Egyptian antiquity; and under his direct orders the Cairo Opera was built by Italian architects in only six months. "My country is no longer in Africa," he once said. "I have made it part of Europe."
    The prominent critic Filippo Filippi, in *Musica e Musicisti* (Milano: Libreria Editrice G. Brigola, 1876), pp. 378–80, describes Ismail Pasha as "a small man, chubby like all Turks, dragging his feet slightly when he walks. His face is alert, gentle, with tiny eyes which do not stare, but speak volumes. . . . He spoke with animation about Italian music, the Cairo theatre, and the artists, saying very sensible things. He referred to Verdi with pride, as an inferior speaking of a superior, with unlimited deference and gratitude."
    Under Ismail's reign, the Egyptian cotton market profited considerably as a result of the American Civil War; and during the Franco-Prussian War, Egypt was to remain neutral. Ismail's love of splendor and luxury, however, and his ambitious though irresponsible undertakings were to destroy the economy of his country. In 1876 the European powers intervened in the affairs of the bankrupt nation by putting Egypt under joint French and British control. On 26 June 1879 Ismail Pasha was forced to abdicate; and four days later he sailed with his harem to Naples, where the King of Italy offered him residence. The former Khedive was permitted to end his days in

Constantinople, where he died on 2 March 1895. In spite of his abdication, Ismail was interred in Cairo.

3. The clock above the proscenium, a common feature in Italian theatres.

4. One hundred and one years later, on 28 October 1971, the Cairo theatre was totally destroyed by fire.

Verdi to Camille Du Locle

Genoa, 23 January 1870

Most Wretched Du Locle!

You have forgotten to send me Wagner's literary writings. You know that I also want to acquaint myself with this side [of the man], and so I ask you to do what you haven't done. [. . .] I continue to think that Nero might be a subject for a grand opera, done in my own way, of course. It would thus be impossible at the Opéra but most possible here. [. . .]

Verdi to Giulio Ricordi

[Genoa,] 3 February [1870]

[. . .] In writing an opera it is not the labor of composition that burdens me; it is the difficulty of finding a subject to my liking, a poet to my liking, and a performance to my liking that holds me back![1]

And, on the other hand, where to write? In France? Poor me! Every time I have set foot in those theatres I have had a fever. I don't know what would happen now that I am more difficult. [. . .]

1. As early as 1 January 1853 Verdi had written to his friend Cesare De Sanctis in Naples: "I should like nothing better than to find a good libretto and with it a good poet (we have such need of one!), but I cannot hide from you that I read with great reluctance the libretti that are sent to me. It is impossible, or almost impossible, for another to sense what I want. I want subjects that are *new, great, beautiful, varied, bold* . . . and bold to the core, with *new forms*, yet at the same time appropriate for music. . . ." Trans. Philip Gossett, "Verdi, Ghislanzoni, and *Aida*: the Uses of Convention," *Critical Inquiry*, 1 (Dec. 1974), p. 291.

Giulio Ricordi to Giuseppina Verdi

Milan, 10 February 1870

[. . .] We live now with the sweet dream that no insurmountable difficulty will fatally prevent the realization of so many beautiful hopes. And I turn to you, Signora Peppina, so that you may help and advise me in this. With an ally like you, I am sure to win everything. Art needs Verdi. It cannot and must not live but for him, and each year that goes by [without his writing] is fatal to all of art — particularly to our poor Italy, to whom by now no other true glory is left. What I say pours spontaneously from my soul. I speak with an open heart, aside from any commercial consideration, which in this kind of thing, however, is fortunately tied to art itself. [. . .]

Verdi to Giulio Ricordi

Genoa, 14 February 1870

[. . .] A drama for music is quite difficult! The more I think about it, the more the obstacles increase. It is certainly not impossible to find a historical event appropriate for a musical setting, but the difficulty lies in grafting the drama or the action to the event. [. . .]

Verdi to Camille Du Locle

Genoa, 18 February 1870

[. . .] The bad weather continues, and consequently my coming to Paris will be delayed because of necessity I must first go to St. Agata.[1]

And what are you doing now? Are you relaxed? And how long will it last? And are you well established at the Opéra-Comique? Are you content with it? We shall talk about these little things at length and in great detail in Paris. [. . .]

1. To care for his farm.

Emanuele Muzio to Giulio Ricordi

Cairo, 5 March 1870

Dear friend,

[. . .] There are many employees in the administration of the theatre but no order whatever. [. . .] This morning I told the Bey [Draneht] that I shall positively leave for Paris on the 19th. I would have come to Italy for a few weeks, but Verdi wrote me that in March he would be in Paris, so we shall meet there.[1] I have not decided whether to return to this city for the next season; I think I shall decide against it. [. . .]

1. The review La France Musicale of 3 April 1870 announced: "M. Muzzio[sic], the conductor of the Italian company in Cairo, has arrived in Paris."

Giulio Ricordi to Verdi

Milan, 11 March 1870

First of all I advise you that we have already written to Madrid twice to get the two plays you requested. They should arrive any day now, and I shall send them to you right away. [. . .]

In the meantime I commend myself daily to God and the devil, to the cherubs and seraphs, to Beelzebub and Baraoth that they may let us find the long-awaited plot. Should we really not pick one out? Must you be silent forever because of this insurmountable difficulty? Good heavens, no! Let heaven and earth come to our aid. Our poor theatre would be dead. Art, the country, the whole world are in need of you. Only Verdi can give life to art! For goodness sake, don't let it die! What would be left to us? I realize this is a little selfish on our part. But vices stand next to virtues! And where do you find perfection? [. . .]

Verdi to Camille Du Locle

Genoa, 26 March 1870

Dear Du Locle,

Two words to tell you that tonight I'll embark on the steamer for Nice and shall soon be in Paris. Upon my arrival in Marseilles I'll send a telegram to you and Léon[1] to inform you of the hour of my arrival. [. . .][2]

1. Léon Escudier, music publisher and opera producer in Paris.
2. Günther, pp. 16, 24, discusses the controversy concerning the length of Verdi's stay in Paris.

Emanuele Muzio to Giulio Ricordi

Paris, 15 April 1870

Dearest friend,

[. . .] Draneht Bey will leave that city [Cairo] on the 19th of the 20th of this month for Brindisi and from there for Naples and Milan; so you can see him in this city [Milan]. [. . .]

Egypt is the country of surprises; my wife and I left some of our health there, and next month we shall go to Verdi in Busseto to rest and recover. [. . .]

I don't see anybody but spend all my days with Verdi. I am sorry that he will leave us next week, but I'll follow him right away to St. Agata.[1] [. . .]

1. On 14 May 1870 Giuseppina Verdi wrote to Clarina Maffei, Verdi's close, lifelong friend in Milan: "In a few days Emanuele will arrive at St. Agata with his wife." (Autograph: Collezione Enrico Olmo, Chiari)

Verdi to Camille Du Locle [1]

Genoa, Saturday [23 April 1870]

Dear Du Locle,

I am dropping you this line simply to tell you that we arrived here last night after an excellent trip and to thank you very, very, very much for the many kindnesses extended to me during our short sojourn in Paris. [. . .]
On Tuesday we leave for St. Agata.

1. By the time of Verdi's visit to Paris, Mariette had probably written to Du Locle from Cairo about his story *La Fiancée du Nil*, which he had developed into an operatic plot. Mariette asked Du Locle to approach Verdi with an offer from the Viceroy to make this plot into an opera for Cairo. Unfortunately this particular correspondence between Mariette and Du Locle is missing as are other important letters from the preceding months. We assume that Du Locle approached Verdi with the Viceroy's offer in December 1869. (See note 5 p. 5) Du Locle again conveyed the Viceroy's offer to Verdi during the composer's visit to Paris, and Verdi again refused to accept it. He did not see the plot, and at that time he was not aware that Mariette had written it. (See Verdi's letter to Du Locle of 26 May 1870.) Du Locle's description of the Viceroy's project must have sounded too vague and fantastic to interest the Maestro, and Muzio's account of the first opera season in Egypt could not have made it any more attractive. Besides, Verdi was used to supervising personally the first productions of his operas, and he disliked the prospect of a sea voyage to Egypt. Meanwhile Du Locle repeated his own requests. About to become codirector of the Opéra-Comique in Paris, he asked Verdi to compose an opera for that theatre. In contrast to the Théâtre-Lyrique and the Opéra (*la grande boutique*, the big shop, as Verdi called it), the Opéra-Comique (*la petite boutique*, the little shop) seemed to promise a more favorable atmosphere for producing his works. On 12 April 1870 Verdi had written Giulio Ricordi: "In the other theatres everything is below mediocrity — except for the Opéra-Comique, which has a good chorus and, above all, a delightful orchestra." (Autograph: Archivio Ricordi, Milano) Upon his return to Italy, Verdi pursued Du Locle's plan for the Opéra-Comique, but he could not find any literary material to his liking.

Verdi to Camille Du Locle

Genoa, 25 April 1870

Dear Du Locle,

In the book *Etudes sur l'Espagne contemporaine* I read a report of a comedy by Lopez d'Ayala [1] which strikes me as being excellent for the Opéra-Comique. Look for the book, open it to page 199, and read beginning with "The first act takes place in the Basque provinces", etc., etc., until the end.

It is certainly difficult to judge from a report, but it seems to me that there is a plot there. If you share my opinion, find the comedy and have it translated. Tomorrow I leave for St. Agata. [. . .]

1. E. Adelardo López de Ayala (1828–79), Spanish playwright.

Auguste Mariette to Camille Du Locle

Boulaq,[1] 27 April 1870

My dear friend,

    I received your two letters.[2] I expected M. Verdi's refusal, which will rather annoy the Viceroy. But try to see our viewpoint. If M. Gounod accepts, we would be very happy. With regard to Prince P.,[3] I think that there are some clouds involved and that the Viceroy would only hesitatingly enter into an agreement.

    In the meantime I am sending you an outline. Don't be shocked by the fancy printing — I have no secretary. I wanted to have four sets of the manuscript copied out; that would have cost 100 francs.[4] So I had four copies printed for 40 francs. This typographical luxury is, therefore, quite a bonus and the result of economy. Consequently regard the enclosed copy as the most modest of manuscripts.[5]

    I need not tell you that the editing is mine. If I have intervened, it is, in the first place, because of the Viceroy's order and, in the second place, because of my belief that I could give the work true local color, which is the indispensable condition for an opera of this kind. Indeed I repeat to you that what the Viceroy wants is a purely ancient and Egyptian opera. The sets will be based on historical accounts; the costumes will be designed after the bas-reliefs of Upper Egypt. No effort will be spared in this respect, and the *mise-en-scène* will be as splendid as one can imagine. You know the Viceroy does things in a grand style. This care for preserving local color in the *mise-en-scène* obliges us, by the same token, to preserve it in the outline itself. In fact, there is a special phraseology for this — a frame of mind, an inspired note which only a thorough acquaintance with Egypt can provide. It is in this capacity that I have intervened and continue to intervene.

    Here, my dear friend, is where we stand.

    Now if the outline suits you, if you agree to write the libretto, if you find a composer, this is what must be done. You must write me that the subject in question is so archaeologically Egyptian and Egyptological that you cannot write the libretto without an advisor at your side at all times and that my presence in Paris is furthermore indispensable for the sets and costumes. I ask no more of you. If I could go to Paris this summer, my goal would be attained.

    It goes without saying that I am not bringing any kind of personal vanity into this matter and that you can change, turn around, and improve the outline as you see fit.

    I forgot to tell you that the Viceroy has read the outline, that he has completely approved it,[6] and that I am sending it to you by his order.

    Don't be alarmed by the title. *Aida* is an Egyptian name. Normally it would be *Aita*. But that name would be too harsh, and the singers would irresistibly soften it to *Aida*. Moreover I care no more for this name than for the other.

For the second scene of the second act and the chant of the priests there is in the *Ritual* a hymn to the sun which exudes poetry and local color. Perhaps it will inspire you.

I know my place, my dear friend, and I would be very happy if in my humble role I may have been able to show you from far away the road we must travel. For the rest I rely on your talent as a poet. With this I press your hand.

1. A suburb of Cairo. See biographical note on Auguste Mariette.
2. These two letters, obviously written during Verdi's stay in Paris, are missing.
3. Joseph Michael Xavier Poniatowski (1816–73), Polish singer and composer, great-nephew of Stanislas Augustus, King of Poland. He was born in Rome, composed a number of Italian operas for Italy, Paris, and London, became the Prince of Monterotondo, and followed his friend Emperor Napoleon III into exile in England.
4. At this time 100 French francs were the equivalent of 20 American dollars and 100 Italian lire.
5. See note 5, Document 1.
6. Note that Mariette mentions only the Viceroy's approval of the outline, not coauthorship. See Du Locle's letter to Verdi of 29 May 1870.

Auguste Mariette to Camille Du Locle [1]

[Cairo,] 28 April [1870]

My dear friend,

This instant I have left H.H., the Viceroy, to whom I have given your letter.

I shall not hide from you the fact that H.H. is extremely annoyed and chagrined by the idea of forgoing the collaboration of M. Verdi whose talent he holds in the highest esteem. [2]

Under the circumstances he makes the offer that rehearsals be held in Paris or in Milan, at the Maestro's choice; the artists of the Cairo Theatre would then receive the order to betake themselves wherever M. Verdi wishes. See if this plan might be agreeable. I have time to write you only these few words in order not to miss the mail.

P.S. One final word. If Maestro Verdi should not accept, H.H. asks you to knock at another door. [. . .] We are thinking of Gounod and even Wagner. If the latter should accept, he could do something grandiose.

1. Du Locle forwarded this letter to Verdi on 14 May 1870.
2. On 19 August 1867, during the Exposition in Paris, the Viceroy had attended a performance of *Don Carlos* at the Opéra. See Günther, p. 29.

Verdi to Clarina Maffei

St. Agata, 30 April 1870

Dear Clarina,

I am really, really at St. Agata,[1] and imagine how pleased I am. It hardly seems true that I may enjoy a little rest after all that noise and fatigue. What an infernal month! And to think that I still don't know for what, or why, I went to Paris! Just like the Picks [2] with their noses in the air and their mouths open, admiring the beauty of the city, which truly becomes more magnificent and lovely all the time. How many new things [have been built] in the two years I have not been there! I visited many theatres: nothing good in the opera houses, except for la Patti [3] who is marvelous. In the prose theatres, little of value. [. . .]

The Maestro [4] is not writing and has no desire to write. It may be, however, that he will do it later for the Opéra-Comique out of friendship for Du Locle, but it is very unlikely, very unlikely.

Sardou [5] told me, in no uncertain terms, that he could not authorize Faccio [6] to do *Patrie*. He's got it into his head that sooner or later he will do a libretto for the Opéra; and, what is strange, he pretends that I shall do the music. *"Bah!! mais oui, mais oui,"* added Perrin, who was present, *"cela doit être!"* [7] *Par exemple*! And there followed one of my long tirades against his *grande boutique* and his singers, etc., etc. All in vain! When they left me, they were convinced that I could not live without breathing the air of Paris or write music without *me fourrer dans la grande boutique*.[8]

Kiss the hand of our great man [9] for me.

Peppina is well, but dead of fatigue, and sends her greetings to you. [. . .]

1. In a letter to Filippo Filippi of 26 September 1865 (Autograph: Museo Teatrale alla Scala, Milano), Verdi wrote about the manor house he built in 1851–53 on his farm named after the hamlet of St. Agata: "Four walls to shield me from the sun and bad weather, a few dozen trees planted, for the most part by my own hand, a puddle, which I might dignify with the name of lake, if I had the water to fill it up with. . . . We never play or even discuss music at Sant'Agata, and you run the risk here of finding a piano which is not only out of tune, but has missing strings." (Franz Werfel and Paul Stefan, *Verdi — the Man in His Letters*, Edward Downes trans. [New York: L. B. Fischer, 1942], pp. 244–45.) Antonio Ghislanzoni, the librettist of *Aida*, describes St. Agata as follows: "Nature has bestowed no charms on this landscape. The plain rolls monotonously on. Rich for the countryman, poor for the poet. In the middle of a long avenue of poplars the eye, surprised and touched with melancholy, rests upon two weeping willows that flank a garden gate. The two giant trees, which would scarcely attract attention elsewhere, tease the mind here like some strange and unfamiliar spectacle. He who planted those trees at this spot can be no ordinary man. . . . He may even be a misanthrope, for a drawbridge furnishes the only communication between his property and the world. . . . If a genius inhabits this house, it must be a genius of pain and passion." (Werfel and Stefan, Barrows Mussey trans., pp. 60–61.)
2. Apparently comic characters of the time.
3. Adelina Patti (1843–1919), Italian soprano. Born in Madrid, she was raised in New York, where she made her operatic debut at the age of sixteen as Lucia di Lammermoor. Two years

later, in 1861, she made a successful debut at Covent Garden in London, where she sang regularly until 1886, including a performance as the first Aida in England in 1876. At the same time she appeared throughout Europe, in Russia, and in South America. Between 1882 and 1885 Mme. Patti toured with Colonel James H. Mapleson's company in the United States; and in 1890 she sang at the Metropolitan Opera in New York. According to Ralph Van Arnam, ("Patti and Tamagno at the Metropolitan in 1890," *Opera News*, 19 April 1948, pp. 21–24), "no singer in the second half of the nineteenth century matched her drawing power or earnings." Patti's second husband was the French tenor Ernesto Nicolini. At the age of seventy-one she made her last public appearance at the Albert Hall in London.

4. Verdi speaks of himself in the third person.

5. Victorien Sardou (1831–1908), French playwright and librettist. Supplying the librettos for such composers as Lecocq, Offenbach, Bizet, Johann Strauss, and Saint-Saëns, he also wrote the original dramas of such operas as *Madame Sans-Gêne* (libretto by Renato Simoni, music by Umberto Giordano), *Fedora* (libretto by Arturo Colautti, music by Umberto Giordano), and *La Tosca* (libretto by Giuseppe Giacosa and Luigi Illica, music by Giacomo Puccini).

6. Franco Faccio, Italian conductor and composer.

7. "But yes, but yes, that must be!"

8. " . . . getting involved in the big shop."

9. Alessandro Manzoni (1785–1873), Italian poet and novelist. In his memory Verdi composed the *Requiem*.

Camille Du Locle to Verdi [1]

Paris, 3 May 1870

[. . .] Thank you a thousand times for having thought and for thinking of me. Nothing can give me more courage and confidence than the thought of producing a work from your hand! [. . .]

1. In answer to Verdi's letter of 25 April 1870.

Camille Du Locle to Verdi [1]

Paris, 7 May 1870

[. . .] This is serious!!! I receive letter after letter from Egypt. The Viceroy cannot resign himself to the thought of not having one of your works. He does not ask you to go to Egypt. He will arrange for all the rehearsals you wish, wherever you wish— in Milan, in Genoa, in Paris, in Busseto, at your choice. He will give you the company you wish. The conditions will be those you wish. I could not refuse to write you this now; look and judge for yourself. Must you absolutely say no!!?? If you should come to Paris in the fall, could you not let a work be rehearsed here at that time — one which would be given down there [Cairo] without you and under the direction of a person you would designate? There is a libretto to which the Viceroy, it seems, is no stranger. It is not absurd — and even contains some beautiful dramatic situations. Would you like me to send it to you? Are you curious to read it? Libretto is an improper word; I should have said outline. Think about it and decide. There might be a nice farm or a nice palace in Genoa for you out of this business, a paradise and something with . . .This is serious!!! [. . .]

1. Du Locle writes having received Mariette's letters of 27 and 28 April 1870. Alessandro Luzio, ed., *Carteggi Verdiani*, IV (Roma: Accademia Nazionale dei Lincei, 1947), p. 7, erroneously dates this letter 7 April 1870.

Camille Du Locle to Verdi

Paris, 10 May 1870

[. . .] I await your reply to the Egyptian proposals in order to transmit your ultimatum to the proprietor of the pyramids. If you ask for one of them as a bonus (the biggest, of course), they may be inclined to give it to you. [. . .]

Camille Du Locle to Verdi

Paris, 14 May 1870

Dear and illustrious Maestro,
        This moment I received your letter,[1] and I have but a minute to answer you. My daughter will be baptized today. . . .
        Here is the plan of the libretto that Egypt proposes. Four copies of this plan have been printed in Cairo. The Viceroy had this one sent to me.
        This very day I shall write to Mariette[2] that you have agreed to have me send you the plan of the libretto and that you may, it is hoped, reach a decision. At the same time I shall ask about the precise financial conditions of the affair.
        Naturally I am maintaining absolute silence about all this, even with Escudier.
        I attach to the libretto a line from Mariette that I received a few days ago,[3] which will show you how much the Viceroy desires that the project be done. [. . .]

1. Missing.
2. Du Locle's reference here to Mariette is the first in his letters to Verdi that are available.
3. Mariette's letter to Du Locle of 28 April 1870.

Auguste Mariette to Camille Du Locle

Alexandria, 19 May [1870]

My dear friend,
        Because of delays I received your letter[1] only today, and I hasten to answer it in order not to miss the courier.
        Thank you for your good intentions concerning my trip to France. Nothing

is taking shape as yet because the business of the opera is not yet sufficiently advanced.

Indeed here is the whole story. The Viceroy is burning with desire to see things take shape. Let's go ahead then. If Verdi cannot do it, get M. Gounod; if necessary, see Wagner. We have full authority. But I must soon be able to tell the Viceroy that his opera will be done, that it is in the works. Until now, unfortunately, we have had only an exchange of letters, whereas the composer should already be at work.

In other words, choose a composer as soon as possible, agree with him on the conditions, inform me by telegraph, and by telegraph I shall send you the Viceroy's official order to begin, your conditions having been accepted.

The Viceroy is ready for any expense; but again he does not wish to wait too long. He talks about the first performance in February of next year. Will this be possible?

I need not tell you that after the opera has been performed in Cairo, the Viceroy would be more than proud to see his opera performed in Paris.

In summation, go ahead. Gounod will do well. Verdi would do better. But the main thing is to lay the first stone and to let the Viceroy know that the work has at least begun. If, afterward, I see that my presence is necessary in Paris, I would at least have a purpose on which to base my request. But for the present, what can I do? [. . .]

[P.S.] In your next letter you should tell me:

The music of the opera will be done by M. ———.

The words will be done by M. Du Locle.

The sets will be painted by M. ———.

The costumes will be designed by ———.

The creative part of the opera (that is, that of the composer and the librettist) will take approximately ———.

With this I shall go to see the Viceroy and shall immediately send you his order to proceed. This is the only way to get us going at last.

1. Missing.

Camille Du Locle to Verdi

Paris, 26 May 1870

Dear and illustrious Maestro,

I am bombarded with letters and telegrams urging me to ask you if there is some chance now that you will accept this Egyptian business. If you do, I am told that your conditions will be accepted no matter what. If you let yourself be definitely tempted, then, and if the Viceroy's libretto does not seem impossible for you to arrange and set to music, just say <u>what you want done</u> and the sum you want to receive. [. . .]

Verdi to Camille Du Locle

St. Agata, 26 May 1870

Dear Du Locle,

I have read the Spanish drama by <u>d'Ayala</u>. It is done by the hand of a master, but . . . one neither laughs nor <u>cries</u>. It's cold and doesn't seem to be made for music. I am terribly sorry you are having it translated. Stop it, if it's not too late.

I have read the Egyptian outline. It is well done; it offers a splendid *mise-en-scène*, and there are two or three situations which, if not very new, are certainly very beautiful. But who did it? There is a very expert hand in it, one accustomed to writing and one who knows the theatre very well. Now let's hear the financial conditions from Egypt, and then we shall decide. Who would have the Italian libretto made? Of course it would be necessary that I myself have it made.[1] [. . .]

1. Günther, p. 48 n, notes that this sentence originally read: "*Il libretto italiano naturalmente chi farebbe fare io.*" Verdi struck out *naturalmente* and covered *io* with a question mark.

Camille Du Locle to Verdi

Paris, 29 May 1870

Dear and illustrious Maestro,

So be it. I shall have the translation of d'Ayala's play stopped. I had a summary made for myself and did not find the subject very musical. Had you liked it, however, I would have produced it with great joy and confidence.

The Egyptian libretto is the work of the Viceroy and Mariette Bey, the famous archaeologist. None else has put a hand to it.[1] It has been edited and printed in Egypt, as I told you.

I hope your next letter will bring me, as I requested, the conditions you desire for the Egyptian business. I shall immediately transmit them by telegraph to Cairo, and I shall send you the definite response, which, after all, is not in doubt. Mariette writes me that the Viceroy passionately desires that this business come about. [. . .]

1. The Viceroy's coauthorship of "the Egyptian libretto" — actually only an outline — was obviously meant to impress Verdi, but it was not true. Verdi expressed his doubts in a letter to Giulio Ricordi of 25 June 1870 and in an undated letter, p. 116.

Auguste Mariette to Camille Du Locle

Alexandria, 29 May 1870

My dear friend,

Since my mail from France ran after me to Cairo and caught up with me only in Alexandria, I received your letter containing Verdi's letter[1] only yesterday.

I have not yet been able to see the Viceroy. But I have been authorized for a long time to tell you to go ahead. Everything will be arranged according to your wishes. The Viceroy is ready for anything, and rather extraordinary circumstances would be required to give you cause to complain about him. Therefore put the opera boldly in the works. The Viceroy will be enchanted with Verdi's acceptance. He was particularly eager that the opera should be written by him, since he is a great admirer of the Maestro.

The opera will be performed for the first time in Cairo in Italian. But I know the Viceroy would be very proud if thereafter the opera were performed in French at our foremost lyric theatre. On this point there is no difficulty whatsoever. To the contrary.

Nothing will be neglected here for the *mise-en-scène*, which the Viceroy wants to be as splendid and magnificent as possible. Everything will be made in Paris, sets and costumes.

As for me, I sincerely hope to leave here one of these days. As soon as I see the Viceroy, I shall bluntly pose the question of my true purpose. I am the one who did the outline; I am the one, of all his employees, who knows Upper Egypt best, as well as the question of costumes and sets. Consequently, I am the one he must send to France. I hope this argument will decide the matter. [. . .] If there is any news, I shall inform you by telegraph.

P.S. The Viceroy is most anxious to have *Aida* performed in Cairo, at the latest during February of next year.

1. Du Locle's letter to Mariette is missing, as is Verdi's letter to Du Locle that was enclosed. Presumably Verdi's missing letter to Du Locle is the one acknowledged by Du Locle in his letter to Verdi of 14 May 1870.

Camille Du Locle to Verdi

Paris, 31 May 1870

[. . .] I have requested from you, in complete confidence, the conditions you desire for the Egyptian business. They write and telegraph me without respite, asking me for these conditions; they declare themselves <u>ready for everything</u>. The Viceroy passionately wishes to conclude the affair. I have already been asked to take charge of the sets and costumes, etc., etc. Nothing is lacking but your <u>yes</u> and a good contract. [. . .]

Verdi to Camille Du Locle

St. Agata, 2 June 1870

Dear Du Locle,

Here I am at the Egyptian affair; and first of all I must set aside time to compose the opera, because this is a work of the broadest proportions (as though it were for the *grande boutique*), and because the Italian poet must first find the thoughts to put into the mouths of the characters and then fashion the verses from them. Assuming that I am able to finish all of this in time, here are the conditions:

1. I shall have the libretto done at my expense.
2. I shall send someone to Cairo, also at my expense, to conduct and direct the opera.
3. I shall send a copy of the score and the music for use only in the Kingdom of Egypt, retaining for myself the rights to the libretto and to the music in all other parts of the world.

In compensation, I shall be paid the sum of 150,000 francs, payable at the Rothschild Bank in Paris at the moment the score is <u>delivered</u>.

Here's a letter for you, as cut and dried as a promissory note. It's business, and you will forgive me, my dear Du Locle, if for now I don't digress to other things.

Verdi to Giulio Ricordi

[St. Agata,] 2 June [1870]

My dear Giulio,

I have a fully developed outline of an opera, with characters, chorus, *mise-en-scène*, act divisions, etc. The dialogue and poetry are missing. If I were to make an opera of it, could Ghislanzoni[1] do the libretto for me? Keep in mind that I would like to see the drama completely developed in prose before the verses are made.

Answer me quickly because I am in a hurry, and this thing should be done very fast.

1. Antonio Ghislanzoni, Italian librettist.

Auguste Mariette to Camille Du Locle

Alexandria, 4 June 1870

My dear friend,

I just spent the morning with the Viceroy. I advise you that the Viceroy speaks of <u>his</u> opera as being well on the way. It's Verdi here, Du Locle there. As for me, all I have to say now, in order to leave, is that the affair has been effectively concluded. The Viceroy wants a rigorously exact *mise-en-scène* and strictly authentic local color. As an added precaution he will send me to Paris. Therefore I impatiently await the letter informing me that things are underway.

I know the Viceroy has been informed of the date on which the new Paris Opéra will be inaugurated;[1] and I had the impression that he was close to writing the Emperor personally, so that his opera might have the honor of being chosen for the first performance. Tell me if we should approach our court.[2] [. . .]

You are busy and I don't want to take your time. *Au revoir* and soon, I hope.

1. By imperial decree of 29 September 1860 the Opéra in rue Peletier (destroyed by fire on 29 October 1873) was replaced by the building which is still in existence. Because of the war in 1870–71 it was not inaugurated until 5 January 1875.
2. The Imperial Court of France.

Giulio Ricordi to Verdi [1]

Milan, 4 June 1870

Illustrious Maestro,

Imagine someone without a penny in his pocket, who learns of an unexpected inheritance! . . . Imagine someone who gets a premium of 500,000 francs from the Bari Loan Association or 600,000 from the Ottoman Loan Association! . . . You can imagine all the degrees of joy, of contentment, of happiness reflected in the faces of those fortunate mortals. . . . Well, all these seem $0 \times 0 = 0$ compared to my stupefaction this morning upon receiving that blessed letter of yours which reopened our heart to the dearest of hopes! . . .

I forgo telling you of our joy and come to the concrete. Ghislanzoni is not in Milan but out in the country. I am authorized to tell you, however, that he is disposed to do for you whatever you want him to do and that he is most happy to put himself under your command. I guarantee this (being authorized by the various discussions I held at various times with Ghislanzoni on this subject): he would be very happy, after all, and I hope that he will devote such care and study that he succeeds in writing excellent verses.

Consequently, in case you consider it useful, I shall simply alert Ghislanzoni. Should our presence not be a waste or a burden, I would immediately, immediately accompany our poet to your home; and you will personally say, do, command, and everyone will obey. [. . .]

1. In answer to Verdi's letter of 2 June 1870.

True and miraculous Effigy
of St. Ovid Big Nose
on the morning of 4 June 1870
half past eight o'clock
at the precious moment he read the letter
from Maestro Verdi

Painted by Titian   Engraved by Morgen[1]

Dedicated to the Most Excellent
Signora Giuseppina Verdi

1. Ricordi's misspelled reference to Rafaello Morghen (1758–1833), one of the most celebrated Italian engravers of his time.

Verdi to Giulio Ricordi

[St. Agata, 5 June 1870]

Dear Giulio,

Slowly, slowly, slowly! Perhaps we won't do anything. In any event, I shall write as soon as I receive a telegram; if you accompany Ghislanzoni, so much the better.

Camille Du Locle to Verdi [1]

Paris, 6 June 1870

Dear and illustrious Maestro,

I sent a telegram to Cairo[2] stating the precise conditions under which you would accept the Egyptian business and requesting an immediate and official reply. All things being equal, the contract is the first thing to be done. As soon as I have had a reply, I shall write you. I dare not use the telegraph while you are at St. Agata, not knowing if there is a line into Busseto. Tell me about this for future reference. [. . .]

If the Egyptian business is concluded, you will probably have to resign yourself to a visit from me for two or three days. On my shoulders, I think, will rest the responsibility for the costumes and sets to be made in Paris. An understanding with you would be needed for the necessary arrangements and changes. [. . .]

Ah, if at the same time we could find something for the Opéra-Comique!

1. In answer to Verdi's letter of 2 June 1870.
2. Missing.

Verdi to Camille Du Locle

St. Agata, 9 June 1870

[. . .] There is no telegraph line here. It only goes to Borgo St. Donnino.[1] If you like, you could send telegrams to Borgo St. Donnino in care of the post office, Busseto, Italy; but you wouldn't gain much time. For example, if you telegraphed at eight or ten o'clock in the evening, I would receive the telegram the next day at noon. In the end twenty-four hours would be gained.

If an agreement is reached with Egypt, you would then come here. That gives me the greatest pleasure. Now I am really desirous for an agreement; and between ourselves we shall quickly agree on the revisions to be made. Only try to give yourself as much time as possible.

Meanwhile I say to you: Until we meet again. [. . .]

1. Borgo St. Donnino lies approximately fifteen miles to the south of St. Agata. Because of its Roman origins (*Fidentia Julia*), the name of this town was changed by royal decree to Fidenza on 9 June 1927.

Auguste Mariette to Camille Du Locle

Telegram   Cairo, 10 June 1870

AM AUTHORIZED TO INFORM YOU THAT PROPOSED 150,000 FRANCS IS AC-
CEPTED — ONLY CONDITION [OPERA] MUST BE READY END JANUARY —
LEAVING SOON.

Camille Du Locle to Verdi

Telegram   Paris, 10 June 1870

RECEIVED FOLLOWING TELEGRAM — AM AUTHORIZED TO INFORM YOU THAT
PROPOSED 150,000 FRANCS IS ACCEPTED — ONLY CONDITION OPERA MUST BE
READY END JANUARY — MARIETTE — PLEASE ANSWER — WILL SEND DEFI-
NITE REPLY TO CAIRO — GREETINGS.

Emanuele Muzio to Verdi [1]

Telegram   Paris, 10 June 1870

ALL YOUR DEMANDS ACCEPTED IN CAIRO — AM ALWAYS AT YOUR DISPOSAL —
THOUSAND GREETINGS.

   1. By sending this telegram, Muzio was not pursuing any interests of his own, since Verdi was
aware that his friend disliked the conditions at the Cairo Opera.

Verdi to Camille Du Locle

Telegram   St. Agata, 12 June 1870

RECEIVED CAIRO CONTRACT — IMPOSSIBLE TO SET DATE IF LIBRETTO NOT
FINISHED — COME SOON — LETTER FOLLOWS.

Verdi to Camille Du Locle

St. Agata, 12 June 1870

Dear Du Locle,

     As I told you in my telegram, I received your dispatch. Before a
completion date can be set, it is absolutely necessary that the libretto be
finished. Otherwise I could find myself in a very embarrassing situation
through no fault of my own. The end of January is time enough, but we must
get to work immediately. If you are authorized to make the necessary revisions, arrange to come here soon and plan to spend as much time as possible.
It will be a double pleasure for us. [. . .]

Camille Du Locle to Verdi

Paris, 13 June 1870

Dear and illustrious Maestro,

I received your telegram in answer to mine, which quoted the one I received from Cairo. The Egyptian affair is thus three-quarters arranged. I am still awaiting some information. I shall then leave to discuss it all with you. The Viceroy cares for this business more than you can imagine. He has sent word to me that he will write to the Emperor to get permission for me to go down there — in your absence — for the last rehearsals of the *mise-en-scène*. Imagine the Emperor's astonishment upon receiving such a letter! Thank God that is none of his business.

I don't think I've been indiscreet by telling M. Muzio that the business is concluded. In talking with him, I saw that he was aware of the situation and that his business with Bagier[1] depended on the Cairo business.

Mariette Bey will come to France for the designs of the sets and the costumes.

Ah, if only, by way of an *entr'acte*, we could find something for the *petite boutique*. As long as you have pen in hand, it wouldn't cost you any more!

Adieu. A thousand affectionate greetings to Madame Verdi and to you. Till later . . . .

1. Director of the Italian Theatre in Paris.

Verdi to Camille Du Locle

St. Agata, 18 June 1870

Dear Du Locle,

I can't wait to see you — first, for the pleasure of seeing you; second, because I believe that in a very short time we shall agree on the modifications that, I think, should be made for *Aida*. I have already given some thought to them and shall submit my ideas to you.

I asked Muzio if he would be disposed to return to Cairo in case I should sign a contract.[1] Now that I know he is negotiating with Bagier, I would not, for all the gold in the world, want him to forgo an engagement in Paris, which is much more useful to him.

I am glad this Egyptian contract has not yet been trumpeted by the newspapers. It seems impossible that *Le Figaro*[2] has not imagined it! Of course we cannot keep it a secret forever, but it will be futile to make the conditions known. We must at least keep the fee secret, since it would serve as a pretext to disturb so many poor dead men. Someone would be sure to point out the 400 scudi for the *Barbiere di Siviglia*, Beethoven's poverty, Schubert's misery, Mozart's roaming about just to make a living, etc., etc. [. . .]

1. If Verdi wrote Muzio on this subject, the letter (like all the others he received from Verdi) was obviously destroyed after Muzio's death.
2. A Paris newspaper still in existence.

Verdi to Emanuele Muzio [1]

St. Agata, 20 June 1870

Dear Emanuele,

I am glad that your business with Bagier is concluded. It's a position that you have earned, and now it's up to you alone to keep it. Bring honor to yourself and show your worth. Now that you are before the public, your fortune and your future depend on you alone; and even if Bagier should leave and his theatre should close, there will be ten other theatres that will ask for you once you are known as a man of ability. Respect others and make yourself be respected; never be unjust and never weak. Treat the highest in the same way as the lowest; don't be partial to anybody. Don't show sympathy or dislike; and don't be afraid even to curse here and there.

1. Thanks to the existence of Verdi's draft at St. Agata, this is one of the few letters we have from Verdi to Muzio. A missing letter from Muzio or an oral account by Du Locle, who supposedly arrived from Paris at St. Agata on 19 June 1870, seems to have brought Verdi the news of Muzio's definite commitment to Bagier.

Auguste Mariette to Camille Du Locle

Cairo, 21 June 1870

My dear friend,

I have the pleasure of informing you that, in all probability, I shall embark from Alexandria on the 29th and shall arrive in Marseilles on the 4th or 5th of July. It goes without saying that I shall try to meet you as soon as I have arrived in Paris.

I have not seen the Viceroy, who is in Alexandria, for several days; and I have nothing new to tell you. The business, of course, is concluded. At any rate, we shall rehash all that soon. [. . .]

Auguste Mariette to Edouard Mariette

[*Probably* Cairo, 21 June 1870] [1]

[. . .] This trip does and does not enchant me. I am quite afraid of repeating the experience with the Exposition. There I was the guiding spirit of everything; I organized the whole thing; and while I burned my paws neatly roasting the chestnuts on the fire, others got to eat them. I gave the Exposition my time, the fruit of my labor, my intelligence; and while I was literally living out of my own pocket, M. C.E. built himself a house and M. D. filled his coffers. [2] Shall I fall back into the same naïveté this time? It's true that I'm not writing the music of the opera in question; it's true that I'm not writing the libretto. But the outline is mine; that is, I have put all its scenes in order, and the opera has essentially come out of my bag. More than that, I am the one who goes to Paris to have the sets executed, the costumes manufactured, to lend everything the local color that must be ancient Egyptian. Now what is happening? V. has already made a contract for 150,000 francs with the Viceroy. You can bet D.L. will take his royalties, the scene painters and costumers will earn their money, Dr. will keep his percentage of all expenses, while my hotel bill in Paris will ruin me. The Viceroy simply thinks I am paid enough with my regular salary. I could refuse, I know; and I could say that, after all, I am asked to do a job there that isn't mine. But how can I give up seeing you all, and how can I answer Joséphine and Sophie when they cry with wide-open mouths: "Daaaaaaddy, when do we leave?"

So this trip is only moderately attractive to me. I know that the Viceroy is aware of what I am doing and that he will do something for me if the opera is successful. I also know that nothing is decided and that H.H. may suddenly tell me he will open a credit for my expenses in Paris. All of that, nevertheless, constitutes a position lacking security. Be that as it may, God's will be done! The pleasure of seeing you all again, of giving pleasure to my daughters, of embracing my poor little boys prevails over everything. There are those who pay for happiness, and I must still consider myself happy if I can procure it with a chance that it cost me nothing. [. . .]

1. Edouard Mariette gives this date for his brother's letter when he quotes it in *Mariette Pacha — Lettres et Souvenirs Personnels* (Paris: H. Jouve, 1904), pp. 84–86.
2. Monsieur C.E. and Monsieur D., or Messieurs C.E. and M.D., cannot be identified. D.L. and Dr. a few lines later, however, obviously refer to Du Locle and Draneht.

Tito Ricordi[1] to Verdi

Milan, 21 June 1870

Dearest friend,

The other day I finally had my last operation (but not [*illegible*]), and the attending physicians have absolved me, so to speak! Thanks to heaven, I got out of this one too!! [. . .]

I do not want to leave, however, without writing my first letter to the dearest of my friends whom I worship more than all others among our great artists! [. . .]

P.S. My Giulio has also suffered for a long time from stomach pains, and the physicians have advised him to go with me to the lake[2] and to San Pellegrino; thus he will leave with me tomorrow. Let's hope that he may at last find a remedy for the illness that has been plaguing him for several years. Of course while he is away from Milan, you can still write him here, since the mail will be forwarded to him wherever he is, and he will always keep himself at your disposal, in writing as well as in person.

1. Music publisher, father of Giulio Ricordi.
2. The Ricordi family spent their vacations at Cadenabbia on Lake Como.

Verdi to Giulio Ricordi

St. Agata, 25 June 1870

Dear Giulio,

Are you taking the waters at San Pellegrino? If you are not, can you delay going there for a few days in order to come here with Ghislanzoni?

This is what it is about: Last year I was invited to write an opera in a very distant country. I answered no.[1] When I was in Paris, Du Locle was commissioned to talk to me about it again and to offer me a large sum. Again I answered no. One month later he sent me a printed outline, telling me that it was written by an influential person (which I do not believe), that it seemed good to him, and that I should read it. I found it to be very good, and I replied that I would set it to music on the conditions etc., etc. Three days after I sent my telegram,[2] he replied: Accepted. Du Locle immediately came here,[3] and, with him, I drew up the conditions;[4] we studied the outline together, and together we made the modifications we thought necessary.[5] Du Locle has left with the conditions and the modifications, which are to be submitted to the influential and unknown author. I have further studied the outline, and I have made and am still making new changes.

Now we must think about the libretto or, to say it better, about writing the verses, since all we need now are the verses.

Ghislanzoni — could he and would he do this work for me? It is not an original work; make that clear to him. It is only a matter of writing the verses, for which, you understand (this I say to you), he will be paid very generously.

Answer me immediately, and get ready to come here with Ghislanzoni. [. . .]

In the meantime, together with Ghislanzoni, study the outline I am sending you. Don't lose it, because there are only two copies: this is one and the other is in the hands of the author.[6]

Don't say anything because the contract has not yet been signed. Besides, it is useless to talk about it now. . . . We'll talk about it in person.

[P.S.] Tell me what it would cost to make a copy of this score with all the parts for chorus and orchestra.

1. We have no record of any correspondence concerning such an invitation in 1869. Verdi might be referring to the Viceroy's message which Du Locle presumably gave him at Genoa in December 1869. See notes 5, p. 5 and 1, Verdi to Du Locle, p. 10.

2. Since Du Locle's telegram to Verdi was dated 10 June 1870, this telegram, which is missing, would have been sent on or about 7 June 1870.

3. Du Locle apparently visited Verdi at St. Agata between 19 and 25 June 1870. Presumably Verdi wrote this letter the moment Du Locle left. See Document III.

4. See Document IV.

5. See Document III.

6. According to Mariette's letter to Du Locle of 27 April 1870 and Du Locle's letter to Verdi of 14 May 1870, *four* copies of this outline had been printed.

Giulio Ricordi to Verdi

Cadenabbia, 1 July 1870

Illustrious Maestro,

I received your letter and it's all right. I can postpone the cure at San Pellegrino indefinitely. Therefore, soon after we receive your order, *en route*, *marche*. I shall be there with our friend Ghislanzoni, with whom I shall meet tomorrow to settle everything.

So you need only command us. My father is most grateful to you for the kind letter you addressed to him;[1] and he is also very happy to hear that, in one way or another, musical art will be enriched by a new masterwork. He leaves tomorrow for the cure at San Pellegrino, where he will remain for some twenty-five days.

My wife sends cordial greetings to you and Signora Peppina, and I am very happy that I am able to close by affectionately saying, See you soon.
[P.S.] Upon my arrival at St. Agata, I shall be able to tell you the price of the score, chorus, and orchestra parts, unless you are anxious to know this right away. Please address your letters to Milan.

1. Missing.

Camille Du Locle to Verdi

Paris, 2 July 1870

Dear and illustrious Maestro,

I arrived in Paris[1] yesterday in good shape, via the Simplon and the Lake of Geneva. [. . .] And now I use my pen and ink, for the first time since my return to the *petite boutique*, to thank you for your excellent reception and your excellent friendship. [. . .]

I found here a letter from Mariette, who is taking the boat on the 29th (June) from Alexandria. He will then be in Paris on the 5th or the 6th. As soon as I have seen him, that is as soon as he has arrived, I shall write you. [. . .]

I personally took your letter for M. Muzio to the Messrs. Ricordi when I left my calling card for them.[2] What a luxurious establishment, and your portrait between the two original scores of *La Traviata* and *Rigoletto*. Hats off, there's a publisher! Compared to this, Escudier is only a gingerbread man. [. . .]

As far as everyone is concerned, I just spent ten days in the country. Hurrah! [. . .]

1. From his visit with Verdi at St. Agata.

2. During a stopover in Milan, Du Locle probably delivered Verdi's letter of 20 June 1870 to Muzio in care of the House of Ricordi.

Giulio Ricordi to Verdi

Cadenabbia, 3 July 1870

Illustrious Maestro,

Just two lines to inform you that Ghislanzoni was here, and I spoke to him about the well-known affair. He accepts and is most happy to be able to serve you.

We are ready, then, for a sign from you; and I, on my part, shall warn you of the day and hour of our arrival.

Ghislanzoni says he will come with a Nubian slave who, upon entering St. Agata, will throw himself as a meal to the dogs, in order to save his [Ghislanzoni's] own legs!!

Meanwhile we send ahead our greetings, illustrious Maestro, very happy to be able to take your and Signora Peppina's hands.

[P.S.] The price — for you, of course — of printing the <u>solo, chorus, and orchestra parts</u> for an opera of four acts is between 500 and 600 lire; the copy of the orchestra score between 150 and 200 lire.

Verdi to Giulio Ricordi

[St. Agata, 4 July 1870]

Dear Giulio,

Come then with Ghislanzoni as soon as you can. Take a carriage at Firenzuola or at Borgo.[1] Of course this trip will be at my expense. . . .

1. Borgo St. Donnino. Like Alseno, Firenzuola, and Piacenza to the north, Borgo St. Donnino was, as Fidenza continues to be, a station on the main railway (opened in 1865), which connects Milan and Bologna. The railway from Fidenza to Busseto and Cremona was not inaugurated until 1908. The Verdis and their visitors traveled by rail to Borgo St. Donnino, Alseno, Firenzuola, or Piacenza, and then by coach to St. Agata, ten to twenty miles away.

Giuseppina Verdi to Clarina Maffei

St. Agata, 6 July 1870

[. . .] Giulio was here for two days like a passing bird and will leave for San Pellegrino tomorrow. [. . .] This year we'll stay in the country very late, because Verdi will perhaps occupy himself with music and so will need solitude and calm. [. . .]

Giulio Ricordi to Verdi

Milan, 8 July 1870

Illustrious Maestro,

Indeed, whenever one has the good fortune of receiving it, there is nothing dearer than a welcome that is always kind and exquisite, one that leaves behind the most agreeable remembrances. Therefore, together with your good Signora Peppina, illustrious Maestro, accept my most sincere and cordial thanks.

I believe it goes without saying that I shall occupy myself in every way with all matters regarding the well-known affair; so great are my satisfaction and joy that I still have to ask myself if it isn't a dream! . . . Fortunately, it is not!

Ghislanzoni, most happy to have the commission, will occupy himself with all his zeal and spirit; and I hope you will be fully satisfied with his work.

I asked Ghislanzoni about his compensation, and, as I had anticipated, he didn't want to say anything, declaring himself completely happy with however much you believed proper.

In the meantime, I shall find out all you want to know about the various historical facts and shall write to you about them. [. . .]

Camille Du Locle to Verdi

Paris, 9 July 1870

Dear and illustrious Maestro,

Mariette is in Paris. He's here as I write you; he comes with the broadest authority on behalf of the Viceroy.

I have asked him, first of all, for the information you desire about the sacred dance of the Egyptians. This dance was performed in long robes and to a slow and solemn rhythm. The music that accompanied it was probably a kind of plainsong, which constituted the bass part, with a very high upper part performed by young sopranos (boys). The instruments that accompanied these dances were twenty-four stringed harps, double flutes, trumpets, timpani, and smaller drums, enormous castanets (rattles), and cymbals.

Above all this hubbub, a thousand fond regards to both of you.

Verdi to Giulio Ricordi [1]

Sunday [St. Agata, 10 July 1870]

Dear Giulio,

Ah, bravo! I am the one who must thank you for having come here in this heat to hear an operatic outline!!! [. . .]

I continuously reread the outline of *Aida*. I see some notes by Ghislanzoni which (just between us) frighten me a little; I would not want us, in order to avoid imaginary dangers, to end up saying something that does not belong in the situation or in the scene; and, likewise, I would not want the theatrical words to be forgotten. By theatrical words, I mean those that carve out a situation or a character, words that always have a most powerful impact on the audience. I know well that sometimes it is difficult to give them a select and poetic form. But . . . (pardon the blasphemy) both the poet and the composer must have the talent and the courage, when necessary, not to write poetry or music. . . . Horror! horror!

Enough: we shall see. In any case you are there to intervene.

1. In answer to Giulio Ricordi's letter of 8 July 1870.

Giulio Ricordi to Verdi

San Pellegrino, 14 July 1870

Illustrious Maestro,

I received your letter. [. . .] I continue to hope for the realization of my ideal — that is, Verdi . . . *Aida* . . . Scala.

You will accuse me of optimism. Never mind. By being optimistic and by pushing ahead resolutely, many beautiful things are achieved — despite some nuisance.

Don't worry in the least about Ghislanzoni. I assure you as fully as possible that he is ready to do, redo, turn over, change a thousand rather than a hundred times until you, illustrious Maestro, are fully satisfied. In this regard, then, you can be at ease, completely at ease. Command and you will be served.

I see with pleasure that as yet nothing has leaked out about this business and that our trip to St. Agata went almost unnoticed.

I am sending you the Fétis book; [1] on p. 187 I found what might be of interest. I read attentively the whole part concerning Egypt. Many things are well known, others are not; but I think, after all, that you too will read it with pleasure. With regard to the other memorandums you left me, I entrusted them to a capable person and shall let you know what he finds out.

I beg you warmly, as always, not to spare me in any way. I am at your disposal in every little thing I can do: command me, ask me, send me backward, send me forward. Who should speak of the heat? We had the happiest trip; and then to see you, to stay with you and Signora Peppina, compensated for any discomfort. As far as we were concerned, there was not the slightest discomfort; so I am entirely in your debt.

[. . .] I hope this cure may restore my old good health so that I can occupy myself, as I would like to, with my affairs and, in particular, with those concerning you.

I found my father in the best of health. He is also calm and of good humor, which pleased me very much. He charges me with his most cordial greetings to you and Signora Peppina, to which I add my own no less cordial ones, and to Corticelli[2] also.

Has it rained? . . . It has here, Heaven be praised!

1. *Histoire Générale de la Musique*, by the Belgian musicologist François Joseph Fétis (1784–1871).
2. Mauro Corticelli, Verdi's personal secretary.

Verdi to Camille Du Locle[1]

St. Agata, 15 July 1870

Dear Du Locle,

I did not write to you earlier because Giulio Ricordi was here with the poet who will set *Aida* in verse. We agreed on everything, and I hope to receive the verses of the first act soon, so that I myself can get to work. We made some modifications in the duet between Aida and Radames in the third act. The betrayal is no longer so odious, without taking anything away from the theatrical effect.[2] I shall send it to you.

Thank you for the instructions you gave me about the Egyptian musical instruments, which may be useful at various points. I would also like to use them for the fanfare in the finale of the third act,[3] but the effect, I fear, will not be great. I assure you that the idea of using Sax's instruments,[4] for example, disgusts me horribly. That is tolerable in a more modern plot . . . but among the Pharaohs!! . . .

Tell me also, were there priestesses of Isis or of another divinity? In the books I leafed through, I found that this function was actually reserved for men.

Give me this information and think seriously about the costumes. Oh, these must be well made and authentic, for they will also be used in Europe. [. . .]

1. In answer to Du Locle's letter of 9 July 1870.
2. At the end of Act III as well, in the three available versions of the original text, Radames does not deliver himself with the words *Sacerdote, io resto a te*. See Documents II, III, IX. See also *Carteggi*, IV, pp. 14, 21, and Guglielmo Barblan, ''Il Sentimento dell'Onore nella Dram-

maturgia Verdiania,'' *Atti del III° Congresso Internazionale di Studi Verdiani* (Parma: Istituto di Studi Verdiani, 1974), pp. 2–13.

3. Unless Verdi had originally thought of a fanfare at the end of Act III, he must have meant the finale of Act II.

4. Saxophones. Adolphe Sax (1814–94) of Brussels had invented this family of instruments around 1840 and had taught the saxophone at the Paris Conservatory.

Antonio Ghislanzoni to Eugenio Tornaghi [1]

15 July 1870 [2]

Dear Signor Tornaghi,

This very day I mailed the first act of *Aida*, accompanied by a long letter, [3] to Maestro Verdi. [. . .] As you can imagine, the libretto occupies me a great deal, since Verdi has requested the utmost haste.

1. Assistant manager and clerk at the House of Ricordi.
2. Like most of Ghislanzoni's letters in this collection, this one was presumably written at his home near Lecco on Lake Como. See Document VII, note 2, and biographical note.
3. Like most of Ghislanzoni's correspondence with Verdi, this letter is missing.

Auguste Mariette to Paul Draneht

Paris, 15 July 1870

My dear Bey,

I received your telegram, [1] for which I thank you, and I hasten to send you the letter I have brought for you.

Since Verdi accepted the offer the Viceroy made to him, the opera (the outline of which you know) will be done. Now this business must be started.

It is toward this end that H.H., the Viceroy, has deigned to send me to France. The Viceroy wants the opera to retain its strictly Egyptian color, not only in the libretto but in the costumes and the sets; and I am here to attend to this essential point.

On my part I am not losing an hour. But it is a difficult thing. In the operas we already know, the task is not as great because one has the traditions to follow. But here everything must be created. Add to this the exotic quality of the *mise-en-scène*. It is in the costumes, above all, that we shall encounter difficulty. To create imaginary Egyptians as they are usually seen in the theatre is not difficult; and if nothing else were needed, I would not be involved. But to unite in proper measure the ancient costumes shown in the temples and the requirements of the modern stage constitutes a delicate task. A king may be quite handsome in granite with an enormous crown on his head. But when it comes to dressing one of flesh and bone and making him walk and sing . . . that becomes embarrassing and, it is to be feared, makes people laugh. In addition, the most consistent principle of Egyptian costume is the absence of beards — a principle observed even more because it was imposed by the religion. Now do you feel up to forcing all your people to cut off their beards? And from another point of view, can you see Naudin[2] dressed as a Pharaoh with a short beard, like the Emperor Napoleon? Obviously the short beard will destroy all the effect and all the harmony of the costumes, no matter how exact we make them. So we must not ignore the fact that the job is difficult and that to mount an opera under the conditions the Viceroy demands is a task to be considered twice. On my part, I am putting my whole heart into it. As for you, I am counting on your arrival in Paris soon. In the meantime I am working vigorously. Verdi has promised to have the opera ready by the end of January. (The Viceroy expressly desires that.) But the costumers and scene painters have declared that they do not have a day to lose. Believe me . . . in order to follow the instructions the Viceroy has given me, to make a scholarly as well as a picturesque *mise-en-scène*, a whole world must be set in motion.

1. Like most of Draneht's correspondence with Mariette, this telegram is missing.
2. Emilio Naudin (1823–90), the leading Italian tenor at the Cairo Opera during its first season. After making his debut in Cremona in 1843, he became the first Vasco da Gama in Meyerbeer's *L'Africaine*, and he sang during several seasons in London.

Verdi to Giuseppe Piroli [1]

[St. Agata,] 16 July 1870

[. . .] I am busy. Guess! . . . Writing an opera for Cairo!!! Oof. I shall not go to stage it because I would be afraid of being mummified; but I shall send a copy of the score and retain the original for Ricordi.

I must tell you, however, that the contract has not yet been signed (and therefore do not talk about it for now); but since my conditions — and they were tough — have been accepted by telegram, it must be considered as done. If anyone had told me two years ago, You will write for Cairo, I would have considered him a fool; but now I see that I am the fool. [. . .]

1. Lawyer and politician, and Verdi's close friend in Rome.

Auguste Mariette to Paul Draneht

Paris, 19 July 1870[1]

My dear Bey,

I received your two letters of 16 and 17 July[2] at almost the same time and I am replying quickly.

You are perfectly correct to demand that you be informed of what is happening in regard to the progress of Verdi's opera; the letter from H.H. that I sent you was meant to keep you posted, and naturally I have nothing to add to it.

Actually a grand opera in the ancient Egyptian style was commissioned by H.H. from Verdi, who has agreed to undertake it. The only condition H.H. made, a condition *sine qua non*, is that the opera must be presented in Cairo at the end of next January. Moreover Verdi is already at work, since all the arrangements have been made with Verdi directly from Alexandria at the personal suggestion of H.H., the Viceroy.

With regard to the mission that now calls me to France, it has as its point of departure the Viceroy's desire to see the opera composed and executed in a strictly Egyptian style. According to the most formal orders that H.H. has given me, I must first place myself at the disposal of the composer and the librettist in order to supply these gentlemen with all the proper information to enlighten them about the local color to be given to the work. Second, I must also take charge of everything pertaining to the *mise-en-scène*, that is, the sets and the costumes. The sets and the costumes, according to H.H.'s orders, must be drawn and executed under my eyes; and for greater accuracy H.H. has directed me to choose the scene painter and the costumer whom I judge the most capable. [. . .] This, in short, is the goal of my mission here — a mission which, with your assistance, my dear Bey, I hope to fulfill to the satisfaction of H.H.

I am quite embarrassed to reply to your second letter on the subject of M. Zuccarelli.[3] When I arrived in Paris you were not here; and since I had the instructions of H.H., I had to get in touch with the scene painters at once and begin the task. What would you have me do now? To find a pretext to put an end to the work already begun is impossible. The task is horribly intricate, and my attention is needed everywhere all the time. The subject is completely new; and at every moment one has to do, undo, and redo, so that I am beginning to believe that we shall only half succeed — even here in Paris with the world's foremost scene painters. I would have to go to Cairo, then, break off the proposals already exchanged, and, in a word, do in Egypt what the Viceroy directed me to come to Paris to do. You will understand that I do not undertake any extra responsibilities.

As for the credit of 250,000 francs that the Viceroy has sent you, it is intended to pay for the initial expenses incurred by the opera in France. If you wish more information on this subject, I shall (to the best of my knowledge) furnish it to you on your return here, which, I hope very much, will not be delayed any longer.

There, my dear Bey, is the information I have been able to furnish you. It is a question of mounting, of creating, a completely new opera. The task will be very difficult and bristling with obstacles caused by the novelty of the subject. But the honor your administration will derive from this will be all the greater. Therefore, I shall be happy to contribute to it to the extent of my abiliites.

1. Mariette wrote this letter on the very day that France formally declared war on Prussia. Like many of his countrymen he was unaware of the consequences of that event.

2. Both letters are missing.

3. Giovanni Zuccarelli, scenic designer at La Scala. Apparently he had worked at the Cairo Opera during its first season. In the missing letter of 17 July 1870 Draneht seems to have questioned Mariette's engagement of other designers for *Aida*.

Auguste Mariette to Paul Draneht

Paris, 21 July 1870

My dear Bey,

I have this instant received your letter of 19 July.[1]

There was no need for you to tell me the contents of the letter from H.H. that I sent you, because, for the good of the mission that I am performing here, H.H. deemed that I should know about it and even charged me to add some less urgent details, which I shall soon be able to communicate to you in person.

You are so right to call the work we are planning a colossal work. As I believe I told you there is really no tradition whatever to follow, and everything must be created. I am not embarrassed to also admit to you that I did not suspect the immensity of the details and that I am literally losing my mind.

Furthermore come to Paris as soon as possible. The two of us are not too many to carry this very heavy burden.

I take the opportunity, my dear Bey, to tell you that you may count on me completely. From now until the end of January, for our dear and illustrious master [the Viceroy], we have to achieve a work of consequence which, to a certain extent, will help to augment the renown Egypt has already acquired for herself. It is essential that we not produce a fiasco. Therefore, just as the Viceroy appealed to the most illustrious living composer, we must do everything possible to make the *mise-en-scène* worthy of this initial step. Until now I have neglected nothing to arrive at that result, and I have proceeded in my research without haste. I hope you will be pleased and that the opera, presented for the first time in Cairo this winter, will bring you great honor. As for myself, I declare in advance that with regard to the libretto and all artistic aspects of the work my name should not even be mentioned.

1. Missing.

Giulio Ricordi to Verdi

San Pellegrino, 21 July 1870

Most illustrious Maestro,

I enclose the answers to the various questions you have asked;[1] they come from a most experienced man of letters, a friend of mine, who is entirely at our disposal for anything further you should wish and who is prepared to shuffle through books, rummage through libraries, etc., etc. [. . .]

What I urge you to do primarily is to secure the designs of costumes, props, etc., etc., in time that I may discuss them with the costumer.[2]

You will laugh, seeing how I chat about all this, as though it were done already! . . . . This is my usual optimism; and then I am actually convinced that I can bring about a most extraordinary and important event at La Scala.

The war,[3] which is destined to break out, cannot last long, considering the present means of destruction. Then, too, such an upset will end at an opportune moment, and it will be closed with an artistic triumph.

Have you received a letter of mine and the book by Fétis?

The waters have really done me good: my stomach ailment has completely vanished, and I hope I am completely healed. My cure will last about eight more days, and then I shall spend the month of August in the country. Thus I hope to be a wonder of health and to occupy myself indefatigably with my affairs, particularly with this business which is more important than any other.

I think it unnecessary to repeat to you that I am always at your disposal, on any day and at any hour. Even if I were in China, I would be ready to fly with the greatest pleasure to Busseto or wherever you may need me, happy to be able to serve you.

My father is very well and sends you and Signora Peppina many greetings, to which I add my most devoted ones.

Excuse the horrible handwriting caused by a most horrible pen!

1. Gaetano Cesari and Alessandro Luzio, eds., *I Copialettere di Giuseppe Verdi* (Milano: Comune di Milano, 1913), p. 637, quote Verdi's "questions" without citing the source of their information. Either Verdi mentioned these questions during Giulio Ricordi's visit to St. Agata between 5 and 7 July 1870 or he asked them in a later letter that is missing. The "answers," which Giulio Ricordi's anonymous friend provided, seem to suggest the specific information Verdi sought. See Document VI.

2. The costumer at La Scala. Giulio Ricordi was concerned about preparations for the production in Milan which was to take place at an undetermined date after the premiere of *Aida* in Cairo.

3. The Franco-Prussian War.

Verdi to Camille Du Locle

St. Agata, 23 July 1870

Dear Du Locle,

Because of your silence, I almost begin to suspect that the delirium of the war has sent even the directors of the Opéra-Comique scurrying to the border! Alas, this war is a great misfortune for everyone; even though it was expected for a long time, I never thought it would suddenly explode like a bolt of lightning out of a clear sky. What do you say about it, my dear Du Locle?

I have heard nothing more about our contract. Perhaps the war also rattles the heads of our Orientals or, better yet, turns them away from theatrical ideas. As for me, I am indifferent; if it can't be done now, we'll do it later or even later yet. Only we need to consider the libretto, about half of which has been completed.

Write me, then. Tell me about yourself first; then about your theatre, then about the war, and then about the Egyptian contract. [. . .]

Camille Du Locle to Verdi [1]

Paris, 26 July 1870

Dear and illustrious Maestro,

Don't think me dead or gone to Berlin, and don't accuse me of having forgotten you! We have lived through ten days of madness, and we all have lost our heads. Our brothers, our friends leave for the border; the *Marseillaise* resounds in all the streets and is sung in the theatres by enraged crowds. [. . .]

Mariette asks me to tell you that you can use as many priestesses of Isis or Vulcan as you please. The costumes and sets are being prepared. I would have sent you the contract long ago, had Mariette not, as a result of this war business, also gone to [. . .] [2] the soldiers in his part of the country. I expect him any day. Perhaps he will be here tonight — I have a first performance. But I didn't want to delay writing to you for another day. [. . .]

1. In answer to Verdi's letter of 15 July 1870.
2. One word is illegible.

Antonio Ghislanzoni to Verdi

Mariaga, 26 July 1870

Most esteemed Maestro,

Here are the fragments of the first act modified as I thought best. [1]

I have developed, as you wished, the first part of the trio, [2] but the situation cannot be much more animated; I fear that by pushing any further we would jeopardize [*illegible*] the effect of the most beautiful scene that takes place in the second act between Amneris and Aida. Besides, I have no doubt [*illegible*] you will achieve with the music what words cannot express. If the tenor's *romanza* is too tightly bound to lend itself to music, see if the strophes I am sending you fit any better. In any case, we shall not tire of redoing it.

[*Illegible*] I see from your letter [3] that you are perplexed and somewhat distrustful. If you want to change, I'll change.

For the time being let me proceed. Sunday or Monday I shall send you the last scene of the act and soon after all of the second act. When the work is finished I shall come, if you permit, to spend two or three days in Busseto,[4] and I shall concern myself with getting all the odds and ends out of the way. [. . .]

1. See Document VII. The "fragments" mentioned here by Ghislanzoni are most likely those later corrected by Verdi.
2. Aida-Amneris-Radames in Act I, scene i.
3. Missing.
4. Ghislanzoni tactfully avoids mentioning St. Agata, where Verdi lived, and refers instead to Busseto, the neighboring town.

Isabella Galletti Gianoli [1] to Paul Draneht

Pesaro, 28 July 1870

[. . .] My friend Signor Lampugnani[2] has confirmed for me that the illustrious Verdi is writing an opera for Cairo. Remember, Excellency, that I want to be the interpreter of the afore-mentioned score. What do you say to this imperative "I want"? But it is self-respect that prompts me, and I hope that you will be willing to consent to my desires. [. . .] I shall relish your kind reply. Please forgive the familiar manner in which I write this; it is only because of your well-known kindness. [. . .]

1. The leading Italian soprano at the Cairo Opera during its first season.
2. Giovanni Battista Lampugnani, theatrical agent in Milan.

Paul Draneht to Riaz Pasha [1]

Lyon, 29 July 1870

Excellency,

I have finally brought to an end all my business involving costumes, props, sets, etc., in Italy, and I have also managed to complete the nucleus of the opera company — all things to my satisfaction. [. . .]

The day after tomorrow I hope to return to Paris and join Mariette Bey, so that I may discuss the affairs regarding the new opera with him.

1. Apparently the Viceroy's treasurer.

Verdi to Giulio Ricordi [1]

Sunday [*Probably* St. Agata, 31 July 1870]

Dear Giulio,

I thank you for the information you have given me about Egypt.

I too have seen in Herodotus that among oriental peoples the cult of the gods was strictly reserved for men; only in Persia were there priestesses, or Dodoneans. But if other authors permit them, we can also permit them without inconvenience. We are all right concerning the locality of Ethiopia. The Ramses we talk about in our libretto would really be the third — that is, Sesostris. Ask your friend once again if it is really only 115 leagues from Memphis to Thebes. I thought it was farther, but my calculations must have been wrong. In *Mondo secreto*[2] I have also read the description of the mysteries of Isis, but they do not concern us. That would be a separate subject — but what a subject and what a spectacle![3]

I received Fétis's book, which I shall return to you right away; it was of no use to me. When he doesn't know something, he invents with an incredible *toupet*. And to think that many consider him a great man! In this book there is a little story (which isn't so lovely) about the Egyptian flute in the Museum of Florence. Using the measurements sent to him, this Fétis had a flute built from which he discovered the ancient tonality!! So many objections could be made, and it seems impossible that no one objects. It may be, however, that the war will send the Cairo affair up in smoke; if so, good night. Is Terziani[4] still at La Scala? If he is, he must stay there; and it would not be wise to propose others. Ghislanzoni sent me almost the entire first act. With a few changes, it will be very good.

1. In answer to Giulio Ricordi's letter of 21 July 1870.
2. Thus far all attempts to learn about this publication have been unsuccessful.
3. Verdi seems not to have been familiar with Mozart's *Magic Flute*.
4. Eugenio Terziani, Italian conductor.

Paul Draneht to Auguste Mariette

Paris, 4 August 1870

My dear Mariette Bey,
        Here are the names of the principal artists of the Opera Theatre in Cairo:

Sopranos	*Tenors*
Mme. Galletti Gianoli	M. Emilio Naudin
" Giovannoni Zacchi	" Guidotti
" Giuseppina Vitali	" Paolo Augusti
" Bettina Capozzi (Comprimaria)	
	Baritones
Altos	M. Luigi Colonnese
Mme. Norina Grossi[1]	" Boccolini
" Lamaire (Comprimaria)	

Basses

M. Paolo Medini
" Giovanni Marè
" Fioravanti (Buffo)

It seems to me absolutely necessary that to assure the success of the new work the principal roles be filled by our best artists; and I recommend, first of all, Signora Galletti Gianoli and Signor Naudin; as baritone, Signor Colonnese,[2] and as bass, Paolo Medini,[3] an artist of the first order for whom we should, if at all possible, enlarge the bass role of that work whose success ought to be entrusted to artists of the first order.

Since yesterday I have been thinking about the divertissement which will be interpolated in *Aida*, but we cannot design the costumes until our choreographer has set the ballets and the divertissement; therefore, he must be sent a libretto as soon as possible. Tell me what should be done in this circumstance.

Here is the address, or rather the addresses, of Cambon, the scene painter: 95 rue de Turenne and 288 quai de Jemmapes.

1. Eleonora Grossi, Italian mezzo-soprano.
2. Luigi Colonnese (ca. 1835–?), Italian baritone. Following his debut in 1860, he appeared regularly at La Scala, where he sang Valentino in the first Italian performance of *Faust* (1862) and Melitone in the first Italian performance of *La Forza del Destino* (1869).
3. Paolo Medini (1837–1911), Italian bass. Popular in opera houses throughout Europe, his best roles were in *Rigoletto, Don Carlos, Les Huguenots,* and *L'Africaine.* Later he became Verdi's favorite bass in the *Requiem.*

Paul Draneht to J. Barrot[1]

Paris, 5 August 1870

My dear Monsieur Barrot,

I received the letter His Highness wrote to me concerning the opera by Maestro Verdi.[2] I was in Italy at the time, but I hastened to get in touch with Mariette Bey; as soon as I arrived in Paris, I paid him a visit.

We are reunited today to obey the desires of His Highness, and our efforts are combined to conclude successfully the work to which His Highness attaches such great importance.

I received the letter of credit for the 250,000 francs that His Highness assigned to Maestro Verdi's opera; I think this sum will be more than sufficient, since the subject of the opera does not require great luxury in the *mise-en-scène.* That is perhaps to be regretted, particularly in our own day and age when the merits of the composer and the librettist do not always suffice and when one is accustomed to see richness displayed in the costumes and grandeur in the sets.

His Highness may be assured that I shall do all I can to satisfy him and that I shall not be the one to keep the work from being a great success.

1. The Viceroy's secretary.
2. The Viceroy's letter, which is missing, that Mariette brought from Egypt and sent to Draneht with his own letter of 15 July 1870.

Raffaele Vitali [1] to Paul Draneht

Ancona per Cerreto d'Esi, 6 August 1870

[. . .] In Italy everyone is talking about the opera Verdi is writing for Cairo and about the reward accorded him by H.H., the Viceroy! If what you told me is true — that in the afore-mentioned opera you will require two sopranos and one contralto — I should be very pleased if you would recommend my daughter to Verdi to perform one of these roles. La Galletti, la Vitali, and la Grossi — that would be an enviable threesome! Please take a hand in this matter, I beg you; it would be a mortification for my Giuseppina if la Giovannoni [2] were chosen in her place!

Even though the "billing" matters little in distinguishing one talent from another, the artistic world nevertheless attributes a great deal of importance to this. In the announcement to the public of the prima donnas, then, I would like la Vitali, rather than la Giovannoni, to come after la Galletti. Although endowed with an uncommon talent, this artist has not yet attained the fame of la Vitali; these are ridiculous little things, I know, but still it is better to submit to certain conventions of the stage!! [. . .]

1. An Italian singer of no especial fame, whose daughter, Giuseppina Vitali (ca. 1855–1915), had sung soprano roles at the Cairo Opera during its first season. She was known particularly for her performances in *Linda di Chamounix* and *Faust*.
2. Ginevra Giovannoni Zacchi (1839–99), the third leading soprano at the Cairo Opera during its first season. After singing *comprimaria* parts in Trieste in the early 1860s she appeared in the principal Italian opera houses and in London, Madrid, and Barcelona in such roles as Lucrezia Borgia and Leonora in *Il Trovatore*.

Giulio Ricordi to Verdi [1]

[*Probably* Cadenabbia,] 8 August 1870

Illustrious Maestro,

I am enclosing more details (which I received today) about the distance between Memphis and Thebes. [2] I am rather late in answering your last letter because I have been very busy these days. You want to know why? You may get a hearty laugh out of it! I was very busy as a result of a quarrel that came about between two summer visitors who are our neighbors! Since it wasn't youngsters who were involved, but two persons of age and married (one the head of a family), the matter was rather serious! In the end, after much weariness as one of our friend's "seconds," I succeeded in having the dispute settled honorably, restoring peace on these shores, which had been threatened by a kind of civil war. If only it were as easy to restore peace between the French and the Prussians! Truly the Emperor was right in anticipating a "long and painful" war; and among 34 million Frenchmen he was the only one to show good sense. Anyway they don't want to submit now to the terms they received, and thus the fight will be prolonged. Is the Latin race really in a state of decline? If it is, let's declare ourselves Chinese, just so this terrible destruction will end quickly.

Ghislanzoni will have sent other parts of the libretto, and I hope that you will be satisfied, illustrious Maestro. If the war does not prevent the realization of such a glorious event in Italian art (which is still alive, at least, thanks to you), I shall be at your disposal — if necessary, by my personal presence — to arrange the printing and copying of the parts and the score, making sure that everything goes in the greatest order. I think that printed copies will also be required of the libretto.

Le Figaro announced your new opera and, in turn, so did all the papers in Italy. Our own Gazzetta,[3] since it has the great good fortune to be of an official nature, naturally awaits an announcement from you.

Our health is excellent. My father is here; in a few days all the rest of the family will also be at the lake.

I shall return to Milan at the end of this month. Next Saturday, however, I'll make a secret excursion to Brescia, because I want to hear, once at least, what this Faccio is like as a conductor. [. . .]

1. In answer to Verdi's letter of 31 July 1870.
2. See Document VI.
3. La Gazzetta Musicale di Milano, a weekly musical journal published by the House of Ricordi from 1842 to 1902. At this time Giulio Ricordi was the publisher and Antonio Ghislanzoni was the editor.

Auguste Mariette to Paul Draneht

Paris, 8 August 1870

My dear Bey,

H.H., the Khedive, has sent me here to watch over the construction of Aida, and I am carrying out this mission with all the zeal I am capable of.

But at every turn I have to make expenditures that in all fairness I should not have to bear.

Thus in the completely unfamiliar matter of the costumes, I have encountered some difficulties I had not foreseen. This business is serious, for we must not fall into caricature; on the other hand, we must stay as Egyptian as possible. That is why, even today, I am obliged to grope, to try on, to do and undo. To this end I am purchasing wretched fabrics and building the costumes through the hands of a dressmaker as best I can. One must also give something to the man who serves as a mannequin. It is not up to me, however, to pay these expenses.

The same consideration applies to the sets. Among these gentlemen I have found some artists highly qualified to design Egyptian architecture of great fantasy. But that is not what we need. Here again, just as I have drawn the costumes myself, I am personally submitting the model for the sets. For that reason I now must have the great work of Prisse, of the Commission of Egypt, of Champollion and Lepsius,[1] and many other illustrations which are ruined once they have passed through the hands of the workmen. So I have bought, or have yet to buy, all of this.

Since H.H., the Khedive, has placed in your hands a letter of credit reserved especially for the expenses of *Aida*, I ask you, by virtue of the preceding reasons, to place at my disposal the sum of 3,000 francs, for which I shall give you an accounting if you wish. The expense is quite justified, since (unfortunately) I am not a capitalist. On the other hand, H.H. himself would be angered if he knew there are certain expenses for *Aida* that I am supporting with my own purse. [. . .]

1. Achille Constant Théodore Émile Prisse d'Avennes (1807–79) and Jean François Champollion le Jeune (1790–1832), French Egyptologists, and Richard Lepsius (1810–84), German Egyptologist.

Verdi to Cesare De Sanctis [1]

Genoa, 10 August 1870

[. . .] If you want to go to Cairo, I'll send you the score of the new opera. You can direct it, and you can receive the applause or boos — assuming that there will be an opera because thus far it is *in mente Dei*. The contract has not even been signed.

1. Most of De Sanctis's and his family's letters to Verdi and his wife are missing. Alessandro Luzio, ed., *Carteggio Verdiani*, I (Roma: Accademia Reale d'Italia, 1935), pp. 3–216, gives only 28 letters, most of them incomplete, from the De Sanctises to the Verdis, versus 237 letters from the Verdis to the De Sanctises (from 28 December 1849 to 3 January 1899).

Verdi to Antonio Ghislanzoni

Genoa, 12 August 1870

Signor Ghislanzoni,

I have been in Genoa for two days, but I shall return home tomorrow; so write to me always at St. Agata.

Corticelli has forwarded your letter[1] to me here, but he did not send me the verses of the finale and the second act. Mariette has informed me that we can use as many priestesses as we wish; so you can add them in the consecration scene.

Of the changes that were made,[2] I have incorporated:

the first recitative;

the *romanza, Celeste Aida, forma divina*;

the recitative with the two strophes for Amneris and Radames. In the little trio that follows it would be better to eliminate the first lines so as not to give Aida too much to say; and I'm not pleased with Amneris' threat either.

The hymn that follows is all right as revised; I only wish that Radames and Amneris would take part in the scene, thus avoiding those two asides which are always cold. Radames has only to change a few words. Amneris could take a flag or a sword or some other old thing and address the strophe to Radames — warm, loving, warlike. It seems to me that the scene would gain by this. Aida is all right as she is; she cannot be otherwise.

Some lines in the aria could be changed,[3] but we shall take care of this when you visit me at St. Agata. I shall write you as soon as I have read the other lines.

1. Missing.
2. See Document VII.
3. According to *Carteggi*, IV, p. 18 n, Verdi added the following words to the text of Aida's aria (*Ritorna vincitor*) as written in Du Locle's scenario: "*Io no posso far voti nè pel padre nè pel amante. Per me è delitto il piangere ed il pregare.*"

Verdi to Giulio Ricordi [1]

Genoa, 12 August 1870

Dear Giulio,

I have been in Genoa for three days, but tomorrow evening I return to St. Agata.

I don't think I shall need any other historical or geographical information about Egypt. I wrote Ghislanzoni that he can use the priestesses, in spite of Herodotus.

Go ahead and announce the Cairo opera. If your official [*Gazzetta*] was the last [to mention it], say that I myself had asked you to be silent. Now you can relate the conversation I had with you when you came to St. Agata with Ghislanzoni. Since *Le Figaro* has told part of it (either Du Locle or Mariette talked to them), you tell the rest. It is useless, however, to mention the fee . . . but . . . you don't know it! . . . Will La Scala work out or not? Either well or not at all. Don't forget that a great artist is needed for Aida and a baritone with a biting voice for Amonasro; and the whole company good, very good, supremely good. Answer to St. Agata.

Ah, this war terrifies me! I have lived so long in France that I must detest French humbug and impertinence; but on the other hand I remember very well that Prussia once declared: the seas of Trieste and Venice should belong to Germany!! And I also remember the contempt with which it treated France after Sadova!![2] If a victorious Prussia meant a well-established German Empire, with Austria driven into a corner and the Adriatic Sea (all the way to the Adige) a part of that empire, our cries of death to the one and long live to the other would be very wrong. Ah, if we [France and Italy] could understand each other for once and, instead of turning away from each other, could look each other well in the eyes, measure our strength, and stand straight on our legs and march, march, march forward. . . . But no; all we do is talk.

1. In answer to Giulio Ricordi's letter of 8 August 1870.
2. France had been defeated by Prussia at Sadova, Bohemia, in 1866.

Paul Draneht to Riaz Pasha

Paris, 12 August 1870

Excellency,

Although I am in no immediate need of the 250,000 francs that His Highness has kindly put at my disposal for the expenses of the opera *Aida*, I wanted to assure myself — in view of the present events in France — that nothing would keep me from getting that sum the moment I should need it. [. . .]

I am asking Your Excellency kindly to take care of this matter, because the most luxurious sets and costumes will be displayed in the production of *Aida*, and nothing like them has been seen in the theatres of Europe.

Paul Draneht to J. Barrot

Paris, 12 August 1870

My dear Monsieur Barrot,

I beg you to forget the remarks I made about the simplicity of the costumes and sets for the opera *Aida*. I have again seen Mariette Bey, who, on his part, had the same fears about this as I. He showed me that he has changed the *mise-en-scène* and the plan of action in order to put great luxury and grandeur into the costumes, which will assure the splendid success of the work.

You are no doubt aware of the law that the French legislature has passed: all unmarried men or widowers without children between the ages of twenty-five and thirty-five will be drafted into the active army. This, of course, will deprive us of the majority of the French theatrical personnel we have engaged.

Since I cannot replace them now, I can do nothing but wait. [. . .]

Giovanni Battista Lampugnani to Paul Draneht

Milan, 13 August 1870

[. . .] Muzio writes me[1] to inform Y.E.[2] that Verdi is writing for la Galletti, la Giovannoni, Naudin, Medini, and Marè.[3] But perhaps you will already have seen him in Paris. [. . .] Here in Milan everything is quiet. Some are for Prussia and some are for France. In this war I am for humanity, which it burdens me to see massacred in such a way. [. . .]

1. Apparently Muzio had been in contact with Verdi to discuss the artists of the Cairo Opera with regard to the various roles being prepared for the new opera. Muzio's letter to Lampugnani is missing.

2. Your Excellency.

3. Giovanni Marè, Italian bass. After appearances in Rome (1865) and Bologna (1868) he was heard during the first season of the Cairo Opera and in Vienna (1872).

Verdi to Antonio Ghislanzoni

St. Agata, 14 August 1870

Signor Ghislanzoni,

When I came home I found your poetry on my desk. If I must frankly state my opinion, it seems to me that the consecration scene did not turn out to have the importance that I expected. The characters don't always say what they should, and the priests are not priestly enough. It also seems to me that the theatrical word is missing, or if it is there, it is buried under the rhyme or under the verse and so doesn't jump out as neatly and plainly as it should.

I shall write you tomorrow when I have reread it more calmly; and I shall tell you what, in my opinion, could be done. Certainly since the scene needs to be done, it must be given all possible importance and solemnity.

I won't talk about the rest of the opera because I need to have this act completely finished so that I too can put myself to work on it.

Verdi to Antonio Ghislanzoni

St. Agata, 16 August 1870

Signor Ghislanzoni,

I think that for the time being it would be better to skip the consecration scene. It must be studied further in order to give it greater character and greater theatrical importance. It must not be a cold hymn but a real scene. I enclose a copy of the French outline so that you may see the full importance of that tableau.

Let's concentrate now on the second act so that I too can work. There is no longer a moment to lose. The first chorus is cold and insignificant. It is an account that any messenger could make. I know there is no action; but with a little <u>skill</u> one can always do something worthwhile. There is no action whatever in *Don Carlos* when the ladies awaiting the Queen are standing under the trees outside the convent; yet with that small chorus and that song which has so much character and color in the French verses, a real little scene was made. Here also it is necessary to make a scene with a good <u>lyrical</u> chorus, with the maidens who are dressing Amneris, and with a dance by little Ethiopian Moors.

I shall explain myself better by writing out the scene:

<u>Room, etc., maidens dressing Amneris. Incense is burning and fans are being waved. Ethiopian boys carry vases, perfumes, crowns, etc. on large basins. They dance to the sound of castanets; meanwhile the</u>

Chorus

Chi è Colui, chi è Colui
che arriva splendente di
gloria, e bello come il Dio   Strophe
dell battaglie?

Vieni, Radames: le figlie
d'Egitto t'attendono ed intuonano
per te inni di gloria,   Strophe
Inni d'amor.

<u>Amneris aside</u> (*Oh vieni,*
Radames. Te sol sospira,   Two lines
te sol ama la figlia del Re.)

Chorus

Dov'è, dov'è il feroce invasor?
Egli resister non potè all'urto
del guerrier. Ei fù disperso come
il vento disperde la nebbia.

Vieni, Radames. Le figlie
d'Eggitto t'attendono, ed intuonano
per te inni di gloria, inni
d'amor.

<u>Amneris, as before</u> (*Vieni,*
Radames etc., etc.)

There should be two couplets of ten lines each. The first four-line strophe of warlike character; the second, also of four lines, amorous. And two voluptuous lines for Amneris.

The second couplet, the same.

And, without seeking rhythmic eccentricities, write lines of seven syllables twice — that is, two lines of seven syllables in one; and if it doesn't upset you too much, write some lines with masculine endings, which are sometimes very graceful in music.

The melody in *Traviata* "*[Di Provenza]*" would be less tolerable if the lines had feminine endings. I shall write you about the duet tomorrow; meanwhile do this little scene for me as soon as possible.

Giulio Ricordi to Verdi [1]

[*Probably* Cadenabbia,] 16 August 1870

Illustrious Maestro,

Forgive the hardly decent half sheet, but the mail leaves in a few moments, and I barely have time to drop you a few lines.

I am enclosing a little article for our *Gazzetta*, but I decided not to send it in before you read it. Therefore, would you kindly look it over, make some observations, if necessary, and then send it back by return mail to Milan so that I can publish it next Sunday.[2] Excuse me for troubling you.

The company for La Scala will soon be complete; I shall keep you posted. Whoever does not work out will be dismissed. Don't worry about this, for *Aida* must be given *non plus ultra* or not at all. Since the "not at all" would be a great calamity for the management, I shall do my utmost in every respect to have an ensemble that satisfies you. [. . .]

We anxiously await the outcome of the next terrible battle, on which France's destiny will depend. May God not allow Italy's fate also to be involved! You are right — if the Germans (I don't say Prussians) should be victorious, who knows where their pride would lead them. [. . .]

1. In answer to Verdi's letter of 12 August 1870.

2. In *La Gazzetta Musicale* of Sunday, 21 August 1870, Giulio Ricordi wrote: "We are making an announcement which will be of the greatest interest for the whole musical world. Verdi is writing a new opera; this means that he will add a new masterwork to his former ones, continuing to raise the name of Italian art.

"Verdi had been repeatedly invited to compose an opera expressly for the new great theatre in Cairo, but he had not wanted to yield to that request. Later Mariette Bey and Du Locle sent him a complete outline of the libretto (in which the Khedive supposedly had a hand); and Verdi found it so interesting, dramatic, and rich in theatrical situations, that he could not resist his wish to compose it. The negotiations were concluded, and thus Verdi's new opera will be performed at the theatre in Cairo next season.

"The illustrious maestro will not go to Cairo; however, he has reserved the right to produce the opera simultaneously in a European theatre. He has already received numerous invitations and the most splendid offers from the most eminent theatres, but until today he has not accepted any of them.

"Our readers would like us to say something about the plot, but we want to leave them a bit of curiosity. Therefore we shall limit ourselves to saying that the title of the new libretto is *Aida*, that the action takes place in Memphis and Thebes at the time of the great pharaohs, and that the verses are written by the prolific genius of our Ghislanzoni."

Verdi to Antonio Ghislanzoni

St. Agata, 17 August 1870

Esteemed Signor Ghislanzoni,

In the duet,[1] there are some excellent things at the beginning and at the end, but it is too long and drawn out. It seems to me that the recitative could be said in fewer lines. The strophes are good until *a te in cor destò*. But then, when the action warms up, it seems to me that the theatrical word is missing. I don't know if I make myself clear when I say "theatrical word," but I mean the word that clarifies and presents the situation neatly and plainly.

For example, the lines

In volto gli occhi affisami
E menti ancor se l'osi:
Radames vive . . .

This is less theatrical than the words (ugly, if you wish):

. . . con una parola
strapperò il tuo segreto.
Guardami, t'ho ingannata:
Radames vive . . .

So also the lines

Per Radames d'amore
Ardo e mi sei rivale.
— Che? voi l'amate? — Io l'amo
E figlia son d'un re.

seem to me less theatrical than the words: *Tu l'ami? ma l'amo anch'io, intendi? La figlia dei Faraoni è tua rivale! —* Aida: *Mia rivale? E sia: anch'io son figlia . . .*

I know very well that you will ask: "And the verse, the rhyme, the strophe?" I don't know what to say. But when the action demands it, I would quickly abandon rhythm, rhyme, strophe; I would write unrhymed verse to say clearly and distinctly whatever the action requires. Unfortunately, it is sometimes necessary in the theatre for poets and composers to have the talent not to write poetry or music.

The duet ends with a typical *cabaletta*, which is also too long for the situation. We'll see what can be done with the music. In any case, I do not think it is good to have Aida say:

> *Questo amore che t'irrita*
> *Di scordare lo tenterò.*

Try to send me this duet — with the finale that follows — as soon as possible, because it is necessary that I work too if I am to finish in time.
P.S. Yesterday you should have received my other letter, in which I speak of the first scene of the second act.

1. Aida-Amneris in Act II, scene i.

Paul Draneht to Isabella Galletti Gianoli

Paris, 17 August 1870

[. . .] Today I received assurance that you will fill the principal role in the opera *Aida*; and, as I am certain of the pleasure this must cause you, and to which I am also susceptible in my own regard, I hasten to inform you of this. [. . .]
P.S. The Maestro, naturally, has not consulted me; only yesterday Dr. Lampugnani wrote to tell me that, upon returning from his visit to Signor Verdi, Muzio had been charged by him to write me that the interpreters of the opera are la Galletti, la Giovannoni, Naudin, Medini, and Marè.[1]

1. Even if Verdi had suggested these artists to Muzio as possibilities for the first performance in Cairo, and even if Muzio had given their names to Lampugnani for Draneht's information, Draneht too hastily accommodated Mme. Galletti in this postscript which he wrote in Italian below the French text he had dictated. Several weeks later Verdi had still not made any definite decisions about the Cairo cast. See Verdi's letter to Ghislanzoni of 27 September 1870.

Paul Draneht to Verdi

Paris, 18 August 1870

My dear Maestro,

I am actively attending to *Aida*, but not until today have I been able to get the costume designs. Even so, that is not enough for me; for to have the costumes made I need the distribution by function of the characters in the opera.

So I am going to ask you, my dear Maestro, to kindly give me, as soon as possible, the exact and detailed distribution of all the roles, including small accessory roles, because I am not familiar with the libretto of *Aida*, except through the French review which is doubtless quite incomplete and indicates only the principal characters.

I am returning to Italy at the end of the month, and before then I would like to be able to have the costumes made to the measurements of the artists who, depending on the types of their voices and their merits, will be called upon to interpret the roles of *Aida*.

Paul Draneht to Giovanni Battista Lampugnani

Paris, 18 August 1870

Dear M. Lampugnani,

I ask you to put the libretto of *Aida*,[1] which I address to you today, at the disposal of M. Monplaisir.[2]

He is in the country, and I prefer that you forward it for fear that it should be mislaid. [. . .]

P.S. [. . .] I also address to you a letter which you will have the kindness to forward at once to Maestro Verdi.

1. Draneht probably sent Lampugnani a copy of Mariette's printed outline and referred to it as a "libretto." He was not to receive the actual Italian libretto until a year later. See Verdi's letter to Draneht of 2 August 1871.
2. Hyppolite-George Monplaisir, French dancer and choreographer.

Paul Draneht to Hyppolite-George Monplaisir

Paris, 18 August 1870

My dear M. Monplaisir,

I have sent to Lampugnani a libretto of *Aida* that I ask you to examine at once.

You will oblige by sending me immediately the exact details of the ballets, their composition and the number of female dancers, as well as the ballet supers and the extras, so that I might know as exactly as possible what I must do to make the costumes. [. . .]

P.S. I must forewarn you that the *mise-en-scène* of *Aida* is splendid — costumes, sets, nothing has been spared for the munificence of this work. [. . .]

Paul Draneht to Riaz Pasha

Paris, 19 August 1870

Excellency,

I have the honor of confirming the fears of my last letter regarding the 250,000 francs that His Highness had kindly deposited through Monsieur Cattavi at the Crédit Lyonnais. In view of the events that are upsetting France at the moment, this credit was refused me.

I did not think I would have to mention the matter again so soon, but

Mariette Bey just brought me the costume designs and the set models; and I find myself facing many more expenses than I had anticipated. Contrary to what I thought, I now believe, as does Mariette Bey, that the luxury displayed in producing *Aida* will oblige us to go beyond the amount of credit granted by His Highness. [. . . .]

Isabella Galletti Gianoli to Paul Draneht [1]

Pesaro, 20 August 1870

Excellency,

Thousands and thousands of thanks for your most amiable letter, from which I learned with the greatest pleasure that the role of Aida in the new opera by the illustrious Verdi will be executed by myself. It has truly been a gift and a courteous thought of Y.E. to inform me, and for this I am immensely grateful to you. [. . .]

1. In answer to Draneht's letter of 17 August 1870.

Raffaele Vitali to Draneht

Ancona per Cerreto d'Esi, 21 August 1870

[. . .] I have seen <u>Muzio's</u> lousy hand in the casting of Verdi's new opera! And particularly in the role entrusted to la Giovannoni! . . . Verdi is blind concerning that man! . . . Muzio and his wife became our enemies at the end of the season in Cairo — simply because we did not defend him sufficiently against the charge that had been leveled against him after the affair of the orchestra player!! . . . But my God, what could one do about his ill-advised behavior in that affair, which made me shudder!! . . . We always used to be very nice to him; but he, and even more so his wife, have an <u>overbearing</u> need to hate and always to do someone ill!!

After la Galletti, only la Vitali should have been chosen and that because of her many qualifications! It is really a <u>most powerful blow</u> to my daughter's morale and one that will certainly cause considerable damage to her professional status. Patience! *Il faut souffrir quelque fois*! I shall prepare my daughter little by little for this unexpected blow! It will be very hard on her; but what can one do! . . . If we did not know how just and good you are, we would fear having to spend a season heaped with disgust and humiliation! . . . You, Excellency, in as much as it is possible, will assist and protect my <u>daughter who is so good</u>;and you will see to it that the inevitable thorns of the theatre do not wound her too grievously! We implore you and we hope. Our character and our conduct always expose us to disgust and intrigues! [. . .]

Giovanni Battista Lampugnani to Paul Draneht

Milan, 21 August 1870

Excellency,

Yesterday I gave the libretto of *Aida* to M. Monplaisir. M. Monplaisir has now returned to Milan. [. . .]

I have sent to M. Verdi, in Genoa, the letter addressed to him.[1] [. . .]

1. Draneht's letter to Verdi of 18 August 1870.

Camille Du Locle to Verdi

Paris, 21 August 1870

Dear and illustrious Maestro,

You have not answered my last letter which contained the agreement on Egypt.[1] I do not know, therefore, whether you have received it; or whether, quite simply, the agreement not being <u>absolutely</u> what we had arranged between us, you have made up your mind not to sign it; or whether you have given up the matter altogether, which is still possible. I did not want to bother you. But as the whole of Egypt is after me to write you again, I do so begging you to tell me openly or, rather, confidentially where we stand. I have no other interest in this matter but to make myself agreeable to you first and then to the Khedive, who was a perfect host to us when we were in Egypt. Since you come first, I wanted to get the orders from you.

The funds are in Paris, the sets under construction. You understand the fears of Mariette and Draneht Bey, whom I have not met but who seems to hold a knife at Mariette's throat.

My wife received Madame Verdi's kind letter. She is in the country and must be answering her this very day. I do not talk to you about our serious and sad affairs. We are full of determination and courage to defend ourselves, if need be, to the death. We spend our days here in training.

Our armies have had better luck these last few days, but how much blood and how much grief!

1. Du Locle had sent Verdi a copy of the Cairo contract, which had been drawn up and signed by Mariette in Paris on 29 July 1870. See Document V. The letter that accompanied the contract is missing.

Verdi to Camille Du Locle

St. Agata, 22 August 1870

Dear Du Locle,

My heart is broken by the news from France, and I wish I were not an individual but rather government and nation at one and the same time in order to do what is not being done . . . and perhaps, alas, what cannot be done!![1]

Yesterday I left myself open to hope; today I am annihilated! There is something fateful about this war which, it must also be said, was undertaken with too much thoughtlessness. Nevertheless French valor will ultimately be victorious over the fate and the misfortune that has thus far befallen you. Dear Du Locle, I wanted to write you a hundred times, and a hundred times the pen dropped out of my hands. [. . .] I don't dare ask for a line from you; but if you wish, and are able, to write me only to tell me that you, your wife, and those whom you love are well, I shall be most grateful to you.

Addio my dear Du Locle. Take heart. [. . .]

1. Verdi apparently hoped for an alliance between Italy and France in the war against Germany.

Verdi to Antonio Ghislanzoni

St. Agata, 22 August 1870

Esteemed Signor Ghislanzoni,

Yesterday I received the finale [Act II]; today, the duet[1] — which is good, except for the recitative which, in my opinion (excuse me), could have been said in even fewer words. But, I repeat, it can very well remain as it is.

This is not the time to write to Mariette; I myself have found something for the consecration scene. If you do not like it, we shall continue to search. But in the meantime it seems to me that we could make a rather effective musical scene of this. The piece would consist of a litany, intoned by the priestesses, to which the priests reply; of a sacred dance with a slow and sad accompaniment; of a short recitative, vigorous and solemn as a biblical psalm; and of a prayer in two strophes, spoken by the priest and repeated by all. I would like it to be profound and quiet, especially the first strophe, unlike the choruses in the finale of the introduction and the finale of the second act, both of which smack a little of the *Marseillaise*.

It seems that the litanies (and, for the thousandth time, excuse my impudence) should be short strophes of one long line and one five-syllable line; or — and perhaps this would be better so that everything could be said — two eight-syllable lines and the five-syllable line, which would be the *ora pro nobis*. They would thus become short strophes of three lines each, six in all, and that is more than enough to make a piece.

Have no doubt, I do not abhor *cabalettas*, but I want a subject and a pretext for them. In the duet in *Ballo in Maschera*[2] there was a magnificent pretext.

After that whole scene, if I may say so, an outburst of love was necessary. . . .

1. Aida-Amneris in Act II, scene i.
2. Amelia-Riccardo in Act II.

Paul Draneht to Hyppolite-George Monplaisir

Paris, 23 August 1870

My dear M. Monplaisir,

The information you gave me[1] suffices completely, for I now know the number of costumes to be made.

As for the colors, we shall adopt those supplied to us in the designs of Mariette Bey in Paris and shall discuss them in Milan.

We shall not be able to establish the style of the dances any further without having an idea of Verdi's music. [. . .]

P.S. Do not be disheartened by the events in France; we are here and we shall defend her without you, since you are not able to come.

1. Monplaisir's letter to Draneht is missing.

Verdi to Antonio Ghislanzoni

St. Agata, 25 August 1870

Esteemed Signor Ghislanzoni,

Yesterday I received the chorus in eight-syllable lines; but twenty-four hours earlier, the other had arrived, and — I don't know if it was fortunate or unfortunate — I had already set it to music.[1] Now we shall have to keep that one in seven-syllable lines, which seemed excellent to me.

You would be doing a blessed deed by coming to St. Agata for two or three days to make a few more little revisions and to clean up these first two acts. Then you will be free to finish calmly the other two acts. I could then finish the first two.

If you decide to make this sacrifice, plan to leave immediately. You can go by train to Firenzuola. When you get off, you will find coachmen in front of the station who can take you to St. Agata. If time should permit, you might notify me [of the time of your arrival], and I would have you met at the station by my horses. But if you can leave right away, it is better; and you will always find a coach at Firenzuola or at Borgo St. Donnino that will take you to St. Agata.

I expect you then. *Addio, addio*. . . .

1. Verdi apparently refers to the consecration scene in Act. I.

Verdi to Camille Du Locle

St. Agata, 26 August 1870

Dearest Du Locle,

In these very sad times that surround us, I would never have dared to mention the Cairo contract. You have asked me for it, and so I am sending it to you with my signature, and with the addition of two articles, which you will find fair and which you will have approved by Sig. Mariette.

I accept the present contract with the following modifications: [1]

1. The payments will be made in gold.

2. If through any unforeseen circumstances whatever, independent of me (that is, through no fault of my own), the opera should not be presented at the theatre in Cairo during the month of January 1871, I shall have the option to have it performed elsewhere six months later. .

You have the kindness, I hope, to collect for me the 50,000 francs, for which I am sending the receipt. From this sum take 2,000 francs and give it as you see fit to aid your courageous and unfortunate wounded. With the other 48,000 buy me Italian Government Bonds. Keep the certificates and give them to me the first time we see each other again; and I hope that will be soon.

I wrote you yesterday.[2] For now I can only take your hand and say that I love you very much. *Addio, addio.* . . .

1. Verdi quotes from the contract in French. See Document V.
2. The letter is missing.

St. Agata, 26 August 1870

Received from H.H. Ismail Pasha, Khedive of Egypt, from the hands of M. Mariette Bey, the sum of 50,000 francs, first installment on the sum of 150, 000 francs, stipulated in my contract for the opera of *Aida* with the representative of H.H.

Signed: Giuseppe Verdi

Camille Du Locle to Verdi [1]

Paris, 26 August 1870

Dear and illustrious Maestro,

I thank you for your kind words and the interest you show in our misfortunes and my poor country. I am very hopeful that by the grace of God we shall pull through, but the ordeal is rough! We all do our best, and I am writing you as one of the national guard, with my fingers still trembling from firing exercise.

I received your letter[2] and saw M. Muzio. I think, as you do, that you would do well to avoid correspondence with Draneht Bey, who by the Viceroy's wish has been kept completely out of this affair. It's Mariette who has been charged with coming to an agreement with you. Apart from Mariette and myself, a benevolent and completely disinterested intermediary, I think you don't have to let yourself be bothered by anyone.

Our letters crossed. Did I tell you about the sets? The one for the last act, I think, will be very beautiful and very novel. I have asked the painter for a sketch for you. [. . .]

My girls are well. They are still in the country. If our Fritz[3] advances too much, they will return to Paris. [. . .]

1. In answer to Verdi's letter of 22 August 1870.
2. Du Locle apparently refers to the missing letter mentioned in Verdi's letter of 26 August 1870.
3. The Germans.

Paul Draneht to J. Barrot

Paris, 28 August 1870

My dear Monsieur Barrot,

Events are quickly marching on as the Prussians march on Paris. In order not to find our affairs thwarted later on, I have invited all the artists here to take an advance payment with the guarantee that they will leave Paris immediately. I see that they all plan to go to Marseilles and that the largest group will go to Egypt on the boats of the 9th and the 19th of next month.

For myself, I shall go to Marseilles in a few days to attend to some business in that city. From there, on the 6th of September, I shall leave for Milan, where I shall spend the rest of the month. [. . .]

Camille Du Locle to Verdi[1]

Paris, 28 August 1870

Dear and illustrious Maestro,

I have but a minute to acknowledge receipt of the contract. It will be done as you wish, and "thank you" from the poor wounded! I deeply appreciate your good and great heart in this!

This morning I went to get my folks in the country. We don't expect the Prussians before Thursday. [. . .]

1. In answer to Verdi's letter of 26 August 1870.

Auguste Mariette to Paul Draneht [1]

[Paris,] 1 September 1870

Excellency,

I received a communication from Maestro Verdi [2] concerning the sum of 50,000 francs which we must pay him. Verdi requests that these 50,000 francs be paid to him in gold, and the way in which he expresses himself proves to me that this is a condition *sine qua non*. Consequently I ask you to secure the sum involved in gold; this will oblige you to make an additional outlay of 500 francs to the account of the opera *Aida*. [. . .]

1. Draneht received this letter shortly before his departure from Paris, and he complied the same day.
2. Du Locle had apparently communicated Verdi's requests to Mariette. See Verdi's letter to Du Locle of 26 August 1870.

Camille Du Locle to Verdi

Paris, 1 September 1870

Dear and illustrious Maestro,

I just received (at five o'clock) your 50,000 francs. Tomorrow I shall make use of them as you indicated to me, and I shall return your copy of the contract.

I have but a minute to write you before the mail leaves. A thousand affectionate greetings.

Camille Du Locle to Verdi

Paris, 2 September 1870

Dear and illustrious Maestro,

Here are some details concerning your affairs, which I could discuss only in general terms yesterday.

Mariette has ratified the two little additions you made in the contract, and I received your 50,000 francs. I immediately ordered my broker to buy 48,000 francs in Italian bonds for you. As soon as I have your securities, I shall deposit them in a safe place, until you come to France or I go to Italy. I don't think it is necessary to make your copy of the contract travel anymore. I shall keep it with your securities in my desk.

I read this morning in *Le Figaro* that you have sent me 2,000 francs for the wounded. I am not the one who put it in there, but it won't hurt. This morning I contributed 1,000 francs in your name to the collection of the *Gaulois*, [1] to which all of us have made an offering. I am keeping 1,000 francs for the field hospital which we are going to establish in the new Opéra, if Paris is besieged. The subscribers of the Opéra will be the first to provide the funds and services for this field hospital, but it will only be opened in case of a siege.[2] If the siege does not take place, your 1,000 francs will be added to the first. I would have written you, or rather my wife would have written to Maestro Verdi to ask him for his offering to the field hospital at the Opéra, had you not anticipated our request. All the composers represented at the Opéra will contribute to this. I think that despite the faults and turmoils of the *grande boutique*, you will not be displeased to have two beds of yours in a field hospital where your name is inscribed and your bust appears.

This, dear and illustrious Maestro, is the way I have used the powers you have entrusted to me.

Still no news, but we are quite courageous and hopeful. If our Fritz comes, he will be well received.[3]

A thousand affectionate greetings to the two of you from the two of us.

Camille

I have a shotgun! . . .

1. A French review published by *Le Figaro*. *La Gazzetta Musicale* of 11 September 1870 quotes a letter from Du Locle to the director of the *Gaulois*. This letter reports Du Locle's intentions precisely as stated in this letter to Verdi.
2. The siege actually began on 19 September 1870.
3. Du Locle wrote this on the day the Germans conquered Sedan and took Napoleon III as their prisoner.

Eugenio Tornaghi to Giuseppina Verdi

Milan, 5 September 1870

[. . .] Tomorrow I expect Giulio and his family from the country. Signor Tito and all are well. Lucky for them that they will not be deafened by the wires from Paris and Berlin. Here we are still bewildered by the enormity of the disaster; this little bit of "republic" was all that was needed. God knows what the consequences will be!

Please pay my respects to the illustrious Maestro and tell him that I shall soon send him the music paper as ordered in the note handed to me by Ghislanzoni.[1]

1. Ghislanzoni responded quickly to Verdi's letter of 25 August 1870, for he visited St. Agata sometime between 27 or 28 August and 3 or 4 September 1870. On his return to Milan he apparently delivered Verdi's request for additional music paper to the House of Ricordi.

Paul Draneht to Auguste Mariette

Milan, 7 September 1870

My dear Mariette Bey,

I have just arrived after a rather troublesome journey — seventeen hours by stagecoach and fourteen by rail.

I found no letters from you or from our contractors. Consequently I must conclude that nothing more has been done since my departure from Paris. I don't know what we shall do if the Prussians advance on Paris and if the capital is surrounded, as is likely to happen.

As far as I am concerned, I think His Highness must be told what has been done until now, so that if we are prevented from going ahead, he will not be deluded until the last moment. You would do well to write him yourself. In my report I shall mention only the difficulties you have encountered in the preparatory work you had to do and your inability to move on more rapidly.

Write me as often as you can, my dear Bey, and accept the expression of my best feelings and friendship.

Verdi to Antonio Ghislanzoni

St. Agata, 8 September 1870

Signor Ghislanzoni,

Since your departure,[1] I have worked very little; I have only done the march, which is, however, very long and detailed. The entrance of the King with the court, Amneris, and the priests; the chorus of the people and of the women; another chorus for the priests (to be added); the entrance of the troops, fully armed for war; dancers who carry sacred vessels, treasures, etc.; Egyptian girls who dance; finally, Radames with the whole shebang — all form but one piece, the march.

You must help me, however, by having the chorus sing a little something about the glories of Egypt and of the King, and about those of Radames. So the first eight lines must be modified; the next eight for the women are fine, and eight more must be added for the priests: "We have triumphed with the help of divine providence. The enemy has surrendered. May God help us in the future." Look at King Wilhelm's telegrams.[2]

I'll explain myself better by outlining the scene.

POPULACE: *Gloria all' Egitto, ad Iside,*
Al Faraon . . . . . .
Luce . . . .

> *Sull' orbe manderà.*
>   *Gloria al guerriero* . . . . .
>
> . . . .
> *S' intrecci al mirto al lauro*
> *Sul crin* . . . . ·

WOMEN: *Cogl' inni, etc.* (as it stands)
           . . . . .

PRIESTS: . . . .

        . . . .

        . . . .

        . . . .

          . . . .

        . . . .

        . . . .

          . . . .

You adjust the sense and the rhyme; in the chorus of the people and the priests, perhaps <u>masculine endings</u> for the fourth verse.

I think the <u>ten-syllable</u> lines you sent me are very good. If the other strophes turn out as well, it will be excellent.

In the recitative that follows, there is a moment in which the situation demands a musical phrase. After the words *Ascolta o Re; tu pure ascolta, o giovane, la parola della saggezza*, finish the eleven-syllable line, then add four *cantabile* lines of either seven or eight syllables. . . .

        . . . .

     . . . .

     . . . .

     . . . .

These lines should be solemn and sententious. It is the priest who speaks. . . .

At the end it would be good to repeat the first strophe from the chorus of the people, *Gloria, etc., etc.*, strophe of four lines; priests . . . strophe of four lines. For all the others, strophe of four lines.

<u>Amen to the finale.</u>

Adjust that line for Radames:

> *Dessa! . . . mia sposa! il folgore.*[3]

It is too broken and cannot be made into a melodic phrase. . . .
Once again, <u>Amen,</u> and a heartfelt addio.

1. On 3 or 4 September 1870.
2. King Wilhelm of Prussia.
3. The line became *D'avverso Nume il folgore*, followed by *Sul capo mio discende*.

Antonio Ghislanzoni to Verdi

11 September [1870]

Most esteemed Maestro,

I confess to you that I have also worked very little because of those damned Prussians and also somewhat — pardon me — because of those mad Frenchmen. On one side as well as the other, what a <u>revolting</u> spectacle! What do they want? I like Napoleon. How much ingratitude in everyone! And how much baseness! It's been a month now that all of France screamed <u>war</u>, <u>war</u> as a single voice . . . and today they accuse the Emperor, the Emperor alone, of the disaster that came about. The betrayed is called the betrayer. . . . We shall see how it will end. Napoleon is alive, and the time will come when history will judge him and the Republicans. Anyway these are things that degrade humanity.

Here are the strophes for the <u>second-act chorus.</u> I have also changed the women's lines so that the meter turns out uniformly. Do as you wish.

POPULACE: *Gloria all'Egitto e ad Iside*
            Che il sacro suol protegge!
            Al Re che il Delta regge
            Inni festosi alziam!
            Vieni, o guerriero vindice,
            Vieni a gioir con noi!
            Sul passo degli eroi
            I lauri e i fior versiam!

WOMEN: *S'intrecci il mirto al lauro*
            Sul crin dei vincitori!
            Nembo gentil di fiori
            Stenda sull'armi un vel.
            Danziam, fanciulle egizie,
            Le mistiche carole,
            Come dintorno al sole
            Danzano gli astri in ciel!

PRIESTS: (to the populace)
            Della vittoria agli arbitri

Supremi il guardo ergete;
Grazie agli Dei rendete
Nel fortunato dì.
Così per noi di gloria
Sia l'avvenir segnato,
Nè mai ci colga il fato
Che i barbari colpì! . . .

Here is the strophe which could serve for Ramfis, in the place you indicated.

RAMFIS: *Ascolta, o Re — tu pure,*
Giovane eroe, saggio consiglio ascolta.
(pointing to the Ethiopian prisoners)
Son nemici e prodi sono . . .
La vendetta hanno nel cuor . . .
Fatti audaci dal perdono
Correranno all'armi ancor!

Tomorrow I shall send you the *concertato*, reduced to ten-syllable lines, and the closing of the act. [. . .]

Verdi to Antonio Ghislanzoni [1]

[*Probably* St. Agata, 12 September 1870]

Dear Ghislanzoni,

I received your letter of the 11th. The verses are good. . . .

The finale [of Act II] is sketched; in fact, I can say it's finished.

The dramatic situation requires a slight revision. Aida recognizes her father too quickly. If a few words were added, Aida would better attract the attention of the audience, and the very important phrase *È mio padre* would stand out clearly. In order to go ahead with the music, I fumbled about with the words, which you will render into good verse for me:

[RADAMES:]   *. . . . . . . a te sien tratti*
i prigionier.

AIDA: *Che veggo! O ciel! . . . Lo salva,*
O Re. . . . Lo salva! . . . È mio padre.

ALL: *Suo padre!*

AIDA: (Would like to speak, but emotion stifles her.)
È lui . . . lui . . .

AMONASRO: (Interrupts his daughter, afraid of being discovered.)
Sì . . . suo padre! . . .

Anch' io pugnai.
Vinceste! . . . *Morte* . . . *non trovai,*
etc., etc.

That *Lo salva* helps the scene, gives the actress some stage action, and allows the music to prepare for *È mio padre.* . . .

It is also good, I think, that Amonasro speaks only when he is afraid of being discovered. . . .

The last line must be broken as much as possible.

E di morir sul campo invan sperai is beautiful, but it is too extended.

1. In response, obviously, to Ghislanzoni's letter of 11 September 1870.

Antonio Ghislanzoni to Verdi

[12 September 1870]

Most esteemed Maestro,

Here are the verses for the second act *concertato*:

AMONASRO:	*Ma tu, o Re, tu signore possente,*
	A costoro ti mostra clemente;
	Oggi noi siam percossi dal fato,
	Doman voi potria il fato colpir.
AIDA — SLAVES — PRISONERS:	
	Si: dai Numi percossi noi siamo,
	Tua pietà, tua clemenza imploriamo;
	Ah! giammai di soffrir vi sia dato
	Ciò che in oggi ci è dato soffrir!
PRIESTS:	*Struggi, o Re, queste ciurme feroci,*
	Chiudi il cuore alle perfide voci;
	Pur dai Numi votati alla morte,
	Si compisca dei Numi il voler.
POPULACE:	*Sacerdoti, gli sdegni placate,*
	L'umil prece dei vinti ascoltate!
	E tu, o Re, tu possente, tu forte,
	A clemenza dischiudi il pensier!
RADAMES:	(looking at Aida)
	Il dolor che in quel volto favella
	Al mio sguardo la rende più bella;
	Ogni stilla del pianto adorato
	Nel mio petto ravviva l'amor.
AMNERIS:	*Quali sguardi sovr'essa ha rivolti!*
	Ed io sola . . . *avvilita* . . . *rejetta!*
	La vendetta mi rugge nel cor.

THE KING: *Or che fausti ne arridon gli eventi,*
             A costoro mostriamoci clementi;
             La pietà sale ai Numi gradita
             E rassicura dei prenci il poter.

THE KING — CHORUS:

             Gloria all'Egitto e ad Iside
             Che il sacro suol difende,
             S'intrecci il mirto al lauro
             Sul crin del vincitor.

RADAMES: *Quale inatteso folgore*
             Sul capo mio discende!
             Ah no! d'Egitto il soglio
             Non val d'Aida il cor!

AMNERIS: *Dall'inatteso gaudio*
             Inebriata io sono;
             Tutti in un dì si compiono
             I sogni del mio cor.

AMONASRO: (*sotto voce* to Aida)
             Fa cor, della tua patria
             I lieti eventi aspetta;
             Per noi della vendetta
             Già prossimo è l'albor.

Are these verses enough? I really did not know anything special the priests and prisoners could say. Don't you think it would be better to blend them into the general chorus rather than have them repeat antiphons or religious laments?

May I begin the third act? [. . .]

Verdi to Antonio Ghislanzoni

[*Probably* St. Agata, 13 September 1870]

Dear Ghislanzoni,

The last sentence of your letter gives me the chills: "May I begin the third act?"

What? Isn't it finished yet? And I had expected it any hour. I have finished the second act. . . . So be sure to send me the poetry as soon as possible. In the meantime I shall do a little polishing here and there.

The lines of the finale are all right, but it is impossible to do without a strophe for the priests at the end. Ramfis is a personality and he absolutely must have something to say. I know well that there is little for him to say and that is why it was necessary to be sure that the priests' strophes at the beginning of the finale could be repeated at the end. It was better, and it would have been better to repeat the strophes of the populace, as I had asked you; but in *Vieni, o guerriero vindice* the *Vieni* makes repetition impossible. Now that it has been done, however, there is nothing to do but add four lines for the priests. Do not be afraid of religious antiphons or laments, etc. . . . When the situation demands it, one must have no scruples. At this point the priests can only invoke the gods so that they may be favorable to them in the future. Take heart then; send me these four lines right away and the third act as soon as possible.

Auguste Mariette to Paul Draneht [1]

Paris, 13 September 1870

My dear Bey,

Before answering your letter I wanted to see all the contractors personally, so that I would be sure of their intentions and not say anything to you carelessly.

They have all agreed to work hard and to commit themselves to being ready by the second half of December. I myself shall give up nothing. I have received an order from the Viceroy, and until I am told to quit, I don't see why I should. After all I am a civil servant of Egypt; and whatever grief the present events may cause me, I don't see why it should keep me from fulfilling my duties.

Therefore do not take it upon yourself to tell the Viceroy that it is impossible to have the opera ready because of me. Unless the rooftops of Paris fall on our heads, we shall somehow go ahead. As for myself, H.H. has put me here to do a specific job, and I shall do it to the end.

You must also consider, first, that if the opera is not performed this winter, it never will be, given that we shall never again be able to organize the hundred thousand details necessary for such an undertaking; second, that we are committed to Verdi, and that, performed or not performed, we must nevertheless pay him 150,000 francs, which would be lost.

Consider, besides, that these are matters of your competence and not mine. As far I am concerned, I am in Paris to do the job the Viceroy has entrusted to me. If the Viceroy wants me to continue, I see no objection to that. If he wants me to quit, he has only to say so. But I do not object, and that is what I wanted to make clear.

Nothing new here. We expect the Prussians, confident that they will not take us. If fate decides otherwise, it will only be another phase of the battle, and the war will continue elsewhere. France is a proud nation. She has been struck broadside, but, thank Heavens, she is not dead yet and still has enough strength to win, now that she is rid of all the weaklings who have caused her to lose.

Au revoir my dear Bey. Let us not lose heart. Paris is not as dejected, as crestfallen, as one in Italy would like to think it.

1. In answer to Draneht's letter of 7 September 1870.

Paul Draneht to Auguste Mariette

Milan, 21 September 1870

My dear Mariette Bey,

I received only yesterday your letter of the 13th of this month.

I have written nothing to Cairo on the subject of our *Aida* business, and I see that I have done well. You tell me in your letter that you have come to an understanding with all of our manufacturers and contractors, who have positively committed themselves to you to deliver at a specified time. So much the better; I remain at your disposal regarding the stand to take.

Madame Baron[1] has written to ask me for an advance of 20,000 francs; I cannot make this remittance without your authorization. I do not know what agreements you have made with her and consequently cannot act according to her wishes. I am staying in Milan until the end of the month, and I embark at Brindisi on 3 October for Alexandria; you can write me accordingly.

Is there a way of knowing what agreements you have made with our contractors?

I do not know whether this letter will reach you in time for you to reply to me in Italy. The mail is subject to great delays; for two days we have received neither letters nor journals. When shall we be rid of this unfortunate war? The Prussians are at the gates of Paris; but it seems to me that with the wise measures taken by the government, Paris will be impregnable. It does not seem possible to me that they can mount a regular siege and maintain [*illegible*] 400,000 men for several months to bombard the capital.

Farewell my dear Bey. I send wishes of good courage and good luck for France and for you, and I hope the end will be better than the beginning.

1. Delphine Baron, costume manufacturer in Paris.

Verdi to Antonio Ghislanzoni

Tuesday [*Probably* St. Agata, 27 September 1870][1]

Esteemed Signor Ghislanzoni,

I was unable to respond to your last letter[2] yesterday nor can I respond today. I am desolated by the news about France. Poor country and poor us! I hope that tomorrow I can harness our horses and look to our business; meanwhile keep working, if you can.

You can reply to *La Gazzetta dei Teatri* that it is not at all well informed, that the old outline has undergone many changes, and that I (who alone have the right) have not yet chosen the artists.

1. Several assumptions point to this date. First, the synopsis of *Aida* must have been published in the review *La Gazzetta dei Teatri*, which is not available, about the same time as it was published in the review *Il Trovatore* on 8 September 1870. See Document IX. Second, Ghislanzoni refers to Verdi's remarks about *La Gazzetta dei Teatri* in his letter to Tornaghi on or about 1 October 1870. Third, the tone of this "Tuesday" letter to Ghislanzoni greatly resembles the tone of Verdi's letter to Clarina Maffei on the following Friday, 30 September 1870. Last, in light of Verdi's letter to Ghislanzoni of 28 September 1870, one can assume that he was able to "harness their horses" and to return to work on the unfinished opera.

2. This letter, which probably accompanied Ghislanzoni's first draft of Act III, is missing.

Verdi to Antonio Ghislanzoni

St. Agata, 28 September 1870

Kindest Signor Ghislanzoni,

This third act is very good, although there are some things that, I think, should be touched up. But I repeat, on the whole it is very good, and I send you my sincere compliments.

I see that you are afraid of two things: of several, shall I say, <u>bold theatrical strokes</u> and of <u>not writing</u> *cabalettas*! I have always been of the opinion that *cabalettas* should be used when the situation demands it. Those in the two duets are not demanded by the situation; and the one in the duet between father and daughter, especially, seems out of place to me. In such a state of fear and moral depression, Aida cannot and must not sing a *cabaletta*. In the outline there are two extremely dramatic points, both true and good for the actor, which are not well realized in the poetry. The first: After Amonasro has said *Sei la schiava dei Faraoni*, Aida can only speak in broken phrases. The other: When Amonasro says to Radames *il Re d'Etiopia*, Radames must hold and control the scene, almost by himself, with strange, mad, highly agitated words. But we shall discuss this when the time comes.

Meanwhile let's analyze this act from top to bottom. For the first chorus the second version seems better to me, except we must not repeat what was said in the <u>litanies</u>:

> *Luce divina eterna,*
> *Spirto fecondator.*

It is better to say, as in the outline, *Iside favorevole agli Amori, etc.* . . . . The recitative and *romanza* are all right. Then *Tu agli occhi miei. Dei Faraon, etc.*, seems weak to me; and I find this sort of enthusiasm by Aida to be false: *Della patria il sacro amor*. After the terrible scene and her father's insults, Aida, as I told you, is left breathless; therefore truncated words in a low and somber voice.

I have reread the outline,[1] and I think this situation is well rendered. I myself would forget about strophic or rhythmic forms; I would not think about singing, and I would render the situation as it is, perhaps even in lines of recitative. At the most I would have Amonasro sing one phrase: *Pensa alla patria, e tal pensiero ti dia forza e coraggio*. Do not forget the words *Oh patria mia, quanto, quanto mi costi*! In short I would stick as closely as possible to the outline.

I shall write you again tomorrow, making some observations about the rest.

1. Verdi's reference to the outline seems to imply that he and Ghislanzoni used Mariette's printed *programma* and/or the Verdis' translation of it rather than Du Locle's scenario for their collaboration on the Italian libretto. A comparison of Documents II and III, however, shows that Verdi means Du Locle's scenario and not Mariette's outline.

Verdi to Antonio Ghislanzoni

St. Agata, 30 September 1870

Signor Ghislanzoni,

I did not write you sooner because I wanted to do the first scene of the third act.

Since the chant of the chorus is solemn, eight lines are too many; six would be enough.

The duet between Aida and Radames is very beautiful in the *cantabile* section, but I think it lacks development and clarity in the dramatic section. I would have preferred a recitative at the beginning. Aida could have been more calm and more dignified, and she would have been able to make certain phrases that add to the scene stand out better — as for example, *Non giurare: t'ho conosciuto prode, non ti vorrei spergiuro*, . . . and further on, *E come potrai sottrarti ai vezzi d'Amneris, al volere d'un re, al voto d'un popolo, etc., etc*. The *cantabile* section should have begun with Radames's *Aida, ascoltami*; only these two words should have been wedged into the preceding recitative.

Following this *cantabile* section the four lines are cold and do not adequately prepare for Aida's beautiful strophes, *Fuggiam gli ardori, etc*. I know well that strophe and rhyme are involved; but why not start out with the recitative so that you could first say everything the action demanded? Note that even in the outline this moment needs greater development. After the eight beautiful lines for Aida, I would have written another eight for Radames. I would have transformed Aida's four lines, however beautiful, into recitative: *Fuggiam, ivi è la patria, etc.* I would also have retained the dialogue that is so lively in the outline, especially the words

> *Va, Amneris t'attende agli altari.*

RADAMES: (underline)(forcefully)(/underline) *Giammai!*

> *Giammai? Allora la scure*
> *Cadrà su me . . . .*
> *Ah! etc. . . . .*

And why did you change the meter of this *cantabile* section, while saying almost the same thing? It might have been better to repeat the first strophes. But now leave these as they are, and we'll see what comes of it.

In the following scene you are afraid to render Aida repulsive. But consider that Aida is justified by the duet with her father and, I would say, almost by the presence of her father, who the audience knows to be hidden there, listening. There is more to it. Aida can naturally stop to ask Radames a question; but after that duet Radames cannot. It seems to me that the situation is not exactly dangerous but that it could be. Therefore I would always prefer the question of Aida, which is more natural and real. But not one useless word must be said. *Ma! . . . onde evitar le schiere qual via terremo . . .* and so on, with a lively and very brief dialogue. Above all try to emphasize Radames. The words of the outline, properly ordered, can provide the opportunity for a good bit of action for the actor!

RADAMES: *Ma no, no, non è possibile!*
AIDA: *Calma.*
RADAMES: *Questo è un sogno, un delirio?*
AIDA: *O Radames, ti calma.*
RADAMES: (with a piercing cry) *Per te, per te ho tradito la patria.*
AIDA: *Sul Nilo amici fidati attendono.*
> *Vieni, sotto altro cielo troverai la gloria e la mano d'Aida*
> *Che ti ama, etc.*

Here you wanted to write a trio; but this is not the place to stop for singing. We must hurry right to the entrance of Amneris.

If you like, keep the lines already written; but take out that *pel mio pugnale*, and, if you can, cut those first four lines to two. For example:

> *Traditor!*
> *Dessa!*
> *Tu!*
> *Incauta!*
> *Muori etc. . . . .*

And it would have been good also to omit the two lines that are useless at this moment:

> *Di salvati è tempo ancor*
>
> . . . .
>
> *Arrestate il traditor.*

At the end, the two lines are very good:

> *Io qui resto, su me scenda*
> *Il tuo vindice furor;*

Yet it would not be more beautiful, but it would be more dramatic, to say simply:

> *Io qui resto, o sacerdote.*
>   Excuse me. . . .

P.S. Please note that in the *stretta* of the finale of the second act we also have a chorus of prisoners on stage; it is impossible to keep them silent (there are at least twenty), and they cannot sing with the populace.[1] So make up any kind of strophe for me.

1. In some of the world's leading opera houses, however, it is common practice to have the prisoners either sing with the populace or not sing at all.

Verdi to Clarina Maffei

St. Agata, 30 September 1870

Dear Clarina,

   This disaster in France brings despair to my heart as it does to yours! It's true that the humbug, the impertinence, the arrogance of the French was — and continues to be — insupportable, despite all their misfortunes; nevertheless France has given liberty and civilization to the modern world. If she falls, let's not deceive ourselves; all our liberties and our civilization will fall. Let our scholars and politicians glorify the knowledge, the sciences, and even — God forgive them — the arts of these victors. But if one looked a little deeper, one would see that the old Gothic blood still runs through their veins; that they are immensely proud, harsh, intolerant of anything that is not German, and rapacious without limit. Men with heads but without hearts. A strong but not a civil race. And that King who always chatters about God and providence, with whose help he is destroying the better part of Europe. He thinks himself ordained to reform the manners and to cleanse the vices of the modern world!! Some missionary! . . . The old Attila (another missionary of the same sort) halted before the majesty of the capital of the ancient world. But this one is about to bombard the capital of the modern world. And now that Bismarck wants us to believe that Paris will be spared, I fear more than ever that at least part of it will be destroyed. Why? I couldn't say. Perhaps, since such a beautiful capital exists nowhere else, because they could not succeed in creating another one like it. Poor Paris — so happy, so beautiful, and so splendid when I saw it last April!

And we? I would have hoped for more generous politics [on our government's part] and the payment of a debt of gratitude.[1] A hundred thousand of our men might have saved France and ourselves. In any case, I would have preferred signing a treaty, and being defeated with France, to this inertia which will make us despised one day. We shall not stay out of the European war, and we shall be swallowed. It will not happen tomorrow, but it will happen. A pretext is found right away. Maybe Rome, maybe the Mediterranean. . . . And isn't there the Adriatic which they have already proclaimed a German sea?

The business in Rome[2] is a big thing, but it leaves me cold; maybe because I feel that it could start trouble abroad as well as at home, because I cannot reconcile Parliament with the College of Cardinals, liberty of the press with the Inquisition, civil code with the Syllabus,[3] and because I am frightened to see that our government goes on haphazardly and hopes . . . for time. Let there be a skillful Pope tomorrow, a shrewd and really crafty one, such as Rome has often had, and he will ruin us. <u>Pope</u> and <u>King of Italy</u> — I cannot see them together even in this letter.

I have no more paper. Pardon this <u>tirade</u>. I am letting off steam. Things look very black to me, and yet I haven't told you half of what I think and fear. [. . .]

1. In 1859 France had come to the aid of Italy against the Austrians. Under Marshal Marie de MacMahon the allied French-Italian armies had won a decisive victory at Magenta on 4 June 1859; and on 24 June 1859 they had defeated the Austrians at Solferino.

Now that Napoleon III was a prisoner at the German castle of Wilhelmshöhe near Kassel, Ghislanzoni expressed himself in his own way on the same subject: "If I knew how one might get something edible into the castle of Wilhelmshöhe, I would like to send a huge *panettone* [Milanese sweet cake] to the Emperor. And I would send a letter along with that *panettone* to tell the prisoner that among the two hundred thousand citizens of Milan who acclaimed him as their liberator and savior in 1859, there is still one who has not forgotten. . . ." (*Rivista Minima*, vol. I, No. 1, p. 27.)

2. On 20 September 1870 Pope Pius IX had withdrawn into the Vatican, as King Vittorio Emanuele's Italian troops took over the city and Rome became the capital of a united Italy.

3. The Syllabus of Errors which accompanied an encyclical issued by Pope Pius IX in December 1864. It "seemed to preclude any accommodation between Church and State in Italy at any foreseeable time. Further, it condemned the premises on which the most liberal states of the time were founded and as such seemed an incredibly reactionary attack on all that was best in the nineteenth century. The Syllabus, strictly speaking, was a private letter addressed to bishops everywhere as a guide for instructing Catholics. It begins: 'A Syllabus, containing the principal Errors of our times' and then lists eighty propositions which Pio Nono considered erroneous. Among those condemning such things as pantheism, Bible societies and communism were others which stigmatized freedom of conscience and religious toleration (No. 77), freedom of discussion

and the press (No. 79), and finally (No. 80) the idea that 'the Roman Pontiff can and should reconcile and harmonize himself with progress, liberalism and recent civilization.' " (George Martin, *Verdi — His Music, Life and Times* (New York: Dodd, Mead & Company, 1963), p. 418.)

Antonio Ghislanzoni to Eugenio Tornaghi

[*Probably* about 1 October 1870][1]

[. . .] Verdi has not attached much importance to the publication of the synopsis of *Aida* in *La Gazzetta dei Teatri* and other papers. In any case, the announcement of the libretto in *La Gazzetta Musicale* would not have been of any use to him. It would not be the least bit similar to that synopsis. But since the matter is over and the Maestro has no longer mentioned it, I would now advise that silence is best.

I shall be ruined if you do not send me 100 lire soon for my November salary. Would you believe it? The trip from Mariaga to St. Agata and from St. Agata to Mariaga cost me 98 lire. . . . How can I manage it? From a talk Verdi had with me, I was able to make out that he thinks I am very rich or at least a stockholder. . . . What a consolation! . . . I am afraid to be re-called to St. Agata from one moment to the next. [. . .]

1. It seems doubtful that Ghislanzoni would have requested an advance on his November salary as an editor of *La Gazzetta Musicale* before this date. Verdi's letter to Giulio Ricordi of 7 October 1870 reveals that Ghislanzoni had, at the same time, also asked for an advance on his fee as the librettist of *Aida*.

Verdi to Antonio Ghislanzoni

St. Agata, 7 October [1870]

Esteemed Sig. Ghislanzoni,

I received your poetry. I don't have time now to talk about the second duet;[1] but tomorrow I shall give you my opinion about it at length. Meanwhile we must make some decision about the first scene so that our work may proceed.

The first chorus and the recitative of Ramfis and Amneris are all right, but I see that Aida has too much to do in this act, and I would reduce the *romanza*, which is rather cold and common. I would shorten this *romanza* in the following manner. I would leave the first five lines of the recitative.

> *Io tremo!*
> *Se a dirmi vieni eterno addio,*
> *Del Nilo ai cupi vortici*
> *Io chiederò l' oblio;*

là in quella tomba gelida
Forse avrà pace il cor.

Arrange the lines and the rhyme any way you like, and if you also want to change the quatrain to recitative, do as you wish. Only, leave the idea of drowning herself in the Nile.

In the following scene I would not be too happy if Amonasro were to call out to Aida. I think it would be better if Aida, turning around, were to see her father: *Cielo! È mio padre. . . .* And I do not care too much for the phrase *Io del tuo cor leggo i misteri* from the mouth of that proud and cunning King; it would be better to say *Nulla sfugge al mio sguardo.*

What follows is all right, but the ending[2] does not correspond to the situation. Perhaps I did not explain myself well in my other letter,[3] but I thought I told you that this is a dramatic moment which must be carefully thought about and worked over. The role of Aida must be better developed and that of Amonasro less so, which seems to me easily done this way:

AIDA:	*Padre! mi uccidono le tue parole.*	
	No, non son la schiava dei Faraoni;	
	Son tua figlia	4 lines.
	Sarò degna di te . . . della patria.	
AMONASRO:	*Pensa che un popolo vinto e straziato*	
	Per te	

If you carefully consider Aida's situation and write me four good dramatic lines, you will see that something plausible and uncommon will come of it.

Try to send me this revision as soon as possible, because I too must work and there is no time to lose. Tomorrow I shall write you about the rest, but meanwhile send me the few lines I have requested.

1. Aida-Radames in Act III.
2. The ending of the Aida-Amonasro scene.
3. See Verdi's letter of 28 September 1870.

Verdi to Giulio Ricordi

[St. Agata,] 7 October [1870]

[. . .] Do you think it would be wise to offer an advance to Ghislanzoni?[1] The libretto is not yet finished. The fourth act and the revisions are missing. Poor Ghislanzoni! I torment him so much, but I can't help it. If it were a question of writing music for salons, there would be no composer more easily satisfied than I; but the stage is such a curious business!!

1. Perhaps Verdi had heard from Tornaghi or Giulio Ricordi about Ghislanzoni's request of 1 October 1870.

Verdi to Antonio Ghislanzoni

St. Agata, 8 October 1870

Dear Ghislanzoni,

Let it be said once and for all: I never mean to talk about your verses, which are always good, but to give my opinion on the theatrical effect. The duet between Radames and Aida has, in my opinion, turned out greatly inferior to the one between father and daughter. Perhaps that is because of the situation or the form, which is more ordinary than that of the preceding duet. Certainly that string of *cantabile* passages of eight lines, each spoken by one and repeated by the other, is not designed to keep the dialogue alive. In addition the interludes between these *cantabile* passages are rather cold.

At the beginning of this duet I still prefer some of the original lines to this recitative, which is too dry. For example, the first eight lyrical lines to *D'uno spergiuro non ti macchiar* would suit me; I don't know if the form would suit you. Then the recitative in the section, *Prode t'amai, benchè . . . nemico; non t'amerei spergiuro*, up to the whole of Radames's solo. After that the lines

> *D'Amneris l'odio fatal saria,*
> *Insiem col padre dovrei morir*

are not theatrical; that is to say they give the actor no chance to act; the audience's attention is not captured, and the situation is lost. There should be greater development, and these words, more or less, need to be said:

AIDA: *E non temi il furore d'Amneris? Non sai tu che la sua vendetta come fulmin cadrebbe su me, sul padre mio, su tutti?*

RADAMES: *Io vi difendo.*

AIDA: *Invan . . . tu nol potresti! Ma se tu m'ami . . . ancora una via resta di scampo a noi.*

RADAMES: *Quale?*

AIDA: *Fuggire.*

You will say, "But this is nonsense, my verses say the same thing." Very true, nonsense, if you like; but it is certain that phrases like *Cadrà su me, sul padre, su tutti. . . . Invan . . . tu nol potresti etc., etc.*, when they are well delivered, always attract the audience's attention and sometimes produce great effects.

Aida's eight lines, *Fuggiam*, are good, as are Radames's first four; but in the four now added, I don't care very much for the idea of the bride. Wasn't it better to say, as in the outline, *Qui dove nacqui e vissi e divenni il salvator della patria*? You left out Aida's outburst

I miei Dei saranno i tuoi,
La patria è dove si ama.

This must be said in the lines already written or reduced to a recitative, as you wish.

Then greater prominence must be given to the interlude that follows:

AIDA:	*Va . . . tu non m'ami.*	These or other
RADAMES:	*Io non t'amo?! . . . Mai gli uomini*	words; it mat-
	in terra, nè gli Dei in cielo ama-	ters little. But
	rono mai di più ardente amore.	let it be a ring-
		ing, theatrical
		phrase.

AIDA:	*Va, va: ti attende all'ara Amneris.*
RADAMES:	*No, giammai.*
AIDA:	*Giammai . . . dicesti?*
	Allor piombi, etc., etc. (until the end of the duet)

Tomorrow I'll write you briefly about the rest.

Verdi to Antonio Ghislanzoni

St. Agata, 9 October 1870

Sig. Ghislanzoni,

It seems to me that Amonasro's words *Si fugga . . . mi segui . . .* are out of place.[1] And it seems that after the line *Tu Amonasro, tu il Re, Numi che dissi,* a phrase spoken by the King with fierce joy would be good: *Anche i miei saranno nelle gole di Napata* or something like that. Then follows:

RADAMES:	*No, non è ver! Sogno, delirio è questo?*	
AIDA:	*Vieni, ti calma, ascoltami.*	
RADAMES:	. . . .	Two full lines;
	. . . .	strong: invec-
		tive against
		Aida.
AMONASRO:	*Era voler del. . . .*	

Then, instead of those two lines for Aida, which do not seem appropriate, I would give four to Amonasro; and here it would be fitting to say: *Sul Nilo fidati amici ci attendono; a te non resta che fuggir con noi. Vieni alla nuova patria,* etc.

The six lines that follow are excellent and very dramatic; only that *Muori* seems too dry to me, and perhaps you should add a pair of lines to say, *Ah! mal per te. . . . Tu vieni a distruggere l'opra mia? Muori*. But do not say, *Pel mio pugnale muori*.

Please hurry.

1. Verdi refers to the end of Act III.

Verdi to Antonio Ghislanzoni

St. Agata, 16 October 1870

Esteemed Sig. Ghislanzoni,

I am terribly sorry that you have been so very ill. Take every imaginable precaution, and I hope to hear in your next letter that you have fully recovered.

To respond to your letter[1] in detail would take some time, and we don't have much to spare at this point. So let's forget about debates and worry about one thing only: success! This is why I would be displeased if the revisions, which I requested, were to weaken, rather than strengthen, the effect.

As for the duet [in Act III] between father and daughter, the revisions do no harm whatsoever. On the contrary, Aida I think, now says what she must say, and it fits the situation.

It seems to me that you are too worried about the character of Radames. Let's not discuss it; it should be as you say. But in this duet, for example, isn't Radames just as interesting as Aida? It seemed natural to me that he should respond to Aida: *Lasciar la patria, i miei Dei, i luoghi ove nacqui, ove acquistai gloria, etc., etc*. But if you don't like these accounts of glory, find something else. Only since we have taken the path of *cantabiles* and of *cabalettas*, we must continue on that path; and it is good that Radames should reply to Aida's eight lines with eight of his own.

I asked you to keep

> *La patria è dove s'ama,*
> *I miei Dei saranno i tuoi,*

because it seemed that it was a good theatrical outburst, which could in no way harm the effect.

As for Aida's *romanza*, let's forgo any concern for the prima donna; certainly, not one of them would complain about it. But if the effort were too great, the duets that follow would be neglected. Then there are other considerations: the first chorus is serious; the scene between the Priest and Amneris is serious; the serious chorus returns. If we add yet another slow and serious scene plus a *romanza*, we shall meet with boredom.

I have composed this *romanza*: I have not succeeded! . . . *Fra il verde dei palmizi, sul Nilo, etc.* should be somewhat idyllic, you say. I entirely agree, but it had to be a great idyll; it had to smell of the odor of Egypt, as Filippi would say, to avoid *l'orfana, l'amaro calice delle sventure,*[2] *etc.* and to find a newer form. . . . But here we are in a debate again. . . . Excuse me.

We are up to the fourth act. When you came here with Giulio Ricordi, you made several notes and some cuts in the duet between Amneris and Radames. The notes and the cuts are quite justified, but something must be substituted for the cuts and the notes because this scene must be very well developed. Perhaps I am mistaken, but the situation seems very good to me, and very theatrical, and Radames's part cannot be colorless. Develop this situation as you see fit, and develop it well; and have the characters say what they must without preoccupying yourself in the least with the musical form. Obviously if you were to send me recitative from beginning to end, it would be impossible for me to write any rhythmic music; but if you were to begin immediately with any rhythm whatever and continue it up to the very end, I would not complain at all. Perhaps, perhaps, it would be necessary to change it, just to write a tiny little *cabaletta* at the end.

Take care of your health, and try to work as much as you can to finish *Aida*. We have no more time to lose.

1. Missing.
2. According to *Carteggi*, IV, p. 24, this is a quotation from a line Ghislanzoni had proposed.

Verdi to Antonio Ghislanzoni

Monday [*Probably* St. Agata, 17 October 1870]

Esteemed Ghislanzoni,

In reading over the scenario[1] of *Aida* I found the fourth act duet between Amneris and Radames revised according to the observations and cuts that you proposed. I am sending it to you, not because you should use it as a guide (I have already told you to develop this scene as you wish), but, rather, because you may find some good phrase or outburst that you can use. I repeat for the twentieth time that I desire only one thing: success. And that is why I take the liberty and find the courage to mention whatever I think useful in reaching that goal. Be patient, then, and here is the duet.

Scene II

AMNERIS:	*Fra poco i Sacerdoti qui*	By beginning
	saranno radunati per giudicarti.	with a recita-
	Grave su te pesa l'accusa,	tive, it would
	grave sarà la pena. Pure,	be difficult to

se davanti ai giudici tu vuoi
abjurare il tuo delitto, io tenterò
d'intenerire il cuor del Re, ed
ottenere il tuo perdono.

RADAMES: No: i miei giudici
non udiranno da me parola
di discolpa. Voi ben sapete
che io sono innocente: che
se il labbro profferì incauti
detti, il cuore è puro.
Puro, è vero, tradii la
patria. Il rimorso che
mi lacera l'anima, le mie
speranze svanite mi rendono
odiosa la vita e ora a me
non resta che un desiderio,
una speranza . . . morire!

AMNERIS: Morire! . . . ma io
voglio che tu viva: intendi?
Ah, tu non sai quanto
immenso sia l'amor mio
per te. Tu non conosci
i miei giorni angosciosi,
le mie notti che non han
fine. Per te rinuncierei
al trono, abbandonerei il
padre, rinnegherei gli Dei.

RADAMES: Ed io pure nel mio delirio
del mio amore per lei
ho rinnegato il dovere,
gli Dei, il Re, la patria?

AMNERIS: (furiously) . . . Non parlarmi
di lei! . . .

RADAMES: E che? Voi volete
che io viva? . . . Voi! . . .
che foste testimonio dell'
onta mia. Voi, sola
cagione d'ogni mia
sventura . . . e forse
della sua morte?

find a place to
start a *canta-*
bile section.
I think we
could begin im-
mediately with
lyrical lines
of any meter,
and continue
with the same
meter to the
end. However,
as the poet
wishes.

If these expres-
sions seem
forced, modify
them. But
Amneris's
phrases must be
passionate and
fiery.

AMNERIS: *Della sua morte? . . .*
Nò . . . . Essa . . . vive!

RADAMES: *Che dite? Vive?*

AMNERIS: *In quella notte il padre*
solo fù colto e nella
lotta ucciso. Essa ne sfuggiva
nè ancora ci fù dato di
rinvenirla!

RADAMES: (aside) *Ah fate, o Dei*
ch'essa raggiunga i suoi
lidi, e scordi l'amor mio
e le mie sventure!

Much feeling in this <u>aside</u> . . . so that a good vocal phrase can be developed. There is no danger of recalling *Norma* to mind, provided that the line is of a different form.

AMNERIS: *Ma, s'io ti salvo, giurami*
che non la vedrai mai piu. . . .

RADAMES: *Non lo chiedete.*

AMNERIS: *Rinuncia ad Aida.*

RADAMES: *Non posso.*

AMNERIS: *Anco una volta:*
rinuncia ad Aida o morrai.

RADAMES: *Morrò.*

AMNERIS: *Insensato! Tu non sai*
che quanto immenso è l'amore,
altrettanto terribile è il mio
furore. Chi ti salva ora?
Và che la giustizia abbia il
suo corso, e la tua morte plachi
l'ira degli Dei.

Only here it would be good to change the meter, to make a strophe of four or six lines for a small *cabaletta.*

RADAMES: *Piombi pure sul mio capo*
tutta l'ira tua. Cara mi fia
la morte se morirò per lei.

<u>As above.</u>

1. Apparently Verdi refers here neither to Mariette's outline nor to Du Locle's scenario. See Document VIII.

Verdi to Tito Ricordi

St. Agata, 18 October 1870

Do me the favor of paying the poet Sig. Ghislanzoni the sum of <u>2,000</u> (two thousand) lire on my account, as part of the compensation due <u>him</u> for the verses he is writing for *Aida*.[1] I shall give him the balance as soon as the libretto is finished.

1. On 20 October 1870 Eugenio Tornaghi (in the absence of both Ricordis) wrote to Verdi that Ghislanzoni's advance was available and that the librettist had been notified. (Autograph: St. Agata)

Verdi to Antonio Ghislanzoni

Tuesday [*Probably* St. Agata, 18 October 1870][1]

Dear Ghislanzoni,

Your last letter from Lecco, on Saturday,[2] promised me for the next day the verses that were missing to complete the third act. I have not received them, and I await them impatiently so that I too can finish this act.

I am aware that you have rewritten Radames's strophe several times. The time was not wasted because

Il ciel de' nostri amori
Come scordar potrem

is very, very, very good. But I tell you, with the same frankness, that I am not very enamoured of the line *È fuoco, è febbre, è folgore.* And I am also sorry that you did not retain *L'are de' nostri Dei* with Aida's response

Nel tempio stesso
Gli stessi Numi avrem.

But we can discuss that in person when I have the pleasure of seeing you here to revise, polish, and clear up the stage directions, etc., etc. Meanwhile keep busy with the fourth act. I have almost finished the third.

1. Ghislanzoni's illness and his letter to Tornaghi of 24 October 1870 suggest this date.
2. Missing.

Verdi to Antonio Ghislanzoni

Saturday [*Probably* St. Agata, 22 October 1870]

Esteemed Sig. Ghislanzoni,

As much as I hate to I must take you away from your work for a moment, but it will only be for a moment. I am sorry you eliminated the line *L'are de' nostri Dei* because it worked well for the piece as a whole. Also I

could not make use of the quatrain *È fuoco, febbre, folgore* because I would
be forced to make of it a kind of *cabaletta*, which would have jeopardized the
other that follows right after. This is what I would have done to finish the
music in this act. The phrases are yours; you need only adjust a few things for
the ensemble.

. . . .

. . . .

. . . .

Il ciel de' nostri amori
Come scordar potrem.

AIDA: *Ivi è la patria ov' è d'amar concesso,*
Gli stessi Numi avrem nel tempio stesso.

RADAMES: (hesitating) *Aida!*

AIDA: *Tu non m'ami . . . và*

RADAMES: *Io non t'amo? . . .*
L'amor che per te sento
Non vale a profferire umano accento

AIDA: *Và và . . . t'attende all'ara*
Amneris

RADAMES: *No, giammai!*

AIDA: *Giammai, dicesti?*
Allor piombi la scure
Su me, sul padre mio

RADAMES: *Ah no, fuggiamo!*

. . . .

. . . .

. . . . .

. . . . .

. . . . .

AIDA: *Ma, dimmi . . . per qual via*
Eviterem le schiere
Degli armati?

RADAMES: *Il sentier scelto dai nostri*
A piombar sul nemico fia deserto
Fino a domani.

AIDA: *E qual sentier?*

RADAMES: *Le gole di Napàta.*

AMONASRO: *Le gole di Napàta!*
A voi sien grazie o Numi!

RADAMES: *Oh! . . . chi ci ascolta?*

AMONASRO: *D'Aida il padre, e degli Etiopi il Re.*

RADAMES: *Tu? Amonasro! Tu! il Re! . . . Numi! che dissi!*
                Nò . . . non è ver! . . . sogno . . . delirio è questo!
AIDA: *. . . ti calma, ascoltami*
RADAMES: *Io son disonorato!*
                Per te tradii la patria!
AMONASRO: *Era voler del fato! . . .*
                Vieni. . . . oltre il Nil ne attendono
                I prodi a noi devoti,
                Là del tuo cor i voti
                Coronerà l'amor

Scena

AMNERIS: *Traditor!*
AIDA: *La mia rivale!*
[AMONASRO:]   *Vieni a strugger l'opra mia!*
                Muori!
[RADAMES:]   *Arresta!*
[AMONASRO:]   *Oh mio furore!*
[RAMFIS:]   *Guardie, olà*
[RADAMES:]   *Presto! fuggite!*
[AMONASRO:]   *Vieni, o figlia!*
[RAMFIS:]   *L'inseguite!*
[RADAMES:]   *Sacerdote, io resto a te.*

If you wish to change these last six lines to eight, because of some rhyme, I can very easily do it; in that case Radames's two lines would be fine.

AMNERIS: *Arrestate i traditor!*
RADAMES: *Sacerdote, io qui resto.*
                In me sfoga il tuo furor.

Do as you please.

Verdi to Camille Du Locle[1]

St. Agata, 24 October 1870

My dear Du Locle,

    A thousand thanks for your letter![2] . . . It surely eases our anxiety to a certain extent, since you wrote on the 24th of September and it is now the 24th of October.

I am trying to send you this line in response. Will you receive it? . . . Oh, this war, this war is quite long and cruel! If only it could have an honorable end for France and a desirable end for humanity. Enough blood and horror!

You have done well to take your dear women to safety. Peppina and I embrace you, and we ardently hope to embrace you in Paris.

Adieu, adieu, adieu.

1. Fearing that censorship might prevent or delay this letter, Verdi wrote it in French. A short note from Giuseppina Verdi was sent with it.
2. Missing.

Antonio Ghislanzoni to Eugenio Tornaghi

Mariaga, 24 [October] 1870

[. . .] The Maestro writes me that he has already finished the third act; the opera will probably be completed in twenty days. Truly this is astounding!

Verdi to Antonio Ghislanzoni

Tuesday [*Probably* St. Agata, 25 October 1870]

Dear Ghislanzoni,

No problem with the seven-syllable lines, either for the *cabaletta* or for the beginning etc., etc. . . . And I really think the duet[1] should begin at once in lyric form. In the beginning of this duet there is (if I am not mistaken) something exalted and noble, especially in <u>Radames,</u> which I would like to have sung. A song *sui generis*; not the usual *romanza* or *cavatina*, but a declamatory song, sustained and exalted. The meter is up to you; but break up the dialogue if you think it would add more life. If in adopting the seven-syllable line you find that the rhyme occurs too frequently, why not use the double line of seven syllables, as in *Trovatore*?

> *Condotta ell'era in ceppi al suo destin tremendo;*
> *Col figlio sulle braccia io la seguia piangendo, etc., etc.*

Allow me to point out that in Amneris's lyric lines there are two or three that slightly diminish her character:

> *Morir? che parli? ah, misero*
> . . . . . .
> *Te spento anch'io morrei*
> *Com'io t'ho sempre amato.*

Morir! must be said, but *che parli, misero* should be changed.

Further on, these two lines are too few:

> *Nol posso . . . a lei rinuncia.*
> *Io l'amo. . . . Ebben morrai!*

This is too brief and does not allow for dramatic action; the situation requires greater development and a little more space.

If we can succeed in writing a good beginning for this duet, you will see the importance it will have for the opera as a whole. Work with spirit; I am expecting, and I am certain of it, one of the best things in the libretto.

If we give lyric form to the entire duet, don't you think the first scene would require greater development? What if we wrote a *romanza*? A *romanza* in nine-syllable lines? What the devil would come out of it? Shall we try?

But now that it [the duet] is under way, continue; and if need be we shall write the *romanza* at the end.

1. Amneris-Radames in Act IV, scene i.

Verdi to Antonio Ghislanzoni

Wednesday [*Probably* St. Agata, 26 October 1870]

Dear Ghislanzoni,

After answering your letter yesterday I studied the duet in the fourth act at length; and I am even more convinced that it must be written, from the beginning, in lyric form. With the very words of the recitative I scribbled some seven-syllable lines; and I saw that a melody can be made of them. A melody, based on words that seem to be spoken by a lawyer, will seem strange. But beneath these lawyer's words, there is the heart of a desperate woman burning with love. Music is splendidly able to succeed in depicting this state of mind and, in a certain way, in saying two things at once. It is a quality of this art hardly considered by critics and held in low esteem by composers.

Here is what the form of this duet should be:

[AMNERIS:]

Arbitri di tua vita i sacerdoti
Si aduneran tra poco.
Grave su te pende l'accusa e grave
Ti minaccia la pena. A te fia lieve
Discolparti se il vuoi. . . . Colle mie
   preci
M'aprirò il varco del paterno core.
E perdonato sarai.

Strophe of eight *cantabile* lines. Write it so the melody can be expanded on the words, *Pregherò il Re, e spero nel perdono*. If eight lines are too few, write ten.

[RADAMES:]

No, non udranno un solo accento mai
Di discolpa i miei giudici. Innocente

Another strophe like that of

Dinnanzi ai Numi ed a me stesso io sono.
Incauti detti profferì il mio labbro,
Ma il tradimento nel mio cor non era.
Pure giusta è l'accusa.

Amneris. Here too the last lines should be written to provide for an expansive melody. . . . Expansive, not screamed.

AMNERIS: *Discolpati, discolpati*
RADAMES: *No. . . .*
AMNERIS: *Ma la tua vita. . . .*
RADAMES: *Io l'odio. . . . Estinta ogni*
              speranza, un sol desio ora
              mi resta . . . morire!
AMNERIS: *Morire. . . .*

And here another strophe of four, of six, of eight lines, as you wish, in dialogue, with whatever words you think best. Do not forget the *morire!* by Amneris; but you can place it either at the beginning of the strophe or at the end of the previous one . . . as you wish.

There follows the strophe of Amneris with the rest, as it is; and perhaps the strophe would turn out better by not starting with *morire*, which should be said in the preceding strophe. . . . But do it however it works out better for you. Only try not to write lines that say little. In this duet every line, I would almost say every word, has to have weight. Instead of the lines

> *Come t'ho sempre amato*
> *Oggi ancor t'amo, ingrato*

put something more important, something that is not useless. I'll tell you again, this duet must be lofty and noble, as much in the verse as in the music. In other words, nothing common.

Verdi to Vincenzo Luccardi [1]

St. Agata, 26 October 1870

I am working like a dog, but in a few days the inventive part will be finished. You are perfectly correct: I shall not go to Cairo. However, I shall send a person I trust with a copy of the score in order to stage it.[2] The original remains with Ricordi, along with the rights for all countries, save the Kingdom of Egypt; and Ricordi will do whatever he likes with his rights; but I shall assist with the *mise-en-scène* the first time it is done [in Italy]. [. . .]

1. Artist and sculptor, and Verdi's close friend in Rome.
2. With the words "to stage it" (*metterla in scena*), Verdi meant that his representative would be in control of the complete artistic direction of the production, as conductor of its performances. No stage director, in today's sense of the term, existed at the time. The *direttore di scena* merely arranged the action as instructed by the conductor. Franco Faccio's own production notes, for example, reveal the conductor's involvement, as *maestro concertatore e direttore*, in the dramatic as well as the musical aspects of operatic production. See Document XI. To this very day the conductor's ultimate artistic authority prevails in Italian opera houses.

Verdi to Antonio Ghislanzoni

Thursday [*Probably* St. Agata, 27 October 1870]

Dear Ghislanzoni,

The duet in the fourth act, the last you sent me, is very good, but it is too agitated and tormented. The lines are too choppy, and there is no way to make a melody out of them, or even long melodic phrases. Furthermore the announcement *Vive Aida* does not stand out as well as in the first lines. Here the last eight lines are excellent

> *Or, s'io ti salvo, giurami*
> *che più non la vedrai*
> . . . . *etc.*
> . . . . .

But in this situation the *cabaletta* is too long. Ah, these damned *cabalettas* that always have the same form and that all resemble one another. See if there is a way to find something more original.

As for the beginning of this duet I really think it would be best to do it as I wrote you yesterday. . . . A beautiful, calm, long, flowing melody for Amneris; another like it for Radames; then, in order to get to Amneris's other solo, some lines of dialogue as in the first lines, but with some adjustments, arriving with those first lines at *Or s'io ti salvo, etc.*

Don't be afraid that such long strophes as these will turn out lifeless. As long as the verse is sustained and beautiful, as you are able to make it, there is no need to worry about this duet.

In the judgment scene it is not necessary to repeat *Radames* three times.

If you want to finish the entire act before revising this duet, go right ahead and I'll touch up what I have done in the meantime.

P.S. I have finished the third act, and I wrote to you about the verses I used and how I used them. I have not received your answer.

Antonio Ghislanzoni to Verdi

31 October 1870

I am sending you the final scene. At a certain point you will find some dots substituted for Radames's words *Ah, vivi! e godiamo un istante di felicità che tra poco sparirà per sempre.*[1]

I don't care much for these words. The situation of the two lovers is so desperate, so terrible, that the *Ah, vivi!* seems out of place to me, and even more the *godiamo un istante di felicità*. These last words could even lead to an erotic interpretation, which would certainly not correspond to the intentions of the author.

We are in the presence of a woman who has not eaten for three or four days . . . and, in truth, how Radames still expects to enjoy a moment of happiness is not understandable. So give me your opinion. Fill in my dots, this one time, with some prose; and I shall write the verse. Since this scene deals with an agony, or rather two agonies, a great many or a few lines might be written according to the wishes of the poet and the convenience of the composer; so I shall leave it up to you.

If the ones I send you are too many, just make cuts; if they are not enough, let me know how and to what extent the strophes must be lengthened.

I hope to finish the duet between Radames and Amneris today, and I shall send it to you tomorrow.

[P.S.] Another question: In the outline,[2] offstage chants of the priests, etc., etc., are mentioned. Must I write verses for these chants?

1. See Document VIII.
2. See Documents II and VIII.

Emanuele Muzio to Camille Du Locle

Brussels, 1 November 1870

Dear Monsieur Du Locle,

Just this moment I received a letter for you from Verdi,[1] which I hasten to send by courtesy of H.E.,[2] the Minister of the United States of America.[3]

The Maestro asks me where Mariette Bey is. I don't know anything, and I think that you can tell him better than I.

Are the costumes and the sets for *Aida* in Cairo or still in Paris? If they are in Paris, I doubt very much that they will ever be able to leave for Marseilles and, from there, for Alexandria. You will know more than I and can give [Verdi] some news.

If you want to send your reply to Verdi through my intermediary, all you need do is take the letter to H.E., Minister Warbur [*sic*][4] of the United States, rue Chialiot 95 [*sic*][5], and address it to M. Muzio, c/o Madame Simons, Hotel de la Poste, Brussels. [. . .]

1. Verdi's letter to Du Locle of 24 October 1870. See Günther, pp. 22 and 37.
2. His Excellency.
3. Muzio's wife, Lucy Simons, was an American citizen.
4. Muzio refers to Elihu Benjamin Washburne, American statesman from Illinois. A friend and political ally of Ulysses S. Grant, he was United States Minister to France between 1869 and 1877. Dale Clifford, in her article "Elihu Benjamin Washburne: an American Diplomat in Paris," *Prologue* (Winter 1970), pp. 163 and 166, writes: "At the outbreak of war, the North German Confederation had withdrawn its ambassador and requested the United States to assume protection of its interests. Washington assented, and Washburne raised the American flag over the German Embassy in Paris. . . . His connection with France's enemy also brought benefits — particularly in the case of American dispatches entering and leaving Paris. German siege regulations prohibited the passage of sealed dispatch bags; when the diplomatic corps protested, Chancellor Otto von Bismarck politely refused to reconsider the order. Washburne, however, received a personal letter, giving the United States permission to send one sealed bag a week. It was the least his government could do, wrote the Chancellor, in view of Washburne's 'zeal and good will' in helping German citizens in Paris — and in return for 'those excellent cigars you have been kind enough to send me.' . . . In the hiatus between the armistice and the announcement of peace terms, Washburne visited his family in Brussels, where they had taken refuge during the siege." Presumably Muzio's American wife met Washburne and/or his family in that city.
5. 5 rue Chaillot.

Antonio Ghislanzoni to Eugenio Tornaghi

[*Probably* Mariaga, 2 November 1870][1]

[. . .] The libretto for Verdi is finished or almost finished; but you know that one cannot say Amen so long as the Maestro has not given the intonation. [. . .]

1. This date is written in another hand on the autograph.

Verdi to Antonio Ghislanzoni

[St. Agata,] 2 November 1870

Dear Ghislanzoni,

I have received the final scene which, on the whole, is all right. The first recitative is a little long and the end is perhaps a little cold, but we shall find a way to warm it up.

Have Radames say whatever you think, and let it be a passionate and *cantabile* little strophe. Nothing is needed for the priests.

Meanwhile let's think about the first duet,[1] which I am anxiously awaiting. Then we'll think about the rest. . . .

1. Amneris-Radames in Act IV, scene i.

Giulio Ricordi to Verdi

Milan, 2 November 1870

[. . .] I repeat what I told you in person,[1] my announcement to the management of the probability of the *Aida* production was received with the greatest satisfaction. The impresario exclaimed: "God be praised, since it is on this opera that we build all our hopes."

Everyone is ready to satisfy your wishes. In two days there will be a meeting of the board of directors and the management, at which I shall disclose everything that is required for the production of the opera, always reserving, of course, the greatest freedom of action on our part. I shall give you at once an exact account of the resources at the disposal of the management and how much it will be able to do so that you may be fully satisfied. It goes without saying that I have recommended the most scrupulous silence, since such an important and delicate business is involved. In short I hope that this beautiful event will come about — so beautiful, so much desired that it seems like a dream to me.

Tomorrow I shall go to the manufacturer of the instruments, and soon I shall tell you about the famous trumpets. [. . .]

My father, to whom I wrote right away concerning *Aida*, is more than happy, as you can believe, and will write you directly.

1. In late October Giulio Ricordi had been to St. Agata on his return from a performance of *La Forza del Destino* in Bologna. Ricordi had suggested this visit in his letter to Verdi of 6 October 1870. (Autograph: St. Agata)

Tito Ricordi to Verdi

Majolica, Lago di Como, 3 November 1870

Dearest Friend,

A letter Giulio wrote me after his return from Bologna and Busseto has filled me with joy. [. . .]

A new work of yours is the most fortunate event that not only the oldest of your publishers but all civilization could desire.

Let me, therefore, express my immense gratitude for such a favor. I also extend this gratitude to your better half, since she probably deserves a little credit too, as a result of her advice and her effect on your soul. [. . .]

Verdi to Antonio Ghislanzoni

[St. Agata,] 4 November 1870

Dear Ghislanzoni,

I have not yet received the revisions of the first duet,[1] but in order not to lose time I am writing about the scene that follows, the judgment. Perhaps I am deceiving myself, but this scene seems to me one of the best in the drama and not inferior to that of the *Miserere* in *Trovatore*. Perhaps you (and perhaps rightly so) are not of the same opinion. But if I am mistaken, it is wise to leave me in my error. However, in my illusion I do not find this piece as great as I had imagined. Let's get to work.

In the first recitative, in addition to the *Morir mi sento*, I need some other broken phrase to be repeated in the course of the piece. Then for the march (which should not be funereal), it is necessary that the words *Ecco i fatali — Gl'inesorati*, *etc.* come at the end of the recitative. We shall see later.

The backstage chorus is beautiful, but that six-syllable line seems short to me for this situation. Here I would have liked a full line, Dante's line, and also in tercets.

The *Taci? Taci?* is so dry that it is impossible to make it musically inter- rogative. I think the <u>tercet</u> form was good because we could repeat *Radames* twice, if we wanted, and because we could write a broken line, for example, like this:

> *Difenditi!*
> *Tu taci? Traditor!*

I know very well that the *ti, tu, ta* . . . *ci* is bad (you will revise it); but this dreadful line says what the situation demands. You want to say, *Nel dì della battaglia*? There was no battle.

Alla patria, al re spergiuro — I would use the ten-syllable line.

Sometime ago I advised you to avoid that meter because it became too bouncy in the *allegri*; but in this situation the <u>three by three</u> accent would pound like a hammer and become terrible.

The <u>solo</u> scene for <u>Amneris</u> is cold, and this kind of aria at this moment is impossible. I have an idea which you may perhaps find too daring and violent: I would have the priests return to the stage; seeing them, <u>Amneris</u>, like a tigress, would unleash the most bitter words against <u>Ramfis</u>. The priests would stop for an instant and reply, *È traditor! morrà!* Then they would continue on their way. Left alone, Amneris would shout, in just two lines of either ten or twelve syllables, *Sacerdoti crudeli, inesorabili, siate maledetti in eterno!* The scene would end at this point. You are perfectly correct in saying the King and maidservants[2] are useless.

To better explain the whole matter, which is really not very complicated, I shall outline the scene; and you can use what is good and revise what is not.

Scene Three

AMNERIS: (alone) *Ohimè!* . . . *morir mi sento!*
           Che feci? . . . *Chi lo salva?* . . . *Or maledico**
           L'atroce gelosia che la sua morte
           E il lutto eterno nel mio cor segnava!
           Che veggo! . . . *Ecco i fatali,*
           Gl'inesorati ministri di morte!

(*Revise the line as you think best. Maintain, however, one phrase that can be repeated later.)

           Oh! ch'io non vegga quelle bianche larve!

BACKSTAGE	. . . .	Twelve-sylla-
CHORUS:	. . . .	ble lines. Dan-
	. . . .	tesque tercet.
AMNERIS:	. . . .	The same, Very
	. . . .	pathetic, an-
	. . . .	guished tercet.

Scene Four

Radames crosses the stage between the guards and enters the subterranean chamber. Amneris cries out upon seeing him. (This is why, in the first recitative, I asked for some phrase to be repeated here: *Ah! chi lo salva!* . . . or something similar.)

VOICE OF	(in the subterranean chamber)	
RAMFIS:	*Radames! Radames!*	Another tercet
CHORUS:	*Difenditi!*	as before.
RAMFIS:	*Tu taci?*	
ALL:	*Traditor.*	
VOICE OF	*Radames! Radames!* . . .	Another tercet
RAMFIS:	*Difenditi!*	as before; it is
	Tu taci?	not necessary,
	Traditor.	however, to re-
		peat *Radames*
		twice. As you
		wish.

ALL:	. . . .	Four or six
	. . . .	ten-syllable
	. . . .	lines.
	. . . .	
AMNERIS:	. . . .	Only two
	. . . .	as before.

The priests return from the subterranean chamber, and <u>Amneris</u>, enraged, at <u>Ramfis</u>:

> *Sacerdote spietato, tu il dannasti a*
> *morte e, tu ben lo sai, non è traditore!*
> *Tu sai che l'amo e tu lo condanni?*
> *Egli non deve morire!*

Strophe of four lines, always with ten sylla- bles. It would be good to be- gin with the word *"Sacer- dote"* or *"Sacerdoti."*

ALL: *È traditor! morrà!* (<u>if it is possible, this seven-syllable line as a refrain</u>.)

AMNERIS: *Sacerdote! e non sai che io regnerò un giorno? E non temi la mia vendetta? No, no . . . lo salva! Egli non deve morir!*

Another strophe as before, always with *"Sacerdote."*

ALL: *È traditor! morrà!*

<u>Slowly the priests leave the stage</u>.

AMNERIS: (<u>alone</u>) *Sacerdote crudel! Maledetta in eterno sia la tua razza infame.* (<u>Two lines only, also of twelve syllables, if you wish</u>.)

The words in these two quatrains are very weak, but you will find the forceful words that the situation requires. The form of the piece, however, is good, uncommon, and I think it could be a good musico-poetic moment. I don't doubt at all that you will write beautiful verse: sustained, noble, sub- lime. I shall do everything possible to come up with something acceptable, and I hope I shall succeed because, I repeat, I think the scene is excellent.

1. Amneris-Radames in Act IV, scene i.
2. See Document VIII.

Verdi to Antonio Ghislanzoni

Saturday [*Probably* St. Agata, 5 November 1870]

Dear Ghislanzoni,

But this duet[1] is very beautiful! — very, very, very! After the one in the third act between Aida and Amonasro this seems to me the best of all. If you can find a slightly new form for the *cabaletta*, this duet will be perfect. In any case, we shall be able to revise it by changing a few lines: *È la morte un ben supremo* and begin *Chi ti salva, sciagurato.*

And try to write one long line and then one short one, for example

a line of eight syllables
a line of five syllables.

or   a line of eight syllables
a line of six syllables.

or   a line of seven syllables
a line of five syllables.

or   a line of ten syllables
a line of seven syllables.

We'll see what the devil comes out of it.

P.S. By now you will have received my letter concerning the judgment scene. Do not be afraid of Amneris's invective against the priests.

1. Amneris-Radames in Act IV, scene i.

Giulio Ricordi to Verdi

Milan, 5 November 1870

[. . .] Today I went to see the instrument manufacturer who will build a sample trumpet for me next week. Then we can see if modifications and improvements, or anything else, are necessary. If you want, I shall send it to you, or bring it to myself, after having tried it out with some able player. Pelitti[1] is my friend, and he will certainly take an interest in this trumpet; he would also be very happy to satisfy you. He fears that the two so-called passing notes, that is, D and F,[2] would not come out well tuned because these notes have to be produced with a certain stress on the lips and because they are

very difficult to hold for a long time. But we shall try that and shall know more when we have the instrument. If the sample works out, he will make six for Cairo at once. He has their diapason,[3] so they will be ready for the 15th of December.

Melzi[4] is away from Milan until Monday night. So, the board of directors and the management cannot meet until Tuesday.[5] Meanwhile, I have good news about the orchestra personnel under contract: the double basses, which used to be nine, this year were increased to ten, so that only two are yet to be engaged. I also felt that the timpani were a little small for La Scala, so I shall see if it is possible to find a larger and more sonorous pair. [. . .]

1. Giuseppe Pelitti (?–1905), manufacturer of woodwind and brass instruments in Milan. His invention of the *pelittone* for symphony orchestras and military bands successfully replaced the *bombardone*; and his *fanfara alla bersagliera* was adopted even by the military bands of Germany.

2. These two notes must be given in my own writing rather than in Giulio Ricordi's because there is no photocopy machine in Verdi's library at St. Agata, where I was privileged to transcribe this and many other autographs. Dr. Gabriella Carrara Verdi generously photocopied all other autographs by Giulio Ricordi in which music examples and diagrams appear.

3. Willi Apel, *Harvard Dictionary of Music*, 2nd ed. (Cambridge, Mass.: Harvard University Press, 1969), p. 231, furnishes several definitions of the word *diapason*: "(1) In Greek and medieval theory, the interval that includes 'all the tones,' i.e., the octave. . . . Derived meanings, chiefly used in French terminology, are (2) range of voice; (3) concert pitch (usually *diapason normal*) . . . ; (4) the main foundation stop of the organ, also called principal." Verdi refers here, of course, to the standard concert pitch. In 1859 a French commission (including Auber, Berlioz, Halévy, Meyerbeer, Rossini, and Thomas) had recommended a standard pitch of 870 vibrations, or 435 cycles, per second. In 1885 an international conference in Vienna was to propose the same pitch. Although Verdi preferred the pitch of 864, adopted by Italian conservatories, he considered unity more important and agreed with the Vienna recommendation. "For my own part," Verdi writes, "I wish that a single pitch were adopted by the whole musical universe. The language of music is universal; why, then, should the note which is called A in Paris or Milan become B flat in Rome?" See Arthur Pougin, *Verdi: an Anecdotic History of His Life and Works*, James E. Matthew, trans. (New York: Scribner and Welford, 1887), p. 285.

4. Alessandro Melzi. According to Giulio Ricordi's letter of 7 November 1870 and to the review in *La Gazzetta Musicale* (11 February 1872) of the *Aida* premiere at La Scala, Melzi was the production supervisor of that opera house and also a capable archaeologist. Pompeo Cambiasi in *La Scala: note storiche e statistiche, 1778–1906* (Milano: G. Ricordi, 1906) mentions him as a member of La Scala's artistic commission.

5. Since Giulio Ricordi's letter to Verdi was written on Monday, 7 November 1870, this meeting apparently took place one day earlier.

Giulio Ricordi to Verdi

Milan, 7 November 1870

Illustrious Maestro,

It really isn't easy to tell you of the enthusiasm with which the management and directors received the news of the likely performance of your new opera, although it's very easy to understand. In order for you to understand it all, I shall simply say [. . .] that I, as a kind of simple messenger, caused a furor; the management and directors are at your command, and everything that is humanly possible will be done to fulfill your wishes.

This much in general. Here is what was said in particular. After the management has put together the best possible company (considering the present times and available means), all of the artists will perform in the first two operas so that, apart from being judged by the public, they can be judged by you or by whomever you will designate. Considering the roster of the artists themselves, however, one can frankly say that no other theatre today offers an overall quality equal to that at La Scala's disposal. [. . .]

Concerning the costume sketches and sets, they [the management] will scrupulously do what you want. Melzi, who sends his regards to you, hopes to have the costume sketches done by Mariette Bey. Melzi is most intelligent and immediately understood the importance of this matter. Meanwhile he is busying himself at once looking for one of Mariette's illustrated works, which he hopes to find in the Brera [Library]. When Heaven finally allows the armistice in Paris to be arranged, Melzi asks you to write immediately for copies of the costume sketches, which will not be difficult to obtain, since it is urgent that Cairo also have them.

I mentioned the double stage in the last scene. It is not difficult to construct. On the contrary, the management is quite happy that there is some spectacle and pomp. [. . .]

All in all, with the likelihood of your coming to Milan, my joy was so great last night that I could barely shut my eyes!!! I imagine you will say with a smile: <u>What a fool!!</u>

A fool, if you like, but in the meantime I shout:
VIVA VERDI — VIVA AIDA! [. . .]

Verdi to Giulio Ricordi

Monday [Probably St. Agata, 7 November 1870]

[. . .] Why is it necessary for the board of directors as well as the management to meet to decide whether or not *Aida* will be given at La Scala? Isn't the management sufficient?

Don't forget that the trumpet in A flat must be straight. The player could perhaps make a crescendo on the high F but not on the D.

Be careful about the twelve double basses; and the second violins, violas, and cellos should be improved. I had forgotten the timpani; the ones you have are impossible. Moreover, good harps are needed. We are in Egypt, and the harps will have to work a lot. The harpist you have can't do it.

Tell me, if you remember, whether la Fricci[1] has the G and the A flat in chest voice for her fourth act melody. . . . If she doesn't, that would be more fatal than whether the high B natural were powerful or weak.

Ghislanzoni has finished, but there is a lot of reworking to do. It is obvious that he is afraid of the ending. I, who am not afraid at all, definitely plan to show Amneris, to have her kneel above the stone of the subterranean chamber, and to sing a *Requiem*, an Egyptian *De profundis*. However, I need to know what their prayers for the dead were. Do me the favor of consulting that friend of yours who once before gave me information about Egyptian matters.

So we shall finish the opera with a very short trio, with the dance and the song of the priestesses inside. What a shock for Ghislanzoni! [. . .]

1. Antonietta Fricci (1840–1912), born Fritsche, Austrian soprano and mezzo-soprano. After her debut in Pisa in 1858 she sang in Italy and also appeared in Lisbon, Moscow, and London in such roles as Norma and Lady Macbeth. In 1863, in London, she married the Italian tenor Pietro Neri-Baraldi (1828–1902). She was Selika in the first Italian performance of *L'Africaine* in 1866 and Eboli in the first Italian performance of *Don Carlos* in 1867. Mme. Fricci was to become the first Amneris in Trieste in 1873, and later she also sang the role of Aida.

Verdi to Giulio Ricordi

Tuesday [*Probably* St. Agata, 8 November 1870]

Dear Giulio,

Promising *Aida* to the public is a more serious matter than it at first might appear to be. The opera is supposed to be performed in Cairo at the end of January. In case of a singer's illness or a fire etc., I cannot give the opera elsewhere before a certain established date; and — damn it all! — I can't even tell you the exact amount of time that must pass, since the Cairo contract is still in Du Locle's hands. I have received several letters by balloon,[1] but so far I have not been able to send any to him. By not advertising *Aida* on the poster, everything is saved. The goal is attained just the same, since, in the end, everything is reduced to one word: success. [. . .]

1. Mail could only be "flown" out of Paris during the German siege of that city.

Verdi to Antonio Ghislanzoni

Wednesday [probably St. Agata, 9 November 1870]

Dear Ghislanzoni,

Except for two or three little things, this judgment scene works marvelously.

The line *Ed io stessa a costor il consegnai* must be left in the recitative. It is in place there; here, it is cold. Omit also that *morrò d'amore*. Instead, we need two lines that are more desolate, written in such a way that I can take some fragments from them and make Amneris repeat them every time she hears an accusation from the subterranean chamber. Hearing those terrible indictments, Amneris cannot remain on stage for such a long time without crying out in desperation. Therefore, a nice tercet along this line:

> *Numi, pietà del mio straziato core*
>
> . . . .
>
> . . . .
>
> *or voi salvatelo dalle unghie*
> *di questi spietati! Ch'io nol vegga*
> *morire*

or something similar; but, I say it again, these must be phrases to be repeated after the line *Ti discolpa. Egli tace. Traditor.*

These two lines are very beautiful:

> *Nè di sangue son paghi giammai*
> *E si chiaman ministri del ciel!*

But here Amneris's terror must be expressed; and, in one way or another, the following must be said: *Ah! sepolto vivo!* . . . Oh, if you could write just two lines for me, something beautiful like:

AMNERIS: (crying out) *Ah! sepolto nell'antro! vivente!*
            E si chiaman ministri del ciel!

Or do you want to write four lines in order to maintain the two already written?

> *Ah! sepolto nell'antro! vivente!*
>
> . . . .
>
> *Nè di sangue son paghi giammai*
> *E si chiaman ministri del ciel.*

Attend to these little trifles for me as soon as possible and send them to me right away.

Tomorrow I shall write you about the final scene, and then Amen.

Giulio Ricordi to Verdi

Milan, 12 November 1870

[. . .] Tomorrow they will bring me the sample trumpet. I shall be able to tell you something about it, and I shall also write you about the Scala business. [. . .]

Verdi to Giuseppe Piroli

St. Agata, 12 November 1870

Dear Piroli,

I am in need of a big favor: have the enclosed letter sent to Cairo by means of the Foreign Ministry. It pertains to the opera written for that theatre. I cannot write directly to the management of the theatre because it was Mariette Bey who, in the name of the Viceroy, signed my contract. Three months ago Mariette Bey was in Paris to arrange for the costumes and scenery for the opera, and I fear he is trapped there, along with the costumes, etc., etc. If that is the case, it will be necessary that the Consul in Cairo have the kindness to deliver the enclosed letter, in Mariette's absence, to the management of the theatre or perhaps better yet to the Viceroy himself. [. . .]

Verdi to Auguste Mariette [1]

Busseto, 12 November 1870

Excellency,

If this unfortunate war does not end soon, the gates of Paris, alas, will remain closed for God knows how long!! Under these very sorry and doubtful circumstances I feel it my duty, Monsieur, to inform you that I have nearly finished my work and that I shall certainly be ready to deliver it at the time established in our contract.

If, in the meantime, the sad circumstances in which France now finds herself continue, it would be absolutely impossible to deliver the score to Paris or to withdraw the money from the designated bank at the appointed time. With this assumption in mind, would you please have the kindness, Excellency, to indicate another city for the delivery of the opera and the name of another banker, from whom I can obtain the remainder of the sum stipulated in the contract. I myself shall send a person I trust to Cairo for the rehearsals of the music and the *mise-en-scène*.

I regret, Excellency, that I must discuss business the first time I have the honor of writing to the friend of my dear Du Locle, to such an illustrious scholar as yourself; but the deplorable disasters force me to deal with this subject directly, and I hope that you will be willing to forgive me.

P.S. Will you please send your answer to Monsieur Verdi, Parma per Busseto, Italy.

1. This letter, enclosed in Verdi's letter to Piroli of the same date, is the only letter on record that Verdi ever wrote to Mariette, whom he apparently never met in person.

Verdi to Antonio Ghislanzoni

Saturday [*Probably* St. Agata, 12 November 1870]

Dear Ghislanzoni,

Amneris's invective is stupendous. This piece is finished too. I shall not go to Genoa[1] until the opera is completely finished. The last piece remains, and I must put the fourth act into the score and orchestrate the opera from top to bottom. It's at least a month's work. Be patient, then, and arrange your affairs so that you can come to St. Agata without being too rushed, because we must put the whole libretto in good order.

Here we are at the last scene, for which I would ask the following modifications.

In the first recitative, which seems to me (as you yourself say) a little ornate, Radames would not want to utter phrases such as

> *Me dai viventi separò per sempre . . .*
> *Al guardo mio non splenderà più mai. . .*
> *Un gemito mi parve udir, etc., etc.*

Then Aida is there, and she must show herself as soon as possible.

After the beautiful lines of seven syllables for Aida, it is impossible to find anything for Radames to say; so I would first write eight seven-syllable lines for Radames, based on the words *Tu morire! Tu innocente, sì bella, si giovane. Nè io posso salvarti! . . . Oh! dolore! Il mio fatale amore ti perdeva, etc. etc.*

At the end I would like to eliminate the usual agony and avoid the words *io manco; ti precedo; attendimi! morta! vivo ancor!, etc., etc.*[2] I would like something sweet, ethereal, a very brief duct, a farewell to life. Aida should sink gently into Radames's arms. Meanwhile, Amneris, kneeling on the stone above the subterranean chamber, should sing a *Requiescant in pacem, etc.*

I'll write out this scene and explain myself more clearly.

Final Scene

[RADAMES:] *La fatal pietra . . . per sempre.*
Ecco la tomba mia. Del dì la luce
Più non vedrò. Più non vedrò Aida. (Revise the line.)
Aida, ove sei tu? Possa tu almeno
Viver felice, e la mia sorte orrenda
Sempre ignorar! . . . Chi geme? Alcuno! Un'ombra,
Una vision! No! Forma umana è questa.
Cielo! Aida! . . .

(I jotted down these lines as best I could, just to have something to work from, and you understand that you must make them beautiful. The same for the following:)

AIDA:	*Son io.*
[RADAMES:]	*Tu qui? ma come?*
[AIDA:]	*Presago il core della tua condanna,*
	Qui da tre dì ti attendo.
	E qui . . . lontana da ogni sguardo umano
	Vicino a te . . . morirò. (One line.)
RADAMES:	*Morire! tu, innocente.*
	Morire, tu? . . . (Eight beautiful *cantabile* lines of seven syllables.)
AIDA:	*Vedi? Di morte l'angelo*
	Radiante a noi s'appressa,
	Ne adduce a eterni gaudi
	Sovra i suoi rami d'or!
	Già veggo il ciel dischiudersi;
	Ivi ogni affanno cessa,
	Ivi comincia l'estasi
	D'un immortale amor.

Song and dances of the priests and priestesses inside the temple.

AIDA:	*Triste canto! . . .*
RADAMES:	*È il tripudio*
	Dei sacerdoti.
AIDA:	*Il nostro inno di morte!*
RADAMES:	*Nè le mie forti braccia*
	Smuovere ti potranno, o fatal pietra.
AIDA:	*Invan! Per noi tutto è finito! Speme*
	Non v'ha! . . . Dobbiam morire!
RADAMES:	*È vero! è vero!*

Together

O vita, addio; addio, terrestri amori;
Addio, dolori e gioie . . .
Dell' infinito vedo già gli albori,
Eterni nodi ci uniranno in ciel!

Four beautiful *cantabile* lines of eleven syllables. But, because they are *cantabile*, the accent must be on the fourth and eighth syllables.

Aida dies in Radames's arms. Meanwhile Amneris, in deep mourning, enters from the back of the temple and kneels on the stone that seals the subterranean chamber.

> *Riposa in pace,*
> *Alma adorata.*
>
> . . . . . .
> . . . . . .

When you have revised this scene and have sent it to me, come to St. Agata two days later. Meanwhile I shall have written the music, and we can occupy ourselves exclusively with what little remains to be done for the stage directions, etc., etc.

1. Between 1867 and 1874 Verdi and his wife customarily spent the winter in their apartment at the Palazzo Sauli, Via San Giacomo 13, on the hill of Carignano in Genoa. Thereafter they occupied an apartment at the Palazzo Doria-Pamphili near the port.

2. Verdi apparently alludes to the last scene of *La Forza del Destino*; Ghislanzoni had collaborated with him on the second version.

Verdi to Antonio Ghislanzoni

Sunday [*Probably* St. Agata, 13 November 1870]

Dear Ghislanzoni,

As soon as I mailed my letter to you yesterday, I began to study seriously the final scene. In inexperienced hands it could turn out either too abrupt or too monotonous. It must not be abrupt; after such an elaborate setting, it would be a case of *parturiens mons* [1] were it not well developed. Monotony must be avoided by finding uncommon forms.

Yesterday I told you to write eight seven-syllable lines for Radames before the eight for Aida. These two *soli*, even with two different *cantilene*, would have more or less the same form, the same character; and here we are back to the commonplace. The French, even in their poetry set to music, sometimes use longer or shorter lines. Why couldn't we do the same? This entire scene cannot, and must not, be anything more than a scene of singing, pure and simple. A somewhat unusual verse form for Radames would oblige me to find a melody different from those usually set to lines of seven and eight syllables and would also oblige me to change the tempo and meter in order to write Aida's solo (a kind of half-aria). Thus with a

> somewhat unusual *cantabile* for Radames,
> another half-aria for Aida,
> the dirge of the priests,
> the dance of the priestesses,
> the farewell to life of the lovers,
> the *in pace* of Amneris,

we would form a varied and well-developed ensemble; and if I am able, musically, to tie it all together as a whole, we shall have done something good, or at least something that will not be common. Take heart then, Signor Ghislanzoni, we are approaching the harvest; or at least you are.

Now see if you can make good verses out of this jumble of rhymeless words I am sending you, as you have done with so many others.

Recitative   . . . .

[AIDA:]   . . . .

E qui, lontana da ogni sguardo umano
. . . . Sul tuo cor morire. (A very emotional
line.)

RADAMES: Morire! Tu innocente?
Morire! . . . Tu sì bella?
Tu, negli april degli anni
Lasciar la vita?
Quant' io t' amai, no, nol può dir favella!
Ma fù mortale l' amor mio per te.
Morire! Tu innocente?
Morire! Tu sì bella?

AIDA: Vedi? di morte l' angelo
etc., etc.

You cannot imagine what a beautiful melody can be made out of so strange a form, and how much grace is given to it by the five-syllable line coming after the three of seven, and how much variety is lent by the two twelve-syllable lines that follow. Nevertheless, it would be good for both to be either truncated or even. See if you can knock some lines out of it and preserve the . . . tu sì bella?, which fits the cadence so well.

For all the rest, as I wrote you yesterday; I would ask only that you write some uneven twelve-syllable lines for the final <u>duet</u>.

1. Verdi quotes from Horace, Ars poetica 139: "Parturiunt montes et nascitur ridiculus mus" (The mountains are in labor, and a ridiculous mouse is born).

Giulio Ricordi to Verdi

Milan, 13 November 1870

Illustrious Maestro,

Here I am to follow up my letter of yesterday. But for goodness sake, Maestro, arm yourself with patience should this letter turn out to be long and make you lose a good deal of your now so precious time. Time is pressing, however, and I take courage. So you can curse me and call me a bore as much as you want.

I too understood that the public announcement of *Aida* was a delicate business, knowing quite well that the contract was in Paris. Without my mentioning this to the management, they brought up the matter themselves and asked me if the opera had to be given at the same time as the Cairo performance or afterward. I said I could not give a positive answer to this, since there is a contract between you and the Khedive, about which I know nothing; but I felt like guessing that the opera could be given at La Scala toward the end of February — a time that you indicated to me, which also happened to be quite suitable to the productions of La Scala.

The management is on tenterhooks every day because *Aida* is being considered at a time when other productions must be organized and, even more so, because a matter of such extraordinary importance as this new opera of yours is involved. The management is not asking for a contract right now, since, once it has had your approval, this would be worth more than any contract or stamped paper.

Following the arrival of your letter I told the management that it would be impossible to put *Aida* on the poster. The management begged and pleaded with me to approach you again; and they insisted so much that I could not deny their request, considering the well-known proverb "Don't blame the messenger." Therefore, here I am to state their reasons:

I. An announcement of *Aida* would mean that, at the very least, 300 more subscribers could be gotten. Calculating these at an average of 100 lire each, this would amount to 30,000 lire that the management would have immediately in cash. With this money they could ward off any possible disaster, satisfy the public, and, in the meantime, quietly prepare everything that concerns your new opera. If the opera were announced shortly before its first performance, these subscribers would be lost; and, because of the half-subscription prices of 30 or 40 lire which would then apply, the resources of the management would be much less, or come in too late, should the season not be successful.

As far as this is concerned, one can very well reply that the performance of a new Verdi opera is an event which of itself will bring the management an incalculable profit. But you must excuse the management if, having been fortunate enough to obtain the rights for the performance of the opera, they attempt to be twice fortunate by announcing it.

II. Either *Aida* can be given no matter what the situation, or circumstances may prevent the performance. Such circumstances might be those that are mentioned in our usual contracts[1] and that concern the interpretation. If something like this happens, it is right that the management pay the penalty for its negligence and inability. But given the possibility that *Aida* will be performed at La Scala, the management must be able to plan ahead for the important obligations involved in such an artistic event. If the size of the orchestra must be increased, there is not much time left to look for good musicians and to sign them up. As for the sets, costumes, etc., etc., at least two months are required, if you want to have a good job done.

If unfortunately, Paris remains under siege all winter long, how can this serious inconvenience be remedied?

Since it has been agreed that *Aida* will be produced, the management will take care of everything concerning the opera. [. . .] They cannot, therefore, see why they should be prevented from announcing the opera, since the personal commitment between the management and the publisher already exists and since the management has already actually begun to prepare for the opera.

These and many other reasons, which I have omitted in order not to annoy you, were given me by the management. [. . .]

I think that if the siege of Paris continues, we must, first of all, think about Cairo. As long as you don't have the Cairo contract, we can't think of La Scala anyway. Is there no way to remedy this very serious inconvenience — by writing, or by having someone else write, directly to Cairo? Or by sending a telegram? Or . . . what do I know?

I have written this as a favor to the management who, after all, appear and disappear like a magic lantern. They are even willing to delay putting up the poster. If there is absolutely no way to do them this favor, I shall give them the most holy benediction, together with a *non possumus*, and they better be content. We shall try to take care of it all.

I would not like you to lose time with a long answer to me. Therefore, in order to explain many things, I think it wise that I come to you. Tell me frankly if I can, because it would be a gift. Perhaps Ghislanzoni must also come to see you? I could come with him and thus spare you so much trouble.

The first part is finished; here comes the second!!!!! What a bore!

If you don't have time, however, you can read this second part another day.

This morning, there was a great trumpet concert in my studio. The sample was brought to me, and I had a good player ready, with whom we made all possible and imaginable experiments.

The tone of the straight trumpet is nice and attractive. It has more sound and clarity than our common trumpet; but as much as we experimented with the mouthpiece, the breath, the strength, it was not possible to obtain sounds

other than the fundamental tone — that is, the following
Trumpet in A flat

After much practice the player also succeeded in producing the F. But it is a mute note, out of tune and very uncertain, since in fifteen tries he succeeded only three times.

Now you need just the D and the F.

The manufacturer could attach a piston to this straight trumpet by means of a twist, in E flat, which would produce the two notes, D and F, in tune. For this he experimented with an old common trumpet with a single piston, made to obtain tonic and produce dominant.

The twist and piston would in no way deform the straight trumpet, since they would be almost completely hidden by the player's left hand; if they were seen, they would look like a kind of "gauntlet" designed to hold the instrument. In a big theatre, then, they would not be visible at all. This twist also has the advantage of reinforcing the trumpet itself, which, to ensure sonority, must be long and constructed of very thin metal. As a result it bends slightly into an arch.

The trumpet in A flat is 1.48 meters long; it's a very beautiful, elegant instrument.

The piston would be attached like this.

The player would hold it in this position.

Thus the appearance of the instrument is unimpaired, and we have the notes you desire — in tune, easily produced, and secure.

If you approve of this idea, the model, with which we can experiment, will be made right away. If I visit you, I can bring it along; otherwise I can send it to you.

Once the trumpet has been approved, the manufacturer will immediately prepare three in A flat and three in B natural for Cairo and will make the ones for La Scala later.

The trumpet in B natural will be 25 cm. shorter than the other and with the piston, of course, will give the notes that you want.

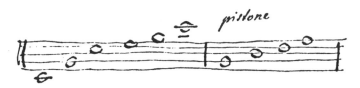

Please be kind enough to drop me a line in answer to this proposal.

I am finished, I am finished, I am finished, and I go to the forty-eight cards,[2] to which you will have sent me several times while reading this endless letter that I dared send you.

1. See, for example, Document XIII.
2. I go to the devil.

Verdi to Giulio Ricordi

Tuesday [St. Agata, 15 November 1870]

[. . .] I must deliver the score at an appropriate time so that it can be performed in Cairo in January.

The score was supposed to be delivered in Paris. Now it will be necessary to find another site for this delivery.

The costumes, scenery, etc. were to be made in Paris. I don't know what has been done.

Two days ago I sent a letter to Mariette[1] through our government; if he is not in Egypt, the letter will be delivered to the Viceroy himself, because I have had nothing to do with the directors of the theatre.

I shall receive some answer; but even if all the difficulties were overcome and everything went normally, there is always the chance of an illness, a fire, etc., etc. Therefore it is impossible to announce the opera on the poster.

I understand that the management wants to play it safe. They have very little faith! But what does it help?

Write Ghislanzoni to come soon, because I have, one might say, finished the opera. First, however, he should send me the revisions for the final scene — but everything as quickly as possible because it all must be put in order before the orchestration is done.

With regard to the curve made in the trumpet, if one can see the movement of the [player's] hand, we defeat the purpose of this effort. It's a question of showing what the trumpets were like in ancient times. If the player's hand covers the curve, it will be all right. Three or four trumpets in B natural would be required to repeat the same motive.

1. Verdi refers to his letter to Mariette of 12 November 1870.

Verdi to Antonio Ghislanzoni

[*Undated*]

Dear Ghislanzoni,

I received the verses,[1] which are beautiful but not at all right for me. To avoid losing time, since you took so long sending them to me, I had already written the piece to the monstrous verses I sent you.

Come quickly; in fact, immediately; we shall fix everything.[2] Don't be afraid of the last scene; it doesn't yet <u>burn</u>. It's cold steel.

1. The verses for the final duet. Verdi had requested them in his letter to Ghislanzoni of 13 November 1870.
2. No record exists of this visit, Ghislanzoni's third during his collaboration on *Aida*, to St. Agata. Apparently it took place during the second half of November.

Antonio Ghislanzoni to Giulio Ricordi

Milan, 28 November 1870

Dear Signor Giulio,

As I already told you in person, I found a suitable investment for the 3,000 lire I have yet to receive from my account with Maestro Verdi. Therefore, I would like to withdraw the entire sum by today or tomorrow; I beg you, however, to act in my behalf. I shall come to you tomorrow night to sign the contract for the transfer of the *Aida* libretto.[1] [. . .]

1. To Verdi and/or Ricordi. Ghislanzoni's manuscript is missing.

Verdi to Giulio Ricordi

St. Agata, 30 November 1870

Dear Giulio,

I received a letter[1] from Du Locle by balloon that tells me: "<u>Mariette</u>

is confined to Paris, as I am. All work on *Aida* has been suspended because there aren't enough workmen. We do only one thing in Paris at this time: stand guard.''

Perhaps in a few days I shall receive a reply from Cairo, which will surely tell me that it is impossible to do *Aida* this year.[2] In the meantime I think it is well to warn you, so that you can inform the management of La Scala. Tell them just how things stand, that there is nothing to be said.

Meanwhile either seal or return to me the copy of the libretto that is in your hands. Also, take the receipt for the sum paid to Ghislanzoni, along with the transfer of the rights, and send it all to me.

1. Missing. Du Locle presumably wrote in answer to Verdi's letter of 24 October 1870, which Muzio had forwarded to him.

2. This season. Verdi's contract with Cairo stipulated that *Aida* could not be given at La Scala, or anywhere else, before its premiere in Cairo. See Document V.

Giulio Ricordi to Verdi

Milan, 4 December 1870

Illustrious Maestro,

As soon as I received your letter yesterday,[1] I hastened to mail you the libretto. I hope you will return it soon, since I still hope for a favorable answer from Cairo. Maybe the Khedive, who has an excellent company this year, does not want to lose a good occasion; he could order the sets and costumes from other first-rate theatres, which in thirty or forty days could furnish all that is necessary for any grandiose production. [. . .]

P.S. Would it not be practical, in any case, to start with the copying of the score?

1. Either *Aida* will be given this year in Cairo and the copy will be required at once.

2. Or it will be given in another year, and then you can be sure that the above-mentioned copy will be sealed and carefully guarded.

3. Or it will not be given in Cairo, and the copy will serve for another theatre. Once the copy has been made, everything can be sent to you, so that it will all remain with you. Once the copy has been printed, however, we shall be ready for any agreement.

You may decide on the best course of action.

1. Although letters between St. Agata and Milan usually arrived the following day, Verdi's letter of 30 November 1870 took three days to be delivered.

Verdi to Giuseppe Piroli

St. Agata, 5 December 1870

Dear Piroli,

I have not yet received a reply from Cairo and that disturbs me considerably, since it has to do with a rather important matter. Perhaps the government did not send my letter[1] immediately, or perhaps the Consul in Cairo did not deliver it with the haste I would have wished. Would I be indiscreet if I were to request that you ask the Minister about it? Please extend my regards.

Now you must know how things stand. I have signed a contract to write an opera for the Cairo Theatre with Mariette Bey, who signed in the name of the Viceroy. The opera was supposed to be delivered (and paid for) in Paris at an appropriate time, so that it could be performed in Cairo by January 1871. The sum of 400,000 or 500,000 francs was deposited by the Viceroy at the Crédit Lyonais in Paris for payment of the [cost of the] score, costumes, scenery, etc., etc. . . . I heard nothing more from Mariette or anyone else, and, thinking that Mariette was in Cairo, I sent him the letter which you know about and which, if he was not there, was to be delivered to the Viceroy.

Two or three days ago I received a letter from Du Locle by balloon telling me that Mariette is confined to Paris, as is Du Locle, and that the scenery for *Aida* is not finished because there aren't enough workmen. That is understandable, but I do not understand why the management of the Cairo Theatre never wrote me a word about these problems.

Now, what is the proper thing for me to do? In the letter I sent through the Minister, I said that the score was finished and, since it could not be delivered in Paris, that they [the Cairo management] themselves should choose another city. Is that enough? Write me. Mind you, I feel perfectly indifferent about whether the opera is performed now or next year, but I would like to make them understand the asininity of not writing to me. Furthermore you must know that I was paid 50,000 francs in Paris when I signed the contract. The rest was to be paid upon delivery of the score.

1. Verdi's letter to Mariette of 12 November 1870.

Verdi to Camille Du Locle

St. Agata, 5 December 1870

Dear friend,

You can well imagine with what joy my wife and I received your news[1] and how much we desire that your overwhelming misfortunes will soon come to an end! You will not forget how much we love you and how much, even though we are foreigners, we love France and your beautiful Paris!

Now, please excuse me, if in the midst of your serious preoccupations, I dare to say a word about my affairs. You tell me that Mariette is confined to Paris. I have no observations to make regarding that, and if he wanted to share the fate of his country, I can only admire him! But I find it strange that the Cairo management has not written me one word. This negligence hurts me, and I could well say: "I have finished my work. I have fulfilled the conditions of my contract, fulfill yours. If the scenery and costumes are in Paris, that does not concern me." I do not want it to come to that declaration; but, I repeat, this negligence of the Cairo management does not satisfy me at all! And it hurts me all the more because, having written to M. Mariette (authorizing [the management] to open the letter, should he not be in Cairo), they did not even take the trouble of acknowledging receipt of my letter. [. . .]

1. Du Locle's letter from Paris. Verdi mentioned this letter to Giulio Ricordi on 30 November 1870 and to Piroli on 5 December 1870.

Emanuele Muzio to Paul Draneht

Brussels, 5 December 1870

Excellency,

It is with the greatest pleasure that I am able to fulfill for Y.E. a commission which honors me highly.

Maestro Verdi, after having made a very mature and diligent study of the matter, has charged me with going to Cairo to stage the new opera *Aida*. This opera was composed expressly for that great stage by commission of H.R.H.,[1] the Khedive of Egypt, Protector and Promoter of the Fine Arts in that city.

I have been able to accept the honor of being the interpreter of this new masterwork of my illustrious and celebrated Maestro, because, at the moment, I am free from the contract that binds me in my capacity as Chief Musical Director of the Italian Theatre in Paris.[2]

Not being able, for the time being, to deliver the score in Paris, Maestro Verdi would like to know to which city to deliver the aforementioned score, so that he can receive the sum still owed him. As soon as I have received Y.E.'s reply, I shall come to Cairo in time for *Aida* to be staged in accordance with the agreement, during the month of January, since thereafter Maestro Verdi must stage it[3] at La Scala in Milan, with la Fricci and Tiberini.[4] I appeal to Y.E.'s well-known kindness to reply with the greatest solicitude, and possibly with a telegram, so that I may undertake my trip in a few days and begin the rehearsals before the end of this year — all parts for the singers, the orchestra, and the chorus having been prepared. . . .

1. His Royal Highness.

2. See Verdi's letter to Du Locle of 18 June 1870.

3. Verdi had personally supervised important productions of his operas — notably, *La Forza del Destino* in St. Petersburg in 1862 and *Don Carlos* at the Opéra in Paris in 1867. His complete control of the artistic direction of these operas relieved the conductor, as *maestro concertatore e direttore*, of his usual responsibilities for the total production.

"In the old days Verdi would have conducted the first three performances himself and then turned the post over to some man whose name often would not even be noted in the program. But as the scores had grown more complicated, requiring larger and better orchestras, conducting had become more of a specialty. Composers less frequently conducted their own works, and when Boito had conducted at the première of his *Mefistofele* in 1868, it had been considered rather unusual and one cause of the opera's fiasco. The change in custom had occurred gradually in the twenty years after 1848 and, at least in Italy, largely because of Mariani [See note 1, Ricordi to Verdi, pp. 118–19], who by the example of his achievements had greatly raised the standard of orchestral playing and conducting everywhere." (George Martin, pp. 460–61.) However, Verdi himself conducted *Aida* in Vienna in 1875, as well as the first performances of the opera in Paris in 1876 and 1880.

4. Mario Tiberini (1826–80), Italian tenor. After a long career in Italy, he sang the role of Don Alvaro in the first Italian performance of the revised *Forza del Destino* at La Scala in 1869.

Verdi to Giulio Ricordi

Friday [St. Agata, 9 December 1870]

Dear Giulio,

I have not yet received any reply from Cairo, but I am rather afraid there is no need to think any further about *Aida* for this year. What a shame! What a beautiful role for la Fricci! What a beautiful role for Tiberini! Only the devil's intervention could have ruined the effect — at least the effect of the scene with Aida and Radames and with Radames and Amneris, of the judgment scene, and of the final scene, including the *Requiem* of Amneris. You understand that I am not talking about the music but only about the dramatic situations, which are undoubtedly good. Meanwhile I have decided to shelve the score and orchestrate it at my leisure during the winter. It's useless to kill myself trying to finish in time.[1] We are about to leave for Genoa. I shall write you when we arrive there.

1. The Cairo premiere had been planned for January 1871, as stipulated in the contract of 29 July 1870. See Document V.

J. Barrot to Paul Draneht

Cairo, 10 December 1870

Monsieur Superintendent,

I have immediately submitted to His Highness, the Khedive, the letter[1] you kindly wrote me under yesterday's date, as well as the letter addressed by M. Verdi to Mariette Bey[2] — in which he requests that Mariette Bey designate another city and another banker, since because of the siege of Paris he cannot deliver his opera in that city and receive the balance owed him according to his contract.

M. Verdi is surely unaware of Mariette Bey's absence from Egypt; and as the latter has sole possession of the contract, His Highness directs me to let you know that he approves completely of your point of view and authorizes you to reply to M. Verdi in the sense indicated by your letter.

I enclose M. Verdi's letter.

1. Missing.
2. Verdi's letter of 12 November 1870.

Giulio Ricordi to Verdi

Milan, 12 December 1870

I too realize that we need not think anymore of *Aida* for this year. You can easily understand what double displeasure this is for us. I say double because apart from not assisting at a musical feast of such importance, we lose the pleasure of your company which truly would have been a feast for us and for Milan! [. . .]

Verdi to Giuseppe Piroli

Tuesday [13 December] 1870

Tonight I shall be in Genoa. [. . .]

Excuse me for the trouble I am giving you about the opera for Cairo.

If I am doing the proper thing, the rest is of little importance to me, although, to tell the truth, I really wish it could have been produced at La Scala with Tiberini and la Fricci.

Paul Draneht to Verdi

Cairo, 16 December 1870

Dear Sir and illustrious Maestro,

In the absence of Mariette Bey I have had to open the letter you addressed to him on the 12th of November. I presumed rightly that it concerned your contract for the music of *Aida*, and this justifies my indiscretion.

I knew of the existence of your contract; that is all. I knew its clauses only vaguely. But your letter informs me that Mariette Bey drew it up, that furthermore it had to be executed in Paris, and that the funds had actually been deposited with a banker of that city to be delivered to you. Now Mariette is confined to Paris, and it is temporarily impossible for us to communicate with him; we are forced, then, to await the lifting of the siege, or its final outcome, in order to fulfill the last clauses of the contract.

When the contract was signed, we were enjoying a peace which seemed to be indefinite, and certainly no one could have foreseen the present events.[1] Consequently, this is a case of *force majeure* before which we are obliged to bow.

I am addressing, by this mail, a letter to Mariette Bey[2] to inform him of your letter; but, unfortunately, he will not receive it until the day communications are reestablished. I am all the more anxious to see this day come, since the costumes and scenery that were ordered for *Aida* are in Paris. The people in charge wrote me by balloon that they were working on them.

This unavoidable delay in the performance of your new masterpiece is quite detrimental to our interests; at the same time it greatly upsets the regular patrons of our opera, all admirers of your genius.

As soon as I was aware of your letter I brought it to the attention of His Highness, the Khedive, and his thoughts were entirely in line with mine concerning the execution of the contract. I have the honor of transmitting his thoughts to you here, and I ask you to rest well assured that on our part we shall hasten, with all our power, to execute a contract which His Highness is happy and proud to have concluded in His own name with the most celebrated musical genius of our time.

1. France had declared war on Prussia on 19 July 1870, however, and Mariette's contract with Verdi was dated 29 July 1870.
2. Missing.

Giulio Ricordi to Verdi

[*Undated*]

[. . .] Some people are going around saying it is the management's fault that *Aida* will not be given. Do you think that out of simple respect for the truth you might put a few words about it in *La Gazzetta*, saying that because insurmountable difficulties prevent the opera from being given this year in Cairo, it cannot be performed at La Scala? If your answer is yes, would you please telegraph me so that I can put it in the Sunday issue. If your answer is no, your silence will be sufficient. [. . .]

Verdi to Giulio Ricordi

[Genoa,] Saturday, 17 December 1870

[. . .] I did not telegraph about *Aida*, because when one must speak to the public it is necessary to dot every "i." Otherwise, the great tyrant shrugs his shoulders, smiles, and doesn't believe. So we must give them a story and say that the negotiations were at an advanced stage — in fact, almost concluded — when I received a letter from Paris by balloon saying that Mariette

Bey (who had signed the contract with me in the name of the Viceroy) was confined to Paris, and that the scenery, costumes, etc., were also in Paris. I had the management of La Scala notified that it was almost impossible to give *Aida* in Cairo and, therefore, simultaneously in Milan. [. . .]

Verdi to Giulio Ricordi

[Undated]

[. . .] I crossed out the part concerning the Khedive[1] because I am not sure he actually did the outline, which was written by such a sure hand.

Now for the Teatro della Scala. That article of yours[2] had the air of a request or publicity. I ask you to guard carefully against one or the other. There isn't any need for La Scala. The opera is doing very well in my briefcase.

1. On the title pages of the libretto and the score. Verdi doubted that the Viceroy actually had a hand in the original outline of *Aida*. See Verdi's letter to Ricordi of 25 June 1870.
2. In *La Gazzetta Musicale*, of 18 December 1870.

Verdi to Antonio Ghislanzoni

Genoa, Wednesday [*Probably* 21 December 1870][1]

Dear Ghislanzoni,

Don't be upset! . . . It's a little thing.

In the second finale when Aida recognizes her father among the Ethiopian prisoners, I have rewritten the two lines of recitative six times.

The situation is beautiful, but it is the characters, perhaps, who do not fit well into the scene; that is to say they do not act as they should.

Be patient, then, and rewrite this little piece for me. Redo it as you wish; don't think about what has been done; get involved in the situation, and write.

As of now it exists as follows . . .

AIDA: *Che veggo! Egli?* . . .
             Lo salva,
             O Re . . . lo salva. . . . È il padre mio.
ALL: *Suo padre.* . . .
AIDA: *Grazia a lui.* . . .
AMONASRO: *Si, padre. . . . Anch'io pugnai,*
             etc. . . .

It's a little thing; but it is a situation and it must be done well.

1. This date is indicated by further remarks about the finale of Act II in Verdi's letter to Ghislanzoni of 28 December 1870.

Verdi to Giuseppe Piroli

Genoa, 21 December 1870

[. . .] I received your last letter[1] at Busseto; but it is strange that the management of the Cairo Theatre has not yet replied to me! By chance could they deny having received that letter of mine?[2] Do you think I should write again? [. . .]

1. Missing.
2. Verdi had not yet received Draneht's letter of 16 December 1870 in response to Verdi's letter to Mariette of 12 November 1870.

Paul Draneht to Verdi

Cairo, 22 December 1870

Dear and illustrious Maestro,

I have just received a letter dated the 5th of this month from M. Muzio informing me that you have chosen him as your deputy to us for the *mise-en-scène* of *Aida*. In this letter M. Muzio tells me, to my great astonishment, of your intention to have the new opera presented at La Scala in Milan, with la Fricci and Tiberini, and this in the near future, supposing without doubt that the first presentation will take place in Cairo during the coming month of January.

I have brought this letter to the attention of His Highness, the Khedive, and He charges me to tell you that if this were so, He would be extremely grieved by your decision. We have done everything possible to present your opera during the coming January, but (as I had the honor of telling you in my last letter of the 16th) because of the declaration of war, unforeseen at the time your contract was signed, events have taken such a turn that the blockade of Paris has made it impossible for our suppliers to fulfill their commitment to us to send the costumes and sets ordered for *Aida* on the agreed date.

Although I don't know the details of your contract with Mariette Bey, it is clear that this is a case of *force majeure*, before which the parties of the contract are compelled to bow.

In choosing you, dear Maestro, to write the score for an unpublished work, in which the action takes place in His own country, His Highness had conceived the idea of creating a national work which would later be one of the most precious remembrances of His reign. Must [this idea] become the victim of a matter of dates, caused by completely unrelated events?

I do not wish to invoke our right of priority or the case of *force majeure*, of which I spoke. It is to your loyalty, dear Maestro, that I wish to appeal, to your tact and to your fastidiousness, which cannot fail you in this circumstance. The delay of the performance of your new masterpiece is more detrimental to us than to you. To deny His Highness the premiere would not only be an injustice; above all it would ever be a cause of genuine grief to Him. I am certain you will want to spare the August Sovereign, who has given you marks of His high esteem and whose thought it is to bring honor to Himself by honoring genius.

P.S. We would be obliged to you for kindly sending us a copy of your contract with Mariette Bey.[1]

1. Verdi did not have a copy of this contract; Camille Du Locle had retained it, for safety's sake, in Paris. See Du Locle's letter to Verdi of 2 September 1870, and Verdi's letter to Giulio Ricordi of 8 November 1870.

Paul Draneht to Emanuele Muzio [1]

Cairo, 22 December 1870

My dear Mr. Muzio,

I just received your letter of the 5th of this month and hasten to answer that, unfortunately, we are not yet ready for the *mise-en-scène* of *Aida* because of an unforeseen circumstance completely beyond our control. The necessary costumes and sets were ordered in Paris before the declaration of war, and the events that led to the blockade of that city make it impossible for us to receive the materials that, above all, are indispensable in putting on the opera.

This is what I had the honor to write a few days ago to M. Verdi; and you will probably receive new instructions from him.

It remains only to congratulate ourselves for the good fortune that the illustrious composer has brought us in choosing you as his interpreter.

1. The existence of this autograph at St. Agata indicates that Muzio probably sent the letter on to Verdi.

Giulio Ricordi to Verdi

Milan, 22 December 1870

[. . .] I can state with a <u>clear conscience</u> that Faccio is a true <u>conductor</u> and <u>director</u>. It's a pity and a shame that he does not hold the position undeservedly accorded to Terziani; but, unfortunately, I can say nothing in the matter because my words would perhaps be badly interpreted. To you, <u>Verdi</u>, I openly speak my mind. Since we were not able to get Mariani,[1] it would be a fortune for La Scala to get this youngster who is full of energy, knows music, and has the conscience of an artist. [. . .]

1. Angelo Mariani (1822–73), distinguished Italian conductor and Verdi's close friend for many years. He made his debut as a conductor in 1844 in Messina and appeared throughout Italy

and in such foreign capitals as Copenhagen and Constantinople. Although at this time he was planning to marry the famous soprano Teresa Stolz, she broke off the engagement early in 1871. See Frank Walker, *The Man Verdi* (New York: Alfred A. Knopf, 1962) pp. 283–392.

Verdi to Tito Ricordi

Genoa, 28 December 1870

[. . .] I was hoping to see you in the course of this winter in Milan, but the devil, that is to say the Prussians, has fouled up everything. What a shame *Aida* could not be given at La Scala!

Verdi to Antonio Ghislanzoni

Genoa, 28 December 1870

Esteemed Signor Ghislanzoni,

The modification made in the finale [Act II] is natural, but it is cold. For example, that *Taci* of Amonasro will escape the audience if it is said rapidly; it cools the action if it is said slowly. The *Suo padre!* sung by everybody must be attached to Aida's words *Padre mio!*

After *che dissi?* there is something cold. Aida does not fit well into the scene (by that I am not referring to the physical grouping of the actors); and she does not, perhaps, say what she should say at this moment.

The *Si, suo padre* of Amonasro was better than the question by the King, *Suo padre?*

In other words we have not gained anything, and this little scene must be redone. It's a matter of a simple ordering of words; but because the situation is so important, it is disastrous if they are not in place or if there are too many. [. . .]

I received a letter from Cairo.[1] The scenery and costumes for *Aida* are being made in Paris; as soon as the siege is lifted the opera will be given. But I don't think the Parisians will surrender yet — several weeks, at least, will pass and perhaps some months.[2]

1. Draneht's letter to Verdi of 16 December 1870.
2. After the German Empire had been proclaimed at Versailles on 18 January 1871, the siege of Paris was lifted on 28 January 1871 and on that day the armistice was signed.

Verdi to Giuseppe Piroli

Genoa, 29 December 1870

Dear Piroli,

I received a reply from Cairo, and it tells me that the scenery, costumes, etc. are in Paris, as is the money owed me (as was agreed), deposited in a bank. I think there is nothing to do but wait until the gates of Paris are reopened. [. . .]

Giulio Ricordi to Verdi

Milan, 29 December 1870

[. . .] The management and the commission of La Scala, who are very sorry not to be able to give *Aida* at this time, hope that you will still be favorably inclined toward this theatre next year. They are already working on preparations for a company suitable for *Aida*. The artists involved would be la Fricci, about whom I think there can be no question, and the baritone Pandolfini,[1] who I think would be an excellent Amonasro. For the tenor part, they are disposed to sign Fraschini[2] or Tiberini, if the latter fully satisfies them during the present season. Meanwhile, however, if neither accepts, they would consider the best after them — that is, Capponi,[3] who is really an excellent artist. [. . .]

1. Francesco Pandolfini (1836–1916), Italian baritone, was a noble singing actor, who belonged to the elite of Italian baritones of the nineteenth century. Following a debut at Pisa in 1859 his fame spread through Italy, France, England, Spain, and Portugal in such roles as Macbeth, Renato in *Un Ballo in Maschera*, and Don Carlo in *La Forza del Destino*.
2. Gaetano Fraschini (1815–87), Italian tenor. After his debut in 1837 he became a leading European singer and distinguished the first performances of Verdi's *Il Corsaro*, *La Battaglia di Legnano*, *Stiffelio*, and *Un Ballo in Maschera*.
3. Giuseppe Capponi (1832–89), Italian tenor. Making his debut as Pollione in *Norma* at Pesaro in 1860, he appeared in Europe's major opera houses and sang in the first Italian performance of *Don Carlos* at Bologna in 1867.

Verdi to Vincenzo Luccardi

Genoa, 30 December 1870

[. . .] My opera for Cairo is finished, but it can't be given because the costumes and scenery are trapped in Paris. It matters little! What does matter a great deal, however, is this horrible war and the superiority the Prussians have achieved; later on this superiority will be fatal for us too.

It's no longer a war of conquest, of ambition; it's a war of race, and it will last a long time. At the moment the Prussians are themselves somewhat exhausted, but they will recover and return. It isn't a question of Rome or the cunning of the priests that frightens me; it's the power of these new Goths that terrifies me.

Farewell for now. Keep well and let us trust in the star that has favored all of Italy until now and not in men.

Verdi to Giulio Ricordi

Friday [Genoa, 30 December 1870]

[. . .] Oh, I would have other ideas for the *Aida* in Milan — colossal ideas! Bang!! It's useless to think about Fraschini! Tiberini has already sung a great deal in Milan! I would be content with a tenor of lesser renown than those two, and I would take two great prima donnas, whom I do not think it would be difficult to sign now, la Fricci and la Stolz.[1] For the latter, it would be necessary to jump up to Venice right away and close the deal before Mariani knows anything about it. Take care and keep this well in mind: Mariani will ruin everything, if he can think of a way.

If only I had those two women and a good tenor . . . and let it even be Capponi. As for the rest, we'll talk about it later, but we'll find [what we want] easily. Meanwhile if Maini[2] is good, sign him for the Priest!

Tell me what you think of this plan. I know the two women will cost us, but [the theatre] will realize a great profit from them. Two years ago they had two tenors at La Scala, one of whom was of very little use. Only I am afraid it is very difficult to sign la Stolz without Mariani knowing about it. And if Mariani knows, then 10,000 obstacles will crop up. [. . .]

1. At this time Verdi was thinking of Fricci as Aida and Stolz as Amneris. Apparently he had considered Stolz for the new opera as early as 24 June 1870, when, while working with Du Locle at St. Agata, he wrote to his friend Carlino Del Signore in Genoa: ''Tell me also whether Signora Stolz is in Genoa and, if so, how long she will stay there. I need to talk with her, or to write her, if you would tell me where she is.'' Umberto Zoppi, *Angelo Mariani, Giuseppe Verdi, e Teresa Stolz in un carteggio inedito* (Milano: Garzanti, 1947), pp. 187–88.

2. Ormondo Maini (1835–1906), Italian bass and bass-buffo of distinction. He appeared first at the Teatro Carcano in Milan in *I Lombardi alla Prima Crociata*, and his best roles were in *Les Huguenots*, *Le Prophète*, and *Lucrezia Borgia*. In 1874 he participated in the first performances of Verdi's *Requiem*.

Giulio Ricordi to Verdi

Milan, 31 December 1870

Illustrious Maestro,

As soon as I received your letter of yesterday, I went to chat with the management, which finds your proposal magnificent and is ready to do everything to please you.

The only thing that keeps us from settling this project is that la Fricci is already signed for Lisbon; but perhaps it would not be difficult to postpone her contract for a year. La Fricci is ready for anything, even a reduction of her salary, as long as she gets to sing in *Aida*. In this regard, then, I have *carte blanche* from la Fricci and the management. Now we must find a way to approach Lisbon in order to reduce the contract to half its length or to postpone it for a year.

Concerning la Stolz, I also have *carte blanche* [from the management], since it is urgent that we also assure ourselves of this artist. Thank you for the advice you have given me in this matter; I shall follow it completely. [. . .]

I await another letter from you in this regard. Then I or someone else from our firm will leave for Venice immediately in order, *ipso facto*, to sign la Stolz. [. . .]

I am really killing myself with work. Therefore, I write in great haste and beg you to pardon the sloppiness of my letter. However, hastily or not, my heart won't let me close without wishing you a happy new year; 1870 was so ugly that, as Arlecchino says, '71 should be most beautiful. [. . .]

Antonio Ghislanzoni to Verdi[1]

[*Probably* Mariaga,] 31 December 1870

[. . .] Could it ever happen that after crossing the ocean, I should drown in a glass of water? Such things do happen; and you know it, you who almost perished in the little lake of St. Agata.[2] Enough! I have rewritten the few verses and send them to you. . . .

I am very sorry that my letter addressed to St. Agata in early December was lost. In that letter I thanked you for the gift of 4,000 lire that you wished to add to the already very great one of having my name associated with one of your operas.

I told you other things that my heart dictated. But the heart doesn't dictate twice, and to repeat today what I wrote then would seem affected.

1. In answer to Verdi's letter of 28 December 1870.
2. Verdi, together with his wife, had capsized their rowboat in July of 1869. See Walker, pp. 277–278.

Verdi to Cesare De Sanctis

Genoa, 1 January 1871

[. . .] *Aida* (not *Haydée*)[1] will not be given in Cairo, because the costumes and scenery remain trapped in Paris. Since it will not be given in Cairo, it cannot be given in Milan either. [. . .]

1. Apparently in a missing letter to Verdi, De Sanctis had misspelled the title of the opera.

Verdi to Giulio Ricordi

Sunday at 4 [*Probably* Genoa, 1 January 1871]

Dear Giulio,

It seems that Mariani would not be unhappy if la Stolz came to Milan. He himself has spoken to me about it.[1] No matter what, I think it is better to make the deal directly. I am writing all this for your guidance, because should you not get a definite answer from la Stolz, I've got Mariani by the tail.

What a beautiful thing: la Stolz and la Fricci for those two beautiful roles.[2] Tell la Stolz, even in my name if you wish, that perhaps she may not like the music but that it will be impossible for her to miss the [dramatic] effects in that role. Tell her I am not saying this to encourage her to sign; I am incapable of deceiving her, and I would never deceive anyone, even if it meant making millions. [. . .]

1. At that time Angelo Mariani was Verdi's neighbor at the Palazzo Sauli in Genoa.
2. Walker, p. 367: "When the production of the opera was put off for another year, the casting, for Milan and for Cairo, had to begin all over again. Giulio Ricordi got busy at once. Verdi's choice of singers for Milan in the following year included Antonietta Fricci, again, as Aida, Teresa Stolz as Amneris. The extensive range of the latter's voice permitted her to undertake either of the two chief women's roles." See Verdi's letter to Giulio Ricordi of 30 December 1870.

Verdi to Giulio Ricordi

Genoa, 3 January 1871

[. . .] Tell me right away how you did with la Stolz. I received the telegram,[1] as has Mariani, who has given his approval to the Scala contract. [. . .]

1. Missing.

Emanuele Muzio to Paul Draneht

Brussels, 4 January 1871

Excellency!

I received the kind and courteous letter that Y.E. sent me.[1] At the same time I also had one from my Maestro and friend Verdi,[2] who informs me that he received your reply. We are then awaiting the opening of the gates of Paris. We shall not have long to wait!

It would be a great loss for art if this opera were condemned to silence.

We hope that the theatre, which Y.E. superintends and directs with so much intelligence, will be fortunate in having this beautiful music resound this season — interpreted by the eminent artists, the principal ornament of this beautiful company, who are assembled with so much intelligence and wisdom.

1. Draneht's letter to Muzio of 22 December 1870.
2. Missing.

Giulio Ricordi to Verdi

Bologna Station, 2:30 a.m. [*Probably* 4 January 1871]
Illustrious Maestro,

This letter of mine will certainly smack of sleepiness! . . . I just arrived from Venice; and while I am waiting for the train to Milan,[1] I hasten to give you news of my trip to Signora Stolz, who has definitely accepted the Scala business, following the telegram[2] of her friend Mariani.

But are they married or not, after all? . . . Enough, let them worry about it; for myself, I am happy to have succeeded in concluding the matter with both of them. [. . .]

1. Because there was not a more convenient railway schedule, Ricordi was forced to take a detour through Bologna.
2. Missing.

Verdi to Giulio Ricordi

Genoa, 5 January 1871

[. . .] Yesterday I saw a letter from la Stolz to Mariani! What difficulties! Forty thousand lire in gold and three performances!! If everyone makes such demands, how will the management be able to get by? How can it give five performances a week? They will have to close shop in the middle of the season! For example, when *Aida* is to be given, if the management gives three performances of it [in a week], who will do the other two? And how will they be done? It will be necessary, then, to give only one performance a week in order to do the other four — two with la Stolz, two with la Fricci. What a mess! I would be very unhappy to find myself with a management that could not function. Another thing: who will be the conductor of the orchestra next year? I would like to know something about it.

Mariani told me he will marry la Stolz in the spring. . . . I don't believe it. [. . .]

Verdi to Paul Draneht [1]

Genoa, 5 January 1871

Excellency,

It is true: I had entrusted M. Muzio with going to Cairo to direct the rehearsals of *Aida*, and I was on the point of signing a contract to give the same opera at La Scala during the month of February, with Mme. Fricci, Tiberini, etc. I was then unaware that Mariette Bey was trapped in Paris, and that the scenery, costumes, etc. for *Aida* were trapped with him. As soon as this news was made known to me, I hastened to inform the management of La Scala to suspend all preparations for the new opera.

At the moment I am in Genoa, and I do not have here the contract signed with Mariette Bey; but this contract (as I remember perfectly) simply says that "I was obliged to deliver the score of *Aida* in good time for it to be given in Cairo during the month of January 1871, and if for some unforeseen reason, independent of me, the opera were not presented in Cairo during the month of January 1871, I would have the right to have it performed elsewhere six months later." That is why I wrote to Cairo [2] the letter Y.E. knows about, in which I said that, the opera being finished, I had made arrangements to send it to Cairo during the month of December 1870, so that the first performance could take place during the month of January 1871.

Now because of the position in which we are placed by the fatal events that are devastating France and Europe, Y.E. can assure His Highness, the Khedive, that I would never have demanded my rights at this time (even if I had any) and that, although with great regret, I forgo my desire to give my opera this season in Cairo and at La Scala.

Nevertheless I must inform Y.E. that the board of directors of La Scala has not forgone [its intention] to give *Aida* during the next carnival season, 1871–72, and, with this end in mind, has already signed several artists suggested by myself. Therefore I ask Y.E. kindly to indicate to me what arrangements you intend to make for the production of *Aida* so that I, in turn, may tend to its future and to my own interests. I would have to know, Excellency, when I should deliver the score and when it will be given in Cairo. [. . .]

P.S. I think it useful to remind Y.E. that for the production of *Aida* two first-rate singers are needed — one a soprano, the other a mezzo-soprano — and a great tenor, a baritone, two basses, etc.

1. In answer to Draneht's letter of 22 December 1870.
2. See Verdi's letter to Mariette of 12 November 1870.

Verdi to Nicola De Giosa [1]

Genöa, 5 January 1871

I received your most esteemed letter of 22 December; [2] before replying in detail to that letter I would like to tell you that there can be no <u>misunderstanding</u> between us, because I have never had the good fortune of dealing with you (except with the question of the <u>diapason</u> in Naples two years ago) and because there can hardly be <u>misunderstandings</u> with me, since I mind my own business and about that I always give my opinion openly, precisely to avoid misunderstandings. It is true, getting back to the question of the <u>diapason</u>, that we did not agree then, and I see even now that we don't. I wanted to propagate the standard <u>diapason</u> and make it as universal as possible; you proposed a compromise which was a remedy worse than the illness. I wanted a single <u>diapason</u> in the musical world; you wanted to add another to the too many already in existence.

It is quite true that I had entrusted Muzio with going to Cairo to stage *Aida* (in accordance with a clause in my contract), and I do not see how you can find his going there damaging to you. Permit me to say, Maestro, that you see only a personal matter here, and I see a matter that is purely artistic. Let me explain: you know better than I that today operas are written with so many different dramatic and musical intentions that it is almost impossible to interpret them; and it seems to me that no one can take offense if the author, when one of his productions is given for the first time, sends a person who has carefully studied the work under the direction of the author himself. I confess that if I had to produce an opera by a colleague for the first time, I would not feel humiliated — rather, I would ask first of all — to know his intentions, whether from himself or from others.

It may be that you are not of the same opinion this time either; but it is not just an opinion for me; it is a deep conviction based on twenty-eight years of experience.

1. Italian conductor. At this time he was engaged in Cairo.
2. Missing.

Giulio Ricordi to Verdi

Milan, 6 January 1871

[. . .] The Stolz affair can be considered finished. Between ourselves, the pettiness of these artists is disgusting. For example, this is the first time I heard about 40,000 <u>in gold</u>. Signora Stolz, always speaking of <u>lire</u>, has lessened herself a great deal in my estimation. [. . .] La Fricci was much more pleasant in this business; she has given me *carte blanche* and is content even to lose money in Lisbon, as long as she can sing in *Aida*. We must take care of this at once. Could you get me a letter of recommendation to some influential person in Lisbon?

When I received your letter this morning, I was just about to write you concerning the conductor.

Can or cannot Mariani come to La Scala? If yes, well, one must know right away; if no, I would propose Faccio. You know me well enough — at least I hope you do — to understand that in such matters friendship does not let me deviate an iota from the truth. I don't know what success *Amleto*[1] will have, but even if the composer fails, an excellent conductor will always remain. I even dare say that in a few years Faccio could be one of the first — not only in Italy but even more so abroad.

At any rate, the way he is now, he is a hundred million times better than Terziani and the usual [*illegible*].

If you have nothing against it, and always provided that Mariani positively does not want to leave Genoa, I would propose to bind the management absolutely to Faccio. That way we cut the legs of Hans von Bülow[2] and company, and of two or three other fools (pardon, Maestro) who covet that position.

Please write me soon about this thing, since it should be decided at once. [. . .]

1. Franco Faccio's opera *Amleto* (*Hamlet*).
2. Hans von Bülow (1830–94), great German pianist and conductor. In 1870 the orchestral concerts under his baton at the Beethoven Centenary in Milan were so successful that the management of La Scala approached him with an offer to become the chief conductor of the famous opera house. His friend and admirer Filippo Filippi warned him in a letter of 22 March 1871, however, that Giulio Ricordi had threatened to withhold the operas under his control, including all of Verdi's works, were von Bülow to be engaged. Filippi concluded: "For the sake of Art, I ardently wish that you accept [the position at La Scala]; but for your own sake, I cannot wish it." See Hans von Bülow, *Briefe* (Leipzig: Breitkopf und Härtel, 1900), IV, pp. 470–76.

Verdi to Antonio Ghislanzoni[1]

Genoa, 7 January 1871

Signor Ghislanzoni,

I really do fear that, after having crossed the ocean, we are drowning in a glass of water. I have written that little fragment[2] twice more (that makes eight times), and I haven't succeeded. It's the King who doesn't fit well into the scene . . . but now it's better that I put this little scene aside and occupy myself with finishing the orchestration.

1. In answer to Ghislanzoni's letter of 31 December 1870.
2. Verdi refers to the finale of Act II.

Verdi to Giulio Ricordi

Genoa, 7 January 1871

[. . .] You can't imagine how sorry I am for having proposed la Stolz. She is too demanding. If they were all like that, the best thing for the management would be to close shop before opening; as for me, I would be most unhappy to find myself with a management that could not function because of too many expenses. When I saw la Stolz's letter to Mariani, I did not think the management would submit to such Caudine Yokes, and I immediately asked about two youngsters who are supposed to be very good — la Pozzoni[1] in *Anna Bolena* in Florence and la De Giuli[2] (the daughter) in Rome. The latter sang *La Forza del Destino* with much success in the fall and was reengaged. I am waiting for particular letters that will tell me about both of them.[3] [. . .]

How can one deal with Mariani? Whatever I propose to him always turns out badly for me. I could say a good many things about this relationship. Impossible in a letter. [. . .]

Before choosing a conductor, think it over very, very, very carefully. The responsibility is immense; and besides, the interests of your firm are at stake, because today two-thirds of the success of an opera depends on the conductor. [. . .]

1. Antonietta Pozzoni (1846–1917), Italian soprano and mezzo-soprano. Born in Venice, but raised in St. Petersburg, she made her debut in 1865 at La Scala as Margherita in *Faust* and subsequently appeared in other Italian theatres, as well as in Spain, Cairo, and Buenos Aires (1873). In 1874 Pozzoni changed to the mezzo repertoire, including the role of Amneris. She was married to the tenor Salvatore Anastasi (1838–1906), who often sang with her.

2. Giuseppina De Giuli, (?–1927), Italian mezzo-soprano. Daughter and pupil of the soprano Teresa De Giuli Borsi, she appeared in such cities as Milan, Venice, and Lisbon.

3. At this time Verdi was thinking that in the absence of Fricci and Stolz either Pozzoni or De Giuli might sing the role of Aida.

Giulio Ricordi to Verdi

Milan, 7 January 1871

I enclose a copy of Signora Stolz's letter and of our reply.

Perhaps I have done badly! . . . Pardon me, Maestro, but I am too susceptible.

This affair concerning Signora Stolz is real dirt; I see Mariani's paw in this matter! . . . And if he were present at this moment, I would give him a kick in the ass! [. . .] He is ruining Signora Stolz's career! . . .

I am writing you with hands trembling with anger! [. . .]

I'd best finish for today, because who knows what I might write. . . .

Excuse my outburst, illustrious Maestro! . . . I couldn't stand it any longer.

Teresa Stolz to Giulio Ricordi

Copy   Venice, 6 January 1871

Kindest Signor Ricordi,

I am writing you according to what was established between us on the 3rd of this month when you were in Venice — that is, to let you know in writing all the conditions I would like put into the contract that would bind me to the Teatro della Scala of Milan during the next carnival season, 1871–72.

1. The first condition would be to have my pay guaranteed either by city hall or by a valid banking firm.

2. The payment of 40,000 francs, without the obligation of paying the agency and any tax whatever.

3. All the operas [to be chosen] by mutual agreement and (if it is possible) to have the right of performing Maestro Verdi's new opera *Aida*.

4. To sing no more than three performances a week.

5. That I be the *prima donna d' obbligo*.

6. To have the right to the customary eight days of sick leave.

Here are all my express conditions. You, kindest Signor Giulio, may now do everything possible to have them accepted, especially the first one, and I shall be ready immediately to place my signature on the contract. [. . .]

Giulio Ricordi to Teresa Stolz

Copy   Milan, 7 January 1871

I confess, esteemed Lady, that never in my life have I experienced such a lively displeasure and such a strong disillusionment as that which your letter of the 6th brought to me.

Accustomed in my many business affairs to holding every word sacred, I cannot help but be highly stupefied at seeing all the conditions stipulated between us broken in an instant.

I am a frank and loyal man, and I hold myself second to none in this. Permit me then, esteemed Lady, to tell you with my usual frankness and loyalty that you were very badly advised!

The conditions you write me, though financially similar to those agreed upon between us, are surrounded by so many other obligations that they change the conditions point blank.

At least, Signora Stolz, for the friendship you claim to bear me, you could have spared me the humiliation of having to tell the management that the commitments, of which I informed them, are no longer honored; better yet, you could have told me outright that you did not care to accept this contract, and I would have left with the pleasure of at least having seen and greeted you.

You will understand, Signora Stolz, that I am not able to propose to any management conditions like those you mention in your letter. I am neither a theatrical agent nor an impresario, and I feel that there are certain things I should not do. Therefore, you had best write directly to Sig. Brunello;[1] I withdraw completely from this affair.

I hope that everything will work out and that the Milanese will once again have the honor of admiring you in a new opera by the illustrious Verdi! [. . .]

1. Giuseppe Brunello and his wife Anna, or Annetta, enjoyed successful careers as dancers during the 1850s, appearing at such theatres as the Teatro Apollo in Rome. In 1860 he managed the theatre in Piacenza; from 1861 to 1863 he was the impresario in Parma and in 1866 codirector of the Teatro La Fenice in Venice. The period of his management of La Scala in Milan could not be determined.

Verdi to Giulio Ricordi

Genoa, [*Probably* 8] January 1871[1]

Dear Giulio,

Oh, I knew well that we wouldn't succeed in making the contract with la Stolz, that the business would be fouled up! I was wrong not to telegraph you to break off all negotiations as soon as I learned from your telegram[2] that her friend's permission was needed.

As I told you in the telegram[3] I sent you this morning, you have done very well to wash your hands of it. Now let the management act; the world won't end if we can't have la Stolz. Meanwhile, as I said yesterday, find out about la Pozzoni and la De Giuli. They are young (which is perfect for a role like Aida), and if they have voice and sentiment, I'll see to it that they sing and move well.

Tell me right away, if you can, how la Stolz answers your letter, which was so neat and so resentful.

P.S. If the management should get in touch with la Stolz, be very careful that they do not promise her the role of Aida. I have never allowed, nor shall I ever allow, any artist (even if it were la Patti) the right to tell me: "Maestro, give me that role, I want it. . . . I have a right to it, etc."[4]

1. The date on the autograph reads 7 January 1871. Since this appears to be Verdi's answer to Giulio Ricordi's letter of 7 January 1870, Verdi obviously misdated this letter.

2. Missing.
3. Missing.
4. Verdi was still undecided whether to offer Stolz the role of Aida or Amneris.

Giulio Ricordi to Verdi

Milan, 8 January 1871

Illustrious Maestro,

Really I cannot find enough words to thank you for the kind idea of sending me a telegram! The fear that I offended you by letting myself go in a moment of anger rather upset me, and I was anxiously awaiting your reply tomorrow. Your telegram saves me twenty-four hours of uncertainty. Thank you, therefore, with all my heart.

Now that I have calmed down, I shall give you some details about the Stolz affair.

Well, after I had made her the proposal for La Scala and for *Aida*, Signora Stolz told me she could not commit herself without first talking to Mariani. I insisted that she see the need to come to an agreement at once, since I could not stay for more than four or five hours. Don't worry, I told her, that Mariani could have anything against it, since the solemnity of the performance of a new opera by Verdi is involved. She realized this performance would be most useful to her, for she would thus add a new opera to her repertoire. I advised her to formulate her principal conditions and telegraph them to the management without commitment, and, at the same time, to telegraph Mariani. Upon receipt of the management's approval, she could then confirm her principal conditions with them.

I won't tell you how much trouble it took to arrange this thing! And what comments and fears, etc., etc. [. . .]

It's a pity you can't attend an orchestra rehearsal conducted by Faccio, so that you could have a good idea [of what goes on.] [. . .]

Faccio has much energy, much musical memory. He is also very severe and reserved with the members of the orchestra who esteem and obey him without a whimper. He maintains the most perfect discipline. To this he adds a secure, calm, and effective beat which brings about a truly commendable performance. [. . .]

Verdi to Giulio Ricordi

Genoa, 11 January 1871

Dear Giulio,

Tell me whether the management has given in to la Stolz and reopened the negotiations. It's an ugly business! [. . .]

Rather than have all <u>this trouble</u> I would prefer not to give the opera. [. . .]

Special reports about la De Giuli are very good. [. . .] At what point are you with la Fricci? Keep me posted on everything.

Verdi to Antonio Ghislanzoni

Genoa, 13 January 1871

Dear Ghislanzoni,

Let's return once again to the finale [Act II] and see how it would be this way, arranging the words as you think best.

AIDA:	*Cielo! che veggo! Mio padre!* (<u>throwing herself at Amonasro</u>)
ALL:	*Suo padre!*
AIDA:	*Schiavo tu pur!*
AMONASRO:	(softly to Aida) *Non mi scoprire!*
THE KING:	(<u>moving slowly toward Amonasro</u>) *Ebbene! Dunque . . . tu sei? . . .*
AMONASRO:	(to the King) *Suo padre! Anch'io pugnai, etc., etc. . . .*

It was easy for me to say *. . . o padre mio . . .* , but the accent, or the strong beat, fell on *mio*, and it is much better on *padre*; that also avoids the three notes of upbeat. If you don't like the accent on the seventh [syllable], write three seven-syllable lines instead, adding a few words aside for Amneris.

AIDA:	*Cielo! È desso! mio padre!*
ALL:	*Suo padre!*
AMNERIS:	. . . . . .

Then I think Aida's phrase *Schiavo tu pur!* is all right, or else *Tu prigionier!*, since it provokes the response *Non mi scoprire*, which is very obvious and explains the situation.

Then we have the King, who must not be forgotten. Whether the words are those or others is of little importance; but the question is natural, and natural too is the reply *Suo padre! . . .*

See what you think. I think as a scene it would be all right.

Verdi to Tito Ricordi

Genoa, 13 January 1871

[. . .] The *Aida* business started so well, but now it's messed up. We have time, it's true, but I think it will be wise not to fall asleep.

Giulio Ricordi to Verdi

Milan, 15 January 1871

Illustrious Maestro,

I am answering your last two esteemed letters and ask you to forgive my long delay.

I informed the management of the Stolz affair, and, as I had foreseen, they declared her conditions impossible. If it were absolutely necessary to get la Stolz, however, the management would try to resume the negotiations — not in the open, of course, so as not to show that they are in absolute need of this artist, who would then insist even more on her pretenses. In any case Toni Gallo[1] could serve in this business very well.

Meanwhile I am not losing time. La Fricci has already written to Lisbon, and now we are waiting for the answer. [. . .]

For next year, then, the seating arrangement of the orchestra will be changed according to your advice, and city hall will definitely provide the theatre with good timpani and a bass drum. When I come to Genoa[2] I shall bring the plan of the orchestra in Milan. [. . .]

1. Antonio Gallo, a friend of Verdi's and Ricordi's representative in Venice, where Stolz was singing at the time.
2. Verdi mentions Giulio Ricordi's visit in a short letter to him of 28 January 1871. (Autograph: Archivio Ricordi, Milano)

Verdi to Giulio Ricordi

Genoa, 16 January 1871

Dear Giulio,

I absolutely do not want to enter into the Stolz business. If Gallo talks to her about it, it is as if we ourselves are talking to her. I don't have any advice to give you, but it seems to me that we should not talk about it anymore at this time. [. . .]

I shall write to you about the seating arrangement of the orchestra when I have more time, because I must show you some ideas of mine that may seem crazy.

Paul Draneht to Verdi

Cairo, 19 January 1871

Dear and illustrious Maestro,

I have just received your very kind letter of the 5th of this month. I submitted it to H.H., who was delighted with the completely gracious manner in which you, upon receipt of my letter, were willing to forgo the presentation of *Aida* at La Scala during this season. He charges me to bear witness to all His gratitude toward you, dear Maestro, and I beg you to accept mine as well.

If the communications with Paris should become free in the very near future (I dare not hope for it), perhaps we would be able, if necessary, to give *Aida* toward the end of the season; but even with this eventuality it would be quite difficult, if not impossible. Since the season is already well under way, it would be best not to dream of this.

As for next season, we shall take all the measures necessary for the first performance of *Aida* to take place in the course of December; you will then be able, dear Maestro, to make your arrangements accordingly, to safeguard your interests.

With regard to the delivery of your score, you know that Mariette Bey is charged with this problem and that he is confined to Paris; as soon as he is free, I shall hasten to communicate our correspondence to him and request that he address himself to you so that he can receive the said score and settle your account.

Paul Draneht to Verdi

Confidential   Cairo, 20 January 1871

Dear and illustrious Maestro,

Aida being the outstanding work of my next theatrical season, I thought I should make the engagements with this production in mind. As a result of this I have released myself from all the engagements that I had made with several artists for next season; I am now entirely free in this respect and, consequently, am in a position to make some expedient choices. Your letter[1] reached me at the moment I was working toward this objective. Two passages of this letter appeared to me to have been dictated by the same thought: one is the postscript, in which you indicate to me the principal personnel necessary for the interpretation of your work; the other is that in which, speaking of La Scala, you tell me that the board of directors at that theatre has already made the engagements recommended by you with regard to *Aida*.

Encouraged by these two suggestions, I am asking you confidentially kindly to indicate for me the artists — either in Europe or among the employees of the theatre in Cairo — from whom I can make my choice. I must tell you, however, that la Galletti has been received most sympathetically here and if the music of *Aida* is within her resources, I would gladly keep her, with your consent.

I beg you, dear Maestro, to accept my excuses for the liberty I take, not having the honor of knowing you personally; but, I repeat, your letter has encouraged me, and, then too, it is a question of a worthy interpretation of your work. Furthermore this is completely confidential and will remain solely between us.

1. Verdi's letter of 5 January 1871.

Paul Draneht to Verdi

Cairo, 2 February 1871

Dear and illustrious Maestro,

A few days ago we received news that an armistice had been concluded between the French and the Germans. Assuming that — as a result of this armistice (which will I hope become a definite peace) — special mail might reach Paris, I hastened to write to Mariette Bey.[1] I brought him up-to-date on our correspondence and, as I told you in my last letter of January 19th, asked him to get in touch with you as soon as possible, in order to carry out the terms of your contract.

If Mariette Bey receives my letter, he will certainly not fail to write both of us at once. In any event, I shall inform you as soon as I receive a letter from him.

1. Missing.

Verdi to Paul Draneht[1]

Genoa, 4 February 1871

Excellency,

Although the fate of Paris is almost decided, I see the impossibility of giving *Aida* in Cairo in the course of this season. Let us not think of it anymore, and let us take measures so that the opera can be given next season. For this reason I am obliged to repeat to Y.E. that I have arranged to give it at La Scala at the beginning of the carnival 1871–72. As for the artists in Cairo, there is none better than Mme. Galletti, if she enjoys the favor of the audience and if her health is not precarious. I would say the same about the others — that is, reengage those who are truly having success and deserve to have it. Therefore, please be so kind, Excellency, to keep me informed about those who will be reengaged; and on my part, if there are any good artists available, I shall make it my duty to indicate them to you.

1. In answer to Draneht's letters of 19 and 20 January 1871.

Verdi to Camille Du Locle [1]

Genoa, 4 February 1871

Dear Du Locle,

You know me, and I know you will believe me if I tell you that I suffer like you and my sorrow equals your own as a result of the great misfortunes that have befallen your country. From far away we clearly saw the situation, and the immense catastrophe could be foretold. In spite of this, the news came to us unexpectedly. One never gives up hope, especially when one is suffering [for others]! What can I tell you? . . . Shall I curse with you? . . . No! You people of Paris, whose resistance was so heroic, you must be great now and resigned in misfortune. Be cautious and the future, I hope, will be favorable to you. I need not tell you that in me you have a friend who loves you very much and on whom you can count in everything and for everything. [. . .]

1. In answer to a letter, which is missing, written by Du Locle on 22 January 1871, six days before Paris capitulated. Referring to that event, Giuseppina Verdi joined her husband in answering Du Locle's letter.

Verdi to Giulio Ricordi

Genoa, 5 February 1871

[. . .] Ah, these conductors are a real scourge! With the music of today, musical and dramatic direction is a real necessity. At one time a prima donna and a tenor with a *cavatina*, a rondo, a duet, etc. could sustain an opera (if it was an opera); not today. Modern operas, good and bad, have very different intentions! Since you have a music journal at your disposal, get busy on this topic which is of the utmost importance. Preach the vital need for capable men as conductors of theatrical music, show the impossibility of successes without intelligent interpretation, and flog the mob of asses who massacre one's operas — asses who are usually impertinent. Do you know that a conductor in Naples dared to write the following words, more or less, about one of Meyerbeer's scores (*L'Africaine*, I think): "This aria is omitted because it is terrible, and written very badly, and one cannot understand how a composer could write such a monstrosity!" Do you understand? [. . .] What a long letter and without saying a thing! . . . A fine talent I have!

Paul Draneht to Verdi

Cairo, 11 February 1871

Dear and illustrious Maestro,

I have the honor to acknowledge receipt of your letter of the 4th of this month, which crossed mine of the 2nd, in which I informed you that I had just written Mariette Bey about your contract.

As I told you in my letter of January 20th, I released myself from engagements I had made with several artists in order to reserve for myself all freedom of action for next season's engagements, which, above all, must be made in view of *Aida*. I am glad you approved of my proposal to engage Mme. Galletti; among the present personnel of the theatre here, I could also find a satisfactory bass and baritone. What preoccupies me a great deal is a dramatic tenor. I have here, for a dramatic tenor, a young talent with whom we are quite satisfied; but with such an important work, I fear he would not be equal to the demands of the role. In addition it might be risky to place him beside la Galletti and other celebrities who will be charged with the interpretation of your work.

I have already requested M. Lampugnani to make an offer to Fraschini; but I am almost certain beforehand that this artist, who refused to come to Cairo last year, will not be anymore disposed to come this year. So I am greatly perplexed, and if you could indicate to me one or two dramatic tenors, I would be infinitely obliged.

Verdi to Camille Du Locle

Genoa, 14 February 1871

Dear Du Locle,

Last night I received your very dear letter.[1]

As soon as I knew the mails were reopened, I hastened in the first days of the month to send you a letter,[2] via Brussels, which I hope you have received. You can well imagine with how much joy I hear your news, and how much I wish you and your family some good luck.

First of all I tell you that you can use those investments, etc., etc., as you request.

As decided in correspondence between Draneht Bey and myself, *Aida* will be postponed until next winter and likewise at La Scala.

When shall I come to Paris? Perhaps sooner than you think! I assure you that if there was ever a moment when I wanted to come, it is this. [. . .]

The Mont Cenis was pierced[3] on Christmas day. The connection was perfect, and they tell me that the joyous emotion of that moment cannot be described. Now they are working on the masonry, the tracks, etc., etc., and soon we shall be able to go from Turin to Paris without moving from our seats.

Goodbye, my dear Du Locle, we embrace you with all our hearts. I wish you all the best possible; we shall see each other soon.

1. Missing.
2. Verdi's letter of 4 February 1871. Like his letters to Du Locle of 24 October 1870 and 5 December 1870, Verdi sent this one through Muzio and his American wife by courtesy of the Minister of the United States, Elihu Benjamin Washburne. See Muzio's letter to Du Locle of 1 November 1870.
3. For the tunnel through the mountain.

Verdi to Camille Du Locle

Genoa, 14 February 1871

My dear Du Locle,

I just sent a letter for you to the post office. But, as usual, I wrote you in Italian; fearing that it may not reach you,[1] I add these few words to repeat that you may use the investments as you requested.

1. Even after the Franco-Prussian War censorship might have prevented or delayed the arrival of the previous letter. Verdi, therefore, wrote a second one in French.

Verdi to Giuseppe Piroli

Genoa, 20 February 1871

Dear Piroli,

In view of the musical conditions and trends of our time, here is what I think should be adopted by a commission called to reorganize instruction.[1]

These are very general ideas, which I have mentioned to you so many times in person and in writing, and which I also pointed out in my letter to Florimo.[2]

I shall speak only about the composer and the singer, because I think that with instrumental performance (which has always produced very good results), there is little need to reform.

For the young composer, then, I would want very long and rigorous exercises in all branches of counterpoint.

Studies of old compositions, both sacred and secular. It must be noted, however, that not everything among the old works is beautiful; therefore, one must choose.

No study of the moderns! That will seem strange to many; but these days, when I hear and see so many works written the way bad tailors make clothes with a pattern, I cannot change my opinion. I know well that many modern compositions, as good as the old ones, can be cited; but so what? When the youngster has gone through rigorous studies, when he has formed his own style and become confident of his own powers, he may later study these works, if he should think it useful, without the danger of becoming an imitator. One might object: "Who will teach the youngster instrumentation? Who will teach him the ideal composition?" His head and his heart, if he has them.

For the singer, I would want a wide knowledge of music, exercises in voice production, very long studies in *solfeggio*,[3] (as in the past), exercises in singing and speaking with clear and perfect pronunciation. Then, without any master teaching him perfect vocal style, I would want the youngster — a secure musician with a trained and flexible voice — to be guided only by his feelings when he sings. That would not be academic singing but inspired singing. The artist would be an individual; he would be himself or, better yet, he would be the character he should represent in the drama.

It goes without saying that these studies must be combined with a broad literary education.

These are my ideas. Can they be approved by a commission? Yes? Then I am ready for the orders of the Minister. No? Then I better return to St. Agata.

1. The Minister of Public Instruction, Cesare Correnti, had invited Verdi to preside over a Commission for the Reform of the Conservatories. Although Verdi had declined the invitation in a letter to the Minister on 2 February 1871, after further discussion and correspondence he finally agreed to head the commission. See *Carteggi*, III, pp. 74–81 and Francis Toye, *Verdi, His Life and Works* (New York: Alfred A. Knopf, 1959), p. 159.

2. Francesco Florimo (1800–88), a composer and a friend of Bellini, was the librarian of the conservatory in Naples. In two letters to Florimo of 4 and 5 January 1871 Verdi declined an invitation to become the director of that institute. See *Copialettere*, pp. 231–233. (Autographs: Conservatorio di Musica San Pietro a Majella, Napoli)

3. *Solfège*, defined by Apel in the *Harvard Dictionary of Music*, p. 786, as "instruction in the rudiments of music, i.e. the study of intervals, rhythm, clefs, signatures, etc., . . . having as its goal the ability to translate symbols (notation) into an aural image immediately and accurately."

Verdi to Giulio Ricordi [1]

[Genoa, 23 February 1871][2]

Dear Giulio,

I wouldn't know what to answer you about la Sass.[3] If the Paris theatres open, it is likely that she will be asked to go there. I believe that Perrin and Du Locle will open their respective theatres immediately or soon after. But I know nothing for certain. At any rate, one can try to find out by telegram if la Sass would like to go to Lisbon.[4]

Mariani returned this morning from Venice. He has talked to me at great length about the Stolz affair. He did all the talking because I never replied with a word. I didn't understand a thing. It seems that sometimes la Stolz gets angry, at other times not. I think, though, that it will not be such an easy business to settle. Write me about all the others.

1. The letter to which Verdi responds is missing.

2. This date does not appear on the autograph, but it is recorded as such in the Ricordi Archives. No reference, however, is made to the existence of a dated envelope.

3. Marie-Constance Sass (1838–1907), Belgian soprano. Enjoying a wide popularity in the opera houses of Europe, she sang Elisabeth in the premiere of *Don Carlos* at the Opéra in 1867. Her name is also spelled Sasse, Sax, and Saxe.

4. To obtain Fricci's release from the contract she had signed with Lisbon, Ricordi was apparently suggesting that Sass replace her there. His plan did not succeed: the Lisbon management did not grant Fricci a release. See Giulio Ricordi's letters to Verdi of 31 December 1870, 6 and 15 January 1871, and Verdi's letter of 11 January 1871 to Giulio Ricordi.

Teresa Stolz to Giovanni Battista Lampugnani

Venice, 25 February 1871

Kindest Doctor,

Forgive me if I have not previously answered your kind letter of the 18th.[1] I, as well as Mariani, have appreciated the good wishes you have so kindly sent us for our marriage;[2] since this news is absolutely devoid of interest to the musical world, it would be better not to mention it in the papers. Let us proceed now to our business. You wish to know my demands, as well as those of Mariani, for the Cairo Theatre. Here they are, briefly: I would ask 30,000 francs per month and Mariani, 45,000 for the entire season. I am certain you will be surprised by such demands, but I had written you in a previous letter[3] that if a good monetary arrangement was involved, I would go to Cairo; otherwise I would stay in Italy. Now that I have made my demands, it is up to H.E., Draneht Bey, to make me his offer. If it is agreeable as such, we shall do business; if not, everything will be over, and I shall no longer bother you with my letters.

1. Missing.
2. There was no marriage.
3. Missing.

Giulio Ricordi to Verdi

Telegram   Milan, 28 February 1871

AGREEMENT SASS MOST DIFFICULT. AGREEMENT STOLZ URGENT. IF YOU THINK IT USEFUL I WOULD WRITE DIRECTLY TO MARIANI. PLEASE TELEGRAPH IMMEDIATELY.

GIULIO

Verdi to Giulio Ricordi

Reply[1]   [*Undated*]

USELESS TO CONSULT ME. DO WHAT YOU THINK. I DON'T WANT TO BE INVOLVED.

VERDI

1. Verdi's reply is written in his own hand on the telegram from Giulio Ricordi.

Verdi to Paul Draneht [1]

Genoa, 1 March 1871

Excellency,

I am as perplexed as you and at this moment would not know which tenor to suggest to you. Fraschini would certainly not agree to go to Cairo. After him, the best are Capponi and Fancelli [2] but both of them, I think, have already been engaged for La Scala. There might be Nicolini,[3] but I have not heard him for a long time, and I don't know if he has kept his voice.

The role of Aida is also very important, and I should be very grateful to Y.E. if you would tell me whether Mme. Giovannoni has been reengaged for next year or whether some other artist is being considered. Also I should very much like to know if you have engaged M. De Giosa to conduct the orchestra once again.

1. In answer to Draneht's letter of 11 February 1871.
2. Giuseppe Fancelli (1833–88), Italian tenor. After singing *comprimario* parts at La Scala and other Italian opera houses in the early 1860s, he graduated to leading roles in such operas as *L'Africaine*, *La Favorita*, *Il Trovatore*, and *Don Carlos*.
3. Ernesto Nicolini, born Ernest Nicolas (1834–98), French tenor. Making his debut in 1857 at the Opéra-Comique he sang such popular roles as Alfredo in *La Traviata*, Edgardo in *Lucia di Lammermoor*, and Riccardo in *Un Ballo in Maschera* at several of Italy's principal opera houses during the early 1860s. In May of 1866 Nicolini appeared for the first time opposite Adelina Patti, as Edgardo to her Lucia at London's Covent Garden. Later he became closely associated with the famous soprano's career; after an extended affair he married her in June of 1886.

Giulio Ricordi to Verdi

Milan, 7 March 1871

Illustrious Maestro,

I see from the papers that you are in Florence.[1] [. . .]

La Pozzoni has had a great new success in *Traviata*. Could you, illustrious Maestro, hear this artist? [. . .]

1. Verdi had traveled with his wife to Florence to meet with the Commission for the Reform of the Conservatories.

Verdi to Giulio Ricordi

Florence [10 March] [1] 1871

Dear Giulio,

Last night I heard la Pozzoni.
Nice figure,
good actress,
much spirit,
true artistic material . . .

but the wobble in the voice and the sagging intonation cause me to fear that her voice is in decline. You who heard her many years ago would know better than I if her voice is in decline. As an artist she certainly must have made very appreciable progress.

Conclusion: if I had to give *Aida* at La Pergola,[2] for example, I would not hesitate for an instant to accept this artist; but in another theatre I would hesitate very much unless she had first secured the sympathy of the audience to such a large extent, as she has here.

For your information, I shall remain here until Wednesday morning.[3]

1. Owing to Verdi's hasty and unclear handwriting, and in the absence of an envelope, this date seems to be the only feasible one. The date of this letter is definitely *not* 1 November 1871, as recorded in the Ricordi Archives and given by Franco Abbiati, *Giuseppe Verdi* (Milano: G. Ricordi, 1959), III, p. 490. This dating ignores Verdi's letter to Giulio Ricordi of 31 October 1871, which is published in Abbiati, III, p. 484. Verdi could not have heard Pozzoni "last night" if he was at St. Agata. Spontaneous and improvised trips were not his habit; and in his available correspondence he indicates no intention of going to Florence at this time. Furthermore Pozzoni informed Draneht by telegram from Florence on 9 October 1871 that illness would delay her departure for Cairo by a few days. See *Genesi dell'Aida*, p. 84. On 1 November 1871, then, she was in Cairo and not in Florence. Even if she had been singing in Florence, Verdi would have had no reason to hear her on 31 October 1871, long after she had been signed for Cairo and Stolz for Milan. In his letter to Giulio Ricordi of 13 March 1871, which includes a dated envelope, Verdi clearly refers to this letter, now dated 10 March 1871. In addition Mario Fabbri, in his article on the "Teatro della Pergola," *Enciclopedia dello Spettacolo*, Silvio D'Amico ed. (Roma: Casa Editrice le Maschere, 1958), V, p. 387, records that Verdi went to the Florentine opera house "on 9 March 1871 to attend the performance of *La Traviata* with la Pozzoni-Anastasi [in the title role]." *La Gazzetta Musicale* of 12 March 1871 also reports Verdi's presence at that performance.

2. The Teatro della Pergola in Florence, where Verdi's *I Lombardi alla Prima Crociata* had its premiere in 1843 and his *Macbeth* in 1847.

3. Instead of leaving on Wednesday, 15 March, however, Verdi waited to leave on Friday, 24 March. See Verdi's letter to Draneht of 23 March 1871. Since Verdi's letter to Giulio Ricordi has been dated 10 March 1871, it must be assumed that his departure from Florence was postponed, although no such change in plans is mentioned in any of the available correspondence. According to Toye, p. 160, the report of the commission over which Verdi presided was drawn up on 20 March 1871. This may explain the delay in his departure. Further proof of this postponement is Verdi's letter to De Sanctis, dated Florence, 22 March 1871, in which he writes: "What will the fruits [of this commission] be? Who knows!!! . . . If one talked less and tried to do more, maybe some good result could be obtained. . . . But we are like our [French] neighbors! . . . Invaded by the We ———. A terrible word, always a sign of ignorance and of decadence. . . . We'll leave the day after tomorrow. Write to me in Genoa. . . . Peppina sends her regards." (Autograph: Accademia dei Lincei, Roma)

Giovanni Battista Lampugnani to Paul Draneht

Milan, 12 March 1871

I have just received your worthy letter of 27 February,[1] to which I hasten to reply. With Fraschini all is finished. He has definitely been engaged in Lisbon, as I have already had the honor of letting Y.E. know. [. . .]

I see the impossibility of dealing with la Stolz and Mariani. I have written to Madame Stolz, seeking to bring her to reason, and I am awaiting her reply. As far as I am concerned, the price for Madame Stolz would be 20,000 francs per month and Mariani's price 4,000;[2] but I am almost certain that Madame Stolz will not accept. Meanwhile I am awaiting her reply; and I will see to what degree Madame Stolz may be disposed to reduce her excessive demands.

We still have at our disposal:

The Marchisio sisters,[3]

Madame Antonietta Pozzoni,

Monsieur Anastasi, tenor, Mad. Pozzoni's husband, and

Madame Sass.

The Marchisio sisters are quite ugly. Madame Pozzoni is very beautiful and has a great deal of talent; I would not hesitate to engage her. Along with Madame Pozzoni you must engage her husband Anastasi, who is a good tenor, somewhere between light and dramatic. As for Madame Sass, you are acquainted with her. I shall write to Madame Pozzoni. [. . .]

I am going to occupy myself immediately with Capponi and Fancelli; but it will take several days before an agreement can be reached, because both of them are engaged by Brunello, and the transfer has to be negotiated. [. . .]

I have written to the tenor Ugolini;[4] he is quite good. And Nicolini? Ugolini gets 7,000 francs a month in Lisbon, and Nicolini 12,000. Returning to Madame Pozzoni, I believe Your Excellency heard her in Rome. Naturally Madame Pozzoni would have to be engaged in place of Madame Zacchi, but her demands are greater. Nevertheless in Florence she is now compared to la Stolz and la Fricci. [. . .]

1. Missing.
2. See Stolz's letter to Lampugnani of 25 February 1871.
3. Barbara Marchisio (1833–1919), Italian contralto, and her sister Carlotta (1835–72), Italian soprano. After separate debuts in the late 1860s, they frequently sang together in such operas as Rossini's *Semiramide*, and *Otello*, *Norma*, *Lucrezia Borgia*, and *Il Trovatore*. Although the two sisters lacked passion and temperament, they were known for their rare discipline and dependability.
4. Giulio Ugolini, Italian tenor. From 1862 to 1884 he was heard in a variety of roles in such cities as Parma, Rome, Lisbon, Madrid, Paris (Italian Theatre), Milan (La Scala), Santiago, Valparaiso, and Bucharest.

Giovanni Battista Lampugnani to Paul Draneht

Milan, 12 March 1871

Just before the mail left I received Capponi's reply by telegraph. His request: 80,000 francs. I am awaiting his letter; and then I shall take care of whatever remains to be done with Brunello.

Your Excellency knows that when one speaks of H.H., the Viceroy, people believe he has gold mines to throw away to satisfy the greed of the artists! As soon as I have settled everything with Fancelli and Capponi, I shall hasten to telegraph Your Excellency.

Paul Draneht to Verdi

Cairo, 13 March 1871

Dear and illustrious Maestro,

I have the honor to acknowledge receipt of your letter dated March 1, and I thank you very much for the interest you take in the performance of your new masterwork in Cairo.

Before receiving your letter I had already made overtures to Fraschini, who expressed his regrets that negotiations had not come about sooner, since he is almost committed now to go to Lisbon. I had also made propositions to Capponi. I was told, in fact, that his services could easily be shared with Brunello, who seems to have engaged him. Upon receipt of your letter I also made propositions to Fancelli; by the next mail I expect the result. Regarding Nicolini I have done nothing; before contacting him I shall wait to find out if we have Capponi or Fancelli.

Unfortunately, Mad. Giovannoni, who is a very distinguished artist and with whom I am pleased in every way, is not liked very much by the Cairo audience. I suppose the comparison between her and la Galletti prevents her from being appreciated as much as she deserves. Whatever the reason, she must be replaced. I have been thinking of Mme. Krauss.[1] I have made her an offer, and I expect an answer by the next mail; but I doubt that I can come to an understanding with her because she is very pretentious.

With regard to the orchestra, I do not intend to reengage Maestro De Giosa; I have contacted Mariani and Bottesini[2] and await their replies.[3]

On the whole nothing has been done as yet, and I would be forever obliged to you if you would give me the names of artists who may be agreeable to you and who might be engaged. In any case you may be assured that all of this will remain completely between ourselves.

1. Gabrielle Krauss (1842–1906), Austrian soprano and great-aunt of the conductor Clemens Krauss (1893–1954). After her debut in *Guillaume Tell* at the Imperial Opera in Vienna in 1859, she became known for her Venus in *Tannhäuser* and her Senta in *Der Fliegende Holländer*. In 1867 she made her first appearance at the Italian Theatre in Paris as Leonora in *Il Trovatore*; and she sang in Italy for the first time during the 1870–71 season at the San Carlo in Naples. She was a member of the Opéra from 1875 to 1887.

2. Giovanni Bottesini, Italian double-bass virtuoso, conductor, and composer.

3. Under contract to Bagier at the reopened Italian Theatre in Paris, Muzio seemed no longer available. See Verdi's letters to Du Locle of 18 June 1870 and to Muzio of 20 June 1870.

Verdi to Giulio Ricordi

Florence, Monday [13 March 1871]

[. . .] I have a good opinion of la Pozzoni's artistic qualities, but I would never dare to take the responsibility of having her signed by La Scala. I told you that if I were to give *Aida* in Florence, la Pozzoni would be fine because the audience is so fond of her. I don't know what success she could achieve at La Scala. Therefore I want no responsibility for the signing of this artist. And if she ever were to be signed, I would first want to put her success with the audience to the test before entrusting a role in *Aida* to her.

Let me also add that, apart from la <u>Stolz</u> and la <u>Fricci</u>, you will not find an artist worthier than she; but it may very well be that she will not be liked in Milan, and it would not then be in your interest, nor in that of the management, nor in mine to sacrifice *Aida*.

Do whatever you think most opportune for the interests of the theatre, but leave me complete freedom of action. Don't hinder me in any manner; this is truly the way to look after everyone's interests.

Paul Draneht to Giovanni Battista Lampugnani

Telegram   Cairo, 16 March 1871

OFFER STOLZ 90,000 WITH BENEFIT BUT DO NOT ENGAGE HER YET. MARIANI 20,000 FANCELLI 60,000 BUT NO BENEFIT. TELEGRAPH IF NICOLINI IS AVAILABLE.

Ernesto Somigli[1] to Paul Draneht

Florence, 19 March 1871

[. . .] Here now are the names of the artists that I <u>guarantee</u> — artists who, I am certain, will be wildly acclaimed in Cairo and with whom, I assure you, I can arrange contracts with an economy you could never obtain through an agency in Milan,

Pozzoni-Anastasi <u>Singing presently</u>	Dramatic soprano at the Royal Teatro Pergola, <u>Florence</u>
Teresa Stolts [*sic*] <u>Singing presently</u>	Dramatic soprano at the Fenice of <u>Venice</u>
Lellá Ricci	Lyric soprano at the Teatro Comunale, <u>Trieste</u>

Emilia Laurati Dancing	Celebrated danseuse at the Fenice of Venice
Gioia Baratti	Celebrated danseuse at La Scala of Milan
Salvatore Anastasi Singing	Lyric tenor Royal Teatro Pergola, Florence
Fraschini	Celebrated tenor
Cotogni	Baritone
Fiorini	Bass
Ferdinando Pratesi	Choreographer

[. . .] Meanwhile I can tell Y.E. that the dramatic soprano this year costs you about 20,000 lire per month; and I pledge myself to let you have the Pozzoni-Anastasi couple for the same amount — that is, 20,000 lire for both of them. [. . .]

1. Theatrical agent in Florence.

Paul Draneht to Gazzetta Teatri Milan

Telegram   Cairo, 20 March 1871

FINAL OFFER STOLZ MARIANI 125,000 WITH BENEFIT. MAKE THEM AP-
PRECIATE BENEFIT. GALLETTI NO MORE THAN 40,000. NICOLINI 80,000
WITHOUT TRAVEL. WOULD ACCEPT FANCELLI'S CONDITIONS. HOWEVER GIVE
ME TIME TO AWAIT ANSWER FROM NICOLINI WHOM I PREFER.

Verdi to Paul Draneht [1]

Florence, 23 March 1871

Excellency,

I am in Florence, but I am leaving tomorrow for Genoa, where I shall again remain for quite some time.

As soon as I have arrived in Genoa, Mariani will tell me whether he is able to accept the engagement in Cairo as conductor. If by some misfortune he should not be able to accept, I beg you to wait a little longer before engaging another, for, believe me, it is quite difficult to find a good conductor . . . and the success of an opera and an entire season can quite often depend on the conductor.

I do not have the time at this moment to speak to you about the artists, but I shall write you again when I am in Genoa.

1. In answer, apparently, to Draneht's letter from Cairo of 13 March 1871. If Draneht had been unaware of Verdi's address in Florence, this letter must have been forwarded from Genoa with unusual speed.

Paul Draneht to Verdi

Cairo, 24 March 1871

Dear and illustrious Maestro,

Forgive me if I should still be bothering you, in the midst of your work, with regard to the subject of the engagements I must make for next season. What encourages me is that, up to a point, this question interests you as well.

I have not been able to conclude anything as yet; in fact I find myself surrounded by excessive demands which are not at all justified. It is true that in the first year, having to make engagements quickly, we were obliged to pay quite dearly; but that was an exception, and we shall now have to return to normal conditions. [. . .]

I have also addressed myself to Mad. Stolz and her future husband, Mariani, but there again I have to contend with excessive demands. I have offered 125,000 francs for the two of them, as well as a benefit which could come to 35,000 or 40,000 francs — conditions which appear quite reasonable to me. If they do not accept, I shall retain Mad. Galletti in spite of her faults; after all she is very pleasing to the Cairo public, which wants her to remain.

I have also addressed myself to Bottesini regarding the orchestra; I await his reply.

Verdi to Tito Ricordi

Genoa, 28 March 1871

[. . .] You will tell Giulio that I no longer know anything about what is being done at La Scala regarding engagements for next year. I need to know something about it, not to give my opinions, but because I have to propose some artists to Cairo. I would not want my proposals to involve artists signed or to be signed by La Scala.

Giulio Ricordi to Verdi

Milan, 30 March 1871

[. . .] I have been occupying myself continuously with *Aida* and our

Scala, since this business is closer to my heart than even my own life. The contracts already made are as follows:

Capponi and Fancelli	tenors
Pandolfini	baritone
Maini	bass

The negotiations with la Stolz have been resumed by the management. The contract would already be signed if la Stolz did not insist on a clause stating that either city hall or a bank must guarantee her pay over their signature. The theatre has not yet considered the matter, since the vote of the Communal Council must come first, and this could take place from one moment to the next. [. . .]

I know that la Stolz would like for us to guarantee her pay! But this is a serious business. In our commercial position it would create such a dangerous precedent that I don't think we can do it. Our relations with artists and managers oblige us not to become involved in matters beyond the sphere of our usual affairs concerning them.

I am still trying all possible means to conclude the business with la Stolz, who, like it or not, I consider necessary for *Aida*. [. . .]

Lucca[1] is doing his utmost to hamper the success of our project; and realizing that he cannot succeed with city hall and the board of directors, he has now brought in Lampugnani, who has offered the management a sumptuous profit to make them give up all the artists they have engaged to the theatre in Cairo. Brunello, however, has stuck to his guns and answered no.

1. Francesco Lucca (1802–72) rival music publisher of the House of Ricordi. See biographical note on Tito Ricordi.

Verdi to Paul Draneht[1]

Genoa, 30 March 1871

Excellency,

As soon as I returned to Genoa, I hastened to speak to Mariani, but I did not find him disposed to go to Cairo. If he doesn't change his mind (which is very possible), we shouldn't count on him; before choosing a conductor, I take the liberty of asking you to wait a little longer, because I may have someone very capable to propose to you.[2]

Regarding the tenors, Nicolini would be the best. I have heard la Pozzoni in Florence; she has talent, a great deal of feeling, and she is very beautiful, which never hurts. There is also another young girl, Mlle. De Giuli, who made her debut in Rome this year with great success. I haven't heard her, but everyone tells me very good things about her. Physically either one would be fine for the character of Aida.

1. In further response to Draneht's letter of 13 March 1871 and probably also of 24 March 1871.

2. Verdi was probably thinking of Faccio, with Mariani as a possibility for the *Aida* premiere at La Scala. See Verdi's letter to Draneht of 1 September 1871.

Paul Draneht to Verdi

Cairo, 3 April 1871

Dear and illustrious Maestro,

I have just received your kind letter of 23 March. I thank you infinitely for the steps you are willing to take regarding Mariani and for your advice about the choice of a good conductor. I understand quite well what you tell me on this subject, since I wished to address myself only to men of the highest order — first Mariani, with whom I am negotiating, and in place of him, Bottesini, with whom I am almost in agreement and with whom I would be well disposed to arrange a contract, if, as I think, I cannot arrive at an agreement with Mariani. I would be very grateful if you would kindly give me your advice on this choice. [. . .]

I have let Mad. Galletti go without renewing her engagement. Her talent is certainly very pleasing, but she is such a capricious character. With her I would be quite afraid that we might not be able to carry out our program. I am in negotiation with Mad. Stolz; from one day to the next I await a definite reply to the proposals I have made her. I shall have the honor to let you know her reply.

I have reengaged Medini and Mlle. Grossi.

Teresa Stolz to Giovanni Battista Lampugnani [1]

Telegram received 7 April 1871   [*Probably* Venice, 7 April 1871]

IMPOSSIBLE TO DECIDE CAIRO AFFAIR. WILL GIVE YOU FINAL DECISION AS SOON AS POSSIBLE.

1. Addressed to "Lampugnani Agenzia Teatrale, Milano."

Angelo Mariani to Giovanni Battista Lampugnani [1]

Telegram received 7 April 1871
[*Probably* Venice, 7 April 1871]

ABSOLUTELY UNABLE TO DEAL WITH CAIRO BUT REASON FOR THAT IS NOT WHAT YOU WOULD SUPPOSE.

1. Addressed to "Dottor Lampugnani, Milano."

Giovanni Battista Lampugnani to Paul Draneht

Milan, 9 April 1871

I understand nothing more. La Stolz and Mariani seem to be in disagreement. Mariani, for his part, after having exchanged three letters and telegrams[1] with me, yesterday sent me the enclosed telegram by which he declares he is unable to accept the contract for Cairo. Madame Stolz, for her part, tells me that we must wait awhile for her decision. I think there is nothing to hope for anymore. I was about to go to Venice; but I have canceled my departure because la Stolz, after having refused the 125,000 francs between herself and Mariani, has signed an option with Brunello for La Scala next winter. I believe that Verdi is somehow involved in this affair.

Aida must be given in Milan, and he probably wants la Stolz to be the first to interpret the role of the protagonist in Italy. [. . .]

1. Missing.

Verdi to Giulio Ricordi

Genoa, 11 April 1871

[. . .] I have read your article on the orchestra, and I am sending it back to you. I believe I should comment:

1. On the aims and on the efficiency of the composers, whom you mention, in matters of instrumentation.

2. On the "intuition" of conductors and on "creation at each performance." This is a principle that leads to the baroque and the false. This is the road that led music to the baroque and the false at the end of the last century and in the first years of the present one, when singers took it upon themselves (as the French still say) to "create" their roles, consequently bungling them and producing all sorts of contradictions. No: I want only one creator, and I am content to hear simply and exactly what is written. The trouble is that one never hears what is written. I often read in the papers about "effects not imagined by the author." But, on my part, I have never, never found them. I know that everything you say is directed at Mariani. We all agree on his worth; but here we are talking not about an individual, no matter how great, but about art. I don't concede the right to "create" to singers and conductors because, as I said before, it is a principle that leads into the abyss.

Do you want an example? Once you praised an effect that Mariani got out of the overture to *La Forza del Destino* by having the brass enter with a *fortissimo* G. Well I disapprove of this effect. In my conception these brass instruments — *a mezza voce* — could not express anything but the religious chant of the Father Superior. Mariani's *fortissimo* completely changes the character, and that section becomes a warlike fanfare, which has nothing to do with the subject of the drama, in which war is but an episodic part. And here we are on the road to the baroque and the false.

3. On the arrangement and distribution of the orchestra, which is, more or less, very bad everywhere. You cite that of the Opéra-Comique as a model. But why ten first violins and eight second?

In Florence[1] we have proposed in the regulations a certain kind of orchestra for the great theatres of San Carlo and La Scala. Since I have been the principal culprit in the formation of that [model orchestra], I would like to adhere to those rules. The work of the commission will be published in a few days.[2] It seems to me that your article, with many modifications (including comment or criticisms of our report), would be welcome then and not now.[3]

At any rate, do what you think best; I speak as I do because you have asked me about it.

1. Verdi had presided over the Commission for the Reform of the Conservatories, which had met in Florence in March.
2. It was published in *La Gazzetta Musicale* of 4, 11, and 18 June 1871.
3. Giulio Ricordi's article was published in the form of a letter signed by L. F. Casamorata to Alberto Mazzucato by *La Gazzetta Musicale* of 18 and 25 June 1871 and of 2 and 9 July 1871.

Paul Draneht to Giovanni Bottesini

Cairo, 12 April 1871

Dear Sir,

I have the honor to acknowledge receipt of your telegram of the 10th and to confirm my own of yesterday, which read:

"Unfortunately cannot give positive answer before arrival Italy. Letter follows."

M. Marini,[1] who has served us as an intermediary in this situation, knew that I was negotiating with another person while he was addressing himself to you. I suppose he did not allow you to ignore this. Until now I have not been able to conclude anything with this person because of his relationship to another artist whom I am also trying to engage. These two persons do not want to come without each other, and I cannot settle this question before my trip to Italy, which will be very soon.

If it were not for this situation, I would be eager to conclude an agreement with you. [. . .]

1. Ignazio Marini, Italian bass and stage manager at the Cairo Opera in 1870.

Paul Draneht to Verdi

Cairo, 13 April 1871

Dear and illustrious Maestro,

I have the honor to acknowledge receipt of your worthy letter of March 30th.

Thank you very much for the steps you have been so kind to take regarding Mariani, on whom, after all, I no longer count.

As I had the honor to inform you in one of my preceding letters, I have also contacted Bottesini, and he has just sent me the following telegram: "Accept engagement offered by your order and received from Marini." I immediately answered him that I could not give him a definite reply until my arrival in Italy, which will be toward the end of this month.

Since, regarding the choice of a conductor, you have requested me not to conclude anything without notifying you, I would be very grateful if you might write at once to let me know your opinion on this subject, so that I can be completely informed in the matter and can give Bottesini a definite answer when I arrive in Italy.

Upon receiving your letter, and in keeping with your advice, I have arranged at once for Mmes. Pozzoni and De Giuli to be approached, but I ask that nothing be settled until my arrival in Italy.

When my most urgent affairs are taken care of, I shall have the honor to pay my respects to you, and we can talk then about the various engagements I shall have yet to make.

Verdi to Paul Draneht[1]

Genoa, 14 April 1871

Excellency,

If, as you say, you want a recognized and unfailing talent as conductor, there is absolutely no one but Mariani. The others, believe me, are all the same; if you haven't been satisfied by the experience of the last two years, you won't be in the coming years either, for you will find virtually the same qualities and the same defects in all the conductors you are obliged to engage. Besides, if you aren't too anxious, Mariani may very well change his mind; in any case a conductor will always be found.

Mme. Stolz has been engaged for Milan, and I think you must now try to get Mme. Pozzoni. I have also spoken to you of Mlle. De Giuli, about whom many good things are said; but I haven't heard her.

I'm afraid that the role of Amneris, which is for a mezzo-soprano, may be a little too high for Mlle. Grossi.

Medini is very good. Who will the baritone be? Would you tell me something about that?

1. In answer to Draneht's letter of 3 April 1871.

Giovanni Battista Lampugnani to Paul Draneht

Milan, 16 April 1871

Madame Stolz has been engaged at La Scala for the winter. I have
done everything possible to secure her. [. . .]

Verdi was involved in the affair, and it is Verdi alone who has blocked the
Cairo engagement — Verdi, the world's foremost Jesuit! [. . .]

Paul Draneht to Verdi

Cairo, 24 April 1871

Dear and illustrious Maestro,

I have the honor to acknowledge receipt of your honored letter, dated
the 14th of this month, which crossed with mine of the 13th.

Having received your letter I realize that you have no one to propose, even
though I understood from your previous letters that you wanted to do this.
Since, according to the latest information from my correspondent, Mariani
cannot be expected to change his mind, and since, apart from Mariani, you
consider all the other conductors alike, I thought I should write and give my
word to Bottesini, who, while not at the height of Mariani, has nevertheless a
certain notoriety. Besides, I found myself somewhat committed to him.

Since I have known I must do without Mme. Stolz, I have begun negotiations with Marie Sass; and I hope to come to an understanding with her for the
role of Amneris. Concerning the role of Aida, as I had the honor of telling you
in my last letter, I requested negotiations with Mme. Pozzoni and De Giuli.
As soon as I am in Italy — that is, in the first days of May — I shall try to
reach an understanding with one of these ladies.

As far as the baritone is concerned, I have made offers to Steller[1] and
Maurel.[2]

I shall have the honor of letting you know the result of the steps I have taken
as soon as I can.

1. Francesco Steller (1826–81), Italian baritone whose most famous role would be Amonasro.
2. Victor Maurel (1848–1923), French baritone. Following his debut in *Guillaume Tell* at
Marseilles in 1867, he appeared at the Paris Opéra in such operas as *Les Huguenots*, *Il Trovatore*,
and *La Favorita*. In 1870 he sang for the first time at La Scala in Gomes's *Il Guarany*. Maurel's
later career was to be distinguished by his performances as the first Iago in Verdi's *Otello* and the
first Falstaff in Verdi's comic opera. He also appeared in Mozart's and Wagner's works all over
the world, including the Metropolitan Opera in New York. Maurel later taught voice and died in
that city.

Paul Draneht to Auguste Mariette [1]

Cairo, 28 April 1871

My dear Bey,

I am keeping the information you have given me regarding *Aida*, and I send you copies, enclosed herewith.

I shall leave for Italy tomorrow. As soon as possible, I shall see Maestro Verdi and get the music. Please tell me if you can come to Italy, or if you must go to Paris, so that we can agree on the [*illegible*] to make for *Aida*. My address is Milan, 22 Corso Vittorio Emanuele.

1. After the German siege of Paris had been lifted on 28 January 1871, Mariette had returned to Egypt.

Paul Draneht to Ignazio Marini

Cairo, 28 April 1871

Dear Monsieur Marini,

The purpose of these lines is to inform you that I have come to a definite agreement with Bottesini; I wrote him on the 24th to give him my word. I requested that he sign the contract you sent him and return it to you. [. . .]

Verdi to Paul Draneht [1]

St. Agata, 28 April 1871

Excellency,

I definitely think it is useless to hope for Mariani as conductor. So engage whomever you think best, although the best may be very difficult to find.[2] I would very much like to speak with you before you engage this conductor; but if you cannot wait, do whatever you think is advantageous for your own interests.

I am in a little shanty in the country, to which I dare not ask you; but I would be very glad to let you in, and I'm always at your service if you need to speak to me. Only since I sometimes go on errands in the neighborhood, it would be wise to inform me on which day you will give me the honor of a visit, to be sure of finding me at home.

1. In response, apparently, to Draneht's letter of 13 April 1871.
2. Verdi might have considered that "the sad events in Paris," which he mentions in his letter to Lampugnani of 1 May 1871, would again postpone Muzio's contract with Bagier and make him once more available for Cairo. See Verdi's letter to Lampugnani of 4 May 1871 and his letter to Draneht of 1 September 1871.

Verdi to Giovanni Battista Lampugnani [1]

St. Agata, 1 May 1871

Esteemed Signor Lampugnani,

You may keep the letter [2] until the arrival of Draneht Bey.

Considering the sad events in Paris, [3] it is not too certain that the letters reach Muzio, and that is why I return them to you, [4] just in case they should contain something important. However, you can send them to this address: Maestro Muzio, 28 rue Tronchet, Paris.

I know that De Giosa will not go to Cairo next year, and I would be happy if Muzio were to return. I did not dare write to the Bey about it, because I get the impression from his letter [5] that some coldness sprang up between them; but if you think it is advantageous and can succeed in getting Muzio to return to that country, I, for one, would be most happy.

1. In response to a missing letter from Lampugnani.
2. Presumably Verdi had addressed his letter to Draneht of 28 April 1871 in care of Lampugnani in Milan.
3. Paris was in a state of civil war at this time, as the Commune of Paris, the city's socialist government established on 18 March 1871, was being suppressed by the Republican government of France. From 13,000 to 36,000 *communards*, including women and children, were executed after the government troops had entered the city.
4. Presumably Lampugnani had sent letters addressed to Muzio in care of Verdi, asking him to forward them.
5. Verdi apparently refers to Draneht's letter of 13 April 1871.

Giovanni Battista Lampugnani to Paul Draneht [1]

[Milan, 4 May 1871]

I just received your telegram; [2] I dare to hope that you have had a good trip, even though you arrived one day late. [. . .]

I await your arrival impatiently in order to conclude the Sass affair. [. . .]

P.S. I don't know if Y.E. can reengage Muzio; Verdi recommends him warmly. Regarding this, I have a letter from Verdi, and I also have one from him for Y.E. Muzio has always been very honest, and I have never come to understand . . . Pardon.

1. Lampugnani writes to Draneht at Ancona, where he had landed following his sea passage from Egypt.
2. Missing.

Verdi to Giovanni Battista Lampugnani

St. Agata, 4 May 1871

Esteemed Signor Lampugnani,

Along with your letter, [1] I today received one from the Bey, [2] in which he informs me that he has signed Bottesini as conductor. That is not a good choice, and for me in particular it is the worst! Since Mariani was out, I had thought of Muzio as the conductor for Cairo; but not knowing what had happened between the Bey and Muzio, I did not dare propose him before learning of these disputes. Meanwhile, I had asked the Bey to wait, telling him that we would always have found a conductor, and that, apart from Mariani, all the others are about the same. By that I meant to say that Bottesini was not superior to the others and that it was useless to be in a hurry to sign him. But the Bey did not wish to understand me, or he understood me too well. I am sorry for Muzio, and I am also sorry for Bottesini who, great musician that he is, is not a good conductor for me or for my operas. There is nothing secret in this or in my previous letter, and you can tell the Bey whatever you think appropriate. The Bey further tells me that he is seriously negotiating with la Sass; that is fine, but I have no use for her — either as Amneris, who is a mezzo-soprano, or as Aida, for other reasons.

1. Missing.
2. Draneht's letter to Verdi of 24 April 1871.

Verdi to Giovanni Battista Lampugnani [1]

St. Agata, 9 May 1871

Signor Lampugnani,

La Pozzoni is excellent for Aida.

I don't know la Viziak,[2] but if she is a mezzo-soprano, and if she is more than a singer, a very dramatic actress, she would be fine for the role of Amneris.

For the other roles there is no problem. Two low basses are also needed — one is Medini and the other?

What I hear concerning la Galletti[3] is not good, with regard to both her voice and her health. Perhaps it isn't true, but I cannot recommend her in good conscience.

1. In response to another missing letter from Lampugnani.
2. Emma Viziak (ca. 1843–1913), Croatian mezzo-soprano and soprano. She was born in Zagreb and died in New York. After studying in Milan, she made her debut in Liverpool in 1866 and then appeared in Italy. She also sang in Cairo, Moscow, Rio de Janeiro, Buenos Aires, Santiago, Valparaiso, and New York. In 1875 she was to replace Teresa Stolz in the title role of the *Aida* premiere in Rome. Her name is also spelled Visjak, Wizjiak, and Wiziach.
3. See Draneht's letter to Verdi of 3 April 1871 and Lampugnani's letter to Draneht of 9 April 1871. Having lost Stolz to La Scala, Draneht might have reconsidered Galletti. Lampugnani apparently suggested Galletti for Amneris in Draneht's name, and Verdi responds here with Draneht's own advice of 3 April 1871 in mind.

Paul Draneht to Verdi

Milan, 12 May 1871

Dear and illustrious Maestro,

I arrived in Milan a few days ago; and I am addressing myself to you, dear Maestro, to ask where and on what day you would be disposed to receive me so that we may discuss the great affair that concerns us.

As far as it concerns me, I am entirely at your disposal; and, after next Tuesday, any day is fine for me, so long as your time and work are not disturbed.

Verdi to Paul Draneht

St. Agata, 15 May 1871

Excellency,

I received your gracious letter, which informs me of your arrival in Milan. If you do not disdain coming to my modest country house, you will always find me at home from Thursday on. Please advise me of the day and hour that you will arrive at Borgo St. Donnino, so that I can have my coach meet you and bring you to my home.

Paul Draneht to Verdi

Milan, 17 May 1871

Dear and illustrious Maestro,

I received your letter of the 15th only this morning, and I hasten to answer. I thank you very much for your kind invitation and for the thoughtfulness of putting your carriage at my disposal. It is an honor, and it also gives me great satisfaction to make your acquaintance; and I am truly grateful to you, dear and illustrious Maestro, for the opportunity you offer me.

Here is what I plan to do: I shall leave Milan on Thursday by train at 9:05 in the evening and spend the night at the Hotel St. Marc in Plaisance.[1] I plan to arrive at St. Agata the day after tomorrow between 10:00 and 10:30 in the morning. I must arrange my itinerary like this because of the luggage I need to continue my trip to Naples. Therefore, dear and illustrious Maestro, you need not send your carriage. It would be difficult, if not impossible, for the coachman to come at such an early morning hour to Plaisance.

Looking forward to the pleasure of meeting you, I ask you to accept the expression of my respectful sentiments.

1. Piacenza, in French.

Tito Ricordi to Verdi

Milan, 19 May 1871

[. . .] In Naples I heard la Waldmann[1] in *Favorita*, but I admit I could not form an absolute judgment of her fitness for the role in *Aida*. I am sorry that I could not hear her as Eboli because rather competent people have assured me that she has performed this role to perfection. She gave the impression of some vocal weakness; there is some defect, perhaps, in her way of singing, but that could be remedied by teaching her the role as it is written. She has a beautiful figure and real dramatic talent, and the audience liked her very, very much. [. . .]

1. Maria Waldmann, Austrian mezzo-soprano.

Auguste Mariette to Paul Draneht

Boulaq, 19 May 1871

My dear Bey,
        When I returned from Upper Egypt, I found your letter of 28 April to which I hasten to reply.
        I ask nothing more than that we come to an agreement regarding the various orders to be made concerning *Aida*. I do not count on leaving before the end of June; but as I shall pass through Milan, we shall come to an agreement during my voyage. I hope that by then the sad affairs of Paris will be ended.
        Meanwhile I wish to send you the complete drawings for all the costumes as soon as possible. I cannot finish this work, however, if I do not have the libretto in front of me. I do not really know what changes Verdi has made in the outline, since Du Locle tells me that an entire scene has even been added.
        Please send me by return mail, then, a copy of the libretto in Italian — that is, of the words of the piece. Once I have this document in my hands, I shall quickly finish my task.

Paul Draneht to J. Barrot

Bologna, 20 May 1871

My dear Bey,
        I am taking the liberty of addressing this letter to you to inform you of the various engagements I have made since my arrival in Italy and also of the difficulties I have encountered in organizing the company.
        [. . .] I am detained by the unreasonable demands of certain artists who, until now, have held their heads high, [*illegible*] thinking I would be obliged

to submit to their will because some of them have learned that Maestro Verdi
has suggested them to interpret *Aida* and others suppose that he will do so.
But I hope to bring all those people to reason. [. . .]

Mad. Sass has not yet signed, but yesterday she finally telegraphed from
London to give her definite approval to the contract I had submitted to her.
The main difficulties with her were that she wanted to appear in *Aida* only if
the role should suit her, to choose the opera for her debut, and, finally, to sing
only the operas in her repertoire. I had to surrender on this last point, adding
La Juive, *Don Giovanni*, *Faust*, *La Figlia del Reggimento*, and *Guglielmo
Tell* to the repertoire I had given you. There would then be seven works for
her in our present repertoire: *Aida*, *Huguenots*, *Trovatore*, *La Juive*, *Don
Giovanni*, *Faust*, and *La Figlia del Reggimento*. [. . .]

Yesterday I saw Monsieur Verdi, who lives near Plaisance, and I reached
an agreement with him on various points concerning *Aida*; but he is not yet
able to give me the music. I must first engage the entire company. [. . .]

Verdi to Tito Ricordi

St. Agata, 22 May 1871

[. . .] Draneht Bey was here, as you know, and after having made
with him many of the arrangements necessary for the production of *Aida* in
Cairo, he asked me to settle our account. That meant "Give me the score and I
shall pay you the stipulated sum," etc., etc. I have taken my time, because
there are two matters which must be tied together in order to guarantee the
rights. First of all, it must be two months since I have heard anything more
about La Scala!! I really shouldn't talk about it, but, considering the urgency,
I ask for a decision and a reply in this matter. If the opera is to be given at La
Scala, there must be a decision soon because the Bey will again be at St.
Agata early in June. If it is not to be given, something will need to be arranged
or invalidated between you and me. At any rate, tell me concisely what your
intentions are so that this matter can be cleared up one way or the other.

P.S. From what I know, and from what you say, Stagno [1] and la Waldmann
might have been excellent for *Aida* at La Scala. They may be inexperienced,
but they are young; and when there is voice and sentiment I am always for the
young; you can always do with them whatever you want.

1. Roberto Stagno (1840?–97), Italian tenor. Following his debut in 1862 as Rodrigo in
Rossini's *Otello* in Lisbon, he appeared throughout Italy and Spain in such operas as *Norma*,
Lucrezia Borgia, and *Il Trovatore*. His later career was distinguished by his appearances in 1883
in the American premiere of *La Gioconda* at the Metropolitan Opera in New York and in the title
role in the South American premiere of Verdi's *Otello* in Buenos Aires (1888), where he met his
wife, the soprano Gemma Bellincioni (1864–1950). Together they sang in the world premiere of
Mascagni's *Cavalleria Rusticana* at Rome's Teatro Costanzi in 1890.

Giulio Ricordi to Verdi

Milan, 23 May 1871

[. . .] Less than fifteen minutes ago Brunello was here with the list of the chorus and orchestra as they were last season. He has asked me to transcribe it for you, so that should *Aida* be performed, you can indicate what might be required and what modifications are necessary.

Orchestra

15 first violins
12 second violins
 8 violas
 7 cellos
10 double basses
 2 flutes
 1 piccolo
 2 oboes and English horn
 2 clarinets and bass-clarinet
 2 bassoons
 4 horns
 2 cornets
 2 trumpets
 3 trombones
 1 bombardon
 1 timpani
 2 harps
 1 bass drum
 1 triangle
 1 cymbals
 1 snare drum

Total: 80 musicians

If necessary, these can be augmented with those of the ballet, namely: 2 clarinets, 2 flutes, 1 oboe, 1 bassoon, 2 horns, 1 tuba.

Chorus

16 first tenors	27	
11 second tenors		
10 bass-baritones	26	53
16 low basses		

2 first sopranos		
2 second sopranos	engaged	
5 contraltos		9

10 first sopranos	students of the	
8 second sopranos	school attached	22
4 altos	to the theatres	

Total: 84

26 musicians of the national band

With this pattern I think some of the string players and the choristers must be augmented.

The artists engaged are la Stolz, the tenors Fancelli and Capponi, the baritone Pandolfini, and the bass Maini.

One woman is missing to complete the company. In any case, I do not know which role you would entrust to Signora Stolz; [1] we ought to know whether the management should engage a soprano or a mezzo-soprano. When I had the honor of talking with you, it seemed to me that you considered la Stolz more suitable for the role of Amneris. But I don't know if you have now changed something. I would be most grateful to you, then, if you could clarify this point for me, so that I can look for an artist suitable for the role that would not be done by la Stolz.

Furthermore the management (which wants to stage *Aida* in the best possible way) has determined to change the scenic designer, replacing Ferrario [2] with some better artist. They have turned to me for advice in the matter. I remember that you spoke to me several times of a famous painter at the theatre in Parma, whose name I do not remember. Could we get him for La Scala? In any case, could you put in a good word of recommendation? [. . .]

(I shall go to Leipzig toward the 15th of June.)

1. See note 1 to Verdi's letter to Giulio Ricordi of 30 December 1870, note 2 to Verdi's letter to him of 1 January 1871, note 3 to Verdi's letter to him of 7 January 1871, and note 4 to Verdi's letter to him of 8 January 1871.
2. Carlo Ferrario (1833–1907), Italian painter and scenic designer.

Giulio Ricordi to Verdi

Milan, 24 May 1871

Illustrious Maestro,

"If you would let me guess, I could tell you what you think." I wrote you yesterday while your letter of the 22nd was on the way. In the absence of my father I have the pleasure of answering it.

If the performance of *Aida* at La Scala is the desire of all the people of Milan, it is for us, in a special way, the most beautiful goal that we could reach. You know that all our endeavors have been directed toward this end. If this has not been mentioned for some time, it was above all due to a feeling of delicacy, since we did not know whether we should insist. Second, we were waiting for the vote on the subsidy, and I wrote you about that in my letter of yesterday.

Your letter, therefore, came just like the cheese on the macaroni! And the decision on this matter will enable us to negotiate even better with the management, also concerning the material aspect of the matter.

You ask about our intentions concerning *Aida*. . . . My God, they are the best intentions in the world — that is, the liveliest desire to add this new masterwork to the many of yours that we have the honor and the good fortune to display gloriously in our library. A year and a half ago I presented to you on my father's behalf a sketch for the composition of an opera.[1] Then came the Cairo business, in all of which I don't know precisely what your ideas may be, what commitments you may have, etc., etc. You need only write us your intentions, however, and according to these we shall draw up a proposed contract, which we shall send for your approval or modifications. After all, and in a few words, it's up to you to command and for us to do as much as will be welcome to you.

Better yet, if you think it beneficial to consider yourself as the stage director for *Aida* at La Scala, we would be able to say something to the management, the directors, and city hall, who are as anxious as we to conclude this business or at least the preliminaries involved.

Another very important matter is copying the score and preparing the parts well and correctly. If the singers' parts could be printed soon with the proper reduction for the piano, which would facilitate and speed up the study of the opera, so much the better.

I am still holding onto the six trumpets for the march; and if these go to Cairo, others must be prepared for La Scala.

As for the artists, I confirm my letter of yesterday. La Waldmann has no extraordinary voice but a beautiful and sufficiently sturdy one; she is very elegant and pleasant, and adapts very well to the stage. I fear, however, that the role of Amneris is somewhat heavy for her; but I would not know how to find a better one at the moment. She has much talent and is very well educated.

In voting for the subsidy to the theatre, our Communal Council decided to nominate a commission that should study ways to restore La Scala's antique splendor, to improve its future, and to make it a great institution truly useful to art. The first one to be nominated by a full vote was Giuseppe Verdi. I don't know whether you can or want to accept, but you will appreciate this homage anyway. When you come to Milan for *Aida*, who knows if you could not offer some precious suggestion and make this idea of our city hall prosper, because it would be a real crime to abandon our greatest theatre. The government doesn't care anymore, and woe to us if city hall should follow the nice example of the government! [. . .]

1. Missing.

Verdi to Giulio Ricordi

St. Agata, 24 May 1871

Dear Giulio,

As I wrote to your father the other day, it is necessary to establish something about the future of *Aida*.

So if it has to be at La Scala,

La Stolz	would do	Aida
Pandolfini		Amonasro
Maini		The Priest
Fancelli or Capponi		Radames

That would leave a second tenor for the

Messenger	
The King	low bass
Amneris	mezzo-soprano

Keep in mind that this Amneris is driven by the devil, has a powerful voice, is very emotional, and very, very dramatic. How about la Waldmann or la Viziak? We must not make a mistake on this role. A mediocre Amneris means a ruined opera.

As for the orchestra, Mazzucato[1] can tell you that the commission in Florence has established that for La Scala the following would be required:

14 first violins
14 seconds
12 violas
12 cellos
12 double basses.

The author of *Aida* could make do with just 10 violins, 10 cellos, and 11 double basses, but the president of the commission[2] must not know that.

As for the chorus, it is the greatest error to reduce the number of middle parts. That way we would never have the full, robust, powerful wave of sound that tempers the high voices. So do it my way — that is:

16 first tenors
16 second tenors
16 bass-baritones
16 low basses
12 first sopranos
12 second sopranos
12 contraltos

It goes without saying that the orchestra and chorus must know how to play and sing. The management must pay them equally and since there is time, must choose well now. Keep in mind that I cannot be content with the kind of chorus and orchestra we had for *Forza del Destino*. More than half of them were bad. Therefore be alert about this. Another most important matter: [*illegible*] Who will be the conductor?

Let us decide, then, on the matters of prime importance:

Find Amneris and the conductor.

The rest goes without saying, as long as there is activity and good will.

The designer in Parma is Magnani.[3] Most excellent!! Perhaps he will not be paid more than the others, but in any case it would even be worth making some sacrifice.

As for the costumes, Mariette Bey is coming to Europe and will come to St. Agata.[4] I shall reach an agreement with him. For the rest, have no fear about the *mise-en-scène*. Think seriously about Amneris, the conductor, and the chorus and the orchestra.

Act quickly because I have no time to lose. [. . .]

1. Alberto Mazzucato, Italian composer and conductor, who had been a member of the commission over which Verdi presided in March of 1871.
2. Verdi himself.
3. Girolamo Magnani, Italian painter and scenic designer.
4. No record exists of a visit by Mariette to St. Agata. See Draneht's letters to Mariette of 28 April 1871 and 10 June 1871, Mariette's letters to Draneht of 19 May 1871, 7 and 19 July 1871, and Verdi's letters to Du Locle of 6 June and 17 June 1871.

Verdi to Giulio Ricordi

Cremona,[1] 25 May 1871

Dear Giulio,

I too had thought about la Stolz for Amneris, but all things considered, it is better to entrust her with the role of Aida.

There is no way out; we must find a mezzo-soprano. If la Waldmann sings

Eboli really well, she would be fine for Amneris, in both her character and *tessitura*; but, unfortunately, one must never rely on what "they say." In any event, if you find no one better, sign la Waldmann, but without promising her the role of Amneris in case she flops in Milan.

I cannot tell you anything about Faccio either. If I had seen him at least once with a baton in his hand, I would give you my opinion. I cannot take the responsibility of having him signed; on the other hand I have nothing against Faccio as a conductor.

I shall write to Magnani today. [. . .]

P.S. Does la Waldmann have good low tones? How low can she go?

1. Verdi apparently wrote this letter during a visit to his wife's sister Barbarina, who lived in Cremona, twelve miles away from St. Agata. See Walker, p. 235.

Verdi to Girolamo Magnani

Cremona, 25 May 1871

Would you be disposed to go to Milan during the coming carnival season as designer for La Scala? Think about it for a moment, and then send me a prompt reply to St. Agata, where I shall be tonight. If you don't want to be burdened with preparing the sets for all the productions, would you like the assignment of doing only those that are needed for my new opera? There are six, maybe seven. [. . .]

Giulio Ricordi to Verdi

Milan, 27 May 1871

Illustrious Maestro,

I received your letter of the 24th in answer to my first letter.[1] There will be at least a couple of good second tenors; and eventually the bass for the role of the King will be found; the management must also sign another first bass.

The difficult obstacle to surmount is Amneris. I have always thought that this role, assigned to la Fricci last year,[2] would be for la Stolz, since one can do what the other does, and they are similar as far as power and wonderful low notes are concerned. To find now a singer other than these two, driven by the devil, as you say, and with a strong voice, is a very difficult business. Among the mezzo-sopranos I have heard during these years, la Waldmann seems to be one of the best because of her dramatic talent and sentiment. She has a rather beautiful voice — even, in tune, sufficiently strong, but not like the voices of la Stolz and la Fricci, which are two exceptions today. La Waldmann, as I wrote you, is young, very pleasant, and intelligent. La Viziak is zero: pretty and graceful but a small, awkward voice, and her low register is poor.

In the role of Eboli, la Waldmann had a truly complete success in Trieste and Naples. But I haven't heard her, and she may have been just adequate.

La Benza[3] is ruined.

Don't you have anyone else to suggest? Have the artists for Cairo been proposed to you? Is there one among them that would do for us?

For the conductor I could not think of anyone better than Faccio. Of course, I am not speaking of Mariani and Costa,[4] both of whom we cannot get, and who would be useless, since you will come to stage the opera. Faccio knows music well, has a good memory and much zeal, and is very much appreciated by the directors, the management, and the orchestra, and has been considered for this post since last season.

What do you say about this, frankly, as I now speak my mind?

As far as the chorus and orchestra are concerned, they will be engaged in conjunction with the publisher, and we shall sternly reject the mediocre.

As I requested before, could you address a couple of words to Magnani asking him whether he is disposed to come to La Scala? If so, I shall advise the management, and they will offer a contract. I don't know how much they paid in the past for each scene. In any event, I shall find out in order to arrange something that will also be acceptable to Magnani.

We must decide soon about <u>Amneris</u>, before the good artists get away from us. I am receiving more information and shall write you at once should I see some new artist come up.

I await your answer to my letter of the day before yesterday, so that we may approach the total definition of this business as quickly as I think you desire.

1. His letter to Verdi of 23 May 1871.
2. No record exists of such an arrangement.
3. Ida Benza (ca. 1844–80), Hungarian soprano and mezzo-soprano. Following her debut in Budapest in 1865, she sang in Vienna between 1867 and 1870, in Lisbon during the 1870–71 season, and at several Italian theatres, including La Scala in 1869. In 1871–72 she appeared with Adelina Patti in Moscow and St. Petersburg.
4. Sir Michael Costa (1808–84), influential conductor and composer of Neapolitan birth, whose career was centered in England. Having become a British citizen, he was knighted in 1869. See Introduction.

Giulio Ricordi to Verdi

Milan, 31 May 1871

Illustrious Maestro,

Yesterday, a serious conference took place with Brunello, and we reviewed all the mezzo-sopranos on earth. Among the young, pleasant (and sane) ladies, Waldmann bore the palm again; and Brunello, very glad to have her, wrote her right away. She sang at La Scala last season and had a decided success as Zerlina[1] in *Don Giovanni* and also in the role of Eboli in Trieste and now in Naples. [. . .] I have heard her sing Eboli in a room, and I liked her very, very much.

It goes without saying that if you don't like her, we are by no means obliged to give her the role. You know that our strict contracts with the management are famous by now and that all details are observed and considered.

At any rate, before making any contract with the management, we can always send you a draft, and you can indicate to us whatever deficiencies there might be.

Concerning Faccio's engagement, neither you nor we need assume any responsibility because the directors and the management are close to proposing it themselves, since he conducted several performances commendably. In Brescia he is reengaged for the third year, and Brunello would have wanted him in Vicenza if that season didn't coincide with the one in Brescia.

Also the greatest care will be taken with the chorus and orchestra. In any event, they will be heard first, and we shall reserve the right to change them, if necessary.

Before I proposed Sig. Magnani to Brunello, he had already written to him. So we are all agreed in this matter, and a word from you now to Magnani would be excellent.

We await your orders, then, so that everything can be arranged.

It really seems like a dream to me, since, unfortunately, the most beautiful things usually do not materialize but in our dreams. Certainly a more beautiful and solemn festivity than the one we are preparing will never happen again in my life.

1. A mezzo-soprano in the role of Zerlina was not uncommon in the nineteenth century. During the 1848 season at Covent Garden, for instance, Pauline Viardot-Garcia sang the role; and so did Marietta Alboni (see note 1 to Verdi's letter to Draneht of 20 July 1871) at Her Majesty's Theatre in 1849.

Verdi to Giulio Ricordi

St. Agata, 1 June 1871

Dear Giulio,

As soon as you tell me that the mezzo-soprano and the conductor have been signed, we shall immediately draw up the contract for *Aida*, with all those guarantees for the production, of course, indicated in your letter of 31 May.

It is necessary that the conductor be appointed because he would have to assume responsibility for the musical aspects of the company. [. . .]

Magnani was here yesterday for a few hours. He has to come to Milan for some personal business. I gave him a few words to pass on to you. You know what you have to do. Get going and quickly. Strike while the iron is hot.

Paul Draneht to Verdi

Milan, 3 June 1871

Dear and illustrious Maestro,

I am finally back here in Milan. Since the day I had the pleasure of paying you a visit in the country, I have gone from one city to another to see and meet artists who are performing at this time; I don't believe I have missed a single one of the theatres that are now open.

I returned to Milan only two hours ago, and I consider it my first duty to inform you that I have finally come to an understanding with the Pozzoni-Anastasi couple and that yesterday I definitely concluded their contracts. Monsieur Anastasi decided to accept the propositions I made him, since he was convinced that we could have chosen someone else if he continued to carry his head so high. I can assure you, dear Maestro, that the result is good, because after having heard Madame Pozzoni in Florence, I had to agree a thousand times with the preference you had given her for the creation of the role of Aida. [. . .]

Now would you please tell me if you have reached a definite decision concerning the role of Amneris, which is of great interest to me. [. . .]

Mariette Bey has written to tell me that he will leave Cairo to come to Milan toward the end of this month, and he asks me for the Italian libretto so that he may find out about the alterations that have been made; he must know them for the final arrangements of sets and costumes. I shall contact Monsieur Ricordi to get the libretto, and I would appreciate your recommending me to him if you should think it necessary.

What a fine man this Monsieur Vincenzo Luccardi is![1] He has given me the most detailed information about [illegible] the artists in question; and he has overwhelmed me with kindnesses. A thousand thanks, dear Maestro, for this precious acquaintance. [. . .]

1. Hermann Baron, the prominent autograph dealer in London, had in his possession (in 1972) a calling card by which Verdi introduced Draneht to Vincenzo Luccardi in Rome: "You, who are not of the theatre, but a fine connoisseur of music, can be more useful to him than any maestro." However, the date attributed to this card, 25 March 1871, is in error. Verdi obviously gave it to Draneht during the latter's visit to St. Agata on 19 May 1871.

Verdi to Camille Du Locle

St. Agata, 6 June 1871

[. . .] Draneht Bey was here for a few hours,[1] and he told me he would return later with <u>Mariette</u>.[2] Oh, if only you could be the third! [. . .]

1. Verdi refers to Draneht's visit of 19 May 1871.
2. In view of the available evidence, it must be assumed that Draneht never returned to St. Agata and that Mariette never met Verdi.

Giulio Ricordi to Verdi

Milan, 7 June 1871

Illustrious Maestro,

While Brunello is negotiating with la Waldmann, I am trying again to find out if there is some other good artist; two names come to mind: la Destinn[1] and la Giovanone.[2] The first is a great actress, a fascinating person of most distinguished ability. Her voice has some strong notes in the middle register (B, C, E, and F); but her upper register is a bit awkward, and her low notes are not very sturdy. She has many defects, then, which are somewhat compensated for by the above-mentioned qualities. She was liked very much in the role of Eboli at La Scala, however, and she had great success during the last carnival season in Cairo and is now singing in Budapest with excellent success. The general word is excellent; but as I said, I have never heard her. Do you know any more about her?

La Waldmann can be signed by telegram immediately; but if we don't risk losing her by waiting a few days, I really think it best to seek out and investigate other names so that from among the good we can choose the best. By doing this I am fighting even myself a bit because I wish I could write you simply that <u>everything is concluded</u>, so that I might arrange the rest with you. But in this instance, indeed, we must apply the old saying: <u>He who walks slowly, walks safely</u>.

Tomorrow, I believe, the contract between Faccio and the management will be signed. Faccio will choose the members of the company, one by one, and they will be arranged precisely according to the guidelines and proportions you have sent.

Magnani was here. I encouraged him to accept, and I offered to draw up his contract with the management myself, so that his interests may be guaranteed. When an agreement is reached, as I hope it will be, I shall present Magnani to the Mayor and the directors so that he may be treated with the regard due such an eminent artist.

My father and my mother left unexpectedly this morning for the lake where my brother Enrico, who is there with his wife and child, fell gravely ill. It concerns a violent attack of the arteries to the heart, a grave and painful illness. Let us hope that he may be able to overcome it! Really there is never a day of peace!

1. Maria Destinn-Löwe, Bohemian mezzo-soprano. First heard in Italy in 1865, she sang at La Scala between 1866 and 1868, and she also appeared as Ortrud in the first Italian performance of *Lohengrin* in Bologna. Later she was to teach Ema Kittlová, who became the famous soprano Emmy Destinn (1878–1930).

2. Ginevra Giovannoni Zacchi. Giulio Ricordi apparently misspelled the soprano's name.

Verdi to Giulio Ricordi

St. Agata, 8 June 1871

Dear Giulio,

La Giovanone[1] is a soprano and could not do Amneris.

La Destinn seems inadequate for that role, and although she made a good showing at La Scala as Eboli, she owes her success mainly to her very elegant figure and to the [Veil] Song. I can't give you a judgment because I have not heard her, just as I have not heard la Waldmann; but from the consensus of the reports I have received concerning these two artists, I think the latter is better. Then, too, la Destinn has very weak low notes. If you decide on la Waldmann, tell me immediately because I shall have la Destinn signed for Cairo. La Pozzoni has already been signed by them. A beautiful Aida!

Don't say anything about la Destinn and Cairo because if it were made known, nothing more would come of it. Quiet then, for Heaven's sake!

Peppina and I are very sad about your brother's illness. I hope it will be less grave than you fear.

P.S. I repeat, do not speak about la Destinn for Cairo.

1. Verdi, in response to Giulio Ricordi's letter of 7 June 1871, obviously repeats the misspelling of the soprano's name.

Verdi to Paul Draneht

St. Agata, 8 June 1871

Excellency,

Since you speak Italian so well, allow me to write you in my native language, in which I shall perhaps explain myself better than by writing in a language that is not my own.

I am most pleased that you have signed la Pozzoni, and I am convinced she will achieve an excellent success in Cairo. The role of Aida, then, will be for her.

The role of Amneris would not be suited to the vocal means of la Sass. It is written too low for her. Furthermore I know her; and I know from experience that it is in the interest of both the management and the composer to give her operas in which she is the only soprano, or at least an opera which has no other role equal or superior to hers.

From what I have heard, la Viziak could not do Amneris well; and since in a few days I myself shall be able to suggest an artist suitable for this role,[1] please wait until that time before making a choice in this matter.

Signor Ricordi does not have the libretto of *Aida*, but soon I myself shall send a copy to Y.E.

1. Verdi obviously wanted to wait for Waldmann's definite commitment to La Scala before suggesting Destinn for Cairo.

Paul Draneht to Verdi

Milan [9 or 10] June 1871

Illustrious Signor Maestro,

I received your kind letter of June 8 and answer immediately.

When I had the pleasure to visit you, it seemed that you were kindly disposed toward my desire to give the role of Amneris to la Sass. But in your esteemed letter, [*illegible*] you embarrass me.

Amneris is within the means of la Sass [*illegible*]. Please do not refuse my request. [*illegible*] The libretto of *Aida* [*illegible*].

Paul Draneht to Auguste Mariette

Milan, 10 June 1871

[. . .] I shall expect you in Milan so that we can come to an understanding about *Aida*. Upon your arrival in Brindisi kindly send me a telegram in care of Dr. Lampugnani, 22 Corso Vittorio Emanuele, to inform me when you will arrive here. This way I can return to Milan as soon as possible, should business call me away during that time.

I wrote to Verdi asking him for the libretto, which I have not yet been able to secure from him, from the publisher, or from anywhere else. He answered by promising me a handwritten copy. I shall deliver it to you as soon as I have it, probably by the next mail.

Verdi to Paul Draneht

St. Agata, 12 June 1871

Excellency,

When I had the pleasure of seeing you here, we spoke at length, it is true, about la Sass; but I never agreed that the role of Amneris should be entrusted to this artist; in fact I think I even told you that la Sass could musically (note that I say musically) manage the role of Aida but never that of Amneris.

As for adjusting this role, either for la Sass or for la Grossi, permit me to say that these arrangements are artistically most reprehensible and are always detrimental to the opera. Finally let me add that Y.E. is not unaware that this opera was written with a role for a mezzo-soprano, as I had the honor of informing you in my letters of 5 January and 14 April.

Giulio Ricordi to Verdi

Milan, 14 June 1871

Illustrious Maestro,

My brother Enrico — having been in very serious and grave danger — is by now on his way to recovery. Unfortunately this heart attack will leave serious consequences. To minimize them he must lead a very quiet life so that another attack, which would be terrible, might be prevented.

Unable to delay my trip to Germany any longer, I must leave tomorrow morning — with great regret that everything has not been determined concerning *Aida*. I shall be gone about fifteen days, and in the meantime the management will conclude everything that concerns the theatre.

Actually la Giovannoni is a soprano, so only la Waldmann remains. The negotiations with her are under way and would have been concluded by now if this artist were not on the way from Naples to Milan. Of course the management wanted to wait for la Waldmann's arrival — certain that it could obtain better conditions in her presence than in writing. Consider this business finished. Another piece of business brought to an end is that of Magnani, with whom I am really most satisfied. I myself presented Magnani to the directors of the theatre, to the Mayor, to various members of the council at city hall, and to Melzi, in the hope that this artist should really get to know Magnani. He was really welcomed in a festive manner and has already signed an agreement with the management which has granted him the increase he requested.

Truly this will be a precious acquisition for our theatre! I must now submit two urgent requests on the part of our Mayor; if only I knew how to present them in a way to obtain your consent.

1. Would you agree to be part of the commission that must study the conditions of our greatest theatre and propose everything that will help to consolidate and improve its destiny? The importance of this action by our city hall will certainly not have escaped you. While the government withdraws its subsidies, while city halls throughout Italy inexorably reduce or refuse their support, only Milan, in an impulse of poetry, wishes to ensure the fate of its theatre and, consequently, of musical art. Not to encourage this most noble

desire now would create a serious threat to the future of La Scala, which (whatever one may say) not only serves the interests of the citizens but has a more noble and lofty purpose — namely, to exemplify and to define all our art. When you yourself come to Milan next winter, you could assist in a few sessions and set forth your ideas, which would be heard with that reverence and respect to which only you are entitled.

2. Next September a great industrial exhibition, in which the government, province, city hall, and private persons compete, will take place in the grandest style in Milan. Everything promises a most excellent success so that the exhibition will be worthy not only of Milan but all of Italy. City hall wants to inaugurate this feast with an enormous festival, which, apart from being in a grand style, should also be of artistic value and interest. The city council has charged me, in complete secrecy, to find out whether you might consent to compose either a cantata or an anthem in honor of industry and the arts. [. . .]

You will say, perhaps: "What a bore!" . . . and so be it. But fame must also pay its taxes to humanity. [. . .]

La Pozzoni and la Destinn![1] A magnificent duet — both fascinating, attractive artists! I am really very glad. You can imagine that I will keep silent about it all. By the way, no less than twenty sopranos, ten tenors, ten baritones, and forty basses have come to me to recommend themselves for Cairo . . . and, of course, I told them to go with God, and good night. You won't mind hearing that among the applicants were . . . La Galletti . . . and . . . Tiberini!

Bona nox.

Draneht Bey (Is his name spelled this way?) was here to get the Italian libretto of *Aida*. I didn't give it to him for thirty-three reasons: the first, because we don't have it; the second, because if I had it I wouldn't have given it to him without your order.

Melzi continuously asks for the costume sketches of *Aida* in order to have them in time.

We had good news from poor Escudier and his whole family

And here I end, sending you as well as Signora Peppina, the most cordial greetings. If I can be of service to you in any way, I shall be in Leipzig, Hotel Hauff, on the 18th.

You can always write me here, however, addressing your letters either in my name or my father's. Tornaghi will answer you about everything.

1. For *Aida* in Cairo.

Verdi to Tito Ricordi

St. Agata, 15 June 1871

Dear Tito,

Giulio must have left for some Germanic stuff, so I address my answer to his letter of yesterday to you. First of all I am very, very happy that your Enrico has overcome a danger which appeared to be grave. May he take care of himself and think of the future.

I am quite pleased that the management has reached an agreement with Magnani, and I hope the audience will be pleased as well.

If la Waldmann is really a good artist, be careful that she is not taken away [from La Scala] as soon as she arrives in Milan. The management must not lose any time. As soon as the management has completed all the necessary contracts, we shall conclude ours as well with a few words. I wouldn't like to waste much time because that blessed Cairo is always involved.

As far as
1. my taking part in a commission, etc., etc.,
2. my writing an anthem, etc.

is concerned, I can do neither one nor the other; and try to spare me letters of invitation such as this. Besides there is enough work as it is. I have an opera that hangs heavy on my shoulders! An opera isn't a trifle, at least not for me.

Verdi to the Mayor of Milan

St. Agata, 17 June 1871

Most illustrious Mayor,

Your having chosen me to be part of the commission concerning the future of the theatres in Milan flatters and honors me very much. Therefore I sincerely regret that I am unable to participate because of my activities and present occupations.

I beg you, Esteemed Mayor, to accept, and to have the City Council of Milan accept, my thanks as well as my excuses.

Verdi to Camille Du Locle

St. Agata, 17 June 1871

[. . .] I also believe I told you that Mariette Bey is coming to Europe,[1] and in case he should go to Paris first, it would be well to tell him how things stand with regard to *Aida*. As you know, Draneht Bey was here for a few hours. He has signed the artist for the role of Aida, la Pozzoni, but a mezzo-soprano for Amneris is still outstanding. He wanted me to adjust this role for la Sass, but that is impossible for a thousand reasons. I wrote him that I have a mezzo-soprano who would suit our needs,[2] and he answered that the financial resources are exhausted![3] Then why sign la Sass when there was no more need for her? Meanwhile time is passing; and later, perhaps, we shall find ourselves in trouble. [. . .]

1. See Verdi's letter to Du Locle of 6 June 1871.
2. See Verdi's letter to Draneht of 8 June 1871.
3. Verdi apparently refers here to the illegible part of Draneht's letter of 9 or 10 June or to a missing response from Draneht to his own letter of 12 June 1871.

Paul Draneht to Auguste Mariette

Montecatini, 17 June 1871

[. . .] The Maestro has still not sent me the libretto for which we have asked. [. . .]

It is regrettable, my dear Bey, that you did not enclose a copy of the Verdi contract[1] for which I have often asked you. The Maestro wants to take over the selection of the artists from me, and I don't know how to deal with him regarding certain claims he raises that don't seem very logical to me. You would be very kind to let me have a copy of this contract as soon as possible. [. . .]

1. The contract drawn up and signed by Mariette in Paris on 29 July 1870. See Document V.

Verdi to Giovanni Battista Lampugnani

St. Agata, 20 June 1871

[. . .] I am surprised that the Bey says nothing at all about the mezzo-soprano for Amneris. He wanted this role to be entrusted either to la Sass or to la Grossi — one a soprano, the other a contralto — although he knew very well from my previous letters that Amneris was written for a mezzo-soprano.

I don't want to insist, since the Bey might tell me: "Here is the Cairo company. I did not make your contract; and if you composed for a mezzo-soprano, that does not concern me." It is true; in that case, however, I would be forced to turn to the person who signed my contract. For now I would like to avoid taking this step; but on the other hand time is passing, and we may very well find ourselves embroiled in the end. Therefore if you think it opportune, you might mention it to the Bey.

Maria Waldmann to Eugenio Tornaghi

Milan, 20 June 1871

[. . .] I see that we cannot agree on anything [for La Scala], since the management's offer is <u>extremely limited</u> — 8,000 lire for the entire season!

I would regret immensely if the matter remained unsettled, but you know only too well that in such a case one must think of one's own interests.

In the hope — and certain — that you, dear Signor Tornaghi, will do what you can to protect a young artist in such a difficult and trying career, I ask you kindly to accept my most sincere regards. [. . .]

Eugenio Tornaghi to Verdi

Milan, 21 June 1871

Illustrious Maestro,

I have the honor to acknowledge receipt of your esteemed letter of the 15th and to inform you that la Waldmann resumed negotiations with the management of La Scala soon after her arrival. They are discussing a little difference in her price, a difference that I hope to straighten out shortly in my desire to announce the accomplished engagement to you as soon as possible. [. . .]

Giovanni Battista Lampugnani to Paul Draneht

Milan, 22 June 1871

[. . .] I am enclosing Verdi's letter.[1] Verdi is wrong to say that the role of Aida [*sic*] suits la Sass <u>musically</u>. The bass Costa[2] wants 1,600 [lire]; he had wanted 2,000 because he said Marini told him that Marè had that sum. At the signing of the contract I think I shall be able to knock that down even below the 1,600. Now it remains for you to tell me what I should do.

[. . .] I am going to write to Verdi that I have received his letter and have forwarded it to H.E., Draneht Bey. Of necessity Verdi has written to me in order to communicate properly with you; not wishing to beat the horse, he has beaten the saddle.[3] I shall wait until the day after tomorrow, however, before I write to Verdi. Since Y.E. does not think I should tell him that I have sent his letter to you, I shall tell him only that I have written to you concerning the mezzo-<u>soprano</u>, so that he may give you an answer.

I feel that Y.E. is annoyed, but this is always much better than finding ourselves in the midst of howling singers and ugly ballerinas, who want to force their way to Cairo.

1. His letter to Lampugnani of 20 June 1871.

2. Tommaso Costa (1836–1909), Italian bass, presumably related to Sir Michael Costa. He was widely known for his *comprimario* roles in Italy, Spain, Buenos Aires, and the United States.

3. "If you can't whip the horse, whip the post."

Paul Draneht to Verdi

Montecatini, 26 June 1871

Dear and illustrious Maestro,

Monsieur Lampugnani has informed me of the letter you sent him on the 20th of this month, in which you complain about my silence regarding the mezzo-soprano whom you want me to engage for the role of Amneris.

In my last letter[1] I had the honor of telling you that this engagement does not depend on me and that — since the funds budgeted for the artists are completely exhausted — I would have to address myself to Cairo to explain the matter and to ask for a subsidy. This is what I have done; and I have been awaiting, and still await, a reply that will, I hope, not come too late. I shall then have the honor to inform you of my course of action and, I even hope, to communicate it personally to you, if, as he wrote me, Mariette Bey should arrive on the first boat expected in Brindisi next Wednesday.

1. Draneht refers either to his letter of 9 or 10 June or to a later one that is missing.

Paul Draneht to Eleonora Grossi

Montecatini, 26 June 1871

Dear Friend Grossi,

I hope this letter still finds you in Naples. But wherever you may be, will you please answer me as soon as possible to enlighten me with regard to the following.

You know that Maestro Verdi does not want to listen to talk about Marie Sass. I don't know exactly what difficulty he has had with her since the premiere of *Don Carlos*, but his grudge developed during that time.[1] I did not want to annoy him too much with this, but he shows me no respect in his obstinacy to keep from you the part of Amneris — the dramatic role that had been composed for Madame Galletti under the pretext that it was written for a mezzo-soprano. I have not yet received the music to submit to you. [*illegible*] The Maestro told me that this role was written for the <u>*tessitura* of</u> [Leonora in] <u>*Favorita*</u> and that any artist who can sing that role can also sing Amneris. Now tell me what you think about this. What are the notes that you doubt? We are not talking about the low notes — you have a cornucopia of those. And in the top notes, I know, you climb high enough. I would also assert that you could sing the role of Adalgisa, a soprano role.[2] In short give me a good idea of your vocal resources, the notes you can execute and those you cannot, so that I may be able to speak knowledgeably with the Maestro, whom I shall go to see upon receipt of your reply.

1. Marie Sass in the role of Elisabeth made faces as her Belgian compatriot Pauline Gueymard-Lauters sang the role of Eboli. See Andrew Porter, "A note on Princess Eboli." *Musical Times*, 1972, 113, no. 1554, p. 751.

2. Adalgisa in *Norma* is a mezzo-soprano role, as Draneht himself states in his following letter to Verdi.

Paul Draneht to Verdi

Milan, 4 July 1871

Illustrious Signor Maestro,

The letters I receive from Cairo[1] are not the kind that authorize me to augment my already too numerous company with further contracts. They do not understand why with such an abundance of artists there is no way to select the artists for *Aida* without resorting to additional large contracts — especially since Signora Grossi has already sung various mezzo-soprano roles, including the Adalgisa in *Norma*, with brilliant success in Cairo.

You will recall, esteemed Sig. Maestro, when I had the pleasure of dining in your hospitable home you told me that since the role of Amneris is written in the range of *Favorita*, it could very well suit the prima donnas who sing that leading role in Donizetti's opera. And I assumed from this assertion that it was your intention to adapt the role of Amneris for Signora Sass, after I had informed you that *Favorita* was in the repertoire of the aforementioned artist. On this subject we had an extensive conversation; and among other things I observed that it was not prudent to allow Signora Sass to make her debut in *Favorita*, after the great success la Galletti had had in this opera. You were kind enough to agree with this observation of mine by saying: "Certainly, her debut in *Favorita* would not be convenient, since la Galletti is a great artist."

The situation being what it is, I hope that you will be kind enough to arrange for Signora Sass to sing in *Aida*; she is the celebrity of the season, and I would be truly displeased to have to replace her. It remains well understood that the role must be perfectly suited to the means of the artist, since, in light of the enormous sums expended and being expended to mount *Aida*, I would under no circumstances act in a way that would impair the success of your grandiose work, whose individual roles must of necessity be sung only by artists of known merit and with ranges adapted to the roles. Actually it seems to me that in my company we have the necessary personnel.

It is in your power to accede to my entreaties, to my desires, which I believe are not at all unfounded. Should you think it absolutely impossible to entrust the role of Amneris to Signora Sass, I would once more beg you to be willing to consign it to Signora Grossi, who — believe me — combines all the necessary qualities to portray the role with dignity. I am so certain of Signora Grossi's talent that I had written her to come to Milan, and I would have taken the liberty of asking you the favor of inviting her to St. Agata; in going over the role with her, you would certainly have been convinced of her distinguished abilities. Unfortunately Signora Grossi had already departed for Cadiz, and I could not see my wish fulfilled.

I shall leave soon for Paris; time is running out, and so I would like to ask that you send me the music and the libretto. I know that changes and additions have been made. Since I must make the necessary dispositions in good time, so that everything is prepared with the requisite grandeur, I must know what these additions and changes are. I thank you in advance.

I have been expecting Mariette Bey these past few days; but he has not arrived, and I have not even received his letters. I suppose, therefore, that he will arrive by steamer on Thursday.

1. Missing.

Tito Ricordi to Verdi

Milan, 5 July 1871

[. . .] Giulio has just returned; he will write you soon.

The engagement of la Waldmann can be considered secure in spite of some little differences that have come up between the artist and the management — differences that will certainly be straightened out because la Waldmann is very anxious to get this engagement and because the management knows I want her. [. . .]

Giulio Ricordi to Verdi

Milan, 7 July 1871

Illustrious Maestro,

Back from my rush through Germany, I hasten to give you news of events at La Scala and to tell you that la Waldmann . . . has not yet been definitely signed. You will exclaim: "What the devil! . . . This is like the building of the Duomo that is never finished." And you are right. It should only be up to us to force the management to sign the contract at any moment. One could do that if la Fricci or la Stolz were at stake, but since la Waldmann is involved, excellent artist that she is, I don't think one should make too much fuss. If the management did not decide to sign her immediately, it was always because (as I had the honor of writing you several times) they figured they could find someone better, or at least equal, who asked for fewer impossible conditions. Apart from a nice little salary, which would be no obstacle, la Waldmann wants the right (by way of a clause in her contract) to make her debut in *Aida* — something to which the management absolutely cannot subscribe.

These past few days I have heard many other women — among them some fairly good ones like la Moro,[1] whose appearance is very distinguished and who sings exquisitely. But even she does not have the vocal strength and volume of la Fricci. I know with what intentions you wrote the role of Amneris, and I really don't know where to turn, since, unfortunately, there is only one Fricci!

Between la Moro and la Waldmann I don't think there is much difference; the first one would be more effective in the upper register, the other in the lower. Their shortcomings and their virtues are about the same.

Tomorrow I must hear some two or three other women — among them one about whom I have heard much praise.

I would think it best to have a conference with you, illustrious Maestro, together with Faccio who has also heard all the prima donnas in question. You would explain to us your ideas, and we would tell you what we have heard; at least we could decide something sensibly and logically.

You wrote us[2] that you would go to Genoa soon. It would be easy, then, to arrange a trip there. Faccio goes to Brescia on the 25th, so we should schedule our trip before that time.

The management intends to open the season with *La Forza del Destino*. They propose: la Stolz (Leonora), Capponi (Alvaro), Pandolfini (Don Carlo), Maini (Priest), Pantaleoni[3] (Melitone), Preziosilla to be engaged. Of course orchestra and chorus as required. What do you think of this project? Can I answer yes to the management?

The company is good, even excellent.

I am really sorry that I must be a continuous annoyance, but you may blame my very intense desire to do everything according to what may be most agreeable to you. [. . .]

1. Angelica Moro, Italian soprano. Between 1861 and 1879 she appeared in Italy and in such cities as Odessa, Budapest, Barcelona, and Nice.
2. Presumably in a business letter to Tito Ricordi on 30 June 1871.
3. Adriano Pantaleoni (1837–1908), Italian baritone and impresario. Following his first appearance in Rome in 1869 he sang a repertoire of over fifty operas throughout Italy, Austria, Spain, and in New York.

Auguste Mariette to Paul Draneht

Boulaq, 7 July 1871

My dear Bey,

I enclose M. Verdi's contract.[1]

At last I have received the order from H.H. to depart. But in connection with certain interests that I must attend to I am obliged to go to Paris by the most direct route. I embark on the 11th; and on the 18th, at the latest, I shall be at my destination.

Since the Viceroy wants us to give *Aida* the greatest possible splendor, and since we do not have another moment to lose, I hope you will come to Paris yourself to put everything in motion. It is almost indispensable that you be there to see the contractors, who will do nothing without you.

I foresee a great task. But I am placing myself completely at your disposal, and I hope we shall come out of it in a manner that will bring honor to your administration.

Do not forget that I am unable to do anything without the libretto. So if you come to Paris, bring it with you. My address will always be 170 rue de Rivoli.

1. See Document V.

Giulio Ricordi to Verdi

Milan, 8 July 1871

Illustrious Maestro,

Today, again, I continued with my job of auditioning artists. [. . .]

Another thing is now necessary: The project to reform the orchestra was acknowledged by the Communal Council but postponed for another year. Together with the theatre's directors, however, I would like it to be done this year so that you may be fully satisfied in this regard! When you write me, could you not cleverly tell me that if *Aida* is to be given this year, a reform in the orchestra will be absolutely necessary, since it is now so very poorly arranged and does not make half the possible effect? If I make the Mayor read these two lines, the business is over and done with, since, for fear that you might not come to direct *Aida*, I think they would even destroy the theatre.

To whom must I consign the six trumpets for Cairo?

J. Barrot to Paul Draneht

Alexandria, 9 July 1871

My dear Bey,

I have the honor to acknowledge receipt of the letter[1] you addressed to me, dated 1 July, concerning the difficulties stirred up by M. Verdi with regard to M. Bottesini and Mlle. Sass. His Highness hopes that you will succeed in convincing M. Verdi; but, in any case, He is unable to solve these difficulties, and He charges me to write that you are free to do whatever is necessary and that He relies entirely on you.

I have read in the newspapers that *Aida* is now being mounted at the theatre in Milan and that it will be presented shortly.[2] I have said nothing of this to His Highness; but I call your attention to this matter so that you will see to it that this project is not carried out. If the news is true, you will easily understand that should this opera be given in Europe before it is given in Cairo, His Highness will not be at all pleased. [. . .]

1. Missing.
2. This was a false rumor.

Verdi to Giulio Ricordi [1]

St. Agata, 9 July 1871

Dear Giulio,

This Scala business is dragging out too long. Some serious, insurmountable trouble will come of it; and I can't tell you if I myself shall be able to wait much longer for a decision.

La Moro is a soprano; she does *Rigoletto*: impossible for Amneris.

La Waldmann makes outrageous demands, and you can tell her that I alone distribute the roles for a new opera. Go ahead and look for someone else, but where will you hear her and how will you judge her? Never depend on [second-hand] reports. [. . .]

P.S. I think we should lay it on the line to la Waldmann. Either she desists in her ridiculous demands or negotiations will cease. [. . .]

1. In answer to Giulio Ricordi's letter of 7 July 1871.

Verdi to Giulio Ricordi [1]

St. Agata, 10 July 1871

Dear Giulio,

You are familiar with the libretto of *Aida*, and you know that for Amneris one needs an artist with highly developed dramatic sensibility who is a mistress of the stage. How can you hope to find these other qualities in a virtual beginner? The voice alone, no matter how beautiful (something very difficult to judge in a room or an empty theatre), is not enough for that role.

So-called polished singing matters little to me. I like to have the roles sung as I wish; but I can't supply the voice, or the soul, or that certain I don't know what, which is commonly called being driven by the devil. Yesterday I wrote you my opinion of la Waldmann, and I reaffirm it today. I know quite well that it will not be easy to find an Amneris, but we shall talk in person about it in Genoa. That's not all, however; you have not yet told me if the conditions I indicated in my various letters have been accepted. You can be quite sure, my dear Giulio, that if I come to Milan it isn't for the vainglory of giving one of my operas; it is to achieve a truly artistic performance. To succeed in this I must have the necessary elements; and I ask you to reply categorically if, in addition to the company of singers,

1. the conductor has been named;
2. the choristers have been engaged in the way that I indicated;
3. the orchestra will be composed as I also indicated;
4. the timpani and bass drum will be changed for much larger instruments than those we had two years ago;
5. the standard pitch will be maintained;
6. the stage band has adopted this pitch to avoid the inevitable discord when playing first on one pitch, then on another;
7. the arrangement of the instruments in the orchestra will be as I pointed out in a kind of diagram[2] as early as last winter in Genoa?

The seating arrangement of the orchestra is of much greater importance than is commonly believed — for the blending of the instruments, for the sonority, and for the effect. These small improvements will afterward open the way for other innovations, which will surely come one day; among them, taking the spectators' boxes off the stage, bringing the curtain to the footlights; another, making the orchestra invisible. This is not my idea but Wagner's. It's excellent. It seems impossible that today we tolerate the sight of shabby tails and white ties, for example, mixed with Egyptian, Assyrian, and Druidic costumes, etc., etc., and, even more, the sight of the entire orchestra, which is part of the fictitious world, almost in the middle of the floor, among the whistling[3] or applauding crowd. Add to all this the indecency of seeing the tops of the harps, the necks of the double basses, and the baton of the conductor all up in the air.

Reply, therefore, in a categoric and decisive manner; because unless I can be given what I demand, it would be useless to continue these negotiations.

1. In answer to Giulio Ricordi's letter of 8 July 1871.
2. Missing.
3. In European and Latin theatres whistling is an expression of disapproval and protest as booing is in American theatres.

Eugenio Tornaghi to Verdi

Milan, 14 July 1871

Illustrious Maestro,

Giulio has gone to accompany his family to the country. He will be in Milan again on Saturday or Sunday and then will go to take the usual cure for his stomach ailment. With regard to your esteemed letter of the 10th, Giulio would like to have a conference with you as soon as possible; and he would hope to visit you along with Faccio on Sunday night or Monday morning to go personally into all those details that would be too difficult to agree to by writing. If Giulio's plan should be inconvenient to you, kindly send me a telegram as soon as you have received this letter.

Meanwhile I can assure you that plans are already under way to have the chorus and orchestra arranged precisely according to your indications and as well as possible. The pitch is, and always will be, the normal one for the stage band as well as for the orchestra. The bass drum and the timpani are stronger and louder. Besides you know that in our contract we can oblige the management to as many clauses as we like, to ensure that we have everything you suggest to us and mention to Giulio.

Signor Tito has left for San Pellegrino after a checkup which gives hope that there is no danger of a stone; but in the meantime he suffers a great deal and is very sad!

Giulio Ricordi to Verdi

Milan, 16 July 1871

Illustrious Maestro,

In view of your telegram[1] I am canceling my trip to you. I now await a note from you to come to Genoa; and if it could be before the 25th, it would be good so that Faccio could also come along. I think it would be very useful for him, as the conductor, to confer with you. [. . .]

1. Missing.

Paul Draneht to Verdi

Milan, 17 July 1871

Signor Maestro,

I am enclosing a letter from Mariette Bey,[1] which I ask you to return to me. You will see that he urges me to obtain the libretto of *Aida*, without which it is impossible to work on the preparation of all the necessities for the *mise-en-scène* of *Aida*. In fact, all I need is the libretto before running off to

Paris, where, as you know, the costumes and accessories must be done, etc., etc., so that the splendor of all this may correspond to the musical importance of the work. Therefore I call upon your courtesy to let me have the libretto by return mail, and I shall be grateful for the favor. Time is passing and woe if we let ourselves be caught off guard. I would also ask you, then, to send me the music, so that I can distribute the parts at the proper time to the artists. As soon as I have it I shall be ready to fulfill the exact obligations of the contract, i.e., the payment of the remaining 100,000 francs.

If you should not now be able to let me have the music of *Aida*, then I would ask you to send only the libretto, and I shall leave with it for Paris at once, to make all the necessary arrangements for the production. I shall then return to get the music.

I am taking this opportunity to inform you of my regret that recent letters from Cairo keep repeating that I absolutely must not increase the costs of the company (which are already rather high) and that I must be satisfied with the artists who have already been engaged. Since a dramatic mezzo-soprano is needed for the role of Amneris, however, I cannot but repeat what I have already communicated to Your Honor in my previous letters — that is, from our point of view Signora Grossi is most suitable. She is now singing *La Favorita* as written [in the original key], and she has also performed the role of Fidès in *Le Prophète* without making any changes. I can assure you that as far as talent goes, Signora Grossi is inferior to no other artist; and I can assure you with a perfect conscience, having admired her for two seasons in more than one opera at the theatre. [. . .]

Would you, illustrious Signor Maestro, be kind enough to favor me with a reply, which my letter of the 4th of this month did not receive. I repeat my request to send the libretto as soon as possible because it is really of the utmost necessity.

1. Mariette's letter to Draneht of 7 July 1871.

Paul Draneht to Auguste Mariette

Milan, 18 July 1871

My dear Mariette Bey,

I have received the Verdi contract, and I thank you for it. Following your request the Maestro was eager to promise us the libretto; in spite of the urgency of my request, however, he has not sent it to me, even though I reminded him in a second letter on the 4th of this month. The illustrious composer has not yet given me the music either, despite the requests I have made on several occasions. So I shall write him again in the most urgent way, telling him that your hands and mine are tied, that we can't do a thing without the libretto, that the time is advancing, and that I beg him, after all, to delay no longer.

I would go back myself to see him in the country were I not a bit upset with him over a little difficulty that has arisen with regard to the interpretation of the role of Amneris, about which he is completely wrong.

As soon as I have the libretto I shall hasten to meet you in Paris. Meanwhile you can continue your preparatory work with our contractors, but I think you should order nothing definitely until this blockhead Verdi sends us the libretto. I cannot explain his insistence on such an unreasonable issue as the one I have mentioned above or his delay in handing over the libretto and the music to us. I forgot to tell you that I asked him for both of these last May when I paid him a visit at his home.

Auguste Mariette to Paul Draneht

Marseilles, 19 July 1871

My dear Bey,

After having changed my itinerary many times, I am at last in Marseilles, enroute to Paris.

The instructions that I received from H.H. on my departure are absolutely the same as a year ago. To summarize, H.H. wishes that the opera be presented in Cairo during the first two weeks of December, something which was, after all, agreed upon a long time ago. Regarding the details, H.H. does not wish to hear about them. He is counting entirely on you and me for what concerns each of us.

Some private letters, and most of the newspapers, have announced that *Aida* is in rehearsal in Milan and is to be presented soon.[1] I have not been involved in this second draft of the contract with Verdi,[2] and I do not know what new things have been agreed upon between you and him. What I do know, however, is that if the Viceroy should learn that the opera has been presented in Milan before being done in Cairo, he would be justifiably astonished, he who is paying 150,000 francs to have a premiere which he would this way no longer have. As far as I am concerned, I would find in this procedure something indecent with regard to me, something that would be difficult for me to explain. *Aida* is, in effect, a product of my work. I am the one who convinced the Viceroy to order its presentation; *Aida*, in a word, is a creation of my brain, and it seems to me that before disposing of it so completely, one should at least have had the courtesy of writing to me about it. Who knows what sort of incongruous things they are going to do in Milan with the costumes and sets. I hope that all of this is only a rumor of the newspapers, however, and that we shall have the premiere in Cairo — a true *Aida*, which will be a serious work of art, in its music as well as its *mise-en-scène*.

The Viceroy has ordered me to return to Cairo as soon as possible, and I do not have a day to lose. The Viceroy also wishes that everything concerning *Aida* be done in Paris. Come promptly, then, so that we may put everything in motion. [. . .]

We must both treat *Aida* as a serious work, worthy of you and me. An opera can be a work of art like any other, and we must not content ourselves with an approximation. [. . .]

1. See Barrot's letter to Draneht of 9 July 1871.
2. We know of no such draft and there was no second contract.

Verdi to Camille Du Locle

Genoa, 20 July 1871

Dear Du Locle,

I know that Mariette Bey is in Paris at 170 rue de Rivoli, and I ask that you go to him and tell him that something is wrong with the *Aida* business. Draneht Bey has not yet found, or rather has not wanted to find, the mezzo-soprano for the role of Amneris, and now he writes me repeatedly that he has no more funds!! Is that my fault? And why didn't he think of that before spending it all!!

Draneht insists on having the libretto of *Aida* in order to transmit it to Mariette; but I cannot send it to him until this dispute is settled. To avoid losing time, however, I am sending the libretto to you; and if you see that Mariette can settle these difficulties, you can deliver it to him so that he can give the orders for costumes and sets.

I shall transcribe below the letter I am writing today to Draneht so that you can see briefly what has happened.

We have been in Genoa since last night and shall stay here for some twenty days. How about it? Will you come here? [. . .]

Verdi to Paul Draneht

Genoa, 20 July 1871

Excellency,

Your esteemed letter of the 17th was forwarded to me in Genoa.

I think that before I send you the libretto of *Aida*, it must be decided who will perform the role of Amneris. As I had the honor of telling you once, neither la Sass nor la Grossi are, or ever were, mezzo-sopranos. You say that la Grossi did *La Favorita* and <u>Fidès</u> in *Le Prophète*; la Alboni[1] once did *La Gazza Ladra*, *La Sonnambula*, I believe, and even the role of <u>Carlo V</u> in *Ernani*!! But what of it? This means only that singers and conductors have no scruples about tampering with, or allowing others to tamper with, the creations of authors.

Permit me to give a little of the history of this *Aida* . . . .

I wrote this opera for the past season, and it wasn't my fault that it wasn't performed.

I was asked to postpone the performance for a year — something to which I readily consented, even though it was rather detrimental to me.

As long ago as January 5 I indicated that the role of Amneris was written for a mezzo-soprano; later I asked that no conductor be named without first notifying me. That way I was always hoping to get Mariani.

While I was in the middle of these negotiations, another conductor was signed, and no one ever thought to sign a mezzo-soprano!! Why is this? And why, when dealing with an opera written <u>expressly</u> for an occasion, did no one think, first of all, to provide all the elements that might be needed for its production? It seems rather strange to me that this was not done, and allow me, Y.E., to tell you that this is not the way to achieve a good production and a success.

1. Marietta Alboni (1823–94), Italian contralto. She had in fact sung the role of Carlo V at the London premiere of *Ernani* at Covent Garden in 1847, when the baritone engaged for that part found it too high. The most famous contralto of the nineteenth century, she assumed physical proportions that prompted Rossini to call her "the elephant that swallowed a nightingale." Nevertheless he greatly admired her, and she sang at his funeral in 1868, five years after having withdrawn from the operatic stage.

Paul Draneht to J. Barrot[1]

Milan, 21 July 1871

My dear Bey,

I thank our August Master, His Highness, for the confidence he has shown in me by letting me solve the question that Monsieur Verdi has brought up concerning the interpretation of Amneris in *Aida*.

His Highness may be sure that I shall uphold his interests to the end, with the understanding that in this affair we are a thousand times right. Monsieur Verdi and I have no feelings of antipathy, rancor, or caprice in this matter; but [*illegible*] he is a thousand times wrong. We shall never find a more suitable person than Marie Sass or la Grossi to interpret the role in question. I shall only surrender in the unlikely event that Verdi would revert to such an extreme measure as refusing to hand over the music. [. . .]

1. Draneht apparently wrote this letter before receiving Verdi's letter of 20 July 1871.

Paul Draneht to Verdi

Milan, 21 July 1871

Illustrious Signor Maestro,
 I am in receipt of your kind letter of the 20th of this month.
 You were pleased to tell me a little story; I could also tell a little story, however, and from that, I am sure, the rather clear result would be that I am not at all out of line in this unfortunate crisis.
 But, quite convinced from your letters that you definitely want to have a mezzo-soprano for the role of Amneris, I shall certainly not be the one to continue a pattern of resistance that might affect the good rapport we have enjoyed until now. I know that by engaging the mezzo-soprano I am acting against the interests of the administration entrusted to me — even, perhaps, against my own rights and against orders to the contrary, which I mentioned to you in my previous letters. But it doesn't matter. I promise you that I shall engage the mezzo-soprano, in the hope that His Highness will come to approve my action; if he does not, I am ready to suffer the consequences.
 With this settled I ask you again to send me the libretto, so that I can leave for Paris and prepare what is needed for the *mise-en-scène* of *Aida*. After the mezzo-soprano has been engaged, I shall await the music.
 I am counting on your courtesy and so shall expect the libretto by return mail.
P.S. I shall occupy myself at once with the engagement of the mezzo-soprano.

Verdi to Paul Draneht

Genoa, 22 July 1871

Excellency,
 I shall not respond in detail to your most esteemed letter of the 21st but shall limit myself to say that it is not enough to sign a mezzo-soprano; this mezzo-soprano must be an artist of great worth. Would you please tell me, before you decide, which artists you are considering for this role originally written for la Galletti?
P.S. The libretto is no longer in my hands; it is in the hands of Du Locle and will remain there until these disputes have ended.

Paul Draneht to J. Barrot

Milan, 24 July 1871

My dear Bey,
 Since my letter of the 21st, Monsieur Verdi has made a pronounce-

ment regarding the role of Amneris in the most absolute and pretentious manner. He refuses to send the libretto and the music if we do not decide to engage a mezzo-soprano to interpret this character. Two contradictions will be more obvious in the contract than in anything I could write you on this subject. Here is the passage in the Verdi contract pertaining to the question:

"M. Verdi will choose the artists who will perform his score from the company of the Italian Theatre in Cairo."

Having now refused Mlle. Marie Sass, he pretends that we have obligated ourselves to engage a mezzo-soprano and that he must approve this artist before she is engaged.

Monsieur Verdi is very rich, and he has staunchly resolved to endure anything that might be done against him. Under Italian law he would be convicted and made to pay indemnities. [. . .]

Paul Draneht to Mariette

Milan, 24 July 1871

My dear Mariette Bey,
        I received your letter from Marseilles, dated the 19th, only yesterday.

The rumors reported in the Italian newspapers about *Aida* are unfounded. We shall have to give the opera in Cairo next December because it will be given here just two months later. Verdi has agreed to this. The Maestro really puts the knife to my throat, and I am obliged to obey or go to court, which I would never want to do. [. . .]

Paul Draneht to Verdi

Milan, 24 July 1871

Illustrious Signor Maestro,
        I have received your kind letter.[1] In Cairo one cannot engage a prima donna who does not have genuine merit corresponding to the importance of the theatre and who is not equal to the rest of the company. In this respect you can be sure of my greatest care. Within two or three days I hope to be able to let you know the mezzo-sopranos to whom I shall give my attention.

    1. Verdi's letter of 22 July 1871.

Paul Draneht to Verdi

Milan, 25 July 1871

Illustrious Signor Maestro,
        Yesterday you were kind enough to advise me through Signor Biondi[1]

that information you received regarding Signora Grossi allowed you to appreciate her talent for the role of Amneris.[2] [. . .] Signor Biondi brought me the pleasant news a few moments after I sent off my letter of yesterday, in which, of course, I told you that I too intended that the artist to be engaged should be one of distinct ability.

Today I went to see Signor Ricordi and was pleased to learn that the first good news was surpassed and that there can be no more doubt about your acceptance of the above-mentioned eminent artist.

While I thank you for your approval, I can once more assure you that in regard to her voice, her manner of singing, and her dramatic acting, Signora Grossi is entirely fit for the difficult task which you are about to entrust to her; and you will be completely satisfied. I know Signora Grossi's convincing talent only too well. Otherwise I would not have taken the liberty to be so insistent with you, to the point of making myself extremely annoying, and to trouble you so.

1. Unknown.
2. See Verdi's letter to Du Locle of 26 July 1871.

Verdi to Tito Ricordi

Genoa, 25 July 1871

Dear Tito,

I see in the newspapers, and Giulio confirms it,[1] that an Egyptian ballet is planned for La Scala. This is a very grave error, which is most harmful to the management and to the production that will <u>follow</u>. Speak about it to whomever you wish; it is something that must be remedied, because, I repeat, in my opinion it is a very serious error — one of the worst that can be committed in the theatre.

1. Apparently in person during his and Faccio's visit to Verdi on the previous day. See Tornaghi's letter to Verdi of 14 July 1871, Giulio Ricordi's letter to Verdi of 16 July 1871, and Verdi's letter to Du Locle of 26 July 1871.

Verdi to Camille Du Locle

Genoa, 26 July 1871

[. . .] The day before yesterday Maestro Faccio was here; and having looked over the role of Amneris, he assured me that la Grossi could do that role very well. Assuming that by now it would be difficult to find an absolutely dependable mezzo-soprano, I think it would be best to entrust the role of <u>Amneris</u> to la Grossi. La Grossi is known there and liked; and even if some passages prove a little high for her, she will always be better than some mediocrity. This is one artist decided upon, and now you can hand over the libretto so that the sets and costumes, etc., can be ordered.

Tell me: are costumes and scenery being made in Paris? Could we have the costume sketches here? Answer me at once with regard to this question.[1] [. . .]

1. See Giulio Ricordi's letters to Verdi of 7 November 1870 and 14 June 1871.

Delphine Baron to Paul Draneht

Paris, 30 July 1871

Excellency,

Monsieur Mariett [*sic*] Bey arrived here a week ago and gave us the order to return immediately to work on the costumes for the opera *Aida*, interrupted during the siege. He informed us that delivery must be made in two months. Consequently we have made arrangements to work very quickly. Monsieur Mariett has informed us of your intended arrival, which we look forward to a great deal. [. . .] Within a week I shall have to accept delivery on a portion of my orders and make some important purchases. The commercial situation, Excellency, being more strained (after the chaos which Paris has had to endure), transactions at this time of crisis are made only in cash. Therefore I am asking you, Excellency, to send me the sum of <u>20,000 to 25,000 francs</u>, as much as you are able, to cover the primary expenses. [. . .]

Verdi to Tito Ricordi

Genoa, 31 July 1871

[. . .] Before settling the contract for *Aida*,[1] I wanted to wait until everything was arranged at La Scala; but things could drag on, and it is better that we come to terms ourselves concerning the score, so that I can send it as soon as possible in order, at least, to make the copy for Cairo.

1. Between himself and the House of Ricordi.

Eugenio Tornaghi to Verdi

Milan, 1 August 1871

[. . .] As Giulio wrote you,[1] we are at your disposal concerning the *Aida* contract as well as copying the score and whatever you would like to ask of us.

Serving as a post office at this time, I am enclosing a letter from Tiberini and also forwarding Draneht Bey's request to kindly let him know your decision concerning la Grossi.[2] [. . .]

1. In a missing letter.
2. Draneht apparently asked Tornaghi to request from Verdi a written confirmation of his decision.

Paul Draneht to Auguste Mariette

Milan, 1 August 1871

My dear Mariette Bey,
    Since the last letter I sent you I find myself at a standstill with regard to our business with Verdi. This gentleman has written neither Ricordi nor myself about his decision on the interpretation of the role of Amneris. I don't think he will come to Paris to hand over the libretto to you; but if he does, please telegraph me. I would leave immediately to meet you.

Verdi to Paul Draneht [1]

Genoa, 2 August 1871

Excellency,
    Although a few passages in the role of Amneris may prove a little high for la Grossi, I confirm what Sig. Ricordi told you in person — namely, to entrust the role of Amneris to that artist, rather than taking a chance at this point with a new artist, since it would be quite difficult to find a talented one.
    As I wrote you before, the libretto is in Paris and at this hour in the hands of Mariette Bey.[2]
    Last year I took the liberty of giving two orders concerning *Aida*,[3] since there was no time to write and to receive a reply from Cairo.
    1. I ordered Sig. Ricordi to copy out all the vocal, choral, and orchestral parts for the *Aida* in Cairo.
    2. I ordered from Pelitti six straight trumpets of ancient Egyptian shape, which are not now in use and therefore had to be specially manufactured.
    If you think I should confirm these orders, I shall pay the total amount, and Y.E. can reimburse me when we settle the account for the score. If not, you can contact Ricordi and Pelitti directly and settle the account with them.

1. In answer to Draneht's request, as conveyed in Tornaghi's letter of 1 August 1871.
2. See Verdi's letter to Du Locle of 26 July 1871.
3. See Giulio Ricordi's letters to Verdi of 13 November 1870 and 4 December 1870. Verdi's reply to Giulio Ricordi of 5 December 1870 is missing. See also Tornaghi's letter to Verdi of 5 August 1871.

Verdi to Tito Ricordi

Genoa, 4 August 1871

Dear Tito,

I mailed only the first act of *Aida*. I hope I can send you the second tomorrow.[1]

The rough draft of the contract[2] is all right, except for one small observation, which you will find reasonable.

Where is Ghislanzoni? Tomorrow I shall send you a letter for him, asking him to write a few more lines in the third act. In the meantime let him know.

Be sure the copy for Cairo is precise and on good paper and made as fast as possible. [. . .]

1. Verdi refers to the orchestral score, which had to be copied for Cairo.
2. Between himself and the House of Ricordi.

Eugenio Tornaghi to Verdi

Milan, 5 August 1871

Illustrious Maestro,

I acknowledge receipt of the orchestral score of the first act of *Aida*, which I have put in a safe and shall hand over to Giulio when he arrives tonight. The copy for Cairo[1] will be made on the identical paper as the one for you; it will be precise and it will be completed as soon as possible. Draneht Bey has confirmed the request for all the vocal, choral, and orchestral parts, and he will take the trumpets which were made last year.

Enclosed herewith you will find a copy of the contract which you will kindly return to me, honored with your signature. I am sending a copy to our Signor Tito for his signature of acceptance, and I know that the conclusion of this business will help to comfort him in his depressed state of mind. Poor Signor Tito is always suffering and fears that he has to undergo yet another operation; that is really a terrible penalty!

Ghislanzoni's address is Lecco pel Porto. As soon as I receive your letter, I shall forward it to him; meanwhile I have advised him that it will be arriving.

It is understood that when *Aida* is given at La Scala, you will receive your share of the rental fees.

P.S. If you would not mind having your signature legalized by a notary, the contract would be more proper.

I am holding Ghislanzoni's transfer of rights to you for the libretto, and that is enough for me.

1. The score for Cairo (see note 3, Verdi's late September 1871 letter to G. Ricordi) was copied by hand from Verdi's autograph (four volumes), which is kept in the Ricordi Archives in Milan. Presumably the other handwritten copy served Verdi for the corrections he made for the

score, which was used for the premiere at La Scala in 1872 and in subsequent performances. The whereabouts of this other handwritten copy is unknown. Verdi may have destroyed it, as he did, according to Dr. Gabriella Carrara Verdi, all his musical sketches of *Aida*.

Paul Draneht to Verdi

[*Probably* Milan, 5 August 1871][1]

Illustrious Signor Maestro,

I acknowledge the receipt of your kind letter of the 2nd, and I am really happy to see the dispute over the artist who will perform the role of Amneris ended in accordance with my wishes. I thank you again for this favor.

I concur with your order to Signor Ricordi to copy all the vocal, choral, and orchestral parts for the *Aida* in Cairo; and I also concur with the order to Pelitti for six straight trumpets of ancient Egyptian shape. Just let me have the bill for both orders, and I shall immediately reimburse you.

I am keeping my funds in Paris to pay the remaining 100,000 francs for the music of *Aida*. Please tell me whether you wish to be paid there or in Milan.

Tomorrow I shall leave for Paris, where, if you should wish to write me, you can address your letters to 91 Boulevard Haussmann. I think I shall be back in about twenty days.

1. This dating is based on Draneht's letter to Barrot of the same day.

Paul Draneht to J. Barrot

Milan, 5 August 1871

[. . .] In view of what I wrote you in my last letter, I should still be upset because of my disagreement with Maestro Verdi. I am pleased to inform you, however, that we have reached a perfect understanding. He has agreed to give the role of Amneris to Mademoiselle Grossi, and, strangely enough, he mentioned that he prefers her to an unknown artist. Consequently I leave Milan tomorrow for Paris to proceed with the final execution of the costumes, sets, props, etc., for *Aida*. [. . .]

Verdi to Tito Ricordi

Genoa, 5 August 1871

Dear Tito,

The second act is also ready. But I want to give it another look, and I don't have the time because I must write to Ghislanzoni about some strophes to be written for the beginning of the third act. In fact, not knowing where he is right now, I am enclosing the letter so that you can forward it to him immediately. The address is missing; please fill it in yourself.

Tomorrow, without fail, I shall mail the second act, and you will receive it Monday morning during working hours.

Verdi to Antonio Ghislanzoni

Genoa, 5 August 1871

Dear Signor Ghislanzoni,

Don't let a letter of mine upset you! . . . It's a matter of a few lines.

I want to rewrite the music for the first chorus of the third act, which doesn't have enough character; and, while I'm at it, I would like to add a little piece for Aida alone, an idyll as you once said. The verses you wrote, however, were not quite suitable for an idyll. It's true that an idyll would not be appropriate for the character Aida at that moment in the opera; but, by digressing a little through <u>memories</u> of her native land, the little piece[1] could be made quiet and tranquil, and this would be a balm at that moment.

This is how I see this scene; if you agree with me, do me the favor of writing the two strophes I need.

ACT III

Scene 1

<u>Offstage chorus</u> and <u>Amneris Ramfis</u> scene as it is.
<u>Aida enters cautiously, covered with a veil.</u>

Qui Radames verrà . . . che vorrà dirmi?
Io tremo! . . . Ah! se tu vieni
a recarmi, o crudel, l'ultimo addio,
Del Nilo i cupi vortici
mi daran tomba e pace forse, e oblio!
*E il padre? . . . Qui prigioniero! . . . E dei fratelli che
avvenne? . . . Oh patria mia . . . mai più ti rivedrò!   Recitative

1st Strophe

Non rivedrò le nostre fresche foreste, i verdi
prati, ed il nostro ciel limpido ed azzurro; nè   4 lines
quelle montagne coronate di neve e splendenti di sole.
Oh patria mia! . . . mai più ti rivedrò.

2nd Strophe

Oh s'egli m'amasse tanto d'abbandonare questi
luoghi, e seguirmi sposo mio nella reggia de'
miei padri.   4 lines
Oh patria mia . . . mai più ti rivedrò.

These are ideas that are repeated later on, but I would not mind this repetition. Besides you can find something fresher and newer; I only wanted to explain myself concerning the form and the character of the piece.

I would like the two strophes to consist of four rhymed, eleven-syllable lines (I like the long line), but I would like them all to have the accent on the fourth syllable; without this they do not lend themselves well to the rhythmic *cantilena*. If you could retain (more or less) *Oh patria mia! . . . mai più ti rivedrò!* at the end of the recitative, it would serve me as the refrain at the end of each strophe . . .

I am waiting anxiously. Address me in Genoa, where I shall be for the entire week.

*I think it is all right that she should remember her father, etc. . . . If you think it is needless, jump directly to the thought of her country, *Oh patria mia!, etc. . . .*

1. See Document III and Verdi's letter to Ghislanzoni of 7 October 1870. In adding "the little piece for Aida alone" Verdi apparently had Teresa Stolz's vocal abilities in mind; but he did not write *O patria mia* to accommodate her. She visited St. Agata only in the fall of 1871, and there is no indication that the *romanza* was requested by her at any time.

Verdi to Tito Ricordi

Genoa, 6 August 1871

Dear Tito,

I have mailed the second act. As soon as Ghis. has sent me the requested change, I shall finish the third, which I hope to mail within a week.

I haven't had time to read the contract.[1] With regard to that, it must be explained that if for unforeseen reasons in Cairo the opera should not be given, the contract is nullified. [. . .]

1. Between himself and the House of Ricordi. See Tornaghi's letter to Verdi of 5 August 1871.

Verdi to Giulio Ricordi

[*Probably* Genoa, 6 August 1871]

Dear Giulio,

Have you returned?

You have also received the second act by now, and thus your copyists can enjoy themselves, especially in the second finale. I shall not send you the third act as quickly, because I want to rework the first piece and I also want to break up some recitatives that are declaimed at the end. I hope I can send it within a week. All right? Or do you want it before or after?

P.S. Put the address on the letter to Ghislanzoni.

Verdi to Antonio Ghislanzoni[1]

Genoa, 6 August 1871

Four more lines and then we'll be finished, absolutely finished.

At the end of the third act, after the duet, there is too much continuous declamation, and some ensemble should be mixed in; not a trio, certainly, but a few phrases by the <u>three</u> to break up the speeches without harming the movement and speed of the action. I shall transcribe the piece for you as it now stands.

After *sogno doloroso è questo*

AIDA: *Vieni . . . ti calma . . . ascoltami.*

RADAMES: *Io son disonorato.*
     Per te tradii la patria!

AMONASRO: *Era voler del fato!*
     Vieni: oltre il Nil ne attendono
     I prodi a noi devoti:
     Là del tuo core i voti coronerà l'amor.

A pair of lines for Aida and Amonasro are needed to do this little concerted passage. Thus:

AIDA: *Vieni . . . ti calma, ascoltami.*

[RADAMES:] *Che feci, ahi sventurato*

     . . . .

(Two lines)

     . . . .

AMONASRO: . . . .

(Two lines)

     . . . .

RADAMES: *Io son disonorato.*
     Per te tradii la patria!

AMONASRO: *No: tu non sei colpevole,*
     Era voler del fato!
     Vieni: oltre il Nil ne attendono
     I prodi a noi devoti:
     Là del tuo core i voti
     Coronerà l'amor.

So you see, there is not much to do. Instead of two there will be three quatrains. Please retain *No: tu non sei colpevole!*, which is very useful to me. It is one of your old lines.

1. Gossett, p. 297n, notes that this letter "has been found among Luzio's papers and was previously published, together with a facsimile of the autograph, in Giuseppe Stefani, *Verdi e Trieste* (Trieste, 1951), pp. 127–28."

Giulio Ricordi to Verdi

Milan, 7 August 1871

The first two acts are in the works and all goes well; no need to assure you that all the precautions have been taken. The chorus parts and the four string parts will be engraved.

I am also arranging for the piano-vocal score so that it may be accurate and, as far as possible, worthy of the importance of the opera.

What you write about the performance of *Aida* in Cairo is all right; I think it unnecessary, however, to mention it in the contract, since your requests in that matter are enough.

It is always better to make the contract in a certain legal form, since copyright laws are so confusing and managers such rascals that all the guarantees one can include will never suffice.

The copy of the score for Cairo will be made with the utmost accuracy; and as you suggested to me, we shall add to the score a dozen librettos in the form of a brochure.

As soon as you have some sketches of the costumes and sets, I beg you to send them to me, because I would like to use them for the title page of the editions.

I shall also send you the subdivision of the various pieces (necessary for the printing), so that you can see if I have guessed correctly and if the acts are not too disjointed. When the time comes I shall also mail you the reduction for the piano-vocal score for your approval.

Of course all of this will not be published before the proper time and according to the understanding we came to in Genoa.

I really think it unnecessary to tell you with what joy the arrival of this new masterwork was received! There really was a celebration, a relief, and also a feeling of pride and satisfaction for our House!

In addition to all this concern for the copying, we are always thinking of La Scala, of the formation of the company, etc., etc., so that everything will be done in a way to merit your approval.

Really, even though the days go by quickly, these months of anticipation seem eternal to me, and I long for the moment when rehearsals will begin and with them the beautiful and holy emotions of real art. [. . .]

Verdi to Giulio Ricordi

Genoa, 10 August 1871

[. . .] The copy of the score[1] must be sent to me as soon as possible because I myself must make the delivery. I think that the Bey,[2] who is now in Paris, will leave for Cairo at the end of this month.

I was hoping, and I am still hoping, that I can send you the third act tomorrow or the day after. But I don't know if I shall be on time because Ghislanzoni's *romanza* did not arrive until this morning.

I am very pleased that you have reached an agreement with Monplaisir about the ballet,[3] thank him on my behalf. I would be very happy if he were willing to choreograph the little dances in *Aida*. I know he is very knowledgeable about the Orient, and he will certainly do characteristic and original things. Have the sheets of the three dances copied, and ask Monplaisir to take care that the tempos be just as indicated by the metronome.

I shall be at St. Agata on Sunday morning. [. . .]

1. Verdi refers to the score for Cairo.
2. Draneht.
3. Verdi apparently refers here to the Egyptian ballet that was planned for La Scala and to which he had objected in his letter to Tito Ricordi of 25 July 1871. Presumably Giulio Ricordi sent assurance to Verdi, in a missing telegram or letter, that Monplaisir had decided against the proposed ballet.

Verdi to Giulio Ricordi

Friday [Genoa, 11 August 1871]

Dear Giulio,

I had hoped I could send you the third act, but it wasn't possible: the meter is missing and also a review to ♯ and ♭ .

I am leaving for Turin.[1] Tomorrow evening I shall be in Piacenza at 10:50. Sunday morning at St. Agata. From there I shall send you the third act.

1. As a Deputy of the Provinces of Parma, Verdi attended regular sessions of the Italian Parliament in that city.

Verdi to Cesare De Sanctis

Genoa, 11 August 1871

Dear Cesarino,

I have had, and I still have, so very, very much to do to put this new score in order that I have never found five minutes of time to respond to your last letter,[1] etc., etc. . . .

I am leaving for Turin in a few moments, and tomorrow evening [I shall be] at St. Agata. Even now I only have time to tell you that I have refused, for twenty years I think, to receive dedications² and that I cannot now waiver in this old resolution.

1. Missing.
2. De Sanctis had apparently asked Verdi to accept the dedication of a new work by an unknown author.

Verdi to Camille Du Locle

Turin, 12 August 1871

Dear Du Locle,

I am passing through Turin, and tomorrow morning I shall be at St. Agata from which I won't budge (at least I hope not) until November.

[. . .] I am sorry not to have seen you in Genoa, but [. . .] we shall be doubly compensated if you come to St. Agata with your wife. I need not tell you how great the pleasure will be that you will give to Peppina as well as to me.

The march is very, very, very long. It will last about eight minutes!!! But don't be terrified; there is a little dance mixed in with it, and that is why it turns out long.

Here is the description:
1. Fanfare on stage with the chorus of the populace; song for the women; song for the priests. Entrance of the King, who goes to sit on the throne, Amneris, Aida, entourage etc., etc.
2. Entrance of Egyptian troops with trumpeters at their head, for whom I have expressly ordered from Milan long, straight trumpets of ancient Egyptian shape.
3. Another procession of troops, also with trumpeters, but with somewhat shorter trumpets which have a different musical modulation.
4. Dance. Dancers who present the treasures of the vanquished, sacred vases, statues, etc., etc.
5. Reprise of fanfare with chorus and a coda, and Radames enters in triumph, etc., etc.

After a short recitative there are a few bars of a march for the entrance of the prisoners. This has nothing to do with the earlier long march.

Ah, bravo! You are translating *Aida*? The verses are not bad, and I think the libretto is theatrically very effective. The duet between Amonasro and Aida in the third act is very good as poetry. [. . .]

P.S. In addition to the dances in the march, there are also the sacred dance in the temple and a little ballet of little Ethiopian Moors at the beginning of the second act while Amneris conducts her toilette.

Verdi to Paul Draneht

Turin, 12 August 1871

Excellency,

Before long the copy of the score of *Aida* that I owe the Cairo Theatre will be ready, reviewed, and signed by me.

In your most esteemed last letter you offered to make the payment in Milan; if you could make that payment in gold, as the contract states, you would do me a special favor. Otherwise the loss would be too serious, and I would prefer to collect the sum in Paris, as was established. If, in any event, you can make the payment in Milan according to the terms indicated by me, I accept with gratitude; and I ask you to tell me to whom I shall have to deliver the score and to whom I must present myself to collect the sum.

The vocal, choral, and orchestral parts will be ready a little later; and I shall have Signor Ricordi send them directly to Cairo, if you have no objections, together with Pelitti's trumpets. [. . .]

Verdi to Giulio Ricordi

Turin, 12 August 1871[1]

Dear Giulio,

Well here I am on a short hop to Turin with my nice little bundle of music in hand. Too bad! If I had a piano and a metronome I would send you the third act tonight.

As I wrote you, I have substituted a chorus and a *romanza* for Aida for a chorus of four voices worked out in the style of Palestrina; this could have gotten me a "bravo" from the bigwigs, and with it (no matter what Faccio says) I could have hoped for a position as a contrapuntalist in any old academy. But I had some scruples about imposing Palestrina on the harmony of Egyptian music. . . . After all, it's my destiny! . . . I'll never be a scholar in music; I'll always be a hack.

The *romanza* for Aida is somewhat refined and delicate. Ah, if I could only get la Stolz in my claws for a few days! I've said it to Faccio; ask him about it. In addition to this *romanza*, there is still a *largo* in the duet with Radames and the entire last scene, both of which are of the utmost importance and of a delicate nature. [. . .]

I shall have mailed the third act by Monday.

1. The date of this letter in *I Copialettere*, p. 676, is 12 November 1871, and in Abbiati, III, 480–81, 12 September 1871. The autograph in the Ricordi Archives clearly reads 12 August 1871.

Verdi to Giulio Ricordi

St. Agata, 14 August 1871

Dear Giulio,

Here is the third act, as I advised you in my letter from Turin.

At the beginning you will find cellos divided with a harmonic note on *G*. Collar some cellist and see if the notes I have written correspond to those I actually want: [1]

Let me hear from you. I shall send you the fourth act in a matter of days.

1. One of the techniques frequently used by string players to produce a certain pitch by means of an artificial harmonic consists of placing one finger soliqly on the note two octaves below the desired pitch and of having another finger touch the string l'ghtly on the perfect fourth above the solid note.

Eugenio Tornaghi to Verdi

Milan, 16 August 1871

Illustrious Maestro,

Having arranged everything for the copying and the reductions of *Aida*, Giulio has made a trip to the country to meet his family. I have the honor to acknowledge receipt of the score of the third act, and I have called upon the Professor of Violoncello, Mazenco, concerning the explanation you need. To get the effect you desire, the stem must be put at the sign of the open string O, which is under the number 3, and this stem indicates the position of the thumb on the fingerboard. [1]

The pages of the three dances are being printed. I have spoken to Monplaisir, who will be very careful to take the tempos according to the metronome markings.

Faccio writes me that when he spoke to Signora Stolz about how useful it would be for her to meet you, she replied that she would be truly happy about it. Faccio will speak of this again to Signora Stolz as if it were his own idea, and he will keep me informed about what will have to be arranged. I shall inform you without delay. [2]

1. Tornaghi refers to the fact that this effect is often achieved by using the thumb (marked by the sign ☥) for the solid note and the third finger for the lightly touching finger (marked by a diamond-shaped note). For example:

Desired pitch   played

2. In an unpublished letter of 14 August 1871 concerning his contract with La Scala, Faccio informed Tornaghi that he had told Stolz that Maestro and Signora Verdi would be happy to receive her at St. Agata. (Autograph: Archivio Ricordi, Milano)

J. Barrot to Paul Draneht

Cairo, 18 August 1871

My dear Bey,

       I have hastened to submit to our August Master your letters of the last days of the preceding month and that of the 5th of August. H.H. was very happy to learn that you have ended all the little difficulties that had cropped up between you and M. Verdi concerning the roles of *Aida*; and he hopes that nothing will further impede the organization of that opera with regard to the *mise-en-scène*, in which he desires that nothing should be neglected, since he has delegated you as well as Mariette Bey, who should be with you in Paris at this moment.

Paul Draneht to Marie Sass

Paris, 22 August 1871

Dear Mademoiselle Sass,

       I just received your letter of yesterday.[1]

      I already knew that you did not care to appear in *Aida*, but that does not at all console me, since I, for one, cared very much. But let us not talk any more about an affair that has caused me a great deal of trouble. A certain Madame Pozzoni will take the role. [. . .]

    1. Missing.

Tito Ricordi to Verdi

Milan, 23 August 1871

[. . .] I still owe you the copy of the contract for *Aida*, which I have signed; you will find it enclosed herewith, and I shall then await yours. Let me assure you in the meantime that this contract of ours has filled me with joy and pride, since apart from what is good for art, I like the splendor of my House.

I have verified that the copies of the orchestral score and the reductions proceed marvelously and quite accurately. [. . .] Our head copyist asks whether in the orchestral parts he should keep the third act all in one piece or divide it, and if so, how. [. . .]

Verdi to Tito Ricordi

St. Agata, 26 August 1871

[. . .] I have finished the fourth act, but I won't send it to you today because I am about to finish the prelude. I shall send you everything tomorrow or the day after.

Tell your copyist that the entire third act, although it includes a choral scene, a solo scene for Aida, a scene with her father, another scene with her lover, and a little trio and a finale, forms but a single scene and therefore a single piece. In the orchestral parts copy everything consecutively as it is in the score; to facilitate performance at the rehearsals, we shall put in the rehearsal letters with A, B, C, etc. I think I myself can put these letters in later on, when you send for my review the score that must go to Cairo.

When Giulio is back in Milan we can correspond assiduously to arrange things for [the performance in] Milan, and we can earnestly see if we can put together something serious and artistic. A little good will on everyone's part and things will go forward. [. . .]

Verdi to Tito Ricordi

[*Probably* St. Agata, 27 August 1871]

I am mailing you the fourth act along with the prelude, which you will have placed at the beginning of the first act.

As soon as two acts of the score that must go to Cairo have been finished, send them to me so that I can review and sign them. The same with the others too.

As soon as Giulio returns to Milan, let me know so that we can decide on the rest for La Scala.

Verdi to Tito Ricordi

[*Probably* St. Agata, 28 August 1871]

Yesterday I mailed you the fourth act, which you should have received. Before you copy it please send me back the little notebook which contains the Chorus of the Priests in the subterranean chamber[1]

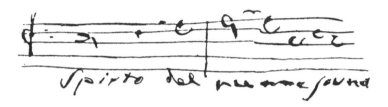

I repeat, send me the little notebook[2] containing this chorus immediately because I must correct a few things.

1. See G. Verdi, *Aida: Partitura d'Orchestra* (Milano: G. Ricordi, 1953), p. 393. (Note that the barline Verdi inserts between *del* and *Nume* is omitted in the orchestral score.)
2. Missing, presumably destroyed by Verdi.

Franco Faccio to Eugenio Tornaghi

Brescia, 28 August 1871

Dearest friend,

[. . .] I shall come to Milan and plunge into the *Aida* score with reverent, affectionate, and most diligent care.[1] Has the copy of the autograph already been made up? And is the reduction for piano and voice already in the making? And is our Giulio in Milan? [. . .] When the occasion presents itself, I won't fail to speak to Signora Stolz of the good a trip to St. Agata would do her health; I think she will undertake it. [. . .]

1. In preparation for the production of *Aida* at La Scala, which he would conduct.

Verdi to Paul Draneht

St. Agata, 29 August 1871

Excellency,

Passing through Turin, I had the honor of directing one of my letters[1] to Y.E., to which I have not had a reply; I think it wise to include a copy of that letter, asking you to favor me with a prompt acknowledgment.

1. Verdi refers to his letter of 12 August 1871.

Verdi to Camille Du Locle

St. Agata, 29 August 1871

My dear Du Locle,

I have time to write you only a few words, requesting you to send someone to Draneht Bey to ask him if he has received a letter of mine written to him from Turin on the 12th of August. Today I am rewriting that letter to him.[1] Perhaps the address is wrong — 91 Boulevard Haussmann — and it is for this reason that I beg you to ask him.

1. This copy is missing.

Paul Draneht to Verdi

Milan, 29 August 1871

Illustrious Maestro,

In Paris, I received your esteemed letter of the 12th to which I did not respond immediately because [illegible]. I have just arrived in Milan and beg you to forgive my delay.

As soon as I have received the music for *Aida*, I shall be ready — according to the terms of the contract — to pay the remaining 100,000 francs to the person you will indicate to me.

I would like to have the solo, chorus, and orchestral parts here in Milan instead of in Cairo as soon as possible because the various artists who are to perform *Aida* urge me to give them their parts so that they may have as much time as possible to study them. We are agreed on the interpreters of your opera, except the role of the baritone, for which you will kindly tell me your intentions — that is, whether you intend to choose the baritone Steller or the baritone Buccolini.[1] While on the subject of casting, I would appreciate having from the very beginning the music of the individual parts, together with the name of each artist to whom they have been assigned.

I would greatly appreciate your kindly writing a letter of recommendation to Signor Ghislanzoni. I would forward this to him, asking him to send me as many major details as possible for the most accurate *mise-en-scène* of *Aida*. I don't want to neglect a single thing, so that the music may scale all the heights which the name of its famous author well deserves.

In the contract you have reserved the right to send a maestro, of whom you approve, to oversee the *mise-en-scène*, the rehearsals, etc., of your opera; and I know that last year Maestro Muzio was to go. I would like to know what you intend to do this year.

Getting back to my desire to receive the parts in Milan (I mean the solo parts), I would like to inform you that Signor Ricordi has already agreed to let me have them as soon as possible, provided I send the chorus and orchestral parts to Cairo in the safest possible way.

1. Cesare Boccolini (1826–9?), Italian bass and baritone. As early as 1855 he was singing in Alexandria, and later he was heard in Vienna, Barcelona, Lisbon, Seville, Cairo, London, Malaga, and Cadiz.

Auguste Mariette to Paul Draneht

Paris, 30 August 1871

My dear Bey,

I am sending you the manuscript of the *Aida* libretto.[1]

You told me you are going to have it printed. Permit me to draw your attention to the fact that this is the business of the authors not of the superintendent. Furthermore it is inevitable that at the dress rehearsals some changes will be made, probably very important ones. Parts that are too long will be excised here, others will be added there. It is always done this way, and the libretto is never submitted for printing before this preparatory work. I urge you, then, to wait. Besides there will always be time to have it printed in Alexandria, where we now have a first-rate printer.[2]

I need to speak to you very seriously about the business of the moustaches and beards of your actors. In France, where great pains are taken with local color and where the *mise-en-scène* is the object of special attention throughout, the question would not even have to be discussed. Contained in each contract, in fact, is a clause that obliges the artists to cut their beards when it is required. But I am afraid it is not the same with your Italian artists, for I know from experience that in Italy they do not pride themselves on great accuracy in costuming. Nevertheless with regard to *Aida* I consider it absolutely necessary that there be neither beards nor moustaches. Of all the arts, Egyptian art is the one where it is easiest to slide into caricature. But since I am taking such extraordinary pains to create costumes that will be elegant as well as correct, according to the period, they must not fail because of a question of moustaches. But that is what will happen if you do not accede to my request. Can you see the King of Egypt with a turned-up moustache and a goatee? Go to the museum at Boulaq and, in your imagination put these appendages on one of our statues. You will see the effect that makes. All harmony disappears, and as handsome as the costume may be, it becomes ridiculous. I go so far as considering this a question of life or death for the opera *Aida*. Without beards, all the figures fit into the framework of Egyptian costume. With beards, the costume becomes literally impossible. For myself, I tell you this very seriously: I shall take no responsibility for the costumes, as far as the critics of *Aida* are concerned, if the actors play it with their beards. That would be as good as playing a role in Louis XIV costume without a wig and with a head of hair like a noncommissioned officer of the guard. Each epoch has its style, and it is not worth the effort to have such beautiful costumes made for *Aida* if we spoil them through the principal part [i.e., the actor's bearded face]. Then dress Radames as a Chinaman. Give me the favor of your opinion on this question to which I attach such great importance.[3]

Our work advances here and will be ready. I have had several costumes tried on, and I tell you that they have great character. Until now no one has seen anything to equal them on the stage, and the Viceroy will be pleased. Not only are the costumes elegant and rich, but they are accurate; men of taste will appreciate them a great deal. The sets are also well under way. The view of the pyramids is completed and crated. It is very lovely, and I am pleased with it. At the raising of the curtain one will truly believe oneself in Egypt.

Count on my zeal, my dear Bey, and be certain that I shall do everything possible so that you should not have a fiasco.

1. The Italian libretto that Du Locle was supposed to give to Mariette. See Verdi's letters to Du Locle of 26 July 1871 and to Draneht of 2 August 1871.

2. The printer Mourès, who printed Mariette's own outline. See Document I.

3. See Mariette's letter to Draneht of 15 July 1870.

Giulio Ricordi to Verdi

Milan, 31 August 1871

Illustrious Maestro,

I take pleasure in advising you that the copy of the first and second acts has been mailed to you today, together with the original of the Priests' Chorus in the fourth act.

I am praying that you will be satisfied with the copy for Cairo. I thought it wise to mail it unbound, since it is easier to read that way; we shall bind it afterward.

All the work is proceeding diligently and well.

Tomorrow I shall write you at greater length. [. . .]

P.S. You try to tell me that you are <u>ignorant</u>! But you certainly don't succeed, and I hope that the prelude will assure you of a professorship in counterpoint at some conservatory, even of second or third class.[1]

1. See Verdi's letter to Giulio Ricordi of 12 August 1871.

Verdi to Paul Draneht

St. Agata, 1 September 1871

Excellency,

The day before yesterday I sent another letter to you in Paris, fearing that my letter of 12 August was lost or that there was a mistake in the address.

A few days ago I sent the last act of *Aida* to Sig. Ricordi (the other three were sent much earlier); I hope it will not be long before the copy of the score, which I want to review and sign, and which I must deliver, is ready.

I shall write Sig. Ricordi today for the vocal parts, so that they will be ready as soon as possible. The parts should be distributed as follows:

Aida	Sig.ra Pozzoni
Amneris	Sig.ra Grossi
Radames	Sig. Mongini [1]
Amonasro	Sig. Steller
Ramfis	Sig. Medini
The King	N.N.,[2] low bass
Great Priestess	N.N., second soprano
Messenger	N.N., second tenor

I shall send someone to Milan, or I myself shall come, to place the score in your hands; and I would appreciate knowing how long you will be there.

The conductor of my choice, the one I would have liked to send to Cairo, would really have been Muzio, and if not him, Maestro Faccio. But I believe that now I shall not be able to count on either of them. That is quite grievous for me, since Y.E. can be quite certain that without direction (I would even say an intelligent, sure, and, I would almost say, devout interpretation), success is impossible, no matter what the music may be like. Furthermore, I do say that when an unknown opera is involved, it is indispensable that the author's intentions be known (let the conductor be as talented as he may). You can take my word for it, which is based on my long experience and, to some extent, my habits regarding this sort of thing. Since all this can in no way hinder the course of affairs, I ask you for more time to reflect on this particular matter.

1. Pietro Mongini (1830–74), Italian tenor. Following his debut in Genoa during the 1852–53 carnival season he quickly became established in Italy, Paris, and St. Petersburg. Between 1858 and 1867 he remained the leading tenor at Her Majesty's Theatre in London, where he sang in such operas as *Guillaume Tell*, *Robert le Diable*, *Norma*, *Lucrezia Borgia*, *Der Freischütz*, *Ernani*, *Il Trovatore*, and *Rigoletto*. He frequently appeared at La Scala and in 1868 sang the title role in *Don Carlos* there.

2. A common European abbreviation for the Latin *non nominatus* or *non nominata* (not named) when a person has not yet been appointed or prefers to remain anonymous.

Verdi to Tito Ricordi

St. Agata, 1 September 1871

Dear Tito,

Draneht Bey is in Milan and asks me for the *Aida* score. Please make a copy of it quickly then. When the first two acts are ready, send them to me so that I may look them over and <u>sign</u> them. The Bey would also like to have the vocal parts as soon as possible. As far as I am concerned, there is no problem once I have delivered the score.

P.S. And what are we going to do about Milan?

Verdi to Opprandino Arrivabene [1]

St. Agata, 2 September 1871

[. . .] Until this very moment I have been quite busy with the opera. I have revised it, cleaned it up, corrected it, perhaps ruined it; and this very day I am sending the last section to Ricordi. . . . <u>Amen</u>, therefore, and *à la grâce de Dieu!* . . .

You say some very wise things about the arts in your last letter, and I think you are right about everything, or almost everything. Only in music one must not be exclusively a <u>melodist</u>. In music there is something more than melody, something more than harmony. There is the music! This will seem like a riddle to you! Let me explain: Beethoven was not a melodist; Palestrina was not a melodist! Don't get me wrong: a melodist in the sense that we understand it.

But I don't want to talk about these things today because (as the Neapolitans say) my head is out of tune. I'm tired.

1. Writer and politician, one of Verdi's oldest and closest friends.

Verdi to Giulio Ricordi

St. Agata, 2 September 1871

Dear Giulio,

I have received the copy of the first and second acts. Very beautiful! Bravo, bravo! I shall review and correct it, should there be need of any correction.

I am returning the piece from the fourth act. The passage of the priests was not to be written in measures. This way the execution will be simple, <u>beating in quarters.</u>[1]

Now that you are in Milan, fire up the engine and let's decide.[2] First of all, the seating arrangement of the orchestra: we shall get more sonority and a better performance. Since it has been decided to do this next year, why not do it this year? That way I can also enjoy it. Talk to the Mayor about it,[3] and make an urgent request for it. It certainly won't mean thousands of lire for city hall. I must come to Milan to settle many things with Draneht Bey and to deliver the score to him; if you want, I could take care of the orchestra at the same time.

Let me know how la Stolz did in Brescia. I heard nothing more about the matter we discussed with Faccio. There are two pieces, the first of the third act and the final duet, which she will never be able to perform well if she does not first study them for a long time with me.[4] What a shame! The final duet is of supreme importance!! [. . .]

1. See Verdi's letter to Tito Ricordi of 28 August 1871, note 1.
2. Verdi refers to the production of *Aida* at La Scala.
3. Traditionally the mayor of an Italian city assumes control of the local opera house.
4. Verdi clearly wanted Stolz to come to St. Agata. See Tornaghi's letter to Verdi of 16 August 1871, Faccio's letter to Tornaghi of 28 August 1871, Giulio Ricordi's letter to Verdi of 2 September 1871, Faccio's letter to Giulio Ricordi of 4 September 1871, Verdi's letter to Giulio Ricordi of 5 September 1871, and Verdi's letter to Faccio of 10 September 1871.

Giulio Ricordi to Verdi

Milan, 2 September 1871

I hope you have received in good shape the music we sent you. The string parts of the orchestra are almost entirely engraved, and we have made a rather accurate part for the piano to facilitate rehearsals.

I am overwhelmed at reading the marvelous, the extremely marvelous things you have created in *Aida*. The trio in the first act and Aida's *romanza* in the second excite me; the duet of the two women exalts me, the love duet between Aida and Radames moves me — well, everything, but everything, brings me one surprise and one pleasure after the other.

Hurray for this magnificent *Aida*! [. . .]

Now you will be the Moltke[1] of La Scala, and I . . . I shall be your <u>drummer boy</u>!

I have checked the reductions. Tomorrow I shall send you one part that has been reduced in two different ways so that you may decide which one seems to be better.

The head copyist asks if in the Prelude the <u>mutes</u> are never to be removed, not even in the *forte* sections.

I think that Faccio has written you about arrangements with la Stolz;[2] and while on the subject of la Stolz, rumors say there is trouble between her and Mariani!!! [. . .]

[P.S.] *Lupus in fabula*: A letter from the management informs me that city hall has asked them to declare which new *opera d'obbligo*[3] it plans to present! [. . .]

1. Count Helmuth von Moltke (1800–91), victorious Prussian field marshal.
2. This letter is missing.
3. The obligatory new opera to be presented each season.

Giulio Ricordi to Verdi

Milan, 3 September 1871

Our letters have crossed. Here is where we stand concerning the copy of *Aida* to be sent to Cairo:

Tuesday 5, I shall send you the third act.

Saturday 9, " " " " the fourth act (provided, of course, I receive the Priests' Chorus in time).

For the 15th, the complete score, the choral, orchestral, and vocal parts, etc., etc., will be ready.

Is it all right to include twelve librettos in the form of brochures?

This morning I was invited by the Commission of the Theatre to its session tomorrow; they want to know at what point the negotiations are between the House of Ricordi and the management with regard to *Aida*.

I shall only be able to say they are in a kind of stalemate at this time.

I shall write you about this immediately to get your instructions on how to act with the management. [. . .]

Giulio Ricordi to Verdi

Milan, 4 September 1871

To return safe and sound from a session of an Honorable Commission of the Theatre is not such an easy thing! Yet here I am, neither dead nor wounded.

As I predicted, I was asked to say something about *Aida*: whether you were happy with the engagements that have been made, etc. I stuck to generalities, without committing myself yes or no. I announced your desire for the re-arrangement of the orchestra, saying that you would probably come to Milan and could then give some explanations, etc., in the matter. This news was received with enthusiasm, and I share in this enthusiasm and celebrate the occasion of your coming here. We wait for your arrival to settle the new plan for the placement of the music stands. I reached an agreement with Melzi and Monplaisir concerning the alterations to be made in the latter's ballet, so that any costumes that might resemble those for *Aida* could be left out. Monplaisir will also do the dances for *Aida*, and I am very glad about it, since he is very knowledgeable in this antique Egyptian style, which, in fact, is the only one he can do well. Your coming here would be very good in this respect. Since Monplaisir must begin his rehearsals soon, you can talk with him and explain your ideas to him, and make him hear the precise tempos as well. This way there will be no deviation, and even if Monplaisir should leave after the performance of his ballet, our dances for *Aida* will be ready and in order, so there will be no obstacles of any kind.

When can we get the sketches for the costumes and the sets?

Tomorrow, as I wrote you, I shall send the third act. I have received the Priests' Chorus which I put in the works right away.

The management has given me the following list of the orchestra. These musicians, as well as the chorus, were arranged precisely according to your list. [. . .]

> Orchestra musicians already engaged at La Scala
> for the Carnival-Lenten Season 1871–72

> 15 first violins
> 1 amateur first violin
> 14 second violins
> 10 violas
> 10 cellos
> 11 double basses
> 4 flutes, including 1 for the ballet
> 3 oboes,   "   "   "   "   "
> 3 clarinets   "   "   "   "   "
> 3 bassoons   "   "   "   "   "
> 5 horns
> 3 trumpets, including the 1st for the ballet
> 2 cornets
> 3 trombones
> 2 harps
> 1 bombardon
> 1 bass drum
> 1 cymbals
> 1 triangle
> 1 timpani
> 1 snare drum

Verdi to Giulio Ricordi

Monday [St. Agata, 4 September 1871]

Dear Giulio,

Tell me if in the *stretta* of the Introduction the chorus responds with the same words as the King:

Su! del Nilo al sacro lido
Accorrete, egizi eroi:
Da ogni cor prorompa il grido:
Guerra e morte allo stranier!

If you could send me a copy of the libretto, it would be a blessing.

[P.S.] I have just received your letter of the 3rd.

The copy of *Aida* is fine. Write up the contract with the management, then, omitting all the conditions indicated in my various letters regarding the performance.

[I need] all the guarantees for the rehearsals.

Don't forget for city hall:

1. Seating arrangement for the orchestra
2. Timpani
3. Bass drum
4. Pitch for the band

Franco Faccio to Giulio Ricordi

Brescia, 4 September 1871

Dearest Giulio,

To explain better my dispatch[1] of yesterday, I am informing you that I have written the Maestro[2] that la Stolz will leave tonight for Florence [. . .] and that from there, toward the end of the month, she will betake herself to St. Agata. [. . .]

1. Missing.
2. Missing.

Verdi to Giulio Ricordi[1]

Tuesday [St. Agata, 5 September 1871]

Dear Giulio,

Here is the title page for *Aida*. I am writing to la Stolz.[2] If she should come here right away, you would have to send me the part of Aida at once and, if possible, also a copy of the libretto that I too can use.

Du Locle will send the costume sketches soon.

The note about the orchestra is all right, as long as the musicians are good. It is understood that the clarinet will also play the <u>bass clarinet</u>, and the oboe the <u>English horn</u>. [. . .]

1. In answer to Giulio Ricordi's letter of 4 September 1871.
2. Missing.

Paul Draneht to Verdi

Milan, 5 September 1871

Illustrious Signor Maestro,

I received your kind letter of the 1st and your other letter, which was forwarded to me from Paris. I am sorry that my delay has caused you the trouble of sending the letter a second time, copying what you had already written me. I beg you to excuse me.

I thank you for the letter of recommendation to Signor Ghislanzoni,[1] as I also thank you for your cast list of the various artists who will perform *Aida*.

I shall be in Milan until the 22nd of this month, and I would be very glad if I could once again meet you and take your hand.

I completely agree with, and therefore completely subscribe to, what you declare concerning the musical direction of a score. It is certainly of primary importance that the conductor should know the author's intentions.

1. This letter, which Draneht requested in his letter to Verdi of 29 August 1871, is missing.

Paul Draneht to Antonio Ghislanzoni

Milan, 5 September 1871

Esteemed Signor Ghislanzoni,

I am honored to enclose a letter from the renowned Maestro Verdi, in which he recommends me to you so that you may be kind enough to send me all the necessary indications — in the greatest possible detail — for the *mise-en-scène* of *Aida*, which (as you know) will be performed during the forthcoming season in Cairo. In Paris I have seen some sketches with figures indicating the various scenic arrangements, the grouping of the characters on the stage, the door through which they must enter, the manner in which they will group themselves, etc., etc. But I would like to have all these things indicated by you as best you can.

If you will do me the favor I ask, I would consider it a token of the greatest kindness and would be infinitely grateful to you.

Paul Draneht to Auguste Mariette

Milan, 6 September 1871

My dear Mariette Bey,

A short absence from Milan has kept me from replying earlier to your letter of August 30th. I shall no longer be involved with the copying of the libretto. I leave it to you to make the alterations you want at your own convenience. As long as they [*illegible*] agree with the music and the *mise-en-scène*, we shall use them. But I must warn you that Ricordi is already printing Ghislanzoni's text. I have told him about the alterations you plan to make; and if you had given them to me, they would no doubt have been adopted. But this does not prevent us from making the alterations you consider necessary.

With regard to the *mise-en-scène*, I am pleased to tell you that I hope to get a first-rate man to help us mount *Aida* in the most splendid fashion. He is a poet himself and has written librettos for several operas,[1] one of which is presently being given at La Scala in Milan. I see, to my regret, that you torment yourself too much over beards, goatees, and moustaches of the artists. You know well that we have the right to make them shave. [. . .]

Here is the final distribution of the roles, which I ask you not to publish:

Aida	Mme. Pozzoni
Amneris	" Grossi
Radames	M. Mongini
Amonasro	" Steller
Ramphis	" Medini
The King	" Costa
Termouthis	second soprano
A Herald[2]	second tenor

I still don't have the music, but they are working hard in the Ricordi shop to hand it over to us.

I plan to finish my business here in order to leave for Egypt on the 26th of this month.

I have written to all the artists, asking them to give Mme. Baron their measurements.

1. Draneht obviously refers here to Carlo D'Ormeville, Italian dramatist and stage director. See Draneht's letter to Mariette of 18 September 1871.

2. See Verdi's letter to Draneht of 1 September 1871 and also Documents II, III, and IX, in which the Priestess still appears as Termouthis and the Messenger as a Herald.

Giulio Ricordi to Verdi [1]

Milan, 6 September 1871

Illustrious Maestro,

I had a conference with the Mayor today. He told me that the council had suspended action on the project to rearrange the orchestra because it was too extensive. With no funds to realize the project, it has been postponed for another year. So I thought I should explain to him that what was questioned for the time being was a better arrangement of the music stands; I did not think that a change in the position of the gas pipes could bring about considerable expense. Furthermore I told him that you would personally make the necessary recommendations. The Mayor told me, then, that he would put himself completely at Maestro Verdi's disposal. He asked me to alert him five or six days before your arrival, so that he could be in Milan — but not on Saturday and Sunday, days on which he is always away. He wants to go with you to the theatre, so that the two of you might agree on all the necessary steps to be taken.

Well this business is also under control. You write, then you come, then you win!

I think the proposal we submitted contained great modifications, which I would call "à la Wagner" and which you have already mentioned to me. Actually these operations must be very expensive, and this year the council has absolutely no funds available.

What concerns us now, however, is that the orchestra be well arranged; the rest will follow for some other important occasion, for example, like the performance of . . . Nerone! . . . Ah! Ah! Ah! . . . what a fool!

Would you, then, illustrious Maestro, please tell me the day on which you will arrive so that I can advise the Mayor in time.

Enclosed herewith is the draft of the contract with the management.[2] I have tried to anticipate all the possible and conceivable situations. But since four eyes are better than two, I thought also of sending it to you, in case I have omitted some important point. I think little is missing, except for the paragraph: "The management will furnish itself with the necessary rope and soap to hang itself on a lamppost each time the Ricordi publishers suggest it."

You see that I have left open the amount of the rent, since I don't know whether this should actually figure as rent or as compensation for your stage direction of the opera. As I have already written, you would do me a great favor by writing me something on this matter, and I shall then be able to make the contract the management is anxious to have. Of course this will always be a private matter between the composer and the publisher. At any rate, a definite sum is necessary.

[. . .] I send you a proof of the libretto. Don't let the errors bother you; it's the first.

Please look at the first piece of the third act, in which there is no indication when the mutes must be taken off. [. . .]

1. See Verdi's letter to Giulio Ricordi of 10 July 1871.
2. Missing.

Verdi to Giulio Ricordi

St. Agata, 7 September 1871

Dear Giulio,

I shall be in Milan the evening of the 18th or the morning of the 19th in order to return here on the 20th or 21st. I am most happy that the Mayor has decided on this small reform in the orchestra which will produce advantages in execution and effect. Pay him my respects and thank him for me.

The libretto is all right, but that margin you leave seems a bit too large. I also would have preferred, as Ghislanzoni wanted, that there be no verses with the first letter outside [the margin] to indicate either the strophe or the meter. The pages 29, 35, 36, and others, etc., etc., are most pleasing to the eye. Well do what you think in this matter.

Another observation, *sotto voce*: on page 40 there is the verse

Morir! si pura e bella

. . . .

. . . .

. . . . . .

Troppo t'amai,
Troppo sei bella . . .

Of course our prima donnas will be very beautiful; but what if, later on, there happened to be one who wasn't? The audience might joke about it, and that would displease me because that moment is too important.

Maybe Ghislanzoni could change the verse? It's easy to change it, but I would not like to lose a certain cadence we have.

On page 41 I would indicate in very bold characters, distinguished from the others: SONGS AND DANCES OF THE PRIESTESSES IN THE TEMPLE.

At the beginning of the third act when Aida enters, delete the four lines

Astri del cielo azzurro,
copritevi d'un vel, m'avvolgi, o notte;

nel lugubre tuo manto
cela a tutti il mio duol, cela il mio pianto.
They prolong the recitative and say nothing.

I have read the contract and actually all the management has to do is buy a few yards of rope to . . .[1] So be as indulgent as possible, never losing sight of the certainty of a good performance.

I want nothing to do with the management, but the House of Ricordi can promise that I shall assist with the rehearsals of *Aida*.

I want nothing for my cooperation on the *mise-en-scène*, since the sum that the management will pay must be considered the first rental fee for the opera.

The stage band should equal that of the other time,[2] but it must be chosen; plus six or eight straight trumpets.

Some time ago I indicated that the following should suffice for the chorus of La Scala, as long as they are well chosen:

12 first sopranos
12 second sopranos
12 contraltos
12 first tenors
12 second tenors
12 first basses
12 second basses . . .

But in special cases like this opera, which requires eight additional basses for the Chorus of the Priests, certain parts must be reinforced.

1. See Giulio Ricordi's letter to Verdi of 6 September 1871, and, for example, Document XIII.
2. Verdi supposedly refers to the *Don Carlos* production at La Scala in 1868.

Verdi to Franco Faccio

St. Agata, 10 September 1871

I thank you for what you have done as a favor to me and to *Aida*.[1] I am correcting the copy for Cairo; and they are working industriously on the rest in Milan. Once this fury has passed, I certainly hope to see you here. If I don't have twenty letters to write today, I have at least nineteen and a half. Therefore excuse the brevity of this one and thanks again!

1. Verdi refers to Faccio's intervention with Stolz. See Verdi's letter to Giulio Ricordi of 2 September 1871, note 4.

Verdi to Camille Du Locle

St. Agata, 10 September 1871

Dear Du Locle,

I am very busy correcting the copy of the score for *Aida* that I must give to Cairo. I shall deliver the score to Draneht Bey in Milan, and it would be a good idea for you to send me the contract, which is still in your hands,[1] and for Mariette Bey to authorize me, in a letter, to settle the account with Draneht.[2] Do this as soon as you can. . . .

Also please concern yourself with getting the *Aida* costume sketches for me. The designer[3] of course will receive whatever compensation you yourself will set. Let me know if I can count on you for this and if so, when they might be finished. I would be so glad to have the same costume sketches for Milan as in Cairo! [. . .]

1. Since the autograph of the original contract (Document V), like most of Verdi's letters to Du Locle, is kept at the Bibliothèque de l'Opéra in Paris, it is doubtful that Du Locle ever returned the contract to Verdi.
2. Such a letter of authorization does not seem to exist.
3. Apparently Verdi did not assume Mariette to be the actual designer. See Verdi's letters to Giulio Ricordi of 31 October 1871, 28 November 1871, and 28 February 1872, and to Du Locle of 21 November 1871 and of 7 January 1872.

Verdi to Paul Draneht

St. Agata, 10 September 1871

E.[1]

On the 19th or 20th of this month, I shall come myself or send someone to deliver the score of *Aida* into your hands.

Please be so kind as to let me know if you will be in Milan on those days.

1. Excellency.

Giulio Ricordi to Verdi[1]

[*Probably* Milan,] 12 September 1871

Illustrious Maestro,

Blessed, then, be the 18th or 19th of this month — I am anxiously waiting for you!

All the corrections of the libretto are fine. I shall see Ghislanzoni, and we shall arrange for the change you suggested. Concerning the format and the arrangement of the text, etc., etc., you need not worry about the copy I sent you, since that is a first printing, and, as such, is pressed on the first piece of paper that happens to be handy, without regard for the margin or the distribution of the pages. All these things will be indicated on the proofs, and the same goes for the beginning of the verses.

I shall advise the Mayor of your arrival at once. Praying, meanwhile, that time may pass quickly until that wonderful moment, I send you and Signora Peppina the most cordial greetings.

P.S. I hope also to see Signora Peppina. It is difficult to find hotel rooms. Please write immediately whether I should reserve some room in the usual Hotel Milano or somewhere else. It would be even better to telegraph.

1. In answer to Verdi's letter of 7 September 1871.

Verdi to Giulio Ricordi

Saturday 16 [St. Agata, 16 September 1871]

Dear Giulio,

I shall arrive in Milan on Tuesday evening at 8:35. [. . .]

You should have received the copies of all three acts. I had hoped to receive the fourth act today! Meanwhile carefully correct the first three acts.

Paul Draneht to J. Barrot

Milan, 16 September 1871

My dear Bey,

Maestro Verdi has written to advise me that he will arrive in Milan on the 19th or 20th to deliver the music for the opera *Aida* to me. Consequently I hope that I shall be able to leave for Alexandria by the English boat from Brindisi on the 26th. [. . .]

Paul Draneht to Auguste Mariette

Milan, 18 September 1871

My dear Mariette Bey,

Today I expect the Maestro, who has promised to hand over the music to me. I hope to leave for Egypt on the first boat from Brindisi on the 26th of this month.

I have asked Monsieur Ghislanzoni to give me a description in writing of the *mise-en-scène* for *Aida*. I shall forward it to Monsieur d'Ormeville, our stage director, who, guided by your advice, will not fail to mount this work to perfection. [. . .]

Verdi's music, which I now know well, is a true masterpiece; the success, then, will be complete.

Verdi to Paul Draneht

[Milan,] 20 September [1871]

E.

The score for Cairo will be ready this evening. Please let me know when and where I can deliver it to you.

Verdi to Paul Draneht

Wednesday evening [Milan, 20 September 1871]

E.

Since you expect to meet me at the Ricordi office, I shall be there tomorrow, Thursday, precisely at 12:00.

Verdi to Paul Draneht

Milan, 21 September 1871

Received from H.E. Draneht Bey the sum of 100,000 lire in gold as total payment owed me for the opera *Aida*, written expressly for Cairo according to the contract drawn up with Mariette Bey in Paris, 29 July 1870.

Antonio Ghislanzoni to Giulio Ricordi

Thursday 21 [September 1871]

[. . .] See if you can persuade Maestro Verdi to leave Radames's lines *Morir! sì pura e bella, etc.* as they are.[1] Apart from the fact that in the theatre all women are beautiful, or at least are made beautiful by musical idealism, I feel that any substitution of words whatever in this place would diminish the effect of the supremely beautiful phrase the Maestro has found. Even if we had a monster from Lapland onstage, the public would go into ecstasies. [. . .]

1. See Verdi's letter to Giulio Ricordi of 7 September 1871 and Giulio Ricordi's letter to Verdi of 12 September 1871.

Verdi to Camille Du Locle

Milan, 23 September 1871

Dear Du Locle,

I have been in Milan for two days to discuss and plan for *Aida*. They are putting great pressure on me for the costume sketches. Tell me, my dear

Du Locle, approximately when can we have them? I am returning to St. Agata this very day. Hurry the designer along, then, and write me as soon as possible at St. Agata. I have settled my accounts with Draneht Bey, and I have delivered the copy of the score which I owed.

Verdi to Giulio Ricordi

St. Agata, [late September] 1871

Dear Giulio,

More mistakes to correct!![1] We'll never finish it.

La Stolz is here.[2] Don't mention it to anyone so that the papers won't gossip.

I am working; you work too, and see that everything be done as indicated.

P.S. Make corrections in the score for Cairo.[3]

1. The corrections, which Verdi presumably enclosed on a separate sheet, are missing.
2. Stolz supposedly arrived at St. Agata on 23 September 1871. See Walker, p. 376.
3. If Stolz actually arrived at St. Agata on 23 September 1871, and if we have dated this letter correctly in accordance with her arrival, then Verdi wrote these lines after he had delivered the score for Cairo to Draneht on 21 September 1871. Draneht had written to Mariette on 18 September 1871 that he planned to leave Brindisi for Egypt on 26 September 1871; and in a letter to his attorney (about the purchase of his villa at Oggebbio) on 20 September 1871, he states his intention to leave Milan for Brindisi on 24 September 1871. It seems unlikely that Draneht left Milan without the score of *Aida* that he had fought so hard to obtain. The only way Ricordi could "make corrections in the score for Cairo" then, was by sending them separately to Cairo, where they could be added to the handwritten copy. The title page of this copy is reproduced in *Genesi dell' Aida*. On this page Verdi wrote: "September 1871. Copy of the original [orchestral score] of *Aida* reviewed by the author G. Verdi." Unfortunately it is doubtful whether this score was photographed in its entirety before it was destroyed by fire in 1971. (See Martin Chusid, *A Catalog of Verdi's Operas* [Hackensack, N.J.: Joseph Bonin, Inc., 1974], p. 10, n. 1.)

Auguste Mariette to Paul Draneht

Paris, 28 September [1871]

My dear Bey,

I hasten to acknowledge receipt of your letter of the 18th. I hope when you receive this, you will have arrived in Egypt in good health.

[. . .] Everything is going well here, and we are proceeding toward a happy solution. I am still not able to tell you anything about the costumes; the work on them has not progressed much. But I shall vouch for the sets, which will be truly splendid, without speaking of their accuracy in imitating the temples of Upper Egypt. These gentlemen[1] have done their work with pride, and they have truly outdone themselves. I believe, in short, that we shall have accomplished a beautiful task, which will bring great honor to your administration.

Next week we shall consign the first cases of scenery to Messrs. Chailan.[2] But a great deal will remain to be done in Egypt, assembling the flats, etc., etc. The sets are very complicated, and the task of putting everything together will be troublesome. However, these gentlemen here have given me all the necessary plans and annotations.

Our jewels are also progressing well, but somewhat slower. Some of them will be very beautiful. I am designing everything myself and am trying as much as possible to make sacrifices to taste and art without losing anything of the antique flavor. You may judge for yourself whether I have been successful.

I plan to embark by boat from Marseilles on 7 October. But the decorators will probably detain me until the next boat leaves.[3] [. . .]

I have seen M. Steller. We have in him a splendid Amonasro, the kind of which I have been dreaming. So let us make him a costume in accordance with his physique.

None of the ladies has sent her measurements to Mme. Baron. [. . .]

1. Messrs. Rubé and Chaperon, who designed Acts I and IV, and Messrs. Despléchin and Lavastre, who designed Acts II and III.
2. Chailan Frères, freight agents in Paris and Marseilles.
3. In a letter to Draneht of 19 October 1871, Chailan Frères noted that Mariette would be departing in a few days. (See *Genesi dell'Aida*, p. 89.)

Verdi to Giulio Ricordi

[*Possibly* St. Agata, September 1871]

Dear Giulio,

In the orchestral score, have the following adjustment made in the *adagio* of the duet for the two women in the second act:[1]

The same also in Aida's solo D flat 3/4 last finale, bars 11 and 12 and 19, as you will see from the attached page.[2] *Addio*.

Take care of the Cairo score.

1. See *Partitura d'Orchestra* (hereafter referred to as *Partitura*), p. 135.
2. Missing.

Verdi to Giulio Ricordi

[*Possibly* St. Agata, September 1871]

Dear Giulio,

In Aida's *romanza* in the third act at the 6/8, place a flat in the key signature [F major]. In the fifth bar of this 6/8 section place an A for the clarinet:[1]

In the repeat of the second couplet of this same *romanza*, in the fourth bar, add to the bassoon[2]

In the duet between Aida and Amonasro, at Aida's words *che mi consigli tu?*, put in a ♮ for the double basses:[3]

In this same duet, at the following 6/8 in the fifteenth bar, add

second violins

and

violas:[4]

In this same tempo, bars 30 and 31, put in ♮ for the second violins

and as follows for the double basses:[5]

   etc.

In bar 46 insert double flats for the trombones:[6]

In the final scene of this act, when Amneris comes from the temple, at the words *Traditor! La mia rival*, put in a flat for the B of the bassoons, trombones, and trumpets.

In the last finale after Aida's passage in G flat: [7]

At the end of this same piece: [8]

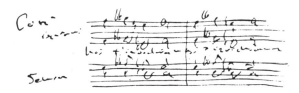

1. See *Partitura*, p. 274.
2. See *Partitura*, p. 276.
3. See *Partitura*, p. 291. (In his handwritten example, Verdi neglects to include a natural sign for the first G to be played by the double basses.)
4. See *Partitura*, p. 295.
5. See *Partitura*, p. 297.
6. See *Partitura*, p. 299.
7. See *Partitura*, p. 436.
8. See *Partitura*, p. 442. (Verdi's notation differs from the *Partitura* in his use of the soprano clef for the high parts and the tenor clef for the middle parts.)

Giulio Ricordi to Verdi

Milan, 4 October 1871

By this hour Bottesini will have visited you; and so this thing has also worked out.

Now there's the other thing at La Scala. Yesterday the managers came here to sign the contract which, tough as it is, was accepted in principle. But they requested one exception, and asked that it be presented to you, which is what I am doing, since I find it sufficiently well-founded.

One of the paragraphs in the contract states that *Aida* can only be performed after the first performance in Cairo. That is fine for December or January; but if *Aida* were to be delayed in Cairo, so that La Scala could not give more than three or four performances, the management would be totally ruined! In another event *Aida* might not be given at all! And that would mean irreparable disaster.

The management has complete faith in you; and they say that if you want them to sign the contract as it is, they will do it, trusting your word for the rest. They also earnestly request permission to put *Aida* on the poster — without suggesting your presence, of course, if you should not want it to be mentioned.

After the promise given to our Mayor, I think there will be no problem with this; and I hope you will authorize me to give the management this permission, which is the same as a stroke of good fortune for them.

While we are on the subject of the Mayor, [let me tell you that] I was called to the theatre today to look at the new seating arrangement of the orchestra. I think it's excellent. Of course the music stands are temporary; everyone begs you to make a short trip to Milan to lend your approval or to suggest alterations that might be warranted. You would have to come here no later than Saturday night or Sunday morning (the 8th), because the city engineer is leaving on Monday morning, and it is urgent to begin the work at once. I know that this is more than a trifling disturbance for you, but it would be very good, even excellent, I dare say indispensable, if you could make this sacrifice. Since you have already made thirty, you might as well make thirty-one. Right now one can make changes, turn things around, and improve; once the floor and the gas pipes have been put in, it will be impossible to touch any of it.

So I am awaiting your arrangements in this respect.

I had news from Clausetti[1] about la Waldmann who really pleased the Neapolitans; her voice was sufficient for that theatre. I was told the same thing by Tornaghi, who heard her in *Favorita*, also at the San Carlo.

P.S. If things should get desperate, would Corticelli not be a good Amneris? *Faust* in Bologna was rather poor.

1. Pietro Clausetti, music publisher, piano dealer, and representative of the House of Ricordi in Naples.

Verdi to Giulio Ricordi

[*Probably* St. Agata, 5 or 6 October 1871][1]

Dear Giulio,

In the *stretta* of the *Introduzione* when Aida says[2]

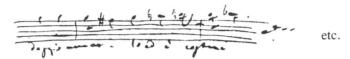   etc.

correct the clarinets

In the same *stretta* when Amneris says[3]

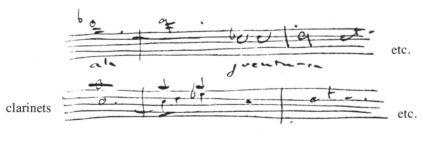

In Aida's following scene when she says[4]

   etc.

clarinets   etc.

After the first chorus of the second act, add the violas to the *Ballabile*[5]

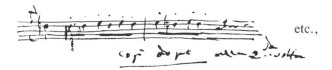

etc.,

so later [?] at the 2nd time.

In the duet between Aida and Amneris at the beginning of the second act:[6]

correct violins
and
violas

Later on in the same duet[7]

correct violins
and
violas

Later on[8] Am.

etc.

correct clarinets  etc.

In the *stretta* of this duet[9]

In the Second Finale toward the end of the March, correct the tenors[10]

At the beginning of the Largo of this Finale in Amonasro's solo[11]

 etc.

in bar 46, put the ♮ to the E of the bassoon and trombones[12]

 etc.

I shall be in Milan Sunday at 2:15 p.m. We shall deposit our traveling bag with the bell captain of the hotel and go straight to the theatre. If we aren't able to do everything before six, we can return at any time from eight until midnight. I must leave on Monday morning at nine. . . . So, in order not to lose time, make sure that everything is ready at the theatre, etc., etc.

1. The dating of this letter is based on the information in the final paragraph. See Giulio Ricordi's letter to Verdi of 4 October 1871 and Verdi's letter to Giulio Ricordi of 10 October 1871.

2. See *Partitura*, pp. 50–51.

3. See *Partitura*, pp. 61–62.

4. See *Partitura*, p. 67.

5. See *Partitura*, p. 112.

6. See *Partitura*, p. 122.

7. See *Partitura*, p. 128.

8. See *Partitura*, p. ·131.

9. As the question mark (added by Giulio Ricordi or his copyist) seems to indicate, there is no trace of this phrase in the published orchestra score.

10. See *Partitura*, p. 196.

11. See *Partitura*, p. 214.

12. See *Partitura*, p. 222.

Auguste Mariette to Paul Draneht

Friday [*Possibly* 6 October 1871][1]

My dear Bey,

The dénouement of *Aida* and this great devil of the subterranean chamber imagined by Verdi prevent me from sleeping. It is 3 o'clock in the morning, and I have not closed my eyes. The matter is worth examining; otherwise we expose ourselves to the disapproval of people of taste, if there are such in Egypt.

Here, indeed, is the difficulty.

The height of the floor on which the female dancers are going to dance and the choristers sing is such that, from the parterre, the audience will see only the top of the characters' bodies. The singers who remain a little in the background will not be seen at all. If the Viceroy were always in his great box, he would find nothing to object to; but when he goes to his lower box, he will certainly find that arrangement quite ridiculous, since he will not see anything at all. It is as if you were at street level, watching people play a scene on the second floor of a house. Evidently to accommodate himself, the spectator would ask them to come down.

Now if I write you, it is because I have a remedy to propose.

This remedy consists of lowering the whole platform considerably, of putting it back a little toward the rear of the stage, and of scattering in front some large painted blocks to resemble the caved-in section of a subterranean chamber. When the curtain rises, M. Mongini could be at the rear and in darkness. From there he will advance toward the audience, extending his arms before him, bending over, raising himself, as if he were walking laboriously through one of those oppressing subterranean chambers, of which the temples of Upper Egypt offer some examples. When he arrives at the point where he no longer has the platform above his head, he will resume his natural posture in order to make a definite entrance onto the stage in the midst of the rocks. As for Aida, she could, from the raising of the curtain, be in a faint on one of these rocks. Hearing Radames, she would raise herself and move about among the rocks to join him.

That is my proposal. I am acquainted with the sets, and I assure you that the thing is as easy as can be. At least in this manner the subterranean chamber would no longer overwhelm us by its mass, and the temple on the ground level above would no longer seem to be perched in the clouds.

So, quite simply, cut off the lower part of the drops on which the subterranean chamber is painted — that will not disrupt any of the lines, since the subterranean chamber is formed by dark arches placed among the mass of rocks. Saw off the lower part of the supports on the platform already built, and push the platform toward the rear of the stage, where plenty of space remains. That is what I request of you.

The more removed the facade of the subterranean chamber is from the footlights, the better the audience's chance to understand at first glance the slightly unusual arrangement of a subterranean chamber and a temple, ideally superimposed.

With that, my dear Bey, I shall try to calm my agitation and sleep a bit. [P.S.] Transmit this letter to M. D'Ormeville and try to bring him around to our opinion. It is impossible that *Aida* end badly; we must bring all chances for a success to our side.

1. As is true of a few other letters published in *Genesi dell' Aida*, the date Friday [2 September 1871] assigned to this letter by Saleh Abdoun is in error, because 2 September 1871 was a Saturday and Draneht had not mentioned Mongini and D'Ormeville to Mariette until his letters of 6 September and 18 September 1871. Presumably while the scenery for the subterranean chamber was being completed in Paris, Mariette realized the problems it might present in Cairo. Since time would not permit changes in Paris, Mariette had the scenery shipped as it was, suggesting that changes be made in Cairo. However, there is no complete date, and it is possible that Mariette expressed his concern in writing as late as in December 1871 during the final rehearsals in Cairo.

Antonio Ghislanzoni to Giulio Ricordi

Lecco, 6 October 1871

[. . .] Tomorrow I shall send you the corrected galley proofs of the *Aida* libretto, which I want to see again. I think it has not been printed as it should have been. Since illustrious [people and things] are involved, they must be honored, beginning with the libretto.

Verdi to Giulio Ricordi

Tuesday [St. Agata, 10 October 1871]

Dear Giulio,

Here I am at St. Agata again; but who knows! Perhaps tomorrow I shall be on the train to Milan. I see that I am destined to travel that route who knows how many times before *Aida* goes on stage. Never mind, as long as things go well.

You will certainly have written to Capponi. Without awaiting his answer, write him a second letter at once and tell him that, in view of my affairs, I can no longer be in Genoa in early November, but only around the 15th. If he could come to Genoa after the 15th, that would be good because la Waldmann can also be in Genoa toward the end of the same month. If Capponi would like to come here, however, he is always welcome; but as I told you in person, we would all be <u>uncomfortable,</u> particularly now that Peppina is not feeling well.

To sum it up, arrange these matters with all the politeness and diplomacy of which you are capable.

Don't neglect the rest — the straight trumpets or the big flute, etc. I want to see all these things personally [*illegible*] on my next trip to Milan.

I shall write the Mayor tomorrow.

Verdi to Léon Escudier

St. Agata, 11 October 1871

Dear Léon,

I am very happy to have news of you[1] and your country, which little by little is regaining its splendor and its old strength. [. . .]

Now for *Aida*. It is more than a year since Ricordi made his first proposal to acquire this opera. Because of the situation in France, however, I did not want to conclude anything, precisely because I thought you would have spoken to me about it, once your war was finished. Having heard nothing from you, I had to believe that, owing to the state of your theatres, it could not have been in your best interests to acquire a score that might perhaps not bring you any profit. All this time having passed, then, about a month ago I reached an agreement with Ricordi, to whom I have ceded all rights to *Aida*. I am very sorry about this; but as you will understand perfectly, I could not do otherwise. If you think I can be of any use to you in this business, all you have to do is say the word, and I shall go right to work and do everything possible for you.

1. Presumably in a letter from Escudier that is missing.

Paul Draneht to Auguste Mariette

Cairo, 12 October 1871

My dear Mariette Bey,

Deprived for some time of your good news, I write to tell you that I have happily arrived in Cairo after a most pleasant sea crossing.[1]

All is proceeding well here, and I hope to open the theatre on the coming first of November, with all the success that our excellent company promises. After the first performances, I shall concern myself at once with our great work *Aida*. I have already distributed the roles to all the artists who will take part in it, so that they may review them in Europe. And, as early as the 10th of November, I shall call for rehearsals; we must be able to bring them to an end no later than the 10th to the 15th of December. Therefore, all the various jobs that are executed in Paris must be delivered exactly according to the terms we have fixed. Please, I pray you, inform me on this point and see to it that the scene painters' models reach me as quickly as possible.

1. Draneht had apparently not yet received Mariette's letter of 28 September 1871.

Giulio Ricordi to Verdi [1]

Milan, 13 October 1871

I wrote immediately to Capponi, trying to make him understand that it would be better to go to Genoa than to Busseto; but from the enclosed letter[2] it seems that Capponi persists in going to Busseto. Anyway look at his letter, and write telling me how I should conduct myself — that is, whether I should simply tell him to come to Genoa around the 15th or should suggest something else.

I am awaiting your letter for the Mayor and hope to receive it tomorrow.

I have seen the flute; it makes a low and decent sound but not a very loud one. Let me know if it is needed for just a few notes or whether it must be a regular flute with holes and keys. The manufacturer says he will figure out how to make as few keys as possible, because the more perforated the instrument is, the more force it will lose. Tell me at once what you need, since the holes can be made right away while the instrument is being drafted. Then it will be ready for your arrival. [. . .]

1. In answer to Verdi's letter of 10 October 1871.
2. Missing.

Verdi to the Mayor of Milan

St. Agata, 13 October 1871

Most illustrious Mayor,

A few days ago I went to Milan to see if the orchestra was doing well in the new seating arrangement that was planned for it. Unfortunately I, together with the members of the commission and the technical director of the theatre, found a very serious defect. The double basses form a kind of barrier, which in certain places prevents the spectator from clearly seeing the performance. This is because of the construction of the old orchestra stalls; but it is deplorable, and I shall be particularly distressed if we are forced to move the double basses back to their old place. If this happens, my plan to make the orchestra more compact, in order to have fuller sonority and to avoid weak and uneven performances, would fail. We would have taken so many pains only to achieve an inconclusive result.

There is a possible solution. In examining the orchestra stalls, I, together with the others, noticed that the floor is in such bad repair that very shortly the patches will not be sufficient and the entire floor will have to be redone. Since this will soon be unavoidable, and since this expenditure is inevitable, could the work not be started immediately, esteemed Mayor, lowering the floor from zero at the entrance to approximately 50 cm. at the footlights?

The orchestra, naturally, would be lowered; and the problem of the double basses solved, it would be arranged as I have indicated. The stage would be more open to view, and with this standard slope, common to all theatres, the spectator would better enjoy the performance. [. . .]

Verdi to Giulio Ricordi

St. Agata, 13 October 1871

Dear Giulio,

Here is the letter to be delivered to the Mayor; accompany it with your eloquence. I did not write him, but you can tell him in person that I am always willing to ride the iron horse whenever there is need.

And don't lose any time with the six trumpets, the flute, the timpani, the bass drum, etc. Mind you, I want to see everything with my own eyes; and I want to see and hear it long before the *Aida* rehearsals begin. I shall come, if you invite me, to the second orchestra rehearsal of *La Forza del Destino*, and at that time I shall hear the orchestra, the chorus, the bass drum and timpani, and I also want to see and hear the trumpets and the new flute.

Mind you well, I shall not accept the usual "We'll do it, it will be done", etc. No. I now loudly declare that I shall not begin rehearsals for *Aida*, if the above-mentioned items are not ready.

So while there is time, don't lose time.

La Stolz left yesterday. She will do well, even in the most delicate things. [. . .]

Tomorrow I shall send more corrections.

P.S. I am awaiting news from Capponi. It's a shame that la Waldmann could not study [her role] as much as I would have liked.

Verdi to Giulio Ricordi

St. Agata, 14 October 1871

Dear Giulio,

To tell you *inter nos*, Capponi's visit here is most inconvenient to me at this moment. [. . .]

I have a mountain of things to do, taking care of my little affairs and giving instructions for the time of my absence. And the house is somewhat disordered. So you see all the problems!

If, instead, Capponi came to Genoa around the 15th of November, I would be quietly and calmly settled there. In addition, la Stolz will come to Genoa at that time before going to Milan. By then Capponi should have a good command of his role, and I could ask la Stolz to go over the many pieces they have together. Even more, if la Waldmann came to Genoa toward the end of the month, the trios, finales, etc., could be gone over with her. You see how wonderful that would be!

If Capponi insists on coming here now, as you say, let him come; but this must not jeopardize the Genoa combination which pleases me very, very much. He can even come right away, if he wants; I shall let him hear the role and hand it over to him; after he has studied it, we shall refine it in Genoa. [. . .]

It is not important that the flute produce a loud sound, as long as it is full. It is particularly needed for the motive of the dance[1]

that is repeated in G flat in the final scene.

Ordinary flutes would not give me the effect I want, unless they were doubled to ten or twelve.

1. See *Partitura*, p. 77.

Delphine Baron to Paul Draneht

Paris, 14 October 1871

Excellency,

I wrote these lines to you at the end of my letter of 15 September:[1] "I am desolate, Excellency, the artists have not sent me their bust sizes or shoe sizes; neither have the starring dancers bestirred themselves." It is now the 13th of October; nearly a month has trickled by, and I am in the same situation, save for a few rare exceptions. [. . .]

We have been able to expend a more considerable sum for the women's costumes. Here is how: Not knowing how the show goes, and judging by the number of costumes that Monsieur Mariet [*sic*] requested for the choristers, there are 64 costumes, as you will notice in the contract. I had counted on furnishing you with 64 pairs of shoes, 64 pairs of trousers, 64 pairs of flesh-colored tights. Since you have only 36 choristers, and since they have a change of costume in the same act, they would not have time to change both tights and shoes. I shall provide you, then, with only 36 pairs of shoes, 36 trousers, and 36 tights, plus 6 red trousers and also 6 red tights for the choristers who have time to change. You will understand, Excellency, that the price of these diverse accessories, together with the sum of 1,530 francs furnished for the squadron of from 5 to 9 soldiers (so insignificant according to the drawings that Monsieur Mariet has decided to eliminate them) will at last allow us to make these poor women's costumes which have heretofore been so overlooked. [. . .] Please, Excellency, tell me by return mail to whom I should deliver and who shall receive the costumes, so that I may be able to account for everything. [. . .]

1. See *Genesi dell'Aida*, pp. 80–81.

Giulio Ricordi to Verdi

Milan, 15 October 1871

I just returned from delivering your letter to the Mayor,[1] who will present the proposal without delay at tomorrow's session and will give it his full support. So your letter has had its effect, as desired, and I hope the council will not deny the necessary funds. [. . .]

Meanwhile the Mayor called at once for the city engineer, who has been studying the project and has raised some very important questions which need to be solved. He fears that nothing at all would be gained by lowering the orchestra stalls, particularly for people in the last row, for whom the height of the double basses would remain the same. For example:

Consequently vision would be impaired for those in the first four or five rows; the advantage comes only in the last rows. In fact, if those in the first rows had been able to see almost the complete figure onstage, they would now, being lowered, see less.

This drawback could be prevented by dividing the difference by one-half — that is, by lowering the orchestra stalls 25 cm. and the orchestra 25 cm.:

And here we must face the great question of sonority. The engineer does not think it would change, but he desires the artist's opinion. He further proposes a placement of the double basses that would be less distracting — that is, against the footlights:

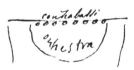

If, in fact, we put the double basses perpendicular to the stage, the line of vision is brought much closer to the spectator, who sees less:

The line of vision would run along line A-B, not along C-B.

But if the double basses are arranged against the footlights, then the line of vision becomes C-B. Here, then, a new and important question arises. You will understand from all of this how necessary your presence is in Milan so that all these things may be decided. If a reform must be made, it is better that it be done well, very well. On Tuesday the council will go to the theatre. I will wire you the result at once; and, if need be, I shall ask you to come to Milan, since there is very little time left if important work must be done.

Don't worry about the orchestra and chorus. The contract with the management is made for both *La Forza del Destino* and *Aida*; so <u>what goes for one, goes for the other.</u> I can't tell you, however, what <u>enormous</u> pleasure it gives me to find you disposed to hear an orchestra rehearsal of *La Forza*. If there should be deficiencies or faults, they can be remedied in time; but I don't know how a remedy could be found after rehearsals for *Aida* have begun in early January. I mailed you the letter from Capponi[2] and await your answer. Of course if you must come to Milan, Capponi's visit will be delayed. If that happens, I shall send you a telegram on Tuesday. Meanwhile I send you a hundred greetings.

How is Signora Peppina?

1. Verdi's letter to the Mayor of Milan of 13 October 1871.
2. Missing, probably thrown away like other messages of no lasting importance.

Verdi to Giulio Ricordi

[*Probably* St. Agata, 15 October 1871]

Dear Giulio,

In the last finale, put back as before:[1]

ran - ti....... volano al

Thus also in the solo of the tenor and when they sing together.

In this same piece, put the ♮ to

at all times.[2]

By now you will have received the letter to the Mayor.

If Pandolfini has arrived, ask Faccio to show him the role. It may be that he will not like it, since it is short and has no arias . . . but I don't know what to say. It cannot be otherwise and must remain as it is. If Pandolfini is intelligent, however, and likes to interpret a character, Amonasro is a character — perhaps the finest, even though the shortest. Anyway I don't want to be bothered. I prefer to have a mediocre artist of good will rather than bad moods at rehearsals. These bad moods always cause bad performances. They paralyze everything. So let's speak clearly from the outset, and if he is not content, go ahead and find someone else for me. [. . .]

P.S. Concerning the flute, you tell me that it has a low, fairly good sound but not a very loud one. What do you mean by very loud? I need an instrument which has notes that are fuller and louder than those of the ordinary flute. Just tell me if the passage of the dance[3]

comes out fuller and louder with the new or the ordinary flute.

1. Since the autograph could not be reproduced clearly, the corresponding musical quotation was photographed from the *Partitura*, p. 435. See also *Partitura*, pp. 441 and 442. (Verdi's original notation differs from the *Partitura* in his use of the soprano clef.)

2. Photograph from *Partitura*, p. 431. (Verdi himself writes again in the soprano clef and *possente* instead of *immenso*.)

3. Photograph from *Partitura*, p. 77.

Paul Draneht to Giovanni Bottesini

Cairo, 17 October 1871

Esteemed Sir,

In reply to your letter dated the 15th,[1] I must advise you that I have not had the slightest intention of diminishing your fame or of wounding your self-respect by contracting a worthy young maestro to conduct occasional performances. This is the custom of the great theatres, and this was incontestably my prerogative. The routine of the theatre is such that this supplementary direction cannot but at times be of prime importance. To provide for the smooth functioning of the performances, I therefore signed the Maestro Signor Angelo Zocchi[2] to a contract as well, without thinking to diminish in the least the importance of your position.

Concerning the order of announcements on the playbill then, I beg you to observe that it was not made with regard to any distinction of rank. You will see Sig.a Sass and Sig.a Allievi[3] on the same line, Sig. De Filippis[4] and Sig. Mongini in the same order, and so forth. If I had made a distinction between you and Sig. Zocchi on the playbill, I would undoubtedly have committed an error.

I am certain that you will consider the reasons I have expounded, and that you will assure yourself that I have not, as you believe, exceeded the limit of my rights, or much less given offense to your reputation as an artist.

1. Missing.
2. Italian conductor.
3. Marietta Allievi had been engaged for the role of the offstage Priestess in Act I, scene ii. Although she had sung in Genoa (1859) and in Parma (1862), and was later to sing at the Teatro Fenice in Venice, no other record of her life and career is available.
4. Unknown *comprimario* not engaged for *Aida*.

Verdi to Camille Du Locle

Milan, 20 October 1871

Dear Du Locle,

I am in Milan again to prepare everything that is necessary for the performance, but one of the most important things is still missing: <u>the costume sketches</u>! For Heaven's sake, my dear Du Locle, do something about these blasted sketches. Time is pressing, since we would like to open about the middle of January. Every day the directors, the impresario, and Ricordi are on my back about this, and I don't know what to tell them. . . . I entreat you, therefore, I entreat you, and I entreat you urgently. At least give me a decisive reply, but it would be a great shame if I could not have those sketches from Paris. Once more, therefore, I entreat you.

Giulio Ricordi to Verdi

Milan, 24 October 1871

[. . .] I am pleased to tell you that the flute in B flat is completely successful. The sound has a more virile timbre than the flute in C, and it is even and pleasant. As a result of this success, we shall now try a flute in A flat. Within three or four days the instruments will be ready, and I shall send them to you right away. [. . .]

Verdi to Giulio Ricordi

[St. Agata, 26 October 1871]

Dear Giulio,

Well were they able to make that damned flute in A as I had asked before? *Non possumus* is not only the motto of the priests but of all poltroons and imbeciles! Make no mistake! When, in such cases, someone says "it can't be done," you can be sure he is an ass. . . . We shall see then how the flute in A flat turns out; the one in B flat, at any rate, should certainly be useful.

I am glad you have found a good cello; do the same for the violas. Be careful with the chorus, be careful with everything. Tell the management not to be too stingy; and warn them that if all is not well with the company, I shall remain in Genoa. A word to the wise is sufficient. [. . .]

Giulio Ricordi to Verdi

Milan, 28 October 1871

I agree with everything you write in your kind letter of the 26th. It will be done as you wish and as it must be. I don't think Pandolfini will cause any problem. On the contrary, once he has seen the role, he will do it with great pleasure. I have already arranged for him to get the part, but Pandolfini will not be in Milan until early November.

The flute in A flat has also come out magnificently. Today, by railway, I am sending you the two flutes in B flat and A flat. Get a player for the flute in C, and you will be able to make the proper comparisons.

Let me warn you that the holes of the flute in A flat are naturally further apart than those on regular flutes. The player, therefore, will have a little difficulty with the positioning of the fingers. But this can be remedied quite simply with some keys, which the manufacturer will make, so that one can play the instrument with the utmost ease.

The manufacturer, thinking, I guess, that you are living in some big city, urges you not to let others of his trade see these flutes — a superfluous request for you at St. Agata. As soon as you have heard them and decided accordingly, however, it is quite urgent that you return them to me immediately so that the ones required for La Scala can be made in time. [. . .]
P.S. The opera is almost entirely engraved; [1] I shall send you the proofs in a few days.

1. That is, the piano-vocal score of *Aida*. According to the House of Ricordi, the first orchestra score of *Aida* for rent was printed in 1894, and the smaller edition of that score was first sold in 1913. Martin Chusid refers also to an earlier printed rental score (ca. 1890) by G. Ricordi (See Chusid, p. 11.)

Verdi to Giulio Ricordi

St. Agata, 31 October 1871

Dear Giulio,

I have received four costume sketches, which I am sending you; I shall also send you the others as they come in. Although Du Locle writes me that "with all his scholarly research Mariette has done rather little,[1] forcing us to do the job ourselves," I think they are very beautiful. What do you think about them?

I have received and tried out the flute, but the player was so embarrassed and tremulous that I learned very little. It seemed to me, however, that the sound of the middle and low notes is better than in ordinary flutes, and that one hears a sound of lamentation, which does not displease me at all. . . . It is certainly almost impossible to cover the third hole, because of the distance, and a key will be needed. I have noticed that some notes are going sharp in the A flat flute; for example, the D

(B flat)

sharpens by almost half a tone. But this is the manufacturer's business.
Let's conclude:
1. The flute in A flat has much more volume and force in the low and middle notes than ordinary flutes.
2. If it is not difficult to make, and if any player can play it, I would say

that three flutes should be built to be used in the Sacred Dance and the last finale.

You may tell the manufacturer that no one at St. Agata will steal his business and that he will have his patent for the invention. Still, that belongs to me . . . but I leave all the glory to him . . . and other glories too, as long as he makes good instruments for me.

Don't forget the trumpets, which I want to see and hear myself.

Don't forget the violas and cellos. Don't forget the Chorus of the Priests.

Still a P.S. Try out the sound of the flute in A flat very carefully, since if it were not really more sonorous than the others, it would not be worth-while. . . .[2]

1. Twenty-four elaborate watercolors of the costumes Mariette designed for the premiere of *Aida* in Cairo are at the Bibliothèque de l'Opéra in Paris. Photographs of these designs are on exhibit at the Istituto di Studi Verdiani in Parma which published them in *Genesi dell'Aida*. Several Italian descriptions of fabrics, etc., by an unknown hand on Mariette's designs suggest that they served for one or several of the early productions in Italy. See letter from Giulio Ricordi to Verdi of 7 November 1870 and Verdi's letter to Du Locle of 10 September 1871, note 3.

2. See Philip Bate, *The Flute: A Study of Its History, Development and Construction* (New York: W. W. Norton, 1969), p. 177: "Of the larger flutes, that in G is probably the most employed in modern orchestral music, but it is interesting to note that in 1871 Verdi originally intended the Sacred Dance finale to Act I of *Aida* to be played on three flutes in A. Instruments were actually made in Milan for the first performance but they did not prove effective and were abandoned."

Paul Draneht to Giovanni Battista Lampugnani

Cairo, 3 November 1871

[. . .] I found M. Ghislanzoni's demands for his work on *Aida* quite excessive.[1] Offer him 200 francs, which, as far as I am concerned, is quite sufficient.

1. See Draneht's letter to Ghislanzoni of 5 September 1871.

Delphine Baron to Paul Draneht

Paris, 4 November 1871

Excellency,

I received your dispatch[1] the day before yesterday. As for the women's costumes, be reassured that three days after I posted my last letter I received the measurements of Mmes. Pozzoni and Grossi. The costumes will reach you complete, except for those of the leading dancers, for whom we have received no measurements. [. . .]

Excellency, now that everything is almost finished, thank God, I can tell you all the difficulties we have encountered in making the costumes for *Aida* — costumes which had to be created under the eyes of M. Mariette and some of which had to be started several times after long experiments. [. . .] All of this, Excellency, has conspired to make the job even more difficult than it was; and with the reduction you insisted on, I truly don't know where I shall end up. Nevertheless, I hope with all the sacrifices I have made in order that everything should be successful, you will be satisfied and, when the occasion presents itself, you will again consider me by giving me an easier order.

1. Draneht's telegram in response to Mme. Baron's letter of 14 October 1871. Draneht refers to this dispatch in his letter of 6 November 1871.

Paul Draneht to Delphine Baron

Cairo, 6 November 1871

[. . .] I confirm for you my telegram of 31 October, which read as follows: "Too late to send lacking measurements for *Aida* roles. Send materials. We shall make costumes here. Consign completed costumes and materials to Chailan at once."

[. . .] I would be grateful if you could send your brother or, should that not be possible, Mlle. Amalie, your first assistant, to Cairo; I would prefer your brother, together with your detailed instructions. I shall pay the costs of his round-trip voyage to Cairo from Paris, second class, and during his entire stay in Egypt, 30 francs per day. His stay in Cairo could amount to fifteen or twenty days.

I had to ask you not to make the costumes for those roles for which the measurements were lacking. Time did not allow me to send you these measurements, and as we are obliged to advance the time of the first performance of *Aida*, I believe the wisest thing to do is to make some costumes here. So send me the materials, along with all the instructions.

Verdi to Camille Du Locle

St. Agata, 7 November 1871

Dear Du Locle,

I had received a first batch of four Egyptians [1] and just now I received a second of six more, for which I thank you sincerely.

The behavior of these good Beys is strange, very strange, and Mariette's surprises me very much!! [2] Since they are dealing with a theatre like La Scala, it seems to me that they would be interested in having everything done well and with a certain uniformity — if not in the musical performance, at least in the *mise-en-scène*. If they do not want that, never mind! We shall do without it. Meanwhile if you can continue to send me the rest of the costume sketches, you will do me a real favor; and tell the designer to continue his work. . . .

As far as I am concerned, *Aida* will be given at La Scala at the end of January, whether or not it is first performed in Cairo. [. . .]

1. Costume sketches.
2. Apparently the Beys were slow to cooperate with the management of La Scala while they were preoccupied with a production of their own in Cairo.

Verdi to Giulio Ricordi

St. Agata, Tuesday [7 November 1871]

Dear Giulio,

Today I sent three more costume sketches (in other words, six) for *Aida*. You have not written to tell me if you received the first four and if you liked them. Let me hear your opinion.

I am here to put things in order on my farm, and it is raining in torrents. [. . .]

Giulio Ricordi to Verdi

Confidential   Milan, 8 November 1871

Illustrious Maestro,

Don't be surprised by my silence, which is caused by a very deep sorrow: For ten days my brother Enrico has been seriously ill with a complicated heart disease involving the aorta and aggravated by arthritic pains. I cannot possibly describe the sufferings of the poor young man. In addition to all the medications, we try to soothe his indescribable torments. My father, who has been under treatment in Turin all the while, knows nothing of this, because in his present state it would hurt him too much and upset him excessively. I am morally and physically exhausted, having also spent some nights at my brother's side. Last evening there was a consultation; for the time being we must not give up hope for his recovery, because the strength of his age will conquer the infirmity. But it is terrible that his health will only be fleeting, for a damaged heart cannot be cured! And so our poor Enrico will be susceptible to those terrible neuralgic attacks which,. should they reoccur, could cause deadly consequences.

You will understand in what state of mind we all find ourselves — distressed on the one hand and worried on the other about my father, whose treatment (thank Heavens) gives us hope, even though it causes him pain. Imagine that father might ask one of us to keep him company, and none of us would dare be away from Milan; imagine the excuses that would follow and the whole mess — oh, what a life!

Why are we in this world, if we must attend to such atrocious scenes. . . .
Excuse this eruption, Maestro.

I like the costume sketches for *Aida* very much; I hope to receive more soon, since they are anxiously awaited by the management.

I shall write to Trieste tomorrow to ask la Waldmann when she can leave.

With Faccio and the timpanist we have had some rehearsals in the theatre, and new timpani have been ordered; I hope you will be pleased.

You will receive the last proof of the libretto. If there is nothing else to be done, I shall print it in order to gain time; please give me your approval. [. . .]

Verdi to Giulio Ricordi

St. Agata, 10 November 1871

Dear Giulio,

I can't tell you how much your letter saddens me! I understand all your sorrows, and I feel them myself as much as an old friend can feel them! Why are we in this world? Tell me! Oh, how many answers there would be . . . but they would result in maledictions and curses! So let's draw a curtain over it; and you, my dear Giulio, take courage. Say a word to your mother on my behalf; the poor woman must be in despair. [. . .]

I am sending you another shipment of Egyptians! Oh, what beautiful costume sketches! The ballerinas are very beautiful, and so is the High Priest! The ballerinas will find the skirts long, but be firm! Amonasro's soldier[1] also has a great deal of character! In other words, to me they look very beautiful. What do you think of them?

As I told you, I shall be in Genoa the evening of the 15th. Write this to Capponi and tell me when he will be there.

P.S. There is nothing to be said about the printing of the libretto. . . . But what if we should find something to change in rehearsals, above all with regard to the staging?

Do as you think, however.

1. In reference, presumably, to a single design for all of Amonasro's soldiers.

Giulio Ricordi to Verdi

Milan, 12 November 1871

Thank you a hundred and a thousand times for your kind and good letter, which has done a great deal for me.

I have already written Capponi and settled with Pandolfini; here is an extract from the latter's reply:

"Glancing through the libretto I have seen that if my role is not big, it is still really beautiful; I have the greatest hopes for the eminently dramatic situation in the duet with the daughter. At any rate, even if the role had been a hundred times smaller, I would have been equally content."

And so be it! Faccio will begin to rehearse with Pandolfini tomorrow.

The costume sketches are very beautiful, even extremely beautiful. I hope they will continue to arrive without interruption. [. . .]

And the overture?

Faccio and I play *Aida* all the time and are more enchanted with it every day. It's an opera that has a mark entirely of its own — a most extraordinary one. It's truly fascinating — really worthy of a Verdi! [. . .]

Verdi to Giulio Ricordi

St. Agata, Monday [13 November 1871]

[. . .] I shall do the overture,[1] if you are sensible — that is to say, if you see to it that everything is done according to my wishes. I shall come to Milan for the second or third orchestra rehearsal of *Forza*; and at that time I want to see and hear the flutes and trumpets, and come to an understanding with Magnani, etc., etc.

I see they are still talking about the *Daughter of the Pharaohs*!![2] That cannot be; make sure that they don't botch things up.[3] [. . .]

1. See Verdi's letter to Giulio Ricordi of 28 December 1871 and to Emilio Usiglio of 26 January 1875. Even though Verdi himself condemned this overture, he did not destroy it, and Arturo Toscanini performed it on 30 March 1940 with the NBC Symphony Orchestra in New York. On 4 June of the same year Bernardino Molinari conducted the overture in the presence of Benito Mussolini at the opening of a Verdi exhibition at the Villa Farnesina in Rome. (See *Carteggi*, IV, p. 25; Carlo Gatti, *Verdi nelle immagini*, [Milano: Garzanti, 1941], p. 236; and *Genesi dell'Aida*, p. XXIVn.) Although the score of this discarded overture is unavailable, a recording of Toscanini's performance reveals Verdi's mastery of counterpoint. Guglielmo Barblan (Teatro alla Scala program 1975/76) associates the polyphonic structure of this *sinfonia* with the prelude to *Die Meistersinger von Nürnberg*, which had been premiered three years earlier. "To the *Aida* prelude that we know," Barblan continues, "Verdi adds the following motives in the overture: Aida's lament '*Numi, pietà*' and the theme of the priests in the triumphal

scene '*Della vittoria agli arbitri supremi*;' another brief allusion to Aida's lament follows at the introduction of Amneris' love motive as it appears in the orchestra on Amneris' first entrance to the words '*Quale insolita gioia*,'; then we hear the motive of Amneris' jealousy as echoed in the orchestra to the words '*Forse l'arcano amore*' (this theme ties in with that of the priests); once more Aida's lament occurs, now interwoven in Amneris' jealousy theme; and finally Aida's theme is heard becoming faster and faster until the *stretta* Verdi describes in his letter to Ricordi. As we see, Verdi wanted to emphasize thematic contrasts by means of the counterpoint, in order to underline the protagonists' dramatic conflicts.''

In an interview with the Milan review *Il Teatro Illustrato* of 1–15 July 1913, Toscanini is quoted as having been entrusted with the orchestral score of this unpublished overture by Signora Maria Verdi Carrara, who had ''jealously guarded'' the manuscript at St. Agata. According to this interview, Toscanini intended to respect Verdi's wish not to perform the overture described as consisting of seventy-six pages apparently neatly written ''all in one breath'' without a single correction, ''dated 23 December 1872 at the top.'' Obviously the interviewer, to whom Toscanini showed Verdi's manuscript, misread the year in the date — 1872 instead of 1871. If the interviewer's reading of the day and month can be trusted, it would appear that Verdi wrote those seventy-six pages in only five days.

2. See Verdi's letter to Giulio Ricordi of 10 August 1871.

3. Giulio Ricordi's answer to this letter is missing as are many others. Tito Ricordi's letter of 6 April 1872 and Giulio Ricordi's letter of 7 April 1872 are the first to close one of the major gaps in the available correspondence of the House of Ricordi with Giuseppe Verdi and his wife.

Verdi to Giulio Ricordi

Piacenza, Wednesday [15 November 1871]

Dear Giulio,

I am on my way to Genoa, where I shall arrive at 11:20.

I expect Capponi at any time. They say in Parma that *Aida* will be performed there for certain, without a doubt!

They say that Rossi[1] visited you in order to reach an agreement and that you did reach an agreement!

They say that the singers will be Capponi, la Waldmann, Pantaleoni, la Pozzoni!

They say: Conductor Mariani!!!!

What is true in all this? Tell me something. Tell me when I shall have Capponi. [. . .]

1. Giovanni Rossi (1828–86), Italian composer and conductor. Since 1851 he had been a conductor in Parma, where first performances of several of his own operas were given.

Verdi to Giulio Ricordi

[*Undated*]

Dear Giulio,

In signing the Parma contract keep in mind that *Don Carlos* was poorly done there. Ferrarini's arm[1] was blamed for that, but that is not at all true. [. . .] The *mise-en-scène* lacked common sense. Therefore, anticipate problems.

1. Verdi refers to Giulio Cesare Ferrarini (1807–91), for many years principal conductor in Parma. A friend of Verdi's as well as of Angelo Mariani's, he had evidently disappointed Giulio Ricordi when he conducted *Don Carlos* in Parma. See Verdi's letter to Giulio Ricordi of 22 November 1871.

Verdi to Giulio Ricordi

Genoa, 17 November 1871

Dear Giulio,

I have been here since yesterday.

I received Radames's part, but why did you send the entire score? At the least that's useless, if not imprudent. Let's avoid the <u>useless</u> then, and send me a part in which there are only the numbers for Radames. The score you sent can be used to correct the remaining errors.

Send me also a part which has only the numbers for Aida. La Stolz has been here for <u>four</u> or <u>five</u> days.

Verdi to Giulio Ricordi

Voghera, Sunday,[1] [19 November 1871]

Dear Giulio,

Last night I received your dispatch,[2] which doesn't appease me at all. You say that the title has been changed! But this is a joke or better yet, a mockery! *The Daughters of Memphis* is the same as *The Daughters of Pharaoh*. There will still be the same set, the same costumes, the same monuments that there are in *Aida*. That cannot be and must not be. Take heed! I warned you two months ago; and before I reach a decision, I warn you again. Once I have made up my mind, nothing will change it. [. . .]

1. It appears that, contrary to his habit of planning ahead, Verdi abruptly left Genoa for Bologna on the morning of 19 November 1871 to hear *Lohengrin*, conducted by Angelo Mariani, that evening. Walker, pp. 380–82, quotes two of Mariani's letters which establish Verdi's arrival at the railway station in Bologna on the afternoon of 19 November and his attendance at the performance of *Lohengrin* in the evening. Verdi obviously writes to Giulio Ricordi on his way from Genoa to Bologna. According to Mariani, Verdi returned to Genoa immediately after the performance. In a vocal score of *Lohengrin*, which is kept at St. Agata, Verdi sums up his impressions: "Beautiful music, and thoughtful, when it is clear. The action moves as slowly as the text. Result: boredom. Beautiful instrumental effects. Abuse of long notes leading to heaviness. Mediocre performance. Much *verve*, but without poetry and subtlety. In difficult spots, always bad." For Verdi's detailed comments see Abbiati, III, pp. 508–11.

2. Giulio Ricordi's telegram, apparently in answer to Verdi's letter of 13 November 1871, is missing.

Verdi to Giulio Ricordi

Genoa, 21 November 1871

Dear Giulio,

Excuse me: but it really seems to me that you are joking in your answers to my questions about the ballet. It's fine for you to say that the ballet has not yet been christened and for the commission to say that the plot and the genre have nothing to do with *Aida*. But this much I know: I am talking to you about the location and the costumes. Now if the ballet is set in Egypt, it will necessarily have the costumes of that country! Then call it *Daughters of the Pharaoh*, *Daughters of Memphis*, or *Daughters of the Devil*; it all comes out the same.

It is a good idea to avoid equivocations, and it is best that we come to a clear understanding at this time. Now I formally ask you: "Where does the action of the ballet which will be given at La Scala take place, and in what period is it set?" Let the response be formal, and for the moment suspend all activities concerning the production of *Aida*.

Verdi to Camille Du Locle

Genoa, 21 November 1871

Dear Du Locle,

Thanks for the costumes sketches you sent me, and please ask the designer to send me the others promptly. Here they[1] want to make the armor of steel (as they do at the Opéra), and we have no time to lose.

Also please have the props designed and send me some kind of chart, etc. [. . .]

1. Verdi refers to the costumers at La Scala.

Verdi to Giulio Ricordi

Genoa, 22 November 1871

[. . .] Well then . . . for your and my peace of mind, couldn't you send me a program of the ballet, which I would send right back to you? You will tell me . . . what, you have no trust? I have trust; I always have trust. But, out of old habits, I want to see and hear with my own eyes and ears when theatrical matters are at stake. Do you want proof? I was in Bologna, and I found the performance of *Lohengrin* totally different from what I had imagined from the reports I had received. So I have reason to want to see and hear for myself.

Send me the program of the ballet if you can, and that way this matter will also be settled.[1]

I am sending you more costume sketches, which I received the day before yesterday. La Stolz wishes to see her costume so that she can send instructions to Paris for her hair style. Therefore, mail me the sketch for Aida, which I shall send back to you right away.

I shall write to Du Locle about the props.

Now let's get to the Parma matter, since you ask me about it. Capponi, la Waldmann, and Pantaleoni are all right, but for Aida!! . . . Do you think this is a role to be entrusted to a near beginner? La De Giuli has had some success in Rome, but there are circumstances which increased the favor she won. She may truly be a talented artist, but we don't know her; and considering the uncertainty, I don't think we should risk the success of the opera. . . . Do you recall the third act of *Aida*? That act can be a success, but only if there is a strong Aida, one with great vocal and dramatic ability. La De Giuli certainly does not have great vocal ability, nor can she be very effective dramatically.

When they wanted to give *Aida* in Parma, the first thing they should have thought about was Aida!!! And when the 1,000 lire for la Stolz shocked them, they should have thought about some other opera.

As for the conductor, I don't think Ferrarini can be ousted (it would be a very nasty move on Rossi's part), but that doesn't concern you. I shall now ask . . . how is Rossi as a conductor? No, no. . . . It is altogether a matter we should not consider without well-founded reasons.[2]

1. In an undated note to Giulio Ricordi, Verdi again insists: "I suppose there is nothing that resembles the *Aida* costumes, but I want to see the program." (Autograph: Archivio Ricordi, Milano) Monplaisir's proposed ballet, *Le Figlie di Cheope*, with music by Constantino Dall'Argine (1842–77), was eventually premiered at La Scala on 31 December 1871. (See Cambiasi, p. 174, and *La Gazzetta Musicale* of 7 January 1872, which called the ballet a "fiasco.")

2. Rossi was eventually assigned to conduct the premiere of *Aida* in Parma, and Ferrarini held Giulio Ricordi responsible for this fatal blow to his own career. In vain he appealed to the Mayor of Parma, the board of directors, and to Verdi himself. Gustavo Marchesi has discovered in the Archives of the City of Parma a great deal of correspondence about this ordeal, as well as the negotiations between the impresario G. B. Lasina and Giulio Ricordi concerning the premiere of *Aida* in Parma.

Verdi to Giulio Ricordi

Genoa, 23 November 1871

[. . .] So Boito[1] has seen the score! . . . and Filippi has also seen it!! You were wrong to show *Aida* to outsiders. Early judgments are worth nothing and do no one any good. Furthermore always mistrust these judgments, whether they come from friends or enemies. I want absolutely no publicity. Good or bad, let the audience judge on opening night. What is done is done. But from this moment on, I ask, and I ask it seriously, that no one speak anymore of *Aida*, and that no one examine or judge it. Don't worry: either *Aida* will make its effect and there will be no need for publicity, or it will not make it and these premature judgments will add to the fiasco.

I have written for the costume sketches, which should arrive soon. I have written for the chart of the props.

I hear that the trumpets work well. I shall see them when I come to the first rehearsals of *La Forza del Destino*. See that the flutes, which I also want to hear then, are ready. Promise that everything will be ready, because I don't have much time to waste.

P.S. Tell your head copyist and your head engraver to have the phrase of the final duet corrected as it was in the original and as I had sent it before,[2]

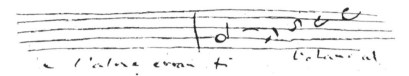

at all times.

1. Arrigo Boito (1842–1918), Italian composer and librettist. His most famous opera, *Mefistofele*, had been given its first performance at La Scala on 5 March 1868. Although he had already furnished the libretto for Faccio's *Amleto* in 1865, his achievements as a poet were more remarkably displayed in Ponchielli's *La Gioconda* (1876), Verdi's *Otello* (1887), and Verdi's *Falstaff* (1893).

2. See Verdi's letter to Giulio Ricordi of 15 October 1871, note 1.

Paul Draneht to J. Barrot

Cairo, 24 November 1871

My dear Bey,

I address to you the enclosed[1] concerning the expenses to date which have been made or are yet to be made for the opera *Aida*.

As you know quite well, H.H. would not like to exceed the original account of 250,000 francs, which he had opened for that opera, by more than 50,000 francs. The account finds itself today exceeded by 70,000 francs, which is 20,000 francs in excess. The increase springs from the amounts that M. Mariette Bey, wishing to do the appropriate things and acting moreover with the consent of H.H., finds himself under obligation to expend for certain items over what he had foreseen at the outset.

Of this total sum of 320,000 francs, I have received 250,000 francs, and I am absolutely lacking the surplus of 70,000 francs. I beg you, then, to kindly pay me this sum of 70,000 francs as soon as possible.

1. Missing.

Verdi to Giulio Ricordi

Genoa, 26 November 1871

Dear Giulio,

You attached too much importance to my last letter,[1] but you did very well to write me so frankly. This way things are always made clear.

There is no need to quibble over this affair, but here is how matters stand. In Bologna, Boito said that he had seen the *Aida* score, or at least various parts of it, and that he had found them to be good, etc., etc. This was related to me by someone who heard Boito's words — I don't know whether at the club or at a party. And Filippi wrote to Clarina that he had seen the *Aida* score and that he liked it, etc., etc. Therefore I naturally had to assume that you had let those two read through the opera.

If this is not so, they were wrong to say it.

But let's not talk about it anymore, and please don't mention it to Clarina, Filippi, or Boito. Consider this matter closed. Only please exercise every precaution in the future, and see that it is spoken of as little as possible.

I have received the other costume sketches,[2] which I am sending right back to you. . . . Ah, those nudes are quite ugly!! We are headed toward the *Duchesse de Gerolstein* or *Belle Helène*, etc., etc. These French imports should definitely be rejected!

Give this [enclosed] letter to Faccio.

P.S. Look at the piano-vocal score of *Aida* on page 20. There are octaves between the bass and the soprano lines. I am quite capable of making mistakes but not that kind. [. . .]

1. His letter of 23 November 1871. Giulio Ricordi's response to this letter is missing.
2. Verdi apparently refers to costume sketches from La Scala. These sketches were probably based on the French designs that Verdi had received from Du Locle and sent to Giulio Ricordi.

Verdi to Franco Faccio

Genoa, 26 November 1871

Dear Faccio,

I hear what you say about Pandolfini[1] with the greatest interest. I don't have the courage to ask him to come here at this time. But if the short trip from Milan to Genoa wouldn't be too difficult for him, I can't tell you how happy I would be to see him; and the other "Egyptians"[2] who come to my home between 1:00 and 3:00 p.m. would also be pleased. If he decides to come, it should be soon; I shall do all I can to conceal my hesitancy.

1. Missing.
2. The singers Verdi coached at his home in Genoa for the *Aida* premiere at La Scala.

Verdi to Camille Du Locle[1]

Genoa, 28 November 1871

Dear Du Locle,

I see that you did not understand the word "props." I think, in fact, that you don't have this word.[2] In our theatres we have, in addition to the word, an employee called the "propmaster," and it is he who provides everything that is needed for the *mise-en-scène* — for example, weapons, shields, helmets, chairs, furniture (*illegible*), etc. . . . I was asking you, then, for a kind of chart depicting all the properties [. . .] needed for the *mise-en-scène* of *Aida*. [. . .]

1. Du Locle's response to Verdi's letter of 21 November 1871 is missing.
2. In the French theatre, props are *accessoires* and the propmaster is the *accessoiriste*. The respective Italian terms are *attrezzi* and *attrezzista*.

Verdi to Giulio Ricordi

Genoa, 28 November 1871

Dear Giulio,

Du Locle writes me that he has sent, more or less, "all the designs drawn according to Mariette's indications." Those costumes that are missing, however, can very well be done by the designer. As far as I can recall (with regard to the principal roles), we are missing a first costume for Amneris and another for Radames. Since you have the costume sketches in front of you, tell me at once which costumes you still want for the masses.

I wasn't able to explain to Du Locle about the "props." They don't have this word, and I can't remember what they call the propmaster at the Opéra. I have already written him indicating the details, however, and he will now perhaps understand what we mean by props.

Keep well in mind that the ancient Egyptians (so Du Locle advises me) did not know about iron or steel; they knew only about gold, silver, and copper (*cuivre*): "All the weapons were made of copper, which they tempered in a way we have lost."

How sorry I am that la <u>Waldmann</u> cannot come! She has two duets of the utmost importance that would give us plenty to do.

<u>Capponi</u> knows the role; la <u>Stolz</u> has known hers for some time, except for the concerted sections. Very well, I think. Let's hope so. . . . In a few minutes I expect Pandolfini.

P.S. Pandolfini has arrived and he has rehearsed his role. Very good.

Verdi to Giulio Ricordi

Genoa, 29 November 1871

[. . .] Pandolfini is here and yesterday he rehearsed. Very good. Capponi leaves tonight, and so the work for *Aida* is finished for the moment.

I am very sorry about la Waldmann. There will be many things to correct, both in her pronunciation and her accent, and we shall be able to do very little at the usual rehearsals in the foyer. What a shame! La Waldmann will never have the accent that la Stolz and Capponi have. [. . .]

Verdi to Camille Du Locle

Genoa, 29 November 1871

Dear Du Locle,

I received the other costume sketches. They, too, are beautiful, but a little less so than the first. I urge you to send me quickly all the others as well. You can't imagine the pressure these people in Milan are putting on me. Also, as I told you, have <u>a chart of the props</u> drawn up for me, and send me everything in the shortest possible time. [. . .]

Verdi to Giulio Ricordi

Genoa, 2 December 1871

Dear Giulio,

I have made another change at the end of the <u>Aida-Amneris</u> duet in the second act. It is the same as it was, more or less, but the few changes that were made require a new copy. So, once again, have patience; <u>this version will remain</u>. I ask you to have it copied as soon as possible and to send it to Cairo immediately, so that it will be performed, if possible.[1] It seems they will open about the <u>18th</u>. All the same, make haste.

I have sent you a telegram that la <u>Waldmann</u> should not come here. There is not enough time, and it would end up that neither her <u>Preziosilla</u> nor her <u>Amneris</u> would be good. The best thing to do is to have her learn <u>Preziosilla</u>

well, very, very well now; and when I come to Milan to hear the orchestra, chorus, trumpets, and flutes, I can stay 48 hours, instead of 24, and let her see and hear the part of Amneris. But I repeat, at that time she must no longer need to study Preziosilla.

At any rate, managers never know what they are doing, and the productions are almost always bad because they don't know how to make them go well. [. . .]

1. After copying the corrections that Verdi enclosed in this letter, Giulio Ricordi presumably forwarded them to Cairo. In 1971 the Istituto di Studi Verdiani in Parma obtained photocopies from Cairo of these changes in Verdi's hand but is withholding them for its own publication which has not yet appeared. (See Chusid, p. 10, n. 1.)

Paul Draneht to M. Grand [1]

Cairo, 3 December 1871

Monsieur,

I have the honor of passing on a letter to you, [. . .] and I beg you kindly to take action on it as promptly as possible. It concerns a gas installation intended to illuminate the Temple Scene in the opera *Aida* and to reinforce the lighting which is at this time insufficient.

1. Monsieur Grand, the commissioner of public streets and highways in Cairo, who was also responsible for the allotments of gas.

Paul Draneht to Delphine Baron

Cairo, 4 December 1871

Madame,

This instant, I received from your brother a letter dated 22 November last, as a consequence of which I hasten to send him the following telegram:

"*Aida* premiere in course of December. Depart therefore without fail by boat on the 9th."

I hope to learn now that M. Baron is presently en route to Cairo, and that we shall have received all the costumes by the time of his arrival. [. . .]

Verdi to Giulio Ricordi

Genoa, 6 December 1871

[. . .] Well did I deceive you by suggesting Magnani? I have known him for a long time, and I know well what he is worth. He is a true artist and of that race whose sacred flame has not been extinguished by the rationalism of our time. He feels, and he feels the right things; he reasons little, and he does much. [. . .]

See to it that la Waldmann learns *La Forza* really well, so that when I come to Milan she has no other preoccupations, and I can go over the role of Amneris with her a couple of times. I don't want her to learn the role with anyone else; make her study the words well, however, the syllables below the notes [in particular] but with no singing.

P.S. I think la Stolz will leave tonight. She will give you her costume sketches for Aida. Have the *stretta* of the duet copied for her at once.[1]

1. See Verdi's letter to Giulio Ricordi of 2 December 1871.

Verdi to Giovanni Bottesini

Genoa, 7 December 1871

Dearest Bottesini,

I am very grateful to you for giving me the news of the first rehearsals for *Aida*. I hope you will give me more when you rehearse with the orchestra and also that you will give me exact, sincere, true news about the success of opening night. Please tell me the whole truth, since I am an old soldier with a chest of armor and have no fear of bullets.

I made a change in the *stretta* of the duet for the two women in the second act. I sent it to Ricordi two or three days ago, and he must have already sent it to Cairo. As soon as it arrives, I sincerely hope you will give it to the two artists and have it sung. The original *stretta* always seemed somewhat ordinary to me. The one I have redone is not; and it will end well if, when the motive of the scene in the first act returns, la Pozzoni sings it while slowly walking offstage. . . .

Paul Draneht to M. Magnier[1]

Cairo, 8 December 1871

Monsieur,

I am going to request of you (though a little belatedly) the service of supplying us with gas today at 1 o'clock precisely for the first orchestra rehearsal of *Aida*.

From now until the performance of this opera we shall be having frequent daytime rehearsals, and I know how bothersome it is for you to supply gas before evening. But in view of the exceptional circumstances we find ourselves in, I am counting on your courtesty to accord us this favor.

1. Monsieur Magnier, representative of the gas company in Cairo.

Verdi to Giulio Ricordi

Genoa, 9 December 1871

Dear Giulio,

When I received your letter this morning, you can't imagine my stupefaction at also receiving one from Filippi, in which he tells me that he has been invited by the Viceroy to go to Cairo. Ahhhhh! . . .

I am transcribing his letter and my reply, which perhaps should be published at the right time and place. Here is his letter: [1]

Milan, 8 December 1871

Esteemed Maestro,

The Viceroy of Egypt has kindly invited me to attend the first performance of *Aida*, and I have consented, because the importance of this artistic event will compensate for the length and discomfort of the journey. [2]

I would think myself remiss in my duty if I did not place myself at your disposal for anything you might need down there. [. . .]

Reply:

Genoa, 9 December 1871

Esteemed Signor Filippi,

What I am about to say to you will seem strange, very strange, but forgive me if I cannot keep from saying everything that is on my mind.

You in Cairo? This is the most powerful publicity for *Aida* one could imagine! It seems to me that in this way art is no longer art but a business, a game of pleasure, a hunt, something to be chased after, something which must be given if not success, at least notoriety at any cost! My reaction to this is one of disgust and humiliation! I always remember with joy my early days when, with almost no friends, without anyone to talk about me, without preparations, without influence of any kind, I went before the public with my operas, ready to be blasted and quite happy if I could succeed in stirring up some favorable impression. Now, what pomposity for an opera!!! Journalists, artists, choristers, conductors, instrumentalists, etc., etc. All of them must carry their stone to the edifice of publicity and thus fashion a framework of little trifles that add nothing to the worth of an opera; in fact they obscure the real value (if there is any). This is deplorable, profoundly deplorable!!!

I thank you for your courteous offers for Cairo, but I wrote to Bottesini the day before yesterday everything concerning *Aida*. For this opera I want only a good and, above all, an intelligent vocal and instrumental performance and *mise-en-scène*. As for the rest, *à la grâce de Dieu*; for so I began and so I wish to finish my career. [. . .]

Listen, my dear Giulio! At this moment I feel so disgusted, so sick to my stomach, so irritated, that I would burn the score of *Aida* a thousand times without a sigh! Shall we? . . . We still have time! . . . The contract[3] isn't signed yet, and if you want to destroy everything. . . . But if this poor opera must exist, for the love of Heaven, no <u>publicity</u>, no paraphernalia; they are for me the most humiliating humiliation.

Oh, everything that I have seen in Bologna, and hear now about Florence, makes me sick to my stomach! No, no. . . . I don't want *Lohengrinianas*.[4] . . . Rather the fire!! [. . .]

1. Verdi copied the entire text of Filippi's letter and of his own reply.
2. See Filippo Filippi, *Musica e Musicisti*, pp. 319 ff. See also Verdi's letter to Giulio Ricordi of 25 December 1871, note 1.
3. With La Scala.
4. Verdi coined the word *Lohengrinate*, referring to the publicity given the first Italian performance of *Lohengrin* in Bologna on 1 November 1871 and its subsequent performances in Florence.

Verdi to Giulio Ricordi

Genoa, 10 December 1871

Dear Giulio,

Taking everything into consideration it would have been better if matters had proceeded as planned and *La Forza* had been performed.[1] It is good that Capponi knows his part, but what he lacks (and does not understand) is a feeling for drama. He will perform very well after a few rehearsals, as he says; but he will perform coldly as far as the drama is concerned. The role of the tenor mainly requires <u>action, action, action.</u> If there is no solution, however, we must resign ourselves to it.

As soon as the first orchestra rehearsal of any opera is finished, let me know if you think the orchestra is producing a <u>fuller sound</u>. The same for the chorus. . . . Also tell me about the bass drum and the timpani. The delay in *La Forza* necessitates a delay of my arrival in Milan. I am sorry for la Waldmann.

Distribute the chorus for the second finale in this manner:

6 first tenors
6 second tenors
6 first basses   for the Chorus of the Priests
6 low basses

---

4 first sopranos
4 second sopranos
4 first basses   for the Ethiopian Prisoners[2]
6 second basses

Keep well in mind that there are 6 low basses in this chorus. The 12 basses in the Chorus of the Priests must be the best, and they will accompany the High Priest in the scene with Amneris in the fourth act. All of these basses, of course, will have to sing in the subterranean chamber. The management should definitely make the sacrifice of signing 6 other basses; not counting the 22 basses who are needed for partial choruses, there would only be 20 (that's not very many) for the large body of the chorus. So try to find some voices that, even if rough, have timbre. Also urge the chorusmaster, to whom you will give my best regards, to be very, very, very alert about the downbeat. It is the common defect of all Italian choruses to miss the attack or to attack weakly. Even those in Bologna, who are praised so much, have the same defect. Tell him also to watch out for the open voices; those Jewish voices that seem to scream "shoe laces and knitting needles"[3] must not be heard at La Scala. Finally, tell the maestro to excuse these observations made only for the purpose of obtaining a truly artistic performance. Should the opera be a fiasco, I want it to be on my account and not because of the performance.

You won't believe it!! But I am still upset by Filippi's letter — poor me!! Many years and a great deal of experience haven't changed me.

1. The revival of *La Forza del Destino*, with Waldmann as Preziosilla, had been postponed at La Scala.
2. See Verdi's letter to Ghislanzoni of 30 September 1870.
3. Verdi quotes from Rossini's *La Gazza Ladra*.

Verdi to Giovanni Bottesini

Genoa, 10 December 1871

Dear Bottesini,

I wrote you two days ago and I did not ask you about something so close to my heart.

What I did not do then, I do now. Therefore I urgently request you to send me news of the final duet, as soon as you have had two or three orchestra rehearsals. I hope you won't mind writing me a few words as soon as you have rehearsed it well with the orchestra and a few more words after opening night, to tell me about the honest effect of this piece. When reading through the score, you will understand that I have given this duet the greatest care; but since it belongs to what I would call the transparent genre, it may be that the effect does not correspond to my wishes. So tell me the whole truth frankly, because this truth could be useful to me. Tell me only about the 3/4 passage in D flat (Aida's song) and about the other song for the two of them in G flat. Tell me about the song and its instrumentation, always with regard to its effect. [. . .]

Verdi to Clarina Maffei

Genoa, 11 December 1871

[. . .] I wrote that letter to Filippi, of which Giulio Ricordi has a copy, in a very sad state of mind. In another letter,[1] which I have just received, Filippi tries to defend publicity under certain circumstances. Not I: it is always a humiliating thing and of no use. At this moment I am so upset, so irritated about this theatrical filth, that I might be capable of making the most grave resolutions. Oh, the years have not yet frozen my blood, and I'm unable to suppress my feelings, whether they be happy or sad!! My poor temperament! Never, never an hour of peace!!

1. Missing, perhaps destroyed in anger.

Verdi to Giulio Ricordi

Genoa, 13 December 1871

Dear Giulio,

I have seen the costume sketches,[1] which I return immediately. They have much character and they are beautiful; nevertheless, I would make a few changes:

1. On those of the little Moors. Why that color? I would like them completely black, and in that way we could also do away with the display of nudity.
2. The insignia bearer. I think you mean to say flabellum bearer. I don't think that is the form of the flabellum, but even if it were, I would modify it, and I would make it more theatrical by likening it to that which (if I remember correctly) they carry in Rome at papal ceremonies.
3. I don't know what effect the other female chorister[2] will produce: it is

somewhat unusual for the theatre. Remember that at the Opéra, which has the reputation for scrupulously preserving the style of their costumes, they are never respected to the letter. There they have an ability to preserve the cut and everything that is uncommon; later they make the modifications that the theatre requires.

4. I would also make Amneris's mourning costume sadder: I would make it more simple by removing several decorative embellishments that make it too cheerful for the situation. I'm just talking, since it's all right as it is.

Let's discuss la Waldmann, who worries me very much. She has defects in pronunciation which I would have made less apparent if I had had enough time. It's not a question of whether Faccio is capable of teaching her the role. He is more than capable, a thousand times more capable than I am; but I would like a few little accents on certain syllables, which no one else could imagine. It is certain, meanwhile, that precious time is being lost and that la Waldmann will delay *Aida*, since that role must be performed just as the other three perform their roles.

If Capponi does not come quickly, my arrival in Milan will be delayed. On second thought, however, I could very well hear the chorus and orchestra in another opera, and go over the role with la Waldmann at that time. I think this might be the thing to do. If Capponi comes quickly (and you will know this tomorrow), I can wait and hear the rehearsals of *Forza*; if not, invite me to hear the chorus, orchestra, trumpets, flutes, etc., in another opera. I say invite me because I never go to someone's home without the consent of the host. The management should not write me, only you, formally, in its name.

1. Verdi apparently refers to costume sketches from La Scala. See his letter to Giulio Ricordi of 26 November 1871.

2. Verdi probably refers to a costume design intended for a particular group in the women's chorus.

Verdi to Camille Du Locle

Genoa, 14 December 1871

Dear Du Locle,

Excuse the trouble I am about to give you, but it has to do with *Aida*, so you will forgive me.

Signora Stolz asks me to send the enclosed letter to Paris and to have it forwarded by someone so that her order may be carried out well by Granger,[1] whom you must certainly know. Please see to it, then, that this commission is properly executed. Signora Stolz knows this Granger, who has previously sent her things for her costume in *Don Carlos*. [. . .]

1. The Paris firm of Leblanc Granger, which manufactured theatrical arms and jewelry.

Verdi to Giulio Ricordi

Monday [*Probably* Genoa, 18 December 1871]

Dear Giulio,

In any event, I shall be in Milan tomorrow evening, Tuesday, at 7. It doesn't matter if you are not ready to stage the opera; it is enough for me to hear chorus, orchestra, the trumpets and the new flutes, and above all to run through la Waldmann's Amneris a couple of times. Since I can only stay a couple of days, see that la Waldmann is at the theatre on Wednesday morning before the orchestra rehearsal (if there is one). I shall take care of the rest later. Arriving at 7, I can be at the theatre around 7:30.

Paul Draneht to Rassik Effendi [1]

Cairo, 20 December 1871

Monsieur,

Conforming to the wish that His Highness has expressed to me, I ask you to kindly do the translation of the *Aida* libretto from Arabic into Turkish,[2] and this without losing a moment, the first performance of *Aida* having been scheduled for Sunday, the 24th of this month. [. . .]

1. Chief editor of *Ruznamez*, the official Egyptian newspaper at the time. *Effendi* is a Turkish title of respect.
2. The translation of *Aida* into Arabic had been done by Abdalla Abul-Soud Effendi.

Paul Draneht to M. Magnier

Cairo, 23 December 1871

Monsieur,

I have the honor of informing you that we are holding the dress rehearsal of *Aida* this evening and that we shall need the same amount of gas as for the performance. Consequently I ask you to please take the necessary measures so that we should have a pressure of 24 m/m on the theatre's meter at 8 o'clock precisely.

Verdi to Giulio Ricordi

[Genoa,] 24 December 1871

[. . .] I still insist on the fourth trombone. That bombardon[1] is impossible. Tell Faccio and, if you wish, consult the first trombonist as well to see what should be done. I would like a <u>bass trombone</u> from the same family as the others, but if it is too tiring or too difficult to play, get one of the usual ophicleides that go to <u>low B</u>. In other words, do whatever you want, but not that devil of a bombardon that does not blend with the others.

Find a solution for the trumpet. He may be your good *professore*,[2] but he has neither attack nor strong sound. Today these instruments are purposely made to blare when necessary.

If I receive a telegram from Cairo, I shall send it to you.

It makes me laugh to think that the Viceroy has invited Reyer.[3] What a choice! Reyer and Filippi!!! Two enemies!! And I enjoy it because <u>Reyer</u> will voice the wrath of God!

Have you heard that the first performance will be by invitation? What pleasure for an artist to study so much and work so hard in order to be applauded as if at a private concert. What a joke! And to think that I am part, and a victim, of it!! [. . .]

1. A wind instrument of the bassoon type.
2. Any player in an Italian orchestra.
3. Ernest Reyer (1823–1909), French composer and music critic of the *Journal de Débats* in Paris.

Verdi to Camille Du Locle [1]

Genoa, 25 December 1871

[. . .] Granger is asking for too much time to make these accessories. The rehearsals here are moving along: the singers already know their roles, the chorus almost; the sets are nearly finished, and we may very well open right on the 20th (which is a Saturday, the usual day for opening nights). Therefore see to it that Granger has everything finished at least by the 15th and that everything is in Milan by the <u>18th</u>. Watch over this because a delay would be absolutely ruinous.

See to it also that the work is carried out as it should be. Write me promptly about this matter. [. . .]

You should have received news from Cairo.[2] I have two telegrams which are good. We shall see if they are confirmed. I learned that the Viceroy had invited Reyer. Oh, bravo! That is really a good friend!!! And the Viceroy has a good nose! Anyhow better this way than to see those nauseating articles of worthless praise. Send me at once the article Reyer will write in the *Débats*. There will certainly be cannonades. But don't worry; my indifference is good armor.

1. Abbiati, III, p. 526, quotes from J.-G. Prod'homme's French translation of this letter rather than giving Verdi's original text in his Italian publication. (See J.-G. Prod'homme, "Lettres inédites de G. Verdi à Camille Du Locle [1868–74]," *La Revue Musicale*, 5 [1928–29], p. 31.
2. The world premiere of *Aida*, conducted by Giovanni Bottesini, took place on Sunday, 24

December 1871, at the Cairo Opera with the following cast: Antonietta Pozzoni-Anastasi (Aida), Eleonora Grossi (Amneris), Pietro Mongini (Radames), Francesco Steller (Amonasro), Paolo Medini (Ramfis), Tommaso Costa (King), Marietta Allievi (Termuthis), Luigi Stecchi-Bottardi (Messenger). Note that the role of the Great Priestess (*Grande Sacerdotessa*) was still listed as Termuthis (the Italian spelling of the French Termouthis) at that time. See Documents II, III, and IX. Luigi Stecchi-Bottardi was supposedly related to Pietro Mongini and had been heard in such roles as Almaviva, Ernesto, and Nemorino throughout the world, including the United States.

Verdi to Giulio Ricordi

Genoa, 25 [December 1871]

[. . .] I too have news from Cairo: "Verdi Genoa: *Aida* enthusiastic success culminating second finale. All artists celebrating. Orchestra very good. Great ovation. Viceroy applauded. Your friend Bottesini." We'll see if [the success] will be confirmed,[1] because one must not put too much trust in telegrams sent after opening night. It seems, however, that the second finale was the piece [applauded most]. So much the better, if that big piece was effective even with insufficient means.

At La Scala, we shall have the necessary means (if you remember the priests), and perhaps we shall achieve the effects we should have had in the finale of *Don Carlos* — a finale, moreover, which has never been performed well in any theatre in Italy, to our greater glory. So, good priests and a good band: I'll take care of the rest. Tell the bandmaster to do the arrangement for his band quickly. Before that march is done at the orchestra rehearsal, I want to listen carefully to it, so that I can fill in what is missing.

P.S. Be sure not to print, or have printed, my telegram from Cairo. Corticelli had asked me for it so he could bring it to *Movimento*[2] . . . but I shouted . . . "By God, I don't want any *Lohengrinianas*." Poor Corticelli ran away and is still running.

1. Filippo Filippi's subsequent review in *La Gazzetta Musicale* of 7 January 1872 reflects the general enthusiasm for the work at its world premiere. In *Musica e Musicisti*, pp. 349–74, Filippi (after giving a detailed description of his journey to Egypt) discusses the Cairo Opera and its staff, the origin, final rehearsals, Mariette's "magnificent" sets and costumes, and the first performances of *Aida*, as well as his meetings with the Viceroy and his visits to archaeological sites.

2. A popular newspaper in Genoa.

Verdi to Giulio Ricordi

Genoa, 26 December 1871

[. . .] La Waldmann frightens me. She has such a curious accent, pronunciation, and sameness of sounds that she can produce the most unpleasant effects. [. . .]

In the event *Forza* should be a fiasco, what would the management decide?

It would be impossible to continue [the season] until *Aida*, and I think it would be wise to find a repertoire opera immediately. [. . .] All this would delay *Aida*, but there is no other solution. [. . .] Think about it then, and let the management think about it, because I shall be immovable and not allow *Aida* to be throttled at any cost.

I am transcribing for you a lengthy telegram from the Bey (obviously the Viceroy paid for it), from which you will see the importance of Amneris and, therefore, how much study la Waldmann will need: "Maestro Verdi Genoa: First performance *Aida* triumphant success. Not one number passed over in silence. First second finales, two duets soprano and tenor, grand march, council scene, total fanaticism. Enthusiastic audience applauded absent Maestro. Congratulations, thanks. Draneht." [. . .]

Verdi to Giovanni Bottesini

Genoa, 27 December 1871

Dear Bottesini,

I don't know how to tell you how grateful I am for your kind thoughtfulness in sending me a telegram after opening night. It is another obligation I have to you (in addition to many, many others) for the loving care you have lavished on this poor *Aida*. In addition to your zeal I am aware of the talent you displayed in leading the rehearsals and the performance — something which I never doubted.[1] Thank you, then, my dear Bottesini, for everything you have done for me in this situation; and please convey my most heartfelt gratitude to all who took part in the performance of this opera.

I am still awaiting a reply to my last letter.[2] I was interested, and am still interested, in having precise, particular information about the effect of the final piece. Mind you, I don't talk about its quality but only about its effect. If you have not written already, write me at length about this, and tell me the whole truth. I want to know about the effects of the orchestra, about those of the song, and above all about the total effect — that is, what impression it produces. I am anxiously awaiting this letter of yours.

1. See Verdi's letters to Lampugnani of 4 May 1871, to Draneht of 1 September 1871, and to Bottesini of 4 March 1883.
2. Of 10 December 1871.

Verdi to Paul Draneht

Genoa, 27 December 1871

Excellency,

Together with the thanks I owe you for all the care you have been willing to give to *Aida*, I owe you particular thanks for your exquisite friendliness in sending me a telegram right after opening night.

I am happy about the success of *Aida*, not only for myself but above all for H.H.; I am aware that his generous sacrifices for the art of music have not been thrown into the sea and that the labor and care which everyone has given for this good success have been repaid.

Thank you again, Excellency; and in my name please thank all those who have contributed to this joyful conclusion.

Verdi to Giulio Ricordi

Genoa, 28 December 1871

Dear Giulio,

I am sending you an overture (the ink is still wet) with which we may perhaps precede *Aida*.[1] I say "perhaps" because I have hardly looked it over and it may be a big mess. By keeping it out of my sight for a few days, I shall be able to look at it when I arrive in Milan, judge it, and tell you if it's worth the expense of having it copied. In any event, we always have the Prelude; I have made some changes in it, and so you can now correct the plates. Watch out for the sheet indicating these changes.[2] You will see that at the end of the overture, when the trombones and double basses shout the song of the priests, and the violins and wind instruments scream the jealousy of Amneris, Aida's melody is played very loudly by the trumpets. That moment is either a mess or an effect. But it cannot be an effect, if the trumpets don't have attack, sound, and brilliance.

Pay attention to what I am telling you, because I have noticed, and I still notice, that I rarely deceive myself with my judgments. [. . .]

When I arrive I don't want to hear any talk about hurrying. So let the management take the necessary precautions. Just *inter nos*, I am not happy about la Waldmann, and I wrote you that even before this failure [of *La Forza*]. It's very difficult to find someone better; but with enough time I'll be able to make her do something good. Yet there are so many things in *Aida*. There is a finale which must be performed and staged better than that of *Don Carlos*. [. . .]

1. See Giulio Ricordi's letter to Verdi of 12 November 1871 and Verdi's reply of 13 November 1871.
2. This sheet is missing.

Verdi to Camille Du Locle

Genoa, 29 December 1871

[. . .] I shall leave for Milan on Tuesday the 2nd to begin the rehearsals for *Aida*. . . . I really hope to open on the 20th. . . . When the rehearsals are well along I'll write to tell you with greater certainty what the date will be. That way you can make plans to come to Milan. How much I want to see you! But alas, poor Du Locle, should you be witness to a fiasco! Oh well, in any event it will be an experience, and you will see how clearly and loudly they whistle in Italy. [. . .]

Paul Draneht to Ercole Tinti [1]

Cairo, 29 December 1871

[. . .] I do not need to give you any details with regard to *Aida*, for the papers are full of those. I can tell you only that they could not exaggerate anything. We have had a success beyond belief. Everything was splendid: music, costumes, sets, etc. I believe that a *mise-en-scène* so rich, so beautiful, and so scrupulously accurate has never been seen in any theatre, thanks to the devoted collaboration of M. Mariette Bey.

1. Theatrical agent in Florence.

Verdi to Giulio Ricordi

[Genoa, 31 December 1871]

[. . .] I'll be in Milan Tuesday evening at 7. Advise hotel[1] for drawing room and little bedroom. Peppina will come next week. Prepare everything for the rehearsal.
P.S. Have a good piano brought to the hotel for me.

1. The still existing Grand Hotel et de Milan, Via Manzoni 29, where Verdi usually stayed in that city and where he died thirty years later.

Verdi to Léon Escudier

Genoa, 1 January 1872

Dear Léon,

Your surprise at my not writing about *Aida* in turn surprised me very much for good reasons. The war and the siege were over, communications completely reestablished, and everyone knew that I was writing that opera.

. . . Therefore it was natural that, just as the publisher in Milan asked about it, the publisher in Paris could also have asked about it. Your not doing so indicated that it did not suit you; and, in addition to the fact that I would never, never have proposed my music, there was a feeling of delicacy in not obliging you to refuse or to accept it at a time when you would have been forced to make a sacrifice, since all the theatres and all business affairs were in a state of stagnation. This is in reply to your letter of last November.[1]

The bells have already rung in the new year! One more to get through!! Alas, alas!! How these damn years are now flowing by!! But as long as our health holds out, let's do our best to pass them with the least possible trouble. [. . .]

I'll be in Milan tomorrow night to start the *Aida* rehearsals. Since the chorus is already studying and the leading artists have gone through their roles, and also because we have good elements in the orchestra and chorus this year, things will go fast. I'll let you know by letter or telegram the precise date, more or less, of opening night.

I have no letters as yet from Cairo, but it seems that they have a success, even though their stage is too small for such a vast subject.

1. Escudier probably wrote this letter, which is missing, in answer to Verdi's letter of 11 October 1871.

Giuseppina Verdi to Cesare De Sanctis

Genoa, 3 January 1872

[. . .] So you will come to Milan for *Aida*? Verdi and I are most happy! . . . But I am terribly sorry to have to tell you that you cannot count on attending the dress rehearsal, because, in spite of all the affection Verdi has for you, he could not work on a double standard, admitting you and leaving others out.

It is an inexorable decision that no one shall be admitted to the dress rehearsal. It was like that for *La Forza del Destino* in Milan and for *Don Carlos* in Paris, etc. Verdi maintains that this is a good idea, since one is free to make corrections, if necessary, and he is not partial to anyone. [. . .]

Paul Draneht to Delphine Baron

Cairo, 4 January 1872

Madame,

By the time this letter arrives, you will already have learned from your brother that we have given *Aida* with magnificent success, a success to which you have contributed with the magnificence of your costumes. Therefore I beg you, Madame, to accept my compliments and thanks for the trouble you have taken with this work. [. . .]

Verdi to Camille Du Locle

[Milan,] 7 January 1872

Dear Du Locle,

I have been in Milan for two days[1] to put everything in order before beginning the regular rehearsals. We have had a misfortune: the tenor is ill, and I think it is serious. One of the better doctors has left to see how things stand! We shall see.

Since Granger doesn't need them, would you please return the costume sketches of *Aida* by mail so that they arrive quickly.

You too will have heard directly from Cairo, and now I am waiting for you to send me Reyer's article in the *Débats*.

Now allow me a question concerning the costume sketches of *Aida*. Filippi writes that Mariette Bey told him that if the *Aida* costume sketches he made had been requested for Milan, he would have been most happy to give them; and that if the costume sketches for Milan were made in Paris, they were invented and neither beautiful nor authentic. I don't understand a thing about all of this! Tell me something that may explain this business to me. [. . .]

1. See Verdi's letters to Du Locle of 29 December 1871 and to Giulio Ricordi of 31 December 1871. Verdi apparently postponed his departure from 2 January to 4 or 5 January 1872.

Verdi to Vincenzo Luccardi

Milan, 9 January 1872

Dear Luccardi,

I can only repeat what I have already told you about *Aida*. It is not an opera that can be done by a company that is already assembled. It is necessary to assemble the company for the opera. Then, too, the *mise-en-scène* must be thought out far in advance. It is better for the opera, for Jacovacci,[1] for everyone, that he forget about this *Aida* for the time being. . . .

1. Vincenzo Jacovacci (1811–81), Italian impresario. The son of a fishmonger, he was the manager of the Teatro Apollo in Rome for some forty years before his death — during a performance of *Don Carlos*.

Antonio Ghislanzoni to Giulio Ricordi

Lecco, 9 January [1872][1]

[. . .] Here are the lines for *Aida*.[2]

AIDA: *Io!* . . .

AMONASRO: *Radames so che qui attendi . . . Ei t'ama . . .*

The two lines you sent me for the ending of the opera seem too dry to me and not very theatrical. I would say it like this:

> *Pace t'imploro — alma adorata . . .*
> *Isi placata — ti schiuda il ciel.*

What if *salma* were used instead of *alma*? Perhaps it would be more Egyptian. Ah! I realize it isn't easy to arrive at the true language of the mummies! [. . .]

Don't count on me too much for the *mise-en-scène*. I shall be able to give some advice, but I don't feel capable enough, or authoritative enough, to direct the masses. You must realize once and for all, Signor Giulio, that I am a big ass!

1. Abbiati, III, p. 430, erroneously dates this letter an entire year earlier, 1871, at which time Giulio Ricordi was not likely to have been concerned with the details of the libretto and with Ghislanzoni's help on the *mise-en-scène*. In January 1872, however, Giulio Ricordi was involved with the staging of *Aida* at La Scala and — if he had heeded Verdi's warning — also with the final printing of the libretto. (See postscript of Verdi's letter to Giulio Ricordi of 10 November 1871.)
2. Ghislanzoni refers to the beginning of the scene between Aida and Amonasro in Act III. Aida's *Io* was later to be eliminated and Amonasro's line slightly changed.

Antonio Ghislanzoni to Giulio Ricordi

[*Probably* Lecco, January 1872]

Dear Signor Giulio,

To make Aida's appearance in the subterranean chamber somewhat more credible, I would have her say:

> *Presago il core della tua condanna,*
> *In questa tomba che per te si apriva*
> *Io penetrai furtiva . . .*
> *E qui, lontana da ogni umano sguardo,*
> *Nelle tue braccia desiai morire.*

This way, I think, everything would be justified. After the priests removed the stone above the subterranean chamber, Aida found an opportune moment to enter furtively, ahead of her lover. What will Verdi say? If these lines are too many, one could also say:

Presago il core della tua condanna,
Qui pel varco a te secluso io ti precessi,
E qui, lontana da ogni umano sguardo,
Nelle tue braccia desiai morire.

This way the line *Qui da tre dì ti attendo* . . . will also be eliminated, and that will be fine, since the specification of time isn't good and makes the situation rather incredible. Also I don't care very much for the line one might substitute: *Qui da più dì ti attendo.*

But I hope Verdi will like one or the other of the two versions I have written above.

Concerning the two

S'intrecci il mirto al lauro
Sul crin dei vincitor

I would, frankly, change them to:

S'intrecci il loto al lauro
Sul crin dei vincitor . . .

The critics, at any rate, who like lotus and live for that, will be satisfied. Make sure to change the verse, not only in the first chorus of the second act but also on pages 29 and 30.

I had to leave Milan because my wife is sick. Besides I had written you[1] that I would not have stayed for more than two or three days as Verdi's guest. I shall return on Tuesday, and if the devil doesn't prevent me, I'll stay until the opening of *Aida*. [. . .]

1. In a missing letter.

Verdi to Camille Du Locle

Milan, 11 January 1872

Dear Du Locle,

I received the costume sketches for *Aida* and your very dear letter.[1] I thank you for the one as well as the other.

Capponi is decidedly ill, and I have to be content with Fancelli. The change is certainly not well-suited, but one must resign oneself.[2] Impossible to open on the 20th or even the 30th. Only today was Fancelli's role sent to him. Go about your business as usual, because the opera will not be ready until at least seven or eight days after the 25th. I shall write you, and if necessary telegraph. In spite of the delay, however, see that Granger sends the material to la Stolz as though we were going to open on the 20th.

Peppina, who is here, sends her greetings to you and your Marie.

1. Missing.

2. Giuseppe Adami, *Giulio Ricordi e i suoi musicisti* (Milano: Fratelli Treves, 1933), pp. 51–52, quotes Giulio Ricordi as having told him:

"The tenor Fancelli could drive one to desperation. This Radames from Tuscany would have been one of the most talented singers of his time, had he had a musical education and intuition similar to his vocal power and range. Well, that poor Fancelli was not only lacking instruction, but also that elementary intelligence which often suffices to crown a tenor with glory. Verdi, of course, was in despair; and he unleashed his anger on Fancelli, when even the most patient admonition fell into the abyss of incomprehension. There wasn't a day on which the Maestro did not occupy himself with him, illustrating even the words and the moods of the role. His time and breath were wasted. On one bad morning, Verdi could no longer control himself. Having made Fancelli repeat the same phrase over and over without obtaining any result, Verdi rose to his feet, seized the tenor by the back of his neck, and, while repeatedly pounding the man's forehead on the keyboard, burst out:

'When will anything ever get into your head? . . . Never!' With that, he furiously left the room. Fancelli did not react and did not utter a word. But the moment Verdi was gone, he turned to the rest of us who were dumbstruck, and looking at all of us one after the other, mumbled with a desolate expression:

'A great Maestro. . . . Yessir! . . . I agree. But he wants the impossible, the impossible! You bet! He wants people to read his music as he wrote it and to sing on pitch and in *tempo*, and even to pronounce the words! How can you do all that stuff at the same time? I couldn't, even if I were the Almighty God himself'!"

See also Gino Monaldi, *Cantanti Celebri del secolo XIX* (Roma: Nuova Antologia, [1907]), pp. 195–98.

Verdi to Opprandino Arrivabene

Milan, 13 January 1872

[. . .] I have begun rehearsals for *Aida*. The devil has stuck his horns in, making Capponi ill, and I have to be satisfied with Fancelli: beautiful voice, but a blockhead. In any case, if they aren't too hard, I'll do everything to break this devil's horns.

You will say I am presumptuous!! No, no. I have good elements in the chorus and orchestra; I have la Stolz and Pandolfini; la Waldmann is intelligent; the secondary roles are good; so something should come out of it. I shall write you about it, and shall tell you the truth. *La Forza del Destino* is going well; I do not listen to the applause, but I look at the full houses. [. . .]

Verdi to Giovanni Bottesini

Milan, 13 January 1872

Dear Bottesini,

First of all I thank you for the very great zeal you showed in the performance of *Aida*, and I congratulate you for your talent in interpreting the work. Then I must tell you that I am most obliged to you for the observations in your latest letters,[1] from which I shall profit. So Amen to that. I thank you again and wish you continued success.

I have begun rehearsals here, but the devil has stuck his horns in, making Capponi ill. We must be content with Fancelli, and there is no other solution. This year we have good orchestra and chorus members — about 120 of the latter and 90 orchestral musicians. One hears a large, round sonority, without the screaming trombones. We shall certainly not have the rich *mise-en-scène* as in Cairo, but it will be suitable; and at last, if the devil doesn't continue to stick his horns in, we shall be able to do something.

I have recently written an overture for *Aida*. Do me the favor of telling Draneht Bey that if it produces some effect, I shall make it my duty to send it to him immediately so that it can be added to the Cairo score. [. . .]

1. Missing.

Auguste Mariette to Paul Draneht

Boulaq, 17 January 1872

My dear Bey,

M. Verdi telegraphs me[1] from Milan and asks me to send him by return mail a photograph showing the barge and the altar which appear in *Aida*. [. . .] It's a matter of simply taking the two objects in question to the courtyard of the theatre. [. . .]

1. Missing.

Verdi to Camille Du Locle

Milan, 18 January 1872

[. . .] I have not received Granger's jewelry; it may be, however, that I will receive it today!! . . . But alas! Ricordi tells me not to hope for it because the connections between the French and Italian railroads are so irregular that they can't be relied upon and there might be a delay of ten or twelve days. Poor us! If that happens, we shall be in a very embarrassing situation. Do me the favor, however, of having Granger tell you (as soon as the jewelry has been shipped): by what means; at what border it will enter Italy.

If it is possible and if there is time, it should be entrusted to someone reliable so that it will not be delayed. As for us, once I know at which border it will arrive, it will be here in a few hours.

Therefore tell me the border and to whom it is addressed.

Reply quickly. Goodbye until we meet again. Two or three days before opening night you will receive a telegram.

Giuseppina Verdi to Cesare De Sanctis

Milan, 21 January 1872

It is nearly midnight, and although my regular time for retiring is past, I want to write you immediately, immediately about the conversation I had with Verdi when he returned from the *Aida* rehearsals, with which he seems rather pleased. He is leaving my room at this moment. He spoke at length of *Aida*, of *Don Carlos*, of La Scala and of Naples. "It's a shame," he said, speaking of the San Carlo, "that this beautiful theatre, in that most beautiful, extremely musical city, should be allowed to go to ruin. If there were only a chance, you see, of getting good resources. If, for example, they gave me, first of all, la Stolz, la Waldmann, a great tenor, etc., I would be disposed to come to an agreement, and to give *Aida*, and to give *Don Carlos* again, under my direction — that is, staging them myself. They couldn't have a true idea of *Don Carlos* the way it was massacred.

"We could stay there for the entire theatrical season. We could make do with one or two domestics, take a nice apartment in a hotel, and enjoy the company of our old friends for several months. Unfortunately the reins of the San Carlo are in the hands of someone who doesn't know how to, or doesn't want to, do well by art, by the country, and by himself, in fair, honest, and loyal terms.[1] Let's not talk about it anymore."

Why? I asked; let's talk about it a great deal more. This simple wish of yours, this attitude of yours delights me more than any other thing you could propose to give me pleasure. But if you are speaking seriously, tell me if you would feel truly disposed to occupy yourself with this business, if you received some proposal from Naples.

"I give you my word of honor, if they ever, I repeat, gave me la Stolz, la Waldmann, and sufficient resources to obtain successes and revive that great theatre, [I would go.] In the meantime, good night; I am going to bed, wishing the San Carlo better days."

Here, word for word, is that which was said between us and which I have been inspired to repeat to you. If you wish to have Verdi in Naples, if you wish to have any good performances whatever, if you have means and influence to move the impresarios and the board of directors, who after all are in charge of those affairs, I believe this to be the opportune moment. Get busy, and I am close to the hope that from Milan you could bring to Naples, in black and white, Verdi's written promise for the next theatrical season. [. . .]

1. Verdi refers to Antonio Musella, Italian impresario. After managing several touring operatic companies in southern Italy, Corfu, Rhodes, and minor cities in South America, he was director of the San Carlo Opera in Naples from 1870 to 1874.

Verdi to Camille Du Locle

Milan, 26 January 1872

Dear Du Locle,

Yesterday la Stolz received her jewels, and she is very happy with them. Please pay Granger and send me the receipt.

I add my most sincere thanks, and I shall reimburse you immediately.

It is almost certain that *Aida* will open on the 3rd of February. I shall write you again. . . .

Giuseppina Verdi to Cesare De Sanctis

Milan, 30 January 1872

From your letter of 26 January, from yesterday evening's telegram, and from Torelli's[1] letter of this morning,[2] I understand that you haven't received my letters of 3 and 22 January.[3] I am sending this one to the old address at Via Concezione, hoping that it will be more fortunate. The others were sent to No. 317 Strada Toledo.

Verdi's good disposition toward Naples has been quite upset by Torelli's letter this morning; for example, Verdi requested reforms in the diapason, the orchestra, and the chorus, in order, actually, to raise the San Carlo to the standards of La Scala. Torelli answers and asks: "What reasonable reforms, but not major ones, [do you want] for the *mise-en-scène*, and will you assist?" He says about la Stolz that Musella has been negotiating with her for a year! . . . But if la Stolz asks for ten and can have ten anywhere, and if the impresario offers her five, she will tell him where to go. What would you have done in a similar situation?

[. . .] I don't know why the artists should have to make sacrifices to sing in

Naples for little money, while they (I am speaking of first-class artists) can get much more in other great theatres! I don't know why they continue to say "Verdi, Verdi, Verdi," and when Verdi shows himself disposed to come, they say: "Be content with that which we offer you!!!" . . . Thus art becomes just another job. It is indecent always to plead poverty in the case of the San Carlo, which perhaps has greater resources than any other theatre in Italy.

This morning Verdi sent me you know where when he showed me Torelli's letter. I didn't know how to answer him! So continue your spectacles with patched-up costumes and the whole mess, until the once great San Carlo dies of consumption. I am sorry, angry, and discouraged; but I foresee that nothing will be done this time, if they are not ready to put aside their humiliating lamentations. As long as no radical reforms are made, Verdi says it is useless to think of a modern lyric theatre. Now it is up to you. [. . .]

1. Vincenzo Torelli, retired journalist and Verdi's friend in Naples.
2. The telegram and letters are missing.
3. The reference to 22 January obviously applies to the letter Giuseppina Verdi wrote late in the evening of 21 January 1872.

Verdi to Vincenzo Torelli[1]

[*Probably* Milan, 30 or 31 January 1872]

My dear Torelli,

Your letter is not likely to sustain my hope of being able to do something good in your theatre. You say: art, art, art, and then you add: reasonable reforms but not major ones. What does it matter, then, whether or not you do my operas if you don't want to make the reforms they require? Either one or the other. Do you want modern operas? Make reforms! You don't want to? Go back to *cavatina* operas, since you have as many as you need — providing you can find the singers. Besides I never did, nor do I now, demand the impossible. I only ask:

The orchestra as it is now arranged at La Scala.

Choristers	The same.
Diapason	The same.
Mise-en-scène	The same.

Even here everything isn't perfect, but it is good, very good; and if this is done in Milan, why can't it be done in Naples, with all its means and such a large population?

Let's conclude then. Do you want to or not? Write immediately, and if you

<u>want</u> to, give instructions and some authority because this deal must be settled soon or not at all.

1. In answer, apparently, to Torelli's letter, which was mentioned by Giuseppina Verdi in her letter to Cesare De Sanctis of 30 January 1872.

Verdi to Giuseppe Piroli

Monday [*Probably* Milan, 5 February 1872]

Dear Piroli,

As you can imagine I am in the middle of rehearsals for *Aida*, which will open Saturday. [. . .]

The rehearsals aren't going badly. The *mise-en-scène* will be good. The choral performance is all right but not the orchestra. It is made up of musicians who are too old and too young, and it is clear that for a long time they have been playing however the <u>devil wishes</u>. Finesse and artistic intentions no longer exist. Sometimes they play the notes well, but many times poorly and nothing more. We shall open nevertheless, but not as I would have liked and as would have been possible a few years ago. [. . .]

Verdi to Opprandino Arrivabene

Milan, 9 February 1872

Dear Arrivabene,

Last night *Aida* excellent;[1] the performance of the ensembles and of the individual roles was very good; the *mise-en-scène*, the same. La Stolz and Pandolfini, excellent. La Waldmann, good. Fancelli, beautiful voice and nothing else. The others good, and the orchestra and chorus excellent. As for the music, Piroli will tell you about it. The audience reacted favorably.[2] I don't want to affect modesty with you, but this opera is certainly not one of my worst. Time will afterward give it the place it deserves. . . .

1. The first performance of *Aida* in Italy, conducted by Franco Faccio and staged by Verdi, took place on 8 February 1872 at La Scala in Milan with the following cast: Teresa Stolz (Aida), Maria Waldmann (Amneris), Giuseppe Fancelli (Radames), Francesco Pandolfini (Amonasro), Ormondo Maini (Ramfis), and Paride Povoleri (King).

Paride Povoleri, Italian bass, appeared between 1870 and 1890 in such cities as Venice, Bologna, Milan, Trieste, Naples, Paris, Amsterdam, Brussels, Berlin, St. Petersburg, and Buenos Aires. In 1875 he sang Verdi's *Requiem* under Muzio's direction in Northern France, Belgium, and Holland.

2. *La Gazzetta Musicale* of 11 February 1872, like the entire Italian press, reported a triumphal success.

Paul Draneht to Verdi

Cairo, 18 February 1872

Esteemed Signor Maestro,

H.H., the Khedive, wishing to offer you further proof of his appreciation for your most beautiful *Aida*, and out of consideration for your high merits, charges me to bestow on you the title of Commander of the Order of Osman and to send you the certificate with the appropriate insignia. It is with the greatest satisfaction of heart that I hasten to execute the gracious decree of my Sovereign, happy to have been chosen by him for such a joyous and distinguished task. On this occasion I take the liberty of advising you, illustrious Maestro, that this order of chivalry, created by the present Sultan, is held in such esteem, here and everywhere, that very rarely are even the lower degrees conferred, and that it is reserved solely for recognition of the highest merits, as is precisely the present situation.

The last mail has brought us the news of the most felicitous success achieved by your *Aida* at La Scala in Milan — news which had been awaited here with unspeakable anxiety, not because anyone had doubted a second success but because we were all longing to rejoice at your new triumph.

With regard to the Cairo theatre, we have already given ten performances of your stupendous musical masterwork, with ever-growing enthusiasm on the part of the audience and with even more lively ovations addressed to you.

Verdi to Giulio Ricordi

Genoa, 21 February 1872

Dear Giulio,

I am here. I won't go into the story of my displeasure at the very moment of my departure from Milan, but I thank you for the care you have demonstrated to me in everything and for everything. Thank you, excuse me, and let's talk business. [. . .]

From this moment on, you must [for Parma]:
1. Find out for sure if Capponi is recovered.
2. Find out about the chorus, since the one they had for *Don Carlos* would be impossible.
3. Come to an understanding at once concerning the diapason and the stage band with Rossi, who will probably be in Milan tomorrow or later.

They write me that as a conductor Rossi is the opposite of Ferrarini. It seems that he rushes the tempos so much that one no longer understands a thing. He would be worse than the other. [. . .]

Verdi to Camille Du Locle

Genoa, 21 February 1872

Dear Du Locle,

You will excuse me, I hope, that I didn't reply from Milan to many of your letters, but you can imagine how much there was to do during the last days of my stay in Milan. As for *Aida*, it seems to be doing well, if we must judge from the enormous box office receipts and from the increased price of admission. Ah, if you had been present at the fourth performance, you might have seen something good, at least in terms of execution. It was a beautiful evening! [. . .]

Verdi to Léon Escudier

Genoa, 21 February 1872

Dear Léon,

I arrived here last night from Milan. [. . .] As for the *Aida* in Milan, it is moving along with the greatest box office receipts. Certainly this is not a sure indication of the quality of a work of art, but it is an indication of a great interest; without that they would not continue to pay a high price to listen at the risk of being suffocated by the heat of <u>Senegal</u>.[1] [. . .]

1. Verdi probably refers to the heat of the gas lights emanating from the stage, particularly during the bright finale of Act II.

Verdi to Vincenzo Luccardi [1]

Genoa, 21 February 1872

Dear Luccardi,

Honest to God, I think that both you and Jacovacci must be half crazy. What second thoughts, what conflicting interests [should keep you] from giving *Aida* in Rome? Certainly without good elements *Aida* cannot be given and will not be given; but whenever a good impresario is able to find these elements, nothing can stand in his way. With the orchestra and the chorus you have in Rome at this time, it would really not be a good performance; but get an orchestra and chorus more or less like those in Milan, get singers like la <u>Stolz</u>, la <u>Waldmann, Pandolfini</u>, etc., a *mise-en-scène* like that of La Scala, and there will be no obstacles. But it is not possible in the fall.

I arrived last night from Milan, and Jacovacci will excuse me if I cannot reply right away; but in any case, I could only repeat the above. Everything depends on him and the possibility of finding the necessary elements.

1. Presumably in answer to a missing letter from Luccardi. The facsimile of this letter is published by Toye between pp. 156 and 157, but the location of the autograph is unknown.

Verdi to Giuseppe Piroli

Genoa, 22 [February] 1872

[. . .] Oh, the newspapers! Even when they want to say something good, they never say anything right! If artists are not guided by their own conscience and sensibility, poor them. For example, put a youngster between D'Arcais[1] and Filippi (who are even among the best critics, although always contradicting each other), and tell me, what should this youngster do, hearing one approve what the other condemns? [. . .]

1. Francesco D'Arcais (1830–90), composer and music critic of the newspaper *Opinione* in Rome.

Verdi to Cesare De Sanctis

Genoa, 22 February 1872

[. . .] I left Musella in Milan, and at the moment of my departure he had settled nothing, neither with la Stolz nor with la Waldmann nor with me, always assuring me that everything had been taken care of. The fact is that Musella would be very happy to find an excuse for calling it all off, casting the blame on one of us or on all of us. Certainly we are demanding, but neither more nor less than one must be in order to do things well.[1] I shall see what Ricordi writes me tomorrow, but I think he will probably tell me, "The negotiations are off."

It is certain that if Musella is forced to sign the Milan contracts, he will do the rest with ill will and badly. . . .

What will happen then? . . .

Then it will happen that I shall go to Naples, and if things are done badly, one fine day I shall say: "I suspend rehearsals and withdraw the scores," since it will be in my power to do so, and I shall return here, and . . . Amen.

Musella couldn't hope for anything better, since he would save both the fees and the very expensive production costs.

But it would mean trouble for the theatre if la Stolz and la Waldmann have signed to do *Don Carlos* and *Aida*.

Speak to whoever is necessary, then, so that in the end we do not have to regret an avoidable mistake. I have warned you, and with this I mean to warn everyone.

1. See Document XIII.

Verdi to Cesare De Sanctis

Genoa, 25 February 1872

[. . .] I know that la Stolz has definitely been signed; and by now Musella must have accepted la Waldmann's conditions (he would be wrong not to) and also Ricordi's. In spite of that the situation is still difficult, because Musella isn't sailing in our waters; unless there is a superior, strong hand to hold the rudder of his ship straight, things will not turn out well. Let me explain. As I have written to Torelli[1] and told Musella himself, Musella secretly despises *Don Carlos*, *Forza del Destino*, and *Aida*. If these operas did not exist, he would be happy; and if he could set a torch to them and to their author, so much the better. But since these damned operas do exist, he was forced — in spite of himself — to go to Milan and accept the conditions imposed on him, always cursing and hoping that a small, partial cataclysm might send us all to hell. With such a disposition on his part and such diffidence on our part, it is quite unlikely that things will turn out well. If Musella were a courageous and farsighted man, the thing to do now would be to forge ahead blindly along the path we have outlined and to produce (as they did at La Scala) a rare spectacle that would perhaps be unique in Italy. By so doing, art and the theatre are honored, and . . . the cash drawer is filled. But since Musella does not seem to be an impresario of that kind, he will try to make impossible savings on the other artists, on the chorus and orchestra, on the costumes, lights, sets, on everything. What will happen then? Then one fine day I shall say enough, withdraw my scores, and return straightway to Genoa. Musella would consider this a lucky break. But it could cause serious trouble. If la Stolz and la Waldmann have signed contracts to do *Don Carlos* and *Aida*, it may be that they would want their agreements upheld, and so it would be necessary to either close the theatre or be satisfied with mediocrity. And this would be a most grave and serious problem. Therefore, one of two things:

Either these artists come to Naples willing to give up *Don Carlos* and *Aida*, and ready to sing in other operas — fine, according to Musella's wishes. . . .

Or my operas will be done in a suitable manner and as I wish.

Advise Torelli, the Baron,[2] and, if you wish, the Mayor about everything.

This is February. There is time to arrange and solve everything. If there is trouble, you will not be able to complain about me, because I have foreseen it almost a year in advance and have warned you about it. All I want is that everything go well and that I be given the necessary materials. I'll take care of the rest.

1. In a letter which is missing, unless Verdi does not recall the exact contents of his letter to Torelli of 30 or 31 January 1872.

2. This important personage is presumably the same "Baron" that Verdi addresses in his letter of 6 February 1873. Although the name of this Baron is not recorded at the San Carlo Opera in Naples, he was probably the president of the board of directors there. He was apparently not the Baron Giovanni Genovese, who belonged to the circle of Verdi's friends in Naples and was suspected by De Sanctis of having joined the San Carlo's Commission in January 1874 to be entitled to a free seat. See *Carteggi*, I, p. 168n. (In quoting De Sanctis, Luzio spells the Baron's name Genovese, but it is Genovesi in the index, *Carteggi*, IV, p. 134.)

Verdi to Giulio Ricordi

Genoa, 28 February 1872

Dear Giulio,

Thank you for the news about *Aida*. [. . .]

Are you well agreed with Rossi concerning the formation of the chorus, the orchestra, and the secondary roles?[1] We need to think at once about the <u>diapason</u>, the straight trumpets, and the two (at least) harps. Answer me in detail about all this.

What else does Rossi want? I shall probably go to St. Agata soon, and then I shall write to Rossi telling him to betake himself to Borgo.[2] How should I address this letter to Rossi?

Again, I repeat, determine as soon as possible

The chorus
The orchestra
The two harps
The diapason
The six trumpets.

In fact it would be well if Rossi were to test the orchestra with the new diapason before beginning rehearsals. [. . .]

P.S. I paid Du Locle <u>200</u> francs for the *Aida* costume designs. They are about 10 francs each; that doesn't seem expensive to me. Put this sum to my credit. [. . .]

1. Verdi refers to the production of *Aida* in Parma.
2. Borgo St. Donnino, today's Fidenza.

Verdi to Alberto Mazzucato

Genoa, 29 February 1872

Dearest Mazzucato,

By now you probably know that *Aida* is to be given in Padua on the feast of the Saint. I would like our Faccio to be the musical director of that production, but I know that his commitments to the Milan Conservatory would not allow him the time. Therefore I turn to you, to whom the direction of that institute has now been deservedly entrusted, so that you may grant him a leave for that period. I ask this warmly of you — a little for myself, a little for *Aida*, but far more for the love of art. Whatever a score's merit may be and to whomever it may belong, I desire, I prefer, I consider it noble and nice that it be interpreted with conscience and intelligence (a very rare thing!). Faccio can completely satisfy this wish of mine, and I hope to receive a favorable reply from you.

Antonio Ghislanzoni to Giulio Ricordi

[*Probably* Lecco, 2 March 1872]

[. . .] Send me *Aida*. . . . I wait for *Aida*. And, along with the score, I want precise news about *Aida*. What do the Milanesi say about *Aida*? When can I come to Milan to hear *Aida*? [. . .]

What did Verdi say about the stupidities of some critics? Did he complain about me and my abrupt departure? I assure you, dear Signor Giulio, that if I had stayed in Milan one day longer, I would have choked to death from the nonsense and the long-winded speeches that I had to listen to. Once again, what do the gentlemen of Milan now say about *Aida*? [. . .]

Send *Aida* for voice and piano.

Send two or three librettos. [. . .]

And send to the devil the whole dog pack of journalists!

Verdi to the Mayor of Parma

Genoa, 2 March 1872

As I had the honor of telling you personally in Milan, I shall venture to take part in the majority of rehearsals for *Aida* in Parma, which is what matters and what is most useful.

I trust that the commission of that theatre will watch over the management to be sure that they provide all the elements suitable and necessary for achieving a good musical and dramatic performance.

You cannot ignore, illustrious Mayor, that the fine success in Milan is due in great part to the excellence and magnificence of the members of the orchestra and chorus, and of the *mise-en-scène*.

Verdi to Giulio Ricordi

Genoa, 9 March 1872

Dear Giulio,

Trouble had to come for the management of La Scala, and it has come! What a pity! But how many times did I shout "Do it, do it, do it . . . don't lose time!!" [. . .] In the theatre it is certainly necessary to try to do well; but rather than doing nothing at all, it is better still to do something poorly. After *Aida* they should not have been afraid of fiascos, and they should have mounted makeshift operas one after the other, at any cost!! But then, how is it possible that in one month, with a company that had nothing to do, they could not give *Freischütz*?!!! It is obvious that no one has any theatrical sense or energy. You will say: "What does it matter to you? . . . " Well, yes, it does matter to me, because in a season in which I played a part, I would have liked, later on, to hear them say: "In such and such a year, the opera did so well that the management earned . . . lire." For me that would have been the most pleasing compensation. This way the obligatory performances will not be given; the Mayor will not pay the quarter-salary, and the season will end like so many others!!! What a terrible pity! My poor wasted breath!

Now let's think about another production — the one in Parma, which, owing to the usual improvidence on the part of the management, board of directors, and conductors, could very well turn out badly if we don't watch out. (Witness *Don Carlos*!) I have written you before about this matter, and you have not answered me or have answered me vaguely. Now let's try to come to an understanding.

At St. Agata I learned from the townspeople that the chorus is poorly directed, old, and terrible, and that they were whistled every night in *Trovatore*, *Poliuto*, etc. (Imagine *Aida*!) I also learned that in the orchestra there are a number of boys who are students at the Carmine School and who are really too young, and that Rossi is in convulsions for fear he won't satisfy me and wants to confer with me about the interpretation, the tempos, the coloring, etc. What need is there of this if I go to Parma? In that event, all he will have to do is follow me. Lasina told Corticelli that he wanted to open on the 13th [of April] in order to give sixteen performances before the termination of the contract on the 20th of May. This is one of the usual managerial bestialities that bring everything to ruin. It is impossible to prepare it all between the 3rd and 11th (the dress rehearsal).

Let me conclude. Send for Lasina at once, and tell him that it will be impossible to open on the 13th, but that [if he wants] to open fairly soon, it will depend on him. He will have to make the following arrangements:

1. If the chorus is old and terrible, find some good young people. If they

are poorly taught, find another [chorus]master. Be sure that the opera is memorized by April 3rd.

2. The orchestra will be composed not of boys but of players, and the new chorusmaster will have experimented with a partial rehearsal before April 3rd. In fact, I would say right now, so that we shall have the necessary time if something should have to be adjusted.

3. The band with the Egyptian trumpets will be instructed by the 3rd.

4. Two or three excellent harps will be ready. Lasina will get together with Maestro Rossi, and there will be no fuss about this thing. This must be done and done at once, to avoid troubles and disorders later on.

You will tell me who will sing the secondary roles; and make sure that Pantaleoni knows his role before going to Parma. Answer me in detail about everything, and make haste. . . .

Verdi to Giulio Ricordi

Saturday [*Probably* Genoa, 9 March 1872]

Dear Giulio,

Just now (at three o'clock) I received your two letters.[1] [. . .]

I repeat again that now, more than ever, it is necessary to watch over the Parma affair, which has become one of prime importance. Tell me all that will be done regarding the chorus; it would be a good idea for Rossi to see to it that their study begins as soon as possible. Tell me who will perform the secondary roles.

Tell Pantaleoni to study the role [of Amonasro] well so he won't lose time in Parma; and if he is going to sing a performance in Milan, tell Faccio to rid him of that usual flabby accent in his singing. Don't forget that he is an Ethiopian king, a kind of Theodorus.

We, after all, shall have to do everything ourselves for Parma, since I have no faith in Lasina's activity and very little in the board of directors' or anyone else's. Certainly if things work out in Parma, it will only be because of our own efforts. No wonder our impresarios always foul things up. It's inevitable! What an asinine world! [. . .]

1. Missing.

Verdi to Vincenzo Torelli[1]

Genoa, 10 March 1872

Dear Torelli,

Fraschini will not work out for the operas or the management if he is under contract for isolated performances. Either the whole season or nothing.

If he does *Don Carlos*, for example, who will then do *Aida*? No, no. A management must not do such things.

Since I propose and insist on la Waldmann, what good is it to talk about la Ferni?[2]

I shall keep you informed about Aramburo.[3] As for the basses, I shall let you know another time.

Don't deceive yourself about the chorus; there is much to do. Everything with regard to the women, much with regard to the men.

Even the orchestra is not what you think. I would not know whom to propose as conductor. But tell me what is Serraro[4] like? [. . .]

Meanwhile allow me to extract a phrase from your letter: "After having toiled all by myself for this agreement", etc., etc.! But let's understand each other well: for whom is any favor being done here? I am also entering into this agreement, but I don't want anyone to toil for me. No, no! I have never asked for any favors, and I don't accept them from anyone. They made me an offer; I accepted. I imposed conditions: among others, the engagements of la Stolz and la Waldmann. La Stolz accepted and exchanged 120,000 francs in Cairo for 65,000 lire in Naples!! I shall spend some of my own!!! These are the favors received.

Let's conclude: Can you get me out of this mess? I shall even go so far to get rid of la Stolz and la Waldmann, who also seems to have signed. . . .

1. Presumably in answer to a missing letter about the season in Naples.
2. Either Virginia Ferni (1849–1934), Italian soprano, or her sister Carolina (1839–1926), Italian soprano and violinist.
3. Antonio Aramburo (1838–1912), Italian tenor. Early in 1872 he made his debut in Florence as Pollione in *Norma*. Later in his career he was to sing with some success in such cities as Milan, Paris, and Madrid.
4. Paolo Serrao (1830–1907), Italian composer and conductor. Since 1863 he had been a professor at the Conservatory of Music in Naples, and among his students were such notable composers as Cilea, Leoncavallo, Giordano, Martucci, and Mugnone. In March 1871 he had also served as a member of the commission over which Verdi presided in Florence. Serrao later aspired to become director of the Conservatory of Music in Parma; but his hopes were in vain, because Boito assumed the position to protect the salary of his dying friend Faccio.

Verdi to Giulio Ricordi

Tuesday [Genoa, 12 March 1872]

Dear Giulio,

It is peculiar that I have not yet received a reply to my most important letter of the 9th, in which I told you at length about the arrangements to be made for Parma. It is even more peculiar since, in your dispatch of the 10th, you told me: "We shall take care of Parma. I shall answer." No answer and no provision!!! Stranger still, [I wrote you] ten or twelve days ago, always about the Parma affair and about an appointment to be made with Rossi, and you never answered me!! What does all this mean? Weather permitting, I shall probably go to St. Agata on Thursday morning. Send me a reply in duplicate, here and at St. Agata. [. . .]

Verdi to Vincenzo Torelli

[Genoa,] 13 March 1872

[. . .] In a few minutes I leave for St. Agata and have little time to write; but I shall return on Monday. Meanwhile I shall discuss some of the more urgent matters.

If Musella is running about like a chicken with its head cut off, so much the worse, or so much the better. . . . What does it matter! Meanwhile it seems to me there is no time to lose. . . .

[. . .] I cannot, and must not, be anything but a composer of operas. As such I can help you put your San Carlo back on its feet and give you a repertoire for two years. [. . .]

Verdi to Paul Draneht [1]

Genoa, 22 March 1872

Excellency,

Together with the insignia of the Order of Osman, which H.H., the Khedive, has seen fit to bestow on me, I have received your esteemed letter, which informs me in the most courteous manner both of the awarding of this order and of the Sovereign's satisfaction with me. I am proud and full of gratitude!

I ask Y.E., who worked with such zeal and intelligence so that everything would contribute to the fortunate success of *Aida*, to deign to convey my gratitude and devotion to this Sovereign, who opens his Kingdom to the arts and sciences, an example worthy of imitation.

1. In answer to Draneht's letter of 18 February 1872.

Verdi to Giulio Ricordi

Genoa, 28 March 1872

[. . .] I see in the *Pungolo* [1] that Pantaleoni tried to make the King of Ethiopia a different type from that of Pandolfini [2] . . . which means he made that fierce character look spineless and flabby, just as I had expected. And this is called creating?!! It's for the critics to say. It's always the same story! And they carry on so much about art and creation whenever some imbecile is given a chance to create!! Long live the critics!! And after the duet he was called back three times? An honor never granted Pandolfini, although he, in spite of a few provincialisms, sang very well! Long live the audience!! What a great thing the theatre is!!! [. . .]

P.S. I received your letter, now that it is three o'clock. I shall leave what I have written above, and if Pantaleoni is a good Amonasro, so much the better. I shall listen to him, but I'm afraid I shall find him soft and flabby, just like his face.

For heaven's sake, find a King for Parma at once. I repeat that the rehearsals must absolutely begin on the 3rd if we expect to open at least by the 20th. Then I want to go to the country!!! [. . .]

1. A newspaper in Naples, with editions in Rome and Milan.
2. Adriano Pantaleoni had replaced Francesco Pandolfini in the role of Amonasro when La Scala gave additional performances of *Aida* following the close of the regular carnival season.

Verdi to Cesare De Sanctis

Genoa, 29 March 1872

[. . .] *Aida* is almost finished at La Scala. I won't say it has been a success, but I will say it brought in a pile of cash!!! It's a historical fact.

That's what it means to do things well. [. . .]

Verdi to Léon Escudier

Genoa, 30 March 1872

[. . .] The performances of *Aida* as part of the theatrical season [at La Scala] ended on the 24th because Pandolfini and Maini left for Seville the next day. The performances were always good, the house was always sold out, and the box office was extraordinary. This is the plain and simple story, apart from the value of the opera. Although the season has finished, the management wanted to give a few more performances, and I think they still give *Aida* tonight and tomorrow night. The opera won't gain anything, but the management will pocket several thousand lire in addition.

You are quite right in saying that *Aida* has its place at the Opéra; but success is impossible with those elements. It's easy for the French to say: "The Opéra . . . the *mise-en-scène*, etc., etc." This is all well and good, but I am ever more convinced that for musical works you must first of all have a musical performance: fire, spirit, muscle, and enthusiasm. . . . All this is lacking at the Opéra; and it will never be there as long as they trot along at the usual pace. You will say to me, "And what would they need?" Very little. A musical person at the head of it all, strong and powerful, as·Costa once was; and the obedience of the company.

Personally I have made enough experiments at the Opéra, and I don't believe in it any more! . . . Trust me that I speak a great truth! . . .

Addio, my dear Léon! Write me at Parma, where I shall be on the 3rd of April. Even in Parma, with more modest elements than those of La Scala and the Opéra, I shall get some result. I am almost certain of this. They have faith in me, and they do what I want. You will see that I am not deceiving myself.

Verdi to Giulio Ricordi

Genoa, 30 March 1872

Dear Giulio,

By God, I'm not the one who believes the newspapers, and you shouldn't even suspect it!!! Certainly if Pantaleoni had interpreted the role differently from Pandolfini, he could not have done it well. But you assure me that he is a perfect copy of Pandolfini, and that is fine. . . . And how was there no time to correct his gross defects? . . . And why didn't you tell me anything about the second performance?

[. . .] When I am in Parma on the 3rd, send me a copy of the contract with Lasina[1] so that I may know how far I can go. . . .

1. See Document XIII.

Verdi to Giulio Ricordi

Genoa, 31 March 1872

Dear Giulio,

For your information I shall be at St. Agata tomorrow morning and in Parma on 3 April!

So this evening is the last for *Aida*!! I can breathe again! Nothing more will be said about it, or at least only a few words. Maybe some new insult, accusing me of Wagnerism, and then . . . *Requiescat in pace*!

And now have the kindness to tell me what sacrifices this opera of mine has cost the management. Don't be shocked by the question; I must assume there were sacrifices, since none of the gentlemen, at least with regard to all the work I did and the many thousands of lire I spent, has said to me, "Thank you, dog!'' Or should I perhaps thank them for having accepted and performed that poor *Aida*, which earned 165,000 lire in twenty performances, in addition to the subscription and the gallery? . . . Ah Shakespeare, Shakespeare! The great master of the human heart! . . . But I shall never learn!!

Tito Ricordi to Verdi

Milan, 6 April 1872

Dearest friend,

I am sending you the first letter I have written since the moment the pains of my grave illness ceased, and I am relieved to inform you of my nearly complete recovery.

I may now have to undergo only one more operation, which, the doctor said, will be done for precaution rather than necessity.

This doctor of mine has managed things so well that he allowed me to enjoy the last two performances of your *Aida*.

I do not recall a similar enjoyment in many a year. These two nights truly crowned the colossal triumph of your great opera, inciting our public to all the manifestations of delirious enthusiasm that can only be stirred by the greatest masterworks.

Let me also express my deepest gratitude, once again, for the endless and extraordinary trouble you took with the *mise-en-scène* of this opera at La Scala, and for the trouble you are now about to undertake in Parma, and later in Naples as well.

Whatever I may do, I shall never be able to repay you for your generosity!

If, as I fear, because of my frequent and serious physical indispositions, I am destined to disappear fairly soon from the face of this earth, please remember that my most ardent prayer is that you may continue to show the same inestimable benevolence toward my Giulio and my other sons as you have always had for your old admirer and friend

Tito Ricordi

[P.S.] Please give my affectionate regards to your excellent and incomparable Signora Peppina.

Verdi to Giulio Ricordi

Parma, 6 April 1872

Dear Giulio,

I received your letter and a copy of the contract.[1] I wanted to know if I could request a closed dress rehearsal. It says nothing about it!

I have heard the band with the six trumpets, and they already play rather well. I think it will be better than in Milan.

The props are also better than those in Milan.

The stage machinery for the last scene is better too.

Capponi is better still. The worst thing will be the secondary roles, and, I fear, the chorus too.

Pantaleoni, well! He'll do, but he should do better!

The orchestra may not have the _fullness_ and the _size_ of the one in Milan, but they will probably play better. Perhaps they are better disciplined and less pretentious!

Once again, I believe the third act is the best in terms of _drama_. I only want to rework the instrumentation of that horrible _cabaletta_, which has attracted so much advice, so much wisdom, and so much benevolence from your critics!! Therefore send me the original of the _cabaletta_. We shall have the parts revised here, since it is such a small matter.

La Stolz received news of her mother's death as soon as she arrived here! So she has not yet rehearsed. . . .

P.S. Note well that in the vocal parts, among other things, the two lines of the recitative added for _Aida_ in the final duet have not yet been revised, nor has the final strophe for Amneris.

1. Both Giulio Ricordi's letter and the copy of the contract for the production of _Aida_ in Parma are missing. Document XIII represents another copy of that contract.

Giulio Ricordi to Verdi

Milan, 7 April 1872

What blockheads we are! It is really true! We have forgotten the clause concerning the dress rehearsal, and we have read and reread the contract without being aware of this omission! I am sorry; but I should think you will be able to obtain whatever you want from the president of the theatre. [. . .]

Faccio is seriously ill and threatened by typhoid fever; I hope this bad news will not be true! [. . .]

Verdi to Léon Escudier

Parma, 15 April 1872

Dear Léon,

I am at the height of rehearsals for _Aida_, and you can imagine how much there is to do! [. . .] We began on the 3rd and it opens on the 20th. It seems impossible, but it's true! And what is even stranger, it will be a good performance musically: one of those live and passionate performances that you never have at the Opéra. Du Locle said he found some fault with the *mise-en-scène* in Milan.[1] . . . Surely if one wants the drama and music to be a pretext for a display of scenery and costumes, he is right. But if the scenery and costumes are to serve the drama (which they should), then the *mise-en-scène* in Milan was more than sufficient. [. . .] For myself and for my music I prefer these performances rather than yours. [. . .]

1. Du Locle probably objected to the presence of such elements as the beards of the priests, which appear in the sketch on p. 567 in Document XII.

Verdi to Giulio Ricordi

Monday [Parma, 15 April 1872]

Dear Giulio,

As I told you yesterday in my telegram,[1] *Aida* cannot be given until Saturday, and it is Magnani's fault. If the sets are beautiful, the entire *mise-en-scène* will be good. I think the costumes are beautiful; the props are very beautiful; the entire technical department is the best. The musical part is more or less like that in Milan, and it would have been much, much better if Rossi had known to put the orchestra into better shape by getting rid of those who are too old and those who are too young. What a shame! I was hoping to produce a truly beautiful orchestral performance, but it will only be mediocre — like that in Milan. Of course you will say "I am satisfied!!" No, no: many, many effects are missing!!

The dress rehearsal will be Thursday evening. Are you still planning to come on Wednesday? If so, at what time? Wire ahead for a room. You won't be able to get one on the first floor, since the best rooms are taken; but you can get an adequate double room on the second floor. Bear well in mind that hotels here are not like those in Milan, but, of course, you spend much less here.

1. Missing.

Verdi to Cesare De Sanctis

Parma, 17 April 1872

Dear Cesarino,

The *Aida* rehearsals have not only begun, but they are finished! The dress rehearsal is left, and we open on Saturday!

[. . .] What bigwigs you are!!! The things you tell me about melody and harmony! Forget about it with Wagner!! On the contrary, if one cared to listen and understand well, one would find just the opposite . . . the total opposite. What can it matter to the public, then, whether or not I am the author of

Rigoletto, *Ballo in Maschera*, or even *Don Carlos* which is more melodious than the other two scores? . . . What do these schools ever mean, these prejudices about singing, harmony, Germanism, Italianism, Wagnerism, etc., etc.?

There is something more in music. . . . There is the music! . . . The public shouldn't concern themselves with the means the artist applies! . . . They should not have academic prejudices. . . . If [the music] is nice, let them applaud. If it isn't, let them whistle! . . . That's all. Music is universal. The imbeciles and pedants wanted to find and invent schools and systems!!! I wish the public would judge from a high ground — not with the miserable views of the journalists, maestros, and piano players, but from their own impressions and nothing else! . . .

You understand, impressions, impressions, and nothing else. . . .

Verdi to Camille Du Locle[1]

Parma, 17 April 1872

Dear Du Locle,

I received your letter a little late because it was forwarded from Genoa . . . and I am answering you a little late because I hardly have time to breathe. We are in the midst of the last rehearsals for *Aida*, and you can well imagine how busy I am. *Aida* will open Saturday, and the performance will be more or less like that in Milan, musically as well as dramatically. [. . .]

You are translating *Aida*? Perhaps for the Opéra? Ahi, ahi! . . . I wouldn't care at all for such an agreement! I accept the *mise-en-scène* in that theatre (although it is too pretentious and <u>gross</u> for me), but I absolutely do not accept what is done there musically. They are bloodless in that theatre! Oh no, no! Let's stay as we are! . . . I am quite happy here! . . .

1. In answer to a letter from Du Locle of 6 April 1872, in which Du Locle wrote that "the translation of *Aida* is proceeding." (Autograph: St. Agata)

Verdi to Cesare De Sanctis

Parma, [21 April 1872]

Dear Cesarino,

Last night, *Aida* excellent.[1] Good *mise-en-scène* and scenery, good orchestra, very good chorus.

In other words, a rare success. So <u>amen</u>.

I received a letter from Musella yesterday, but I won't reply because I don't like that sloppy tone he assumes with me. Please tell him, however, that a <u>full agreement</u> with Ricordi concerning the signing of the artists absolutely does not exist. Ricordi has suggested some names and proposed signing them, but, after all, they must be <u>accepted</u> by me. Furthermore, in the list of names sent to me the following are missing:

    1. The baritone.

    2. Two basses.

    3. The tenor, since I shall not accept Bulterini[2] until I have heard him.

[. . .]

    1. The cast of the first performance in Parma, conducted by Giovanni Rossi and staged by Verdi, included Teresa Stolz (Aida), Maria Waldmann (Amneris), Giuseppe Capponi (Radames), and Adriano Pantaleoni (Amonasro).

    2. Carlo Bulterini (1839–1912), Italian tenor. Between 1863 and 1888 he sang a wide range of leading roles in Italy and in such cities as Lisbon, Seville, London, Buenos Aires, Rio de Janeiro, St. Petersburg, Santiago, and Warsaw.

Giuseppina Verdi to Franco Faccio

Calling Card   Parma, 23 April 1872

    Thank you, dear Faccio, for the interest you have taken in *Aida* . . . and in <u>Amneris!</u> . . . Even though a bear, my bear[1] is deeply grateful as I am for this proof of affection. I have heard from the Ricordis how you have overcome the danger of a grave illness. I congratulate you and wish you the health, fortune, and happiness you deserve in every way. We are leaving in a moment. Verdi greets you, and I cordially take your hand.

    1. Giuseppina Verdi's affectionate characterization of her husband.

Camille Du Locle to Verdi[1]

Paris, 26 April 1872

    [. . .] Yes I am working on the translation of this beautiful *Aida*. At least in this manner I can still be a little with you. Once translated, *Aida* will become whatever you wish, and I shall not be the one to torment you with entrusting it to the *grande boutique*. [. . .]

    1. In answer to Verdi's letter of 17 April 1872.

Verdi to Cesare De Sanctis

St. Agata, 26 April 1872

    [. . .] I do not want to <u>excuse myself</u> for being the <u>follower</u> of anyone. I am what I am! Everyone is perfectly free to think of me as he wishes.

You are, I repeat, the bigwigs with your Italian music! . . . No, no, there is no Italian music, or German, or Turkish . . . there is only MUSIC!! Don't bother me, then, with these definitions. It's useless. I write as I see fit and as I feel. I believe in neither the past nor the present. I detest all schools, because they lead. to conventionalism. I idolize no individual, but I love beautiful music when it is truly beautiful, whoever composed it.

"Progress of art" — another empty phrase!! It goes without saying! If the author is a man of genius, he will make art progress without seeking it and without willing it. [. . .]

Verdi to Opprandino Arrivabene

St. Agata, 27 April 1872

[. . .] As you know, *Aida* did well,[1] and they write me that the third and fourth performances went very well with packed houses. Therefore let's leave in peace the *cabaletta*[2] that bothers you so much. It is certainly no masterwork, but there are many, many others much worse. Only today has it become fashionable to shout and to want no *cabalettas*. It's just as much a mistake as in earlier times when they wanted nothing but *cabalettas*. They shout so much against the conventional, and yet they abandon one convention only to embrace another! Oh! the big sheep!!

Besides, this *cabaletta*, which was disliked in Milan, makes a certain effect in Parma; and in Cairo it was repeated over and over every night *Aida* was performed. [. . .]

1. Verdi refers to the production in Parma.
2. Verdi refers to "*Si, fuggiam da queste mura*" from Act III.

Verdi to Giuseppe Piroli

St. Agata, 27 April 1872

Dear Piroli,

You were wrong in not coming to Parma. Apart from the music it is a good production. More or less as in Milan. Scenery better than in Milan. Chorus a little less so. Orchestra is all right, although very much deteriorated. They are old and they play old. Taken as a whole it's good, and they write me that the third and fourth performances were very good with the house fuller than on the first night!! [. . .]

I shall remain here until it's time to go to Naples. Ah, how very, very much there will be to do there!! In Milan they understand and they go ahead. In Parma they are somewhat like dunces; but once goaded they also go ahead. In

Naples they are like the French in politics and war — they think they are the best in the world, they are petulant, and they holler loudly. They can holler as much as they want, but I am going to tell them the bitter truth; and if they were once the first in music, their vanity has blinded them, and they have not seen, and do not see, that we have come a long way. [. . .]

Antonio Ghislanzoni to Giulio Ricordi

Lecco, 30 April 1872

Dear Signor Giulio,
First and foremost I thank you for having sent me a telegram from Parma to inform me of the splendid success of *Aida*. As it goes from theatre to theatre, this opera will be received with growing enthusiasm; and when it is given again in Milan, the same will happen to it as happened to *Ballo in Maschera* and *Forza del Destino*. It will earn even the vote of the obtuse and malignant few who did not understand or did not want to understand it. Please let me know where Maestro Verdi is staying so that I may send him my congratulations. [. . .]

Giulio Ricordi to Verdi

Milan, 1 May 1872

[. . .] To get precise news about Bulterini, I asked Monti[1] to go and hear him. He went to Ferrara at once, accompanied, I believe, by two adjutants in the field, Liverani[2] and Ivanoff.[3] Here is his report:
"Powerful voice, good intonation, intelligent phrasing. He takes half a dozen b naturals and holds them as long as he wants. He looks good on the stage . . . [*illegible*]. He has lungs of steel; he is better than Capponi. He enjoys drinking."
This seems to be a good account, and if it is so, we can be satisfied.
The measurements of La Scala are as follows:

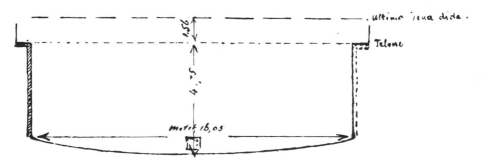

With regard to your well-taken remarks, we have broken off the negotiations for Trieste, and we have not entered into those for Florence, which have just been presented to us.

But there are others I consider most important — those for Germany. For some time the Baron de Loën, intendant of the theatre in Weimar, has been asking me through Maestro Raff[4] for permission to give *Aida* in that theatre. I seized upon this occasion to clearly tell off these German gentlemen, who have always mishandled our music. I detailed the artistic necessities for *Aida* and expressed my doubts that they would be able to give it well. It's useless to dwell here on what I wrote and rewrote, and what they answered me. All my conclusions were that *Aida* could not be given in Germany without serious artistic guarantees to ensure a perfect performance, which would be a true artistic event, worthy of the opera and its author. Judging from the answers received, it appears that they want to consider the matter seriously. They would like to give the opera in September, on the occasion of the wedding of the Crown Prince.[5] In six or seven days Raff will come to Milan so that he can tell me more about the resources of that theatre, which actually ranks among the first in Germany. I understand the supreme and immense importance of the first production of *Aida* outside Italy, yet our consent will be out of the question if the quality of the performance cannot be ensured. If the artistic means are good, do you think we should settle with Weimar? . . . I would send Faccio to supervise the performance; and, if you think it useful, I would also go to oversee the *mise-en-scène* so that the excellent production one has the right to expect can really be achieved. A true success would be such a beautiful thing!

Kindly honor me with your thoughts about this so that I may know how to conduct myself with Raff when he comes to Milan.

Meanwhile I beg you to give a thousand greetings to Signora Peppina and to continue your very dear benevolence toward me.

1. Luigi Monti, representative of the House of Ricordi in Bologna.

2. Domenico Liverani (1805–77), Italian composer, conductor, and clarinetist. A close friend of Rossini, who nicknamed him "Menghino" and on 12 November 1842 warmly recommended him to his friend Sir Michael Costa in London, Liverani was appointed professor of clarinet at the Liceo Comunale in Bologna in the same year. See Herbert Weinstock, *Rossini* (New York: Alfred A. Knopf, 1968), pp. 227–28.

3. Transliteration of Nikolày Ivanov (1810–77), Russian tenor. With Glinka, he won a scholarship to study in Italy and Ivanov remained there. Following his debut at the San Carlo Opera in Naples in 1832 he enjoyed a successful career during the 1830s and 1840s — especially in operas by Bellini, who held him in high esteem. So did Rossini, who affectionately addressed him as "Nicolino" and on 28 January 1845 thanked Verdi with a check of approximately $700 for an *aria di bravura* he had composed for his friend. See Weinstock, pp. 233–34.

4. Joseph Joachim Raff (1822–82), Swiss composer and conductor, and a close friend of his prominent German colleagues Hans von Bülow and Ferdinand Hiller.

5. This wedding was apparently postponed. On 26 August 1873 Carl August von Sachsen-Weimar-Eisenach (1844–94), heir to the reigning Grand Duke, married a relative, the Princess

Pauline von Sachsen-Weimar-Eisenach, daughter of Prince Hermann von Sachsen-Weimar-Eisenach and the Princess Auguste von Württemberg.

Verdi to Giulio Ricordi

Thursday [St. Agata, 2 May 1872]

Dear Giulio,

I have received the measurements of La Scala. Now let me know if the Padua contract requires the usual pitch and if there will be a closed dress rehearsal with costumes, scenery, etc. [. . .]

For my own part I am not at all anxious to see *Aida* done in Germany at this time, and I would heartily renounce that high honor. Keep this in mind and consider it as gospel: In Germany *Aida* will be interpreted (I say "interpreted") terribly — as my operas have always been and as all Italian operas usually are. If it is done later, fine; but at this time it would displease me. To tell you the truth I am sorry it is being done in Padua before Naples. I am not worried about the [production] elements in Padua, but I am worried about the lack of discipline and the disorganization of the company. In Parma I have just now seen what the problem is! No one has courage; no one is capable of controlling the company! It must be worse yet in Padua, judging by what even the members of the commission and city hall told me when they visited me the other day.

My idea, then, would be not to do *Aida* anywhere else before Naples (and, if I were able, I would even avoid Padua). After Naples you can do whatever you want. I would never be in favor of sending Faccio to Germany. That would reawaken a horde of wounded feelings! They also make a lot of demands for the *mise-en-scène*. In that respect you would do more harm than good; but you could be most helpful, if, having seen the rehearsals, you could (provided the contract is well made) cast an absolute veto, should the circumstances require it.

But is this affair of interest to your firm? Even if it were, this doesn't seem to be the opportune moment — on the occasion of the wedding of a prince!

I think it's something to discuss later on, and perhaps I could also suggest some ideas to you. Meanwhile our interest is to see that *Aida* is done in Padua and Naples as it was in Milan and Parma.

Verdi to Giulio Ricordi

Thursday[1] [*Probably* St. Agata, 3 May 1872]

Dear Giulio,

Night gives good counsel, but I have not changed yesterday's. Today more than ever I approve of what I wrote you yesterday. No, no. *Aida* would not be performed in Germany with the emphasis and intentions that I want and that are indispensable to my music. I am aware of some little details which many times bring about the desired effect. At any rate I have often heard my operas in countries other than Italy and in Germany itself. I know what to believe. I heartily renounce this glory.

1. Verdi was apparently in error; he seems to have written this letter on Friday.

Verdi to Giulio Ricordi

St. Agata, 10 May 1872

Dear Giulio,

Yesterday I received from Reggio (Emilia) a letter which is so amusing that I am sending it to you, asking you to carry out the commission I am about to give you. Here is the letter:

Signor Verdi *Gentilissimo*

Reggio (Emilia), 7 May 1872

On the second of this month, attracted by the sensation your opera *Aida* was making, I went to Parma. Half an hour before the performance began I was already in my seat, No. 120. I admired the scenery, listened with great pleasure to the excellent singers, and took pains to let nothing escape me. After the performance was over, I asked myself whether I was satisfied. The answer was in the negative. I returned to Reggio and, on the way back in the railroad carriage, I listened to the verdicts of my fellow travelers. Nearly all of them agreed that *Aida* was a work of the highest rank.

Thereupon I conceived a desire to hear it again, and so on the fourth I returned to Parma. I made the most desperate efforts to obtain a reserved seat, and there was such a crowd that I had to spend 5 lire to see the performance in comfort.

I came to the following conclusion: the opera contains absolutely nothing thrilling or electrifying, and if it were not for the magnificent scenery, the audience would not sit through it to the end. It will fill the théatre a few more times and then gather dust in the archives. Now, my dear Signor Verdi, you can imagine my regret at having spent 32 lire for these two performances. Add to this the aggravating circumstance that I am dependent on my family, and you will understand that this money preys on my mind like a terrible specter. Therefore I address myself frankly and openly to you so that you may send me this sum. Here is the account:

Railroad: one way	2.60 lire
Railroad: return trip	3.30 "
Theatre	8.00 "
Disgustingly bad dinner at the station	2.00 "
	15.90 lire
Multiplied by 2	×2 "
	31.80 lire

In the hope that you will extricate me from this dilemma, I am yours sincerely,

Bertani

My address: Bertani, Prospero; Via St. Domenico, No. 5.[1]

———————

Imagine, if to protect a child of a family from the horrible specters that disturb his peace, I should not be disposed to pay that little bill he has brought to my attention! Therefore by means of your representative or a bank, please reimburse 27.80 lire in my name to this Signor Prospero Bertani, 5 Via St. Domenico. This isn't the entire sum for which he asks me, but . . . to pay for his dinner too! . . . No. He could very well have eaten at home!!!!! Of course he will send you a receipt for that sum and a note, by which he promises never again to go to hear my new operas, to avoid for himself the danger of other specters and for me the farce of paying him for another trip. [. . .]

1. Prospero Bertani's letters of 7 and 15 May 1872, published in *La Gazzetta Musicale* of 19 May 1872, are given in Edward Downes's translation. Courtesy Vienna House Publishers, New York.

Giulio Ricordi to Verdi

Milan, 16 May 1872

As soon as I received your last letter I wrote our correspondent in Reggio, who found the famous Signor Bertani, paid the money, and got the proper receipt!!! I am copying the letter and the receipt for the newspaper, and I shall return everything to you tomorrow. Oh, what fools there are in this world! But this is the best one yet!

The correspondent in Reggio writes me: "I sent immediately for Bertani, who came to me right away. Advised of the reason for my invitation, he first showed surprise, but then he said: 'If Maestro Verdi reimburses me, this means that he has found what I wrote him to be correct. It's my duty to thank him, however, and I ask you to do it for me.' "

This one is even better!!

Pleased to have discovered this rarity of the species, I send the most cordial greetings to you and Signora Peppina.

Prospero Bertani to Verdi

15 May 1872

I, the undersigned, certify herwith that I have received the sum of 27.80 lire from Maestro Giuseppe Verdi, as reimbursement of my expenses for a trip to Parma to hear the opera *Aida*. The Maestro felt it was fair that this sum should be restored to me, since I did not find his opera to my taste. At the same time it is agreed that I shall undertake no trip to hear any of the Maestro's new operas in the future, unless he takes all the expenses upon himself, whatever my opinion of his work may be.

In confirmation whereof I have affixed my signature,

Bertani, Prospero

Verdi to the Mayor of Padua

St. Agata, 18 May 1872

In truth the letter it pleased you to write me[1] was so beautiful, dignified, and courteous that I was moved by reading it; and, unable to reply as you wished, I had to wait a few days to find the courage to reply negatively. Asking your forgiveness for that delay, I confess that I am mortified and sad that I cannot accept your invitation, so graciously expressed, to come to Padua to assist with the rehearsals for *Aida*. But how can I allow a change, so to speak, in my habits of so many years without a special reason? That is why, Your Honor, I ask you to accept, with my apologies, my gratitude for the exquisite consideration shown for me.

1. Missing.

Camille Du Locle to Verdi

Paris, 21 May 1872

[. . .] Nuitter[1] and I are working on the translation of *Forza*, and we are preparing that of *Aida*. Oh how happy I would be if *Aida* could be given one day, and soon, in Paris, as I imagine it! [. . .]

1. Charles Nuitter, French librettist and archivist of the Opéra in Paris.

Giulio Ricordi to Verdi

Milan, 21 May 1872

Raff was in Parma to hear *Aida* and is enthusiastic about it. Today he was here, and we talked for <u>three hours</u> continuously about his *mise-en-scène* in Weimar. If I had to tell you the thousand reasons given me by Raff, it would take <u>six</u> hours and you would send me to the devil!!!!! . . .

I can tell you frankly that I am convinced of our German's true enthusiasm and his desire to produce this opera splendidly. Do they have the means? . . . I think they do. [. . .]

You opposed the production in Weimar . . . and now I have the courage to talk to you about it again! . . . What are you going to say about me? Consider, Maestro, that if I have this courage, it's because I am sure that we shall never again have such a favorable chance to launch *Aida* in Germany. [. . .]

Verdi to Giuseppe Piroli

St. Agata, 5 June 1872

You were wrong not to go to Parma, because you would have seen a beautiful production and heard a beautiful performance! The crowd was immense, such as has never before been seen in Parma. [. . .]

As for the *Aida* to be performed in Rome, Luccardi is not behaving like a good friend. He knows how operas are massacred in Rome, and he should not insist on this one. When theatres are in as poor shape as the ones in Rome are, reforms are not made overnight. Jacovacci is from the old school and thinks that successes can be had by putting two or three well-known names on the playbill. That was true once with *cavatina* operas, but not now. He doesn't realize that the successes in Milan and Parma were due in great part to the chorus and the orchestra and to the splendid *mise-en-scène*. [. . .]

Verdi to Vincenzo Luccardi

St. Agata, 5 June 1872

My dear Luccardi,

I am sorry that you are taking so much interest in this *Aida* to be given in Rome. But don't you think that if Ricordi saw [the possibility of] a success, he would be happy to [let them] do the opera and make money? A controversy has arisen over this matter, and that is very irritating, because in the final accounting, as long as the right of ownership exists, everyone must be the master of his own stuff. If Ricordi has withheld *Aida*, it means that he believes it is in his best interest not to give it now. They scream about monopoly! . . . But monopoly of what? . . . By God, what a monopoly that must be! The monopoly of a shopkeeper consists of his selling his own merchandise and Ricordi's of making his <u>rentals</u>. If he sometimes refuses, it is because he is afraid of jeopardizing his property. That's all.[1]

Up here we have the lowest opinion of the manner in which productions are mounted in Rome (after all, look at the papers), and that is the real motive for the refusal of *Aida*. I know well that Jacovacci promises the sun and the moon, but when theatres have been in bad shape for so long, when there are no longer good choruses or good orchestras, improvements are not made overnight. He thinks that once he has put two or three well-known names on the playbill he has done everything. But he doesn't know that successes in Milan and Parma are due mainly to the imposing chorus and orchestra, to the perfect performance of the ensembles, and to the splendid *mise-en-scène*. [. . .]

It isn't fair to compromise our opera to accommodate an impresario, just because he may have addressed a few words about his particular interests to some authority. When *Aida* has played two or three other theatres, then, *à la grâce de Dieu*, they can massacre it in Rome too.

Addio, my dear Luccardi, and tell me if I'm right or wrong. Besides, why all this mania to hear *Aida*? What if I hadn't written it? And then, why should I, the owner, not do with it according to my own judgment? How about that? Are we artists to serve the moods of the managers?

1. In *La Gazzetta Musicale* of 3 March 1872 Giulio Ricordi published a letter he had addressed to Vincenzo Jacovacci in Rome on 28 February 1872 in answer to a missing letter from that impresario. "First and foremost you must realize," Ricordi writes, "that I do not buy operas with the idea of burying them in my archives; and that if I am careful in permitting their performance, I am not doing it out of caprice but out of love for art, out of respect for the authors, and to protect my own interests. [. . .] It must be in my interest and it is the illustrious Maestro's wish to achieve perfect performances of his *Aida* [. . .] at least in the first productions. [. . .] And the production of *Aida* in the capital of Italy is too important for the Maestro and for me to run the risk of a performance not being under his personal supervision. [. . .]" In the same issue of *La Gazzetta Musicale* Giulio Ricordi counters the Roman critic Franco D'Arcais's arguments in favor of an *Aida* production in Rome.

Giulio Ricordi to Verdi

Milan, 7 June 1872

You may have thought I went to live on the moon. Please forgive my long silence, the result of a thousand silly little things!

I would be very sorry to let *Aida* be massacred in Rome, especially after its production in Naples. It will certainly be massacred with those ——— talents and the artistic means at the disposal of the Italian capital! In any event — to get rid of so many nuisances — if you want to appease Jacovacci, then let us do this business too.

In Weimar they were very sorry not to have gotten what they wanted;[1] now we have a request from Berlin, but our answer is that they should wait a while. I am secretly convinced, however, that the time has now come for Italian art to claim the part of real glory that awaits it in Germany. I shall try to conclude something quite good for next year.

Faccio writes me many details about the orchestra and chorus in Padua, and he seems to be rather pleased. When things are on the way, he will write you directly. You absolutely do not want to burden yourself with another sacrifice by going to Padua? On the one hand, you have a thousand, even two thousand reasons. On the other, you are Verdi!

    1. On the third page of this letter Verdi writes: "I go to Veimar [*sic*]! You must be crazy!"

Verdi to Giulio Ricordi

Tuesday [St. Agata, 11 June 1872]

Dear Giulio,

    I have received your *Gazzetta*![1] More about *Aida*!! Oh this opera is certainly upsetting them in Bologna![2]

They come to Milan to hear *Aida*, and they needlessly write three big articles.

Pedrotti's[3] opera is given in Modena — and they bring *Aida* into it!

L'Africaine is given in Reggio — and more about *Aida*!

They even take a bow to Bertani!!!!!!!

For the love of God don't talk about it anymore, and don't defend me anymore. Rather say that if *Aida* is an abortion, [*illegible*], the shabbiest opera in existence, it's of little importance. The world won't come to an end because of that! All that will suffer will be the reputation of the author. Certainly neither the management in Milan nor the one in Parma have suffered any damage. I hope, then, you won't suffer because of it either. So? . . .

    1. *La Gazzetta Musicale* of 9 June 1872.

    2. Verdi refers to Angelo Mariani and his followers in Bologna, where *Lohengrin* had been given in November 1871 and where *Aida* was not to be performed until 4 October 1877.

    3. Carlo Pedrotti, Italian composer and conductor, whose *Olema la Schiava* (with a libretto by Piave) had received its first performance in Modena on 4 May 1872.

Giulio Ricordi to Giuseppina Verdi

Milan, 11 June 1872

[. . .] Now, Signora Peppina, a few words seriously and in secret.

The Weimar project, although suspended for this year, is still alive, and they would like *Aida* for next year. At the same time requests are made by Berlin and Vienna. If I considered material interests, the Weimar arrangement would be settled right away and so also, perhaps, the requests from Berlin and Vienna. But I would like to make of it a truly artistic event, a glorious one for our dear Verdi and all of Italy. The timing would be favorable; besides it isn't we who are asking, but we who are being asked and wanted.

I for one would always prefer Weimar to the other theatres. The opera house in Berlin is small and dull; Vienna doesn't have a perfect ensemble, whereas in Weimar they would assemble the finest one can get for an extraordinary season. [. . .]

I addressed myself to you instead of to the Maestro, for fear of receiving a letter from him which would begin and end like this:

I go to Veimar! . . . You must be crazy! . . . G. Verdi[1]

With this in mind, and to spare myself the nervous tension involved, I am pleading with you.

1. Verdi writes these same (italicized) words from the previous letter into an open space between the last two paragraphs of this one. His comment is italicized in order to distinguish it from Ricordi's text.

Verdi to Giulio Ricordi

[*Probably* St. Agata, 12 June 1872]

My original opinion has not changed concerning *Aida* in Germany. Let's not discuss the taste of various countries or good and bad faith; but it is certain that a half success at this time would be fatal. By giving *Aida* in Germany we have nothing to gain and we jeopardize the future of the opera. To quote, then, from a trivial proverb: "He who was burned by hot water is afraid of the cold." And I am afraid of the cold water.

I have already told you I would be glad if we could avoid giving *Aida* in Padua, not because I fear a fiasco but because until the Naples production the success of *Aida* should be on the same level as in Milan and Parma. After Naples *à la grâce de Dieu.*

I know what I say neither pleases nor persuades you. But mind you I am rarely mistaken in this sort of thing. Let me remind you of the fiascos that many of my operas had in Milan at one time — fiascos I had predicted:

Vespri, *Macbeth*, *Boccanegra*, *Ballo*, etc., etc. (I speak of their first performances.) Let me also remind you that about this year's[1] *Forza* revival — which, among its good elements, also had many to be feared — I always said: "There is still enough good left for a success." After that unfortunate dress rehearsal, I telegraphed you: "Don't have any fear." Therefore if I see the successes, I also see the defeats.

This German business might not be a defeat, but it might just be. Let's avoid it; this seems wise to me.

1. The past season's *La Forza del Destino*.

Franco Faccio to Giulio Ricordi

Padua, 13 June 1872

[. . .] The chorus is good, but in the orchestra there are some rotten eggs which must be eliminated for *Aida*.[1] [. . .] The first flute, the first bassoon, and the first clarinet must be changed. [. . .] Among the orchestra members I have already acquired the reputation of being very severe. [. . .] I hope [. . .] I shall not encounter difficulties in fulfilling my duties; if I do, I shall not fail to solicit your intervention. [. . .]

1. Faccio refers to the musicians in Padua.

Franco Faccio to Giulio Ricordi

Padua, 16 June 1872

Dear Giulio,

I am writing you with the pleasant feeling of satisfaction. The modifications I have found it necessary to make to ensure a good performance of *Aida* have resulted in the dismissal of some inept persons. [. . .] Inform the illustrious Maestro of all these things; tell him that I don't write him in order not to bore him with the account of these details. [. . .]

Verdi to Giulio Ricordi

St. Agata, 19 June 1872

Dear Giulio,

Right now I would send all baritones and perhaps even the theatres to the devil. Those baritones I know (from the list you sent) I don't care for at all! One is like the other, so let's wait a while longer before deciding!!! Or better yet, do whatever you want.

Quintili Leoni[1] writes that Tornaghi told him I don't want him in Naples.

Why does Tornaghi have me saying something I never said? In any event, let's not quibble about it, and never mention my name when the signing of artists is involved.

I don't know anything about Padua, except what I saw in the *Gazzetta*! [. . .] You don't tell me anything at all about the *Aida* rehearsals! You don't tell me whether or not Faccio is pleased with the [production] elements in Padua! And yet it is rather interesting and could be serious with regard to the results, very serious!!!

1. Vincenzo Quintili-Leoni (?–1896), Italian baritone. From 1861 to 1886 he sang in Italy, Spain, England, and Mexico City where he died as a professor of voice.

Franco Faccio to Verdi

Padua, 21 June 1872

You may have heard that to ensure a good performance of *Aida* I was compelled to dismiss some members of this theatre's orchestra and chorus, whose incapability was evident during the *Dinorah*[1] rehearsals. I can't deny that these actions weren't the most unbiased in the world, since my objections (with few exceptions) hit persons who had, with audacity and intrigue, been making themselves referees in this theatre for many years. Thus anonymous personal threats, fears of a strike that even upset the police, and other troubles that I don't want to bore you with; but I held on tight, and the public, which had become aware of all this dirt, applauded my behavior. [. . .]

I closed a corrupt little bar, located below the stage and habitually tolerated by the management of this theatre, where choristers and supers went between the acts to get indecently drunk. Imagine the kind of performance the chorus could give, for instance, in five-act operas. I thought of the fourth act of *Aida* and insisted that the room in question be nailed shut. Later on we'll see if my shoulders don't bear the consequences of all these disorders; for the time being I go ahead with confidence and serenity, because my conscience tells me that I'm doing my duty. The changes in the orchestra are the following: the first violin (excuse me if that's all), the first flute, the first bassoon, the second trumpet, the second horn, the bass drum, and some string instruments. The first violins are now excellent; the remainder of the strings, altogether very good; the brass, the first flute, the first bassoon, excellent; the rest, all right.

Midnight, after the orchestra rehearsal. . . . Good, good, good. The first two acts were given with a love, with a fire, that assure me now of an excellent *Aida* performance. Oh how right I was to rid chorus and orchestra of those wicked elements! How happy I would be if in this circumstance you too could be pleased with me. I hold your hands with the love of a son and pupil.

1. The alternate title of Meyerbeer's opera *Le Pardon de Ploërmel*.

Giulio Ricordi to Verdi

Milan, 22 June 1872

I received your kind letter and must tell you frankly that it greatly upset me. How could you ever think that Tornaghi told Sig. Quintili-Leoni that you were the one who did not want him? . . . It is our <u>general, absolute, immovable</u> rule always to assume the entire responsibility for the refusal of artists, without ever involving your name. We neither wrote you about the matter, I must add, nor were we told by you that you did or did not want Sig. Quintili. [. . .]

If I gave you little news about Padua, it's because at this point I myself don't have much; but we are agreed with Faccio that he will let me know when it is the right time to go there. We have corresponded and telegraphed a great deal, asking for orchestral players and choristers to replace unsuitable ones. Faccio was threatened because of his dismissals but was applauded at the theatre when this became known in the city. Faccio will not fail to give you news about the rehearsals as soon as they have advanced, and I shall also write you as soon as I hear something. [. . .]

Verdi to Camille Du Locle [1]

St. Agata, 22 June 1872

Dear Du Locle,

You are quite right to complain that I haven't written you in ages. It's really all my fault, because for the last few days I have had almost nothing to do. I am living in complete leisure. No one disturbs me, and even the Po, which has ruined so many villages near Ferrara, has left us in peace. So much the better for us, but those poor people!! How much has been ruined!! Nothing less than a hundred square kilometers are involved, all flooded! And the most fertile land one can imagine! [. . .] Think how much wealth has been lost!

What are you saying? Reyer!!! Reyer convinced [of *Aida*]? This is greater than the Ferrara flood. . . . Only it is less ruinous! So much the better! And so much the better if *Aida* appeals to the intellectuals. I don't think it will lose anything in production if it is performed as I wish. But that is most difficult in Paris!

And how are you? Is your *petite boutique* still prospering? . . . And how did the translation of *Aida* turn out? . . . Put modesty aside, because one must always tell his friends what is in his heart. [. . .]

1. Presumably in answer to a missing letter (written after 21 May 1872) in which Du Locle referred to Verdi's silence.

Verdi to Léon Escudier

St. Agata, 23 June 1872

Dear Leon,

I haven't written you for a long time, and if you are a bit mad, you have a right to be. You understand very well, however, that he who has worked hard should beware of relaxation, for he will end up not being able to stand on his feet anymore. Since my return from Parma on 21 May[1] one might say I haven't gotten up on my feet anymore. I have been in complete leisure and I still am; I just can't persuade myself to do something, not even to raise two fingers to write a few silly letters. I notice, however, that sometimes I am worn out by this laziness, so I'll soon resume my usual trot. [. . .]

1. After the first performance of *Aida* in Parma, Verdi had returned to St. Agata on 23 April 1872. See Giuseppina Verdi's card to Faccio on the same date. Apparently Verdi went back to Parma for one or more of the eighteen *Aida* performances given during April and May of 1872.

Franco Faccio to Giulio Ricordi

Padua, 23 June 1872

[. . .] I am writing to tell you that the first person to prevent the opening of *Aida*, should it not be performed as it must be, would be myself. Your telegram displeased me because it had about it an air of doubt concerning my firmness in respecting the conditions of your contract. [. . .]

Verdi to Franco Faccio[1]

St. Agata, 25 June 1872

Dear Faccio,

Excellent, excellent! One must not hesitate or compromise when art is involved. I highly praise your behavior with the orchestra in Padua. Do not fear anything. Even the greatest scoundrels always end up respecting forceful actions, when they are just. [. . .]

P.S. In the *mise-en-scène* of the *Aida* in Parma, I had the platform for the final scene placed further downstage than it was in Milan. That was a mistake. Although the theatre in Padua is smaller than La Scala, I think it is a good idea to maintain the distances as they were in Milan. The temple will be seen better and will be more mysterious, and the lovers' scene (allow me the word) more poetic.[2] [. . .]

1. In answer to Faccio's letter of 21 June 1872.
2. See Mariette's letter to Draneht of 6 October 1871.

Franco Faccio to Giulio Ricordi

Padua, 27 June 1872

[. . .] Wednesday, first performance of *Aida*.[1] [. . .] Maestro Verdi
has written me a good and very dear letter; I can't wait to describe the success
of his opera to him. I am calm and tranquil, but I try to set the devil after all
the asses of the company so that they may do their duty well, but really well.
[. . .]

1. The cast of the first performance in Padua included Teresa Stolz (Aida), Maria Waldmann
(Amneris), Giuseppe Capponi (Radames), and Francesco Pandolfini (Amonasro).

Giulio Ricordi to Verdi

Milan, 27 June 1872

[. . .] Germany continues to ask for *Aida*; how shall I proceed?
Saturday I'll leave for Padua and return immediately after the opening night
of *Aida*. [. . .]

Verdi to Giulio Ricordi

St. Agata, 28 June 1872

Dear Giulio,
My opinion is that we show no opposition to La Scala and give them
all the operas they want, with the exception of *Aida*, as long as the performances are good.
Bickering serves no purpose. Then, too, one must be an <u>artist</u>. After all, a
monument such as La Scala must be supported.
After Padua we'll talk about Germany. To tell the truth I am most unfavor-
ably disposed toward the people there. Contrary to the whole world's opinion,
I am not for their kind of <u>art</u>.

Giulio Ricordi to Verdi

Milan, 8 July 1872

I am confirming the enormous success of *Aida* in Padua; a dispatch I
just received informs me that last night at the third performance the theatre

was overcrowded and the enthusiasm literally indescribable. I would have
given you major details about the performance, if I had not been indisposed
upon my return from Padua; if at all possible, I'll leave tomorrow morning for
San Pellegrino where I hope to find the cure as beneficial as in former years.
I'll be away for only a few days — not more then twelve or fourteen —
because of a great deal of-business. I assure you that the performance of *Aida*
has given me the greatest pleasure. The company with Maini and Pandolfini is
admirable; the evening one spends there really leaves unforgettable impressions. Go there, Maestro; it's a production worthy of you. [. . .]

Verdi to Giulio Ricordi

Monday [St. Agata, 8 July 1872][1]

Dear Giulio,
        I received your letter. I already knew about the success of *Aida*, and I
shall be most happy if the cash drawer is filled.
    Me go to Padua? To show myself off? Never, never.
    I wish you would return soon to Milan, to occupy yourself very, very
seriously with Naples!

1. Verdi apparently wrote these lines on Tuesday, 9 July 1872.

Eugenio Tornaghi to Verdi

Milan, 11 July 1872

        [. . .] Some of the best choristers, who were in Parma and are now in
Padua, are being signed for Naples. [. . .]
    In Rome the press is making a fuss, because Jacovacci can't get *Aida*. I had
an official letter from no one less than the Mayor, and I answered him with a
long letter, confirming our refusal and presenting reasons which no one in
good faith could refute. [. . .]

Verdi to Giuseppe Piroli

St. Agata, 16 July 1872

        [. . .] Yes, *Aida* also went well in Padua, and those people in Rome
are quite wrong to think that they can do it better or as well as it was done in
Parma and Padua. The performances in Parma and Padua were truly exceptional because they had the most favorable circumstances.
    After the success in Milan the company was free, for the most part, and it

was possible to sign almost all of them for those two cities. In this region it is easy to find all the choristers and instrumentalists that might be needed; not so in Rome. We had on hand the best set designer in Italy, machinery, props, excellent costumes, plus two most able conductors, which you certainly don't have in Rome. Now they tell me they want to sign the company from Naples and perform *Aida* later. The company is not enough. I don't think Ricordi will be satisfied with this; in any event, I shall certainly not come to Rome to assist with *Aida* in a theatre that is run in that manner. [. . .]

Franco Faccio to Giulio Ricordi

Padua, 22 July 1872

[. . .] The receipts for *Aida* are fabulous for this theatre. One must tell this to the Maestro who understands success only [in terms of] the box office. [. . .]

Giuseppina Verdi to Giulio Ricordi

St. Agata, 22 July 1872

[. . .] You may say that forty days are plenty, but they are not too many to ensure success in a business of such importance as the German one. I casually mentioned a few words to Verdi in the beginning, but I saw that the time to sow and harvest was not right. I thought it better, therefore, for the common good, to do as the farmer who patiently waits for time and some straw to ripen his pears and apricots.

With regard to *Aida*, to its successes, to the questions exciting the musical world at this time, etc., etc., I felt the opportune moment to push forward and attack, in the hope of victory, had arrived on Saturday. [. . .]

1. The request must come from Germany itself and in the proper terms.
2. Verdi would personally conduct the first three nights.
3. [. . .] All vocal and instrumental elements, scenery, costumes, etc. would have to be furnished for Verdi, without restriction and without obstacles, in order to obtain a model performance.

Weimar would be the first theatre, then Berlin and Vienna. This way it would be a true artistic event and would implant our music, I hope, solidly in Germany, with personal glory for Verdi and general glory for Italy.

But . . . (and without this we need not talk about it) the two women would have to be the same who have performed *Aida* in Italy [1] — because they perform it admirably, because as Germans they would also serve Verdi as translators, and because, while retaining their German qualities, they have intermingled Italian ones. [. . .]

1. Stolz and Waldmann.

Verdi to Giulio Ricordi

St. Agata, 27 July 1872

[. . .] I think now it would be better to go to Veimar [*sic*] immediately, as long as this thing is still a secret. The greatest secrecy and the utmost haste are extremely important in this whole affair. [. . .]

Also, give a thought to Naples which is a pressing matter, and for me much more so than Germany. If it fails in Naples, the opera will be jeopardized in Germany. [. . .] We've made our own bed, so we must lie in it. As for me, I shall never again make such a <u>bed</u>. [. . .]

Verdi to Léon Escudier

St. Agata, 7 August 1872

[. . .] I am pleased to hear that Halanzier[1] did not dislike *Aida* in Padua. So much the better, but he should not get the idea to do it at the Opéra! It would be a sacrificed opera, more so than all the others, and that would displease me and do him no good. [. . .]

1. Olivier Halanzier-Dufrenoy, director of the Opéra, who hoped to introduce *Aida* to France in the translation prepared by Du Locle and Nuitter. See Du Locle's letters to Verdi of 26 April and 21 May 1872, and Verdi's letter to Du Locle of 22 June 1872. All performances at the Opéra had to be given in French; operas in Italian were confined to the Italian Theatre in Paris, the *Théâtre des Italiens*.

Verdi to Vincenzo Torelli

St. Agata, 22 August 1872

Dear Torelli,

Excuse me, but I don't want to get at all involved with *Aida* in Rome! Whether they do it or not makes no difference whatsoever to me. Ricordi is the proprietor, and Ricordi will certainly let them have it if there are <u>good elements for the performance</u>. And let's understand each other for once, if that is possible. By good elements for the performance, I don't mean to speak of the singers alone, but of the orchestral and choral masses, the costumes, the scenery, the props, the <u>stage movement</u>, and the <u>subtlety of coloration</u>. I am also sorry to hear from you, who are so intelligent, that the Apollo[1] is the equal of Parma and Padua. Not a chance. In Rome they will never have an orchestra like Parma's, never the chorus that was there on that occasion, never that scenery, never those costumes, never that *mise-en-scène*, and, above all never that SUBTLETY of performance. It must have been the same in Padua, because there were the same, the very same elements as in Parma. You can say this softly or loudly to whomever you wish and however you wish. In Rome, as in Naples, you are completely out in the cold so far as mounting a production in the way it should be done and in the way *Aida* was done in Milan, Parma, and Padua! And, I repeat again, it isn't enough to have two or three good singers. . . .

As for Musella, I have suggested various things, and he has always replied that they know how to manage in Naples and they will manage better!!!!! We shall see.

As for the choristers, the addition of twenty-one makes me laugh. There were so many bad ones, what do you expect twenty-one more to do!!! Then, too, one hundred choristers are not enough for *Aida*! They must be good — as good as in Milan and as the contract states!

Are you kidding about the diapason? There is no need for money; there is need for good will! [. . .] Well, what will be will be. I shall go to Naples, and if the elements are good, I shall exert myself in every way and for everything, as I did in Milan and Parma, so that there can be a good performance. If not, I shall withdraw the scores, even at the dress rehearsals! You can be certain of that. No one will persuade me to do *Don Carlos* as you have done it before or to do *Aida* as you are used to doing your operas. [. . .]

1. Verdi refers to the Teatro Apollo in Rome.

Eugenio Tornaghi to Verdi

Milan, 24 August 1872

I consider it my duty to give you a summary of Giulio's letters and telegrams. In Augsburg he met with the Baron de Loën to discuss Weimar, but the trouble is that the season in Weimar begins on the 8th of April, Signoras Stolz and Waldmann are engaged in Naples until the 15th of April, and Signora Stolz would also like a little rest after Naples. We are very sorry about this conflict, because Baron de Loën was completely sold on *Aida*, about which he is enthusiastic, having heard it played and sung by Liszt, another admirer of the opera. [. . .]

Verdi to Olivier Halanzier-Dufrenoy

Busseto, 24 August 1872[1]

Sir,

I thank you very much for the most courteous manner with which you have proposed to enter into business relations with me. I am also especially flattered that you have thought the score of *Aida* worthy of the Opéra. But, in the first place, I am too imperfectly acquainted with the personnel of the Opéra; and second, permit me to confess that I have been so little satisfied each time I have had to deal with your great theatre that at present I am not disposed to risk a new attempt.

Possibly later, if you preserve your good intentions toward me, I may change my mind. But at present I do not have the courage to face again all the trickery and opposition which rule in that theatre, of which I have preserved a painful recollection.

Excuse me, Sir, if I have explained my ideas with perhaps too much candor; but I was desirous of speaking to you frankly, to leave no uncertainty. This does not prevent me from having for you, Sir, personally, a feeling of gratitude for the courteous expression with which you have been good enough to honor me in your letter.

1. Arthur Pougin, *Verdi: histoire anecdotique de sa vie et ses oeuvres* (Paris: Calman Levy, 1886), pp. 256–57, gives 24 August 1873 as the date of this letter, whereas it was obviously written one year earlier. After Halanzier had "enjoyed *Aida* in Padua" (see Verdi's letter to Escudier of 7 August 1872), he had apparently written a letter to Verdi, which is missing. Besides, on 24 August 1873 Verdi was in Paris and not in Busseto (St. Agata), where this letter is dated. Except for two minor corrections, James E. Matthew's translation of this letter could not be improved. See Pougin, *Verdi: An Anecdotic History of His Life and Works* (New York: Scribner & Welford, 1887), trans. James E. Matthew, p. 237.

Verdi to Giulio Ricordi

St. Agata, 26 [or 28] August 1872

Dear Giulio,

I think <u>Aida</u> in Trieste before Naples is a mistake. I don't have much faith in la <u>Viziak</u> and la <u>Vogri</u>,[1] but even if la <u>Stolz</u> and la <u>Waldmann</u> were in Trieste, I would be of the opinion not to do *Aida*. I think you still don't wholly appreciate my fears. I don't believe in their musical and dramatic interpretation. [. . .] Once it has been performed in Naples, *Aida* could be left to its own destiny. [. . .]

1. Fanny Vogri, Hungarian mezzo-soprano and soprano. From 1870 to 1879 she appeared in Budapest, Madrid, Valencia, Vienna, Italy, and Mexico. From 1892 to 1898 she taught voice in Brussels. Her name is also spelled Vogry.

Verdi to Tito Ricordi

St. Agata, 28 August 1872

Dear Tito,

I am aware of the difficulties involved in doing *Aida* in Germany the way we would like to. But otherwise it would be very easy for it to be compromised. Look at *Don Carlos*! If things are not arranged soon, however, it will be difficult to hold on to the two artists! [. . .]

I advise that there is also a telegraph line in Busseto, and now telegrams can be sent directly here! It's unbelievable but true!

As for Musella, I have little to say, and I only repeat that if I don't find everything as it should be in Naples, and as I want it, I shall return without taking part in or listening to a lot of chatter, and I'll take the scores with me. . . .

Verdi to Opprandino Arrivabene

St. Agata, 29 August 1872

[. . .] I have tried to revive some of our theatres and to give them productions that are somewhat suitable. Where for many years one fiasco followed another and the final quarter-salary could not be paid, in the four theatres where I conducted or rather commandeered the performance, the crowds poured in and the profits were enormous. You will say: "And what do you care about profits?" Yes I do care, because they prove that the production was interesting, and thus they show us how to do well in the future. You know that I myself was in Milan and in Parma; I was not in Padua, but I sent them the same choristers, the same scene designer, the same technical director, props, and costumes we had in Parma. I sent Faccio, who had conducted the opera in Milan. I corresponded daily about what was going on, and the opera went well. Crowds at the theatre and profits.

Yesterday the impresario came all the way out here to thank me and not, apparently, because he had to. [. . .]

Perhaps you will again say: "This is something that others, too, know how to do." No and again no: they don't know. If they did, they wouldn't do such scandalous productions!

Now I shall get busy with Naples . . . where it's a little more difficult. In Naples, as in Rome, because they have had Palestrina, Scarlatti, and Pergolesi, they think they know more than anyone else.

Yet they have lost their bearings, and now they know very little. They are somewhat like the French: *Nous, nous, nous,* and they let themselves be applauded. So excuse this chatter, which can't interest you very much. But I would really like for our theatres to rise a bit to the surface. And they could!

Verdi to Girolamo Magnani

[St. Agata,] 2 September 1872

Dear Magnani,

Oh, what imbeciles, waiting so long before writing you.

I really would have liked you to do the scenery for *Don Carlos* and *Aida* in Naples; but, unfortunately, we can no longer give any thought to *Don Carlos*.

I thank you for your offer for after December and hope I can at least arrange to have you do the scenery for *Aida*.[1]

1. Supposedly Magnani did not design the scenery for the first production of *Aida* in Naples. See Verdi's letter to Du Locle of 27 February 1873.

Verdi to Vincenzo Torelli

St. Agata, 13 September 1872

Dear Torelli,

Do you think I am so crazy, and such a poor artist, that if I were to see the chance for a good performance of *Aida* in Rome, I would not immediately give my approval?

I repeat that it is now too late to do in Rome what was done in Milan, Parma, and Padua.

I shall put aside Milan and Parma because I was there and tell you only about Padua. For that city I requested [. . .]:

1. So and so as singers . . . . .Yes
2. So and so as conductor . . . . .Yes
3. Add to the choristers all those that I had added in Parma . . . . .Yes
4. So and so as set designer .Yes
5. So and so as technical director . . . . .Yes
6. Same props as in Parma . . . . .Yes
7. Same costumes as in Parma .Yes
8. So and so as choreographer . . . . .Yes
    etc., etc., etc. . . .

Everything I asked was done. And then Faccio, strengthened by my support, had no less than the first violin, the first cello, and the first flute replaced after the first rehearsal. Three pretentious old men from the past . . . there are such everywhere, especially in Rome.

I repeat that it is too late to do things well in Rome; and even if it were possible to <u>find</u> the right elements, not for all the gold in the world would I now want to do such a <u>hateful thing</u> as object to <u>Tom, Dick, or Harry</u>, etc., etc. When you want to do things well, you must begin at the beginning; and when you wanted to produce *Aida*, you should have asked me right away what elements were required. (That would be the beginning!) It takes more than just having the newspapers trumpet: "First-rate theatre, first-rate company, first-rate orchestra, first-rate chorus, sublime *mise-en-scène*!!!!!!" I know all these firsts only too well, and I have known for a long time this sacramental phrase of Jacovacci: "<u>I have the best company in the world</u>." Those are words, just words.

For the opening of *Trovatore* (always with those words of Jacovacci) I could get only two good singers, a very inadequate chorus, a bad orchestra, terrible sets and costumes. For the opening of *Ballo* (always with the usual words) I had only good male singers, the rest as in *Trovatore*.

In spite of the success I couldn't help but tell him after the third performance: "<u>You see, you dog of an impresario, what a success there would have been had I had a good ensemble.</u>" You know what he answered? "Heh, heh! <u>What, what more do you want! The theatre is filled every night. Next year I shall find good female singers, and that way the opera will still be good for the audience. Half this year, the other half later!</u>" . . ." You can well understand that an artist could not accept this shopkeeper's reply.

You are too intelligent not to understand that I have a thousand reasons. The time will come when it will be necessary to leave this poor *Aida* in the hands of the . . . But meanwhile, since it must be given in Naples, I want it to be produced once more (at least I hope) as it should be.

Verdi to Vincenzo Torelli

St. Agata, 19 September 1872

Dear Torelli,

Oh no I shall not be the one who suggests to la Stolz that she sing during the month of October. First of all she is obliged to be in Naples on November <u>15th</u>, and I think Musella is trying to get her to open in early November. In any event it's a good idea for la Stolz as well as for la Waldmann to rest during these two months. They have sung a great deal this year, and they have a great deal to sing in *Don Carlos* and *Aida*. So let's not talk about these two women.

As for giving *Aida* next year, you will do what you want, as they will. After Naples I think *Aida* can stand on her own two feet; and so you may sign whom you wish and give it as you wish — always provided, of course, you have Ricordi's permission and approval. [. . .]

Verdi to Tito Ricordi

St. Agata, 4 October 1872

[. . .] Please have a small diagram made of the present orchestra in Milan (Giulio must have it) and send it to Musella. [. . .]

I don't want to go to Naples to be annoyed. Everyone should do what he is supposed to do in enough time. As for me, I shall do whatever I have to do; but I warn you, I shall not tolerate anything. Therefore tell Musella to be sure to do what must be done. [. . .]

Verdi to Tito Ricordi

St. Agata, 7 October 1872

Dear Tito Ricordi,

A friend writes me, in the name of Cesarò,[1] that Musella dismissed this artist because I refused him!

It's about time for people to stop bringing my name into the middle of things all the time! I think that all the pains and efforts I devote to these damned operas should be enough!

Since no one ever mentioned this Cesarò, I want these rumors of my refusal denied, and I ask you to do so by writing to Musella or by taking some other course of action which you might think better.

1. Salvatore Cesarò, Italian bass. Between 1863 and 1873 he built his reputation around the Verdi repertoire in Italy. The San Carlo Opera in Naples had engaged him for the 1872–73 season.

Verdi to Cesare De Sanctis

St. Agata, 7 October 1872

No, by God!! We'll never get along with that Musella of yours! [. . .] Oh if there were a way to get rid of that beastly contract I signed with him!

Please go to him in person, and ask Torelli to come along (it's better that there be two of you), and tell this Sig. Musella in my name the toughest things about this Cesarò affair. [. . .]

Verdi to Vincenzo Torelli

St. Agata, 18 October 1872

Dear Torelli,

I thank you for your letter[1] and for the haste with which you went to see Musella on my behalf. Musella was absolutely wrong in saying that I rejected Cesarò, when I never even mentioned him; but *Fanfulla*[2] says of Musella: "Already they are beginning to accuse him of acting in bad faith, he who usually is not offended by that accusation. . . ."

And you, to tell the truth, are a bit offended because of the Rome affair? . . . You are wrong, because you already know that the theatres in the South do not do, do not want (or know how) to do, what I want. [. . .] For them it is enough to put two or three names on a poster, and they think they have done well. For me that is absolutely not enough. Difference of taste and opinion! . . . After so much preaching, however, I was hoping to get something more out of Naples. Such a small number of new choristers have been signed that it's laughable. But they say "most excellent." We shall see. . . . In the orchestra no improvement whatsoever has been made! This, too, they say is "most excellent"! We shall see, we shall see; and we shall see about all the rest. After all I have informed Musella in every way possible; I am almost ashamed that I have talked so much and asked so many times! So much the worse for him if I do not get everything that I have a right to demand according to the contract with Ricordi. Do you know that contract? Ah if I had signed such a contract, I would take things much more seriously than Musella does!

He will think about it in the end. I shall certainly have no remorse that I didn't warn him about everything.

Excuse the endless chatter, and *addio, addio*.

1. Missing.
2. A newspaper in Rome.

Verdi to Tito Ricordi

Genoa, 24 October 1872

[. . .] It is necessary that you tell me: "You can now leave for Naples; everything there is running smoothly." If you, you yourself, do not give me this assurance, I don't leave. I want to find things quite clear and clean, because it's impossible to find a bigger swindler than Musella. Three days ago he wrote me, asking me to be in Naples at the end of this month, because he had agreed with la Stolz that she would also be there on the 1st of November. Instead he wrote a rather discourteous letter to la Stolz, saying "if you come, I'll pay your board at the hotel for the fifteen days, etc., etc." Imagine the sharp eyes of la Stolz! I think she answered him that she doesn't need anyone to pay for her meals and that she'll be in Naples at the time stated in the contract. [. . .] So this swindler, who is also an ass, will pay all the other artists for fifteen days without being able to do a thing. [. . .]

Giulio Ricordi to Giuseppina Verdi

Milan, 1 November 1872

Kindest Signora Peppina,

Your letter [1] has been a true <u>oasis</u> in the desert, and I hastened to sip the beneficent water from your consoling pages. Without digressing too much, I tell you I think it's a very good idea to send Faccio to hear the artists in Vienna: four eyes and four ears are worth more than two, and then he can also hear other operas instead of those I heard. I mentioned this to Faccio, without going into the reasons, and only vaguely suggested the need of a trip to Vienna to get the Maestro some information. He answered me that for the Verdis he would go to the end of the world. I am now finding out what productions they are giving in Vienna, so we can see if this trip would be useful to us at this time.

Here now I should interject a litany of eternal thanks!! . . . But you must be very busy, and I don't want to bore you; besides, I dare believe you will be convinced of the immense gratitude I feel for innumerable favors! . . .

1. Missing. But there is the following draft in Verdi's handwriting (Autograph: St. Agata):
"As soon as I learned from your reply of Verdi's decision about the Vienna affair, I hastened to telegraph you not to break off the negotiations as yet, in hopes of seeing this affair materialize. It's not an easy matter, because Verdi does not like the theatres abroad in general and is of the opinion that all of them have orchestras and choruses like those in Germany. Nevertheless, speaking of Vienna, he agrees that their theatre must be exceptionally well equipped and that there must be a chorus and orchestra that could perform any foreign opera very well, as long as no racial dislike is involved. But he has a very low opinion of the singers, and if this so highly praised <u>Vills</u> [see note 3, Faccio's letter to Giulio Ricordi of 26 November 1872] is that same <u>Vilda</u> who sang a few years ago in Venice, she must be rather poor.
"How then could one get reliable information about the singers of that theatre? And if those singers are vocally and emotionally suited to the roles in *Aida*? Whom to trust?
"Faccio, for instance, might go to hear them and inform Verdi by letter?
"I'm just thinking aloud; these ideas are crossing my mind at the moment. But work out something better."
Below this draft by her husband Giuseppina Verdi noted:
"Written on the 28th of October 1872
"Wrote also to Giuditta" [Giulio Ricordi's wife].

Verdi to Giuseppe Piroli

Naples, 23 November 1872

Dear Piroli,

Tell me if there is an agreement between Germany and Italy regarding artistic and literary rights. It's a question of doing *Aida* in German at the big theatre in Vienna. . . . I would go there to stage it, and I would like to know if, according to our laws, I am entitled to the so-called *droits d'auteur*.

You have heard that the theatre here is a shambles. It's natural. . . . Do you know why? Because the 250,000 lire that city hall provides as a subsidy is not enough to cover the initial expenses; and when a minor mishap occurs (such as la Stolz's illness), the poor impresario runs around like a chicken with its head cut off. When the accounts are cleared and the management has paid the company, plus 40,000 or 50,000 lire (Think of that!) in tax to the government, all of the subsidy he has left is about 30,000 lire!!! Now I ask you if, with nothing but box office receipts and 30,000 lire, it is possible to pay all the artists and the dancers, to pay for props, technical apparatus, etc., etc., costumes, the *mise-en-scène* of three large ballets (The first one alone costs 80,000!), and five operas, among which are some very expensive ones such as *Don Carlos* and *Aida*? Ah the government has been quite guilty! To abandon the arts in Italy is like blocking out the sun! It amounts to this! At least, the government should have been more logical; if it abandoned music, it should have abandoned all the arts. . . . Why does it spend money for [. . .] academies of design, painting, etc., etc.? It would be better to deal one good blow and turn this nation, which will always be primarily and essentially artistic, into a race of nonentities, babblers, and finally, imbeciles! . . .

Excuse me; and may God better inspire these leaders of ours . . . to at least do worse, if nothing else . . . to make us starve to death. . . . We are headed that way! . . . But, you will say, you aren't starving to death? . . . Oh no! But, by God, I certainly don't owe that to the government, of which I fortunately have no need. No, no, I don't owe it anything. . . . I owe it some crosses which I must bear and a few sword thrusts, which, however, did not wound me.

Franco Faccio to Giulio Ricordi

Vienna, 26 November 1872

Dearest Giulio,

Here are the explanations promised in the telegram you will have received. I have been welcomed with great deference by Herbeck[1] as well as by Lewy,[2] the Inspector of the Imperial Theatre. In their presence I read the draft of the contract concerning *Aida*. They accept all the artistic conditions set down in the draft and all others that might occur to Maestro Verdi with the purpose of guaranteeing the perfect performance of his opera. The difficulties lie in the question of money. [. . .] Tonight I shall begin to hear artists that Herbeck intends for *Aida*; they are la Wilt[3] and Beck[4] — soprano and baritone. [. . .] Thursday, in *Rienzi*, I shall be able to judge the mezzo-soprano to whom the role of Amneris would be assigned. The tenor would be a certain Müller,[5] but he doesn't sing until Sunday in *L'Africaine*. [. . .]

I am enchanted with the city and the theatre. [. . .]

1. Johann Herbeck (1831–77), Austrian composer and conductor. He was a Wagnerite and ardent exponent of Schubert, whose Unfinished Symphony he discovered; but his own compositions are not well known. From 1870 to 1875 he was director of the Imperial Opera in Vienna, where he was to conduct the first German *Aida* in Austria on 29 April 1874.

2. Gustav Lewy (1824–1901), Viennese music publisher and theatrical agent.

3. Marie Wilt (1833–91), Austrian soprano. After making her debut in 1865 at Graz in *Don Giovanni*, she sang with some success (under the name Marie Vilda) at London's Covent Garden in such operas as *Norma*, *Les Huguenots*, and *Il Trovatore*. In 1867 she appeared for the first time in Vienna, where she was to become the first German Aida. Marcel Prawy, *The Vienna Opera* (New York: Praeger Publishers, 1970), p. 36, writes: "Her voice was phenomenal, but her ample proportions gave rise to a certain amount of ribaldry (such as 'Round the Wilt in 80 Days') which could hardly help coming to her ears. She ended her life by jumping out of a window."

4. Johannes Nepomuk Beck (1827?–1904), Hungarian baritone. In 1856 he first appeared on the operatic stage as Riccardo in *I Puritani* in his hometown of Budapest. Singing for the first time in Vienna in 1858, he remained a favorite there for three decades, giving the city first performances of Telramund, Wolfram, the Flying Dutchman, and Hans Sachs. In 1874 he became the first German Amonasro in Vienna.

5. Georg Müller (1840–1909), German tenor. Singing a wide repertoire of roles, from Mozart to Wagner, he was to become the first German Radames in Vienna, where he also sang Turiddu in 1892, with Mascagni conducting his own *Cavalleria Rusticana*.

Verdi to Franco Faccio

[*Probably* Naples, 8 December] 1872

Many, many thinks for the information[1] you have given me about the singers at the Vienna theatre. But it isn't enough for me, and I would like more details. I would like you to tell me, for example, if la Wilt sings good low notes. I have already heard that neither la Wilt nor la Materna[2] has good low notes, but I would sincerely like to know from you whether this deficiency would impair the effects which are in *Aida*.

La Waldmann tells me there is a young mezzo-soprano, la Tremorel,[3] whose voice is steady even in the low notes. Have you heard her? Is she the one you told me about, the one Herbeck would not prefer to Materna for now? Are there perhaps two good basses for Ramfis and the King? Finally, *somme toute*, tell me in all sincerity and good conscience, like the true artist you are, if la Wilt, la Materna, Labatt,[4] and Beck, along with two good basses, would form a good company and one that would represent *Aida* well.

1. Faccio's letter is missing.

2. Amalie Materna (1844–1918), Austrian soprano and mezzo-soprano. Making her operatic debut in 1869 as Selika in *L'Africaine* at the Imperial Opera in Vienna, she quickly established herself as a leading German singer. With an extraordinary vocal range and power, she was the first German Amneris in Vienna; and in 1880 she alternated there between the roles of Aida and Amneris. She appeared in the role of Brünnhilde in the first *Ring* performances at Bayreuth in 1876, as well as Kundry in the first performance of *Parsifal* in 1882, and was known as the foremost Wagnerian soprano of her time.

3. Wilhelmine Tremmel, Austrian mezzo-soprano. She was engaged by the Imperial Opera in Vienna from February of 1872 until January of 1878. In Rome (1879) and elsewhere she appeared

under the name Tremelli. After several seasons in St. Petersburg, London, Paris, and Barcelona, she returned to Vienna as a guest. In 1880 she sang the role of Amneris to Materna's Aida in Vienna. In 1885 Tremmel, alias Tremelli, sang at La Scala, 1886–87 in Budapest, and 1891–92 with the Minnie Hauk Grand Opera Company in the United States.

4. Leonard Labatt (1838–97), Swedish tenor. Making his debut in Italy under a pseudonym, he appeared at the Opéra in Paris as M. Labat in 1861. Engaged in Dresden and Stockholm, he was a standing guest at the Imperial Opera in Vienna, where he had sung the role of Tannhäuser under Wagner's direction. In 1888–89 he toured the United States.

Verdi to Giulio Ricordi

Naples, 12 December 1872

Dear Giulio,

I am quite surprised to have received no answer to a letter of mine[1] in which I asked you to send me the designs and quantity of all the props for *Aida*.

It seems impossible! But as far as this poor theatre in Naples is concerned, nobody cares or else everything goes wrong! And yet this could become a great theatre, because this town still has orchestral resources that are far better than those in Milan.

Perhaps my letter got lost, or you forgot about it, or you lacked the time to compile the information I asked of you. Let me sum things up — I want to have:

The list of all the props,

The quantity,

The size,

What the height and bulk of the God Vulcan was.

Send me, then, a penciled design of all these props and write under each one:

The numbers,

Height,

Length, etc.

They say that the financial crisis of the theatre here has ended. We shall see if it has. Others will arise (1) because this impresario (like all impresarios) does not know how to put on productions and (2) because the illnesses, especially la Stolz's, have really been fatal [to the theatre].

Ask Faccio immediately if it would be possible for him to go to Ancona, should they do *Aida*.

We must decide absolutely and at once about the business of Germany, Berlin, etc. You were very wrong not to have said a few words to la Stolz and la Waldmann when you were here. Reply to everything by telegram, because there is no time to be lost.

P.S. Also tell me if there are the additional four or six female choristers.[2] You haven't said anything more to me about them either!!!!

1. The letter to which Verdi refers is missing; but its receipt probably caused Giulio Ricordi to send the prop list to Verdi on 9 December. See Verdi's letters to Giulio Ricordi of 26 December 1872.
2. See Verdi's letter to Giulio Ricordi of 14 January 1873.

Verdi to Léon Escudier

Naples, 20 December 1872

Dear Léon,

From your dispatch[1] I learn with immense surprise that you did not receive a letter, written after the performance of *Don Carlos*, in which I spoke of its success. In the same letter I told you that it is almost certain that I shall go to Vienna to direct *Aida* in German. That is why I asked you to see Peragallo,[2] so that you could inform me how they handle the *droit d'auteurs* in that theatre. I hope this letter reaches you and that you will do me the favor of going to see Peragallo. . . . Let me repeat once more that it would be *Aida* in German. . . . .I urge the greatest solicitude. . . .

1. Missing.
2. Agent of the French Society of Authors.

Giulio Ricordi to Giuseppina Verdi

Milan, 25 December 1872

Kindest Signora Peppina,

Although forced to stay in bed, and still indisposed with a rheumatic fever, I cannot possibly ease my mind without writing you at once that the Maestro's last letter[1] has deeply hurt me because of his reproaches, which I honestly do not deserve. Since I have always found so much goodness in you, such kindness of the heart, and such polite indulgence toward me, I hope you will forgive me for addressing this most confidential letter to you as a relief of my great affliction.

First of all, please tell me what makes the Maestro think that I am less interested in the business of Naples than in the others? . . . This lack of faith in me is an indisputable fact; I did not receive any letter from the Maestro, and instead of simply thinking that his letter could have been lost, he doubts my zeal and good will. But how can the Maestro ever imagine that I would not answer one of his letters or that I would be late in carrying out his orders? . . . And how can he ever think that Naples is less important to me than La Scala? . . .

If certain things work out better at La Scala, it is because it is better organized. The San Carlo is a ruin today, and what the Maestro has already done to raise it to its present artistic conditions is a miracle. [. . .]

As I said before, the designs of the *Aida* props were sent to the House of Ricordi in Naples on the 9th, that is perhaps even before the Maestro wrote me the letter that got lost. [. . .]

My head is so confused that I don't even know what I wrote. You will read between these lines far better than I and guess how much was on my mind to tell you. With all these lovely things, the Christmas holidays have been quite sad for me! . . . Now that I have written you, however, I feel more calm and cheerful, also because I flatter myself that you will forgive this outburst and know how to justify me before the Maestro. In a moment of bad humor he did not remember how devoted I am to him and how fond of him, and that whatever his interests may be, they are the supreme law for me.

I hope the *panettone*[2] did not take the same road as the letters and that it arrived safe and sound, together with a few Milanese sweets you will have distributed among friends and Signoras Stolz and Waldmann. [. . .]

1. Missing.
2. A traditional Christmas gift from the Ricordi family.

Giulio Ricordi to Verdi

Milan, 25 December 1872

Forgive me if I answer briefly your letter of the 22nd,[1] since I have been sick in bed for four days. I am very sorry that you did not immediately attribute my silence to the fact that I did not receive any other letter from you. [. . .]

1. Missing.

Verdi to Giulio Ricordi

[Naples,] 26 December 1872

Dear Giulio,

I definitely did not receive the prop list you sent me (according to your telegram) on the 9th. How did you send it? Didn't you insure it? Inquire about it at the Milan post office; I shall ask Clausetti about it tomorrow morning. . . .

Verdi to Giulio Ricordi

Naples, 26 December 1872

[. . .] Clausetti just gave me the prop list, but the annotations aren't sufficient or clear enough for this place. I have asked Clausetti to return them so you can give more explanations.

Things here couldn't be any worse. The improvidence and the bullheadedness of the management and board of directors have been such that now it is impossible to go on. [. . .] It is no longer decent to remain here. Unless there is an unexpected provision, or something short of a miracle, I shall give up Naples soon!

Not only one letter but several got lost. And perhaps also the *panettone* has been eaten, but not by us! Who knows if it will arrive? I'll let you know.

I can't tell you anything about Usiglio,[1] whom I don't know; anyway do what you think best. Be sure to lower the pitch of the tuning fork. *Aida* would be enriched by many effects, such as la Waldmann's beautiful chest E and the F sharp of la Stolz. And while on the subject, what is the diapason in Germany? Their ancient tuning fork would be a serious problem.

I repeat again that I don't know if we shall give *Aida* here. [. . .]

1. Emilio Usiglio, Italian composer and conductor.

Verdi to Opprandino Arrivabene

Naples [*Probably* 29 December 1872]

[. . .] You know that things are going to the dogs at the theatre in Naples. Misfortune is half responsible, but the ignorance and improvidence of the management and the municipal commission are beyond belief. With a kind of malicious pleasure I am waiting for the disorder and crisis that seem inevitable, so that I can get out of here. . . .

Verdi to Clarina Maffei

Naples, 29 December 1872

Dear Clarina,

Good morning and a happy new year — that is to say, good health and peace! Peace! The best thing in this world, and the thing that I desire most at this moment. What devil ever put it in my head to dirty myself with theatrical affairs again! I, who for many years have enjoyed the blessed life of a peasant! Now I'm at the ball and must dance, and I assure you this is quite a dance here. I knew about the disorder at this theatre, but neither I nor anyone else could have imagined what it is like. It's indescribable: the ignorance, the inertia, the apathy, the disorder, the lack of concern on the part of everyone for everything. It's unbelievable. It almost makes me laugh when I stop and think about all the trouble I cause for myself, about all the agitation I suffer, about my obstinancy to want and to want at any cost. I feel as if they were all watching me, laughing and saying: Is he crazy?

Oh my vanity has been well punished; I must confess to you I really had a moment of vanity. Let me explain. When the government withdrew its subsidy from the theatres, I said, well then, let's show this government that it is wrong and that we can also do something without it. Then I went to Milan for *Forza del Destino*. Much was said against the music, but the production itself and the performance by the company were impressive. That was what I wanted. Then I went for *Aida*. The usual story about the music (by that time *Forza del Destino* had become good), but once again the production and the performance were successful. A brilliant house and great box office. I went to Parma, and the outcome was also excellent: always a brilliant house and great box office. I watched Padua from far off, and, thanks to Faccio's care, once again success and box office. I came to Naples in the hope of an equal success, but here, wham! The rug has been pulled out from under me, and I don't know where to turn.

It serves me right.

My vanity has been well punished.

Now I am quite disillusioned; and if, unfortunately, I had not (like an imbecile) made other commitments to Giulio, I would leave at once and go plow my fields, even at night, just to completely forget about music and theatres.

Verdi to Camille Du Locle

Naples, 2 January 1873

[. . .] I am afraid that we shall soon leave Naples ourselves, because the theatre will probably close. The management, lacking foresight, was caught by surprise with the illness of la Stolz, which lasted three weeks. Meanwhile the performances of *Don Carlos* had to be suspended, the bills are due, and the management is in hot water. Unless city hall comes to the rescue, the management will not be able to save itself; but city hall won't help because of personal hatred for the management.

Oh well, in one sense so much the better. I'll wear myself out less and be able to contemplate leisurely the beauties of Naples and enjoy the warmth of this climate. [. . .]

Verdi to Tito Ricordi [1]

Naples, 3 January 1873

Dear Tito,

If the Vienna business is lean fare for you, it's quite a bone for me, and one that is hard to gnaw on. Let me also say that if, as you write, " the first idea to do *Aida* in German was Giulio's, etc." . . . then the thing becomes much too humiliating and not very dignified, since we would be the ones who offered *Aida* to those gentlemen and not they who sought it. [. . .]

With regard to the question of glory, [. . .] for the love of Heaven, let's not talk about it. You see how I have been treated by the press during all these years that I have gone to so much trouble, spent so much money, and worked so hard! Stupid criticisms and even more stupid praise; not one noble, artistic idea; not a single one who tried to discern my intentions. . . . Always absurdities and nonsense, and beneath it all a certain spiteful attitude against me, as if I had committed a crime by writing *Aida* and by having it performed well. No one, finally, who tried at least to discern the obvious fact of an uncommon performance and *mise-en-scène*! Not one who said to me, "Thank you, dog." [. . .]

So let's not talk anymore about this *Aida*, which, if it has given me a tidy sum of money, has also caused me endless annoyance and great artistic disillusions! Would that I had never written it or published it! If it had stayed in my briefcase after the first performances, and if I had had it performed only under my direction where and when I pleased, it wouldn't have been such food for the wickedness of the curious and the analyses of your critics and petty maestros, who know nothing about music except the grammar, and even that but poorly. Speculation would have lost something, but art would have gained immensely.

1. In answer to a letter that is missing.

Verdi to Giulio Ricordi

Naples, 14 January 1873

[. . .] We must absolutely find these [additional] choristers in order to remedy as best we can the indecencies of this women's chorus. The other night in *Favorita* they were whistled at quite loudly. Keep searching, keep searching; they must be found.

La Stolz and la Waldmann are signed for Cairo; no use to talk about Trieste. La Waldmann is signed for Ancona, but la Stolz is very reluctant. Usiglio may very well be a good conductor; la Stolz doesn't doubt it, but she would prefer a conductor who has already done *Aida* in another place. Write them directly, because I don't want to bother anymore with this *Aida*. [. . .]

Verdi to Léon Escudier

Naples, 18 January 1873

Dear Léon,

What the devil ever prompted you to say that I received a letter from the Emperor of Austria asking me to go to Vienna to stage *Aida*!![1] . . . That's much, much too much, and it would be wise to deny it.

This is how things went: As early as six or seven months ago, the management of the Vienna theatre asked Ricordi very insistently if they could do *Aida* in German. (Herbeck had come to hear *Aida* in Milan and also, I believe, in Parma or Padua.) They also asked that I betake myself to Vienna to stage the opera and conduct it the first three or four nights. At first they wanted me to do the opera during the carnival season, but because of my commitment in Naples it was impossible for me to go to Vienna. Their management then requested the opera for the spring, which displeased me since the performance would have fallen at the time of the Exposition. The negotiations continued anyway, and Ricordi sent Faccio to Vienna, specifically to examine the theatre and to see if they had suitable elements for the production of *Aida*. At last, after having pondered and calculated everything, I told Ricordi that I would not go to Vienna; and Ricordi thought it best not to do the opera without my assistance. That is the whole and entire truth! No one wrote me directly. I did not impose anything on the Vienna management; it was the management itself that requested the opera and my assistance. That's all. What pleases me about all of this is that there (having a great director) they realize that the author's assistance can enhance the performance and success of the opera . . . quite apart from you Frenchmen, who believe that any old musician can interpret an opera. That is why my operas have never been performed [as they should be] and never will be as long as you maintain those mistaken notions. (You can tell that to Halanzier with regard to *Aida*.) [. . .]

1. Verdi apparently refers to a press release by Léon Escudier to his review *L'Art Musical* or another publication.

Verdi to Léon Escudier

Naples, 25 January 1873

[. . .] As for the Italian Theatre [in Paris], if you want my opinion, nothing is certain about the artists. La Stolz and la Waldmann are going to do

Aida in Ancona as soon as the present Naples season is finished. During the fall and the following carnival season, they are both going to Cairo. I would not suggest any of the other prima donnas to you. They say there are two youngsters who are just starting, but I have not heard them: la Pantaleoni[1] and la Mariani (Mariani the soprano, not the contralto)[2]. . . . In a few days I shall begin the *Aida* rehearsals and shall write you about them.

1. Romilda Pantaleoni (1847–1917), Italian soprano. The sister of the baritone Adriano Pantaleoni, she made her debut at the Teatro Carcano in Milan (1868). Following appearances in several Italian cities, she was particularly successful in the role of Margherita in Boito's *Mefistofele* (Turin, 1875). As a leading artist of La Scala, she was chosen by Verdi for the role of Desdemona in the *Otello* premiere at La Scala in 1887; but he rejected her for the *Otello* performance in Rome, and she withdrew from the stage until, in 1888, she reconquered it at Genoa in *La Gioconda*. In 1889 she appeared in the first performance of Puccini's *Edgar* and in 1891 as the first Santuzza at La Scala. She was a close friend of Faccio and retired shortly after his death in 1891.

2. Maddalena Mariani Masi (1850–1916), Italian soprano. After a brief career in provincial Italian theatres, she had distinguished herself as Agathe in *Der Freischütz* at La Scala in September of 1872. Later she excelled as Elena in *I Vespri Siciliani*, as well as in the title role in *La Gioconda*, a part given her by Ponchielli himself in the first productions of both versions of that opera (1876 and 1880). Mariani Masi was heard in all of Italy's major theatres, in Buenos Aires (1875), and in Madrid (1885). Her sister Flora (later Mariani-De Angelis) was a soprano until 1877 and thereafter appeared in mezzo-soprano roles, frequently with her sister, in Italy and Madrid. Both retired in 1890. See Verdi's letter to Waldmann of 14 April 1877.

Verdi to Baron ———[1]

Naples, 6 February 1873

Yesterday it was established (between myself and the representative of the House of Ricordi) that the roles for *Aida* would be distributed by the management and rehearsals would begin this morning. I do not know what may have happened afterward, but I do know that neither the distribution nor the rehearsal announcement came about!!

Judge for yourself whether or not it is possible to always proceed in this manner!! Let the Mayor know, and tell him that if things continue like this, we shall certainly not be able to perform *Aida*. Tell him also that this opera requires much care, as much in the *mise-en-scène* as in the musical performance, and that I shall never permit this opera to be performed the way all other productions are performed at the San Carlo.

My opinion is still not to give *Aida*. It is the best thing to do under the present circumstances. . . .

1. The name of this Baron is unknown. See note 2, Verdi's letter to De Sanctis of 25 February 1872.

Verdi to Giulio Ricordi

[Naples,] 16 February 1873

[. . .] Peppina is pestering me to send you the two acts of the *mise-en-scène*. Allow me to keep them a little while longer since they might be useful to me.[1]

In the prop designs the shapes of the lances and the axes are missing. Design them quickly and send them to me right away. Tell me also what metal they should be made of, because, if I remember correctly, I think they were not of steel.

Mentioned in the march are two ballet-supers carrying on their back a small [*illegible*] for the golden vases, etc. Send me the design for these [*illegible*], which will be a small litter, basket, etc., etc . . . and tell me how many golden vases and how many idols. And tell me if there are heaps of gold, silver, stones, etc., etc.

All this as quickly as possible. . . .

1. Verdi probably refers to Giulio Ricordi's production book of *Aida*, which had apparently not yet been printed. See Document XII.

Verdi to Giulio Ricordi

Tuesday [*Probably* Naples, 25 February 1873]

Dear Giulio,

I am sorry that the costume sketches were lost. . . . How the devil did you lose them? . . . In your next to last letter[1] you told me you would send me the completed costumes, and I have not received anything. . . . Of all the costume sketches, I am particularly sorry to miss the one of the King's Officer. It was very beautiful — in fact, one of the most beautiful in *Aida*. We have gotten another one and have made some changes, but I am not satisfied. . . .

How dirty the Egyptian trumpets are. Weren't they ever cleaned? . . . And they were packed in such a way that it's a miracle they didn't arrive broken. . . .

1. Missing.

Verdi to Camille Du Locle

Naples, 27 February 1873

Dear Du Locle,

The orchestra rehearsals for *Aida* have not yet begun. As soon as the first rehearsal is over I shall write or telegraph you, and that way you can be almost certain the opera will be performed ten days later. Are you really planning to come to hear *Aida*?[1] But don't expect a performance like that in Milan. Except for the two women, you won't find the artists equal to those, nor the chorus, nor any of the rest. The orchestra is good, however, and will certainly equal the performance in Milan. As far as the *mise-en-scène* is concerned, we shall be a thousand miles away from the one in Milan. That means a lot to a Frenchman. You who are accustomed to the luxury of the Opéra will hardly be satisfied with our shabbiness. As for me, I certainly would have liked to have had in Milan the props and the scenery they had in Parma, and I was satisfied with the rest. I like a beautiful frame very much, but I do not like it to distract me from the painting. And that is why I am not too enthusiastic about the splendors of·the Opéra. [. . .]

1. Verdi wrote to Escudier on 27 March 1873 that "Du Locle has come for a few hours to Naples." (Autograph: Bibliothèque de l'Opéra, Paris)

Verdi to Giulio Ricordi

[Naples,] 8 March 1873

[. . .] I can't tell you if the *Aida* rehearsals are going well or badly. I don't understand anything. I only understand that given the terrible organization of this theatre, I am still not entirely certain whether *Aida* will be given or not. . . .

Verdi to Camille Du Locle

Naples, 12 March 1873

Dear Du Locle,
The orchestra rehearsals for *Aida* have begun and we can open on the 20th or 22nd. [. . .]

Verdi to Léon Escudier

Naples, 20 March 1873

[. . .] The rehearsals for *Aida* are in a very advanced stage, and it would have opened already had la Waldmann not fallen ill and been in bed for a fortnight. She is better now, and I hope to be able to open in another eight or ten days. The musical performance of the company and of some of the principal roles will be good, and they will have that fire and that verve which is always lacking at the Opéra. I don't know about the *mise-en-scène*, which will be inferior to that in Milan, but I think it will be such to satisfy my demands.

You already know I am not easy [to please], but I don't like a *mise-en-scène* that overwhelms everything and becomes the principal object. I like the *mise-en-scène* at the Opéra, but I wish they would sing better at that theatre and that the chorus and orchestra would perform with more fire, with more . . . and more artistically. For them it's business not an art. [. . .]

Verdi to Opprandino Arrivabene

Naples, 22 March 1873

[. . .] Regarding *Aida*, you are aware that the Naples contract was made when *Aida* had not yet been performed in Italy.[1] I thought it prudent, therefore, to supervise its performance here, above all, where there is no capable direction and where they know nothing, absolutely nothing, just as in Rome. [. . .]

Ricordi told me that he had a little quarrel with D'Arcais over not doing *Aida* in Rome and that D'Arcais was surprised one could not get in Rome a performance like that in Parma. No, and again no, a thousand times no. In Parma, with the old musicians and with the reinforcements that can easily be brought in from Milan and Bologna, they can put together an orchestra and a chorus the likes of which they will never have in Rome. In Parma, too, there is the best set designer in Italy, the best technical director (not only in Italy, but one of the best in Europe), one of the best propmasters, the most beautiful stage lighting you can imagine. Add to this a conductor who understood and followed all my intentions perfectly! Now you tell me if you could have all of this in Rome, and you will see that the first *Aida* in your theatre would be a great fiasco.

Aida will open here Saturday, if la Waldmann is well.

1. From Verdi's letters to Torelli of 30 or 31 January 1872, to De Sanctis of 22 February 1872, and his further correspondence about *Aida* at the San Carlo Opera, it appears that the contract was not signed before the Italian premiere of *Aida*, but between 22 February and 10 March 1872.

Verdi to Giuseppe Piroli

Sunday, [Naples, 30 March 1873]

Dear Piroli,

Aida opens tonight[1] and perhaps it won't go badly. There are some good things, both in terms of the musical performance and the *mise-en-scène*. [. . .]

1. The cast of the first performance in Naples, conducted by Paolo Serrao and staged by Verdi, included Teresa Stolz and Maria Waldmann.

Verdi to Clarina Maffei

Naples, 9 April 1873

[. . .] The success of *Aida*, as you know, was outspoken and decisive, untainted by <u>ifs</u> and <u>buts</u> and such cruel phrases as <u>Wagnerism</u>, the <u>Future</u>, the <u>Art of Melody</u>, etc., etc. The audience surrendered to its feelings and applauded. That's all! . . .

It applauded and even surrendered to a hysteria that I don't approve of; but, after all, it expressed its feelings without inhibitions and without *arrière-pensée*! And do you know why? Because here there are no critics who act like apostles; no mob of maestros who know about music only what they have studied in the <u>copybooks</u> of <u>Mendelssohn, Schumann, Wagner,</u> etc.; no aristocratic dilettantes who are fashionably attracted to something they don't understand, etc., etc. And do you know the result of all this? The confusion and corruption of young minds.

Let me explain. Imagine, for example, a youngster of Bellini's temperament in these times: not very sure of himself, hesitant because of his insufficient studies, guided only by his instinct, harassed by the Filippis, Wagnerites, etc.; he would end up with no faith in himself and perhaps he would be lost. . . .

Verdi to the Mayor of Naples

Naples, 9 April 1873

I am very sorry I was not able to shake your hand and say <u>goodbye</u> today before leaving — particularly, Your Honor, since you took so much interest in this *Aida*. I need not tell you how glad I am about its success and about all the manifestations with which the public saw fit to honor me; and I am glad not so much for myself as I am for the sake of art. I am most happy that the performance and the *mise-en-scène* have produced some impression. Let's not talk about the music, which others could do much better; what is important now is to revitalize the theatre, which has been so wrongly abandoned, with worthy and complete productions. My greatest satisfaction would be to hear that these carefully prepared performances had left some marks. This alone was my goal and the reason I went twice to Milan, then to Parma, and now to Naples. You, Your Honor, could do the greatest good by bringing about the reforms at the San Carlo that modern art demands; the carelessness and the ignorance [displayed] in performing operas these days are no longer possible. Only [through such reforms] can this great theatre regain its ancient splendor.

Verdi to Giulio Ricordi

St. Agata [*Probably* 12 April 1873]

Dear Giulio,

I have been at St. Agata for two days.

You sent me a note to Naples[1] concerning Usiglio. I haven't done anything you recommended because it would have been a waste of time. In this sort of thing one must do either a great deal or nothing at all. Running with Usiglio to an *Aida* performance would have done nothing but give him an excuse for all his crap: "This is the way the Maestro wants it."

1. Missing, like most of Giulio Ricordi's letters during this period.

Verdi to Opprandino Arrivabene [1]

St. Agata, 16 April 1873

[. . .] In moments of leisure in Naples I wrote a quartet.[2] I had it played one night at my home,[3] without giving the slightest importance to it and without any invitations whatsoever. Only seven or eight persons, who usually came to me, were present. If the quartet is beautiful or ugly, I don't know. . . . I know, however, that it is a quartet!

Whoever gave you such a fastidious description of the *Aida* production in Naples didn't tell you the truth. Nothing is perfect, but on the whole this production was better than the ones in Milan and Parma. Orchestra, superior to the other two. Chorus, inferior only to that in Milan. Costumes, as in Milan and better than Parma. Scenery, props, stage machinery as in Parma. Altogether, more life and greater effect.

You are wrong to think about the substantial expenses for the "sauce" of this score. First of all, it remains to be decided if this is nothing more than sauce or if there was a roast in the former scores. By the same token the merit of this or that singer remains to be decided and what is meant by melody, harmony, and all the other crap that doesn't mean anything. For example, if someone should tell you that the old masters, first of all Palestrina, didn't know what melody was, that there is no melody in *Il Barbiere di Siviglia* (aside from *Ecco ridente in cielo*) . . . *solfège* yes, melody no . . . would that seem to you a great blasphemy? [. . .]

1. In answer to a letter that is missing.
2. For years, Verdi did not allow this quartet — his only string quartet (in E minor) — to be published and performed in public. See Verdi's letter to Tito Ricordi of 3 June 1876, Abbiati, III, pp. 624–28, Charles Osborne, *Letters of Giuseppe Verdi* (New York: Holt, Rinehart and Wins-

ton, 1971), pp. 203–4, Joseph Wechsberg, *Verdi* (New York: G. P. Putnam's Sons, 1974), pp. 162–3, and other biographies.

3. The Albergo delle Crocelle in Naples, later named Hotel Hassler, which no longer exists.

Giulio Ricordi to Verdi

Milan, 30 April 1873

[. . .] Theatres, impresarios, directors, and city halls besiege us with requests for *Aida*; among the most insistent are Rome and Genoa. I would like to have your opinion in this matter, even if you should declare me the biggest bore in the world! [. . .]

Verdi to Giulio Ricordi

Milan, 2 May 1873 [1]

Dear Giulio,

I have no faith whatsoever in the productions of *Aida* in Genoa and Rome. [. . .] What frightens me most about this opera is the stinginess of impresarios and the poor interpretation of conductors. Considering all of this, I think you must do what you did for *Forza del Destino*: Do it everywhere, but do it simultaneously in different theatres. That is my opinion.

I have received four telegrams from Ancona. [2] All of them speak of success, but one of these telegrams says: "Company excellent. The rest less than mediocre." It's true that the author of this telegram is a little hostile to that theatre, but I see he is right. [. . .]

1. In all probability Verdi wrote this letter from St. Agata, although "Milano" is clearly legible in the autograph.

2. According to Marcello Conati, in *Genesi dell'Aida*, p. 158, the first performance of *Aida* in Ancona took place on 3 May 1873, with a cast including Stolz, Waldmann, Capponi, and Pantaleoni, conducted by Emilio Usiglio. The date of this letter, however, is clearly legible on the autograph as 2 May 1873. The telegrams from Ancona, which are missing, could possibly have been in response to a successful dress rehearsal of the new production.

Verdi to Giulio Ricordi

St. Agata, 5 May 1873

[. . .] I am a stone's throw away, and yet I know nothing about [the revival of *Aida* in] Parma. I think there is applause but small crowds. They like la Mariani and Pandolfini . . . but the opera is poorly produced. That's not my opera; they won't understand that a musical and dramatic ensemble is necessary today, not just a singer who makes them applaud the piece. [. . .]

Verdi to Giulio Ricordi

St. Agata, 23 May 1873

Dear Giulio,

I am deeply grieved by the death of our Great One.[1] But I shall not come to Milan tomorrow because I would not have the heart to attend his funeral. I shall come soon to visit his grave, alone and without being seen, and perhaps (after further reflection and after having considered my own powers) to propose something in honor of his memory.[2]

Keep the secret, and don't say a word about my coming because it's so painful for me to hear the papers talk about me, telling me what I haven't said and haven't done. [. . .]

1. Alessandro Manzoni.
2. Verdi alludes here to his personal tribute, which was to become the *Requiem*.

Verdi to Giuseppe Cencetti [1]

[*Probably* St. Agata, June 1873]

My dear Cencetti,

I know that in Rome they hope to reorganize the theatre, and I wish these reformers were fully impressed by the fact that modern melodrama (that is to say, the opera) has requirements very different from those of former times[2] and that to obtain success it is indispensable to have a perfect ensemble. Consequently, the direction must be entrusted to two men only, both capable and energetic: to one, all the musical department — singers, orchestra, chorus, etc., etc.; to the other, the scenic department — costumes, props, settings, *mise-en-scène*, etc., etc. These men alone should be the arbiters of everything and should assume the completest responsibility. It is by these means only that good performances and success can be obtained.

I hope that the cares of the stage direction will be entrusted to you, whom I have known for so many years,[3] and who, I am persuaded, will make every effort to present the operas according to our intentions.

1. Stage director at the Teatro Apollo in Rome, where he directed the Roman premiere of *Aida* on 17 February 1875, but unknown even at the archives of the Teatro dell'Opera in that city. Pougin gives this letter in French translation on pp. 311–12 of his *Verdi: histoire anecdotique*. He writes (p. 311) that this letter was published by several Italian newspapers in the month of July 1873; the autograph of the letter, however, is missing, and in the absence of any copy of the Italian text, I translated this letter from Pougin's French publication.

2. See Verdi's letter to Luccardi of 26 October 1870, Muzio's letter to Draneht of 5 December 1870 and note 3 to that letter, and Draneht's letter to Mariette of 6 September 1871.

3. In a letter to De Sanctis of 1 January 1853, Verdi mentions a meeting with Cencetti. See *Carteggi*, I, pp. 16–17.

Verdi to Camille Du Locle

St. Agata, 24 June 1873

Dear Du Locle,

We'll leave for Paris tomorrow, but shall stop over for a day in Turin and not arrive until Saturday. I'll let you know the hour. . . .

I beg you, I implore you, I entreat you: don't go to any trouble for me, and above all, don't tell anybody that I am in Paris. I shall not go to any theatres, especially the musical ones. I come to see friends, to visit Paris, and to stay quiet — something I need very much.

Verdi to Giulio Ricordi

Paris, 24 August 1873

Dear Giulio,

La Waldmann wrote me about a month ago[1] and offered to sing in the *Mass* for Manzoni.

I replied[2] that it would make me most happy, but that if it were true she had been signed by Florence for April and May, it would be impossible, since the *Mass* must definitely be performed on the 22nd of May.

She wrote back,[3] asking me to help her find a way to work things out. [. . .]

I don't remember well, but I think she is supposed to do Amneris in Florence! And who will be Aida? And Radames? And then that chorus and that orchestra and that disregard for the drama! It will certainly be the worst of all the *Aidas* done until now.

1. Missing.

2. Actually, Signora Verdi replied in her husband's name on 12 August 1873: "Verdi . . . sends you fifteen hundred greetings and thanks for your offer to participate [in the *Mass*], and he accepts this offer with all his heart. You must only give him an explanation. You say that you will sing in Florence in the months of April and May. The question is on how many days in May will you be free, because the *Mass* must be performed without fail on the 22nd, the anniversary of Manzoni's death. Will you, then, answer as soon as possible in regard to this, and address your letter, as always, to Maestro Verdi, Hôtel de Bâde, Boulevard des Italiens, Paris." (Autograph: Conservatorio di Musica "G. B. Martini," Bologna)

3. Missing.

Giulio Ricordi to Verdi

Milan, 27 August 1873

[. . .] I still have not heard from Signora Waldmann about the affair you mentioned to me, but the moment I do I shall take care of it at once. I don't think it's difficult to reach an agreement with the impresario; Signora Waldmann could always remain in Florence until the 5th or 10th of May and then go to Milan for the rehearsals. All of this would be subject to your approval, of course, and to our agreement with the impresario, who will hardly wish to give up Signora Waldmann, important as she is to the role of Amneris.

Regarding your observations about the production in Florence, you know, illustrious Maestro, how many and what kind of cautions we are now taking in the contracts for *Aida*. In Florence, too, they can't even engage the doormen without our approval! And since all or almost all theatres are very bad — especially as far as the orchestra, chorus, and ballet are concerned — we would have to refuse *Aida* to them all, which, I believe, would not be even your intention. In writing up a contract, therefore, we aim at controlling the bad parts of a theatre as much as is humanly possible; and what we are able to obtain will always be much better than what the audience of that theatre is used to hearing. [. . .]

Concerning *Aida* [for Naples], do you think that last year's unique, indescribable success would allow us to grant them the opera this year also, though in a production which certainly will not be comparable to the first? . . . If you say yes, so much the better. Let the management get through it as best they can; for us it will mean one more affair. If you feel, however, that we must not give them the opera, we shall reply accordingly.

At La Scala, I think, *Aida* can have a very good production that should ensure it of a lasting and financial success. There is a general desire to hear this masterwork again. The orchestra, chorus, and ballet will not be good, but excellent, and perhaps better than before. Many have been fired and replaced with fine voices and good players. If we don't have a Stolz and a Waldmann in the company, there still are sufficient elements for a very good ensemble. [. . .]

Of course, if I had more courage and aplomb, and if I didn't have a cursed fear of the looks a certain Maestro might give me, I would risk many questions and requests. Among these I would ask you to direct at least the rehearsals for *Macbeth*. [. . .]

Verdi to Giulio Ricordi

Paris, 31 August 1873

[. . .] I don't have time today to respond in detail to your letter and to give you my opinion about the future performances of *Aida*. [. . .] For next year, sign whatever artists suit you best, but don't count on me for now. [. . .]

Giulio Ricordi to Verdi

Milan, 4 September 1873

I received your esteemed letter and see that what I wrote you in general does not appeal to you. Let's no longer talk about the *Macbeth* rehearsals, then, or of anything for Milan. But in the meantime I cannot refrain from exclaiming: poor Milan and poor Scala, if you really abandon them! . . . and why? . . .

You will do me a real favor, illustrious Maestro, if you tell me how to proceed with *Aida*, especially in Milan and Naples, in accordance with what I wrote you. Here one doesn't talk about or want anything else, and I think that, as long as you are not against it, the reproduction of *Aida* will be a real fortune for the management.

Today I saw the impresario from Florence, who, though protesting that he wants to do everything possible, hinted at many problems in the Waldmann affair, since his season lasts from 15 April until early June. After many tergiversations I understood that this impresario would be disposed to let Signora Waldmann off for ten days, provided that he gets the contract with la Stolz who until now did not want to accept it. He would then let both these artists off for ten days of rehearsals and the performance of the *Mass*, after which they would return to Florence for the final performances of *Aida*. He is too pleased to have signed Signora Waldmann to release her altogether. If the combination with Signora Stolz were possible, there would be two advantages: to have a very beautiful *Aida* in Florence and the two women for the *Mass* in Milan. [. . .]

Verdi to Giulio Ricordi

Paris, 6 September 1873

Dear Giulio,

You must be joking when you say, "Poor Milan, and poor Scala, if you abandon them. And why?" Why, do you say why!!

No one is necessary to the world, and if La Scala existed for so long without me, it can do without me again. And all for the better!

As for *Aida*, I think it should now be made popular. After five successes, I think severity is excessive at this time. Nothing must ever be exaggerated. And your demands could now become exaggerated, if they are pushed too far. The scenes that occurred in Trieste[1] were not nice. From now on, then, be a little more easygoing with *Aida*; do it wherever you think best (taking some indispensable precautions, however), and do it in many theatres at the same time. If it fails in one place, it will succeed in another. [. . .] So loosen up — to a certain point — and don't tyrannize these poor impresarios too much; they don't know where to turn anymore.

———————

Let's now get to the *Mass* business and to la Waldmann, whom I would be most anxious to have. Without her I could not write for contralto. (I have no faith in the others.) And in an important work, it would be bad not to have a complete quartet of voices.

La Stolz has been in Milan for several days; I have a letter from her dated Milan, 31 August.[2] When I heard about the business in Florence, I wrote and asked her to arrange it so that she, along with la Waldmann, would be free at the time of the *Mass* and both of them would arrive in Milan on the 8th of May. The impresarios never understand anything. (And as a result, they have so many fiascos.) The proposed ten days for rehearsals and performance is a real stupidity! I have written la Stolz to arrange matters so that she will be in Milan on the 8th of May. I hope she will be firm. You help her as well, because even if it does not concern *Aida*, it concerns something which artistically is of equal or perhaps greater importance. [. . .]

P.S. Mind you, in this business I don't want to be mentioned in any way whatever to the Ronzis.[3]

I received a letter[4] from the president [of the theatre] in Trieste, who has invited me to go there for the first performance of *Aida*!!! By God in Heaven, I must be thought of as a charlatan, a clown, who enjoys displaying himself like a Tom Thumb, a Miss Baba, an orangutan, or some other freak!! Poor me! Poor me!

Neither the impresarios nor the directors realize yet that if I took part in the preparation of *Aida* three times, it was because I was certain I could bring about a better performance than they could! So many believe (and it is an old hoax that should be destroyed) that there are people who are able to interpret and direct better than the author. They are all imbeciles a thousand times over!

I for one, by God, have never found effects that I had not imagined! Damn the theatre!

1. Verdi seems to refer to Giulio Ricordi's negotiations for the first performance of *Aida* in Trieste on 4 October 1873 under Faccio's direction. See Faccio's letter to Giulio Ricordi of 6 October 1873.

2. Missing.

3. The Ronzi brothers. Luigi Ronzi was the impresario of the Teatro della Pergola in Florence, and Waldmann had signed a contract with him to sing Amneris at this theatre in the spring of 1874.

4. Missing.

Verdi to the President of the Teatro Comunale, Trieste

Paris, 6 September 1873

Most illustrious President,

For artistic reasons, I thought it necessary to help with *Aida* at two or three large theatres, which is what I did in Milan, Naples, and Parma. I also went to this last city because I am a native of that province and consequently almost a compatriot. Now *Aida* is started on its way, and I have surrendered it to its destiny, hoping only that it be produced with care and intelligence, and above all, according to my intentions.

I thank the Theatrical Directors of Trieste for the courteous invitation to attend the first performance; but, in addition to the fact that my presence would be of no advantage to the performance of the score, I do not care to go to theatres purely and simply to have myself exhibited as a curiosity. [. . .]

Verdi to Camille Du Locle

Turin, 13 September 1873

Dear Du Locle,

We have been here in Italy for a few nights following an excellent trip. The tunnel[1] is really sensational! Splendid gas illumination inside and profound darkness outside. Fresh air, without being suffocated by the smoke — it's a most beautiful thing! And then, three thousand meters of earth and rocks above your head!!

We'll not leave Turin before twelve; we'll have lunch in Piacenza, and we'll be in St. Agata around seven o'clock.

And now, what to tell you, my dear Du Locle? How can I thank you for all the kindnesses bestowed on us, my wife and myself, during our all too long sojourn in Paris? Your courtesy and kindness truly cannot be surpassed; and I, blushing a bit, can only say thanks to you . . . a thousand times, thanks. [. . .]

1. The Mt. Cenis tunnel. See Verdi's letter to Du Locle of 14 February 1871.

Verdi to Giulio Ricordi

St. Agata, 22 September 1873

Dear Giulio,

The day before departing from Paris I wrote you a letter asking you to find a way to dissolve la Waldmann's contract with Florence, etc. On the same day of my departure I saw Tornaghi in Paris who told me that tomorrow I would receive the answer to that letter. <u>Tomorrow</u> has not yet arrived. I have never received your letter. So may I ask you to drop me a line.

Giulio Ricordi to Verdi

Milan, 25 September 1873

In answer to your most esteemed letter of the 22nd, which I received only today, I sent you not one, but two letters to Paris about the affair of the *Mass* and in answer to your last letter.[1] Now I hasten to inform you that I talked not only with Ronzi, but also with Signora Stolz whom I had the pleasure of seeing in the best of health in Milan.

Since Ronzi now wants Signora Stolz, I don't think it's difficult to arrange what you want. Besides, we are only somewhat committed to these Ronzis and have the right to determine the artists. This morning Ronzi came to see me, precisely to tell me that Signora Stolz was not opposed to singing some performances of *Aida* in Florence (which I already knew). He asked me then to tell him the exact period of time [for the *Mass*] and how many days of leave Signora Waldmann needs to combine the one with the other. The *Mass*, I believe, must be performed on 22 May more or less; be kind enough to tell me then precisely, illustrious Maestro, from which day onward you plan to have the artists at your disposal. I figured just for myself that one might calculate the time that is necessary for an opera, that is about fifteen days; but it's up to you to give me the precise dates. Is there a tenor and a bass? . . . Of whom might you have thought? [. . .]

1. Giulio Ricordi presumably refers to Verdi's letter from Paris of 6 September 1873. Giulio Ricordi's answer to that letter is missing.

Verdi to Giulio Ricordi

St. Agata, 29 September 1873

Dear Giulio,

Forgive me if I haven't answered your letter of the 25th until today.

I think that the business of la Stolz in Florence is a difficult one to settle since it would be necessary for that management to agree to these conditions:

1. To open with *Aida* around 18 or 20 April.
2. To release la Stolz and la Waldmann around 6 May so that they will be in Milan on the 7th, since the *Mass* has to be performed on the 22nd.
3. To allow the above-mentioned artists to return to Florence around the 25th or 26th to do a few more performances.

This way, they could do about fifteen or sixteen performances. Otherwise, I don't think an agreement can be reached.

Now we come to *Macbeth* and *Aida* in Milan. [. . .] I want no praise and no blame, and I also ask you not to let them say such things as your correspondent said in *Opinione* — that Ricordi and Verdi had approved la Singer[1] to do *Aida* at La Scala. I would then be forced to deny the report and to say, even, that in *Aida* there are so many problems of diction and action that I don't think a young girl singing in Italian for the first time could do that opera well. [. . .]

1. Teresina Singer (ca. 1850–1928), Moravian soprano. After her debut in 1870 at Vienna's Imperial Opera in *Faust* and *Die Zauberflöte*, she established her career in several German theatres. On 4 October 1873 she made her Italian debut at Rome's Teatro Apollo in *Faust*. On 18 October 1879 she sang the first Aida in St. Louis, Missouri, and on 18 April 1880 she was the first soprano to perform Verdi's *Ave Maria* (at La Scala in Milan). Toward the end of her career she frequently appeared in the role of Amneris.

Giulio Ricordi to Verdi

Milan, 2 October 1873

I received your most esteemed letter and will call for Ronzi to find out if and how the Stolz-Waldmann business might be arranged; and I shall hasten to inform you about it. [. . .]

What D'Arcais said in *Opinione* is not at all my fault, because it has and will always be my policy not to give anyone, journalists in particular, such information about what we are planning to do. If we cared about all the nonsense they say every day in the papers, we would require a special office of rectification!! . . . We are lucky, though, that the Italian public doesn't lend any importance to all these stories of the journalists, but takes them for what they are worth! . . . Besides, since I don't receive the *Opinione*, I didn't know at all that D'Arcais had written in one way or another of la Singer. [. . .]

Franco Faccio to Giulio Ricordi

Trieste, 6 October 1873

Dearest Giulio,

I have not written you because I have been occupied with the utmost diligence and energy in the well-being of *Aida*. (Of course, I have only done my duty.) The result has exceeded the greatest expectations: the success of *Aida*[1] was immense, not to be surpassed. Hallelujah! Hallelujah! Hallelujah! Really the performance I was able to achieve, thanks to an indefatigable chorus and orchestra and to stage rehearsals (all of which I directed), is even better than the one in Padua.

The orchestra — the <u>strings</u>, excellent; the rest, very good — was enthralled by the beauty of the music and has great admiration for me. (Mind you, I wouldn't say this to others: I know better!) [. . .] When I appeared in the pit, I was received with such general and prolonged applause that I almost lost the calm I needed at the moment. [. . .] The effect of the *largo* in the finale was also immense. Here too, I received a special ovation from the audience, which wanted this piece to be repeated; but the lazy Capponi intoned his *O re, pei sacri numi* and pulled himself forward. [. . .]

In the third act the audience was enchanted with the beauty of the music and the quality of the performance. I say nothing about Pandolfini and Capponi, whom you know; but I must tell you that in the aria and in the *adagio* of the duet with Radames, la Mariani surpassed la Stolz. Naturally this is not so in the *allegro* of the same duet, in the phrases of the duet with the father, and in the great finale where the vigorous and piercing voice of la Stolz has no competition. [. . .] I have told you enough about la Mariani; I must add, however, that in the final duet as well, I prefer her to la Stolz. I can only say a world of good about la Fricci: stupendous voice, accent and action stir the audience to enthusiasm; but she does not succeed in making me forget la Waldmann. (We know this already.) Anyway she is a most valuable Amneris, and if I had to choose between one or the other . . . I would choose both of them. [. . .]

1. The first performance of *Aida* in Trieste took place at the Teatro Comunale on 4 October 1873.

Eugenio Tornaghi to Verdi

Milan, 24 October 1873

In Giulio's absence I have the honor to address these lines to you, to inform you without delay of the result of the negotiations with the management in Florence to obtain the leave you had proposed for Signora Waldmann. I am sorry that the result does not correspond to our wishes. I am enclosing a letter from the management,[1] and it goes without saying that I am ready for your orders regarding if and how it should be answered. [. . .]

1. Missing.

Verdi to Eugenio Tornaghi

St. Agata, 25 October 1873

Esteemed Signor Tornaghi,

I think I should have been left out of the *Aida* business in Florence, and it was useless to drag my name between *Aida* and Sig. Ronzi.

I have asked the House of Ricordi to arrange it so that in signing a contract for *Aida*, la Waldmann might be free to rehearse and sing the *Mass*, etc., etc. [. . .]

I don't know Sig. Ronzi, except that last year he pulled a mean trick on me in Naples when he ordered the bass Monti[1] to refuse, at the dress rehearsal, to sing the role of the Friar in *Don Carlos*, which Monti had accepted.

Sig. Ronzi's offer to give me all the artists on the 19th to sing the *Mass* on the 22nd is not only a joke, but a jeer! I am not used to having music performed under my direction in the manner it is performed at the Pergola in Florence.

I have not requested anything or accepted anything from Sig. Ronzi. I have asked, and I still ask, the House of Ricordi (as I said above) to arrange the signing of the contract for *Aida* so that la Waldmann may be free to rehearse and perform the *Mass*. That's all! [. . .]

1. Gaetano Monti, Italian bass. Singing at the San Carlo Opera in Naples between 1872 and 1874, he later was to appear at La Scala and other major Italian theatres, as well as in London, the United States, Berlin, Stuttgart, and Odessa. In 1873 he had sung the King in the first Neapolitan production of *Aida* under Verdi's direction.

Verdi to Eugenio Tornaghi[1]

St. Agata, 3 November 1873

Signor Tornaghi,

In terms of art, opera will always be massacred in Naples. This year, with the exception of la Krauss, they have the worst company, and *Aida* will not do well. [. . .]

I am still of the opinion that *Aida*, like *Forza*, must be done, but in many theatres simultaneously. It's bad if *Aida* is done only at La Scala and in

Naples. It will go very badly in Naples; and in Milan success is not sure except in a few parts.

As for Vienna and Berlin, do whatever you think best, but don't count on me. [. . .]

1. Presumably in answer to a letter that is missing.

Emanuele Muzio to Verdi[1]

New York, 8 November 1873

[. . .] This week I shall begin the ensemble rehearsals and the stage rehearsals with chorus for *Aida*; and since I don't trust la Nilsson,[2] I have had la Torriani[3] study and rehearse the role. [. . .]

1. Muzio was in New York to conduct the fall season of Italian opera at the Academy of Music, under the management of Maurice Strakosch (1825–87).
2. Christine Nilsson (1843–1921), Swedish soprano. After studying in France, she made her debut at the Théâtre-Lyrique in 1864 as Violetta in *La Traviata*. She quickly became Adelina Patti's most dangerous rival, with a repertoire encompassing Donna Elvira, the Queen of the Night, Lucia di Lammermoor, Elsa, and Mignon. Best known for her Marguerite in *Faust*, the role in which she appeared at the opening of the Metropolitan Opera on 22 October 1883, she was at the height of her career in the early 1870s. Muzio's concern was probably caused by Mme. Nilsson's concentration on lyric and coloratura parts.
3. Ostava Torriani (ca. 1847–?), born Sophia Ostave-Tornquist, German soprano. The daughter of the United States Consul in Hamburg, her mother came from a prominent German family. After studies in Paris, she made her debut in 1867 (under the name Sophia Tornquist) as Gilda at the Teatro Carcano in Milan. In 1872 she appeared at the Italian Theatre in Paris and during later seasons in England, Italy, Germany, and the United States.

Verdi to Giulio Ricordi

St. Agata, 9 November 1873

Dear Giulio,

I don't hear any more talk about *Aida* in Florence! What has happened, or what will happen?

And are they going to do *Aida* in Milan? If it is done, I would like it to be done well, because it will be massacred in Naples! The company, with the exception of la Krauss, is the worst! So tell me for sure who the artists will be [in Milan]! [. . .]

Verdi to Giulio Ricordi

St. Agata, 19 November 1873

Dear Giulio,

At the beginning of last week I asked you to tell me which two women will sing in the *Aida* in Milan. I positively must know, so please tell me immediately by telegram. [. . .]

Giulio Ricordi to Verdi

Milan, 20 November 1873

By this hour you will have received my dispatch.[1] This letter will explain my delay in replying to your last letter because of my desire to give you definite news about everything you requested to know.

As a result of la Mariani's great success in Trieste, the management of La Scala repeatedly asked the impresario Ciaffei[2] in Warsaw to negotiate her release. Ciaffei always refused. [. . .] The company of *Aida* remains then as it was originally established. [. . .]

The famous Ronzi [. . .] finally came to see us yesterday, and I told him that the free days the Florence management proposes to arrange for la Waldmann will not suffice. He will write again to Florence, but I think that nothing will happen that way. As I wrote you already, and to get to the point, we have not signed the contract for *Aida*; this is the only way to get what we want. [. . .]

1. Missing.
2. Unknown.

Franco Faccio to Eugenio Tornaghi

Trieste, 20 November 1873

[. . .] I shall insist that the management of La Scala [. . .] not miss the opportunity to have la Mariani sing *Aida*. [. . .] With this I don't mean to say that la Singer is insufficient for this opera; but really she doesn't offer me the guarantees of a sure success that la Mariani does. [. . .]

Verdi to Giulio Ricordi

St. Agata, 21 November 1873

Dear Giulio,

What you tell me about *Aida* and la Waldmann in Florence is fine.

La Mariani would have been better for the *Aida* in Milan, rather than risking a beginner . . . but she [la Singer] will still be acceptable for Aida, even though I am not as hopeful as you. . . . While *Aida* may hold up, *Macbeth* will unpardonably fail. [. . .]

Emanuele Muzio to Verdi

New York, 22 November 1873

[. . .] The rehearsals for *Aida* are going well, and on Wednesday the 26th we shall give the first performance. I shall send you a telegram, which you will use as you wish and which I hope you will communicate to Ricordi. The opera makes a great impression on the orchestra members, who play it with much love; the chorus is animated and full of good will, and the artists are most zealous. All that is left for me to do is one more stage rehearsal with all the crowds (including the supers), the first dress rehearsal, and the final dress rehearsal. It will be a great success, financially too. [. . .]

Franco Faccio to Eugenio Tornaghi

Trieste, 24 November 1873

[. . .] So it isn't possible to have la Mariani? A pity, really a pity. Since there is no remedy, however, it's better not to think about it and to turn all of our attention to la Singer, who is facing the grave task of making her debut in *Aida*. [. . .]

Emanuele Muzio to Verdi

New York, 27 November 1873

My dear Maestro,

Last night at half past eleven, I sent you a telegram to announce the immense success of *Aida* [1] to you. Today I shall mail the newspaper reports, which my wife will read and translate for you. The best article is perhaps the one in the *Tribune*; [2] the rest of the papers have written without expressing any ideas and without having understood a thing. The success is assured, and I am happy that my labors have been appreciated and rewarded. [. . .]

The preparations for the war [3] continue, but today the news is peace, since Spain will give the requested satisfactions. Perhaps you will no longer be at St. Agata and will have looked for a milder climate; we are in the cold and will soon go on to the West, [4] where there is plenty of ice and snow.

1. The first American performance of *Aida* was given at the Academy of Music in New York, with a cast including Ostava Torriani (Aida), Annie Louise Cary (Amneris), Italo Campanini (Radames), and Victor Maurel (Amonasro).

Annie Louise Cary (1841–1921), American contralto. Born in Wayne, Maine, she received her initial vocal instruction in Portland and studied in Boston. Following further studies with distinguished teachers, including Mme. Viardot-Garcia, in Europe, she made her debut as Azucena in Copenhagen (1868) and was heard in other Scandinavian countries, as well as in Hamburg and Brussels. In 1870 she appeared under the name of Cari at Covent Garden in London and was so successful that Maurice Strakosch brought her back to the United States. Until 1873 she also sang at Covent Garden and between 1875 and 1877 in Russia. She retired at the height of a brilliant career in 1881 and died forty years later in Norwalk, Connecticut.

Italo Campanini (1845–96), Italian tenor. Following his debut as a *comprimario* in Parma, he appeared as a leading tenor in Odessa. After three years of engagements in Russia, he sang at La Scala and, in 1871, was the first Italian Lohengrin under Mariani's baton in Bologna. He also sang this role under Faccio's direction at La Scala (1873). Applauded in a vast repertoire, he was heard throughout Italy, in Spain, Portugal, Austria, and Russia, and he was particularly admired in England and the United States. When he sang Faust in the inaugural performance of the Metropolitan Opera on 22 October 1883, his voice was already in decline. Three years later he was whistled in *Mefistofele* at the San Carlo Opera in Naples; but in New York and London his performances were enjoyed as late as 1894.

2. A review by Henry E. Krehbiel (1854–1923) in *The New York Daily Tribune* of 27 November 1873.

3. Muzio refers to the differences between Spain and the United States over the possession of Cuba. War was averted at this time; but in 1898, the same differences were to erupt in the Spanish-American War.

4. The same Strakosch Italian Opera company performed *Aida* on 12 December 1873 in Philadelphia, on 20 and 23 January 1874 in Chicago, on 27 January 1874 in Milwaukee, and on 5 February 1874 in Boston. Giuseppe Del Puente replaced Maurel in Chicago, Milwaukee, and Boston.

Giuseppe Del Puente (1843–1900), Italian baritone, began to establish himself in the roles of Macbeth and Renato in Seville. From 1872 to 1888 he was heard throughout Italy; but, like Campanini, he enjoyed his greatest successes in England and the United States. His vast repertory included such roles as Papageno, Melitone, and Jago. In 1878 Del Puente sang Escamillo in the first English production of *Carmen*; in 1883 he appeared as Valentin in the *Faust* performance inaugurating the Metropolitan Opera and, on the same stage, in the first American performance of *La Gioconda*. Later he taught voice in Philadelphia, where he died.

Verdi to Franco Faccio

[*Probably* St. Agata, 29 November 1873][1]

Dear Faccio,

I would have liked ten contraltos rather than ten sopranos. But leave things as they are, if you have no more time to change them for the better. Like this, for example:

First tenors	14	First sopranos	8
Second tenors	14	Second sopranos	8
Bass-baritones	14	Contraltos	8
Low basses	18		

A total of 84 choristers. That would be only two more, and the proportion would be better.

In the second finale I would want the chorus to consist of the following:

For the chorus of priests:

First tenors	5
Second tenors	5
Bass-baritones	5
Low basses	5

For the chorus of the Ethiopian slaves:[2]

Sopranos or mezzo-sopranos	3
Contraltos	3
Bass-baritones	3
Low basses	4

Both for the chorus of the priests and for that of the slaves, choose the freshest and most beautiful voices. Use everyone else for the chorus of the populace, which will consist of:

First tenors	9
Second tenors	9
Baritones	6
Basses	9

With 18 or 20 women. That isn't too much, but it's enough.

Be sure to also arrange the members of the orchestra in proportion. If you have twelve violins, have twelve seconds with eight violas and eight cellos. This way, you won't have a shrill, noisy sound, but one that is robust and full. [. . .]

1. The transcription of this letter in *Franco Faccio e Verdi*, Rafaello De Rensis ed. (Milano: Fratelli Treves, 1934), pp. 133–35, is inaccurate, and the date given to the letter (''29 November from Genoa'') cannot be trusted. Verdi's advice to Faccio in the letter suggests that he wrote it before rehearsals began for the revival of *Aida* at La Scala on 26 December 1873.

2. See Verdi's letters to Ghislanzoni of 30 September 1870 and to Giulio Ricordi of 10 December 1871.

Teresa Stolz to Verdi

Cairo, 5 December 1873

Dearest Maestro,

Infinite thanks for your kind letter.[1] [. . .]

On the 2nd of December we opened with *Aida* [. . .], the fifth opera of the season.

What shall I tell you about the performance of this stupendous music? There were good things, also mediocre things, and even bad things!!!! First of all, the *mise-en-scène* was the worst, even though it was changed last year after D'Ormeville had seen the *mise-en-scène* in Parma.

The sets here are as pretty as a picture, but they are not theatrical; the painter wanted to make an effect, without thinking that he had to serve the theatre. [. . .]

Bottesini conducted the opera with great zeal, with much accuracy, but he is cold and soft (yet always a thousand times better than the conductors in Naples). [. . .]

I and la Waldmann have made the greatest impression on the audience, and on the Viceroy, who never tired of applauding. [. . .]

1. Missing.

Verdi to Giulio Ricordi

St. Agata, 16 December 1873

[. . .] How are the rehearsals for *Aida* going?[1] A word between the two of us. . . . Would it be possible to let me hear the first dress rehearsal without a soul in the world knowing? . . . I mean, strictly speaking, not a soul in the world — including, dare I even say, your wife! [. . .]

1. Verdi refers to the revival at La Scala.

Verdi to Giulio Ricordi [1]

St. Agata, 19 December 1873

Dearest Giulio,

I was quite right in saying that *Aida* should not be done at La Scala, because that opera can only be reproduced with a secure company. Now I ask how it could be secure when it had as protagonist an artist making her debut, since that is what la Singer was at that time. I admit she has plenty of talent and that she might even become another Patti one day; but for the time being, no matter how favorable the judgment in Rome has been, it was very unwise to entrust her with such a burden, having also to depend on her physical strength, which it appears you yourself had doubts about. For theatres like La Scala, you need a *pièce de consistance*.

The best thing to do now is to change the opera or close the theatre until her recovery, as I told you in my telegram.[2] [. . .]

It was a mistake to give *Aida*, and these are the consequences! But I am a little like the old Cassandra, and I am wasting my breath. [. . .]

1. Presumably Verdi wrote this letter under the influence of a bad rehearsal, or having received bad news from Giulio Ricordi about the *Aida* rehearsals at La Scala.
2. Missing.

Giulio Ricordi to Verdi

Milan, 21 December 1873

Illustrious Maestro,

Although forced by one of my wintry rheumatisms to stay in bed, I do not delay even for a moment in replying to your esteemed letter, anxious as I am to explain the situation well and thus to justify myself to you. Before arranging for *Aida* at La Scala, I did not fail to turn to you, as was my duty, and your answers really did not give me the impression that you were against the reproduction of this opera. [. . .] After Faccio had urged Ciaffei to release la Mariani, we learned that the board of directors in Warsaw flatly refused to let Ciaffei release her. We were more at ease when we had news about la Singer from Rome. Then she arrived, the rehearsals began, and we realized that she was tired or sick, or has lost her voice!! . . . And now we think of every means to find another artist; the only one available is la Pozzoni, who arrived from America only last night. So, if la Singer does not improve today, we are already agreed with Faccio and the management to replace her with la Pozzoni, provided that she accepts the contract. [. . .]

Verdi to Giulio Ricordi

St. Agata, 23 December 1873

Dear Giulio,

I have never been hostile to giving *Aida* again at La Scala; but I have said and written a hundred times that I would have wanted it to be done simultaneously in many theatres. As long as it could only be given in Milan and Naples, it was absolutely necessary to have definite guarantees of its success. Now I ask if a success in Naples is possible with Barbacini,[1] Colonnese, Sanz,[2] etc., etc.? In Milan it was imprudent to entrust the longest role to a beginner. It's true the Brescia theatre could have served as an experiment; but since the cholera prevented it, it would have been wise to withdraw the score from La Scala. You talk to me about the success in Rome! But what does that success prove? It proves that la Singer will be able to sing the *romanza* and the final duet extremely well, even better than they have ever been sung! . . . We can hope for this; I might say, if you want, we can be certain of it. But are you certain about the rest! What about the Hymn of War? What about the Invocation, which requires a big voice, one that carries?[3] What about the Great Finale? What about the third act? What, after all, about the role as a whole? The role and the character: all that is uncertain!

This is the unknown which neither you nor I can know. Well then, I say that this was not the moment to trust the unknown.

Mind you, I am not passing judgment . . . later on we'll see. . . .

1. Enrico Barbacini (1834–1905), Italian tenor. Having sung at the Teatro Canobbiana in Milan for several years, he appeared at La Scala for the first time in *Don Carlos* in 1868, as a replacement for Mongini who had fallen ill. In 1879 he was to sing performances of the *Requiem* there.

2. Elena Sanz (1850–98), Spanish mezzo-soprano. After studying in Madrid and Paris, she

made her debut in 1869 in Warsaw. She was heard during several seasons at the Italian Theatre in Paris, but she also sang in Italy and in both Americas. She had two sons by King Alfonso XII of Spain. Her sons sued him for nonsupport, but their mother died in poverty.[1]

3. Since the time of his letter to Draneht of 1 September 1871, in which he lists a second soprano for the role of the Great Priestess, Verdi changed his mind and assigned the offstage Invocation in Act I, Scene 2, to the artist performing the role of Aida. An apparently added note in the autograph score requests her to sing the strophes of the Great Priestess, *Possente Fthà*. The *New York Herald* of 27 November 1873 reports that at the first American performance of *Aida*, under Muzio's leadership, "the second scene . . . began with a very quaint theme of an Oriental character, chanted by Mlle. Torriani, and afterwards taken up by the chorus." See also note 2, Verdi's letter to Du Locle of 25 December 1871 and Document XII.

Verdi to Giulio Ricordi

St. Agata, 26 December 1873

Dear Giulio,

I am glad to hear better news and that the dress rehearsal went well. As the telegram[1] will have told you, keep sending dispatches to me here and a detailed letter about opening night. Also send me the box office receipts until after the sixth performance. [. . .]

1. Missing.

Verdi to Giulio Ricordi

St. Agata, 28 December 1873

Dear Giulio,

I am happy that my guess was wrong!

I am happy that when I wasn't there the management and the directors found a way to acquire good props, good stage machinery, a good stage band, good *mise-en scène*, and thus to achieve the effect that I couldn't and didn't know how to achieve.

So much the better, so much the better; and I repeat, I am happy, and I shall be even happier if I can finally convince you that my guess was only half right in Milan and that it's in everyone's best interest I don't get involved with the matters of that theatre. [. . .]

Verdi to Giulio Ricordi

Genoa, 23 January 1874

[. . .] I have received three telegrams from Naples.[1] Musella says wonderful things about everyone. Cesarino[2] says: "Success. La Krauss good. Others inadequate." A third says: "Music highly enjoyable. Artists all equal.

Few moments for la Krauss and la Sanz. On the whole weak. Excellent performance for the music only.''

An ugly word, that "only." It means a token success and a meager house. [. . .]

1. *Aida* had also been revived in Naples.
2. Cesare De Sanctis, who in a long letter of 23 January 1874 had given Verdi a detailed account of the *Aida* reprise at the San Carlo Opera on 22 January 1874. See *Carteggi*, I, pp. 167–69.

Verdi to Cesare De Sanctis

Telegram   Genoa, 17 February 1874

WRITE ME AT LENGTH HOW THEATRE DOES. TELL ME RECEIPTS.

Verdi to Eugenio Terziani

[*Probably* Genoa, February 1874]

Your letter[1] troubled me, especially since I could not provide you an escape in the sense that you wanted. If you are shot at on one battlefield, I am under fire on another. I seldom read the newspapers, and I am even less concerned with the rumors that might be spread about me. I know in general, however, that I am made to say and do whatever suits the interests and passions of those who make me speak and act without my knowledge.

Nothing is going to drag me into the *Aida* business in Rome. . . . When I stage and assist [in the preparation of] my operas, I want to know everything, and I take the responsibility for everything. [. . .] When I don't stage them myself, I never take charge of my operas, and I grant complete freedom to the publisher-proprietor to do and undo as he sees fit. [. . .]

1. Missing. Abbiati, III, p. 674, claims that Terziani had pleaded for Verdi's permission to direct *Aida* in Rome.

Verdi to Giulio Ricordi

Genoa, 25 February 1874

Dear Giulio,

This Florence business is absolutely indecent! Every day a new proposition!! Now, suddenly, the production is to be in the fall!!!! But you, you who know about these dealings, don't you see that this agreement is almost impossible? How is it possible that those two artists[1] haven't received an offer to return to Cairo next year? And how is it possible that perhaps both, but certainly one of them, will not accept those fat contracts? In short, we are only wasting time, and we shall be ridiculed in the end. [. . .]

So you haven't at all understood what I told you in my last letter:[2] that one absolutely must decide, because apart from the answer I should give la Waldmann, there are so many other things for me to arrange thereafter.

So don't hesitate any more; make up your mind.

Tell the Florence management that if they have not decided by ———, they can keep la Waldmann, but count no longer on *Aida*, either now or in the fall.

It seems impossible to me that you could have agreed to this new proposition for the fall! You know well that, first of all, we must write to la Stolz and la Waldmann, and that it takes three weeks to get an answer from Cairo. How, then, can this affair be arranged at this hour?

There would be a way, however, to take care of everything, namely:

1. The management would agree to give us la Waldmann for the *Mass*.
2. You would agree to give *Aida* in the fall.
3. If la Stolz and la Waldmann can and want to go there, so much the better, and these two first of all. If not, you will still allow *Aida*, with la Mariani, and also la Singer, if you wish, la Fricci, or some other mezzo-soprano whom I could not suggest to you.

Anyway make up your mind, because, I repeat, I don't like to be led around by the nose. [. . .]

1. Stolz and Waldmann.
2. Missing.

Verdi to Maria Waldmann

Genoa, 27 February 1874

Dearest Waldmann,

Who would believe that nothing has been decided yet about *Aida* in Florence? It's impossible to reach an agreement with those Messrs. Ronzi. Never in my career, long as it is, have I seen so much hesitation, so much uncertainty! Every day there's a new project! A few days ago there was the project to begin the season after the *Mass*, that is, at the end of May. Now they would like to switch the season from the spring to the fall. . . .

But would you and la Stolz be free; could you, and would you, go to do *Aida* in the fall? Worst of all, time is passing, and I have not succeeded in getting the Ronzis to release you at the time of the *Mass*. . . . Please drop me a line immediately, immediately upon receiving this letter, and tell me:

1. If you have signed with the Ronzis in Florence on the condition that *Aida* is done or if you have signed without it.
2. If you would be disposed to changing the contract and doing *Aida* in the fall? I say if you <u>would be disposed</u>, but it's always understood that it would be convenient for you to do it.

I ask you again to reply as soon as you receive this, because time is running out!! A couple of words are enough.

I inform you once more that Capponi has signed in Florence on the condition that *Aida* is done. If Ricordi does not give *Aida*, Capponi is free and would most likely sing in the *Mass*. Therefore if the Ronzis accept and agree, possibly, to reschedule *Aida* after the *Mass* or in the fall, leaving you the necessary free time to rehearse and perform the *Mass*, then they can do *Aida*. If not, it is impossible!

Forgive me if I have bored you with my <u>chatter</u>, but I need these clarifications from you as soon as possible. [. . .]

Goodbye then, my dearest Maria, [. . .] and believe me the most sincere of your friends. [. . .]

Teresa Stolz to Verdi

Cairo, 28 February 1874

[. . . Bottesini] amounts to very little in the orchestra pit and, unable to impose himself on the company, tolerates indecent performances that are really shameful!!! [. . .]

Verdi to Cesare De Sanctis

Telegram   Genoa, 1 March 1874

TELL CLAUSETTI IMMEDIATELY TO PROTEST TO MANAGEMENT. SURPRISED HE PERMITTED SUCH A THING.[1]

1. Verdi refers to cuts made in the *Aida* revival in Naples.

Verdi to Tito Ricordi

Genoa, 1 March 1874

Dear Tito,

Read this little article from the *Pungolo* in Naples!

How can *Aida* be performed on several evenings in that manner, and the

House of Ricordi looks the other way? And the firm's representative allows things to run in that manner?

According to the terms of our contract, I formally demand that a claim for damages and penalties be made to the Naples management and that these penalties must be claimed by the author. The owner, having gotten his rental fee, suffers no damage. It is art that is abused, and I make it my duty to vindicate this.

No concession, no compromise in this matter! [. . .]

Verdi to Giulio Ricordi

Genoa, 1 March 1874

Dear Giulio,

As I telegraphed you,[1] I don't think la Waldmann will give up her contract in Florence. I think it's enough of a sacrifice to come to Milan for the *Mass* and return to Florence. If la Waldmann were disposed to breaking that contract, I wouldn't be the one to propose it to her. And if la Waldmann is now a burden to the Ronzis, let them think of a way to extricate themselves.

I wrote to your father today about the *Aida* in Naples, and it deeply saddens me. [. . .]

1. This telegram is missing.

Verdi to Tito Ricordi

Genoa, 4 March 1874

[. . .] How about this Naples business? The fourth act was cut! It's come to that! And Clausetti said nothing?

Verdi to Tito Ricordi

Genoa, 6 March 1874

Dear Tito,

No, no, with regard to this Naples business, I am not going to be sweet as sugar like you. Clausetti is certainly guilty because he should have stopped the performance that very night. Not only did he not stop it, but he permitted them to do *Aida* with a mutilated last act for several nights. In our contract, after all, there exists a clause that states the opera must be performed as in the original. Since the clause is there, it must be fulfilled. Wouldn't it be nice if there had to be a trial between me and you over this!! [. . .]

Tito Ricordi to Verdi

Milan, 7 March 1874

Dearest friend,

I received your dear letter of yesterday and hasten to answer you about that damn trouble in Naples.

From what Clausetti writes me, it seems that Musella acted without warning and that he did not have time to protest. Clausetti replied to my very severe reproaches; he confessed that he let himself be taken in for fear of entangling me in a long and difficult lawsuit and that he took steps instead to make sure it would not happen again.

This will teach me a lesson for the future: to find a way to eliminate the danger of a lawsuit and, thus, to make the repetition of similar cases impossible.

Be this as it may, it is clear that you are not only right one time but a thousand; and I assure you that I am extremely mortified by what has happened. I understand that I am responsible for my representatives' actions; nevertheless I do not want to think that (if only out of a purely personal regard for me) you will not grant me your pardon. [. . .]

Verdi to Léon Escudier [1]

Genoa, 7 March 1874

Dear Léon,

The *Aida* and *Forza* business is most delicate. First of all I must tell you frankly that neither in the kind of music nor in the style of production are these two operas suited to the Italian Theatre in Paris. The Italian Theatre requires operas with a simple *mise-en-scène*, operas that rely mainly on singing and a small orchestra. [. . .]

Ricordi is the owner of the score. The management should address itself to him; he knows best how to do things so that there is at least a probability of success, in which I do not believe.

To conclude: I am in no way opposed, but I don't want to cooperate either. So do whatever you think best. [. . .]

1. In response to a missing letter, in which Escudier had requested permission to give *Aida* and *La Forza del Destino* at the Italian Theatre under his management.

Verdi to Tito Ricordi

Genoa, 8 March 1874

Dear Tito,

I do not at all intend to pass over the Naples business.

It could not have been a surprise to Clausetti that *Aida* was mutilated on several evenings.

At any rate, either Clausetti or Musella is at fault. So it must be remedied by a good <u>trial</u>, and this is what I <u>formally</u> demand as an <u>author</u> of the <u>House of Ricordi</u>.

It is not a matter of personal gain for me, it is the dignity of art. If I had cared so much for personal gain, no one could have stopped me from writing an opera a year after *Traviata* for enormous profits; instead, since that time (<u>twenty-one</u> years!), I have almost abandoned the theatre, having written only two operas for Italy.

If, four years ago, I convinced myself to go to Milan for *Forza del Destino*, it was still because of a feeling for art. I knew that for many, many years at La Scala, operas had been produced and performed horrendously. (I saw it myself one evening with *Don Carlos*.) So I said to myself, pardon my vanity, "Let's try to succeed in achieving a production worthy of that theatre," and I resolved to go to Milan to stage *Forza*.

At the time it seemed as if there was a result; but afterward it didn't seem fair to make me pay for it with all sorts of prickings. Never mind! Let's get back to the subject. I repeat, the Naples business is an offense to art which must be amended! [. . .]

Verdi to Tito Ricordi

Genoa, 11 March 1874

Dear Tito,

I understand nothing, absolutely nothing, about this entire Naples business!

But why? Was the contract with Musella drawn up so carelessly that, in a way, he had the right to do what he did?

And, further, you accepted Musella's explanation?

But what about me? What does that make me then? A worker, a day laborer, who brings his goods to the <u>firm</u> and who is exploited by the <u>firm</u> as it sees fit! That is not what I want. I told you before that if I had wanted to be a merchant, no one could have stopped me from writing an opera per year after *Traviata* and making for myself a fortune three times greater than the one I have! I had other ideas about art (as proved by the care I have taken with my last operas), and I would have accomplished something if I had not encountered opposition, or at least indifference, from <u>everything</u> and <u>everyone</u>!

I want to distinguish between Tito Ricordi and the publisher, and that is why I ask Tito Ricordi to tell me frankly how things stand. Even though the publisher's agents have not cared for my interests, I would not embarrass Tito Ricordi with a lawsuit; but permit me to say once more that the <u>publishing house</u> has treated me with a total lack of consideration.

Eugenio Tornaghi to Verdi

Milan, 13 March 1874

Illustrious Maestro,
    Signor Ricordi informed me of your letter of yesterday. Therefore I must tell you with the greatest embarrassment, yes, illustrious Maestro, the fault of the Naples affair is entirely mine and Sig. Clausetti's. I was wrong not to have seen to it that in the contract with Musella the danger of his doing what he did was not explicitly and definitely avoided. Sig. Clausetti admits to his failure in not warning me before the damage was done. And, in fact, had I been advised in time, I could have prevented it, because even though the clause concerning the performance is not strong enough (unfortunately, my fault alone) to assure us of victory in case of a suit, it was nevertheless sufficient to keep Musella from doing what he did.
    Sig. Clausetti has his excuses in a series of extraordinary coincidences, among them the serious illness of his chief clerk, etc. I shall not make up any reasons; I am most distressed that an innocent oversight has caused you and my Signor Tito so much displeasure; I am guilty, I admit it, and humbly ask for your pardon.
    As far as the future is concerned, you can be quite sure that what has happened will be a lesson for me to adapt myself with all my powers, weak as they are, so that you and Signor Ricordi may never again have reason to complain about my conduct or that of my colleagues.
[P.S.] Signor Tito, hoping to see you here soon, reserves for himself the opportunity of answering you in person.

Verdi to Tito Ricordi

Genoa, [*Probably* mid-March] 1874

Dear Tito,
    Out of consideration for you, and wishing to grant the request you made in your letter, I agree this one time to forget about and draw a veil over the *Aida* controversy that has arisen in Naples. Art now has other needs; and if I stated the condition in my contract that I did not want any mutilations or changes in the performance of my scores, I did it because I know the impre-

sarios and the thousand indecencies they are capable of committing because of a misunderstanding or because of their greed for a few francs.

Verdi to Maria Waldmann

Genoa, 14 March 1874

Dear Waldmann,

I am most grateful to you for having replied immediately[1] and doubly grateful for your having done so right after the performance of *Aida* — after midnight! Thank you!

I am happy that you can take part in the *Mass*, and I must also tell you, for your peace of mind, that if you had signed the contract in Florence only to do *Aida*, you wouldn't have gained anything, since it was impossible for Ricordi to give them the score. The Ronzis had not thought about, prepared, or done anything except sign you and Capponi — and this only conditionally. They had not secured an Aida. They had not thought about the company or about the conductor, etc. Great people, these Ronzis! But that's not the way to do business!

It may be that this deal will be changed to the fall, but don't give it a thought! . . . I shall talk with and give instructions to Ricordi so that this mess isn't repeated.[2] As for the business with La Scala, don't be in any hurry! There is time! [. . .]

1. Waldmann's reply from Cairo to Verdi's letter of 27 February 1874 is missing.
2. *Aida* was eventually given its first performance in Florence at another theatre, under another management, and without Stolz, Waldmann, or Capponi. See note 2 to Verdi's letter to Tornaghi of 10 October 1874.

Verdi to Giuseppe Piroli

Genoa, 16 April 1874

[. . .] Your theatre in Rome goes along as it can and as it must. And I have known for some time that, sooner or later, serious scandals had to occur with those people.[1] Was Ricordi not right then to refuse *Aida*? And why didn't the newspapers, which unleashed themselves so heavily against us, get after those who were guilty of those indecencies? That would have been justice, and maybe they would have considered remedying the evil earlier. [. . .]

1. Verdi apparently refers to Jacovacci's management of the Teatro Apollo and other Roman theatres, but the particular scandals that occurred at that time are not known.

Verdi to Giulio Ricordi

[*Probably* Genoa, 16 April 1874]

[. . .] How many effects of sonority, rhythm, and coloring, which I was sure I had written into *Aida*, I missed in Milan and later found in the modest orchestra in Parma and in the one in Naples. And I'll bet that if Trieste still has the same decent orchestra it had many years ago, Faccio will have found some effects that were lacking in Milan. Ask him privately, and he will tell you it's true.

Giuseppina Verdi to Cesare De Sanctis [1]

Milan, 6 May 1874

[. . .] *Aida*, they say, went well in Berlin[2] and very well in Vienna.[3] I consider this a piece of good luck, because I can guess what a rendering they have given that inspired music. The Germans know a great deal about science, art, literature, everything; but they do not feel Verdi's music, and until now they did not know how to perform it. [. . .]

1. Signora Verdi writes at the time Verdi was rehearsing for the first performance of the *Requiem* on 22 May 1874 at the Church of San Marco in Milan.
2. The first performance of *Aida*, in a German translation, was given at the Royal Opera in Berlin on 20 April 1874.
3. The Austrian premiere, in German, took place at the Imperial Opera in Vienna on 29 April 1874.

Verdi to Giulio Ricordi

[*Probably* Paris, 1 July 1874][1]

Do what heaven inspires you to do, and don't consult me anymore. I am not always of your opinion; and with last winter's *Aida* and *Macbeth*,[2] you discovered that I was wrong. What does it matter if the roles of Aida and Amneris were performed well or badly, since the audience applauded! And what did it matter that two years ago I went to so much trouble for the coordination of the production and for the *mise-en-scène*, since this year it was done better without me, and your own *Gazzetta* saw fit to ridicule that *mise-en-scène* of mine! . . .

But these are things of the past. . . . I did not mention them to you then, and I only mention them briefly now to prove to you that I don't understand anything or that I understand things in my own way. [. . .]

I have read the article on the *Aida* in Vienna! I am not at all upset by it!

What does it prove? . . . That they are impertinent, and that their national arrogance has always rendered them blind and stupid! How marvelous!!! . . . When one of them comes to us, what a delight! . . . It is human wisdom that comes to us! There are no adulations we fail to heap on them! There are no insults they fail to hurl at us! [. . .]

1. Since the autograph of this letter contains no date or salutation, it must be assumed that the first part is missing. The postmark on the envelope reveals only that it was mailed in July. Abbiati, III, p. 703, for incomprehensible reasons, dates it 1 July 1874 and describes it as Verdi's reply to a long letter from Giulio Ricordi, in which he writes about a proposal to perform the *Requiem* in Bologna and about the success of *Aida* in Vienna. Along with this letter, which is missing, Giulio Ricordi had also sent a translation of a clipping from an Austrian newspaper, which, he thought, would amuse the Maestro. If Abbiati's information is correct, Verdi received Giulio Ricordi's letter upon his return to Paris from London. In June he had conducted performances of the *Requiem* at the Opéra-Comique.

2. The productions of these operas at La Scala during the past season.

Verdi to Opprandino Arrivabene

St. Agata, 21 July 1874

Dear Arrivabene,

I have been at St. Agata since the fifth of this month! So you see how poorly you are informed of my affairs. [. . .] Do you think that all, or almost all [of the critics], know and understand anything? . . . Do you think that all, or almost all of them, penetrate the guts of a composition and comprehend the aims of the composer? Never, absolutely never!

But it's useless to talk about it. Art, the true art that creates, is not the labored art the critics preach to us; after all, they don't even agree with one another. I wish they would define for me two words that are always on their lips, melody and harmony! Do you know what they mean? I really don't. . . .

There's no news here. We are well, and if it weren't so hot, I would run through the fields all day long, without reading or writing, and, above all, without listening to music!! [. . .]

Verdi to Opprandino Arrivabene

St. Agata, 15 August 1874

[. . .] I know nothing about the *Mass* in Rome, as I have never known anything about *Aida* in the past; and now I only know what the papers say. I think I told you before that when I take charge of my operas, I do so completely and assume all the responsibility; when I cannot or don't want to take charge of them myself, I leave all the responsibility to whoever is around.

You will see that in Rome they won't even know enough to do what little is now being done in Perugia,[1] and *Aida* will fall flat on its face in the capital.

1. On 8 August 1874 *Aida* was given its first performance in this city, with Pozzoni and Waldmann and conducted by Usiglio.

Verdi to Vincenzo Luccardi

St. Agata, 18 August 1874

[. . .] I know nothing officially about the *Aida* in Rome, because I did not care for the idea, and I shall never care for it; but I hear that it will be done. It will be done badly, because Jacovacci is an impresario after his own fashion, and because the Apollo Theatre has been so neglected that it is now incapable of doing an opera well. [. . .]

Verdi to Léon Escudier[1]

St. Agata, 30 September 1874

[. . .] Now you tell me about *Aida* at the Opéra and *Forza* at the Italian Theatre. As for me, I tell you frankly that I have no opinion about the elements of either the Opéra or the Italian Theatre. Furthermore I add that I absolutely do not wish to face the ———— gentlemen at the Opéra again. (You find the right word.) You will say, I am sure, that there will be new contracts and that new artists will be discovered; but beside the fact that I don't have faith in you, these would not be enough. Everything else is what cannot be agreed upon. Therefore let's not talk about either the Opéra or the Italian Theatre. [. . .]

1. Presumably in answer to a missing letter in which Escudier had proposed productions of *Aida* and *La Forza del Destino* in Paris. See Verdi's letter to Escudier of 7 March 1874.

Verdi to Eugenio Tornaghi[1]

St. Agata, 10 October 1874

I too have received news from Florence,[2] and mine agrees with yours. My letter, however, is blacker than yours, and it speaks poorly of the performance in general. It makes some exceptions, though, with high praise; but it ends by saying that if the female roles did not compromise the opera, they came very close to it.[3]

In other words it's a success of individual numbers, and that's not enough to make an opera. If there is no <u>real opera</u>, the theatre won't be filled. You will see that this is so; and for the first time, *Aida* will not make money. . . . As for the *Aida* and the *Mass* in Bologna, I have no opinion to give; and I cannot and don't want to get involved in anything!

1. In answer to a missing letter.

2. The first performance of *Aida* in Florence was given at the Teatro Pagliano on 6 October 1874. See Verdi's letters to Giulio Ricordi of 24 August 1873, 6 and 29 September 1873, 9 and 21 November 1873, and 25 February 1874, to Tornaghi of 25 October 1873, and to Waldmann of 27 February and 14 March 1874.

3. Teresina Singer sang the role of Aida and Rosina Vercolini-Taj, Amneris. Rosina Vercolini-Taj, Italian mezzo-soprano, was heard between 1864 and 1879 throughout Italy and in Buenos Aires, Barcelona, Valencia, Montevideo, and Porto Alegre. In a letter to De Sanctis of 1 March 1874, Verdi had inquired about this artist, whom he remembered as Eboli in Naples, but without recalling her name. De Sanctis answered Verdi on 4 March 1874 that Vercolini-Taj was wildly applauded as Amneris, despite her obesity and the fact that she was nine months pregnant. See *Carteggi*, I, p. 171.

Verdi to Giulio Ricordi

St. Agata, 20 October 1874

[. . .] As I have said before, I wouldn't be so strict about *Aida*, and I would do it in many theatres at the same time. You can't always have secure companies, and what good is it to have artists like the ones now in Florence, who are applauded for a *romanza* and a little bit of singing but are incapable of doing the rest? What does it matter if the *romanza* of the third act and the *adagio* of the duet with the tenor are applauded? Take away those two pieces, and the opera is still what it is. Meanwhile the first two acts are considered zero in Florence. Do you really think they are very inferior to the other two? I don't care about singers who know how to be applauded for a solo. . . . The whole is what matters, even a modest whole. In that way, both art and the opera gain. Otherwise, go back to *cavatina* operas. A chorus, a *cavatina* for the soprano, one for the tenor, another for the baritone, a finale with a soprano-tenor *adagio* at the octave, together with violins. . . . A second act with a duet, a chorus, a rondo for the prima donna, and that's that. [. . .]

Verdi to Giulio Ricordi [1]

Genoa, 18 November 1874

[. . .] The greatest obstacle will be our most kind and gracious Maria [Waldmann]. In any event, let's not fool ourselves; both for the *Mass* and for Amneris, better her than all the others put together. [. . .]

1. Concerning a proposed tour of *Aida* and the *Requiem*.

Verdi to Giuseppe Piroli

Genoa, 21 November 1874

Dear Piroli,

I received your letter[1] informing me of my nomination for senator.
[. . .]

The dispatch [from the Prefect of Parma] says I should go to be sworn in at
the Royal Session. I would go at once, but you know that they are doing *Aida*
as the first opera at the Apollo, and they are perhaps in rehearsal at this hour.
If I were to go to Rome, it would be very difficult to escape those musical
bores, and I don't want to meddle in the performance of *Aida* at this time.
[. . .]

  1. Missing.

Verdi to Giulio Ricordi

Genoa, 16 December 1874

Dear Giulio,

I telegraphed you yesterday that my reply to Rome was that la Galletti
could do the role of Amneris well. She won't drum up any business for the
management, but she will always be better for the opera than la Pozzoni (How
could la Pozzoni ever do that role?) or la Marchisio!!! or la Viziak, as
D'Arcais suggests. By God, our music critics should talk about everything
except music and theatre! [. . .]

Verdi to Giulio Ricordi

[*Probably* St. Agata, 20 December 1874]

I received the telegram![1] Be careful not to fall from the frying pan into
the fire.

Withdrawing the score is the only thing to do! . . . How can you manage
it? If there are no prima donnas, you can do nothing else. [. . .]

  1. Giulio Ricordi apparently sent word about the production of *Aida* in Rome.

Verdi to Maria Waldmann

Genoa, 26 December 1874

[. . .] I want to hear the news about *Aida*[1] from you — from you and
no one else. And I want it all the more because I was surprised to learn that la

Fricci had agreed to do Aida. La Fricci certainly has great qualities, but I never thought that she, a soprano of limited range, could hit the high notes with ease and flexibility, and sustain them with long breaths, as Aida requires. [. . .]

1. Verdi refers to the revival in Cairo.

Verdi to Carlo Pedrotti [1]

Genoa, 1 January 1875

In the newspapers I read a letter they want to send me from Turin, inviting me to attend one of the performances of *Aida*. Assuming there is some truth in all of this, and hoping it is in your power to prevent them from sending this letter, I ask you please to do so, that I may avoid the displeasure of refusing such a courteous invitation.

You will understand, dear Maestro, that I can, and perhaps must, present myself to the public when I compose or assume responsibility for the performance of one of my operas; but this is not true for Turin. Why would I be going there? I would go for the sole purpose of showing myself off and being applauded! No: this was never one of my habits, even at the beginning of my career. . . . Imagine if I could or should do it now! . . . So please try to persuade those gentlemen to give up their plan, assuring them at the same time that I am aware of the esteem they intend to show me. [. . .]

1. The draft of this letter, in Giuseppina Verdi's handwriting, is in the possession of Sig. Natale Gallini of Milan. Abbiati, III, p. 217, publishes this text, but refers to the slightly different version of the same letter, as published by Pougin, *Verdi: histoire anecdotique*, pp. 301–02, *I Copialettere*, p. 682, and *Genesi dell'Aida*, p. 131. The second version seems to represent the actual letter, which Pedrotti received. This text is translated here.

Verdi to Giulio Ricordi

Genoa, 2 January 1875

Dear Giulio,

Perhaps you have heard that some people in Turin were signing a letter to invite me to attend a performance of *Aida*. When I learned about it I wrote to Pedrotti so that he might prevent the sending of that letter; but, alas, the fatal letter arrived this morning with some 200 signatures! It's a real nuisance and an embarrassment; but in any event I won't go!

I am sending you a copy of the letter I wrote to Pedrotti yesterday, so that you can have it published, if it becomes necessary. We are agreed, then, that if you receive a telegram from me tomorrow morning saying, "Publish the letter,'' I ask you to have it published the same day in some big paper — but in the *Pungolo*, first of all, because this paper printed the letter those gentlemen of Turin sent me.

All of this will depend on the letter I receive from Pedrotti. If he is able to handle the thing to avoid any squabbling, then we'll say nothing more about it; if not, I repeat, I shall send you the telegram, and you will have my letter to Pedrotti printed as soon as possible. [. . .]

Verdi to Giulio Ricordi

Genoa, 3 January 1875

Dear Giulio,

This morning I received Pedrotti's letter in which he asks me "if he might publish my letter as my entire reply." I immediately sent him a telegram authorizing him to print this letter — mainly because I am so embarrassed by this nuisance and, then, because I wish these impresarios and directors would leave me in peace for a while. Just think, there isn't a village where *Don Carlos*, *Forza*, or *Aida* is given to which I am not invited to attend a performance, so I can do four pirouettes on the stage! [. . .]

Verdi to Giulio Ricordi

Genoa, 4 January 1875

Dear Giulio,

The letter was printed in the *Gazzetta di Torino*. It was poorly printed, and Pedrotti is either an imbecile or . . . It is not "Senator Verdi who refuses to betake himself to Turin," but Maestro Verdi who refuses to play the clown. Do me the favor of publishing a little introductory comment to that effect with my letter.[1] If it pinches or stings, so much the better because, I repeat, Pedrotti did not do well by me. [. . .]

1. See *La Gazzetta Musicale* of 10 January 1875.

Verdi to Maria Waldmann [1]

Genoa, 9 January 1875

[. . .] Without speaking of the success, what surprises me is that la Fricci was able to sing the role of Aida right up to the end. La Fricci's artistic qualities are not to be doubted, but here it is a question of having a true soprano voice — one that is facile and secure — and plenty of breath! Enough; let it be as she wishes, but it is really deplorable to see a famous artist allow herself to do what she can't do and to pocket 100,000 francs! Money is all right, but a little conscience and dignity is worth more than 100,000 francs!

In the Italian theatres, as usual, things go well here, badly there. In Milan, very coldly; in Genoa, so, so; in Venice, not very well; in Turin, *Aida* is doing beautifully; in Mantua, the same. [. . .]

1. In response, apparently, to a missing letter that Waldmann had written from Cairo.

Verdi to Tito Ricordi

Genoa, 25 January 1875

Dear Tito,

Many, many little jobs kept me from answering your letter of the 20th[1] before now.

I am sorry to hear about the difficulties with Berlin and Vienna; if this project[2] were to go up in smoke, I wouldn't have much interest in the London deal. With London, Berlin, and Vienna together, and then Paris again, the plan had some significance and it meant something for art. London alone means a concert and nothing more.

I can't answer you about the *Aida* in Vienna,[3] since I hardly understand a thing about that paltry sum of 8235.50 lire you sent me.

What kind of contract did you make?

By what authority was that sum paid?

By whom was it paid?

Who collected it?

I think there is nothing to do but return to our *Aida* contract. I don't have it here; but, if I remember correctly, the author's rights in Germany are mentioned in it. You can consult it, and from that you will see how much is owed me.

1. Cesari and Luzio, in *I Copialettere*, p. 297, give the 23rd as the date of Tito Ricordi's letter to Verdi, which is missing.
2. Verdi refers to a proposed tour of the *Requiem*.
3. Verdi refers to royalties paid by the Imperial Opera in Vienna, where *Aida* had been performed in German since 29 April 1874. See Giuseppina Verdi's letter to De Sanctis of 6 May 1874.

Verdi to Emilio Usiglio[1]

Genoa, [*Probably* 26] January 1875

First of all I must say that one has to deal with Ricordi for everything concerning *Aida*, since he is the sole owner and proprietor.

It is not that I give any importance to the *romanza*[2] that you ask me to lower (just as I give no importance to any other piece of *Aida*), but it is for a principle of art that I find it repugnant to allow any alteration. Unfortunately this has been the established practice for a long, long time, but it is a reprehensible practice which should be remedied once and for all. This should primarily be the obligation of the artists themselves, not, if you will, out of respect for this particular opera or that particular composer, but out of reverence for art, for true art.

I know Nicolini, and I don't understand how the *tessitura* of that *romanza* can be high for him. If it were changed by half a tone, it would definitely be the *tessitura* of a baritone; and without the A any baritone could sing it. I perfectly understand that if the final two measures in B flat were reduced to an A, the sound would become fuller, rounder, and more supple; but for the sake of one effective note, is it worth turning all the rest upside down?

I also understand that it is difficult to sing if we leave the B flat the way it is written, but I have remedied this myself by adding these three notes for Capponi:[3]

[. . .] There is no overture[4] for *Aida*. Perhaps you have heard that at one of the rehearsals for *Aida* in Milan I had the orchestra play a piece that had the air of an overture. The orchestra was good, ready, and obedient, and the piece might have turned out well if its construction had been solid. But the excellence of the orchestra merely served better to illustrate the silliness of that supposed overture. [. . .]

1. Luzio publishes the draft of this letter in *Carteggi*, II, pp. 42–43, but he gives no indication of its correct date and admits that he does not know to whom it was addressed. Mario Rinaldi, *Verdi critico* (Roma: Ergo, 1951), p. 297, declares that Verdi wrote this letter to an "until now unknown friend." Abbiati, III, pp. 578–79, records that Verdi wrote the letter to Ghislanzoni. Verdi's letter to Giulio Ricordi of 26 January 1875 provides the correct answer.

2. *"Celeste Aida."*
3. Aware of most tenors' inability to sustain a *pianissimo* B flat, Toscanini followed Verdi's advice in his recording of *Aida*.
4. See Giulio Ricordi's letter to Verdi of 12 November 1871 and Verdi's letters to Giulio Ricordi of 13 November and 28 December 1871.

Verdi to Giulio Ricordi

Genoa, 26 January 1875

Dear Giulio,

First of all I tell you in a great hurry that Usiglio writes from Rome,[1] asking me to lower the tenor's *romanza*. This is the kind of thing that infuriates me, especially since the point of all this is merely to insert an <u>A</u> instead of a <u>B flat</u>. I replied that they should contact the publisher, and if they write you about it, considering how badly things are going in that theatre, you may allow it. But let this be an <u>exception</u>, since it is really necessary to put an end once and for all to these alterations and to the abominable abuses that are so harmful to art. [. . .]

1. Missing.

Verdi to Giulio Ricordi

Genoa, 13 February 1875

Dear Giulio,

Yesterday morning — no, the other morning — I received the telegram[1] in which you announced a letter concerning the Vienna matters.[2] Today, Saturday, at 4:00 p.m.: *nix*![3] What does it mean?

I read in the *Opinione* that la Pozzoni will do Amneris in Rome! But how can she do that role without the low notes?

1. Missing.
2. Verdi refers to a proposal to go to Vienna with the *Requiem* and *Aida*.
3. "Nothing" in Viennese dialect.

Verdi to Giuseppe Piroli

Milan, 24 February 1875

[. . .] Thank you for all the news you give me about *Aida* and the dissolution of la Stolz's contract.[1] That is unfortunate, but I think she did very well under the circumstances. I just learned from a telegram that last night's repeat of *Aida* went beautifully. It surely isn't, nor could it ever be, the *Aida* I want; but if they like it, so much the better. For my part I am quite happy about it — especially if I never hear another word about that miserable theatre.

1. On 17 February 1875 Usiglio conducted the first performance of *Aida* at the Teatro Apollo in Rome, with Viziak as Aida, replacing the indisposed Stolz, and Pozzoni as Amneris, replacing the indisposed Sanz.

Verdi to Giulio Ricordi

Genoa, 27 February 1875

Dear Giulio,

I feel sorry for Faccio!!![1] La Waldmann will be married — following the Count's year of mourning — in the spring of '76, at the close of the season in Cairo, where she will return, almost certainly, next year. [. . .] And then, good night. Good-bye, then, to our beautiful Eboli and Amneris, who now has no equal in those roles. [. . .]

1. See Giuseppina Verdi's card to Faccio of 23 April 1872. Faccio had apparently been enamored of Waldmann, who was now engaged to Count Galeazzo Massari of Ferrara.

Verdi to Maria Waldmann

Genoa, 27 February 1875

[. . .] On the one hand I rejoice for you; on the other I deplore your leaving the stage. But if you are happy, I rejoice with all my heart. [. . .] If la Fricci does poorly in *Aida*, she will do worse in the *Mass*, which even more than *Aida* requires certainty of voice, intonation, and the greatest breath control. [. . .]

Verdi to Giulio Ricordi

Genoa, 3 March 1875

Dear Giulio,

I reply:

1. That if we go to Vienna to do the *Mass*, I shall conduct *Aida* at the theatre, provided that all the singers are Italian, which means that it will be sung in Italian.
2. Be careful about the Amneris from Darmstadt;[1] and, for La Scala, be suspicious of all German women unless they have spent three or four years of their career in Italy. [. . .]

Don't even consider my old operas [for La Scala]. The only one I would always be inclined to do would be *Aida*, but it would require la Waldmann.

Then, too, it's an opera that can be done for only a few nights, which isn't profitable for the management. [. . .]

Above all, don't rely on operas that evoke a lukewarm response. [. . . In the theatre] it's better to have a great fiasco, even a scandalous fiasco, than successes of that kind.

1. Verdi probably refers to a certain Frau Taide, who had appeared in the first performance of *Aida* in Darmstadt on 29 November 1874.

Verdi to Giulio Ricordi

Genoa, 21 March 1875

[. . .] I hear that *Aida* is being torn to shreds in Rome. I am writing today to find out what is going on; but meanwhile I wish to say to the House of Ricordi that I absolutely cannot allow such abuses. I do not think that the House of Ricordi will reply, as it did once before, that it knew nothing about it! . . .[1] That would not be a good reason; in fact, it would be a kind of mockery! [. . .]

1. See Tito Ricordi's letter to Verdi of 7 March 1874.

Verdi to Vincenzo Luccardi

Genoa, 21 March 1875

[. . .] I see from certain newspapers that they slaughter *Aida* in Rome. That is to say, one night they cut one piece, another night another piece; there are some who can sing, some who can't. In other words, it is no longer the whole opera I wrote, which has been performed scrupulously and always intact until now.[1]

I know you are frank and sincere, and I ask you to tell me what is going on. Please tell me absolutely everything, with the understanding that this will remain between us and that you will never be named — never, never, never! [. . .]

1. Note that Verdi does not mention the events in Naples at the time of the *Aida* reprise a year before. See Verdi's telegram to De Sanctis of 1 March 1874, his letters to Tito Ricordi of 1, 4, 6, 8, 11, and mid-March 1874, and Tito Ricordi's letter to Verdi of 7 March 1874.

Verdi to Antonio Ghislanzoni

Genoa, 24 March 1875[1]

Dear Ghislanzoni,

I am very happy to hear from you, and I thank you from my heart for your good wishes.[2] I would have been even happier if you had told me something about yourself, your works, and those dramas you are working on at the moment. You have been deceived: as far as I am concerned, I do nothing, nothing, nothing. It's easy for them all to say, "Write." And then what? . . . Do you think it's very pleasant for us to work only for the satisfaction of having (apart from a success or nonsuccess) a pile of crap? [. . .]

1. In Verdi's handwriting the last number of the year could be a 7, but the contents of this letter seem to suggest that he wrote it in 1875.
2. Verdi's name day fell on the 19th of March, the feast of St. Joseph. Ghislanzoni's letter is missing.

Verdi to Giulio Ricordi [1]

Genoa, 25 [March 1875]

Dear Giulio,

Performance!!!!

Nicolini has always omitted his piece!!!
Aldighieri[2] has omitted the third act duet at various times!!
Even the second finale was cut one night!!!!!!!
In addition to taking the *romanza* down, they changed several bars.
A mediocre Aida!!
A soprano for Amneris!!
And what's more, a conductor who takes the liberty of changing the tempos!!! [. . .] We don't need conductors and singers to discover new effects; for my part, I declare that no one has ever, ever, ever been able, or known how, to draw out all the effects conceived by me. . . . No one!!! Never, never . . . neither singers nor conductors!! But it is fashionable now to applaud even conductors, and I feel sorry for the few I esteem; even more, I feel sorry for those who pass on indecencies in the opera house from one to the other without end. At one time we had to endure the tyranny of prima donnas; now we'll also have to endure that of conductors!

Well? You who talk to me about composing . . . about Art, etc.!! Is this Art?

Let me finish by asking you to tell the House of Ricordi that I cannot tolerate the above-mentioned improprieties; if it wishes, the House of Ricordi can withdraw my last three scores (and that would give me great pleasure), but I cannot allow them to be subjected to alterations. Whatever will happen will nappen; but I repeat again, I cannot allow . . .

1. Verdi reacts to the performances of *Aida* in Rome.
2. Gottardo Aldighieri (1824–1906), Italian baritone. He made his debut in *La Traviata* in 1858 and sang Barnaba in the world premiere of *La Gioconda* at La Scala in 1876.

Verdi to Giulio Ricordi

Friday [Genoa, 26 March 1875]

Dear Giulio,

I received the telegram.[1] You have taken care of the future . . . but what about the past?

1. Missing.

Verdi to Giulio Ricordi

Genoa, 30 March 1875

[. . .] What is certain and historical is that *Aida* in Rome is a real puppet show. Tenors who sing baritone and sopranos who sing contralto; a conductor who lowers the notes and changes the tempos; an artist who refuses to continue singing her role: these things are intolerable. Don't speak to me about the effect, which, after all, is not what it could have been; and, above all, don't speak to me about the effect of the judgment scene in the fourth act, which is precisely what desolates me. When a piece, or even an entire section, stands out too much, that is harmful to the whole. It is no longer a drama, but a concert. Let the artist have his piece, if the drama calls for it; but he must be more or less consistent throughout and contribute to the totality of the musical structure. For these reasons (which I have never been able to make understood), I never wanted to write for la Patti.

Finally I repeat what I said before: "This is not art." According to the contract that exists between the House of Ricordi and myself, my last operas and the *Mass* must not be performed as *Aida* was performed in Rome. [. . .]

It is said that *Aida* will be done here. (I am sorry because that banishes me from Genoa for a while.) It is also said that they want to sign Ponchielli[1] and Berini.[2] No: that's impossible. They are two sopranos, and Amneris must have the voice and character of a contralto. La Waldmann, for example, can sing high A's and B's as much as she wants, but she will always be a contralto. [. . .]

1. Teresa Ponchielli-Brambilla (1845–1921), Italian soprano. She was commonly called Teresina to distinguish her from her renowned aunt, Teresa Brambilla, who had sung the first Gilda in *Rigoletto*. Making her debut in 1863 in Odessa, she sang at the Italian Theatre in Paris in 1873, at La Scala in 1874, in several other Italian theatres, in Lisbon, Madrid, and supposedly St. Petersburg. In 1874 she married the composer Amilcare Ponchielli, and in 1875 she was the first Aida in Genoa.

2. Enrichetta (Henriette or Helène) Berini, French soprano. Following studies in Paris and in Milan, she appeared from 1856 to 1877 in Warsaw, Nice, Bucharest, Lisbon, and Italy. She was married to the bass Ormondo Maini.

Verdi to Giulio Ricordi

St. Agata, 4 April 1875

Dear Giulio,

Excuse me if, in spite of all your arguments, I continue to believe that the *Aida* in Rome was performed much worse than in any other place thus far and that it was done in a patchwork. I know quite well that perfection does not exist and that elsewhere there were very deficient parts. But at least the parts were in place. [. . .]

I have said several times, it's true, that *Aida* should now be launched more often — but, of course, with artists suited to their respective roles and without changes of any kind. [. . .]

You speak to me about the results obtained!!!!!!!!! Where are they? . . . I'll tell you. After an absence of twenty-five years from La Scala, I was whistled after the first act of *Forza del Destino*. After *Aida*, endless chatter: that it was no longer the Verdi of *Ballo* (of that *Ballo* whose premiere at La Scala was whistled); that it was a good thing the opera had a fourth act (so wrote D'Arcais); that I didn't know how to write for the singers; that the second and fourth acts had some tolerable moments (nothing in the third); and finally that I was an imitator of Wagner!!! What a fine result after a career of thirty-five years — to end up as an imitator!!!

Certainly this chatter does not — and never did — make me budge an inch from what I wanted to do, because I have always known what I wanted. But having arrived at the point where I am, be it high or low, I can well say: "If that's the way it is, do as you please." And when I want to write music, I can write it in my room, without hearing the pronouncements of the scholars and the imbeciles.

I can only take as a joke your statement: "The total salvation of the theatre and of art rests with you!!" Oh no, have no doubt; there will always be composers. And I repeat what Boito said in a toast to Faccio after his first opera: "Perhaps he who will sweep clean the altar is born."[1]

Amen. [. . .]

1. This toast kept Verdi and Boito apart for several years.

Verdi to Giuseppe Piroli[1]

Paris, 6 May 1875

[. . .] In Vienna, in addition to the *Mass*, the direction of that theatre would like to hear one or two performances of *Aida* by the same singers, to understand the way in which this opera should be performed. This is not so easy because some time is necessary for a few rehearsals, and we don't have much time. We'll see what can be done. [. . .]

1. At this time Verdi was on tour with the *Requiem*, seven performances of which he led at the Opéra-Comique between 19 April and 4 May 1875. On 15 May 1875 he conducted the *Requiem* at the Albert Hall in London, and on 11 June 1875 he led the work at the Imperial Opera in Vienna.

Verdi to Giulio Ricordi

London, 25 May 1875

[. . .] I think it wise to remind you that the rehearsals for the *Mass* and *Aida* [in Vienna] should be arranged very carefully, especially those for the two most difficult pieces, since I would not put up again with what happened in London.[1] I would leave Vienna immediately.

We shall leave for Paris the evening of Wednesday, 2 June. Take care of finding us apartments in the Grand Hotel. I don't like these big hotels like the de la Paix and the Louvre, because there is so much coming and going in them that one is uncomfortable and the room service [. . .] is bad. Therefore I want a more modest hotel — that is to say, one that is smaller, but dignified and quiet, where the service is certainly better.

I shall need two bedrooms and a drawing room. This is what is absolutely necessary, but if there is something more spacious, all the better.

La Stolz needs a bedroom, a parlor, and another room for her maid. We shall take our breakfasts and lunches in the apartment: breakfasts and lunches for three . . . the maid, as usual, with the other domestics.

I want whatever kind of piano is available in my drawing room. It would really be providential if there were a French or Italian waiter at the hotel.

If you can take care of finding these apartments for me, let me know the conditions and write me from Vienna. If you can't, write me immediately.

As for the train compartments from Paris to Vienna, if there are four places, reserve a compartment for me for Wednesday evening, 2 June.

The last time I was in Milan to collect [my fees] for the previous six months, the German accounts had not been settled. If it's not too much trouble for the office to send the German *Aida* contracts (together with my own contract) to Vienna at once, we shall examine and ponder them together, since (in passing) I don't think that these contracts were made [. . .] according to the express spirit of my own contract.

P.S. La Waldmann asks you to reserve another train compartment for her to Vienna, Wednesday evening, 2 June. [. . .]

1. Presumably Verdi was annoyed about Giulio Ricordi's arrangements in London, as well as disappointed by the box office receipts of the four *Requiem* performances he conducted at that

city's Albert Hall. Giulio Ricordi's cancellation of projected performances of the *Requiem* in Berlin and Verdi's suspicion that the House of Ricordi had shortchanged him in his receipt of royalties added to this ill feeling. See Abbiati, III, pp. 751–55.

Verdi to Maria Waldmann

Vienna, 5 June 1875

Dear Maria,

You have received, or you will receive, the announcement of your rehearsals. Monday at eleven in the morning will be the first rehearsal of the *Mass*. Then it will be necessary to get busy right away with *Aida*,[1] for which I think there will be much to do. I also think it would be a good idea for you to stay in the city after Monday. Be patient, keep well, good-bye for now till Monday morning.

1. Abbiati, III, p. 753, notes: "The artists stayed in Vienna until the 25th of June — three more days than originally planned, because of an additional performance of the sacred work and a reception given by the Emperor Franz Josef, who wanted to bestow on the Maestro the highest Austrian decoration for cultural merits. About an *Aida* in Vienna, however, nothing more was said; the time was lacking for adequate preparation." Marcello Conati, however, in *Genesi dell'Aida*, p. 161, lists a performance of *Aida*, in Italian, at the Imperial Opera on 19 June 1875, with a cast including Stolz, Waldmann, Masini, and Medini — the quartet who had just sung the *Requiem*. Verdi was the conductor and the *mise-en-scène* was that of the Viennese premiere on 29 April 1874. Like several other writers, Prawy, pp. 40–41, 44–45, describes these events and even reproduces the Viennese posters of the *Requiem* and *Aida*, on which a second *Aida* performance is listed on 21 June 1875. Ferdinand Pfohl, in his biography, *Arthur Nikisch: sein Leben, seine Kunst, sein Wirken* (Hamburg: Alster Verlag, 1925), pp. 24–26, tells of the famous conductor's enthusiastic participation as a young violinist in these rehearsals and performances which were reviewed by Eduard Hanslick and other critics.

Angelo Masini (1844–1926), Italian tenor. Born in poverty, Masini made his debut in 1867 in the Italian provinces and gradually progressed to a career of international fame. His great success in the role of Radames in Florence (1874) attracted Verdi's attention and led to Masini's engagement for the *Requiem* and *Aida* tour under the composer's direction. Until Masini's final appearance in 1905 he was heard in most of the world's major opera houses, except in the United States.

Verdi to Opprandino Arrivabene

St. Agata, 16 July 1875

Dear Arrivabene,

I have been at St. Agata for ten or twelve days, quiet and tranquil, without thinking of music. I don't know if this tour has been good or bad for the others, and I don't know if the enthusiasm is shared by and inspires the talented, as you say. I couldn't even tell you how we are to escape this musical ferment. Some want to be melodists like Bellini, some harmonists like Meyerbeer. I don't want either the one or the other; I wish that the youngster starting to write would not think of being a melodist, a harmonist, a realist, an idealist, a futurist, or any of the devils who care for these pedantries. Melody and harmony must be, in the hands of the artist, only the means to make music; and if the day should come when they no longer talk of melody and harmony, German and Italian schools, the past and the future, etc., etc., etc., then perhaps the kingdom of art will begin.

Another trouble of our time is that all the works by these youngsters are the products of fear. Nobody writes with abandon; when these youngsters start to write, the thought that predominates in their minds is how not to upset the public and how to win the favor of the critics!

You tell me that I owe my successes to the fusion of the two schools. I have never thought of that. But this is an old story, which is repeated for others at a certain time! Nevertheless, my dear Arrivabene, keep calm: art will not perish. Be assured, after all, that the moderns have also done some good things. . . .

Franco Faccio to Eugenio Tornaghi

Trieste, 28 September 1875

[. . .] I am here now on the eve of the opening of *Aida*.[1] I am most content with everything and everyone . . . except for la Sanz. A most singular artist, this beautiful lady from Spain! At the piano rehearsals she satisfied me and her colleagues; but the painful notes began with the orchestra rehearsals. There is no way to make her sing on pitch, and that is a rather serious and disquieting calamity. [. . .]

1. A reprise in Trieste.

Franco Faccio to Eugenio Tornaghi

Trieste, 6 October 1875

[. . .] You already know of the most felicitous success of *Aida*. [. . .] At the first performance, to tell the truth, most of the applause was directed at your humble servant. [. . .] La Stolz is always a stupendous artist, vocally and dramatically, but in this opera she does not have the charm that la Mariani projected two years ago. [. . .] And la Sanz? She acquitted herself with sufficient honor, but in my opinion she is no good for La Scala. [. . .] Since a better Amneris cannot be found, therefore, I would advise you not to give *Aida* at La Scala.

Verdi to Léon Escudier [1]

St. Agata, 28 December 1875

Dear Léon,

I really have not heard from you for ages, but I understand very well that your usual occupations — and now the worries of an impresario — have deprived you of the will and the time to write. Oh it's an ugly business to be an impresario! [. . .]

And since we are talking from the impresario's point of view, have you arranged things well, have you made all your plans, have you calculated well your business, which is much bigger than at the Italian Theatre in the spring [of 1875]? I hear that the expenses grow overnight; but I did not expect that the orchestra would somehow grab you by the collar. . . . Anyway, consider it well . . . The worst thing would be to lose money. . . . As far as I am concerned, I have no desire whatever to show myself with an unknown opera. . . . The artists you signed are the kind who don't need another contract. . . . Perhaps it is not too late for you to let it all go in the event you should not see a sure thing. [. . .]

1. As producer and manager of the Italian Theatre in Paris, Escudier planned to give the first performance of *Aida* in France during the spring of 1876.

Verdi to Léon Escudier

St. Agata, 20 January 1876

[. . .] If you think it is better to have the costumes made in Paris, I have no objection. For myself, in particular, I would be satisfied with the costumes from Milan — mainly because of the lower cost and, then, because all the artists who did *Aida* in Cairo say that the Milan costumes were more theatrical and characteristic. . . . But be careful not to overdo it, since that is a common fault in Paris.

[. . .] The six trumpets must be played on stage, while [the players are] marching. Remember these trumpets don't exist and must be made for this purpose; it would be better, however, to rent them from Ricordi, who usually delivers them along with the score. [. . .]

Verdi to Clarina Maffei

Genoa, 30 January 1876

[. . .] Monday I shall go to hear *Color del Tempo* by Torelli.[1] Everyone has been attacking this poor Torelli for some time; but I wouldn't be surprised if he proved them wrong. When a young artist permits himself to have two or three successes before he is thirty, you can be sure that the public will be bored with him thereafter; it resents having applauded the rascal and picks the slightest occasion to show him its disdain. If the artist has the strength to face this current and to go straight along his path until he is in his forties, he is safe. By then, the public no longer disdains him, but impertinently keeps a rifle aimed at him, always ready to take a good shot.

An author may have genius, talent, all the knowledge in the world — it doesn't matter. It's a battle that only ends with life itself — a nice consolation for the author! But he will not fall if he is armed with a good breastplate of indifference and conviction. Woe to him if he fears. Everything that is produced today is born of fear. One no longer thinks of following one's own inspiration, but is preoccupied with sparing the feelings of the Filippis, the D'Arcaises, and all the others. [. . .]

1. Achille Torelli (1841–1922), Italian playwright, son of Vincenzo Torelli.

Verdi to Opprandino Arrivabene

Genoa, 5 February 1876

Dear Arrivabene,

Of those I know, the one who can do the best is Ponchielli; but, alas, he is no longer young (I think in his forties), and he has seen and heard too much. You know my opinions about hearing too much. . . . I told you in Florence. When the youngsters realize they need not search for the light in Mendelssohn, Chopin, or Gounod, then perhaps they will find it. It's strange, however, that they take composers who are not dramatic as their models. You'll be surprised that I speak that way about the composer of *Faust*! What do you want me to tell you? Gounod is a very great musician, the first maestro of France, but he has no dramatic fiber. Stupendous music, pleasant, magnificent details, the word almost always well expressed. . . . The word, mind you, not the situation. He doesn't delineate the characters well, and he doesn't impart a particular color to the drama or the dramas.

This, *inter nos*. The repertoire theatre [in Italy] would be an excellent thing, but I don't think it is practicable. The examples of the Opéra and Germany are of very little value to me, because the productions in all those theatres are deplorable. At the Opéra the *mise-en-scène* is splendid, superior to all other theatres because of the exactness of the costumes and good taste; but the musical side is awful. The singers are always very mediocre (except Faure [1] for some years), the orchestra and chorus lax and undisciplined. I have seen hundreds of productions in that theatre, and never, really never, a good musical performance. But in a city of 3,000,000 inhabitants, and some

100,000 foreigners, there are always 2,000 persons to fill the house, even when the production is bad.

In Germany the orchestras and choruses are more attentive and conscientious; they perform correctly and well. In spite of this I have seen deplorable productions in Berlin. The orchestra is big and sounds big. The chorus not good, *mise-en-scène* without character and without taste. Singers . . . oh the singers are awful, absolutely awful. This year[2] in Vienna I heard la Meslinger[3] (I don't know if I spell it correctly) who passes for the Malibran[4] of Germany. God in Heaven! A miserable, tired voice, awkward and coarse singing, indecent acting. Our three or four standard prima donnas are infinitely superior in voice and style of singing, and at least equal in their acting.

In Vienna (the leading theatre in Germany today), things are better on the side of the chorus and orchestra (most excellent). I have attended several productions and have found the performance of the major groups to be very good, the *mise-en-scène* mediocre, the singers less than mediocre. But the production usually costs very little. The audience (which sits in the dark during the performance) sleeps or is bored, applauds a little at the end of each act, and goes home at the end of the performance, without disgust and without enthusiasm. And that may be very well for those northern natures; but try to bring a similar performance to one of our theatres, and you'll see what a symphony the audience will compose for you! Our audience is too restless and would never be content with a prima donna who, as in Germany, costs 18,000 or 20,000 florins a year. They want the prima donnas who go to Cairo, Petersburg, Lisbon, London, etc., for 25,000 or 30,000 francs a month. And how, then, are we to pay them? Look at this example: this year at La Scala they have a company that couldn't be better. A prima donna with a beautiful voice, who sings well, who is most animated, young, beautiful, and even more, one of ours. A tenor who might be the first, but is certainly among the first. A baritone who has only one rival, Pandolfini. A bass who has no rivals. Still the theatre does a meager business. Last year they spoke very well of la Mariani. This year they have begun to say that she is a little tired, which, mind you, isn't true. Now they say that she sings well but doesn't draw, etc., etc. If she returned next year, everyone would say: "Oh always the same. . . ." [. . .]

Now I ask you whether, with our audiences, it is possible to have a permanent company for at least three years! And then do you know what it would cost to have a company like the one now at La Scala? [. . .]

1. Jean-Baptiste Faure (1830–1914), French bass-baritone. A member of the chorus at the Italian Theatre in Paris in 1850, he made his debut at the Opéra-Comique in 1852 in Massé's

Galathée. In 1861 he made his first appearance at the Opéra in Poniatowski's *Pierre de Médicis*, and he remained the leading baritone there for seventeen years — during which time he sang the first Nelusko in *L'Africaine* (1865), the first Posa in *Don Carlos* (1867), and the first Hamlet in Ambroise Thomas's opera (1868).

2. Actually it was the previous year, during June of 1875.

3. Probably Mathilde Mallinger (1847–1920), Austrian soprano. Making her debut in Munich as Norma in 1866, she was chosen by Wagner to perform the role of Eva in the premiere of *Die Meistersinger von Nürnberg* on 21 June 1867. She appeared regularly in Berlin after her debut in 1869 as Elsa in *Lohengrin*, and her successful career brought her to Vienna, Italy, Russia, and America. Later, after 1890, she was to become a renowned vocal teacher in Prague and Berlin, where Lotte Lehmann was among her students. See Aldo Oberdorfer, *Giuseppe Verdi: Autobiografia dalle lettere* (Milano: Rizzoli, 1951), p. 336. A certain Fräulein Meisslinger, about whom Eduard Hanslick wrote to Ferdinand Hiller on 13 December 1882, does not answer Verdi's description. See Reinhold Sietz, *Aus Ferdinand Hillers Briefwechsel* (Köln: Arno Volk Verlag, 1966), V, p. 28.

4. Maria Malibran (1808–36), Spanish soprano of legendary fame. Her father was the tenor Manuel Garcia; her brother, the baritone Manuel Garcia, Jr.; and her sister, the contralto Pauline Viardot-Garcia.

Verdi to Giulio Ricordi

Genoa, 12 February 1876

Dear Giulio,

I would like to know, if possible, the price Zamperoni[1] asked from Escudier for the costumes for *Aida*. If there are no difficulties involved, please tell me <u>exactly</u>; and also tell me if the price he demanded included the jewelry, travel, and expenses for the workers, etc., etc. [. . .]

1. Luigi Zamperoni, owner and director of the costume department at La Scala.

Verdi to Giulio Ricordi

Genoa, 29 February 1876

[. . .] At the end of the week we shall return to St. Agata to prepare and arrange everything before leaving for Paris.

[. . .] For my part, I declare that I would not go to Bologna; and if I have to give you my entire opinion, I would not be very edified if *Aida* were done in that theatre. They would make a weapon of it at all costs.[1] To struggle!! To struggle now at my age!!! [. . .]

1. Verdi refers to the ardent Wagnerites in Bologna, where *Lohengrin* had been presented in 1871 and where *Aida* was not to be given until 4 October 1877.

Verdi to Léon Escudier

St. Agata, 12 March 1876

[. . .] I know that now you are almost exclusively concerned with the *mise-en-scène*. That's fine, but I wouldn't want it to be too much. I am an enemy of excess, and I don't always admire your *mise-en-scène* because it can be too contrived. Quite possibly you found what was done in Milan detestable, but I would be completely satisfied with something like that.

Enough . . . do whatever you think best; but permit me to tell you that I shall not allow the stage to be cluttered by <u>platforms</u> and <u>machinery</u>, which always happens with the painters at the Opéra. The final scene should be a <u>subterranean chamber</u>, and not a <u>cave</u>, as it was in Cairo. Finally there should be a good band of musicians who do not disdain to appear before the audience. The orchestra should be complete, and pay special attention to the choristers, especially the women. All this is more necessary than a fastidious *mise-en-scène*, which, although pleasing to the eye, cannot cover the defects of a bad musical performance. [. . .]

Verdi to Opprandino Arrivabene

St. Agata, 15 March 1876

I perfectly agree that the theatres of Italy must have regular orchestras and choruses, salaried by the government and the city halls. As early as '61 I proposed the following to Cavour for the three principal theatres of Italy (in the capital, Milan, and Naples): chorus and orchestra salaried by the government; evening classes in voice for the people (gratis), with the obligation that they lend their service to the local theatre; the three conservatories of the above-mentioned cities tied to the theatre, with mutual obligations between theatre and conservatory. The program could have been realized, had Cavour lived; with other ministers it's impossible.

Why in the world do you speak to me about writing again? Listen, my dear Arrivabene, I don't mean to make a resolution, but it is unlikely that I shall ever write again. . . . You will say, why? I really couldn't say why . . . but perhaps it bothers me to see that the public no longer has the courage to either applaud or whistle frankly, loyally. [. . .]

I shall leave for Paris in eight or ten days[1] and shall do everything possible to see that *Aida* goes well; I want that not so much for myself, but because a success might revive our theatre,[2] which is falling into total ruin. The Italian Theatre in Vienna[3] will also be restored, and I have something to do with that. Let's hope. Since they no longer want Italian music in Italy, we'll take it abroad.

1. Carlo Gatti, *Verdi*, II (Milano: Alpes, 1931), p. 286, gives 20 March as the date of the Verdis' departure for Paris. See Verdi's letter to Emile Perrin of 23 March 1876 and note 1 to that letter.

2. The Italian Theatre.

3. The artists of the Italian Theatre in Vienna were supported for many years by the court and performed at the old Kärntnertor Theater, usually between May and July. After the Imperial Opera was inaugurated in 1869, the Kärntnertor Theater was razed in 1870 and replaced by the Hotel Sacher. Consequently the Italians had to move to the Karltheater or the Theater an der Wien.

Verdi to Emile Perrin

Paris, [*Probably* 23 March 1876][1]

Seeing how generously you endeavor to set straight the affairs of M. Du Locle, I am forced to address myself to you, although regretfully, about a rather serious matter concerning Du Locle and myself.

When I signed the *Aida* contract for Cairo, Du Locle received in my name the sum of 50,000 francs from the management of that theatre. Of that amount I asked him to donate 2,000 francs to the hospital of the Opéra and, with the remaining 48,000 francs, to buy me shares of Italian Government bonds. . . .[2] He sent me a letter by balloon, dated 24 October 1870,[3] in which he said: "Your Italian stock certificates are deposited in care of Countess Mollien[4] at the Banque Magnard André e C., as of today, 24 October. The certificates, totaling 77, are valued at 48,000 francs. Keep this note in case something unexpected should happen." A short time thereafter Du Locle asked me to leave these certificates on deposit for him, since they would be a great help to his management in those very difficult times. I agreed to this request[5] and left the certificates on deposit, while he paid me the interest regularly through the end of 1874.

Last year before leaving Paris I asked him to give me the stock certificates, which I needed. With a certainty that now seems incredible, he replied that I should name the day, and he would bring the certificates personally to my country home in Italy. We decided on the end of October of last year; but he failed to keep his promise, which left me in a rather embarrassing situation.[6] We exchanged several letters,[7] but with no result.

Now, here in Paris, I understand the situation rather well, and I turn to you first of all to ask you in all fairness if it is in your power, and if you believe there is a way, to settle this matter without a scandal. It is so far known to no one and is a secret among you, Du Locle, and me. Please drop me a note with regard to this at the Hôtel de Bâde, so that, if necessary, I may take the proper measures.

1. Abbiati, III, p. 803, dates the draft of this letter and Giuseppina Verdi's French translation 23 May 1876, but Günther convincingly dates it 23 March 1876, the day after the Verdis' arrival in Paris. See Ursula Günther, "Der Briefwechsel Verdi-Nuitter-Du Locle zur Revision des 'Don Carlos', Teil I," *Analecta Musicologica*, Band 14 (Köln: Arno Volk Verlag Hans Gerig KG, 1974), p. 426.

2. See Verdi's letter to Du Locle of 26 August 1870.

3. Missing.

4. Du Locle's aunt.

5. See Verdi's letter to Du Locle of 14 February 1871.

6. Verdi had needed these stock certificates for a substantial payment, which was due 11 November 1875.

7. Not having paid Verdi any interest since 1874, Du Locle had admitted to him on 5 October 1875 that he was unable to pay his debt and was immobilized by a heart attack. In November and December 1875 Du Locle sought to restore his health on a trip to Egypt, while his friend Charles Nuitter temporarily replaced him as director of the Opéra-Comique. Aware of Du Locle's problems, Verdi did not remind him of his debt and the outstanding interest until 15 February 1876. At that time, however, Du Locle was not even able to pay the salaries of his company at the Opéra-Comique; Emile Perrin took care of the payroll but not of his son-in-law's debt to Verdi. On 10 March 1876 Verdi had written another letter on the subject to Du Locle, but again to no avail. See Günther, "Der Briefwechsel, Teil I," pp. 424–26.

Giuseppina Verdi to Cesare De Sanctis

Paris, 4 April 1876

[. . .] We would be obliged to you if you would send to Borgo St. Donnino for Busseto the same amount of pasta that you sent last year. But send less of the largest macaroni and more of the medium-sized macaroni and vermicelli.

Having ended his unspeakable suffering, may God have mercy on Piave![1] Let his soul have peace! His was, I can assure you, a delicate and honest soul.

Even Du Locle is not well. We have not seen him yet, because he went to take the cure at Hyères.[2] I don't know to what science dear Du Locle has entrusted himself, since I know him only as a poet . . . and, perhaps, a poet in the full meaning of the term: he is not a practical man in the face of life's hard realities. Let's hope he will soon recover and resume occupations more suitable to him than those of the past.

I hear that you hope soon to start settling your accounts with Verdi. I hope so, for your sake, and for the affection I bear you; for myself, I wish it from every point of view. You will understand what I mean without my going into greater detail.

The rehearsals for *Aida* at the Italian Theatre will begin soon, and we hope it will have the same success in Paris that it has had everywhere else. [. . .]

Courage, energy, my dear Cesarino! Where there's a will, there's a way.

Not always (but many times), wanting something is being able to do it. With these qualities, you will be respected by friends and enemies. [. . .]
P.S. Instead of 90 kg. of long pasta and 10 kg. of pastine, send 85 kg. of long pasta and 15 of pastine. Verdi, who sends his best, likes the pastine a great deal.

1. Francesco Maria Piave (1810–76), Italian librettist, who had furnished the verses for Verdi's *Ernani, I Due Foscari, Macbeth* (with Andrea Maffei), *Il Corsaro, Stiffelio, Rigoletto, La Traviata, Simon Boccanegra, Aroldo*, and *La Forza del Destino*. During Piave's illness, and following his death in Milan on 5 March 1876, Verdi helped to support the poet's family.

2. On the same day Giuseppina Verdi wrote these lines to De Sanctis, she reassured Marie Du Locle, who had accompanied her husband to Hyères on the French Riviera, in a warm letter of Verdi's and her own continued friendship and sympathy. See Günther, "Der Briefwechsel, Teil I," pp. 426–27.

Verdi to Léon Escudier [1]

Sunday [Paris, 16 April 1876]

What I said last night in a moment of anger I now repeat with the clearest head: I will not return to the theatre unless I am sure, materially sure, that the indecencies of the scenery in the fourth act have been amended. You have time, and if you know how to give clear, precise orders and to have them carried out at any cost, you will repair the most shameful disorders.

Any light whatever must be avoided in the subterranean chamber. . . . The curtain must be still and not flutter about.

Make a ceiling (not a loose drop) to prevent the temple from being seen, etc., etc.

Finally the intermission must not last more than twenty minutes.

Another rehearsal is necessary, and for the last time I formally request it for tomorrow night. A complete stage rehearsal with everything and for everybody, with not a single thing left out. If you can succeed in this, fine; if not, I know that . . . I am ashamed to expose myself once more to a humiliation like last night's.

1. Luzio, *Carteggi*, IV, p. 233, and, in a slightly different version, Abbiati, III, p. 794, give this text, which is obviously a draft of the following letter written on the same day. Luzio notes that a part of this draft is in Giuseppina Verdi's handwriting.

Verdi to Léon Escudier

Sunday [Paris, 16 April 1876]

Dear Léon,

Once more, and for the last time, I request a complete stage rehearsal with everything and for everybody tomorrow night, with not a single thing left

out in the fourth act. [. . .] If you can succeed in this, fine; if not, I know
what I shall have to do.
N.B. In order to rehearse and find out how much time is needed for the
intermission, it is necessary to set up the third act.
P.S. Perhaps I shall come to the theatre later and you can give me an answer.

Giuseppina Verdi to Giulio Ricordi

Paris, 22 April 1876

[. . .] At this time you will be in possession of the telegram[1] announcing the outcome of *Aida* at the dress rehearsal. This dress rehearsal can
be considered as good as the first performance, so far as its impression on the
listeners, made up mainly by the press, who last night in the theatre and this
morning in the newspapers showed their enthusiasm for *Aida*. We shall see a
little later. The performance of the orchestra was excellent, notwithstanding
weaknesses in several of the strings. The harps sounded like guitars. The
timpani, too, were extremely poor.

Less satisfying was the performance of the chorus, which, it is true, usually
has a small sound but makes up for it with a great lack of discipline! Consequences and fruits of the Commune! You know all the leading artists and how
they are able to perform *Aida*. They had, more or less, a most brilliant
success.

As for the *mise-en-scène*, with regard to the costumes, I shall repeat along
with *Le Figaro*, "everything is of gold" and so much gold that the old
employees of the Italian Theatre don't say *Aida*, Verdi, Escudier, but *Aid-or*,
Verd-or, and *Escudier-or*. This *mise-en-scène* has and will have an effect on a
certain kind of public; it is less so for that class which, not allowing itself to be
dazzled by the tinsel, condemns the lack of respect for and faithfulness to the
true history of the times that are being represented. The sets [. . .] oh there
have been many good intentions for these; but as the proverb says, "The road
to hell is paved with good intentions"!

First of all, the Italian Theatre is too small a house for the triumphal scene
of *Aida*. Then, without taking into consideration the space available, they
ended up assembling the sets in many disconnected pieces, putting one in
front of the other, which is fine perhaps at the Opéra, but which takes up too
much space on a stage as small as that of the Italian Theatre. In addition they
made little effect and were very pretentious. The stage machinery is complicated, misunderstood, and badly directed; it requires a long time for preparation and necessitates interminable intermissions. Fortunately it seems that the

music has made such an impression that, combined with the stupendous performance, all will be saved. [. . .]

1. Missing.

Giuseppina Verdi to Mauro Corticelli

Paris, 22 April 1876

[. . .] You will have received some of the journals Emanuele [Muzio] sent; and you will have seen that even though the opera and its performers were praised to the skies, the opinion concerning the *mise-en-scène* was not the same. I could write twenty pages on this subject, but I lack the time and the inclination to do it. It will be a topic of conversation upon our return.

Verdi was rather angry, but in spite of his quite justified and needed severity, he was not and will not be able to obtain what he should have obtained for the good of all. [. . .] I shall not close this letter until tomorrow, so that I can add a word about the first performance, which will take place this evening.[1] For several nights we have not retired until two in the morning! . . . Verdi's activity, energy, and foresight are incredible; he is immune to colossal fatigue!! . . . He really has a privileged nature, in the broadest sense of the word! [. . .]

Sunday morning, 23 April

In spite of all the bestiality of the stagehands and the stage managers, the opera had one of those frank, enthusiastic successes, which make an epoch in the history of art and especially in the musical-theatrical history of Paris. The singers were acclaimed in the theatre, lauded and censured in the journals; but it was Verdi who was really given the crown of glory. In spite of the habitual coldness of the Parisian public, women, men, orchestra musicians, everyone abandoned themselves on this occasion to an expression of enthusiasm that I can't remember being equaled, except in the *Requiem*. But that technical department and those stagehands! . . . One would think they were being paid to mess everything up; they didn't succeed, however, and that money was wasted, because the success was colossal! Tonight we shall sleep at last. [. . .]

1. For the premiere of *Aida* in France at the Italian Theatre (Salle Ventadour) in Paris on 22 April 1876, Verdi conducted and staged the work with the same four artists he brought with him to Vienna in 1875, together with Pandolfini as Amonasro and the young Edouard de Reszke in the role of the King.

Edouard de Reszke (1853–1917), Polish bass and brother of the celebrated tenor Jean (1850–1925) and the soprano Josephine de Reszke (1855–91), who appeared in the role of Aida at London's Covent Garden in 1881. Edouard de Reszke was trained by his brother Jean, studied in

Warsaw and Italy, and made his debut in the above-mentioned performance of *Aida* in Paris. Following great successes in that city, as well as in Milan and London, he made his American debut in Chicago as the King in *Lohengrin* (9 November 1891), and — together with his brother Jean in the role of Romeo — as Frère Laurent in *Roméo et Juliette* at the Metropolitan Opera 14 December 1891. He selected his greatest role, Méphistophélès in Gounod's *Faust*, for his last appearance at the Metropolitan Opera on 21 March 1903.

Emanuele Muzio to Katinka Evers [1]

Paris, 26 April 1876

[. . .] I had to conduct the orchestra rehearsals of *Aida* until the first dress rehearsal and then take charge of all the onstage music; but on Saturday I myself shall begin to conduct. The success of *Aida* is immense, without precedent. La Stolz and la Waldmann were liked much better last night (second performance) than at the first, and they really sang like two angels. Masini had more success at the first than at the second; he is an uneven artist who has no rhythm, and to accompany him one must have — as Verdi says — holy oil in his pocket. Pandolfini, immense success; Medini good, even though his voice has suffered and he always sings flat. The receipts of the first night were 18,223 francs. Second night, 17,790 francs. The theatre is almost completely sold out until the sixth performance, and seats are selling for the seventh and eighth performances. [. . .]

1. Widow of Giovanni Battista Lampugnani, who directed his theatrical agency in Milan after his death.

Verdi to Giuseppe Piroli

Paris, 28 April 1876

Dear Piroli,

I didn't want to write you after the first night, so that I could tell you about the audience's judgment with greater certainty. You will have read the newspapers and telegrams, and you will know the story about the dress rehearsal (which was a first performance) and the premiere. The other performances confirmed the success of the first, as I surmise from the box office receipts, which were about equal:

1st performance	18,200 fr.
2nd performance	17,500 fr.
3rd performance	17,796 fr.

If it continues like this, even with some decline, it will be a real success.

The press somewhat mistreated the ladies, especially la Stolz. It spoke well of the rest. An excellent musical performance. *Mise-en-scène*, rich but not beautiful. They tried to do too much, and they overdid it. Amen. [. . .]

Verdi to Tito and Giulio Ricordi

Paris, 28 April 1876

Aida

1st performance receipts	approx.	18,000 fr.
2nd performance	"	approx. 17,700 fr.
3rd performance	"	17,796 fr.

The receipts would have reached 20,000 and maybe more if Escudier had had the courage to eliminate completely the free press passes. On the basis of the receipts, then, it is a success. The press has harassed the ladies somewhat, especially la Stolz, but it has been most favorable to the rest. Here, of course, as in Germany, I have only learned to write well in the last three or four years; but at least they have not accused me of Wagnerism, as the Italian press did so graciously, especially in Milan.

In spite of all that, it is obvious to me that Escudier will not revive the Italian Theatre, and in the future his fortune may very well be swallowed up. Meanwhile my goal has not been achieved here, as it was not in Italy. I think that in '70, *Forza del Destino* in Milan was a success. The next year, *Aida*: success and money. The following year, rather poor performances and not much money. Last year, a bad season and not much money — in fact, a huge loss. This year (despite the last few nights), a terrible season and a loss again.[1] And next year? Perhaps the closing of the theatre.

What a sad picture! The same elsewhere. *Aida* was a great success in Naples. Result: closing of the theatre. In Rome the theatre is closed! Conclusion . . . effort wasted and time lost! [. . .]

1. Verdi apparently refers to the Italian Theatre in Paris. (The autographs of this letter, as well as of Verdi's letters to Tito Ricordi of 17 and 30 May 1876, are not in the Ricordi Archives. They may belong to Sig. Natale Gallini's collection, which he claims was accessible to Abbiati, who published these three letters in volume III, pp. 798–800.)

Verdi to Tito Ricordi

Paris, 17 May 1876

I am sorry, but I cannot act as arbiter in the dispute between you and Escudier, especially since the conditions you have given him are so miserable that I am humiliated! Five thousand francs for three years for all of France! Better nothing. [. . .]

I want to know from you, positively and clearly, if Escudier has the right to make a French arrangement [of *Aida*] for publication. Considering the infamous translations of my operas (translations that change the dramatic meaning and the musical phrasing), I had thought, from the time I was writing *Aida*, to reserve the right to do the translation myself, together with a French poet. I am doing this work with Nuitter,[1] at any rate, but I would hate to give [Escudier] this translation. Let me know by return mail, I repeat, if Escudier has the right to print a French translation. . . .[2]

1. Note that, as in his letter to Tito Ricordi of 20 May 1876, Verdi does not mention Du Locle's previous collaboration on this translation. See Du Locle's letters to Verdi of 26 April and 21 May 1872, and Verdi's letter to Du Locle of 22 June 1872.
2. See Verdi's letter to Escudier of 19 May 1876 and his letters to Tito Ricordi of 20, 24, and 30 May 1876, and of 3 June 1876.

Verdi to Léon Escudier

Paris, 19 May 1876

Dear Léon,

"What can I do? Tell me . . ." Those are the last words of your letter!

During these three years that I have come to Paris, I have never asked you for anything; and even now I only ask for what I think I have a right to expect.

I don't know how you understood my words concerning the *petits droits* . . . but if, during these years, you had collected the sum of 3,900 francs, you should have written me about it or at least told me about it as soon as I arrived — especially since this is not an account [. . .] but a deposit for me. You must agree that not mentioning it at all was treating me a little too much *sans façon*.

And since you speak of tact, I ask you if it is tactful to negotiate with Marseilles and to promise them *Aida* in French without telling me a word about it?

But these are all matters of minor importance; there are others, much more serious.

1. I understand that you must go about your business as a publisher; but that you should use my name to negotiate for *Aida* and to acquire it under humiliating terms — that is what I cannot tolerate! If Ricordi accepted those terms, it was because you told him: "I shall pay Verdi the complete *droit d'auteur*, as if *Aida* were done in French!!"
2. "*Aida* in France and England. . . . It's the same situation as that of *Trovatore*"! No. . . . My publisher in France for so many years should never have pronounced these words!

I could add much, much more, but what use are words? For the time being, at least, we must get ourselves out of a position that is embarrassing for everyone. It is impossible to reply at length to everything in writing, but we could, if you like, discuss it in person. Therefore I propose a meeting for the purpose of clearly defining:

1. The *droit d' auteur* with Peragallo.
2. The question of the French translation.

I think that two people we trust should be present at this meeting. For my part there will be Muzio, who is fully informed of this dispute. For your part it seems to me that the most suitable person would be your son-in-law.[1] [. . .]

1. Unknown.

Verdi to Tito Ricordi [1]

Paris, 20 May 1876

Dear Tito,

I haven't made myself clear. I don't want to know about your contracts or your business. I simply asked you if Escudier has the right to have a French translation of *Aida* made for publication! Yes or no?

I ask this because Nuitter has done a French translation that is terrible since it fails to take into account the stage and the music. Naturally a poet who is not watched by the composer thinks only of his verse, rhyme, phrasing, etc. But this is not what is needed for a good translation; basically one needs to say what must be said with the accents in the right place. Without that the musical phrase is altered and becomes something else.

Now I myself, together with this same Nuitter, am doing the translation that should be used for the performances whose rights I own. It will not be a good translation stylistically, but it will be excellent dramatically and musically. I would be very unhappy if, in addition to the one I am doing, there happened to be other translations around. But tell me, why did you have a French translation done without telling me a word about it, since you know that the performance rights belong to me? I say this *en passant*, and I'm not making a big thing of it, because I hope you will now agree to my translation.

Answer immediately but decisively (without going into unnecessary words) what you intend to do and what Escudier must do, because he urges me to make haste so that he can publish his translation.

P.S. Reply by telegram if I can give Escudier the translation I am having Nuitter make, so that he can do a piano-vocal score. What a mess! Why not make clear, precise contracts? Yes or no? Sell or don't sell. Now you see how much trouble it is even for me!!!

Escudier has just arrived; and at this very moment he is telling me that you can do as many French translations as you want, but only he has the right to do or sell a French translation in <u>France</u>. [. . .]

1. Tito Ricordi's reply — possibly by telegram — to Verdi's letter of 17 May 1876 is missing.

Verdi to Tito Ricordi

Paris, 24 May 1876

Dear Tito,

I am sorry that the *Aida* contract is not as clear about the French translation and performance as I had first imagined and wished. It was done in a hurry (following the performance of the opera, I believe); and since I signed it shortly before leaving Milan, I did not pay much attention. Now doubts arise at every instant.

After I received your telegram, I delivered part of the translation that I am doing to Escudier. With an eye to the performances in the French theatres, my translation requires a score. To perform the opera, of course, the orchestra parts and a score are needed. I ask you, in all <u>fairness</u>, who should provide this score? The theatres in France don't pay the so-called rental fees, as you know, but only some very small amount for the copying. So once again I ask, according to the contract, <u>to whom does the score translated into French belong?</u>

Reply quickly while I am here.

Verdi to Tito Ricordi

Paris, 30 May 1876

Dear Tito,

This *Aida* business is a real mess — what with all the divided property rights. What do we do now? We have to think about doing the opera in those theatres that ask for it, now that the translation is finished; I shall send it to you as soon as possible. What are your rights? What are your intentions? Must the orchestra parts (with the French words) be purchased from your firm? That way Escudier would be cut out, and I think that would be unsuitable for a thousand reasons.

Do you want to establish a price for your parts (always in French), both for the rental fee and for the sale, authorizing Escudier to draw up the contracts, so that whatever money might be realized beyond your price would be divided between Escudier and myself? He would be paid for his administration and for the <u>piano-vocal</u> score for the singers; I would be paid for my translation of the score.

Or would you rather draw up a single contract, with a single amount to be divided among us into three equal parts? I have not yet spoken to Escudier, but I would like to establish something clear and precise before leaving Paris. You decide . . . anything that is fair, and I'll accept it from now on; in fact, it is already accepted.

Tonight is the first performance of the *Mass*; and even if I decide to conduct it for three nights, Saturday will be the last, and I shall leave here Sunday or Monday.[1]

1. On 4 or 5 June 1876. According to Gatti, II, p. 287, the Verdis returned to St. Agata "in June." Abbiati, IV, p. 3, dates their departure from Paris "toward the middle of June." See Verdi's letters to Escudier of 20 June 1876 and to Maffei of 1 July 1876.

Verdi to Tito Ricordi

Paris, 3 June 1876

Dear Tito,

Escudier would buy not five but ten copies of *Aida* in French: five immediately at the price of 1,000 francs each, and five in September of next year at the same price. Altogether 10,000 francs. . . . Those terms seem most reasonable to me; and if you accept, my troubles will also be over, since I shall authorize him to have the opera performed. [. . .]

The day before yesterday the Quartet, which you heard in Naples, was played in my home. [. . .] On Tuesday at three p.m. it will be played in the theatre at a private performance attended by some one hundred persons, including many journalists, of course. Escudier wants to print it and has asked me for all property rights. I thought it wise to keep the Italian and English rights for you. Escudier has offered me 3,000 francs for those countries. [. . .]

Emanuele Muzio to Katinka Evers

Paris, 8 June 1876

[. . .] We still have six performances of *Aida*, and on the 20th we'll give the last.

La Krauss has canceled her contract with the Opéra in light of the publicity the French newspapers have given her divorce suit against the Duke of St. Onorato on grounds of adultery.

La Stolz says that she does not want to sing anymore. . . . I don't believe it — does she? [. . .]

La Waldmann will definitely become Count Massari's wife in August; the bridegroom's mother has already been in Paris for three weeks. [. . .]

Verdi to Léon Escudier

St. Agata, 20 June 1876

[. . .] So tonight is the last performance of *Aida*. I shall be very happy to hear that everything has gone smoothly, with no illness or mishap. . . . Oh you have been most fortunate in this! Twenty-six performances in a row without a hitch or an illness that caused you to cancel any performances. That kind of luck doesn't come twice!

Verdi to Clarina Maffei

St. Agata, 1 July 1876

Dear Clarina,

At last I am in Italy. I am not <u>emotionally</u> exhausted (as you say), but I am worn out by a number of little annoyances on all sides. This is all over, however, so let's not talk about it anymore.

What do I plan to do? It's my duty, you say, to keep writing!! But no, I definitely plan to do nothing. What good would it do anyway? It would be a useless thing, and I prefer <u>nothing</u> to something <u>useless</u>. I don't want to make any resolutions, but tell me, of what use was all the trouble I went to these past few years? Pretentious as I am, I thought of reviving our theatres and, at least, of showing how operas should be done. I began in Milan with *Forza del Destino*. At that time the theatre had a terrible chorus, a poor orchestra, and a *mise-en-scène* that lacked common sense. I changed things a little, and *Forza del Destino* was rather well performed. For *Aida* the next year I made improvements in the chorus and orchestra, and *Aida* (although musically I was criticized as though I had committed a crime, and I was even accused of not knowing how to write for singers, and Filippi dared to suggest that I should change my method of rehearsing) *Aida*, I repeat, put the theatre back on its feet and made a lot of money for the management. Then what happened? For two years, in spite of an excellent company, they put on dreadful productions and the management lost many thousand lire. . . .

In Paris, the Italian Theatre had fallen into such discredit that it was generally believed it could no longer survive. But this was not so; there are people in Paris who love that theatre and who will rush to it as soon as something decent is offered. Proof of this is *Aida*, which filled the theatre for twenty-six nights, even though it was late in the season. . . . Do you think this example will be helpful? No they will do just what was done in Milan; and next year, if the management doesn't stop its <u>downhill</u> course, it will lose 200,000 francs. So what good does it do to write? Besides if I want, I can do it at home for my own pleasure, but as far as the public and the managers. . . . Let's talk about something else. [. . .]

It seems that la Stolz really intends to give up her career — at least that would seem to be the meaning of her refusal of some very important contracts, such as Petersburg, Cairo, etc. You can ask her about it, however, since she should be in Milan now, and she will certainly see you. La Waldmann is getting married after this summer, and she will bid farewell to the stage. [. . .]

Verdi to Maria Waldmann

St. Agata, 10 July 1876

Dearest,

You have probably been in Venice for several days . . . calm and happy, and busy with rehearsals for the opera this season, which will be the last for you. . . . The last! It's a sad word that holds a world of memories and embraces a life of excitements — some happy, some sad, but always precious to those who have the stamina of an artist. You are lucky, however, because you will be greatly compensated in your change of fortune. It's not so for others, to whom this word "last" means: All is finished!!

But, my dear Maria, why do I keep repeating painful things to you? The last evening I saw you in Paris I told you more or less the same things! I regretted it then, and here I am doing it all over again! Excuse me for that. Since I cannot give you cheerful news about myself, tell me about the many good things in your life — young, beautiful, and at the height of your happiness as you are.

Write to me, then, not only to give me news of *Aida* and the *Mass*, but to tell me about yourself.

We pass the time here quietly, and, if not cheerfully, well enough. Peppina joins me in sending greetings to you and your sister.

Verdi to Léon Escudier

St. Agata, 10 July 1876

[. . .] I know you have been in London, and I am sure you found the English better musicians than they used to be. So many theatres! So many concerts! So many classic masterpieces! They say that *Aida*[1] is doing well and making money. But, except for la Patti, I don't know how well it is being performed. A few days ago I met an intelligent Frenchman who had heard it almost every night in Paris. He said plagues upon this *Aida* in London. So which is the truth? [. . .]

How is the Du Locle affair going? It is sad, very, very sad![2] [. . .]

1. The premiere of *Aida* in London had taken place at Covent Garden on 22 June 1876.

2. When his letter to Perrin of 23 March 1876 brought no results, Verdi contacted the Paris attorney Ernest Cartier and requested Escudier's intervention, in order to recoup the Viceroy's downpayment, i.e. one-third of his fee for *Aida*. Complications arose as a result of Marie Du Locle's concern that the inheritance expected from her husband's aunt the Countess Mollien (who died on 26 February 1878) could be diminished by her payment of Du Locle's debt to Verdi. With Escudier and Cartier's assistance, however, the suit was handled with such discretion that it is not known whether it was settled in or out of court. The case was supposedly judged to Verdi's satisfaction in August, and he received the first installment of Du Locle's repayment in October 1876. Years later Nuitter brought about Verdi and Du Locle's reconciliation. See Günther, "Der Briefwechsel, Teil I," pp. 428–36, and also Teil II: "Die Dokumente herausgegeben von Gabriella Carrara Verdi (Sant'Agata) and Ursula Günther (Paris), Einleitung und Anmerkungen von Ursula Günther," *Analecta Musicologica*, Band 15 (Köln: Arno Volk Verlag Hans Gerig KG, 1975), pp. 398–401.

Verdi to Antonio Ghislanzoni

St. Agata, 3 August 1876

Dear Ghislanzoni,

Forgive me, forgive me, forgive me![1] You are fifty thousand times right, and I am a hundred thousand times wrong. If I tried very hard, I could probably find some reason that would somewhat lessen my guilt; but since I am convinced that I deserve a sentence, I can only give myself up. Before hurling the sentence at me, however, tell me about you and your activities.

I'll tell you nothing about myself, because all I could say is that I'm not doing anything and that I don't want to do anything! What good would it do to act differently? To entertain and amuse the public (an ugly word, "entertain"), to give the papers more food for slander, and to hear my music badly performed (Oh this is certain!) — I don't care for these things anymore! [. . .]

1. For his long silence.

Verdi to Léon Escudier

Genoa, 21 January 1877

Dear Léon,

In your telegram from the first of the year,[1] you told me that you would send me a promissory note within a week. I see once again that your big affairs have made you forget your little ones. I am obstinate about this trifle because I want to put my affairs in order, and I think that you yourself would not want to leave such a paltry item as 4,000 francs outstanding. I call it a trifle because it concerns only the contract that expired last November since I don't want to mention the other 15,000 francs; if I do mention it now *en passant*, it is only because you said, almost publicly, that you wanted to pay me something for my trip to Paris! Although I may be vain enough to think that my presence last spring was not entirely useless and that my journey and my lodging expenses were worth something, I state that I would not now accept compensation. I had wanted the Italian Theatre to revive itself, and for that reason I was prepared to make any sacrifice; but I no longer have the hopes I had before. I know that now you have some successes. (I am not talking about *Aida*, which you have prostituted by trying out all your new-comers in it — something which you, you above all, should never have done.) In spite of that, I believe, as I always have, that individual successes benefit only the individual and not art; and I, as an Italian and as an Italian composer, was hoping first and foremost for the revival of our theatre. You may have other partial successes and other good nights; but forgive me if I take advantage of the good relations we have had and dare to tell you that you will not resurrect the Italian Theatre and that it will swallow your entire fortune in the long run. [. . .]

1. Missing.

Verdi to Maria Waldmann [1]

Genoa, 9 March 1877

[. . .] I am going to save you from a bad move. You know that it takes two to sing a duet. Your part, of course, would be divine. . . . But the other?

Now I ask you as a favor (and I would be most desolate if you took this in the wrong spirit) not to perform this duet. Tomorrow I shall tell you why.

1. In response to a missing letter in which Waldmann supposedly informed Verdi of her intention to sing, with Flora Mariani, the Aida-Amneris duet at a benefit concert in Ferrara. At that time Mariani was changing from the soprano to the mezzo-soprano repertoire. See note 2, Verdi's letter to Escudier of 25 January 1873.

Verdi to Maria Waldmann

Genoa, 10 March 1877

Dear Maria,

I shall begin by repeating the words I wrote yesterday, asking you not to take this in the wrong spirit, if the circumstances (the interests of art, I would even say the conscience of art) have obliged me, in the contracts of my latest operas, to impose certain terms which are perhaps a bit hard and severe,

but which are necessary to prevent, in part, the monstrosities that have occurred in our theatres. It's true that these clauses aren't sufficient to guarantee
good performances; but at least they help to apply a brake on the alterations,
the cuts, transpositions, etc., etc., which happened all too frequently in our
operas. This is the reason there exists the clause that the operas can only be
performed in their entirety and as they were performed the first time.
. . . Accept my reasons as being justified, therefore, and write me a few
lines to tell me that you are not angry with me. [. . .]

Verdi to Tito Ricordi

Genoa, 10 March 1877

It's an old habit of the House of Ricordi to involve me in things that
don't concern me.

There are the contracts.

Each of us has his own part.

I write the operas.

Your firm administers them.

And just as the House of Ricordi (acting within its rights) did not ask my
authorization to do *Forza del Destino* now at La Scala, so it should not have
saddled me with the hateful duty of replying negatively to a request from an
old friend, whom I love and respect, to do the *Aida* duet at a benefit in
Ferrara.

Verdi to Maria Waldmann

St. Agata, 14 April 1877

Dearest Maria,

Let's say no more about the quibbling that arose over the concert in
Ferrara. It's easy to understand why Ricordi did not refuse the duet immediately, as he was obliged to. He thought it was a good occasion to show
off Flora Mariani, who, for all I know, could be a soprano, contralto, tenor, or
bass; I only know that everyone says very bad things about her. [. . .]

Verdi to Giulio Ricordi

St. Agata, 5 October 1877

Dear Giulio,

I am reading the letter[1] you wrote to Corticelli, and I reply. I don't understand if by engaging la Patti they[2] mean to do *Aida*. If this were so, imagine for yourself whether I would be pleased; but with the rest [of the company], no.[3]

A success, then . . . great . . . it really had to be! You heard her ten years ago, and now you exclaim: "What a change." You are mistaken! La Patti was then what she is now: perfect organization, perfect balance between singer and actress, a born artist in the fullest sense of the word.

When I heard her for the first time in London — she was eighteen years old — I was stupefied not only by her marvelous performance but by several dramatic traits in which she revealed herself to be a great actress. I recall her chaste and modest demeanor when in *La Sonnambula* she lay down on the soldier's bed, when in *Don Giovanni* she left the libertine's room as though contaminated. I recall a certain byplay in Don Bartolo's aria in the *Barbiere* and, most of all, in the recitative that precedes the quartet in *Rigoletto*, when her father shows her her lover in the tavern saying *E l'ami sempre* and she replies *Io l'amo*. Nothing can express the sublime effect of this word as spoken by her. This, and more, she knew how to say and do over ten years ago. But many people didn't agree then, and you thought just as your public did — you wanted to give her your blessing first, as though the entire European public, which was going mad for her, didn't understand a thing! But "we are what we are — Milan has the foremost theatre in the world!"[4] Don't you think all this is a little too close to that detestable *chez nous* of the French? The world's foremost theatre! I know five or six of these foremost theatres, and actually it's in those places that lousy music is most often produced. So *inter nos*, go ahead and admit it: six years ago, what a mediocre orchestra,[5] what a poor chorus, the worst technical equipment, a horrible lighting system, impossible props, and a *mise-en-scène* — for better or worse — was then unknown! Today things are a little better, but not much, just a little! Meanwhile having been persuaded to come to the highest temple of art, our good public sits in judgment! Always ignorant when it doesn't judge by its impressions, this public — which tomorrow, for example, will greet a poor thing like la Fossa[6] with a cordial salute — will remain cold at la Patti's appearance. This public, which has repeatedly applauded its approval of so many mediocre mediocrities, will hardly grace la Patti with one call after the *cavatina* in *Traviata*. An incomparable performance. . . . Ah public, public, public!!!

If you see la Patti, give her my very best regards and also my wife's. I don't send her the usual congratulations, because it really seems that for la Patti it would be the most useless thing in the world; and then you know, and know very well, that I did not wait for her success in Milan, but since the first time I heard her in London (almost as a child), I have judged her a marvelous singer and actress, an exception in art.

Give her my regards then and nothing else. . . .

1. Missing.
2. The management at La Scala.
3. Adelina Patti had sung her first Aida in the London premiere of the opera on 22 June 1876, with tenor Ernesto Nicolini, her future husband. He was apparently appearing with her at La Scala, and Verdi supposedly could not forget the reports about Nicolini's Radames in Rome. See Verdi's letter to Giulio Ricordi of 25 March 1875. Quite possibly Verdi also thought that the prima donna's large salary (presumably the largest any star received at that time) would leave no money in the budget for any supporting artists of quality.
4. Verdi quotes in a Milanese dialect: "*nun sem nun . . . Milanes . . . el primer teater del mond!*"
5. See Verdi's letter to Usiglio of 26 January 1875 and other contradictory comments he made on the orchestra in Milan.
6. Amalia Fossa (1852–1911), Italian soprano. After her debut in *Un Ballo in Maschera* in Lisbon in 1870, she sang throughout Italy and at La Scala between 1876 and 1878. In 1876 she had sung the first Margherita in Boito's *Mefistofele* in Trieste.

Verdi to Gino Monaldi [1]

Genoa, 5 December 1877

Sir,

At my farm near Busseto several copies of your writing[2] have arrived, and now here I have received five others that you had the kindness to send me.

From a meager subject you have wanted to extract a large work, and I am, in every respect, grateful to you; but permit me to tell you neither my impressions nor my opinions. It is an old habit of mine not to pass judgment, not even in music. I believe so little in that of others! Can you imagine that I have faith in my own?

1. Writer and music critic.
2. One of Monaldi's many biographical works on Verdi.

Verdi to Opprandino Arrivabene

Genoa, 8 February 1878

Dear Arrivabene,

I too have read, or at least looked over, Monaldi's booklet. It's full of inaccuracies! It goes without saying that such writing cannot be but a bundle of errors, even when one is inspired by the protagonist, because there is always an *amour propre* involved, or at least a vainglory, which hides what is bad and enlarges what is good. There are so few honest men, so few high-minded men. And, as a result, those writers copy what others have said on the same subject; and what they don't know, they invent. So did the Grrrreat

Fétis, the ultimate authority for all musicians, but actually a mediocre theorist, the worst historian, and a composer of Adamic innocence. I detest this big charlatan, not because he spoke so badly about me, but because he made me run to the Egyptian museum in Florence one day (You remember? We went together.) to examine an antique flute,[1] by which, in his History of Music, he pretends to have found the system of ancient Egyptian music . . . a system equal to ours, except for the tonality of the instrument!!! Son of a bitch! That flute is but a pipe with four holes like those our shepherds have. That's the way to make history! And the imbeciles believe. . . .

P.S. But they will never stop this bullshit, our "repairmen." In truth we are falling from bad to worse!

1. See Giulio Ricordi's letter to Verdi of 14 July 1870.

Verdi to Giulio Ricordi

Genoa, 12 March 1878

Dear Giulio,

"Did not make any observations, but think it wise to inform you"!! So you say in our telegram.[1] It would have been better, however, not to inform me and instead to make some observations. . . .

La Patti, in fact, told me something about *Aida*.[2] But it was at my home. . . . I didn't want any discussions, so I interrupted her, saying precisely these words: "*Aida* no longer concerns me. . . . Speak to the gentlemen in Milan about it." Now I hear that a cut in the third act is involved. That poor third act, which was worthless according to the first judgment of the Milanesi, is destined to suffer! . . . And yet there is nothing to cut, not even the ugly *cabaletta* of the tenor-soprano duet. It is part of the situation, and it must, or should, remain; if not, there is a hole in the canvas. You know that I am the greatest enemy of cuts and transpositions.[3] It's better not to perform the operas. If la Patti finds this role difficult, why does she do it? What need does she have to do *Aida*? And as I have said to her personally many times: "Why a new opera when you have so many old ones to choose from?" La Patti has no need for new operas, for *Aida*, or for other operas. Didn't the world admire her before? And I myself didn't need to be baptized by the audiences to realize what a marvelous actress-singer she was at eighteen when I heard her for the first time in *Sonnambula, Lucia,* the *Barbiere,* and *Don Giovanni!* She was then what she is now — except for some changes in her voice, especially in the low register, which was then somewhat empty and infantile and is now very beautiful. But the talent, the dramatic instinct, the singing — perfectly equal, equal, equal, equal.

To return to us, however, we must not now provoke any petty quarrels, so let it be. But I state that not this, nor the *Mass* in the Duomo, nor some other things suit me at all. I further state that I shall henceforth not answer telegrams of this sort and that . . . for now I say nothing else. [. . .]

P.S. You believe in a complete production, but mind you, you live in a deceptive atmosphere . . . La Scala! A great word! But to look within!! When I think that you had the best designer and the best technical director!! And they are no longer there.

1. Missing.

2. Verdi apparently refers to a visit of the famous prima donna, after she had sung the role several times. There is no indication that Verdi ever coached her, as Hermann Klein relates in *The Reign of Patti* (New York: Century, 1920), p. 186: "She had, while in Italy, visited him at his villa at Brussetto [*sic*] and carefully gone through the part with him. Mr. Gye [the impresario Ernest Gye] had duly announced the fact in his prospectus, together with the proud statement that 'The exclusive right of performance of *Aida* in England has been secured by the director of the Royal Italian Opera.'"

3. On 30 November 1883 the critic of *The Evening Post* in New York, reviewing "the best performance of the season at the Academy of Music," wrote: "When Mr. Mapleson [the impresario Colonel James H. Mapleson] repeats *Aida*, as he will most certainly do, we trust that Mme. Patti will refrain from the *Traviata* cadenza with which she marred the closing bars of *O Cieli azzurri*. As a bit of vocalization it was perfect, but its introduction upon the banks of the Nile would have made Verdi's hair stand on end." *The New York Daily Tribune* of 1 December 1883, quotes Colonel Mapleson: "I noticed that one critic [in *The New York Times*] used very harsh language in criticizing what he calls the 'abominable cadenza she saw fit to introduce.' I wonder whether it would surprise the writer to learn that the 'abominable cadenza' was written by Verdi himself. Madame Patti has the original manuscript and will, I am sure, be happy to show it to her intelligent critic."

Teresa Stolz to Verdi and Giuseppina Verdi

Milan, 18 March 1878

[. . .] As everywhere; *Aida* has again worked miracles. [. . .] La Patti interprets certain things stupendously well, but either does not care for others or cannot interpret them. A very strange thing, her high notes are now forced. [. . .]

Verdi to Clarina Maffei

Genoa, 19 March 1878

Dear Clarina,

Really, really, really!!! They miss the power and the passion of la Stolz!! But if then she couldn't sing that part . . . if then she was sacrificed . . . if then I did not know how to write, etc., And five years later!! . . . You see . . . Time's little jokes!

You, even you, advise me to write? But let's talk seriously. For what reason should I write? And what should I write? And what would I gain from it? The result would be quite miserable. I would hear all over again that I don't know how to write and that I have become a follower of Wagner. Some glory! After a career of almost forty years to end up as an imitator! [. . .]

Verdi to Adolphe Dennery [1]

Busseto, 19 June 1878

Monsieur Dennery,

If I feel reluctant to write again for the Opéra, it is not, I beg you to believe me, because of the directors, with whom I have always been on the best terms. My repugnance or, better, my dislike results from a certain opposition on the part of the personnel based on habits and systems that are not mine, and on what you might call an exact but generally flabby, nerveless, and colorless execution. Maybe this is just my own particular way of looking at it, but I cannot think differently than I do. If (to my collaborator's and my own misfortune) I were to decide to write once more for this theatre, I would be obliged to demand certain conditions that would most probably not be accepted by a director. I hasten to add that I find myself at this moment very little disposed to write for the Opéra or for any other theatre. In the meantime, however, before speaking of conditions and before speaking to the director, don't you think, M. Dennery, that it would be more to the point and more opportune to speak about the poetry? It would be useless to do business if the poetry — even though very beautiful, as I do not doubt — were not to my taste. I don't ask you to send it to me, but I simply ask you for a few sketched-out pages to give me an idea. Excuse the frankness of my speech. [. . .]

1. A French playwright whose letters to Verdi are missing.

Verdi to Adolphe Dennery

Busseto, 9 July 1878

[. . .] I, too, enjoy the *mise-en-scène* [in the theatre], but on the condition that it does not go beyond certain limits and become technique.

I really wanted to read a little sketch of your poetry on my own, but you fear that I might not understand it. This is perhaps so; but, on the other hand, the reading of a poem by the author — his very presence, I am afraid — might influence me toward an impression which might then be less when I reread the poem in the silence of my room. That would be a pity (I dare say, a very grave pity), because I am incapable of doing anything, even with the most beautiful poetry in the world, if it does not appeal to me. To the contrary, let the poetry be as full of faults as you wish, like *Rigoletto, Ballo, Aida,* and so many others, so long as I feel it.[1] [. . .]

But tell me, M. Dennery, is there really no way of having, if not a sketch, at least an outline that would suggest to me the genre, the period, etc., and if it is historical, the subject? Have no fear, for you can be sure that I won't say a word to anyone in the world! This way we can either forget it right away or go ahead with greater confidence. At any rate, it isn't necessary for you to undertake a trip to Italy, because I shall probably have to make a trip to Paris later on, for business as well as for the Exposition. [. . .]

1. Amid the French text of this letter Verdi wrote these three words, which he underlined, in Italian (*io lo senta*).

Verdi to Adolphe Dennery

Busseto, 23 July 1878

[. . .] I should have the power to withdraw the score, if, in the course of rehearsals (even the last), things should not go according to my wishes. [. . .]

This condition, I admit, is a tough one! But the past makes me fear the future, and for all the gold in the world I would not want to find myself in the middle of troubles and turmoils such as I have had to undergo at other times. [. . .]

Verdi to Antonio Ghislanzoni

Genoa, 26 December 1878

Dearest Ghislanzoni,

Thank you for your greeting, which among the many, is one of the dearest to me. I heartily reciprocate your greeting, together with my wife, wishing you all the best and health above all, which is the greatest happiness, as you say so well, that one can have in this very sad world. [. . .]

Verdi to Clarina Maffei

Genoa, 21 February 1879

[. . .] Thank you for the newspaper clippings you sent me. [. . .] Among them was one that said some very harsh things . . . telling of intrigues, cliques, etc. Whether there is any truth in all of this I don't know and don't want to know; but I do know that all this excitement and agitation over an opera,[1] all this praise and adulation remind me of the past (everyone knows that old-timers always praise their own times) when, without any publicity, without knowing anyone at all, we showed our face in public. If they applauded, we said (or didn't say), "Thank you." If they whistled, "We'll see you some other time." I don't know if that was better, but it certainly was more dignified.

Corticelli had me read one of those newspapers that really made me laugh. That newspaper proposed that a tablet be engraved at La Scala:

"In the year 1879 a foreign composer came here, and great festivities were given in his honor, including a dinner which the prefect and the mayor attended. In 1872 a certain Verdi came in person to stage *Aida*, and he was not even offered a glass of water."

What glass of water, I said; I was lucky they didn't stone me! Don't take that statement literally, since all it means is that I bickered with everyone about *Aida*, and everyone looked at me askance as if I were a ferocious beast. I hasten to say the fault was mine, all mine, since, to tell the truth, I am not at all polite inside the theatre (nor outside of it either), and since I have the misfortune of never understanding what others understand, precisely because I am never able to proffer those sweet words, those phrases that send everyone into ecstasies. No I shall never, for example, be able to say to a singer: "What a talent! What expression! It can't be done any better! What a heavenly voice! What a baritone . . . you have to go back fifty years to find such a voice! What a chorus! What an orchestra! This is the foremost theatre in the world!!'' Oh things are becoming quite confusing. Time and again I have heard them say in Milan (even when I staged *Forza del Destino*, of all things):

"La Scala is the foremost theatre in the world."

In Naples: "San Carlo, the foremost theatre in the world."

In the past they used to say in Venice: "La Fenice, the foremost theatre in the world."

In Petersburg: "Foremost theatre in the world."

In Vienna: "Foremost theatre in the world." (And I would agree with that.)

In Paris, of course, the Opéra is the foremost theatre in two or three worlds!

And I remain stunned, goggle-eyed, my mouth open, saying, "Mulish as I am, I don't understand anything,'' and I end up by saying that among so many foremosts, a second will be better. [. . .]

1. Verdi refers to the production of Massenet's *Le Roi de Lahore* at La Scala on 6 February 1879.

Verdi to the Orchestral Society of La Scala [1]

Genoa, 4 April 1879

Gentlemen,

I regret that I cannot accept the honorable title you gentlemen offer me. As you rightly say, I am by nature alien to this sort of position, and even more so in today's chaos of ideas, in which trends and studies contrary to our character have upset Italian musical art. This chaos, which may very well bring forth a new world (though no longer ours), but more likely nothingness, is something in which I wish to take no part at all. It is my ardent wish, however, that this orchestral branch of art may turn out well. I also earnestly desire that the other branch be equally cultivated, to give back to Italy that art which was ours and was once distinguished from the other.

It's all right to educate the public to great art, as the scholars say, but to me it seems that the art of Palestrina and Marcello is also great art . . . and it is our own.

With these words I do not mean to pronounce a judgment (God forbid) or to express an opinion. My only purpose is in some measure to justify my decision.

I beg you, gentlemen, kindly to accept my excuses, and I wish the new institution splendid success.

1. Verdi was apparently asked to become president of this newly established organization under Faccio's direction.

Verdi to Giulio Ricordi

St. Agata, 2 May 1879

[. . .] Yesterday I received a large package, which I assume contains the score of *Simone*! If you come to St. Agata in six months, a year, two, three years, etc., you will find it intact, just as you sent it to me. I told you in Genoa that I detest useless things. It's true that everything I have ever done has been useless, but there were extenuating circumstances in the past. There would be nothing more useless to the theatre at this time than one of my operas. . . . And then, and then, it is better to end with *Aida* and the *Mass* than with a rehash.[1]

1. However Verdi did revise *Simon Boccanegra*, with Boito's assistance, for a production at La Scala which opened on 24 March 1881. (Verdi's revision of *Don Carlos* was first performed at La Scala on 10 January 1884. *Otello* was premiered there on 5 February 1887, and *Falstaff* on 9 February 1893. Three of the *Quattro Pezzi Sacri*, Verdi's final creations, were first performed at the Opéra in Paris on 7 April 1898.)

Verdi to Clarina Maffei

St. Agata, 2 May 1879

[. . .] Reading your letter[1] I wondered as you did, "Why these sad thoughts?" It's true that the times are very sad in every respect, and if you add to this your own personal troubles, the weight becomes crushing. Life is nothing but a sequence of misfortunes from which only the egotist can escape. One must have courage (which you certainly do not lack) and have faith in the friends who remain, among whom you may count me in the first rank. [. . .]

La Stolz writes me every once in a while, and I am aware of her brilliant life. She does very well: she has a fortune, she is free, still of a good age, popular, and esteemed. Nothing could be better. . . . La Waldmann, on the contrary, is in the depths of sadness. Yesterday she wrote me a devastating letter,[2] prompted by the death of her father who was over eighty years old. Time will heal the wound! [. . .]

1. Maffei's letter, which is missing, might have reflected Verdi's own disillusion following the Risorgimento and Italy's political and economic deterioration.
2. Missing.

Verdi to Emanuele Muzio

St. Agata, 7 October 1879

Dear Emanuele,

Seeing how far things had gone, I realized I could not refuse *Aida*;[1] but *inter nos*, I am not very pleased. Either I don't go to Paris and the opera is performed in a feeble, lifeless manner, without any effect, or I go and destroy myself, body and soul.

Escudier is always the same, always himself. This latest *Aida* contract is another dirty trick. If only Heugel[2] had been able to acquire the rights to *Aida*, I would be free of Escudier forever. That man makes it even more difficult for me to go to Paris. After an association of more than thirty years between publisher and composer, it is difficult to break if off. All those who are now saying he's a scoundrel would condemn me if I were to change publishers. That's the way the world is!

The Italian newspapers don't approve of my condescension regarding

Aida.[3] Even yesterday the *Corriere della Sera*[4] reported that after the re-peated discourtesies I had received, I would not allow *Aida* to be performed. Who knows what they will say when they find out that I have actually given my permission. The best part of it is that I am basically in total agreement with them. [. . .]

Such a mess! Such an annoyance! Such trouble! Even at St. Agata one can't live in peace!!

1. Verdi refers to a proposed production at the Opéra in 1880. Cesari and Luzio, *I Copialettere*, pp. 312–13n, remark: "During Halanzier's direction of the Opéra in Paris, Verdi was consistently opposed to a performance of *Aida* in that theatre and had also published his reasons for this opposition." See Verdi's letter to Halanzier of 24 August 1872. Halanzier understandably resented Verdi's preference for the Italian Theatre in Paris, and Halanzier's absence from the *Aida* premiere in that house on 22 April 1876 had not been unnoticed by the Maestro (See Gatti, II, p. 286). Auguste Emanuel Vaucorbeil succeeded where Halanzier had failed. Soon after his installation as director of the Opéra on 16 July 1879, Vaucorbeil set out for St. Agata. According to Cesari and Luzio, and to Gatti, II, p. 321, Vaucorbeil arrived at St. Agata on 3 October 1879 and accomplished his mission. Pougin, *Verdi: An Anecdotic History of his Life and Works*, pp. 236–41, also gives a detailed account of Vaucorbeil's visit to St. Agata.

2. Jacques Leopold Heugel (1815–83), music publisher in Paris.

3. His permission for *Aida* to be given at the Opéra.

4. A prominent newspaper in Milan, still in existence.

Verdi to Ferdinand Hiller

[*Probably* St. Agata, October 1879]

[. . .] I never wanted to allow this performance in the past; and now circumstances have forced me to grant my permission — not only that, but also to go there and take part in the rehearsals and perhaps conduct it. . . . What can I say? One never does what one would like to do. [. . .]

Verdi to Giuseppi Piroli

St. Agata, 8 November 1879

Dear Piroli,

For the time being I am not leaving for Paris; and I may not go later on, as I had planned, precisely because *Aida* will be done in French. You know that, in spite of myself, I gave permission for this opera to be done at the Opéra. I would not deny the performance, as I have at other times, because they would have thought it a matter of personality, antipathy, etc., etc. . . . Imagine!! Anyway what's done is done. As an artist, however, I am extremely sad about it, because it will be a very mediocre performance. I haven't yet decided if I'll go; more likely, I won't.

Verdi to Ferdinand Hiller

St. Agata, 11 November 1879

[. . .] You know that *Aida* will be done at the Opéra and that Saint-Saëns seems to be antagonistic about it. If they only knew how I feel about it! But many times in life there are circumstances that force you to do something you don't want to do, and I had no desire whatsoever to do *Aida* at the Opéra at this time.

Auguste Emanuel Vaucorbeil to Verdi

Paris, 18 November 1879

[. . .] I believe it would be useful to augment the number of special trumpets in the procession and also the number of musicians placed on the stage; the fourteen indicated in the score would be insufficient for my large house. The processional trumpets in A flat and B? Do you absolutely want me to have them sent from Italy? Or better, do you not think that Sax could make us some of a superior quality? [. . .]
P.S. Permit me one simple observation. I fear that the playing time of *Aida* is a little short, according to the customs of the Opéra. Would you not be disposed to adding several airs to the ballet so that I may employ all of my large dance personnel, which would only add to the splendor of the spectacle? [. . .]

Verdi to Auguste Emanuel Vaucorbeil

Milan, 24 November 1879

My dear Monsieur Vaucorbeil,

With many thanks for your gracious letter I answer the questions you pose for me.

I believe that the six trumpets for the march, three in A flat, three in B, will be sufficient. La Scala and the San Carlo in Naples are larger than the Opéra, and the six trumpets were completely sufficient there.

Sax could make the instruments quite well, but I would have you notice that in this instance the refinements of Sax are useless. If you put keys and valves [on these instruments], you no longer have the ancient grand trumpet, in shape or in sound. You know that the march is built around the natural notes[1]

As for the number of musicians on the stage, the 14 indicated by the score is an error in figuring. There are supposed to be at least 24 or 30. At La Scala there were 28.

As for the ballet, the matter is more serious. I know well that *Aida* is a little short for your theatre, but I could not, and I would not, know where to put an [additional] ballet. What can I say? It seems to me (if you will allow something for an author's vanity) that *Aida* must be what it is and that in adding something you would spoil, pardon the phrase, the architecture of the whole. [. . .]

1. In the absence of the autograph, I have transcribed these notes as Ursula Günther did on p. 581 of her article "Documents inconnus concernant les relations de Verdi avec l'Opéra de Paris" in *Atti del III° Congresso Internazionale di Studi Verdiani* (Parma: Istituto di Studi Verdiani, 1974).

Verdi to Auguste Emanuel Vaucorbeil

Genoa, 4 January 1880

My dear Monsieur Vaucorbeil,

Away from Genoa for several days, I have not been able to answer your gracious letter,[1] for which I thank you a great deal.

[. . .] I do not doubt that the *mise-en-scène* [of *Aida*] will be superb at the Opéra. That is not the weak side of this theatre.

Concerning Nicolini, I could not give you my opinion. It has been a long time since I have heard that tenor, and I don't want to take the responsibility of having you engage an artist whom, strictly speaking, I could almost say I don't know. As for the other artists, I shall tell you only that for the roles of Amonasro and Amneris they must, above all and before anything else, have feeling, feeling and still more feeling! Remember la Waldmann and Pandolfini. . . . Two singers! But they also had the devil inside them! That is what is needed for these two roles. Without this, success is not possible! [. . .]

1. Missing.

Verdi to Ferdinand Hiller

Genoa, 7 January 1880

[. . .] First of all let me tell you that it is not certain that I shall go to Paris. I have so little desire to get involved in the Babel of that pretentious Opéra, where music is performed so poorly, that as of now I really don't know if I shall make this journey. [. . .]

Verdi to Antonio Ghislanzoni

Genoa, 13 January 1880

Dearest Ghislanzoni,

Nothing could have been more welcome to me than to receive your news,[1] accompanied by your beautiful, interesting, most charming little volume,[2] for which I am doubly grateful to you, since you mention my name in it with indulgence.

As far as I am concerned, it's quite true that there have been projects to write more <u>notes</u>; but I, to tell the truth, have never felt more inclined to let anyone write them who wants to, and I really, really don't know what I shall do in the future. [. . .]

1. Missing.
2. Probably *Reminiscenze artistiche*. See biographical note on Ghislanzoni and note 1, Verdi's letter to Maffei of 30 April 1870.

Verdi to Auguste Emanuel Vaucorbeil

Genoa, 31 January 1880

Monsieur Vaucorbeil,

I regret that you have been ill for several days. They write me, however, that you are on the way to a full recovery, and I hope this letter finds you completely well again and in a condition which will allow you to assist with the rehearsals for *Aida*.

I don't know how to inform you of the precise day of my arrival in Paris, for it seems impossible for me to leave Italy without making a trip to St. Agata. Be quite calm and <u>certain</u> that the premiere of *Aida* will suffer no delay on my account. [. . .]

Verdi to Giuseppe Piroli

Genoa, 10 February 1880

Dear Piroli,

On Thursday I shall leave with Peppina for Paris. Alas! Alas! I am going to stage *Aida* at the Opéra!!! It's something I didn't want, that I always refused, but circumstances have forced me to renounce my resolutions. People have told me, and written me, and have been prompted to write me that this could appear to be an Italian's antipathy for the French!!! Imagine if I have, or have ever had, such notions in my head!! I'm going . . . I'm going. . . .

And what do you think about this trip? . . . Oh you say I am doing the best thing, but you don't know about the annoyances, the bothers that I shall have to put up with . . . and at the end of all this, perhaps a <u>fiasco</u> . . . .

Verdi to Clarina Maffei

Paris, 7 March 1880

Dear Clarina,

I should have written you before, and now I should write you a long, long letter, but I don't have the time. I think I must spend <u>twenty-six</u> hours a day at the Opéra! I want to know everything, and also see everything they do for my opera in that theatre. I am killing myself with work this way, perhaps to end up with a fiasco. . . . No: I don't think it will be a big <u>fiasco</u>; but it could be a *fiaschetto*. . . . It could also be a success. . . . Who knows! The theatre, that is the audience, is such a curious thing that one must expect anything. However, all is going smoothly, and I have nothing to complain about. After the first performance I shall write you the whole truth, absolutely the whole truth. [. . .]

Teresa Stolz to Katinka Evers

Paris, 13 March 1880

[. . .] I wanted to write you after the first performance to make my letter more important. [. . .] I am in the company of my dearest friends, the Verdis, a great deal, and we speak of you many times, my good and dear friend.

Well Monday the 15th will be the premiere of the long-awaited *Aida*.[1] The dress rehearsal was Thursday, and they closed the doors to everyone, but the Maestro permitted his wife to bring me along. [. . .] From a box we were able to hear and see <u>everything</u>. The rehearsal went very well. The orchestra and chorus were stupendous, never out of tune, altogether stupendous. In the orchestra one could detect certain subtleties of execution which I have never heard in our Italian orchestras. Among the artists who surprised me were the baritone Morel [*sic*]; he is a wonderful artist of great intelligence. La Kraus [*sic*] did not sing her entire role in full voice, but what she sang was perfect, as far as expression goes, and well interpreted. The voice is not of such beautiful timbre. But she sang very well, and she is an artist of the greatest resources. La Bloch[2] is a most beautiful Amneris; she may not be an "<u>eagle</u>," but in any case, she is much better than our two Milan Amnerises (of this year). The tenor <u>Selier</u>[3] [*sic*] has a beautiful voice and interprets many things extremely well, but in my opinion he is still a beginner. The basses were excellent. What shall I tell you about the staging and the costuming — everything stupendous, splendid. A great success is predicted. La Kraus is held in great esteem here, and I really believe her to be a true artist. [. . .]

1. The cast of the first performance of *Aida* (in French) at the Opéra, conducted and staged by Verdi, included Gabrielle Krauss (Aida), Rose Bloch (Amneris), Henri Sellier (Radames), and Victor Maurel (Amonasro).

2. Rose Bloch (1848–91), French mezzo-soprano. Between 1865 and 1879 she had appeared at the Opéra in Paris, where she made her debut as Azucena, and between 1875 and 1879 at the Théâtre de la Monnaie in Brussels. Verdi had her in mind for Princess Eboli in *Don Carlos*, but ultimately he cast Pauline Gueymard-Lauters for that role.

3. Henri Sellier (1849–99), French tenor. Discovered at the age of twenty-eight, he studied at the Paris Conservatory and made his debut in 1878 at the Opéra, where he remained a leading tenor until 1892. He also sang in Marseilles, Brussels, and St. Petersburg.

Verdi to Maria Waldmann

Paris, 20 March 1880

Dearest Maria,

Among the various telegrams I received, yours,[1] as you can well imagine, is one of the dearest. I thank you and the Count, and Peppina adds her thanks.

Perhaps you know that the premiere of *Aida* has been postponed for eight days because of Maurel's sore throat. Monday, at least I hope, will be the real premiere of *Aida*. I am dead tired, but I'm going along as best I can. . . . I shall conduct the orchestra for three nights. On the whole the production is good. Stupendous *mise-en-scène*.

23 March. . . . I did not mail this letter the other day so that I could tell you something about last night's *Aida* at the Opéra. It's not too bad. La Krauss and Maurel are excellent. The tenor is good. *Mise-en-scène*, chorus, and orchestra — superlatively good. On the whole a very good performance. It may be a success. We shall see. [. . .]

1. Missing.

Verdi to Clarina Maffei

Paris, 24 March 1880

[. . .] It seems to me that twelve or fourteen years ago I wrote that *Don Carlos* was not a success. Now, with the same sincerity and not much modesty, I tell you that *Aida* is a success. Let me quickly add, however, that there was a favorable current in the theatre the other night that made everything turn out well. We'll see if it lasts.

Meanwhile I tell you that la Krauss and Maurel were stupendous; the tenor good; Amneris mediocre; chorus and orchestra excellent; *mise-en-scène* beyond comparison. That is the truth. Don't believe everything you read or hear. After the third performance (Monday) I shall leave for Milan. [. . .]

Teresa Stolz to Katinka Evers

Paris, 25 March 1880

Dearest Friend,

I know well that my news of the *Aida* performance will be the last to arrive. . . . I shall tell you only a few words which will equal so many pages of the newspapers.

Aida and Maestro Verdi have made a triumphal entrance at the Operà [*sic*]. The success for the grand Maestro could not have been greater. Here everyone is saying that this spontaneous success of the opera and the celebrations honoring the Maestro are exceptional. . . . One can see that the public, the press, and the entire musical world have combined to celebrate Maestro Verdi; and, in fact, at his appearance there was such a hurricane of prolonged applause as to almost terrify one!!!!

The performance in certain sections was very beautiful, superior to all other performances I have heard before. The orchestra, enthusiastic about the Maestro (which they haven't been in the past), now works wonders; there are certain superb colorations which stand out strikingly in each section of the opera. La Kraus [*sic*], without having a voice of great volume, is a great artist; she sings with great mastery and makes one forget even the rather unpleasant timbre of her voice. She is an Aida full of passion; if she possessed more volume in her lower range, she would be perfect. Probably the duet between the two women is the piece that fails here, precisely because neither la Kraus nor la Bloch possesses a low range. Morel [*sic*] is superb!! Selier [*sic*] is a young beginner, but the voice is beautiful and he interprets a good many things extremely well. La Bloch wasn't bad, but she enjoys so little popularity here that the press is more severe with her than it should be.

The staging is simply superb; the grand march succeeds very beautifully here, first because the famous trumpets play extremely well and then because the total effect fascinates the audience. [. . .]

Oh! What a world! With the exception of some envious composers, all are now proclaiming Verdi a composer of great genius. As if, some years ago, he hadn't done anything!!!! [. . .]

Verdi to Giuseppe Piroli

Paris, 26 March 1880

[. . .] It really seems that *Aida* is a success. We'll see later. The production was magnificent. La Krauss and Maurel, very, very good. The tenor, good. A little less so, Amneris. All the other roles were excellent, as was the chorus. And the orchestra was superior to my expectations. I had promised to conduct three nights, but the season-ticket holders complain because their performance will not be until Friday, 2 April, which would be the fifth performance. It is possible that I shall have to remain here longer and that I won't leave for Milan until the 4th. [. . .] Then? Ah then I'll fly to St. Agata, because I really need to relax. [. . .]

Verdi to Ferdinand Hiller

Paris, 27 March 1880

I am so grateful, my dear Hiller, that you remembered me in these circumstances. All I shall tell you about *Aida* is that the production was splendid. La Krauss and Maurel are truly uncommon artists. The others very good, some excellent. Chorus good. Orchestra splendid. I won't speak of the *mise-en-scène*, which is always exceptional at the Opéra. [. . .]

Camille Du Locle to the Editor of L'Italie [1]

[Rome,] 28 March 1880

Since the history of the *Aida* libretto raises a polemic in the Roman press, and since I am here in Rome, I can give you precise information on this subject. You have been well informed; the poem was first the idea of Mariette Bey, the famous Egyptologist. I wrote the libretto, scene by scene, line by line, in French prose at Busseto, under the eyes of the Maestro who took part to a large extent in this work. The idea for the finale of the last act, with its two superimposed scenes, belongs entirely to him.

The translation of this prose into Italian verse was the task of M. Ghislanzoni. He very correcty indicated this by simply writing on the score: "Verses by Ghislanzoni." After the music had been written, these verses were translated in turn for the French performances.

Here, my dear editor, is what one might say was the genesis of *Aida*, since there is no law against investigating paternity in such matters. But what singular fantasy did the *Bersagliere* [2] have in trying to involve the self-respect of two nations in the making of the libretto? At any rate, isn't Italy assured of keeping for herself that part of *Aida* which is good and even all-embracing? Last year I saw *Aida* played without music in a marionette theatre here; the work suffered considerably. I admit this without false modesty for France, as much as for Mariette and myself. [. . .]

1. French newspaper, published in Rome, which printed this letter in its edition of 30 March 1880.
2. Italian newspaper, published in Rome.

Camille Du Locle to Marie Du Locle [1]

Capri, Wednesday [2]

My dear Marie,

For the love of God, don't send me these sad papers. What should I do with them? The whole world will always be lined up against me and I against the whole world.

We must resign ourselves to that. I would gather only insults and rumors around my sad name. Here is the absolute truth about *Aida*. The true author of the libretto is Mariette Bey who, having invented an Egyptian story, put it into the Viceroy's head to have an opera made of it for the opening of the Isthmus [of Suez].[3] This story by Mariette, printed in Cairo in a small number of copies, is in Nuitter's file,[4] because I gave him the copy I had. The idea was to make an opera out of it. That is what I did, constructing and reducing a scenario with Verdi, then writing it completely in French — not only the scenario, but the whole play, piece by piece, line by line.[5]

Verdi had the play put into verse by Ghislanzoni, and the latter claimed such a small part in the authorship that the posters read: "Verses by Ghislanzoni." Not "libretto," as is usually the case. There you have the real truth. I did this work in Busseto, where Verdi had summoned me. All this can be established by the letters and telegrams. A curious telegram to me, which can be found,[6] is one in which I was given the choice of the composer for *Aida* among Verdi, Gounod, and Wagner! Verdi never knew of that telegram. And I was poorly rewarded. I, who always find that the whole world is lined up against me, how can I excuse Verdi for having taken, on top of the bargain, the rights of the translation from poor Nuitter?

1. In the wake of *Aida's* greatest triumph, in which Du Locle had no share, his wife apparently urged him to set straight the record of the decisive role he had played in the creation of the opera. Whichever papers Marie Du Locle sent to her husband, they were obviously intended to prove that he was instrumental in bringing about *Aida*.
2. The final sentence of this letter suggests that it was written before Nuitter's letter to Verdi of 13 May 1882. Günther, "Der Briefwechsel, Teil II," p. 401, assumes that Du Locle wrote this letter in early 1878.

3. If Mariette and the Viceroy had such a plan, it had not materialized in time for the opening of the Suez Canal on 17 November 1869. See note 1 to Verdi's letter to Du Locle of 8 December 1869 and Günther, "Zur Entstehung von Verdis *Aida*," pp. 17–18n.

4. No such copy exists in Nuitter's file.

5. Document III corresponds only in part to this description. No evidence is available in the correspondence or elsewhere to show that a complete play was ever written in French.

6. No such telegram is available. Du Locle apparently confused it with Mariette's letter to him of 28 April 1870, which he forwarded to Verdi on 14 May 1870. Verdi's knowledge of the letter is proven by the fact that the autograph is kept at St. Agata, while all other letters to Du Locle are in Paris.

Verdi to Giulio Ricordi

Genoa, 9 April 1880

If the Italian rights to *Aida* [1] have been transferred to Escudier, I think there is no further need to consult attorneys. Naturally the House of Ricordi will have transferred the rights according to the conditions established between composer and publisher — that is, that *Aida* must be performed not in fragments, or with cuts, transpositions, etc., but in its entirety. If this were not so, it would be a <u>matter</u> concerning composer and publisher. French law would have nothing to do with it. [. . .]

1. For performances with the original Italian text in France.

Verdi to Eugenio Tornaghi

Thursday [Genoa, 13 January 1881]

Signor Tornaghi,

I don't write to Giulio or Tito because I know they are both sick. I turn to you so that you might do something about the outrages that occur all too often. Again last night, here at the Politeama [Theatre], *Aida* was mutilated. You know the terms of our contract. They must be respected. Send a strong telegram suspending *Aida*. [. . .]

Verdi to Giulio Ricordi

[Genoa,] Monday, 21 February 1881

[. . .] I have never had the fortune of seeing one of my operas done well at La Scala. Even *Aida* was performed better in a small provincial city, Parma, than in Milan. [. . .]

Charles Nuitter to Verdi

Paris, 13 May 1882

Dear and illustrious Maestro,

You are the owner of the French translation of *Aida*, made by Du Locle and myself.

You have let me know that you voluntarily renounce, by your own actions, your rights to this translation, and that consequently, as of 1 May 1882, all the author's rights proceeding from performances of *Aida* in the French language will be divided equally between the composer on the one hand and the authors of the translation on the other.

I hasten to tell you that this arrangement is acceptable to me, in my name and in that of Camille Du Locle, for whom I have power of attorney; and I have the honor of thanking you in this respect.

Verdi to Giovanni Bottesini

Genoa, 4 March 1883

Dear Bottesini,

I have been very busy for several days in the country, so I could not reply at once to your letter of February 24.[1]

They are very wrong, those who take the liberty of using my name to have me say things about you that I have never said or never could have said. You know, and everybody knows, how highly I esteem your talent as a composer and instrumentalist. This truth, known to all, should have stopped tongues too quick to lie.[2] [. . .]

1. Missing.
2. See Verdi's letters to Lampugnani of 4 May 1871, to Draneht of 1 September 1871, and to Bottesini of 27 December 1871 and 13 January 1872.

Verdi to Giulio Ricordi

Genoa, 26 December 1883

[. . .] You know, as well as I, there are people with good eyesight, and they like clear, sharp, natural colors. There are others who have a little cataract, and they like faded and dirty colors. They are in fashion. I don't disapprove of following fashion (because we must keep up with the times), but I would like it to be accompanied always by a bit of judgment and good sense. Therefore neither the past nor the future! It's true I have said, "Let us return to the past,"[1] but by the past I mean that which is basic, fundamental, solid. I mean that past which has been pushed aside by modern exuberance and to which, sooner or later, we must inevitably return. For now, let the torrent rush over the banks. The dikes will be built later. [. . .]

1. On 4 January 1871, Verdi had written the much publicized sentence to Francesco Florimo (see note 2, Verdi's letter to Piroli of 20 February 1871): "Let us return to the past, and it will be progress."

Verdi to Opprandino Arrivabene

St. Agata, 10 June 1884

[. . .] I have heard very good things about the musician Puccini.[1] I have seen a letter that tells nothing but good about him. He follows the modern trends, which is natural, but he remains attached to melody, which is neither modern nor ancient. It seems, though, that the symphonic element predominates in him! Nothing wrong with that. Only one must walk cautiously in it. An opera is an opera, a symphony is a symphony. I don't think it's nice to write a symphonic passage in an opera for the sole pleasure of making the orchestra dance. I talk just to talk, without giving it any importance — not at all certain that I've said the right thing, yet certain that I've said something contrary to the modern trends. Every age has its mark. History later tells us which age is good and which is bad. [. . .]

1. On Boito's recommendation, Puccini's first opera, Le Villi, was premiered at the Teatro Dal Verme in Milan on 31 May 1884.

Verdi to Eugène Ritt[1]

Genoa, 24 March 1887

Sir,

I thank you for the good news; should the success of Aida[2] continue and should the management take in good box office receipts, I shall be delighted. It is not because I am interested in the material aspect, as you say, but because I believe that the true thermometer of a theatrical success is the cashbox.

1. In answer to a missing communication from Eugène Ritt, director of the Opéra from 1884 to 1891.
2. Verdi refers to a revival of Aida at the Opéra.

Verdi to Giulio Ricordi

Genoa, 9 January 1889

[. . .] Here, as in Milan, the seating arrangement or distribution of the orchestra was done, I think, especially for Aida. It went well; but these blessed conductors are always doing something, and their vanity isn't satisfied unless they tear something apart, even if it's going well. It's not enough for them to be applauded onstage like other prima donnas or to thank the audience from the podium when it applauds four measures of the prelude — as if they had composed it themselves! All that is ridiculous! I mention it now only because I no longer have anything to do with it; I am merely a simple amateur. [. . .]

Camille Du Locle to Verdi

Rome, 3 December 1891

Dear and illustrious Maestro,

A few days ago Nuitter and I received a complaint concerning *Aida* from Mariette's son,[1] who demands an explanation. We notified Ricordi, to whom this M. Mariette must have also written. Today your Paris agent, Roger, asked us to notify you as well, and we are doing that, asking pardon for the annoyance we are afraid we shall give you. This Mariette, who was totally estranged from his father, is an evil character who has had all kinds of adventures. [. . .]

1. We do not know the name of this son who had apparently claimed some rights to *Aida* because his father was the author of the original plot. Possibly this son was Alfred Mariette. See biographical note on August Mariette, Document I, and Ursula Günther, ''Zur Entstehung von Verdi's *Aida*,'' p. 21.

Verdi to Camille Du Locle

Genoa, 9 December 1891

Dear Du Locle,

When I arrived here last night, I found your very dear letter of 3 December.

Ricordi, in fact, has spoken to me about this claim of Mariette's son. That's a bolt from the blue!

You know how things went: I think you will recall that you yourself gave me four little printed pages, without the name of the author, telling me that the Khedive would like the opera to be on that subject, since it was Egyptian; and I supposed that the author of those little pages was the Khedive himself.[1] As for Mariette Bey, I knew only that he was responsible for the costumes, etc., etc. That's all. I can't tell you anything else, and I don't understand what claims this Mariette can have.

And now that we are here in our winter quarters, I hope to see you sometime, either passing through or staying awhile. You would be doing me and Peppina, who sends you her very best, a great favor.

I hope you will, and I take your hand.

---

1. See Du Locle's letter to Verdi of 29 May 1870, and Verdi's letters to Giulio Ricordi of 25 June 1870 and (undated) on p. 116.

DOCUMENTS

DOCUMENTS

I	Excerpts from *Mariette Pasha* by Edouard Mariette	435
II	*Synopsis by Giuseppe and Giuseppina Verdi (SA)	440
III	*Scenario by Camille Du Locle (SA)	448
IV	Giuseppe Verdi's Terms for the Contract with Cairo (OP)	472
V	Auguste Mariette's Contract with Giuseppe Verdi (OP)	473
VI	*Information on Egyptian Antiquity by an Unknown Scholar (SA)	475
VII	*Sketch of the First Scenes of the Libretto by Antonio Ghislanzoni (SA)	483
VIII	*Sketch of the Fourth Act Dialogue by Giuseppe Verdi (SA)	487
IX	Synopsis in the Review *Il Trovatore*	494
X	*Production Annotations by Giuseppe Verdi (PM)	499
XI	*Production Notes by Franco Faccio (CM)	554
XII	Production Book by Giulio Ricordi (SC)	558
XIII	*Contract for Parma by Tito Ricordi (AS)	619
XIV	*An Anonymous Letter	622

*First publication.

DOCUMENT I

Excerpts from

Mariette Pasha

Letters
and
Personal Memories

by
Edouard Mariette

Paris
H. Jouve Publisher
15 rue Racine
1904

Even if we can accept some of Edouard Mariette's story only with great reservations, it does seem to suggest that, despite striking similarities, *Aida* is not related to Pietro Metastasio's drama *Nitteti* or to any of its offspring, as suspected by Mary Jane Matz and assumed by Charles Osborne (Mary Jane Matz, "An ancestor for Aida," *Opera News*, 1955, 20, no. 8, pp. 4–7, 26–28, and Charles Osborne, *The Complete Operas of Verdi* [New York: Knopf, 1970], pp. 377–82). Matz and Osborne seem to base their theory on a hypothesis formulated by Matteo Glinski in the review *La Scala*, May 1954, p. 17ff., who, however, oddly enough, fails to mention F. Pérez de la Vega's article "La Prosapia de Aida" (Mexico City, 1950) on the same subject. See also Franco Abbiati, *Giuseppe Verdi* (Milano: Ricordi, 1959), III, pp. 529–530, and Guglielmo Barblan, "Aida," Teatro alla Scala program 1975/76, p. 22, n. 5.

There is no evidence that Auguste Mariette or the Viceroy knew of *Nitteti*. Camille Du Locle, who was more likely to have been acquainted with Metastasio's work, never referred to it and credited only Auguste Mariette with the invention of the Egyptian story. (See Camille Du Locle's undated letter to Marie Du Locle on p. 424) Siegfried Morenz's theory that Mariette was inspired by Heliodorus' fourth-century novel *Theagenes and Chariclea*, however, deserves consideration. (See Siegfried Morenz, *Die Begegnung Europas mit Ägypten* [Zürich: Artemis, 1969], p. 155, n. 87.)

Certainly no one has shared Mariette's life as much as I, except his wife and daughters, long gone, and also Vassali Bey,[1] deceased, I believe about 1885. Intermittently from the year 1856 to the year 1861, in the closest way from 1861 to 1875 and then less frequently from 1875 to 1881, the date of his death, I visited my brother; in Cairo, Paris, and Boulogne, I lived under the same roof, ate at the same table, sometimes collaborated in his work, and always shared his sorrows as well as his joys. [. . .] Because I was twenty years younger than he, he certainly did not always consider me a person whose every word of advice had to be followed. [. . .]

When I began writing Mariette's biography, one duty became apparent to me immediately, and I have painstakingly complied with it — that of respecting the entire truth. Consequently [. . .] there is no fact for which I have not made an effort to furnish proof. Everything has been faithfully reported as I have seen it with my own eyes, without exaggeration or attenuation. Besides, my remarks refer to already distant events and to men who have long since disappeared. It was therefore very easy for me to stay faithful to the truth, since neither *amour-propre* nor anger was to be feared. [. . .]

One of several fields in which Mariette proved himself, although he had never practiced it before, is the so difficult and so special art of the theatre. This relates to the conception of the libretto of *Aida*, about which so many inaccuracies have been spread.

For the sake of simple rectification, and if one will kindly submit to it, I shall succinctly relate the genesis and the series of facts concerning this matter, being absolutely convinced beforehand that this has never been told in detail.

From June to the end of October 1866, we made several important sojourns in Upper Egypt — at Abydos, Gournah (Thebes), and Philae, and on the way back at Sakkara. The idea was to collect assorted documents for the Exposition of 1867 in Paris, where Mariette was to represent Egypt and for which I was to draw up the plans. [. . .]

Now during those months of a wandering life spent in trips on the river or in long stopovers on isolated spots of its shores, I amused myself by jotting down on paper the outline of a novel; it was inspired by local legends, and I gave it the title *The Fiancée of the Nile*. I shall not tell the very romantic story in great detail. I shall simply speak of the subject, since it relates to the most remote traditions of Egyptian society and seems to be one of the last traces of these religious and public customs.

To begin with, here is the present-day custom: when the Nile rises to the height of seventeen cubits, the dams of the canal, which cross it in Cairo, are opened; that is the signal for the opening of all the other irrigation canals. In memory of the ancient rites, in which a sacrificial offering of a young virgin was made to the river to render it favorable, it is still the custom to parade on the Nile an effigy dressed as a woman and called *Mahroussa* or fiancée, and finally to hurl it into the waters.

Taking advantage of what I already knew of the Pharaonic civilization, I divided into scenes the principal episodes of an operatic libretto based on ancient times. I had already given particular care and even set to verse several situations that, in my opinion, are very moving. This entire literary lucubration, in the making at the time, was spread out in the form of notes, rough drafts, and copies on the table of the room I occupied for the more than six weeks of our uninterrupted stay in Sakkara. Mariette certainly read this material, none of which was hidden, and he was undoubtedly struck by the possibilities that the immense resources of Egyptian solemnities offered in a work of that kind.

Such a thought must later have suggested to him the idea to propose to H. II. Ismail Pasha an operatic production of Egyptian character to inaugurate in a fitting manner the recently built Grand Theatre of Cairo. An opera with a plot, *mise-en-scène*, sets, and costumes conceived by an archaeologist, who was at the same time a man of letters, and with music by an illustrious composer, was certain to bestow new glamour to the young Egypt and also to attract an ever-increasing flow of travelers.

As a matter of fact, on 8 June 1869, the eve of his return to France where he wanted to spend the summer months, my brother wrote me the following letter:[2]

"Nothing is new here regarding my departure. There is quite a story behind this, which I shall tell you one day. Imagine that I have written an opera — a grand opera for which Verdi is about to finish the music, which is to be performed in Cairo. The Viceroy is spending a million. Don't laugh. This is serious. Details in another letter.[3] As usual, I am in a hurry and have only time to shake your hand. It's because of the *mise-en-scène*, the sets, and the costumes that I must go to Paris."

The very day of his arrival two weeks later[4] he gave me a copy of his outline, nicely printed in ten copies by Mourès,[5] and asked for my evaluation. To tell the truth, in glancing through the text I was somewhat surprised to recognize not an identical story (Mariette's imagination was too lively for him to lower himself to the rank of plagiarist) but certain similarities, certain analogies to my *Fiancée of the Nile*. Involuntarily, without his being conscious of it, the same sky, the same horizon, the same period, the same race of people, the same customs, had brought to his pen scenic combinations more or less resembling those I had imagined.

"Well!," I said simply, after reading the outline, "I too had that kind of dream except for this difference, and still others, that my two lovers threw themselves into the Nile instead of dying, as did Romeo and Juliet, in the depths of a subterranean chamber."

He did not react to my remark.

"It will be very beautiful," he resumed, "because the Viceroy seems enthusiastic."

"That is exactly what I think."

I did not feel like saying anything more — and for good reason. Such surprises happen every day in literary arenas. Besides, what good would it have done to complain? My brother's work, had it not already taken shape quite a while ago? Was it not in the process of realization, given that Verdi was about to "finish" the music? Wasn't it true that a credit of one million francs had been arranged for this gigantic undertaking; that soon the sets and costumes would be designed and executed in Paris; and, finally, that the first performance was, so to say, announced for the following February? I would have been justified to invoke in this circumstance a sort of owner's right, while my poor brainchild, scarcely born, was still fast asleep in the darkness of my files.

The new outline, in the form of a brochure and without the author's name on it, carried the now so famous title *Aida*. Mariette had offered me that brochure with the dedication "To my brother Edouard," contrary to his habit. Needless to say, he took the brochure back later, supposedly only for a while. During his incessant travels he could not, of course, carry all his books with him. Only a very few of those he authored, and which he needed at times, have remained in my hands. Sometimes for one reason, sometimes for another, he asked me for those he had given me and he often neglected to return them to me. The *Treatise on the Mother of Apis* and the outline of *Aida* are among the works I have in vain asked him to return.

Verdi, the great Italian composer, was then contracted by the Egyptian government to embroider on the canvas furnished him by Mariette the skillful arabesques and marvelous ornaments with which he has endowed the lyrical works that have sprung from his brain. He succeeded, as is well known, in a truly superior manner. By way of remuneration he was to be paid 150,000 francs. By special arrangement Camille Du Locle, who was in Italy at the time, had been charged to put into everyday language all the dramatic developments. Once accomplished, this secondary work, in the form of a draft,[6] was delivered to the Italian librettist Ghislanzoni, whose versification the composer used to write his score. These same verses were later translated into our language by Du Locle and Nuitter, and this translation constitutes the French edition of *Aida* — without, as always, any mention of the name Mariette. [. . .]

As he had foreseen, Mariette drew no profit, besides his regular salary, from the masterly work for which he had suggested the idea and conceived the plan, and for which he had traced the whole theatrical figuration, based on the most unquestionable scientific documentation. No more than I, the putative father of a stillborn opera, did he get as much as a penny. It is not only in the toilsome world of the bees that the *sic vos non vobis* is and always will be true.

NOTES TO DOCUMENT I

1. Unknown.

2. The autograph of this letter, apparently written one year later on 8 June 1870, is missing.

3. See Auguste Mariette's letter to Edouard Mariette of 21 June 1870. Also, Auguste Mariette's letter to Draneht of 19 July 1871.

4. Auguste Mariette apparently reached Paris in early July 1870. See his letters to Du Locle of 21 June 1870 and to Draneht of 15 July 1870.

5. Until recently all copies of this outline were missing. In his letter to Du Locle of 27 April 1870 Auguste Mariette mentions only four copies, which were more likely to be missing than were the ten copies his unreliable brother recalls. In this letter Auguste Mariette does not name the printer of his outline; but Du Locle wrote to Verdi on 14 May 1870 that "four copies of this plan have been printed in Cairo," and on 29 May 1870 that "the Egyptian libretto [. . .] has been edited and printed in Egypt." Actually "the four little printed pages" to which Verdi refers in his letter to Du Locle of 9 December 1891 were printed by the Mourès firm in Alexandria, with which Auguste Mariette dealt on other occasions as well. In 1891 Verdi obviously confused the number four (four copies) with the number of pages. This apparent lapse of memory — insignificant in itself — has resulted in most of Verdi's biographers referring to *quattro paginette*, "four small pages," or a "four-page scenario." See Carlo Gatti, *Verdi* (Milano: Alpes, 1931), vol. II, p. 206; Francis Toye, *Verdi: His Life and Works* (New York: Knopf, 1959), p. 151, and several other publications.

According to all indications, a booklet of 18×13 cm. containing twenty-three pages and titled *Aïda, Opéra en quatre actes et en six tableaux* (without mention of the author and the printer) is actually the "four little printed pages." (See Document II.) Dr. Jean Humbert of Paris discovered this long-sought document and sent a copy of it to St. Agata. I am most grateful to Dr. Gabriella Carrara Verdi for this information and for having made available to my research what appears to be Auguste Mariette's own text.

6. See Document III and comments to Document VIII. Charles Osborne (p. 377) states that "Mariette's story [was] expanded by Du Locle into a libretto which was translated by Ghislanzoni for Verdi, who also had a hand in the Italian text."

DOCUMENT II

Synopsis

by

Giuseppe and Giuseppina Verdi

The autograph is on both sides of seven sheets of legal-size paper. Acts I and II are described in Verdi's handwriting, Acts III and IV in his wife Giuseppina's, both in ink. Verdi and his wife wrote only on the left half of the pages, leaving blank the right half, except for listing the cast and providing information about the sets. The few words that Verdi struck out on these pages are struck out in this English translation; also, the Verdis' inconsistent spellings and capitalization of the names of the characters have been retained.

The Verdis' synopsis is an exact translation into Italian of the French *programma*, as Verdi referred to the original outline by Auguste Mariette. A copy of this outline, which Du Locle sent Verdi on 14 May 1870, inspired him and his wife to translate it before Du Locle's arrival at St. Agata on or about 19 June 1870.[1] Abbiati's contention that Verdi and his wife wrote this synopsis *after* Du Locle's visit is in error.[2] Verdi's letter to Du Locle of 18 June 1870 suggests that he worked on the synopsis *before* Du Locle's arrival at St. Agata.

Programma is translated as "outline" in English (Auguste and Edouard Mariette referred to it as *scenario* and Du Locle as *plan du libretto* or *libretto*) to distinguish it from Du Locle's *scenario* (Document III).

This document, published here for the first time in its entirety, precisely corresponds to the French text of the outline attributed to Auguste Mariette — the *programma* (misnamed "four little pages") — discovered by Dr. Jean Humbert, which *La Société Française de Musicologie* intends to publish in 1977. (See note 5 to Document I.)

AÏDA
Opera in four acts

Characters

The King
Princess Amnèris, his daughter
Aïda, Ethiopian slave ~~and maid~~ in the service of the princess

440

Rhadamès, captain of the guards
Amounasro, father of Aïda and king of Ethiopia
Ramphis, head of the college of priests
Termouthis, high priestess of the temple of Vulcan
A Herald
      Priests, Civil Servants, Soldiers, Populace

The setting is on the banks of the Nile during the reign of the Pharaohs.

Act I
The setting is Memphis

The set represents a hall in the palace of the king. The doors, windows, walls, and ceilings are covered with brilliant paintings. On the right and the left extends a colonnade in which are interspersed statues, flowering shrubs, and pieces of furniture decorated in the taste of the period. The hall is open at the back. In the distance can be seen the temples, palaces, and houses of Memphis. On the horizon, the pyramids.

The officers of the palace prepare themselves to see the king. Among them are the college of scribes in charge of the interior, flabellum[3]-bearers carrying long fans of ostrich feathers, guards of the king's stables, ensign-bearers with shields displaying the royal coat of arms, generals in command of chariots of war, captains of the guard, tonsured priests wearing long white vestments with scarlet trim. Rhamphis [sic] and Rhadames are lost in the crowd.

At the end of the chorus, as soon as the cortège has disappeared beneath the colonnade to the left, Amnèris enters. Her imperious look detains Rhadames. The proud and impassioned princess is deeply in love with the young captain. She would like him to have the rank, title, and magnificence that surround her. But Rhadames responds coldly and can hardly conceal his agitation. He does not wish to admit anything as yet, but his mind, his heart, his soul are elsewhere. For him the world lies in the lovely eyes of Aïda. A hundred times more beautiful, a hundred times more attractive than the daughter of kings, the slave girl has captured his heart, which now belongs only to her. Amnèris is assailed by cruel doubts at Rhadames's coldness. A rival is certainly contending for Rhadames's heart. Who is it? Aïda, the Ethiopian slave who fell into the hands of the Egyptians after a recent victory, appears at the rear of the stage. An ardent look from Rhadames, a long sigh from Aïda threaten to reveal everything. Some instinct tells the princess that her rival is the slave she sees before her. At the moment when they, to themselves, are expressing their love, their lamentations, their displeasures, their sorrows, an officer of the king's household announces that his majesty is coming to the hall to receive a messenger sent by the governor of the Egyptian provinces bordering on Ethiopia. The king appears, preceded by his guards and followed by his court. A herald in battle dress is introduced. He announces that the black Ethiopians have violated the Egyptian frontier, burned the cities, devastated the countryside, and, emboldened by their success, dare to march on the capital. An invincible warrior is at their head — Amounasro. At the mention of this name Aïda turns pale and almost faints. This formidable enemy is her father. The king orders immediate repressive action to stop the invaders' advance. Remember, he cries, the glory and the greatness of the Pharaohs who have carried the name of Egypt to the ends of the earth! Remember these always victorious armies, upon whom the Gods of Thebes and Memphis have for centuries laid their protective hands. It is one of these armies that will confront the fierce Amounasro. Rhadames, the young captain to whom the oracles assigned a high destiny, will be its leader. Rhadames is to go immediately to the temple of Vulcan and, according to the prescribed rites, have his weapons blessed and invoke for Egypt the protection of the omnipotent. The king reenters the palace. Aïda, alone, torn by her love for the two leaders who are about to meet on the battlefield, laments; whether the victory is won by her father or by her lover, whatever the outcome of the campaign, the poor slave girl who has been abandoned by the Gods will have only tears and sorrows.

Change of scene

The interior of the great temple of Vulcan in Memphis. The stage is barely illuminated by a mysterious light that shines from above. Long colonnades, superimposed one upon the other, fade into the darkness in the background. Here and there are statues of the divinities. In the center of the stage above a platform covered by a carpet rises the altar, surmounted with sacred emblems. Incense is burning on golden tripods.

The college of priests has gathered. Ramfis [sic], dressed in stately vestments, stands at the foot of the altar steps. In the distance one hears the sound of harps ~~that accompany~~ mixed with the voices of the priestesses of the temple.[4] Rhadamès is brought in. He is unarmed. As he approaches the altar, the priestesses perform the sacred dance to the sound of a drum. A silver veil is placed over the head of the young captain. Ramfis pronounces the solemn rites of the invocation. May the God who sees all, the God who determines the fate of empires as he pleases, grant strength to Radames's [sic] heart and victory to his arm. Radames rises, filled with fierce pride. He, in turn, invokes the Gods who have made Egypt the queen of nations. He will be conqueror of the black Ethiopian and destroyer of the enemies. The religious chants resume. The harps play beneath the dark arcades ~~far away. All respond with the greatest sonority while~~ To the shrill sound of the voices and the instruments Ramfis dresses Rhadamès in his battle armor.

Act II
The setting is Thebes

The set represents one of the entrances to the city. ~~In the foreground~~ Downstage is a group of palms. A platform surmounted by a purple canopy is to the audience's left. At the rear is a triumphal portal. In the background can be seen the pillars of the great temple of Ammon.

The populace has gathered. They await the king, who will come to see the troops file past, returning victorious from the Ethiopian campaign. The enemy paid for the audacity of his first attacks with a bloody defeat. Amounasro has disappeared or is dead. The young hero is all-triumphant. Princess Amnèris appears. Her love for Radamè [sic] has grown with all the glory with which the conqueror of Amounasro has covered himself. But terrible suspicions have assaulted her heart once more. It is not she whom Radames loves. Prey to devouring doubts and jealous torments, she will see that the girl she regards as her hateful rival is killed. But first she wants to be sure that it is Aïda whom Radames prefers. She has the young slave called to her. She feigns great sorrow and announces that a messenger who has just arrived has brought news of the captain's death. Aïda bursts out sobbing. Her father and her lover are dead. Life is now nothing but torment for her and she is ~~almost~~ barely able to conceal her agitation from the Princess. From this moment there are no more doubts. For Amneris, the lover of Radamè is Aïda. Aïda will die.

The King enters. He takes his place on the throne, situated to the audience's right.[5] A distant sound announces the arrival of the troops.

Grand march to the sound of a fanfare. Foot soldiers bearing many kinds of weapons, and chariots of war appear in succession, entering the city through the triumphal portal.

Radames is seated beneath a canopy carried by sixteen of his officers. At the moment he passes before the King, the cortège stops and Radamès steps down. The King embraces him and proclaims him savior of the nation, conqueror of conquerors. He orders that a feast be celebrated in honor of the victory. The soldiers mingle with the populace in various parts of the stage. The King mounts his throne.[6] Dancers in elaborate Egyptian costumes perform before the enthusiastic spectators. At the end of the ballet the trumpets sound again, and soon the last soldier has disappeared beneath the triumphal portal.

The King remains alone with Amneris and her entourage, which includes Aïda. At a sign from him the soldiers lead in the prisoners taken in battle. Among them is Amounasro, disguised in the uniform of a simple officer of his troops. As soon as Aïda sees him, she ~~throws~~ cries out. "Oh omnipotent King," she exclaims, "may the Gods open your heart to clemency: this man who stands before you, a submissive slave, is my father!" But at the moment she is about to reveal that her father is the terrible Amounasro, he stops her and tells his daughter that he is disguised as an officer of his own troops so that he can carry out the vengeance he has planned. Won over by Aïda's pleas, the King grants the prisoner's life; the defeated Ethiopian will take his place among the slaves assigned to guard the palace.

Act III
The setting is Thebes

The set represents a garden of the palace. At the left, the oblique facade of a pavilion — or tent.[7] At the back of the stage flows the Nile. On the horizon the mountains of the Libyan chain, vividly illuminated by the setting sun. Statues, palms, tropical shrubs.

As the curtain rises, Aïda is alone. More than ever her heart is filled with thoughts of Ramadés [sic]. The trees, the sacred river that bathes her feet, those distant hills where for centuries the ancestors of her loved one have been resting, she calls everything to witness her loyalty and faithfulness. Ramadés is going to come. She is waiting for him. May Isis, protectress of love, guide him to her who wants to belong only to him.

But it is not Radamés who comes. A doorway of the pavilion on the left opens and the somber figure of Amonasro [sic] appears. The conquered king wears a slave's costume, which accentuates his sharp features and fierce bearing. He wears his beard interlaced in the Ethiopian fashion; his black hair is pulled back and held off his forehead by a small red band. He informs his daughter that Ethiopia has once again raised the flag of revolt and that Radamés will once again march against him. In a touching speech he reminds her of her native soil, of her disconsolate mother, and of the sacred images of the Gods of her ancestors. The love Aïda has inspired in the young Radamés has not escaped her father's clairvoyance. He tells Aïda that she should take advantage of this love to wrest from Radamés the secret of the march by the Egyptian troops. Then, in the midst of the turmoil, Aïda and he will flee, and Radames, captured following the encounter, will be taken as a slave to Ethiopia where eternal bonds will forever ensure their common happiness. Won over by her father's entreaties, by the memories of her childhood, by the joy to possess the one she loves, far from the land where, for too long a time, she has undergone the torment of slavery, Aïda promises.

The following scene deals with Radames and Aïda. Aïda in turn threatens and pleads. She fascinates her lover, she wins him over, she captivates him. Lost in love, Radamés throws himself at her feet. Not his country, nor the world, nor the sacred vows that bind him are worth one look, one smile from her. Honor calls him in vain. He will betray his king, he will betray the sworn faith, and in exchange he asks nothing of the Gods but the love of her for whom he would die.

Amonasro arrives. At his sight Radamés feels duty reawaken in his heart. He trembles, he hesitates, he staggers. Aïda lifts her beautiful, imploring eyes to him. It is decided, he does not resist. Near Napata are some dark gorges leading into impenetrable forests. That is where the Egyptian army will pass. That is where the Ethiopian army can easily ambush the Egyptian phalanxes and destroy them in a few moments.

Amonasro, Aïda, and Radamés have barely left the stage when the princess Amnéris, pale and trembling, emerges from a grove of trees which, until now, have concealed her from view. She has heard everything. A terrible vengeance will now be hers. Aïda will perish and with her the faithless captain who has scorned the wiles of a princess.

Act IV
The setting is Memphis

First Scene

The set represents a hall in the palace of the king. To the right, a low door leads into the hall of judgments. Toward the rear of the stage is a <u>platform</u> or <u>pulpit</u>,[8] to which one ascends by a double stairway. In front of the platform, on two granite pedestals, stand two bronze statues, one representing justice, the other truth.

The officers of the royal household are speaking among themselves. Having been informed by the princess of Radamés's betrayal, the king himself marched against the rebellious Ethiopians. The Gods once again favored the Egyptian armies, and the King has returned triumphant to his palace. Both Amonasro and Aida had fled as the fighting began. Amonasro was killed in battle, but there is as yet no news about the fate of his daughter. As for Radames, he awaits in chains the punishment reserved for traitors.

The courtiers retire. Améris [*sic*] enters. Radamés's betrayal has not diminished her love. Anxiety increasingly agitates her heart. Radamés must come to her! If he is willing to repudiate his crime before the assembled judges, she will attempt to persuade the king to pardon him. By order of the princess, Radamés is brought in. But Amnéris's pleas and threats are futile. Radamés rends the veil. It is Aïda he loves. For Aïda he is happy to die. May the wrath of the Gods be calmed, exclaims Amnéris, and let the justice of [. . .][9] take its course.

The priests and the judges, Ramfis at their head, file by upstage and disappear through the low door situated at the audience's right. Some soldiers seize Radamés and drag him away. Amnéris anxiously awaits the result of the judgment. Soon the cortège returns. The judges and priests solemnly take their places on all parts of the stage. Ramfis is on the platform, or, rather, in the pulpit,[10] holding the golden scepter. Radamés is brought in again. Ramfis pronounces the rite of anathema. A traitor to his king and to his country, a traitor to his oath, Radamés will die an infamous death. As a just punishment by the angry Gods, he will be buried alive in one of the subterranean chambers of the temple of Vulcan. The scene changes.

Second Scene

The set represents a subterranean chamber. Long vaults fade into the darkness at the rear of the stage. To the right and left one can barely make out the entrances of the galleries or dark, mysterious corridors. Colossal statues of Osiris, with hands crossed on his chest, lean against massive pillars that support the vault.

Radamés is alone. The fatal stone has been sealed, closed[11] above him, and he awaits death as the end of his woes. In the midst of his grief the image of Aïda crosses his heart. Fear, hunger, and the horror of the place create in his troubled mind a strange vision. There seems to be a vague noise; he thinks he sees a figure appear and move about in the shadows. From the rear of one of the corridors Aïda seems to be approaching, pale and already dying. Is it a dream? No! At the moment his hand touches Aïda's the vision ends; it is without doubt his adored lover, whom he presses to his heart. Anticipating the fearful death reserved for the young captain, Aïda hid in the subterranean chamber; for four days she has awaited the happy moment when she could die with him, far from all human view. Cries, sobs, and the sorrow of Radamés. The two bewildered[12] lovers see the heavens open and an eternity of blessedness begin for them. At the moment the dying Aïda falls upon a rock, vague sounds are heard of the priests' invocation, harps, and the rhythmic drum to which the priestesses dance. The divine service is being celebrated, as in the first act, in the hall of the ritual temple above the subterranean chamber. The ruffled echoes of the religious chant are like a murmur in the background as Aïda bids Radamés her final farewell; soon the captain holds to his heart, which is about to stop beating, the already cold hand of the woman he had loved more than his honor and his life.

NOTES TO DOCUMENT II

1. See comments to Document III and note 3 to Verdi's letter to Giulio Ricordi of 25 June 1870.

2. See Abbiati, III, p. 375, where he refers to Alessandro Luzio, *Carteggi Verdiani* (Roma: Accademia Nazionale dei Lincei, 1947), IV, p. 13. On pp. 8 and 13 of this volume Luzio mentions the existence, but not the location, of ''4 copies printed in Cairo'' of Mariette's outline. Luzio claims that ''assisted by the precious and constant collaborator, his consort Giuseppina, Verdi had translated Mariette's '*programma*' into Italian.''·On p. 11, note 2, Luzio suggests that he had seen Mariette's outline, ''since Mariette's plan included a moving and eloquent page about the death of the two lovers.'' On p. 20 Luzio writes ''As I said before, Giuseppina had already translated the second half of the *programma*,'' and he quotes two of its paragraphs.

3. A fan, especially one used ceremonially.

4. Verdi failed to translate two somewhat repetitious sentences that follow here in Mariette's text: *C'est Rhadamés qu'on amène. Sur un ton grave et presque plaintif, les prêtres récitent les litanies saintes*. (Rhadamés is led in. The priests recite the holy litanies in a grave and almost plaintive tone.)

5. Mariette wrote *à gauche du spectateur* (to the audience's left). In all subsequent versions of the libretto the throne is situated to the audience's right. (See Documents III, IX, X, XI, and XII.)

6. Obviously the King was meant to descend from his throne to embrace Radames and to mount it again thereafter. (See Documents III, X, and XII, in which the King descends but does not return to his throne.)

7. In her Italian translation of Mariette's text, Giuseppina Verdi added and underlined ''or tent'' (*o tenda*).

8. Giuseppina Verdi added ''or pulpit'' (*o pulpito*) in her translation of Mariette's French word *chaire*. The underlining of ''platform'' and ''pulpit'' is hers.

9. Giuseppina overlooked the French word *hommes* (men) in the original text.

10. Uncertain of her translation of *chaire*, Giuseppina Verdi added ''or rather, in the pulpit.''

11. Giuseppina Verdi added ''closed'' (*chiusa*). The underlining is hers.

12. Giuseppina Verdi wrote the original French word *éperdus* over the Italian equivalent (*smarriti*), which she underlined.

DOCUMENT III

Scenario
by
Camille Du Locle

The autograph, four title pages and thirty-four almost fully covered sides of legal-size paper, shows Verdi's initials in a watermark. The writing, in pencil, is in French and appears to be entirely Camille Du Locle's.

The autograph has been followed closely in the transcription, the translation, and the printing of this document. The text struck out by Du Locle has been transcribed and translated when it was decipherable; when it was undecipherable, it is marked [illegible]. Du Locle's excitement when drafting these pages is reflected in the many inconsistencies in spelling and punctuation, and in the frequent use of lower case rather than capital letters, etc. The translation is also as faithful as possible to Du Locle's often careless French. No attempt has been made to improve his sketchy writing, but commas have been added wherever warranted to make the text more readable. "Right" and "left" in the stage directions are the actor's right and left.

This scenario, on which Verdi collaborated[1] during Du Locle's visit to St. Agata (presumably 19 to 25 June 1870), is based on Auguste Mariette's French outline and the Verdis' translation of it (Document II).

Luzio, *Carteggi* IV, pp. 11–14, discusses and quotes a few parts of this document; but, as with Document II, the complete text is published here for the first time.

Aïda

Act I
Scenario

1-1.

Act I
1st tableau

Scene 1
Rhadamès, Ramphis

A courtyard planted with trees, in the palace of the king at Memphis. To the right, a portico.

448

Rhadames

Venerable priest of Isis, what news is spreading? The Ethiopians, these cruel enemies of Egypt, dare, it is said, raise their heads again with Amounasro, their king, ~~one~~ pressing hard upon the valley of the Nile and Thebes loved by the Gods. speak . . does your wisdom bring the king the counsel of Isis who governs the world? .

Ramphis (*purposefully*)

Oh Rhadames!
/Isis watches over Egypt. she will designate the one who shall fight the Ethiopians and save this sacred soil. .

Rhadamès

Fortunate is he! though he should die shrouded in his triumph!

Ramphis

The Gods have spoken . . from their venerable lips has come the name of a young and valiant hero, and I shall convey their supreme will to the King!

Rhadamès

whom
Fortunate, though he should die, is he ~~whose~~ the Gods have appointed to defend his country!   (the priest enters the palace)

Scene II

Amneris comes out of the palace — Ramphis² salutes her and goes under the portico.

Amneris, Rhadamès

Amneris

such brilliance in your eyes, Rhadamès? such pride on your face. She would
    fortunate   glances
be [~~illegible~~], the one whose presence puts this fire in your ~~eyes~~, these rays of joy on your face!

Rhadames

daughter of the pharaohs, .
/~~Egypt is threatened but the Gods have spoken. A warrior has been ap-~~
               has appointed a warrior the enemies of Egypt.
~~pointed by~~ Isis /to fight and to defeat /why am I not that warrior? this thought alone makes my hand tremble and my heart beat faster!

Amneris

Is there in the world no greater happiness than the joy of victory, no fate more fortunate than that of a soldier in the field. Could Rhadamès indeed leave Memphis without a regret or a hope?

Rhadamès (*aside*)

ah! does she read in my heart? has she discovered my secret thoughts, has she guessed

~~read in my heart~~ my love for her slave?

Amneris (*aside*)

This coldness! this scornful indifference. there is in his heart a secret he hides from me. Despite him, I shall penetrate it.

Scene III

Amneris, Rhadamès, Aïda

Aïda appears under the portico, descending toward Amneris. at
              hadames
the sight of ~~Ramphis~~ she stops and is troubled. Amneris per-
              looks
ceives it and ~~turns towards~~ at Rhadamès who turns away his
      eyes
~~glances.~~ Movement.

Amneris (*aside*)

This rival whose name I seek in vain . . . Could it be she . . Could it be Aïda he loves!! (*to Aida*) Come now, my favorite slave, you whom I ~~Trio ensemble~~ protect above all others and whom I treat like a sister, why this trouble in your glances and these tears that shine despite yourself in your eyes?

Aïda

Alas! War will break out again between the beloved land where I first saw the day and this country where I am a prisoner. how could the poor captive hold back her tears and control the disturbance of her heart?

Ensemble (*trio*)

Aida

> may the Gods forgive me! my misfortune and those of my country do not alone weigh on my troubled heart. alas! at the sight of Ramphis [*sic*] I feel myself trembling and dying ~~my eyes become clouded~~ and my confusion shows in my eyes!

Rhadamès

~~Ramphis~~

> how beautiful and touching she is! Under the raiments of a slave, how noble and proud she is, one would say a Captive Queen. who would not be happy to dry the tears in these ravishing eyes.

Amneris

> Yes, 'tis she he loves. ah, I shall destroy this unworthy rival, I shall revenge myself! But no, to win I shall need only my love, my youth, and my beauty!

Scene IV

The same — a Herald — then the King

Ramphis — noblemen of the King's retinue

The Herald

I come from the distant provinces which touch the burning hot Ethiopia.

implore

I come to ~~speak to~~ our glorious King.

Noblemen

Here he comes, advancing toward us . .

(*the king appears under the portico, with Ramphis and the noblemen of his retinue*)

The King

herald

speak . . /   what news do you bring me?

The Herald

Great King, Thebes is threatened. the fierce Ethiopians, Amounasro at their

they burn the towns, they lay the country waste.

head, have invaded Egypt./ The people of Thebes implore you and entreat your assistance! .

The King

They do not implore me in vain. tomorrow our phalanxes, whom victory follows, will take to the road. The land of the Rhamsès has not degenerated.

the Gods still protect it. they have appointed the one who shall deliver Egypt and chastise the fierce Amounasro. may he gird his Sword and go to the temple of Vulcan, there to take the sacred armor. The warrior appointed by the Gods, Rhadamès, is you!

Rhadamés

Great Gods! oh you fill my heart with joy!

Aida and Amneris

Alas, he will leave . . he will go perhaps to meet his death.

The king and Ramphis

Go Rhadamès. go to put on the sacred armor, leave and return victorious! . .

Amneris

Return victorious . . .

The noblemen and the priests

Return victorious!

Rhadamès bows and leaves with Ramphis. The king, followed by the noblemen, returns to the palace with Amneris.

Scene V

Aida alone

dramatic aria

return victorious Rhadamès! . ah! what blasphemy my lips dare pronounce . . what? return victorious over my father who has rekindled this war only to return to take away from the depths of this palace his daughter whose illustrious origin no one knows!! return victorious over my country, covered with the blood of my family, dragging my father chained to your triumphal chariot!!! ah, immortal Gods, disperse this deadly army! . . give the victory to my father . . to my country . . what am I saying, wretched woman. Rhadamès whom I hold dearer than my life . . defeated . . wounded . . dead perhaps . . . ending his miserable existence in the depths of a dark dungeon. Gods, take my life! . Through death deliver the miserable Aïda from her torments and her grief! ———

Act I

2nd tableau

The temple of Vulcan in Memphis
   Chorus of the priests.
   Entrance of Rhadamès

prayer of Termouthis and Ramphis ———
Sacred dance.
Veil spread over the head of Rhadames
He puts on the sacred armor
Hymn to Isis
   (As in printed program)

Hospital[3]

~~Aida~~

~~act II~~

———

~~Scenario~~

~~1st tabl~~

~~Chorus of the women.~~
~~recit of Amneris.~~
~~duet of Amneris and Aida~~
   ~~Exeunt~~

========

~~2nd tab~~

{
~~Chorus.~~
~~march~~
~~ballet~~
~~march~~

{
~~Septet — recit of Amounasro~~
~~finale~~

========

Act II
1st tableau

Act II

1st tableau

A room in the apartments of the princess Amneris

========

S. I. Amneris — her women

Joyful chorus. The princess is being adorned for the festivities about to take place. Her slaves add finishing touches to her attire. They burn perfume at her feet, they wave large fans in the air around her.
Day blessed by the Gods. Day of feast! The sons of Osiris have won! Their

annihilated

enemies, the black Ethiopians, are dispersed and ~~have vanished~~. As the wind
of the desert disperses the sand and strews it far away, so the glorious
Rhadamès has seen their black phalanxes vanish before him. Glory to
Rhadamès, glory to Isis the Virgin mother! —
Silence, says Amneris. the beautiful Aïda, my slave, advances toward us.
she belongs to the defeated nation, let us respect her sorrow —
Aida enters with downcast eyes, slowing bringing the crown to the princess.

affected

Amneris welcomes her with ~~a smile~~ kindness, and with a gesture she
sends her women away.

S. II. <u>Amneris Aïda</u>

The suspicion that has already crossed Amneris's heart is awakened more
sharply when she sees her beautiful slave appear. This love which Rhadamès
refuses her, does he not give it to this pale Aida? The glance between them
filled with fire, which she had caught by chance, did it not reveal the cause for

coldness

the ~~disdain~~ of Rhadamès, ~~the victor, the hero~~!

<u>Amneris (to Aïda)</u>

The fate of battle has run contrary to your people ~~says Amneris to Aida~~, the
enemies of Egypt are chastised; but do not fear, my protection is forever
yours, and you shall live happy at my side.

<u>Aida</u>

I

Happy? alas, ~~Aïda. yes, I would be~~ if can / forget the beloved country where
I first saw the light of day! . . can I forget my father and my young sisters

are dead or who

who / weep there over my slavery?

<u>Amneris</u>

A God will comfort you ~~answers Amneris~~, a god who causes a smile to be

virgins

born again on the pale lips of the ~~young girls~~, a powerful and mighty God . .
Love! . . you blush . . . some young son of Egypt, has he known the art
of touching your heart? tell me . . I am your friend . . . maybe a young

warrior, one of those returning after the victory . . . ah! not all have had the
fatal destiny of their glorious chief whom death has seized at the very moment
noble
his triumph was decided! . of the ~~illustrious~~ and unfortunate Rhadamès.

Aida (dazed)

Rhadamès, cries out ~~Aida~~ [illegible] ~~herself~~ . . . he is dead!! Gods! . .
pitiless
I feel myself dying, too! . ah! strike me, ~~cruel~~ Gods . . . that the daughter
of the king of Ethiopia may not survive her victorious enemy! .

Amneris

What is the matter? you turn pale? your hand trembles? a veil descends upon
your eyes . . . would you be weeping for Rhadamès, the hero fatal to your
country! . .
I weep for everything I love, replies Aïda, everything I loved the ~~implacable~~
Gods have taken from me. Allow your plaintive slave to hide her anguish
and her tears in the depths of the palace, do not make her attend the triumph
of the enemies of her country and her King.
[Amneris] Rhadamès is dead! the Gods have avenged you!
The Gods! . . . the Gods are without pity for me! replies Aïda in despair.
No longer any doubt, says Amneris to herself. Rhadamès loves this slave and
ah! I want to observe her when Rhadamès appears.
this slave dares to love him. /she must perish. why do not my eyes, like those
/if my jealousy has not deceived me
of the Basilisk, have the power to kill the one who defies them! He is dead,
[Amneris]   (No, he is alive, but you are my rival . .)
says Aida to herself . . / I shall destroy you. [Aida] I dared to love the enemy,
the destroyer of my country. the Gods have punished my sacrilege. all is over,
ah, why am I still alive, why do I tarry to follow my beloved to the infernal
shores!

She   [Amneris] forces her to follow her.

Scene III. Amneris — Aïda — women

~~Music is heard from inside. Amneris's women return. the festivities are about
to begin. Amneris leaves to go there, followed by her women and with a gesture
ordering Aïda to stay at her side.~~

The scene changes

Act II
1st tab
2.

Aïda

I weep for everything I love. everything I loved the Gods have taken from me! .

Amneris (*watching her*)

The Gods have avenged you . . Rhadamès is dead! .

Aïda

The Gods! alas! they are without pity for me!

Amneris (*violently*)

 and tremble.
Listen/ I have read in your heart. you have dared to raise your eyes to Rhadamès . . you loved him . . .

Aïda (*very disturbed*)

I! . a slave! . .

Amneris

why the lie? with one word I shall wrest your secret from you. look at me . . . I have deceived you . . . Rhadamès is alive.

Aïda (*falling to her knees*)

oh Gods!

Amneris

you love him! do you still dare deny it . . but I love him, too, do you hear! . the daughter of the Pharaohs is your rival!

Aida (*beside herself*)

He is alive! . oh merciful Gods! . .

Amneris

break your heart, slave, or fear my vengeance!

Music outside

Do you hear? the triumph of Rhadamès is being readied . . .

Aïda

ah! let me hide my grief and my shame in the depths of the palace . . have pity!

Amneris

Come! I want the Conqueror of ethiopia to see you at my side, humble and trembling, when he enters Thebes in state and receives the triumphal crown from my hands!

They leave

Act II

2nd tableau   1st Scene

One of the entrances to the city of Thebes — in the back the great pylons and the obelisks of the temple of Ammon. to the right a triumphal portal, to the left a throne under a purple canopy.

Ramphis, Thermoutis [*sic*]

The King is sitting on his throne, the princess Amneris at his side — somewhat farther down, Aïda among the slaves — populace, guards, priests, etc., etc. etc. — general chorus

---

A herald comes to ask the king if he will receive in his sacred city the warriors who were victorious over his Ethiopian enemies and who return loaded with their spoils . .

The king gestures — great march — the foot soldiers bearing many kinds of weapons — the chariots of war — the treasures of the defeated carried by girl dancers who mingle their steps in front of the throne of the pharaoh — finally,

on their

Rhadamès on a triumphal chariot, surrounded by chained prisoners / his foreway to death,

head adorned with the triumphal crown.

and wants to run toward him

At the sight of Rhadames, Aïda lets out a cry/. Amneris, watching her, rises

(one word, she had deceived me)

and stops her with a threatening expression/. the King descends from his throne to welcome Rhadamès, whom he embraces and clasps in his arms. One of the Ethiopian officers, a prisoner of Rhadamès, turns aside and looks at Aïda intently; it is Amounasro, Aïda's father and king of Ethiopia.

Grand ensemble with Septet.

At the end of the Septet, Amounasro, in chains, draws nearer to Aïda and
throws himself at her feet, beseechingly. Aïda looks at him and cries out
Septet. Amounasro begins
. . . my father! . . /
ah! she cries, glorious king, and you, victorious heroes, save this man who
is marching to his death, beseeching me, he has just kissed my tunic . . .
he is of my race . . . he is of my blood! . . . . save him! . it is . . .
keep quiet, says Amounasro to his daughter. if I am hiding behind these
attempt
clothes, it is to assure my vengeance. Save me, [illegible] don't betray me.
speak, says Rhadames/: who is this man . . do you ask for his life? . The
to Aïda   I shall address to him
King has sworn to fulfill the first request / this day! . .

the septet.

He loves her, says Amneris! ah! this woman must perish . . .
Conqueror of my race, says Amounasro, spare us . . The Gods have struck
us in their anger yesterday. they can strike you tomorrow. teach them mercy
if they do not know it. Bent over the soil and toiling, rowing for you on the
waters of the Nile, we shall still keep the greatest of all gifts . . Life! teach
the Gods mercy! .

Aida ah I [illegible]
daughter of
Aïda adds her entreaties to those of the prisoners. /Amneris alone. So be it,
Amounasro
says the king, your wishes shall be fulfilled, and you, Aida, be happy. Be
happy like my daughter Amneris whom tomorrow I shall give as spouse to
the most valiant warrior, the glorious Rhadamès, as price for his victory!
Vivats from the populace and the priests. Joy of Amneris, despair of Rha-
to whom
damès and Aïda whom Amounasro promises a swift revenge . . The king
unites the hands of Rhadames and Aida [sic].

Curtain

Aïda

Act II
2nd tableau

[illegible]

Scenario

Act II
IInd tableau
1.

Act II.

2nd tableau

[illegible]

One of the entrances to the city of Thebes. In the back the pylons and obelisks of the temple of Ammon. to the right a triumphal portal, to the left a
throne under a purple canopy.

Amneris at his side
The King is sitting on his throne./ Ramphis and Thermoutis are near her.
below, Aïda among the slaves. populace, guards, priests, etc, etc., etc.

General Chorus

Glory to our glorious King whom Isis protects! Glory to Egypt dear to Am-
Our King
mon! ~~Amneris~~ ~~always~~ ~~victorious~~ unites in his hands the lotus of the Delta
with the palm trees of Upper Egypt! Glory to the son [illegible] of Rhamsès
Merämonn!

A herald

Mighty King
~~Mighty~~ ~~Queen~~, do you wish to receive in the sacred city of Thebes [illegible]
your soldiers who return victorious to put at your feet the spoils of your annihilated enemies!
The King gives a signal, the parade begins.

Grand March

The Clarions — the foot soldiers bearing many kinds of weapons — the chariots of war — the insignias — the sacred vases, the statues of the Gods — the
treasures of the defeated carried by girl dancers who mingle their steps in
   King's   Rhadamès triumphal
front of the [illegible] throne. finally / appears on a ~~triumphal~~ chariot, ~~Rha-
damès, his forehead adorned with the triumphal crown~~. The King descends
                he
towards Rhadamès [illegible] ~~kneels before her~~ who / opens his arms to
him and embraces him. ~~throws himself at her feet and puts the hand she~~
         places the triumphal crown on Rhadamès, then
~~offers him to his lips~~. Amneris / throws a challenging glance at Aïda who
staggers.

The King (to Rhadames)

Victorious warrior, ~~says Amneris~~, upholder of my throne, hero chosen by
the Gods, speak. By my sacred crown, by the veil of Isis, what you ask for
I shall grant, however high your wish may rise. speak . . you may obtain
everything! . .
    and looks at Aïda, Amneris watches him. is heard. An-
Rhadames keeps silent/at this moment a lugubrious march/ enter the Ethio-
nounced by a herald,
pian prisoners in chains who follow the chariot of the Victor and march to
their death. the last one is Amounasro.

Aïda

crying out, throws herself into the arms of Amounasro.
Almighty Gods! my father ·. . . (to the King) ah have pity, save him! .
save . . .

Amounasro (interrupting Aïda)

Save, if your good fortune opens your heart to mercy, the unfortunate
ones on whom fate has exhausted its blows. the Gods have struck us in their
anger, they can strike you tomorrow! teach the Gods mercy! . The King
of Ethiopia is dead. may that just vengeance suffice to your anger! . spare us.

Aïda (aside)

  you oh
Gods! I was about to betray / my father, oh my king! wanting to save you I
almost lost you!

Amounasro

keep quiet, so that I may live for vengenace. .

Septet

~~The King~~

<u>The King</u>	In the ~~Septet~~ days of prosperity the Gods advise us to use indulgence, and I feel my heart opening to mercy!
<u>Amneris</u>	is all jealousy. she sees that Rhadamès does not take his eyes off the trembling Aïda. she swears to avenge herself of her insolent slave.
<u>Amounasro</u>	pleads for his life and that of his companions. bent over the soil and toiling, rowing on the blue waters of the Nile, we ask for only one gift: to live. teach the Gods mercy!
<u>Aida</u>	joins her entreaties with those of her father, calling in turn upon The King and Rhadamès.
<u>Amounasro's Companions</u>	entreat with Amounasro and Aida.
<u>Ramphis</u> ⎫	no mercy for the enemies of Egypt.
<u>Thermoutis</u> ⎬	the gods want
<u>The priests</u> ⎭	their death.
<u>The populace</u> ⎫ _____ ⎬	soften your wrath, oh great King. You, priests of the angry Gods, open your heart to mercy.

Act II.
IInd tableau
2.

[illegible]

after the ensemble

Rhadamès (*to the King*)

You have sworn by the veil of Isis to grant me my first request. . my first request is this. give these prisoners life and liberty! .

Amneris (aside)

ah! How he loves her! . .

The priests

No . . . no mercy!

The populace

mercy! mercy! . .

The King

I have sworn. . let them be free! But you, Rhadamès, valiant hero in combat and merciful in peace, do you know to what the Gods inspire me? they have

after me I want
opened my heart to you, ~~they want that at my side~~ you to reign over the fer-
the hands of my daughter
tile Egypt and the sacred Nile. . let the priests unite [~~illegible~~] / in holy
and yours   my son and
betrothal! Come, Rhadamès, and tomorrow you shall be /~~united~~ the husband of my beloved daughter.

Great ensemble. The populace   the priests

the King
Glory to ~~The Queen~~! glory to Rhadamès!

The king

may this be the reward of the heroic savior of Egypt whom the Gods have
sent us!

Rhadames

Oh heavens! I am thunderstruck. . if I speak, I lose Aïda. . she dies with
me!

Amneris

The Gods have spoken to my father's heart! let the slave now dare to raise
her eyes to the one I love!

Aida (to Amounasro)

I love Rhadamès. .
My father! ~~I love him~~   and I am dying! . .

Amounasro (to Aïda)

I
I shall avenge you, my daughter! If / hide myself, if I humiliate myself like
this, it is to prepare our revenge! .

The priests

(joining the hands of Rhadames and Amneris)
Awaiting the wedlock, you shall be bound by a holy promise. Glory to the
Gods of Egypt. glory to Isis who holds the heart of men in her hands. (reprise
of the 1st chorus)

The populace

the King!
Glory to Rhadames — Glory to ~~the Queen~~

Cad. la Tela [The curtain falls]

<u>Aïda</u>

Act III

Scenario

Act III

At night on the shores of the Nile. . rocks of granite on which palm trees
         half-
grow. a little temple/hidden and silhouetted against the sky. Very brilliant
moonlight.

~~Prelude painting the splendor and calm of the night. Religious chants in~~
    ~~A boat appears. Amneris steps from the boat followed by Ramphis~~
~~the temple. and women carrying flowers. she goes up to the temple~~ X
        ~~appears~~
~~As the curtain rises~~ Aïda enters alone, listening and weeping. These rocks,
this sacred river ~~these distant hills where for centuries the ancestors of
her loved one have been resting,~~ she calls everything to witness her loyalty
and faithfulness. Rhadamès is going to come, she is waiting for him. he has
asked her to meet him at the foot of this solitary, little temple, the temple of Isis
propitious to love. — if Rhadamès, smiling at the fortunate wedlock with
Amneris, only wants to bid her farewell, she will find death in the sacred
river.
A man appears. It is not Rhadamès, it is Amounasro who has followed
his daughter. he informs Aïda that behind the steps of Rhadames's victorious
departure the Ethiopians have once again raised the flag of revolt. once again
[~~illegible~~] Rhadamès will march against them. In a touching speech he reminds her of her native soil, of her disconsolate mother, of the sacred images
of the Gods and her ancestors. But the love Aïda inspires in the young Rhadamès has not escaped his fatherly clairvoyance. Aida should take advantage of this love to wrest from Rhadamès the secret of the march by the Egyp-

---

                    she goes up to the temple
X She will beseech Isis to open Rhadamès's heart to her./ and enters, the boat
                         withdraws

tian troops. while he and Aida take flight, Rhadamès will be captured and taken as a slave to Ethiopia where, far from Amneris, eternal bonds will forever ensure their common happiness. Won over by her father's entreaties, by the memories of her childhood, by the joy to possess the one she loves, Aïda promises.

Rhadamès appears. He swears to Aïda that he loves only her./ Aida thereupon

And I, too, am the daughter of a King.

in turn threatens and entreats, she fascinates her lover, she wins him over,

And I, too, am the daughter of a King.

she captivates him. overwhelmed by love, Rhadamès throws himself at her feet. not his country, nor the world, nor the sacred vows that bind him are worth one look, one smile from her. honor calls him in vain, he will betray his king, he will betray the sworn faith!!!

Amounasro arrives. at his sight Rhadamès feels duty awaken in his heart, he trembles, he hesitates, he staggers. Aïda lifts her beautiful imploring eyes to him. It is done (near Napata are some dark gorges) leading into immense

there is a boat, leave.

forests. that is where the Egyptian army will pass. . . . /Amneris and Ramphis have come out of the temple. they have heard the last words of Rha-

I have not been deceived, says Ramphis.

damès./ He is a traitor, says Amneris, staggering!

Yes, he is a traitor! . . repeats Ramphis. . he must die.

No, he shall live, I love him, priest . . . and I want to save him! .

He shall die, replies the priest!

General Chorus

Scene for 2. ———

Scene for 3 ———

Big ensemble. Messenger.

Air of Aïda

A vestibule in the Palace

Rhadamès and Ramphis

News is expected.

Entrance of Amneris.
Scene for two

Scene for 2.

Scene for 3 ———— appearance

— Rh   Herald —

    Aida

Appearance of Aïda

Scene for III

The King the priest, the messenger

Air of Aïda

———————————————

2nd tableau

the temple of Vulcan

———————————————

Act III

———————————————

At night on the shores of the Nile. rocks of granite on which palm trees grow. on top of the rocks, a little temple half-hidden in the leaves and silhouetted against the sky. Splendid moonlight.

———————————————

distant

Chorus — (*in the temple*)

Isis Virgin and mother together, Isis Goddess of Nature, Isis propitious to Love, hear our voices, harken to us! you through whom everything is born and renewed, Wife and mother of the resplendent Osiris, Isis, be favorable to our prayers! . .

A boat appears on the Nile. it carries   ~~and~~   ~~appear,~~

~~A boat appears on the Nile. it carries~~ Amneris, Ramphis / priests and of their retinue. they wear dark veils over their cloting — they step women/~~the~~ [illegible] ~~follow they disembark, they step down, the boat withdraws.~~ down — the boat withdraws.

Amneris

Why, priest, do you lead me in the middle of the night to this secluded temple where one implores Isis propitious to Love? why these veils which conceal from all eyes the daughter of Pharaoh and the priest of Isis?

Ramphis

Who dares say that he has nothing to ask from the Gods! who can disdain their
          pious
help. The /princess Amneris on the eve of her wedding, can she neglect to

the soul

implore the counsel of Isis, of Isis who reads in ~~the heart~~ of men and for
their designs

whom [~~illegible~~] have no mystery!

Amneris

It is true, priest, Isis holds the heart of men in her hands . . and I want to
implore her . . . (aside) may she, oh Rhadamès, give me your whole heart
all of

as she has given you/ mine.

*Amneris, Rhadamès, [sic] and their retinue go up to the temple and
enter it.* —

Distant Chorus (*in the temple*)

Isis, Virgin and mother together, Isis Goddess of nature, Isis propitious to
Love, hear our voices, harken to us!! you through whom everything is born
and renewed, wife and mother of the resplendent Osiris, Isis, be favorable
to our prayers!

---

3. (1. bis)

Scene II
Aida. alone

Shadows of the night, hide me, ever-veilless star who reigns resplendent in the implacable azure of the sky, turn your rays from me! . . Vague
voices raise from that solitary temple. . A boat has passed on the sleeping
Nile . . . but all is quiet. Rhadamès must come here . . I await him!!

Romanza

Oh Rhadames, you my love and my life, what do you want from this torn
heart that beats only for you? The crown of Egypt is offered to your glorious
brow, the beautiful Amneris whose heart belongs to you will be your wife
tomorrow. . ah! Rhadames, if you come to bid me an eternal farewell . . I
shall sleep tomorrow, pale and cold, among the tall reeds of the Nile!

etc., etc., etc.

Scene III
Amounasro   Aïda

Amounasro

Aïda! . .

Aïda

God! . it is not Rhadamès . . . and yet this voice pronouncing my name
is also dear to me. . . my father!! my beloved father! . .

Amounasro

Oh my dear daughter! .

Ensemble

{ Joy to find each other again . . . to hold one another.
all their miseries forgotten . . the Gods have reunited them! .

Amounasro

Listen . . your country, your king, your father expect from you heroic
assistance. Rhadamès, the conqueror of Ethiopia, the betrothed of Pharaoh's
daughter, loves you and will be taken from you. Save your love and your
country at the same time. Remember the Gods veiled in mourning, the dese-
                                                        our
crated tombs of your ancestors. Remember, too, ~~the~~ beautiful fragrant for-
        our glittering palaces   free and glorious,
ests ~~of your country~~, / where your life,/would be so sweet next to a beloved
spouse! .

Aïda

                    one day
what can I do? one day,/ of that life . . and die, if I must! . .

---

3. — (2.

Amounasro

Our heroic people raise their heads again. they meet, they arm themselves
in the shadows. all is ready for vengeance. Wrest from Rhadames the secret
                                                we
of the march by the Egyptian troops. while ~~Aïda and he~~ take flight, Rhadamès will be captured and taken to Ethiopia where, far from Amneris, eternal bonds will forever ensure your happiness and his.

                                (Ensemble Amounasro and Aïda)

Aida

Yes! may it be thus! may the army of haughty Egypt perish, may our Gods
be avenged, may I live happy and proud at the side of my beloved!! —
            (Rhadamès appears, Amounasro withdraws)

Scene IV

~~Rhadamès appears, Amounasro withdraws~~
Rhadamès, Aïda

Rhadamès

Oh my beloved, I find you again. Yes, you are the only one I love, the only one to whom my heart belongs. For you I disdain the love of Pharaoh's daugh-
you, lovely

ter and the crown of fertile Egypt! for a̶ slave, I scorn the daughter of a king! . .

Aïda

Listen . . I, too, am the daughter of a King. . The terrifying Amounasro is my father. . . he is the one you saved yesterday. . . he owes you his
But

life. . / for us, ~~you as well as me~~ Rhadamès . . everything here is a trap and a peril, death hangs over our heads, the abyss [opens] under our feet. . . Come . . . let us flee. . . come reign with us in my beautiful country. far from these desolate sands! . . . from these shores seared by an implacable sun. . in our cool forests at the foot of our verdant mountains crowned by the snow . . . it is so sweet to live and to love! . . But you are silent! [illegible] . . . no doubt your soft words were a trap! you scorn me, you flee from me!! you sacrifice me to the proud Amneris! . ah strike me. . plunge your sword into my heart, cruel man! . that at least I may have the joy to die by the hand of the one I love!

Rhadamès

No, Aïda! I love you and love you alone. . . . but what . . . to desert forever my Gods and my country! . .

3 — 3.   ### Aida

Our Gods will be yours, and our country is where we are loved! . .

Rhadamès

Well then, let us flee. . I am yours. let us flee! . .

Aida

Do one more thing! . (*Amounasro appears in the back without being seen by Rhadames*)

Rhadamès

what do you want from me. . . ah! my love makes me yours entirely! . . .

Aïda

Confide the secret march of the Egyptian troops to us so that my country may be delivered from its implacable enemies.

Rhadamès

never! what do you dare demand from me! . .

Aïda

Rhadames . . . there is death for us here! over there, happiness and life!!

Rhadamès

Aïda! . .

Aïda

oh

speak, Rhadamès. . . I love you! . . .

falls at Aida's feet. he

(*Rhadamès / is about to speak. he notices Amounasro who approaches. suddenly he / draws back frightened. .*)

(*Silent Scene. Aida leans on her father and stretches her arms out to Rhadamès, raising her eyes to him entreatingly. she bows down, she falls on her knees imploring Rhadames who hesitates and trembles. finally, with a gesture of despair she rises, hides her head in her hands and falls weeping in the arms of her father. Ramphis [sic], overcome, rushes to her*)

Rhadamès

Near Napata are some dark gorges leading into impenetrable forests. that is where the Egyptian army will pass. that is where the Ethiopian army can easily ambush the Egyptian phalanxes and annihilate them.

(*Ramphis [sic] stops and is crushed by his shame. Aida throws herself into his arms.*)

Ensemble	Amounasro

let us flee. . a boat is there on the nile! . . my companions await us. . cursed Egypt, farewell. we will be avenged! .

3 — 4.	Aida

Oh my beloved! what horizons open for us! what eternity of love and joy! . land of Egypt, farewell! may your memory forever be driven from us.

Ramphis [sic]

Aida, I adore you! I am yours. I give you all my life and all my blood . . and more than my blood, my honor! turn your eyes away from me, and you, my country . . farewell! farewell forever.

They leave

Scene V
Amneris — Ramphis

Rhamphis

Do you still dare to scorn Isis's counsel. . you have heard him. . . he is a traitor!

Amneris (*crushed*)

He is a traitor!

Rhamphis

He must die!

Amneris

No. . . he shall live. . . I still love him and I want to save him! .

Ramphis

He is a traitor. . he shall die!!

Amneris swoons. . upon a sign from Ramphis several priests rush off on the side where Aida, Amounasro, and Ramphis [sic] have left. the curtain falls.

Act IV[4]
2nd tableau

Set divided in 2.
Above, the temple of Vulcan.
Below, the crypt where Aida and Ramphis [sic] die.

At the moment when Aida dies . . Amneris enters the temple and kneels in tears on the sealed stone of Ramphis's [sic] tomb.

NOTES TO DOCUMENT III

1. See Verdi's letter to Giulio Ricordi of 25 June 1870 and Du Locle's letter to the editor of *L'Italie* of 28 March 1880 and his undated letter to his wife on p. 424. See also Ursula Günther, "Zur Entstehung von Verdis *Aida*," *Studi Musicali* (Firenze: Leo S. Olschki, 1973), Anno II, n. 1, pp. 18–19, 31–33. Also in a letter from St. Agata of 24 June 1870 to his Genoese friend Carlino Del Signore — part of which was published by Frank Walker, *The Man Verdi* (New York: Knopf, 1962), p. 362 — Verdi confirms Du Locle's presence at that time ("Du Locle is here.") A few letters Du Locle wrote to his wife from St. Agata during those days were recently discovered by Dr. Ursula Günther but were not made available for this publication. When these

letters are published, they may shed additional light on Du Locle's collaboration with Verdi at St. Agata.

2. Du Locle certainly meant Rhadamès, not Ramphis. Apparently in haste, he frequently confused these two names, and at the end of Act II he even confused Amneris with Aida.

3. This seems to be a personal note, unrelated to *Aida*.

4. Luzio, *Carteggi*, IV, p. 19, assumes that Act IV, scene 1 of Du Locle's scenario is lost. Judging from the last page of the autograph, it seems more likely that Du Locle and Verdi were so rushed and involved with the ideas of the divided set and Amneris's appearance at the end of the opera that they decided to forgo working on the judgment scene.

DOCUMENT IV

Giuseppe Verdi's Terms
for the Contract with Cairo

During Camille Du Locle's visit to St. Agata in June 1870, Verdi made two undated copies of this document in his own hand. (See his letter to Giulio Ricordi of 25 June 1870 and Günther, p. 34.) Du Locle took one copy to Paris, where it served as a basis for Auguste Mariette's contract of 29 July 1870 and is kept in the Bibliothèque de l'Opéra. This copy is translated here from the Italian. The other copy, Verdi's draft in a slightly different version, is at St. Agata.

    With this private document between ——— and the composer of music G. Verdi, the following is agreed:

    1. Maestro Verdi will compose an Italian opera with music entitled *Aida* (drawn from an outline, etc.) to be performed at the Italian Theatre of Cairo during the month of January 1871. The verses will be written by an Italian poet chosen by the above-mentioned Maestro.

    2. The rights to the score and libretto remain for use only in the Kingdom of Egypt with ———. Maestro Verdi will retain the rights to the aforesaid score and libretto in all other parts of the world. In due time a copy of the score will be sent to Egypt, and the vocal and orchestral parts will be taken from that copy.

    3. Maestro Verdi will not be obligated to go to Cairo for the rehearsals, but he will send a person he trusts so that the opera will be performed according to his intentions. The services of this person shall be paid by ———; likewise, the services of the poet who will write the libretto will be paid by ———. The amount they will receive can at present be set at 20,000 lire.

    4. While the opera is being performed in Cairo, Maestro Verdi can have it performed simultaneously in another great theatre of Europe.

    5. Maestro Verdi will indicate the artists who will perform the score.

    6. For this work Maestro Verdi will be paid by ——— the sum of 150,000 lire, payable at the Rodschild [*sic*] Bank in Paris as soon as the score is delivered.

DOCUMENT V

Auguste Mariette's Contract
with
Giuseppe Verdi

Camille Du Locle forwarded a copy of this agreement, written in French by Mariette, to Verdi on or about 29 July 1870. (See Du Locle's letter to Verdi of 21 August 1870.)

Verdi waited to sign and return the contract to Du Locle until 26 August 1870. Contrary to Verdi's terms of June 1870 (Document IV), the salaries for "a person he trusts" and the poet are no longer mentioned. Furthermore Auguste Mariette limited Verdi's choice of the artists to the members of the Cairo company. (See Draneht's letter to J. Barrot of 24 July 1871 and Verdi's correspondence with Draneht in the summer of 1871.) The two extra clauses that Verdi added to the contract were obviously prompted by the culminating events of the Franco-Prussian War.

Auguste Mariette finally sent a copy of the contract to Draneht on 7 July 1871, and Draneht acknowledged its receipt on 18 July 1871.

Between the undersigned

M. Auguste Mariette Bey, acting in the name of and with the authorization of H.H. Ismail Pasha, Khedive of Egypt, on the one hand,

and M. Giuseppe Verdi, composer of music, on the other hand,

the following has been agreed:

M. Verdi promises to compose the music for an opera in four acts, entitled *Aida*, the plan of which he has accepted (with the exception of modifications in detail which may be judged necessary).

This opera will be presented at the Vice-Royal Theatre of Cairo during the month of January 1871.

The Italian verses will be written by a poet chosen by M. Verdi.

M. Verdi will not be obligated to come personally to Cairo for the rehearsals of this work; should he judge it useful, he may send a person of his choice to direct the performance of the work in accordance with his intentions.

As soon as the opera *Aida* has been presented in Cairo, M. G. Verdi will be free to have it performed in Europe at the theatre or theatres of his choice.

M. Verdi will choose the artists who will perform his score from the company of the Italian Theatre in Cairo.

The libretto and the score of *Aida* will be, for Egypt, the absolute property of H.H., the Khedive.

M. G. Verdi reserves for himself the rights to the libretto and to the score for the other parts of the world.

At an opportune time, M. Verdi will send to Egypt, or will submit to an agent of H.H. in Paris, a copy of the orchestral score of *Aida*.

M. Verdi will receive for this work the sum of 150,000 francs.

This sum will be paid in two installments: 50,000 francs on the day of the signing of the present contract, 100,000 francs on the day that M. Verdi will submit, or will have submitted, to H.H. the score of *Aida*.

Made in duplicate in Paris, 29 July 1870.

Document approved

Signed: Auguste Mariette

I accept the present contract with the following modifications:[1]

1. The payments will be made in gold.

2. If through any unforeseen circumstance whatever, independent of me (that is, through no fault of mine), the opera should not be presented at the theatre in Cairo during the month of January 1871, I shall have the option to have it performed elsewhere, six months later.

Signed: Giuseppe Verdi

NOTE TO DOCUMENT V

1. These clauses (written in French) are *not* part of Verdi's letter to Du Locle of 26 August 1870, as it appears on p. 227 of Gaetano Cesari and Alessandro Luzio's *I Copialettere* (Milano: Comune di Milano, 1913) and in subsequent publications. I discovered this falsification only when the autograph of Verdi's above-mentioned letter became available after the present volume had gone to press. The text to be omitted on p. 57 is indicated in bracketed ellipses.

DOCUMENT VI

Information on Egyptian Antiquity
by
an Unknown Scholar

The autograph consists of fourteen 13 × 20 cm. pages on four folded sheets of thin blue paper. Twelve of these pages are almost completely covered, and two of them are partly covered with a very clear, handsome, Italian writing in ink.

This document represents "the answers to the various questions" Verdi had asked Giulio Ricordi to provide.[1] Ricordi enclosed twelve of these little pages in his letter to Verdi of 21 July and two in his letter of 8 August 1870. Since Ricordi did not identify the author, but only mentioned "a most experienced man of letters, a friend of mine, who is entirely at our disposal," the scholar deserving credit will perhaps never be known; an extremely delicate sense of tact and modesty might have prompted him to remain anonymous.

In briefly discussing and quoting from this document, Luzio, *Carteggi*, IV, pp. 15–16, surmises that the informant was "probably Michele Lessona, who had lived for a long time in Egypt." Thus far, however, I have been unable to learn anything else about him.

Luzio refers to only *tre azzurri foglietti* (three little blue sheets), whereas there are four, comprising the above-mentioned fourteen pages, which have not been published before in their entirety.

Enclosure in Giulio Ricordi's Letter
to Verdi of 21 July 1870

It cannot be asserted with absolute certainty that the cult of the gods in Egypt was exclusively reserved for men; although no author positively admits to priestesses, none rules out the possibility. More probably women played a secondary role in the cult of the gods; that is, they were not excluded from the rites and religious mysteries but were limited to dancing in the sacred processions, preparing the food, and being custodians of the sacred animals. In Pythagoras' rites, which call to mind the principal features of the Egyptian religious system, the women play a distinct role. One author — I no longer remember his name — tells the tale of a priestess who tore out her tongue in order not to betray the secrets of her religion.

Here is an important note by Creuzer[2] on the subject:

Herodotus formally denies that there were priestesses. Juvenal and Persius, however, affirm that there were (Sat. VI, 488, V, 186), and the inscription on the Rosetta stone suggests the existence of priestesses.

Other evidence, for example, is a figure in the bas-relief of Médinat-Abou; and certain passages from ancient writers on the subject of Zeus's priestesses in Thebes cause us to believe that women were employed in the temples of the ancient Pharaohs as well, although not precisely as priestesses.

Music of the purest and most ethical character, in which the sound of the string instruments accompanied a grave and majestic chant, was exclusively reserved to the priestly cult, whereas the people's cult, completely materialistic and sensual, required songs and instruments appropriate for its noisy orgies. (Creuzer, *Religion of Egypt*, III, p. 7.)

Egyptian power and civilization, which increased under each king of the XVIIIth dynasty, after the expulsion of the Hyksos, reached its highest degree under the kings of the XIXth dynasty.

Fifteen kings were known by the name of Ramses during the periods of the XVIIIth, IXXth, and XXth dynasties — from Ramses I, who reigned from about 1613 B.C., to Ramses XV, who should have reigned around the year 1000.

We are not concerned with Ramses I.

Ramses II (Bathotis) erected a magnificent palace in Thebes, and nothing else is remembered of him.

Hence the great king you ask about should be Ramses III, called the Great.

In none of the writers I consulted did I find that he was known by the name of Teramon.

On the contrary, it seems that I can eliminate this hypothesis with some certainty, since the name Teramon does not appear on any of the known Egyptian monuments. Therefore it does not seem to be a part of Egyptian history.

Ramses III is generally known to all historians by the name of Sesostris; and this would be precisely the Sesostris of whom Herodotus speaks and to whom he attributes half-legendary deeds.

The Hyksos renewed their invasion of Egypt during the reign of Amenophis III, so that he was forced to withdraw into Ethiopia; from there, however, he returned victoriously with the help of his son Ramses III.

The story goes that this son was educated by his father in every manner of military discipline along with 1,700 youngsters who had been born on the same day — an impossible figure, since Egypt had no more than sixteen million inhabitants. Thus when he succeeded his father, he was surrounded by a group of strong and educated people who were completely devoted to him. With a powerful army — some historians say 624,000 men and add a fleet to it

— he subdued Ethiopia, moved into Asia, penetrated India beyond the Ganges (further than Hercules and Bacchus), attacked the Scythians and Colchis, and moved toward Europe through Thrace. But a conspiracy recalled him to his homeland after nine years. Having returned there after abandoning the conquered lands that were impossible to rule, his only thought was the prosperity of his kingdom, which bordered on Ethiopia to the south, on the Mediterranean to the north, on Lybia to the west, and on the Arabian Gulf to the east. Until that time this land had been divided into approximately thirty-six provinces.

He erected temples and monuments and had his statue — thirty elbows high — as well as those of the queen and his four children put into the temple of Vulcan in Memphis. He established a network of canals that brought fertility to the country and connected Memphis to the sea. For these works he used only the labor of slaves and foreigners; when he went to the temple, he had his wagon drawn by subdued princes. He promulgated excellent laws, which he claimed were suggested by Mercury, and he divided territories among his subjects and raised regular taxes.

The grateful Egyptians erected monuments to him as if to a semigod; and his memory was so revered almost two centuries later that the high priest of Phta did not want to put the statue of Darius before that of Sesostris in Memphis.

Having been crowned about 1565 B.C., he reigned approximately sixty years. Then he apparently killed himself in order to end such a beautiful life with dignity; it is said that he had become blind.

In Nubia, Belzoni discovered a temple dedicated to Isis by the wife of Ramses III. Before that he surveyed the temple of Ipsambul, on the facade of which were four seated giants, each sixty-one feet high, that supposedly represented this Ramses. His victories are commemorated by reliefs scattered throughout the entire sixteen-room monument as well as in a sanctuary at the back — supposedly the tomb of Sesostris — where there are four more large statues.

Concerning the deeds of this Sesostris, Cautà observes that he was certainly the greatest of Egypt's kings; that he restored independence to the country by driving out the Hyksos; that he very likely invaded Ethiopia and Asia as far as Babylon, Thrace, and Persia, and perhaps also the Indian peninsula; that he was an absolute ruler; and that the great works attributed to him were probably begun by him alone.

Ramses the Great is also known as Egyptus, Sesostris, Sesoosis, and Sethos, perhaps from *soos*, meaning impure, because he drove out the Hyksos, who were considered impure.

Thebes is 115 leagues from Cairo.

An <u>original Egyptian</u> funeral prayer is impossible to find, particularly since it is not certain that the Egyptians recited <u>requiems</u> in memory of their dead. I think an <u>imitation</u> would be easy, however, if it is based on the following principles — principles which are certainly not gospel but which have been derived from the research of a hundred different, and sometimes contradictory, interpretations of profound writers in this field.

The Egyptians believed in the immortality of the soul. They believed that near the places of burial (Necropolis) there existed a vast, eternal empire, governed by Osiris and Isis. The souls of the dead remained there for a long or short time, depending on their individual circumstances — from nine to three thousand years. This funeral kingdom, known as Amenthis, was a place of purification; the souls were cleansed there. No one could escape from this kind of purgatory, because no one was spotless. But the most virtuous were the first to be freed. They did not go through the whole fatal circle, and they returned to the celestial spheres from which their souls had descended after only nine years. Before entering Amenthis, the soul presented itself to the sacred tribunal of Osiris, the supreme judge and the sovereign of the dead, who, having examined the vices and virtues of the dead one, decreed the length of the purgation.

This purgation consisted of the passing of the souls into the bodies of various animals. If the souls did not obey the exhortations and the laws of the merciful Osiris, a thousand years were not enough to complete the fatal circle, which had to be started again a second or even a third time, so that some souls achieved a perfect purification only after three thousand years. It must be noted that the soul began its transmigration only after the body had disintegrated into dust. The Egyptians, therefore, took the greatest care to preserve the bodies (mummies) of their dead, believing that the longer the body remained intact, the shorter the period of transmigration would be.

When the souls were completely purified, they rose again to the higher spheres, crossing the stars and the signs of the heavenly zodiac. The most virtuous arrived at the fixed stars — that was the perfection and the highest glorification of the soul. The less virtuous arrived at the errant stars. The sun was the most sublime abode.

The Egyptians were not much concerned with the specific time assigned to life, which was a simple pilgrimage for them. Far more important was the time after death, which perpetuates the remembrance of virtues. The houses of the living were <u>inns</u> to them, whereas the tombs of the dead were considered to be perpetual, eternal dwellings.

The Egyptians associated ideas of happiness and joy with the kingdom of the dead. It was the Elysium where all the sorrows and needs of man came to an end.

I found a recorded prayer that was said in the preparation of the mummy; it begins as follows:

"Oh Sun God, and all Gods who have given life to men, receive and transmit me to the eternal Gods, that I may partake of their abode. . . ."

For the chorus of the priests, I think it is useful to remember that Egyptian music had a grave and solemn character — the simple chant, accompanied by the sound of multistringed harps.

In the funeral prayer, I think, the following concepts could be developed, barring particular circumstances:

Nothingness of life.

All human sorrows and needs end in Amenthis.

The brief stay that makes the soul virtuous under the rule of the merciful Osiris.

The possible encounter of Amneris's soul with the soul of the other [Radames?] and with the same fate [after death?].

The splendor of the ascent to ethereal regions.

Complete bliss in the flaming Kingdom of the Sun.

The mysteries of Isis were probably celebrated in the subterranean chambers of temples, palaces, places of burial (Necropolis), etc.

The candidate was introduced by the initiator. Having taken off his clothes and jewelry, he was ritually clothed in the outer court of the sacred buildings. With a flickering torch, he descended into a deep, dark, and humid well. The dangerous stairs had been driven into the wall, the steps scarcely protruding. At the bottom stood two doors — one to the north, one to the south; one was bolted shut, the other open. Through the first, a long and magnificent arcade with torches and lamps could be seen. Entering the other, which immediately closed with great noise, the candidate found himself at the entrance of the majestic sacred vault, which was very deep and was covered with inscriptions. Then the candidate reached a gate guarded by three men in armor, with shining helmets topped by emblematic animals. These men warned him that there was still time to retreat; that he must never look back and never hesitate; and that, if he failed the trial, he would remain forever imprisoned in the subterranean city. The first trial was that of fire — vast blazes from everywhere; two pyres of burning aromatic branches were placed in the middle of a marble hall. The smoke rose inside thin pipes. A grating of red-hot iron covered the floor, with openings, however, through which one could put one's foot.

The second trial was that of water — rumbling in a vast, dark, and frightening canal. The candidate was required to swim through it while firmly holding a lighted lamp above his head to lessen the darkness.

The third trial was that of air. The candidate walked across a small drawbridge, whereupon a little door of ivory came into view. He tried to open it while holding onto two large iron rings. The drawbridge was suddenly raised, the wind blew out the lamp, and the candidate found himself suspended in space and complete darkness and there was a deafening, terrible noise caused by a hundred rotating machines. Finally the ivory door opened; and the candidate found himself in a magnificent, brilliantly lighted temple, where a large number of priests were assembled in two rows with the high priest at the head.

All of the temple was decorated with the serpent that vomits an egg (the universe), the bent cross, a serpent that holds onto its own tail, etc.

Among the priests, the torch-bearer held in one hand a golden vase shaped like a ship, from which arose a sparkling flame — the symbol of the sun. The altar-bearer represented the moon. A third priest carried the golden palm and the Caduceus of Mercury. Others carried the hand of justice, a vase in the shape of a breast, the mystic sieve, a vase filled with water, the sacred sieve, a vase in the shape of an egg with a serpent winding around it, etc.

The master of ceremonies encouraged the candidate to advance close to the high priest, who gave him a goblet filled with water and made him kneel before the triple statue of Isis, Osiris, and Horus. After the priests repeated an invocation to Isis ("Isis, great Goddess of Egypt, instill strength into the new priest, who through your love has overcome the three trials. Make him now victorious in the trials of the soul, and make him so obedient to your laws that he may become worthy to participate in your revered mysteries"), the novice rose again and drank from the vase which the high priest gave him, saying: "Here is the drink of memory that will impress on your mind the rules of wisdom that we shall teach you."

When the hymns and chants had ceased, the novice went to far-off rooms where further trials awaited him for a period of not less than eighty-one days of fasting, silence, religious and moral instruction, prayer, and complete isolation.

When he was allowed to speak once more, the twelve days of the manifesta-tion began. At dawn of the first day he was taken to the temple and vested in the twelve sacred stoles and the Olympic mantle, with a crown of palm branches and a torch adorned by the sun in his right hand. After being sworn in, he was introduced to the most secret area of the sanctuary, where he

learned the meaning of the mysterious figures and the mysteries of the Hermet-
ic doctrine.

The triumph of the initiated followed. On the previous evening priests of an
inferior order, sumptuously dressed, announced the procession. Flowers were
strewn in the streets, and the houses were decorated. In the temple the treasures were uncovered; and between the dances of the priests' daughters an
offering was made to a precious image of Isis, which was doubly veiled. Then
came the procession.

It was led by the cantor with a symbol of music and two books of Hermes.
Then came the horoscope with the clock and the palm branch, and, in front of
it, the four books of Hermes about the stars. Then came the sacred scribe with
feathers on his head, a book and ruler in his hand, and [in his other hand] the
ink and the writing reed. Then came the stole-bearer with the cubit of justice
and the cup for the libations. At last came the prophet with the sacred urn,
visible to all.

After the mysteries of Isis and Horus, the candidate was admitted to those
of Serapis and then to the lesser known of Osiris. Those of Isis were the minor
mysteries.

The temple of Serapis at Canopus is near the sea, on the western bank of the
tributary of the Nile, which carries its name and was built by the Ptolemies.
The immense ruins of Canopus are not far from Abouquir.

———————

Temple of Luxor and ruins of Thebes = Champollion,[3] *L'Egypte sous les
Pharaons*, p. 204.

The priests: white vestments of linen, shoes of papyrus, the head completely shaved — special rules of life. See Creuzer.

Isis: I am the one that is, was, and will be: no mortal has lifted the veil that
covers me. To you, who is one and all, Goddess Isis.

Statue of Isis: a woman with seven breasts, surrounded by a lion, a dolphin,
an eagle, and a salamander in black stone.

Ruins of Naisi: one league from the Nile, to the east of Bhabeit or Beibeth.

Enclosure in Giulio Ricordi's letter
to Verdi of 8 August 1870

The author, from whom I have taken the information concerning the distance between Memphis (Cairo) and Thebes, says that Thebes is located
precisely at 115 French leagues S.S.E. of Cairo. On Volney's geographical
map of Egypt, which was published in 1799 and is rather well known, I

followed as best I could the windings of the Nile — the most natural route between Memphis and Thebes — and measured the above-mentioned distance. I came up with some two leagues more. Therefore it appears that one can positively establish the distance between Memphis and Thebes at 115 French leagues, or about 511 kilometers, since the common French league equals 4.444 kilometers. I find some differences, however, in the various geographical treatises. But apart from the fact that only ten or fifteen kilometers are more or less involved, these differences are caused by the various locations assigned to ancient Memphis. Shaw[4] puts Memphis at Giza where the pyramids rise. Savary[5] places it eighteen miles to the south of Giza, where the village of Memf is located on the western bank of the Nile. Bruce[6] and Metraine[7] put Memphis in the Sahara Desert; others place it close to Saggarah and Mil-Raineh in Central Egypt to the left of the Nile and four leagues south of Cairo, etc.

Calculating the distance between Memphis and Thebes in a magnificent old atlas published in Vienna, I find about 72 geographical miles or roughly 530 kilometers.

NOTES TO DOCUMENT VI

1. In view of the great pains Verdi took to inform himself about Egyptian antiquity it seems strange that he — and even Auguste Mariette — either ignored or did not object to certain historical discrepancies in Mariette's outline. Guglielmo Barblan (Teatro alla Scala program 1975/76, p. 21, n. 3) gives the following examples from an article by Adriano Vargiu, ''Il libretto dell 'Aida,'' *Rassegna Musicale Curci*, 1968, 21, no. 3, pp. 148–150: ''The pharaohs never charged an officer with the defense of their country (as in Radames's case), but always led their troops themselves; Vulcan is a Roman god unknown to the Egyptians; the Egyptians did not erect arches of triumph like the Romans; the famous *Aida* trumpets are Roman; the Egyptians did not attack by surprise, and thus Amonasro's wish to learn their secret plan for such an attack is historically unfeasible; the custom to wall in traitors alive is only known from medieval literature, etc., etc. It goes without saying that all these scholarly reservations do not at all affect the 'truth' of this work of art.''

2. Georg Friedrich Creuzer (1771–1858), German classical philologist.

3. Jean François Champollion le Jeune (1790–1832), French archaeologist and the founder of Egyptology.

4. Thomas Shaw (1694–1751), English traveler and antiquary.

5. Possibly Felix Savary (1797–1841), French astronomer and mathematician.

6. Probably James Bruce (1730–94), Scotch traveler.

7. Unknown.

DOCUMENT VII

Sketch of the First Scenes of the Libretto
by
Antonio Ghislanzoni

The Italian autograph consists of both sides of three sheets of legal-size paper, that are fully covered with Ghislanzoni's and Verdi's handwritings in ink. All cancellations in the text appear to be Verdi's, and the changes he made are underlined. Words underlined by Ghislanzoni are italicized. Additional pages of this sketch, which Ghislanzoni probably sent to Verdi, are missing.

Presumably these pages are "the fragments of the first act" that Ghislanzoni mentioned to Verdi on 26 July 1870. Strangely enough Verdi seems to refer to these fragments only in his letter to Ghislanzoni of 12 August 1870. Apparently at least one or two letters that Verdi wrote to Ghislanzoni before 12 August 1870 are missing: Verdi no doubt acknowledged receipt of and commented on "the first act of *Aida*, accompanied by a long letter," which Ghislanzoni mentioned to Eugenio Tornaghi on 15 July 1870. In his missing answer to that letter and its enclosure, Verdi seems to have requested the changes embodied in this document, which is published here for the first time.

Luzio, *Carteggi*, IV, p. 17, quotes different texts by Ghislanzoni and Verdi, which apparently preceded this fragment.

Ghislanzoni's address near Lecco appears in Verdi's handwriting in the upper left corner of the first page of this document.

Ghislanzoni
a Pusiano per Mariaga   **Aida**
Lombardia   **First Act**

Courtyard in the palace of the King at Memphis —
Trees — To the right, a portico.

Scene I
Radamès — Ramfis

ardisca

Ramfis.   Si: corre voce che l'Etiope ~~insano~~
Sfidarci ancora e del Nilo la valle

483

~~Anco una volta diffidarci ardisca,~~
~~E del Nilo la valle~~
E Tebe minacciar — Fra breve un Messo

Recherà il ver

~~Qui giunger deve, e tutto il ver fia noto.~~

Rad.   ~~La sacra Iside ancora~~ La sacra

Iside consultasti?

~~Non consultasti?~~

                     ha nomato

Ramfis.   Ella ~~già diè il responso,~~
Delle Egizie falangi

~~E il guerrier designò cui della guerra~~
Il condottier supremo

~~Si affidino le sorti.~~
Rad. (aside)   Oh Lui felice!
~~Oh foss io quello!~~ . . .
Ramfis.   Giovine e prode è desso . . . Ora del Nume

~~Il decreto del Nume~~

                                   (exits)

Reco i decreti al Re

~~Io reco al Re — vado a nomargli il prode,~~
~~Il giovane guerrier che alla vittoria~~
~~Guiderà l'armi nostre.~~   (exits)

Scene II

Radamès alone

                        Se quel guerriero

                     ~~Ah! perchè il cuore~~

Io fossi . . . . ! Se il mio sogno

~~Mi palpita costì . . .~~ ~~Che il sogno mio~~
Si avverasse . . . ! Un esercito di prodi
Da me guidato! . . . e la vittoria! . . e il plauso
Di Menfi tutta . . . . ! E a te, mia dolce Aida,
Tornar di lauri cinto . . .
Dirti: per te ho pugnato e per te ho vinto!

                [*undecipherable canceled passage*]

Romanza tenore
Celeste Aida, forma divina,
   Mistico serto di luce e fior —

Del mio pensiero tu sei regina —
  Tu di mia vita sei lo splendor.
Il tuo bel cielo vorrei ridarti,
  Le dolci brezze del patrio suol —
  Un regal serto sul crin posarti
Ergerti un trono vicino al sol.

(and one could repeat the
preceding strophe)

(Alternative)

~~Rosa di cielo, eterea~~
  ~~Forma di luce e fiori,~~
  ~~Astro in cui tutti splendono~~
  ~~Dell'iride i colori,~~
  ~~Io t'amo, Aida, io t'amo,~~
  ~~O prigioniera bella —~~
  ~~Meta dei passi e stella~~
  ~~Tu sei del mio destino.~~
~~Della perduta patria~~
  ~~Vorrei ridarti i cieli,~~
  ~~Le valli, i sogli liberi~~
  ~~A cui piangendo aneli.~~

  ~~Godrei nel tuo sorriso,~~
  ~~Nel contemplarti il viso,~~
  ~~Nel carezzarti il crin.~~

Chorus   Sorgiam tutti! all'armi! all'armi!,
  ~~Dell' Egitto il sacro lido~~
  ~~Non eccheggi che un sol grido~~
  ~~Guerra e morte allo stranier!~~

_____[undecipherable canceled passage]

  Via d'Egitto gli stranieri . . .
    <u>ai</u>   <u>i</u>
  Morte ~~al~~ barbaro invasor!
~~Quanti ha il mattino raggi e splendori,~~
  ~~Quanti hanno vezzi le [illegible] e i fiori,~~
  ~~Tutto in te adunasi, forma divina,~~
  ~~Astro di vita, astro d'amor.~~

Qui sei straniera — sei prigioniera —
Pur la regina sei del mio cor.
Sulle mie braccia chè non poss'io
Recarti, o bella, nel suol natio?
Tornarti all'estasi dei dì felici . . . .
Di lunghi amplessi bearmi il cor!
Ah! tu sei figlia de' miei nemici,
Ma pure io t'amo d'immenso amor! . . .

Scene III

Amneris — Radamès

Amneris.	Quale insolita fiamma Nel tuo sguardo! Di quale Nobil fierezza ti balena il volto! Degna d'invidia oh quanto Saria la donna il cui bramato aspetto Tanta luce di gaudio in te destasse!
Radamès.	D'un sogno avventuroso

O figlia del mio Re, di un lieto sogno
Si beava il mio core.

Mi perdea la mente — Oggi la Diva
Profferse il nome del guerrier che al campo
Le schiere egizie condurrà . . . S'io fossi
A tale onor prescelto
Alla impresa proscelto . . .

Amneris.   Armi e battaglie . . .
Nè un'altro sogno mai

Stragi e vittorie . . . Nè altro sogno mai
Più gentil . . . più soave

Più mite . . . più gentile
Al cuore ti parlò? . . . Non hai tu in Menfi
Desiderii . . . . speranze . . . ?

Radames.   Io? . . . Quale inchiesta? . .
(aside) Forse . . . l'arcano amore
Scoprì che mi arde in core . . . .

DOCUMENT VIII

Sketch of the Fourth Act Dialogue

by

Giuseppe Verdi

The Italian autograph consists of seven sides of four sheets of legal-size paper. Except for information about the sets and stage directions, Verdi wrote (in ink) only on the left half of the pages, leaving the right half empty. Ghislanzoni's comments (underlined twice) and a few hurried annotations, all of which seem to be Verdi's, appear on the right. These annotations are written in pencil and could not be completely deciphered. The few words Verdi struck out are also struck out in this English translation.

Presumably this autograph is the last part of the 37 pages mentioned by Luzio, *Carteggi*, IV, pp. 16 and 18. According to Luzio (pp. 13 and 16), Verdi left hundreds of sketches in prose for the Italian libretto, changing Du Locle's French scenario (Document III), neatly rewrote the entire libretto in prose on 37 pages, and gave it to Ghislanzoni to be versified. (The divided set and Amneris's appearance at the end of the opera are not mentioned in this sketch.) If the present document, from which Luzio quotes on p. 19, is truly part of those 37 pages, from which he quotes on pp. 21–22, then 30 of the 37 pages are missing like the hundreds of sketches Luzio claims to have seen at St. Agata.

This document has not been published before, except for Luzio's quotation on p. 19 of *Carteggi*, IV.

Fourth Act

The set represents a hall in the palace of the King. To the right, a low door leads into the hall of judgments. Toward the rear of the stage is a platform, to which one ascends by a double stairway. In front of the platform, on two granite pedestals, stand two bronze statues, one representing <u>Justice</u>, the other <u>Truth</u>.

<u>Amneris alone</u>

~~Amonasro~~ The father alone
was captured as they fled.
Aida, my rival, has
escaped me. Meanwhile, Radames,
in the hands of the priests,

487

awaits the punishment of the
traitors! No! . . He is not
a traitor! . . (*She cries*.)
And yet he revealed ~~to the enemy~~
a high secret . . . and fled
with her . . . Traitors all!
To death, to death!! . .
Ah, what do I say! . . I want him
to live . . . I love him always,
I love him desperately . . .
And how to save him? . . Let us try. (*She thinks for a moment*.)
Radames shall come to me!

Scene II

Radames and the above

Am. Soon the priests
will assemble here to
judge you. The charge weighs heavily
on you — heavy will be the punishment.
Yet, if you want to deny your
crime before the judges,   ~~Avoid~~
I shall try to soften
the King's heart and obtain   ~~Norma and Pollione~~
your pardon. But you will renounce
Aida and swear to me   ~~duet~~
that you will never see her again.
Rad. I desire no pardon,
and I do not hope for it. My
sorrows, my vanished
hopes, the remorse that
tears my heart
make life hateful to me.
To me is left but
one hope, one desire — to die.
Am. To die! . . . But I want
you to live; you hear? . . You
do not understand the immensity
of my love. For you I would
renounce the throne, forsake
my Father, repudiate the Gods . . .

Rad. In the rapture of
my love for her, have I
betrayed my duty, the Gods,
my King, the country?
Am. Do not speak to me of her . . .
Rad. Forgive a demented one. . .
Yes, I am ungrateful . . . but
I love Aida . . . I love her . . .
and her alone . . .
Amn. Ah be silent!   Less crude

Rad. . . . If I had treasures,   warmer
thrones,
all would I give to see her   I would omit and go to the sign +
a moment . . . to
rejoice a moment
at her sight . . and to die
happily thereafter.
Amn. You are crazy! You do not know   +
that as my love is immense, also
my furor is terrible;
one word of mine saves you,
one word of mine kills you.
And you do not tremble?
Rad. No: I do not tremble. Avenge yourself.
Amn. Once more:
renounce Aida.
Rad. I cannot.
Amn. Renounce Aida
or you will die! . . .
Rad. I will die!
Amn. Well then! Let the Gods
be placated and may justice
take its course. Guards!
Rad. (*with exaltation*) Death will
be welcome to me if
I die for her. (*He leaves between the guards.*)
     Amneris alone
~~Ungrateful~~! . . . . . Ah me! . .
I feel I am dying! (*At this moment, to the sound of a religious march, the
                    Priests file by upstage. Ramphis is at their head, and they*

disappear through the low door situated at the audience's right.)

Ah, here they are! . . . The fatal ⎫
priests . . . . the merciless! That ⎬   Rec.
I might not see those white ghosts! ⎭

       (She covers her face in her hands and, after some silence,
       exclaims:)

And I! . . It was I myself . . . .
who turned him over to them . . . *(silence)*
Oh, atrocious jealousy that
will be the cause of his
death and my eternal despair.

       (Meanwhile, the Priests will have disappeared. A low
       murmur of voices will be heard — it is the Chorus of the
       Priests in the subterranean chamber:)

Gods, descend upon
us. You enlighten us,
You guide us, so that   [*Illegible*]
justice may be given promptly
and securely.

       (Amneris bursts into tears, crying:)

Almighty Gods, have ⎫
pity on him!   ⎬   Phrase
   The Voice of Ramfis in the subterranean chamber: marked by +
                                    repeat =

Radames! Radames! Radames!
~~I accuse you of having sold~~   + I accuse you of having revealed
~~your honor to the enemy of the~~   a high secret to the enemy
~~country!~~ . . . Defend yourself. You are silent!!   of the country.
       Traitor!
  All   Traitor!

  Ramfis as above

~~You wanted to deliver our~~   I accuse you of having abandone
~~army at the Gorges of Napata~~   our army on the
~~into the hands of the enemy!~~   eve of the battle.
Defend yourself. You are silent!!
       Traitor!
  All   Traitor!

  Ramfis as above

You have betrayed your vow, the   Last part
King, the country. You will   chorus
die an infamous death.   more extended

<u>All</u>

You will die an infamous death.

<u>Ramfis</u>

You will be buried
alive in the subterranean chambers of the temple
of Vulcan. (*The chorus repeats.*)

Amn. (*in despair*)

Ah no! Hold! . . . Buried alive!
Horror! (*The voices disperse, repeating:*)

Traitor!

Traitor!

(*Silence!*)

All is silent! . . Buried
alive!! And I . . . I, the
omnipotent daughter of
the Pharaohs, cannot save him!   <u>Rec.</u>
And my desperate love
cannot tear him away from the   <u>Warmer</u>
claws of the priests
of blood! What good,   <u>and perhaps faster</u>
then, is that golden seat they
call the throne, if it cannot
save the one I love
more than anything on earth!!

Scene III

<u>The King enters</u>

<u>Am</u>. Oh my father! Save him!

<u>King</u>. ~~It is true, then! You love him.~~ So great is your love for him?

<u>Am</u>. I love him desperately.   <u>useless</u>
Save him.

<u>King</u>. You beg in vain. He is
condemned: he will die . . .

Rec.

(*Amneris cries out and breaks down. The King calls
the maids who carry her off, etc.*)

Scene IV

*The subterranean chamber. Long lines of arcades fade into the darkness at
the rear of the stage. To the right and left one can barely make out the
entrance of the gallery. Colossal statues of Osiris, with hands crossed, lean
against the pillars that support the vault.*
Radames is alone *on the steps by which he descended.* We still hear the blows
that seal the stone above the subterranean chamber.

The fatal stone is closed
above me! Forever
it is closed. In this
eternal night I am condemned
to die of hunger! I shall   Aria [?]
not see the day again! . . I shall not
see Aida again!! . . Oh my Aida,
where are you? May you at least
be happy and forever
ignore my cruel
death! But . . . what
a strange noise! . . . Somebody! . .
It is a vision! . . Ah . . . it is a human
shape! . . . Heaven! . . Aida,
Aida . . .
Aida. It is I . . .
Rad. You here? But how?
Aida. I anticipated your sentence
and ~~hid~~ could hide   [*undecipherable canceled passage*]
in this darkness. For
four days I have awaited you to
die with you, far from all
human view.
Rad. Oh, my Aida! But you, to die!
You, so innocent, so young,
so beautiful! . . Damnation,
and I cannot save you!
Aida. Calm yourself. Death is all
that is left to us. Look! the Angel
of Love flies above
us with his golden wings, and
he awaits us to take us
to a better world. The
Heavens open up; the sorrows end.

An eternity of blessedness
begins for us.
Rad. You are delirious, Aida . . . listen to me.
You are living, still living, so
let us enjoy a moment of
happiness that will soon vanish
forever. (*At this moment one vaguely hears the Invocation of the Priests, the sound of the harps*, and [the music accompanying] the dance of the Priestesses.)
Rad. The feast of the Priests!
Aida. Our hymn of death!
Rad. (*with despair*) And these strong arms
of mine cannot move
this fatal stone!
Aida. I am fainting . . . I precede you.
Rad. Await me. I do not want to live
a moment without you.
Aida. On the threshold of heaven . . .
There you will see me . . . I shall await you . . .
then we shall never be divided
again . . . .
Rad. Ah, my Aida . . . await me!
Aida. Ah, I precede you . . . Farewell! . . . (*She dies.*)
Rad. Aida! . . .

The curtain falls

DOCUMENT IX

Synopsis
in the Review
Il Trovatore

This synopsis, published in Italian, was, like others at that time, based on Auguste Mariette's original outline. See Verdi's letter to Ghislanzoni of 27 September 1870 and Ghislanzoni's letter to Tornaghi of 1 October 1870.

Milan, Thursday 8 September 1870

Il Trovatore
Literary, Artistic, and Theatrical Review
with caricatures and illustrations

published every Thursday

Il Trovatore also has a Theatrical Agency which could do much
business . . . if needed.

Aida by Verdi

We give a resumé of the story of this new opera which the illustrious maestro must write for the Viceroy's theatre in Cairo; publishing the entire outline would take too long.

Characters

The King.
Princess Amnèris, his daughter.
Aida, Ethiopian slave and maid of the Princess.
Rhadamès, Captain of the Guards.
Amounasro, father of Aida and king of Ethiopia.
Ramphis, head of the college of priests.
Termouthis, high Priest [*sic*] of the Temple of Vulcan.

A Herald.

Priests, Civil Servants, Soldiers, Populace.

The action takes place on the banks of the Nile during the reign of the Pharaohs.

First Act — Scene One

Palace of the *King* in Memphis. Officers, scribes, flabellum-bearers, guards, ensign-bearers, priests, etc. prepare themselves to see the *King*. *Ramphis* and *Rhadamès* are lost in the crowd. When the cortège disappears, *Amnèris* enters and detains *Rhadamès* with her look. The proud Princess *Amnèris* is deeply in love with the young Captain who does not respond because he loves another woman, *Aida*, the Ethiopian slave. *Rhadamès*'s coldness rouses *Amnèris*'s jealousy; she suspects a rival. At this moment *Aida* appears at the rear of the stage; the uneasiness of the two lovers makes the Princess suspect that the slave is her rival. An officer comes to announce that the *King* is about to betake himself into the great hall to receive a messenger. The *King* enters with his entourage; a *Herald* is introduced; he announces that the Ethiopians have violated the Egyptian frontiers and burned the cities, and that they are moving toward the capital of Egypt; *Amounasro*, an invincible warrior, is at their head. At the mention of this name, *Aida* falters; *Amounasro* is her father. The *King* orders an army to move against the enemy; *Rhadamès* will be its commander; he is to go to the Temple of Vulcan and have his weapons blessed. *Aida*, left alone, torn by her love for the two leaders who are to fight each other, expresses her grief. The scene changes.

Scene Two

Interior of the Temple of Vulcan; a dim light shines from above; colonnades, statues of divinities; the altar in the center of the stage; incense is burning on tripods. The college of priests is assembled. *Ramphis* stands at the foot of the altar steps; one hears the sound of harps and the voices of the priestesses; the priests recite the litanies. *Rhadamès* is brought in unarmed; as he advances toward the altar and the priestesses perform the sacred dance to the sound of the drums, a silver veil is placed over *Rhadamès*'s head, and *Ramphis* pronounces the rite of the invocation. *Rhadamès* vouches to conquer the enemy. The chants resume. To the sound of the voices and instruments *Ramphis* dresses *Rhadamès* in his armor.

Second Act

One of the entrances to the city of Thebes; a throne to the left, at the rear a triumphal portal. The populace has gathered. *Rhadamès* was victorious;

Amounasro has disappeared and is probably dead. Princess *Amnèris* enters; her love has grown with the triumph of her loved one, but jealousy assaults her once more; she wants to be certain of her suspicions; she summons *Aida* and, feigning sorrow, she announces to her that *Rhadamès* has died. *Aida* bursts out sobbing; her father and her lover are dead; life does not matter to her anymore. The Princess no longer doubts. *Rhadamès* loves *Aida*, and *Aida* will die. The *King* enters and ascends the throne; a distant sound announces the arrival of the troops who file in to the sound of fanfares; *Rhadamès*, carried in triumph, steps down before the *King*, who proclaims him savior of the nation and orders a feast to celebrate the victory. Egyptian dances are interpolated; when they are ended, the trumpets are heard and the populace disperses. The *King* is left alone with *Amnèris* and the maids, including *Aida*; he orders the prisoners to be brought in. *Amounasro* is among them in the costume of a simple officer. *Aida* sees him, cries out, and implores the *King* to have mercy on her father. *Amounasro* prevents his daughter from revealing his true identity and secretly tells her that he is in disguise in order to avenge himself. The *King* has mercy on the prisoner who will become one of the slaves assigned to guard the palace.

Third Act

Garden of the royal palace; the Nile in the distance. *Aida* is alone; *Rhadamès*'s love agitates her heart; she awaits *Rhadamès*; she wants to belong only to him. *Amounasro* appears, dressed as a slave; he tells his daughter that Ethiopia is rising once again and that *Rhadamès* will again move against their country; he reminds her of her birth, her mother in tears, the Gods of her ancestors; he knows that *Aida* loves *Rhadamès*; she should take advantage of this love to wrest from the Captain the secret of the march by the Egyptian troops; father and daughter will escape at night, *Rhadamès* will be captured and taken as a slave to Ethiopia where an eternal bond will join the two lovers. The father's pleading, the memories of childhood, the joy of possessing the man she loves deprive *Aida* of her senses. There follows a discussion between *Rhadamès* and *Aida*; she pleads and threatens and fascinates her lover, who, madly in love, throws himself at her feet; his country, the world, vows, honor — all he will sacrifice for the woman he loves. *Amounasro* appears. *Rhadamès* feels his devotion to duty reawakening; he trembles, he hesitates, he staggers; *Aida* supplicates . . . he is conquered. An ambush by the Ethiopians in the dark gorges near Napato [*sic*] can annihilate the Egyptian phalanxes in a few moments. *Amounasro*, *Aida*, and *Rhadamès* have barely left when suddenly the princess Amnèris reveals herself; she has heard everything; a terrible vengeance will be hers.

Fourth Act — Scene One

A hall in the palace of the *King* at Memphis; a pulpit at the rear. Officers of the household are speaking among themselves. Aware of the betrayal, the *King* himself has moved against the Ethiopians and won; he enters his palace triumphantly. *Amounasro* and *Aida* had fled the palace, but *Amounasro* was killed and there is no news of his daughter. *Rhadamès* awaits the punishment of his treason. The courtiers retire. *Amnèris* enters; she loves *Rhadamès* even more; he must come to her; if before the assembled judges he is willing to repudiate his crime, she will ask the *King* for mercy. *Rhadamès* is brought in; but *Amnèris*'s pleas and threats are futile; *Rhadamès* confesses his love for *Aida* and is happy to die for her. "Let justice takes its course," *Amnèris* cries. The priests and the judges, *Ramphis* at their head, file by upstage and disappear through a door that leads to the hall of judgments. *Rhadamès* is dragged away by the soldiers. *Amnèris* anxiously awaits the result of the judgment; the cortège reappears, *Ramphis* steps on the pulpit and pronounces the rites of anathema; *Rhadamès* will die an infamous death: he will be buried alive in one of the subterranean chambers of the temple of Vulcan.

Scene Two

Dark subterranean chamber. *Rhadamès* alone; the fatal stone has sealed his tomb and he awaits death; in his grief *Aida*'s image crosses his mind; cold and hunger create a vision; he thinks he sees *Aida*, pale and dying. Is it a dream? No. It really is his beloved, whom he presses to his heart. Anticipating the death reserved for her beloved, *Aida* had entered the subterranean chamber and for four days awaited the moment to die with him. Sorrow of *Rhadamès*; when the dying *Aida* falls upon a rock, one hears the vague sounds of the invocation of the priests, the harps, and the dance of the priestesses to the sound of the drums; the divine service is being celebrated in the temple. The last farewell dies on *Aida*'s lips; *Rhadamès*, dying, embraces only a corpse.

DOCUMENT X

Production Annotations

by
Giuseppe Verdi

In a copy of the first Italian libretto of *Aida* printed by Ricordi, Verdi sketched out some of his staging of the first three acts of the opera in ink, presumably before directing the rehearsals for the production at Parma in April 1872. No other libretto containing Verdi's handwritten stage directions of *Aida* is known.

This document was copied and edited by the Italian musicologist Gino Roncaglia "through the courtesy of a friend." Roncaglia did not disclose the location of the autograph, which he transcribed and partly reproduced in the form of a booklet published by the *Società Tipografica-Editrice Modenense* in 1956. See also Abbiati, III, pp. 546–552. Mary Jane Matz discusses some parts of Roncaglia's booklet in her article "Aida without tears," *Opera News*, 1957, 22, no. 4, pp. 4–8. See also Spike Hughes, "The look of the thing," *Opera News*, 1968, 33, no. 7, pp. 8–12.

In 1969 the Mary Flagler Cary Music Collection of the Pierpont Morgan Library in New York acquired this unique document and has kindly permitted me to reproduce it in its entirety for the first time. Translations of Verdi's handwritten annotations appear on the pages opposite. Some of Roncaglia's transcriptions and diagrams are incorrect and misleading. The following pages accurately show Verdi's intentions.

Apparently Verdi sketched out this staging only as a guide to himself and therefore did not have to describe every situation. His diagrams are meant to be seen from the viewpoint of the audience, but in his text he refers to the right and left of the actor.

~~~~~~

ATTO PRIMO

SCENA PRIMA.

Sala nel Palazzo del Re a Menfi.

A destra e a sinistra una colonnata con statue e arbusti in fiori. —
Grande porta nel fondo, da cui appariscono i tempii, i palazzi di Menfi
e le Piramidi.

Radamès - Ramfis   *in scena conversando fra loro, in faccia l'un dell'altro senza guardare*

RAMFIS

Si: corre voce che l'Etiope ardisca   *il pubblico —*
Sfidarci ancora, e del Nilo la valle
E Tebe minacciar — Fra breve un messo
Recherà il ver.

RADAMÈS   *prestarci molta attenzione alle parole di Ramfis*

La sacra
Iside consultasti?

RADAMES — RAMFIS   on stage conversing with each
other, facing one another without
looking at the audience.

RADAMES   pays close attention to Ramfis's words.

8

RAMFIS

   Ella ha nomato
Delle Egizie falangi
Il condottier supremo.

RADAMÈS

    Oh lui felice!

RAMFIS

(con intenzione, fissando Radamès)

Giovane e prode è desso — Ora, del Nume
Reco i decreti al Re.

       (esce)

RADAMÈS *solo.*

     Se quel guerriero
Io fossi! se il mio sogno
Si avverasse!... Un esercito di prodi
Da me guidato... e la vittoria... e il plauso
Di Menfi tutta! — E a te, mia dolce Aida,
Tornar di lauri cinto...
Dirti: per te ho pugnato e per te ho vinto!

Celeste Aida, forma divina,
Mistico serto di luce e fior;
Del mio pensiero tu sei regina,
Tu di mia vita sei lo splendor.
Il tuo bel cielo vorrei ridarti,
Le dolci brezze del patrio suol;
Un regal serto sul crin posarti,
Ergerti un trono vicino al sol.

Amneris
e detto.

AMNERIS

Quale insolita fiamma
Nel tuo sguardo! Di quale
Nobil fierezza ti balena il volto!

RADAMES

Oh lui felice!   turning slightly toward the
                                    audience, as in an aside.

Un esercito di prodi [. . .]   with enthusiasm.

AMNERIS   has heard the final words.
                                    Radames, who has turned and
                                    seen Amneris, makes a respectful
                                    low bow, raising his right hand
                                    almost to his forehead.

9

Degna di invidia oh ! quanto
Saria la donna il cui bramato aspetto
Tanta luce di gaudio in te destasse !

RADAMÈS

D' un sogno avventuroso
Si beava il mio cuore — Oggi, la Diva
Profferse il nome del guerrier che al campo
Le schiere egizie condurrà... S' io fossi
A tale onor prescelto...

AMNERIS

Nè un altro sogno mai
Più gentil... più soave...
Al cuore ti parlò ?... Non hai tu in Menfi
Desiderii... speranze ?...

RADAMÈS

Io !... (quale inchiesta !)

(Forse... l' arcano amore
Scoprì che m' arde in core...
Della sua schiava il nome
Mi lesse nel pensier !)

AMNERIS

(Oh ! guai se un altro amore
Ardesse a lui nel core !...
Guai se il mio sguardo penetra
Questo fatal mister !)

AMNERIS

    [. . .] *Non hai tu in Menfi*
Desiderii . . . speranze? . . .

she says these words with much
intent and smiles maliciously.

RADAMES

    Io! . . . (quale inchiesta!)

<u>Radames</u> does not understand
and moves downstage right, far
from Amneris.

10

Aida

e detti.

RADAMÈS   *(vedendo Aida)*

Dessa!

AMNERIS

(Ei si turba... e quale
Sguardo rivolse a lei!
Aida!.. a me rivale...
Forse saria costei?)

(dopo breve silenzio, volgendosi ad Aida)

Vieni, o diletta, appressati...
Schiava non sei nè ancella
Qui dove in dolce fascino
Io ti chiamai sorella...
Piangi?... delle tue lacrime
Svela il segreto a me.

AIDA

Ohimè! di guerra fremere
L'atroce grido io sento...
Per la infelice patria,
Per me... per voi pavento.

AMNERIS

Favelli il ver? nè s'agita
Più grave cura in te?

(Aida abbassa gli occhi e cerca dissimulare il proprio turbamento)

AMNERIS

(guardando Aida)

(Trema, o rea schiava, ah! trema
Ch'io nel tuo cor discenda!..
Trema che il ver mi apprenda
Quel pianto e quel rossor!)

RADAMES (seeing Aida)
   Dessa!

cannot suppress a faint indication of uneasiness.

AMNERIS
   (*Ei si turba* . . .)

Amneris is aware of this, and from this moment she is jealous.

   Vieni, o diletta, appressati . . .

with a fast change of expression and with a smile on her lips.

   (*Trema, o rea schiava* [. . .])

very far from one another.

ii

AIDA

(No, sull' afflitta patria
Non geme il cor soltanto ;
Quello ch' io verso è pianto
Di sventurato amor.)

RADAMÈS

(guardando Amneris)

(Nel volto a lei balena
Lo sdegno ed il sospetto...
Guai se l'arcano affetto
A noi leggesse in cor!)

Il Re, *preceduto dalle sue guardie e seguito da* **Ramfis,** *dai*
Ministri, Sacerdoti, Capitani, *ecc., ecc. Un Ufficiale*
di Palazzo, indi un **Messaggiero.**

IL RE

Alta cagion vi aduna.
O fidi Egizii, al vostro Re d'intorno.
Dal confin d' Etiópia un Messaggiero
Dianzi giungea — gravi novelle ei reca...
Vi piaccia udirlo...

(ad un Uffiziale)

Il Messaggier si avanzi!

MESSAGGIERO

Il sacro suolo dell' Egitto è invaso
Dai barbari Etiópi — i nostri campi
Fur devastati.... arse le messi... e baldi
Della facil vittoria, i predatori
Già marciano su Tebe...

THE KING
Alta cagion vi aduna [. . .]

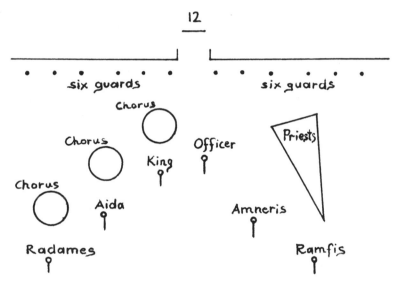

MESSENGER
Il sacro suolo [. . .]   bows before the King, raising his right
hand to his forehead. He has a bow in
his hand and a quiver at his side.

13

RADAMÈS

        Sien grazie ai Numi!
I miei voti fur paghi.

AMNERIS

       (Ei duce!)

AIDA

        (Io tremo.)

IL RE

Or, di Vulcano al tempio
Muovi o guerrier — Le sacre
Armi ti cingi e alla vittoria vola.

Su! del Nilo al sacro lido
Accorrete, Egizii eroi;
Da ogni cor prorompa il grido:
Guerra e morte allo stranier!

RAMFIS e SACERDOTI

Gloria ai Numi! ognun rammenti
Ch'essi reggono gli eventi —
Che in poter dei Numi solo
Stan le sorti dei guerrier.

MINISTRI - CAPITANI

Su! del Nilo al sacro lido
Sien barriera i nostri petti;
Non eccheggi che un sol grido:
Guerra e morte allo stranier!

RADAMÈS

Sacro fremito di gloria
Tutta l'anima mi investe —
Su! corriamo alla vittoria!
Guerra e morte allo stranier!

THE KING
Or, di Vulcano al tempio   makes a sign to Radames who
Muovi o guerrier [. . .]   bows and approaches Ramfis.

14

AMNERIS
(recando una bandiera e consegnandola a Radamès)

Di mia man ricevi, o duce,
Il vessillo glorïoso;
Ti sia guida, ti sia luce
Della gloria sul sentier.

AIDA

(Per chi piango? per chi prego?...
Qual poter m'avvince a lui!
Deggio amarlo... ed è costui
Un nemico... uno stranier!)

TUTTI

Guerra! guerra! sterminio all'invasor!
Va, Radamès, ritorna vincitor!
(escono tutti meno Aida)

AIDA

Ritorna vincitor!... E dal mio labbro
Uscì l'empia parola! — Vincitore
Del padre mio... di lui che impugna l'armi
Per me... per ridonarmi
Una patria, una reggia! e il nome illustre
Che qui celar mi è forza — Vincitore
De' miei fratelli... ond'io lo vegga, tinto
Del sangue amato, trionfar nel plauso
Dell'Egizie coorti!... E dietro il carro,
Un Re... mio padre... di catene avvinto!...

L'insana parola
O Numi sperdete!
Al seno d'un padre
La figlia rendete:
Struggete le squadre
Dei nostri oppressor!

ALL

    Guerra! guerra! [. . .]   at the final *Più mosso*, everyone moves
                                                  about rapidly downstage.

At the end of the Introduction the chorus separates, and the King, extending his hand to Amneris, crosses upstage with her and they exit into the right
wing, followed by the Messenger, the Officer, and the chorus. Ramfis makes
a sign to Radames, and together with all the Priests, they leave by the door in
the rear.

16

SCENA SECONDA.

Interno del Tempio di Vulcano a Menfi.

Una luce misteriosa scende dall'alto. - Una lunga fila di colonne, l'una all'altra addossate, si perde fra le tenebre. Statue di varie Divinità. Nel mezzo della scena, sovra un palco coperto da tappeti, sorge l'altare sormontato da emblemi sacri. Dai tripodi d'oro si innalza il fumo degli incensi.

Sacerdoti e **Sacerdotesse** — **Ramfis** ai piedi dell'altare — A suo tempo, **Radamès** — Si sente dall'interno il canto delle **Sacerdotesse** accompagnato dalle arpe.

SACERDOTESSE (nell'interno)

Immenso Fthà, del mondo
Spirito animator,
Noi ti invochiamo!

—

Immenso Fthà, del mondo
Spirto fecondator,
Noi ti invochiamo!

—

Fuoco increato, eterno,
Onde ebbe luce il sol,
Noi ti invochiamo!

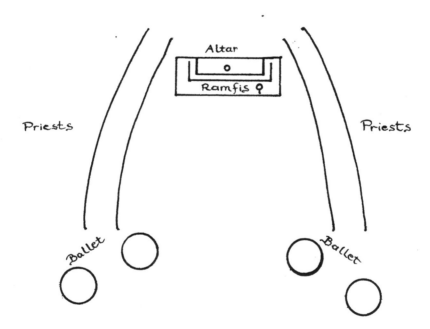

During the invocation, complete immobility is necessary, both of the Priests and the Priestesses. The hands on the chests but not crossed.

17

SACERDOTI

Tu che dal nulla hai tratto
L'onde, la terra e il ciel,
Noi ti invochiamo !

—

Nume che del tuo spirito
Sei figlio e genitor,
Noi ti invochiamo !

—

Vita dell' Universo ,
Mito di eterno amor ,
Noi ti invochiamo !

(Radamès viene introdotto senz' armi. Mentre va all'altare, le Sacer-
dotesse eseguiscono la danza sacra. Sul capo di Radamès vien steso
un velo d'argento.)

RAMFIS

Mortal, diletto ai Numi - A te fidate
Son d'Egitto le sorti. - Il sacro brando
Dal Dio temprato, per tua man diventi
Ai nemici terror, folgore, morte.

(volgendosi al Nume)

Nume, custode e vindice
Di questa sacra terra,
La mano tua distendi
Sovra l'egizio suol.

RADAMÈS

Nume, che duce ed arbitro
Sei d'ogni umana guerra,
Proteggi tu, difendi
D' Egitto il sacro suol!

(Mentre Radamès viene investito delle armi sacre, le Sacerdotesse
ed i Sacerdoti riprendono l'Inno religioso e la mistica danza).

At this point the dancing stops. Radames bows before the god. Ramfis commences the recitative *Mortal* on the steps of the altar. At the end, after the word *morte*, he hands the sword to Radames and walks downstage.

At the *pppp Noi t'invochiamo* all put their hands on their chests, as before, bowing to the ground. In replying to the offstage invocation of the Priestesses, the Priests are already in position, and on the second *Noi t'invochiamo* they move about extensively, put their hands on their chests, and remain in this position until the *fff Immenso Ftà*.

N. B. In tutta questa scena del
Giuramento si deve conservare la
più completa immobilità tanto
dai Sacerdoti che dalle Sacerdotesse
Ballerine. Tutti devono ascoltare
il canto religioso che viene dall'
interno. Tutti pure atteggiati e rivolti
verso il Dio Vibsano. Soltanto all'
ultime battute della terza Invocazione
le ballerine depongono i ventagli più
tiepidi e si preparano per incominciare
la danza sacra al suono di tre
flauti ed arpa — Radames entra
alle ultime battute prima della ripresa del
motivo. Al ballabile termina in modo
che le ballerine si trovan di nuovo aggruppate
intorno ai quattro tiepidi — Quando il corpo
musica si spinge al ff. della musica le
ballerine prenderanno i loro ventagli e lentamente
si ritireranno in fondo lungo l'ottava sul
gruppo finale — all'ultimo forte di tutti
immenso. Stà le ballerine intorno all'altare
agitando tutti i ventagli formando come un
solo immenso ventaglio

N.B. Throughout this Scene of the Invocation, absolute immobility must be maintained by the Priests as well as the Priestesses — ballerinas. All must listen to the religious chant that comes from offstage. All are turned toward and facing the God Vulcan. Only on the last bar of the third Invocation, the ballerinas put their fans on the tripods and prepare to begin the sacred dance to the sound of the three flutes in the orchestra. Radames enters a few bars before the refrain of the motive. The dance ends in such a way that the ballerinas are again grouped around the four tripods. When the chorus unites on the *ff* of the music, the ballerinas take their fans and quietly move to the rear, in front of the altar, for the final grouping. On everybody's last *forte Immenso Ftà* the ballerinas around the altar raise their fans, forming what appears to be a single enormous fan.

[Act II, Scene 1]

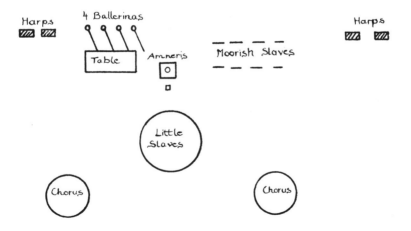

ATTO SECONDO

SCENA PRIMA.

Una Sala nell' Appartamento di Amneris.

Amneris *circondata dalle* **Schiave** *che l' abbigliano per la festa trionfale. Dai tripodi si eleva il profumo degli aromi. Giovani schiavi mori danzando agitano i ventagli di piume.*

SCHIAVE

Chi mai fra gli inni e i plausi
Erge alla gloria il vol,
Al par di un Dio terribile.
Fulgente al par del sol?
Vieni: sul crin ti piovano
Contesti ai lauri i fior;
Suonin di gloria i cantici
Coi cantici d'amor.

AMNERIS

(Vieni, amor mio, mi inebbria...
Fammi beato il cor!)

2

Amneris seated on a large, very tall chair,
about 1.60 m. high. Its seat is about 90 cm.,
the footrest about 40 cm. high.[1]

22

SCHIAVE

Or, dove son le barbare
Orde dello stranier?
Siccome nebbia sparvero
Al soffio del guerrier.
Vieni: di gloria il premio
Raccogli, o vincitor;
T'arrise la vittoria,
T'arriderà l' amor.

AMNERIS

(Vieni, amor mio, ravvivami
D'un caro accento ancor!)

Silenzio! Aida verso noi si avanza...
Figlia dei vinti, il suo dolor mi è sacro.
(ad un cenno di Amneris tutti si allontanano)
Nel rivederla, il dubbio
Atroce in me si desta...
Il mistero fatal si squarci alfine!

—————

Amneris - Aida.

AMNERIS
(ad Aida con simulata amorevolezza)

Fu la sorte dell'armi a' tuoi funesta,
Povera Aida! — Il lutto
Che ti pesa sul cor teco divido.
Io son l'amica tua...
Tutto da me tu avrai — vivrai felice!

AIDA

Felice esser poss'io
Lungi dal suol natio... qui dove ignota
M'è la sorte del padre e dei fratelli?...

AMNERIS

Silenzio! Aida verso noi si avanza . . .
Figlia dei vinti, il suo dolor mi è sacro.
(at a sign from Amneris all withdraw.)   at this sign everyone
starts to go to the left,
and Aida enters carrying
the crown, which she
places on the table.

26

SCENA SECONDA.

Uno degli ingressi della Città di Tebe.

Sul davanti un gruppo di palme. A destra il tempio di Ammone - a sinistra un trono sormontato da un baldacchino di porpora. - Nel fondo
una porta trionfale. — La scena è ingombra di popolo.

Entra **il Re,** *seguito dai* **Ministri, Sacerdoti,** *Capitani, Flabelliferi, Porta insegne, ecc., ecc. Quindi,* **Amneris** *con*
Aida e Schiave - Il Re *va a sedere sul trono.* **Amneris**
prende posto alla sinistra del **Re.**

POPOLO

Gloria all'Egitto e ad Iside
Che il sacro suol protegge;
Al Re che il Delta regge
Inni festosi alziam!
Vieni, o guerriero vindice,
Vieni a gioir con noi;
Sul passo degli eroi
I lauri e i fior versiam!

DONNE

S'intrecci il loto al lauro
Sul crin dei vincitori;
Nembo gentil di fiori
Stenda sull'armi un vel.
Danziam, fanciulle egizie,
Le mistiche carole,
Come d'intorno al sole
Danzano gli astri in ciel!

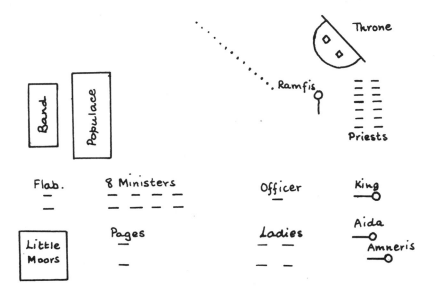

As the scene changes a few of the populace
are on the stage. From various points and
in small groups enter
    first the Priests
    then the King
    the King's Officer
    then the ministers
    two flabellum bearers
    8 ministers (supers)
As the women's chorus begins to sing, Amneris enters,
followed by Aida, then 4 or 6 women, 2 pages,
little Moorish slaves in a group.

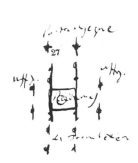

SACERDOTI

Della vittoria agli arbitri
Supremi il guardo ergete;
Grazie agli Dei rendete
Nel fortunato dì.
Così per noi di gloria
Sia l'avvenir segnato,
Nè mai ci colga il fato
Che i barbari colpì.

*(Le truppe Egizie precedute dalle fanfare sfilano dinanzi al Re
- Seguono i carri di guerra, le insegne, i vasi sacri, le statue
degli Dei - Un drappello di danzatrici che recano i tesori dei
vinti - Da ultimo, Radamès, sotto un baldacchino portato da do-
dici uffiziali.)*

IL RE

(che scende dal trono per abbracciare Radamès)

Salvator della patria; io ti saluto.
Vieni, e mia figlia di sua man ti porga
Il serto trionfale.

*(Radamès si inchina davanti Amneris che gli
porge la corona)*

IL RE   *(a Radamès)*

Ora, a me chiedi
Quanto più brami. Nulla a te negato
Sarà in tal dì - lo giuro
Per la corona mia, pei sacri Numi.

RADAMÈS

Concedi in pria che innanzi a te sien tratti
I prigionier...
*(entrano fra le guardie i prigionieri Etiopi, ultimo Amonasro,
vestito da uffiziale)*

AIDA

Che veggo!... Egli?... mio padre!

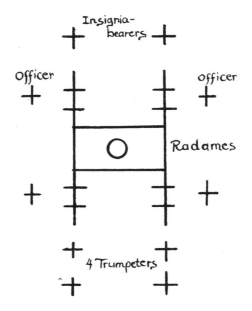

[illegible]

[illegible]

28

TUTTI

Suo padre!

AMNERIS

In poter nostro!...

           AIDA   *(abbracciando il padre)*

Tu ! Prigionier!

          AMONASRO   *(piano ad Aida)*

Non mi tradir!

         IL RE   .   *(ad Amonasro)*

               Ti appressa...

Dunque... tu sei?...

         AMONASRO

              Suo padre — Anch'io pugnai...
Vinti noi fummo e morte invan cercai.

          (accennando alla divisa che lo veste)

Questa assisa ch'io vesto vi dica
Che il mio Re, la mia patria ho difeso;
Fu la sorte a nostr'armi nemica...
Tornò vano dei forti l'ardir.
Al mio piè nella polve disteso
Giacque il Re da più colpi trafitto;
Se l'amor della patria è delitto
Siam rei tutti, siam pronti a morir!

      (volgendosi al Re con accento supplichevole)

Ma tu, o Re, tu signore possente,
A costoro ti volgi clemente...
Oggi noi siam percossi dal fato,
Doman voi potria il fato colpir.

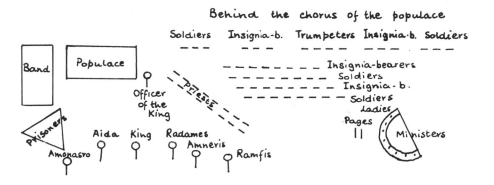

As he recounts his story, Amonasro takes a step toward the King and is situated like this

29

AIDA, PRIGIONIERI, SCHIAVE

Si: dai Numi percossi noi siamo;
Tua pietà, tua clemenza imploriamo;
Ah! giammai di soffrir vi sia dato
Ciò che in oggi n'è dato soffrir!

RAMFIS, SACERDOTI

Struggi, o Re, queste ciurme feroci,
Chiudi il core alle perfide voci.
Fur dai Numi votati alla morte,
Si compisca dei Numi il voler!

POPOLO

Sacerdoti, gli sdegni placate,
L'umil prece dei vinti ascoltate;
E tu, o Re, tu possente, tu forte,
A clemenza dischiudi il pensier.

RADAMÈS   *(fissando Aida)*

(Il dolor che in quel volto favella
Al mio sguardo la rende più bella;
Ogni stilla del pianto adorato
Nel mio petto ravviva l'amor.)

AMNERIS

(Quali sguardi sovr'essa ha rivolti!
Di qual fiamma balenano i volti!
E a tal sorte serbata son io?...
La vendetta mi rugge nel cor.)

IL RE

Or che fausti ne arridon gli eventi
A costoro mostriamci clementi;
La pietà sale ai Numi gradita
E **rafferma** dei Prenci il poter.

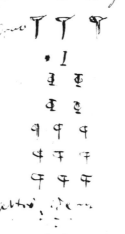

First the Priests

2. King, Officer, <u>8</u>
   ministers, 2 flabellum-bearers

3. Amneris:
   Aida, 4 Ladies,
   2 Pages, Little Moors

The March, etc.
3   Trumpeters
1   Officer
4   Insignia-bearers
9   Soldiers with axes

Trump. [?]

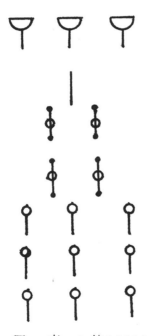

The others the same

32

RADAMÈS

(D'avverso Nume il folgore
Sul capo mio discende...
Ah no ! d' Egitto il soglio
Non val d'Aida il cor.)

AMNERIS

(Dall' inatteso giubilo
Inebbbriata io sono ;
Tutti in un dì si compiono
I sogni del mio cor.)

AMONASRO   (ad Aida)

Fa cor: della tua patria
I lieti eventi aspetta ;
Per noi della vendetta
Già prossimo è l'albor.

POPOLO

Gloria all' Egitto e ad Iside
Che il sacro suol difende!
S' intrecci il loto al lauro
Sul crin del vincitor!

AMONASRO

Fa cor: della tua patria [. . .]   After this <u>solo</u> sung to Aida in a low
voice, at the moment when the <u>chorus</u>
takes up the <u>Hymn</u> once more, the
entire company onstage takes four
steps forward. Only the chorus and
artists must raise their arms on *Gloria
ad Iside*.
All the <u>insignia-bearers</u> raise their
insignia very high, and the soldiers
raise their weapons. The eight ministers on the <u>platform</u> of the throne,
together with the two flabellum-
bearers, raise their fans. The four
ladies or the two pages occupy the
steps of the throne.

[*Verdi's writing on the left side of this page at the end of the printed text is
illegible.*]

1. – Esaminare il Trono di Radames...

2. Far fare la Corona ~~del Augusto~~ colla quale arrivati incorona Radames. –

3. Avvertire che le *Insegne* della Marcia sieno distribuite in modo che alla fine dell'Inno finale non abbino ~~od~~ opera le più alte da un lato, e le più basse dall'altro, come avvenne ieri sera

4. Esaminare la spada da Vulcano che mi sembra meschina e senza carattere.

5. Sarebbe bene nel Terzo carro di guerra cacciarvi alla rinfusa armi rotte, scudi, lance et et —

6. Oltre l'Invocazione provare anche le prete battute del Duetto finale

7. L'Uffiziale del Re (nel Finale secondo) starà fra il Coro del Popolo e quello dei Sacerdoti

[Between the second and third acts in the printed libretto a sheet of paper is inserted, which contains the following notes by Verdi.]

1. Examine the throne of Radames . . .
2. Have the crown made with which Amneris crowns Radames.
3. Be sure that the insignia for the march are distributed in such a way that at the end of the final hymn the tallest are not all on one side, and the smallest all on the other, as happened last night.
4. Examine the sword of Vulcan, which seems to me cheap and without character.
5. It would be well to throw broken weapons, shields, spears, etc., helter-skelter into the third war chariot.
6. In addition to the Invocation, also rehearse the few bars of the final duet.
7. In the finale of the second act, the King's Officer will stand between the chorus of the populace and that of the Priests.

ATTO TERZO

Le Rive del Nilo.

Roccie di granito fra cui crescono dei palmizii. Sul vertice delle roccie il tempio d'Iside per metà nascosto tra le fronde. È notte stellata. Splendore di luna.

CORO   (nel tempio)

O tu che sei d'Osiride
Madre immortale e sposa,
Diva che i casti palpiti
Desti agli umani in cor;
Soccorri a noi pietosa,
Madre d'eterno amor.
(Da una barca che approda alla riva, discendono Amneris, Ramfis, alcune donne coperte da fitto velo e Guardie)

RAMFIS   (ad Amneris)

Vieni d'Iside al tempio - alla vigilia
Delle tue nozze, implora
Della Diva il favore - Iside legge
Dei mortali nel cuore - ogni mistero
Degli umani a lei noto.

(Amneris, Ramfis, some women covered
by thick veils, and guards descend
from a boat that lands at the shore.)   two women and 4 guards

38

AMONASRO

Non fia che tardi — In armi ora si desta
Il popol nostro — tutto pronto è già...
Vittoria avrem... Solo a saper mi resta
Qual sentiero il nemico seguirà...

AIDA

Chi scoprirlo potria? chi mai?

AMONASRO

Da un rapido sguardo attorno di Montenari ? Ò diapasii

Tu stessa!

AIDA

Io!...

AMONASRO

Radamès so che qui attendi... Ei t'ama...
Ei conduce gli Egizii... Intendi?...

AIDA

Orrore!
Che mi consigli tu? No! no! giammai!

AMONASRO   *(con impeto selvaggio)*

Su, dunque! sorgete
Egizie coorti!
Col fuoco struggete
Le nostre città...
Spargete il terrore,
Le stragi, le morti...
Al vostro furore
Più freno non v'ha.

AIDA

Ah padre!...

AMONASRO   *(respingendola)*

Mia figlia
Ti chiami!...

AIDA   *(atterrita e supplichevole)*

Pietà!

AMONASRO   looks about quickly, and moving a few feet
   Tu stessa!   away

39

AMONASRO

Flutti di sangue scorrono
Sulle città dei vinti...
Vedi?... dai negri vortici
Si levano gli estinti...
Ti additan essi e gridano:
Per te la patria muor!

AIDA

Pietà !...

AMONASRO

Una larva orribile
Fra l'ombre a noi s'affaccia...
Trema! le scarne braccia
Sul capo tuo levò...
Tua madre ell'è... ravvisala...
Ti maledice...

AIDA   *(nel massimo terrore)*

Ah! no!...
Padre...

AMONASRO   *(respingendola)*

Va, indegna! non sei mia prole...
Dei Faraoni tu sei la schiava.

AIDA

Padre, a costoro schiava io non sono...
Non maledirmi... non imprecarmi...
Tua figlia ancora potrai chiamarmi...
Della mia patria degna sarò.

AMONASRO

Pensa che un popolo, vinto, straziato
Per te soltanto risorger può...

AMONASRO
Una larva orribile [. . .]   suddenly seizes Aida by
                                                the left arm[2]

AMONASRO (pushing her back)   with such violence that
Va, indegna! non sei mia prole . . .   he throws her to the
Dei Faraoni tu sei la schiava.   ground.

AIDA
[. . .] *Della mia patria degna sarò.*   Amonasro gradually
                                                calms down, looks at
                                                his daughter, and says
                                                solemnly

AMONASRO
Pensa che un popolo, vinto, straziato [. . .]

40

AIDA

O patria! o patria... quanto mi costi!

AMONASRO

Coraggio! ei giunge... là tutto udrò...

(si nasconde fra i palmizii)

———————

Radamès - Aida

RADAMÈS

Pur ti riveggo, mia dolce Aida...

AIDA

Ti arresta, vanne... che speri ancor?

RADAMÈS

A te dappresso l'amor mi guida.

AIDA

Te i riti attendono d'un altro amor.
D'Amneris sposo...

RADAMÈS

Che parli mai?...
Te sola, Aida, te deggio amar.
Gli Dei mi ascoltano... tu mia sarai...

AIDA

D'uno spergiuro non ti macchiar!
Prode t'amai, non t'amerei spergiuro.

RADAMÈS

Dell'amor mio dubiti, Aida?

AIDA

O patria! o patria . . . quanto mi costi!

AMONASRO

Coraggio! ei giunge . . . là tutto udrò . . .

has meanwhile looked to the right and seeing Radames approaching he runs to Aida.

43

AIDA

Va... va... ti attende all' ara
Amneris...

RADAMÈS

No!... giammai!...

AIDA

Giammai, dicesti?

Allor piombi la scure
Su me, sul padre mio...

RADAMÈS

Ah no! fuggiamo!

(con appassionata risoluzione)
Sì: fuggiam da queste mura,
Al deserto insiem fuggiamo;
Qui sol regna la sventura,
Là si schiude un ciel d'amor.
I deserti interminati
A noi talamo saranno,
Su noi gli astri brilleranno
Di più limpido fulgor.

AIDA

Nella terra avventurata
De' miei padri, il ciel ne attende;
Ivi l'aura è imbalsamata,
Ivi il suolo è aromi e fior.
Fresche valli e verdi prati
A noi talamo saranno,
Su noi gli astri brilleranno
Di più limpido fulgor.

AIDA - RADAMÈS

Vieni meco - insiem fuggiamo
Questa terra di dolor -
Vieni meco - io t'amo, io t'amo!
A noi duce fia l'amor.

(si allontanano rapidamente)

Only on this <u>resolve</u> by Radames does Aida cheer up
and with all the enthusiasm of love, etc., etc.

44

AIDA   *(arrestandosi all'improvviso)*

Ma, dimmi : per qual via
Eviterem le schiere
Degli armati?

RADAMÈS

    Il sentier scelto dai nostri
A piombar sul nemico fia deserto
Fino a domani...

AIDA

    E quel sentier?...

RADAMÈS

        Le gole

Di Nàpata...

Amonasro - Aida - Radamès.

AMONASRO

    Di Nàpata le gole!
Ivi saranno i miei...

RADAMÈS

    Oh! chi ci ascolta?..

AMONASRO

D'Aida il padre e degli Etiopi il Re.

RADAMÈS   *(agitatissimo)*

Tu! Amonasro!... tu il Re? Numi! che dissi?
No!... non è ver!... sogno... delirio e questo...

RADAMES

> *Il sentier scelto dai nostri*
> *A piombar sul nemico fia deserto*
> *Fino a domani . . .*

AIDA

> *E quel sentier? . . .*

RADAMES

> *Le gole*
> *Di Nápata . . .*

Here Amonasro
appears cautiously
and listens to the
last words

AMONASRO

> *Di Nápata le gole!*
> *Ivi saranno i miei . . .*

Radames backs up
three or four steps
and moves down-
stage right, and
they will be situ-
ated like this

RADAMES

> *Oh! chi ci ascolta? . . .*

AMONASRO

> *D' Aida il padre e degli Etiopi il Re.*

RADAMES (most agitated)

> *Tu! Amonasro! . . . tu il Re?*
> *Numi! che dissi?*
> *No! . . . non è ver! . . . sogno . . .*
> *delirio è questo . . .*

Meanwhile Amon-
asro has made a
sign to Aida to take
heart and moves
downstage left.

45

AIDA

Ah no! ti calma... ascoltami,
All'amor mio t'affida.

AMONASRO

A te l'amor d'Aida
Un soglio innalzerà.

RADAMÈS

Per te tradii la patria!
Io son disonorato...

AMONASRO

No : tu non sei colpevole –
Era voler del fato...
Vieni: oltre il Nil ne attendono
I prodi a noi devoti,
Là del tuo core i voti
Coronerà l' amor.

Amneris *dal tempio*, indi **Ramfis, Sacerdoti,**
Guardie, e detti.

AMNERIS

Traditor !

AIDA

La mia rivale!...

AMONASRO
(avventandosi ad Amneris con un pugnale)

Vieni a strugger l'opra mia !
Muori !...

Aida

AIDA

Ah no! ti calma . . . ascoltami [. . .]

AMONASRO

seizes Radames by the arm, and Radames offers no resistance	[. . .] + *Vieni: oltre il Nil ne attendono i prodi a noi devoti . . .*	+ At this point Amneris [appears] and notices the three from above. She cannot believe her eyes. She comes partway down the platform. When Amneris cries out, Radames frees himself from Amonasro, who runs abruptly to his daughter.

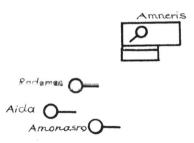

On the word *Muori* he is about
to hurl himself with a dagger
at Amneris, but Radames
steps between them.

46

RADAMÈS   *(frapponendosi)*

Arresta , insano!...

AMONASRO

Oh rabbia !

RAMFIS

Guardie, olà !

RADAMÈS   *(ad Aida e Amonasro)*

Presto !... fuggite !...

AMONASRO   *(trascinando Aida)*

Vieni , o figlia!

RAMFIS   *(alle Guardie)*

Li inseguite !

RADAMÈS   *(a Ramfis)*

Sacerdote, io resto a te.

RADAMES (stepping between them)
Arresta, insano! . . .

At this moment Ramfis appears
and calls for the guards

RAMFIS (to the guards)
Li inseguite!

who have come out[3] of the
temple, run after Amonasro and Aida
Only Amneris, Radames, and Ramfis
remain onstage. Radames approaches
them and, turning to Ramfis, he
says firmly to him *Sacerdote*, etc.

NOTES TO DOCUMENT X

1. See Document XII, pp. 573–74.
2. The two struck-out words are illegible.
3. The struck-out words on this page are illegible.

DOCUMENT XI

Production Notes
by
Franco Faccio

Faccio probably made these notes, previously unpublished, at the time of the first *Aida* production at La Scala in February and March 1872. They apparently served him for the productions he directed in Padua (1872) and Trieste (1873).

(*Right* and *left* always of the spectator)
Memorandum
for the *mise-en-scène* of *Aida*

First Act: Ramfis — Radamès. After the dialogue Ramfis exits through the door located upstage a little to the left. Later Amneris from the right wing. Aida later from the same side. Entrance of the King from the left wings, preceded by the guards and followed by Ramfis, priests, ministers, captains, etc.

 A flabellum-bearer goes to receive the Messenger who enters from the right wings. On the *stretta* of *Guerra, guerra* all rush downstage; then they leave in the same manner in which they entered. Aida alone, then an *a vista* change of scene to the Temple of Vulcan.

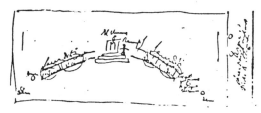 Harps and priestesses remain behind the columns.

After the litany follows the dance in which the ceremony of Radamés's investiture takes place. After the words *Folgore! Morte!*, repeated by the chorus during the four bars of the orchestra preparing the g minor, all come downstage in the following manner:

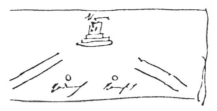

The priestesses withdraw to prepare themselves for the final grouping. At every musical entrance the four groups of the chorus separately take a step forward toward the God, and at the *messa di voce* (D)[1] preceding the reprise of the prayer all unite in a single line downstage. When the priestess begins to sing offstage, they open up as before and turn toward the god, allowing us to see the group of dancers (who conceal the fans) formed on the altar steps. At the second *Immenso Fthà!* all bow and remain in that attitude until Ramfis and Radames's *ff* invocation, to which they respond by raising their arms. The dancers extend their fans.

The curtain falls.

Second Act: Small scene arranged in the following manner:

The chorus ladies then group themselves upstage to make room for the dance of the little Moors, after which Amneris dismisses all, remaining alone with Aida who enters from the left wing. The duet follows, after which the scene changes *a vista*. At the opening of the curtain, the populace, already on stage, moves downstage left, concealing from the spectators the platform for the stageband. At the *crescendo* of the march, enter Ramfis and the priests; they place themselves next to the throne located half way up to the right. At the other *crescendo*, the King enters with his entourage and takes his place on the covered throne. On the women's *ritornello* Amneris enters, followed by Aida, etc., and takes her place to the right of the King. Then through the triumphal arch in the background enter the trumpeters, followed by a squad of victors who march past the King and turn to the left. Other trumpeters and other victors follow. Then the dancers, then the chariots of war, etc., and at the end of the march, Radames under a canopy carried by twelve officers. Thus the scene is arranged as follows:

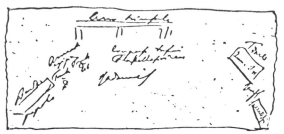

The Ethiopian prisoners enter from upstage and move downstage left in front of the populace. This is the arrangement during the *Adagio concertato*:

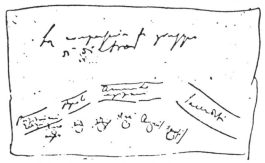

At the final reprise of the three strophes, the insignia are raised, and all move still further downstage. The curtain falls.

Third Act: The boat comes to a landing from the left: Ramfis, Amneris, two veiled women, two guards alight. All enter the Temple, which is located to the right. Do not forget the concertina to support the offstage chorus. Aida from the left; Amonasro from the left, and then he hides behind the palm trees on the right; Radames from the left; at the end of the act: Amneris, Ramfis, priests, guards of the Temple of Isis.

Fourth Act: The set has an opening to the left, through which the priests eventually enter on their way to Radames's judgment, an opening in the center leading to the subterranean chamber, and a small opening to the right that leads to Radamès's prison. Between the opening on the right and the one in the center, an idol atop a pedestal on which Amneris is sadly leaning at the opening of the curtain. N.B. The steps from which Ramfis and the priests descend (after the Amneris-Radamès duet) must be placed like this

 stage floor

so that their descent may be visible to the spectators. As soon as the scene ends, the gas of the chandelier in the auditorium must be turned down immediately.[2] The scene change is made *a vista*.

Arrangement of the last scene:

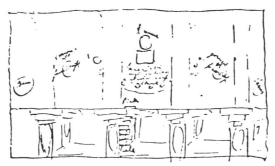

At the opening of the curtain Radames is seated on the steps of the staircase, turned toward the audience; two priests in the temple are still in the process of sealing the stone above the subterranean chamber. The priests rise when the priestesses (concealed behind the pillars of the subterranean chamber so that they can see the conductor) intone the religious chant. Then they remain immobile for the rest of the scene. The curtain falls slowly.

NOTES TO DOCUMENT XI

1. The almost imperceptible *portamento* or slide that precedes the resolution to the E flat major chord.

2. Until the early twentieth century houselights were not extinguished during performances in Italian theatres. However, they were turned down when darkness was required onstage, as in the last scene of *Aida*. Verdi's letter to Arrivabene of 5 February 1876, in which he remarks that in Vienna "the audience (which sits in the dark during the performance) sleeps or is bored," points up the customs inspired by Richard Wagner. "The introduction of gas to replace candles, which occurred in most of the larger theatres during the 1870s," George Martin writes in *Verdi: His Music, Life and Times* (New York: Dodd, Mead, 1963), p. 479, "was a major revolution in theatre construction and affected even the kind of operas composed. For the first time the house lights could easily be dimmed and the auditorium made much darker than the stage. In another twenty years electricity would make it possible to put the auditorium in total darkness and relight it easily and safely. Dimming the house lights greatly emphasized the musical side of a performance over the social parade connected with it. Under candles, which once lit had to remain so, the audience visited in boxes for an act or two because they could be seen the whole time. The opera house was as much a social as musical center of the city. Gas and later electricity changed this. With the audience sitting in darkness unmusical Kings and Emperors decided the intermission was simply not worth the agony of the music, and society began to go elsewhere, to show itself off where it could be seen. Music lovers rejoiced, for the gabbling noise of society had always been infuriating. But the cost was great, and part of the financial difficulty of the opera houses in Italy arose from the fact that they were losing part of their audience. Verdi's operas reflect the change and span it. His early operas were lit by candle, *Aida* by gas, and *Falstaff*, his last, by electricity."

DOCUMENT XII

Production Book

by
Giulio Ricordi

Giulio Ricordi published this production book after the *Aida* premiere, in which he had assisted Verdi at La Scala in 1872.

The House of Ricordi has no record of these pages, which have no publication date and have been out of print for many years.

This document reflects the style and taste of times past and, therefore, in spite of imperfections — including inconsistent capitalization — it should be of lasting interest. It is published here for the first time in English translation.

Production Book
for the opera

AIDA

Verses by A. Ghislanzoni
Music by
G. Verdi

compiled and arranged according to the production
of the Teatro alla Scala

by
Giulio Ricordi

CAST

THE KING — about 45 years: majestic, imposing bearing.

AMNERIS, his daughter — 20 years: very vivacious, impetuous, impressionable.

AIDA, Ethiopian slave: olive, dark reddish skin [*sic*] — 20 years: love, submission, sweetness are her principal qualities.

RADAMES, captain of the guards — 24 years: enthusiastic character.

RAMFIS, High Priest — 50 years: strong-minded, autocratic, cruel, majestic
  bearing.
AMONASRO, King of Ethiopia and Aida's father: olive, dark reddish skin — 40
  years: indomitable warrior, full of love for his country, impetuous, violent
  character.

The directions are intended to be given to the right and left of the stage
facing the auditorium.

Impress upon the chorus, especially the men, that they must not appear as
an insignificant mass of people, but that each of them represents a personality
and must act as such; he must move on his own account, according to his own
feelings, preserving with the others only a certain unity of action to ensure the
best musical execution.

Explanation of Signs

♀ ACTOR   Arrows indicate the direction
                                  in which the characters should face.

♀ CHORUS

♀ BALLET

♀ SUPERS etc.

☿ BAND

•-•-•-•-•→   Indicates a cross made on the stage before taking a
             certain position.

∿∿∿∿→   Indicates a cross to be made.

FIRST ACT
First Scene

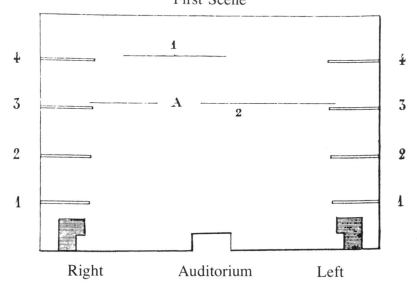

Right   Auditorium   Left

Hall in the Palace of the King at Memphis[1]

To the right and left a colonnade with statues and with shrubbery in bloom. Large door in the background through which appear the temples, palaces of Memphis, and the pyramids.

1. Backdrop representing the pyramids in the distance; the temples and the palaces of Memphis are closer.

2. Large drop representing a colonnade with statues and with shrubbery in bloom: very rich and lively colors and a great deal of light.

A. Large open doorway.

———————

The curtain rises on the next to last bar of the prelude.

Ramfis and Radamès are very far downstage, engaged in conversation. The beginning of the recitative *Sì: corre voce che l'Etiope ardisca* must appear as a continuation of their discussion.

All of Ramfis's words must be spoken with the intention of raising Radamès's joyous hopes, the latter paying the greatest attention to what the

High Priest has to say. Therefore the two characters must not look at the audience, but must observe each other while standing in diagonal positions.

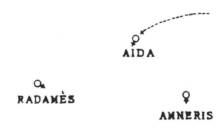

On the words *Oh lui felice!* Radamès turns toward the audience; as soon as he has said *Reco i decreti al Re*, Ramfis exits to the right into the chambers of the King. Radamès remains still and speaks his recitative becoming increasingly excited. On the words *Per te ho pugnato e per te ho vinto!*, which he says very forcefully, he takes two steps downstage. Then he sings the *romanza "Celeste Aida"* with great passion.

At the commencement of the ALLEGRO ASSAI MODERATO in B flat, Amneris enters from the left rear; perceiving Radamès, she expresses satisfaction and moves hastily toward him; he turns at the same time and, seeing Amneris, makes a respectful low bow, raising his right hand almost to his forehead. Amneris speaks the recitative with much grace, gazing fixedly at Radamès; she must say *Non hai tu in Menfi desideri . . . speranze? . . .* with obvious intent, smiling maliciously and advancing a little toward Radamès.

Perturbed by this question, Radamès withdraws slightly from Amneris, and both sing the ALLEGRO AGITATO E PRESTO in e minor with great excitement.

When the ANDANTE MOSSO in G begins, Aida enters from the left rear; Radamès perceives her and cannot suppress a faint indication of uneasiness, exclaiming: *Dessa!* Amneris is aware of this and says, at first suspiciously, *Ei si turba . . .*; but her suspicion changes almost to certainty and, taking a step downstage, she exclaims with concentrated anger: *a me rivale . . . forse saria costei? . . .*

AIDA

RADAMÈS   AMNERIS

Meanwhile Aida has come almost to center stage; with a sudden change of expression Amneris turns to Aida and, the anger gone from her face and with a smile on her lips, says to her *Vieni, o diletta, appressati . . .* Aida comes closer, bowing, but not without having first glanced amorously at Radamès, who tries to hide his feelings.

AIDA

RADAMÈS   AMNERIS

After the words *nè s'agita più grave cura in te?*, Amneris turns toward the audience and takes a step downstage. Aida also steps forward and so does Radamès, the one quite apart from the other.

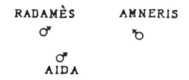

RADAMÈS   AMNERIS

AIDA

In this position they sing the ensemble of the little ALLEGRO AGITATO E PRESTO trio. The moment it ends the trumpets sound, while the three characters, aware of the arrival of the King, turn around. Amneris moves toward her father to the left, Aida and Radames withdraw to the right.

RADAMÈS   AMNERIS

AIDA

As soon as the trumpets sound, the Priests enter in double file through door A. Diagonally crossing the stage, they group themselves on the left.

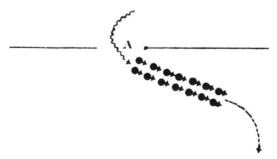

Immediately thereafter, twelve guards enter from the right rear and come to stand at attention at the sides of door A; following them enter in order the King, Ramfis, the Officer of the King, Ministers, Captains, etc. etc. All the artists and the entire chorus must be well placed in the wings, the Priests upstage of the large drop, so they can make quick and orderly entrances in the short time allowed by the music; at the end of the ♫ chord all must be grouped as follows:

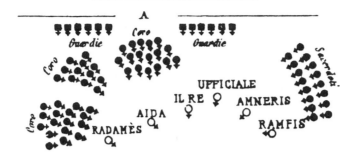

The stage director must agree with the chorus master on a good distribution of the voices in the three choral groups; these groups must be quite different and therefore stand approximately three feet apart from each other. All the choristers must pay serious attention to the words of the King. The stage director must impress on them that they represent elevated personalities and not just any mass of sonorous voices; by the same token, he must not let them make the same gestures and movements but must have each of them naturally express his own feelings. In the beginning it will not be easy to accomplish this, but by effectively playing on their pride, by clearly explaining to them their actions and the various sentiments that motivate them, one will succeed in having a perfect ensemble, which will attract the attention and approval of the audience.

The King turns to the officer, telling him *Il messaggier si avanzi!* The officer bows, exits to the left and reenters immediately, followed by the Messenger. Meanwhile everyone has turned a little in the direction of the officer's exit, anxious to see the Messenger, who advances toward the King and salutes him, bowing and raising his right hand to his forehead. The Messenger has a bow in his hand and carries a quiver at his side; as soon as he has saluted the King, he begins his account *Il sacro suolo.* He is quite perturbed but tells his story clearly. At the words *i predatori già marciano su Tebe . . .* all express surprise, some by raising their hands, others by turning to their companions and angrily shouting *Ed osan tanto!* The entire chorus must realize that they must pay the greatest attention to this account, and therefore EVERYONE'S eyes must be turned toward the Messenger.

At the words of the King, *Sì: guerra e morte il nostro grido sia*, the various groups of the chorus respond forcefully *Guerra!* At this word, all groups turn to the King, extending their right arms toward him and taking very small steps forward. When the King indicates that Radamès is the supreme commander, all are surprised; the various groups of the chorus exclaim the word *Radamès* and repeat it *mezza voce*, but with very clear pronunciation. While saying *Radamès*, several members of the various groups turn slightly to each other, imparting this news; others point with a small motion of the hand at Radamès. The choral groups are placed so that the word *Radamès* is pronounced first by those on the right, then by those on the side, and last by those in the rear, i.e. by the first and second tenors, the first basses, the second basses.

At the same time, Aida and Amneris express surprise at the unexpected news, animated by various and contrasting sentiments. The stage director should pay careful attention to this detail, especially concerning the chorus. If properly executed, this entire scene makes the most realistic impression.

At the words *Le sacre armi ti cingi e alla vittoria vola*, the King motions Radamès to place himself next to Ramfis; Radamès bows and, crossing the stage, assumes a position near Ramfis. The characters will be placed thus

The King turns to his entourage and forcefully intones the Hymn of War, *Su! del Nilo al sacro lido*. Ramfis responds, taking a step toward the King, and then the chorus enthusiastically takes up the hymn, moving another step forward. Aida and Radamès cross rather far downstage; she says with much passion and sobbing *Per chi piango? per chi prego?*; he joyfully exclaims *Sacro fremito di guerra*. Meanwhile Amneris crosses upstage, exiting to the left, where she will take the flag and then return onstage in time to intone *Di mia man ricevi, o duce*, while surrendering the flag to Radamès. Then all forcefully intone the hymn while taking another step forward. One must take care, however, that all these movements should not be too obvious; and the chorus must not crowd the actors. Also, the latter must not be too close to the footlights because of the general movement at the end of the piece. At the word *Guerra!* in the PIÙ MOSSO, the various groups in turn extend their hands to swear. Precisely at the end of the 4th bar of the PIÙ MOSSO, ALL choristers, actors, priests, etc. take three very definite steps forward, raising their arms toward heaven, and shout with a truly savage howl, *Guerra, guerra sterminata!* Well-coordinated and precisely timed, this movement will be very effective. For the sake of absolute clarity these are the bars involved:

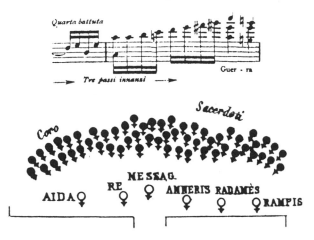

At the last *guerra!* everyone remains motionless. Amneris takes a step backward and, turning to Radamès, says to him *Ritorna vincitor!*; everyone repeats these words, also turning toward Radamès. Immediately thereafter the chorus separates in the middle, and the King, extending his hand to Amneris, crosses upstage with her and they exit into the right wing, followed by the Messenger, the Officer, the entire chorus, and the guards. Ramfis motions for Radamès to follow him and, leading the Priests, exits through door A upstage. These exits occur very quickly, and the chorus must not block the wing but must make room so that the stage will be empty by the end of the few instrumental bars that close the piece.

Meanwhile Aida has remained aside, immersed in deepest sorrow. Suddenly, recalling the previous scene, she exclaims, *Ritorna vincitor!* . . ., and then continues her whole scene in which the music and words will more effectively suggest the appropriate action to the artist than will any specific directions. At the end of the piece, on the words   (eighth bar before the end) Aida staggers, anguished and afflicted, toward upstage left, so that on the last word, *soffrir*, she will be in the wings.

NOTE: During Aida's scene *the entire male chorus* must change to priests' costumes; since there is not much time for this, the costumes must be ready backstage, behind the backdrop of the temple. Many dressers will be required to help the choristers with this change. The stage director must arrange everything to avoid confusion, so that the choristers will be ready and in their positions on time. A delay in the scene change would spoil the musical effect.

Second Scene

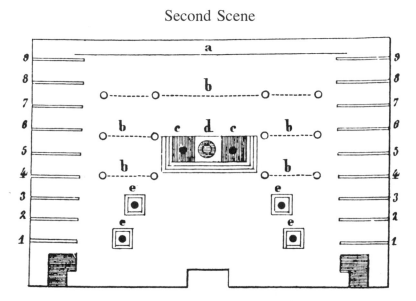

Interior of the Temple of Vulcan at Memphis

A mysterious light shines from above. A long row of columns — statues of various divinities. Center stage, on a platform covered with rugs, is the altar of the god. From golden tripods rises the smoke of incense.

a. Large drop upstage represents the continuation of the temple.

b. Cutouts which form the large high cornices and the columns of the temple. At the top of the upstage drop, the bright, very clear sky.

In the center a large altar at the top of three steps; on the sides, at *c*., two enormous vases smoking with incense; at *d*., a colossal golden statue of the God Vulcan.

e. Four small steps, on which golden tripods are placed, also smoking with incense. (In theatres in which no other means are available, the smoke can be made by using large terra-cotta vases filled with quick lime into which water may be poured during the scene change.)

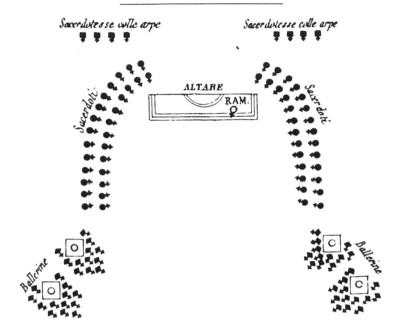

Sacerdotesse colle arpe   Sacerdotesse colle arpe

ALTARE
RAM.

Sacerdoti·   Sacerdoti·

Ballerine   Ballerine

At the opening of the scene Ramfis is on the left steps of the altar, holding Radamès's sword in his hand. All the Priests stand in double file at the sides of the altar. On the steps around the four golden tripods stand the ballerinas, forming four groups in the shape of pyramids. They hold large fans of white feathers.

Offstage left two harps accompany the offstage women's chorus; the solo lines of the invocation are sung by the prima donna soprano.

The Priests hold their hands on their chests, but not crossed, i.e. the right hand on the right chest and the left hand on the left.[2]

During the entire triple invocation to the god, complete immobility of the Priests as well as the Priestess-dancers is an ABSOLUTE NECESSITY.

On the last bars of the third invocation, the ballerinas deposit the fans on the steps of the tripods and come slowly downstage in preparation for the *sacred dance*. There must be no interruptions between the invocation and the dance, except those called for by the music.

The choreographer must arrange a quiet religious dance in which the usual modern steps are replaced by simple graceful movements, contemplative poses, genuflections, etc., etc. The most ancient dances should be imitated, of which the Eastern peoples still preserve some traditions.

At the attack of the bars in c minor  Radamès is

brought in from the left, weaponless, by four Priestesses; he walks to the altar and turns to it with a small bow, while the four Priestesses place a silver veil over his head.

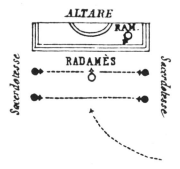

Radamès remains in this position until the fourth to last bar of the dance, in which the four Priestesses remove his veil and group themselves at the sides of the altar. Radamès takes a step backward, turning to Ramfis.

The dance ends with the ballerinas again grouped around the four tripods.

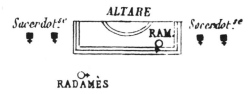

Ramfis, always on the steps of the altar, commences the recitative *Mortal,
diletto ai Numi* and during the reprise of the chorus hands the sword to
Radamès. Then he descends the steps and crosses toward the footlights, with
Radamès. As soon as they have sung the word *morte!*, the Priests also cross
toward the footlights, always in double file and turning to each other as soon
as they are in position.

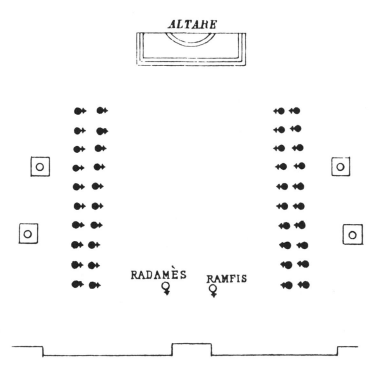

At the end of Ramfis and Radamès's invocation, the chorus responds with a
brief imitation in A flat, *Nume, custode e vindice*, and at the entrance of their
individual parts, each group of the chorus takes two steps downstage, raising
their hands and turning almost toward the statue of Vulcan.

PRIMA ENTRATA

SECONDA ENTRATA

TERZA ENTRATA

QUARTA ENTRATA

On the held D the entire chorus unites in a semicircle, advancing considerably and forcefully intoning the invocation *Nume, custode e vindice*.

When this semicircle is formed, the ballerinas descend from the tripods, take up their fans again, and QUIETLY move to the rear close to the altar to prepare the final grouping.

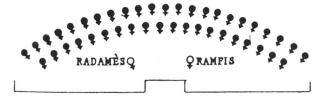

They remain in this position throughout the chorus, and at the bar all take a step forward, raising their arms to heaven.

At the ppp   they bring their hands to their chests, as before, bowing a little. Then, dividing in the center, they all move upstage, turning their backs to the audience, facing the altar. Before the chorus divides in the center, the ballerinas form a group in the shape of a pyramid and a fan around the altar of the god and on its steps; they lower all their fans toward the ground so that the fans cannot be seen.

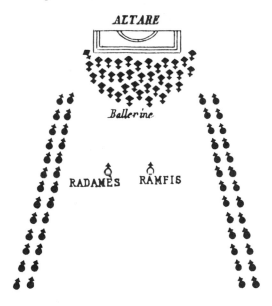

While the chorus crosses to this position, they respond humbly to the offstage invocation of the Priestesses *noi t'invochiam!* At the second *noi t'invochiam*, they have already reached their positions and, bringing their hands to their chests, *all* bend QUITE to the ground in an act of adoration.

It is necessary that the chorus remain motionless until after Radamès and Ramfis's exclamation *Immenso Fthà*. Radamès and Ramfis have turned toward the audience, taking four steps downstage. Precisely at this moment all the Priests quickly stand erect; turning toward the audience and raising their outstretched arms above their heads, they respond *fortissimo Immenso Fthà!* Simultaneously the ballerinas around the altar raise their fans, forming what appears to be a single enormous fan.

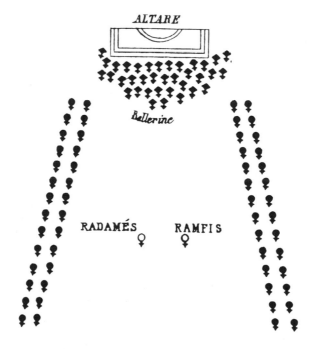

The curtain falls rapidly.

Properties for the First Act[3]

1 Heraldic emblem with white feather for the Officer of the King.
1 Flag.
4 3-step risers of about 1.50 square meters.
1 Large riser with three steps on which the altar of Vulcan is placed.
2 Very large vases of bronze and gold, about 1 meter high and 65 cm. in diameter.
6 Terra-cotta vases in which chemicals will be burned to make the smoke of the incense.
1 Large gold statue of the God Vulcan; height 2.50 meters.
40 or 50 white feathers fans for the Corps de Ballet.
8 Harps for the ballet supers.

SECOND ACT
First Scene

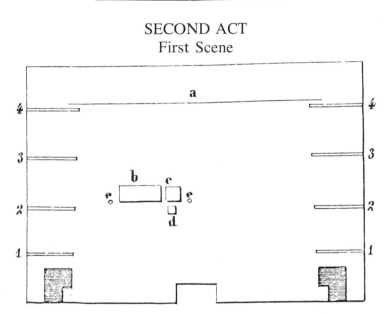

A Chamber in the Apartment of Amneris

a. Large backdrop representing an elegant chamber, with graceful columns of wood and a ceiling of wood decorated in gold; rich tapestries, placed between two columns, form a wall.

b. Table, *c*. chair, *d*. footstool.

NOTE: The chairs[4] must be very high so that to be seated one must climb up

using a footstool, which will then be used as a footrest. The chair should be
1.60 meters from the ground; the smaller chair, 90 cm.; the footstool, 40 cm.

 e. Small cups of bronze and gold in which perfume is burning.

The curtain rises as the music begins. The women's Chorus of slaves and
the ballerinas will be positioned as follows:

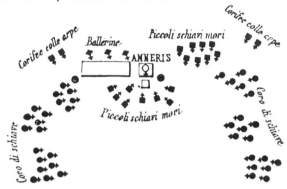

During the Chorus of the slaves, *Chi mai fra gl'inni e i plausi*, four ballerinas finish dressing Amneris, putting bracelets on her wrists and her ankles,
earrings in her ears, and offering her mirrors, etc., etc. Five or six little
Moorish slaves are kneeling around Amneris, slowly moving feather fans;
other Moorish slaves are grouped upstage. The women's chorus of the slaves
form six various small groups. Amneris sings the phrase *Vieni, amor mio, mi
inebbria . . .* with great expansiveness, but remains seated. While the
chorus is singing, the four ballerinas are moving around Amneris to finish
dressing her. On the reprise of Amneris's phrase *Vieni, amor mio, mi inebbria . . .* the ballerinas have finished dressing her; and the little Moorish
slaves kneeling around her rise, put the fans on the table, and join the other
group of little slaves; all of them come downstage to begin at once and *a
tempo* the dance in g minor PIÙ MOSSO. Simultaneously the women's chorus
reunites and withdraws to the edges of the stage very close to the wings. The
dance of the little Moorish slaves (ballerinas) must be very lively and rather
grotesque, without many complicated steps which could not be executed
considering the speed of the music.

As soon as the dance is over, the Moorish slaves withdraw upstage left and
exit. During the reprise of the Chorus, Amneris finishes dressing, leaves her
chair, and, advancing toward the audience, repeats the phrase *Vieni, amor
mio, mi inebbria . . .* At the end of this phrase, she turns toward upstage

right and, seeing Aida in the wings, addresses herself to the Chorus, saying
Silenzio!, and motions them to withdraw. The chorus moves left and exits
there, while Aida enters upstage right, holding Amneris's crown, which she
places on the table. Amneris says to herself softly *Nel rivederla*, and then,
turning lovingly to Aida, motions her to advance, adding *Fu la sorte dell'armi
a' tuoi funesta*.

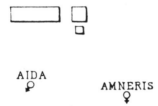

After *Un Dio possente* . . . Amneris takes a small step toward Aida and
tells her with obvious intent and great sweetness *amore*. Aida, shocked by that
word, takes two steps downstage and, deeply moved, advances three steps,
exclaiming *Amore! amore!* Amneris also takes three or four steps to the left
and downstage, and says with suppressed anger, her eyes fixed from time to
time on Aida, *Ah! quel pallore*.

AIDA
♀

AMNERIS
♀

At the beginning of the POCO PIÙ LENTO Amneris approaches Aida again.
The actress must distinctly portray her action: she is a jealous woman who is
aware of her power and makes every attempt to tear from her rival, a slave,
the secret of her heart. She must therefore continually study the effect of her
words in Aida's reactions. When Aida learns from Amneris that . . . *il duce
impavido cadde trafitto a morte*, she makes a gesture of sorrow, exclaiming
Che mai dicesti! ahi misera! . . . Amneris draws still nearer and says to her
Sì . . Radamès da' tuoi fu spento . . .

AIDA   AMNERIS

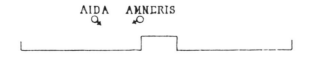

Aida exclaims *Avversi sempre mi furo i Numi* . . . Hearing these words
Amneris can no longer control herself and, drawing even nearer to Aida, says
to her furiously *Ah! trema!* Aida, terrified, takes a step backward, exclaiming

Io! . . . Amneris charges toward her and, her voice choked with anger, answers *Non mentire!* . . . and forcefully announces *Vive!* . . . Now Aida, transported by joy, can no longer pretend; with the greatest enthusiasm she takes three steps forward toward the right, falls to her knees, and exclaims *Ei vive!*

Amneris, at the climax of her fury, screams *E mentir speri ancora?* Then, rushing toward the kneeling Aida, hurling contemptuous glances like lightning, she tells her *Son tua rivale* . . . *Figlia dei Faraoni* . . .

At that point Aida rises and turning with pride to Amneris she answers *Mia rivale!* . . . Meanwhile Amneris has taken some steps toward upstage left; Aida, on the words *Pietà, perdono*, follows her a little; then, beginning the CANTABILE ESPRESSIVO *Pietà ti prenda del mio dolore*, she is in the following position:

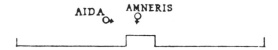

In the meantime the Chorus and the stage-band will be ready offstage to immediately begin the ALLEGRO MARZIALE *Su! del Nilo al sacro lido*. Also the entire ballet, supers, ballet supers, etc., etc., will be prepared upstage right in the order which will be explained later. The great second scene of the second act will be ready, and the throne set in position immediately behind the scene that is playing downstage. The stage director must make certain that absolute silence is observed at all times, so that the duet being sung downstage is not disturbed.

Upon hearing the triumphal hymn, Amneris turns to Aida, and with the utmost pride, says to her *Alla pompa che s'appresta*. At the end of the piece she gives her an imperial command to follow her and exits very quickly to the right. Aida, in deepest sorrow, has almost no strength left to follow Amneris; after having said *Numi, pietà del mio martir*, she walks with great effort in the direction of Amneris, so that she has disappeared by the last note of *pietà*.

Meanwhile the Chorus (populace) has remained behind the set; the band, however, immediately positions itself in the right downstage wings to be ready to ascend the platform as soon as it is in place.

Fast scene change.

Second Scene

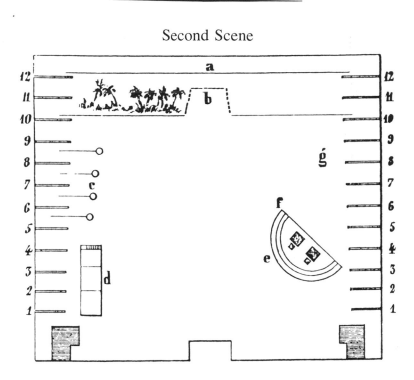

One of the Gates of the City of Thebes

Downstage a grove of palm trees. To the right the temple of Ammon. To the left a throne surmounted by a purple canopy. In the background a triumphal arch.

a. Large backdrop, representing the distant pyramids, with the enormous avenue of the sphinxes leading to them; to the right, temples and grandiose buildings, to the left, palm trees.

b. Arch, representing a great gate of Thebes in the middle, leading into the wings with large columns to which poles of bronze with flags are attached. The left side of this arch will be entirely cut out so that the upstage backdrop can be clearly seen; on the right, however, the arch will be cut only four meters above stage level; these four meters represent a thick grove of palm trees behind which the personnel participating in the march can be placed.

c. Temple of Ammon.

d. Bandstand, about 1.25 meters high and 2 meters wide; divided into three sections, it can easily be pushed quickly out of the wings during the scene change. The band is requested to ascend this platform very quickly to be in position to sound the trumpet calls. A prolonged delay would be harmful to the action and the music.

e. Semicircular riser, with three steps — two very rich chairs and two footstools in gold and purple — very rich canopy also in purple and gold. The riser, the steps, and about one meter of the stage floor surrounding them will be covered with an enormous carpet of purple cloth with border and fringe.

f. Back of the canopy.

g. Palaces.

The lighting is extremely bright, especially upstage.

There were 107 choristers at La Scala, distributed for the finale of the second act as follows:

POPOLO	– Soprani primi . .	9	} 28			
	Soprani secondi .	7				
	Contralti . . .	12			65	
	Tenori primi . .	10	} 18			
	Tenori secondi .	8				
	Baritoni. . . .	8	} 19			
	Bassi.	11				107
PRIGIONIERI	– Soprani primi . .	4	} 8	18		
	Soprani secondi .	4				
	Bassi.	10				
SACERDOTI	– Tenori primi . .	6	} 12		24	
	Tenori secondi .	6				
	Baritoni. . . .	6	} 12			
	Bassi.	6				

Other theatres will make proportionate arrangements.

At the scene change, part of the populace occupies the downstage area; others enter from the wings on the right and left, form a tight group, and all move close to the bandstand to take up the least possible space. As the Chorus begins to sing *Gloria all'Egitto, ad Iside*, Ramfis, followed by the Priests in double file, crosses the stage from upstage right, and they group themselves to the left of the throne.

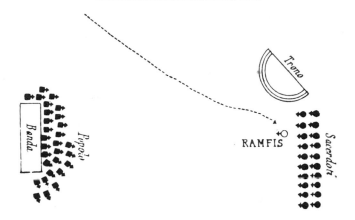

At about the 16th bar of the chorus, the King, followed by Officers, Ministers, Flabellum-bearers, etc., etc., also enters from upstage right, only from one wing further downstage. The King's entourage will be composed as follows:

The King crosses the stage and mounts the throne, seating himself on the left chair — 4 Ministers to the left, 4 Ministers to the right of the throne, some on the steps, some on the ground; the two Flabellum-bearers behind the throne.

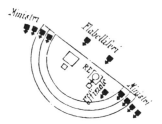

The 8 ministers are dancers.

As the women's Chorus begins to sing *S'intrecci il loto al lauro*, Amneris and her entourage also enter from the right, from one wing further downstage than the King; she crosses the stage and mounts the throne, helped by the King, who rises and gives her his hand.

Amneris's entourage is composed as follows:

One of the pages carries a crown of lotus. The little Moorish slaves (ballerinas) are in a group, not in a line.

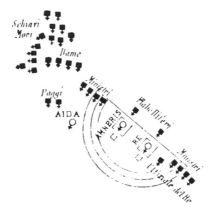

The stage director need not observe too strictly the timings that are indicated here for these three entrances, but he will arrange them according to the size of the theater, the area to be covered, etc., etc., and therefore will either anticipate or delay them so that there is continuous movement on the stage. Everyone must then be in place for the beginning of the march.

All participants in the march are upstage right, according to the space and the resources of the various theaters, of course; the order is as follows:[5]

Sequence of entrances

 3 Trumpeters (Band)   1
 2 Officers (dancers)   2
 6 Insignia-bearers   3
18 Soldiers with axes   4
 3 Trumpeters (band)   5
 2 Officers (dancers)   6
 6 Insignia-bearers (black soldiers)   7
18 Soldiers with lances   8
 2 Ballet supers: they carry a small litter on their
   shoulders, covered with golden vases, idols, etc.   9
 2 Ballet supers: carrying an identical litter   10
The Corps de ballet   11
 2 Soldiers: they pull a chariot of war   12
 2 Insignia-bearers   13
 4 Soldiers: they carry an idol on their shoulders   14
 2 Insignia-bearers   15
 2 Soldiers: they carry the statue of the Ox Apis on their
   shoulders   16
 4 Flabellum-bearers   17
 2 Soldiers: they carry an idol on their shoulders   18
 2 Insignia-bearers   19
 2 Soldiers: they pull a chariot of war   20
 2 Insignia-bearers   21
 4 Trumpeters (supers)   22
 4 Soldiers to carry the throne of Radamès   23
 4 Officers   24
 2 Insignia-bearers   25
Chorus of Ethiopian slaves and prisoners   26
 6 Soldiers   27

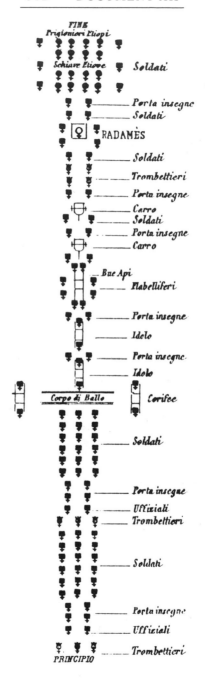

All the entrances should be arranged as follows:

At the last bars of the chorus *Grazie agli Dei rendete nel fortunato dì*, the three trumpeters of the band of the first group of soldiers (trumpets in A flat) hold their instruments ready to play at once and *a tempo*; at the beginning of the march, they enter through the large door upstage, followed by the Officer,[6] insignia-bearers, and soldiers; marching in a well-marked step they turn a bit to the left and file past the throne; two steps before arriving before the King, the Officer turns to the soldiers, making a sign with his sword; precisely at their arrival before the throne, the insignia-bearers raise their standards perpendicularly and with outstretched arms, and the soldiers raise their axes with their right arms:

(Method of carrying axes and standards)

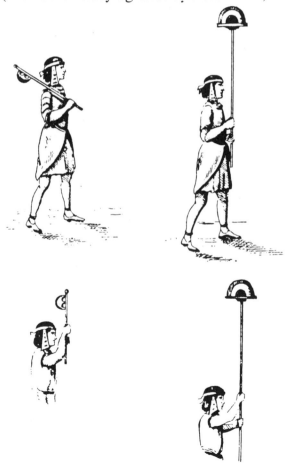

After passing before the throne, the first squadron of troops turns right about 4 meters upstage of the footlights, crosses the stage, and groups itself on the right; the trumpeters stop before the chorus of the populace and let the soldiers pass.

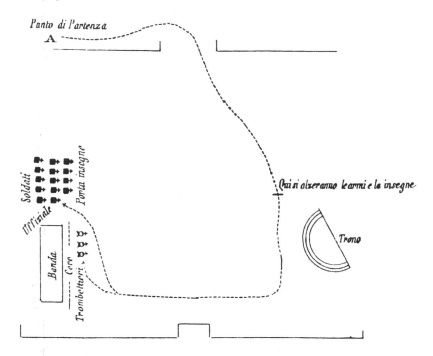

This entire movement must be calculated so that at approximately the 18th bar of the march the trumpeters are standing in their places and at the end of the 22nd bar the soldiers should be grouped in their position. One must arrange the entrance of this squadron according to size of the stage, either delaying it a measure or two or accelerating or retarding their steps. Therefore neither rehearsals nor efforts should be spared, since all the different entrances of the supers are set by the music, which would lose all its effect if there was a delay on the stage.

At the entrace of the first squadron of troops, the second squadron (trumpets in B) advances to occupy, behind backdrop *a*, the place of the first; and the trumpeters, marking time, are able to play their motive in B on time. This second squadron of troops repeats identically the movements of the first; the three trumpeters line up to the left of the other three, and the soldiers line up to the left of the first.[7]

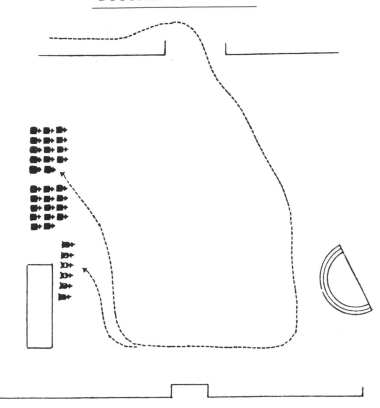

The six trumpeters must be chosen from among the best players, and they must learn to play the long ancient trumpet, according to the established model, well in advance.

The three trumpeters of the second squadron of troops have only 11 bars to reach their proper place; therefore they must march faster than the first so that they are standing still to securely execute the "hammered" D sharps with the others. Since the six Egyptian trumpets are very long, the officer, the insignia-bearers, and the soldiers must become accustomed to making their last turn at least 2 meters away from the place where the trumpeters turned. Thus one avoids the danger of their hitting the instruments and upsetting the whole march.

The second squadron of troops is armed with lances and shields; the lances are carried as the axes are, and they are raised in the same manner before the throne. All the soldiers and insignia-bearers, having reached their places, put their weapons and insignia in the parade rest position.

On the final bars of the trumpets, the corps de ballet comes onstage through the upstage door; at its sides the ballet supers carry idols, trophies, etc., etc., on their shoulders. The Moorish slaves of Amneris's entourage also join the corps de ballet to begin the dance, after which the ballerinas withdraw to upstage left. If the stage is large enough they can remain; otherwise they gradually exit into the wings, leaving the stage to the rest of the supers.

This dance must also be meaningful [and is performed] around the idols captured from the enemy; the Moorish slaves participate in the dance, precisely at the beginning of the motive in f minor.

As soon as the dance ends, the ballerinas withdraw to the right and left, leaving the stage free; immediately thereafter the remainder of the march files in along the route the soldiers took. The insignia that accompany the idols are also raised when the bearers pass before the King; the two idols and the Ox Apis are carried to the right and held at the side of the soldiers; the two chariots of war, after crossing the stage, go to the left; as the RITENUTO COME PRIMA begins, 27 bars after the dance, everyone stands still in place. At this point the men assigned to carry Radamès raise to their shoulders the throne on which he is seated and enter four bars before the PIÙ ANIMATO; they cross downstage in a straight line, turn left in front of the King's throne, and set down the triumphal throne. Radamès entourage is composed according to the numerical listing of the march and is arranged as follows:

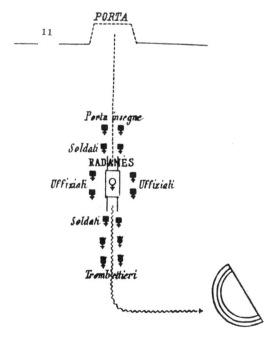

The moment Radamès reaches the ground his entourage assumes the following positions:

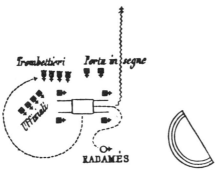

The trumpeters and the four Officers make a circle to the right on their way behind Radamès's throne. The four soldiers who carry Radamès back up a little immediately after they set down the throne to make room for Radamès who leaves it at once, coming forward and turning to the King. The men replace Radamès's throne on their shoulders and leave through the center door in which a moment later the Ethiopian prisoners appear between soldiers. The two insignia-bearers move upstage left.

This entire movement must be calculated so that on the sixth bar before the end of the piece everyone will be standing *still* in his or her proper place, as follows:

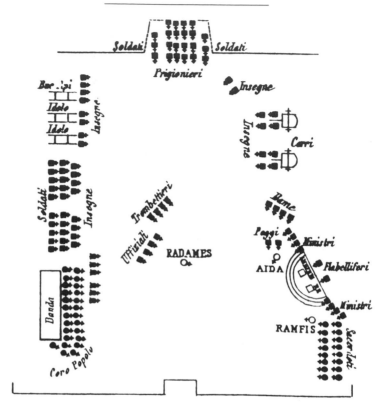

At the end of the march there is a short pause, during which the King descends from his throne, crosses towards Radamès, and, placing his hands on the hero's shoulders, exclaims *Salvator della patria, io ti saluto*.

RADAMÈS   RE

Then the King motions Radamès to go to Amneris, who gives him a crown while he kneels on the steps of the throne. Radamès hands the crown to a page and again approaches the King to tell him *Concedi in pria che innanzi a te sien tratti i prigionier*. When Radamès signals to the soldiers upstage, they advance four steps, bringing in the Ethiopian prisoners, who cross to the right and place themselves near the chorus of the populace. The moment Radamès signals the soldiers, the Officers and Trumpeters of his entourage back to the right to make room for the prisoners.

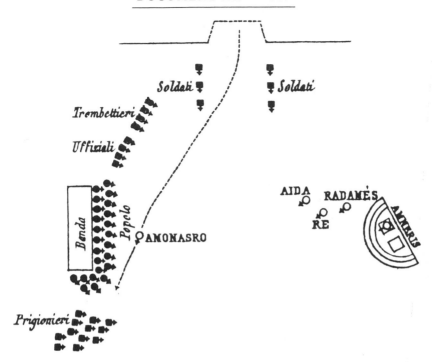

Last among the prisoners, Amonasro comes forward with a gloomy expression, restless, anxiously looking about, realizing that his daughter is a slave among the Egyptians. When he has crossed past the upstage half of the stage, Aida recognizes him and cries out *Che veggo! . . . Egli? . . . mio padre!* Whereupon, excitedly, she crosses the stage and throws herself into Amonasro's arms. All react with surprise, saying *Suo padre!*, and draw near Amonasro. Amneris descends the throne, and Ramfis, the King, and Radamès cross down to center. The Priests close in from the left, the populace from the right, as follows:

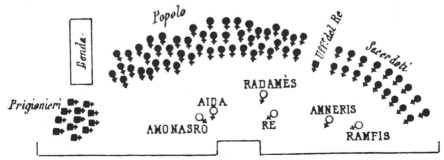

This movement must be carried out most naturally, without noise and confusion, and without giving the audience the impression that the Chorus is taking its place to sing the finale. Instead, it must be emphasised that everyone is curious to see Aida's father and to hear his story. The Ethiopian prisoners remain artistically grouped on the right, rather distant from the Populace, and they anxiously observe Amonasro.

As soon as this movement is completed, the remainder of the personnel onstage will take the following positions:

The four insignia-bearers of the first squadron of soldiers and the four insignia-bearers of the second squadron form a single line behind the Chorus.[8] Behind them the first platoon of soldiers with the axes, then the second platoon with the lances. Further back, the eight insignia-bearers who accompany the idols. Upstage right and left, on both sides of the entrance door, three insignia-bearers and three of the soldiers who accompanied the Ethiopian prisoners. The four trumpeters who preceded Radamès stand at the upstage door. The soldiers, who carry the idols on their shoulders, place them on the ground. This entire movement must be executed without noise and confusion so the audience will not be aware of it.

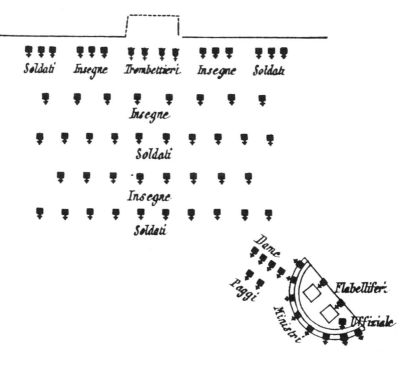

The eight ministers stand about the steps of the throne; the two flabellum-bearers of the King step behind the two thrones. All the insignia, fans, and weapons are held in perpendicular position, resting on the floor.

In answer to the King's interrogation, Amonasro takes three steps downstage and begins his account *Quest' assisa chi'io vesto*. Aida crosses a little toward downstage right.

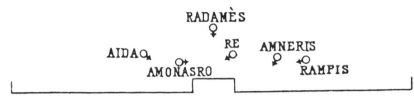

After the account and plea of Amonasro, Aida takes a small step toward the King; the Ethiopian prisoners also turn toward him and beg for mercy with outstretched hands, *Sì: dai Numi percossi noi siamo*; then Ramfis and the Priests take a small step forward toward the King, and with great force, pointing at the Ethiopian prisoners, exclaim *Struggi, o Re, queste ciurme feroci*. Then all begin the *ff*. At the *p*

the principals turn to the audience and come a little bit downstage.

The finale thus continues and, at the *forte*, when the Priests cry

they advance toward the King; the prisoners also take a step forward toward center stage; the Populace takes another step forward, so that the heightening of the action corresponds to that of the music, while everyone bursts into the expression of the various emotions that dominate them. All these movements must be made gradually, without exaggeration, so that the principals will not be pressed for space. A small step, a small movement of the arm, executed together by various groups, produces the best effect, without exaggeration. At the end of the piece, all take two or three steps upstage, thus enlarging the circle and leaving the principals more isolated. The King occupies the center. Radamès, taking a step toward him, says *O Re: pei sacri Numi*. Amonasro approaches his daughter.

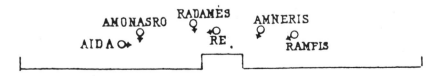

At the words *Morte ai nemici della patria!* the Priests take a step forward, extending their right arms toward the Ethiopian prisoners. The Populace responds, imploring *Grazie per gli infelici!* Then Ramfis advances toward the King to tell him *Ascolta, o Re.* Amonasro and Aida attentively observe all that is happening.

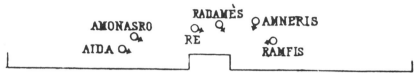

At the King's announcement that Amneris is to be Radamès's wife, Aida remains stricken with sorrow, while Amneris, bursting into a cry of joy, takes three steps toward the audience, saying *Venga la schiava*; then all intone with force and enthusiasm *Gloria all'Egitto, ad Iside.*

Meanwhile Amonasro inconspicuously mingles with the various groups of the populace on the right; passing behind them, he approaches the Ethiopian prisoners and comes to stand in the middle of them. The prisoners surround their king who speaks to them in a low voice. This group must be most artistically composed, and the choristers must take the greatest interest in what Amonasro says to them.

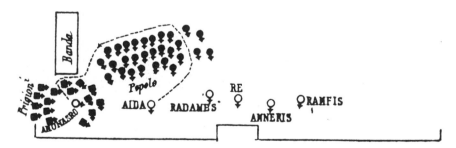

Two or three bars before the MOLTO PIÙ MOSSO, QUASI TEMPO DOPPIO, Amonasro, leaving the center of the Prisoners' group, brings himself into the first line and then suddenly, approaching Aida from the side, says into her ear in a low and moving voice *Fa cor: della tua patria*.

Meanwhile the stage director gives all the dancers, supers, and ballet supers a warning cue, and on the second to last bar of the crescendo, before the commencement of the SOSTENUTO COME PRIMA, all take four steps forward; the Chorus and artists take two steps, and raising their arms, intone with the utmost force and enthusiasm *Gloria all'Egitto, ad Iside*.

I am marking the exact point [see sign at the end of the second measure in the illustration] where the masses must make this downstage movement.

At the same time they step forward, all the insignia-bearers raise their insignias very high and the soldiers raise their weapons; the eight Ministers step up on the platform of the throne at the same time as the two flabellum-bearers raise their fans. The four women and the two pages occupy the steps of the throne. The other soldiers raise the idols on their shoulders. This whole movement should be executed with perfect timing and above all without noise; it should be arranged so that at the sign [see sign at the beginning of the fourth measure in the illustration] everyone is immobile in their proper places.

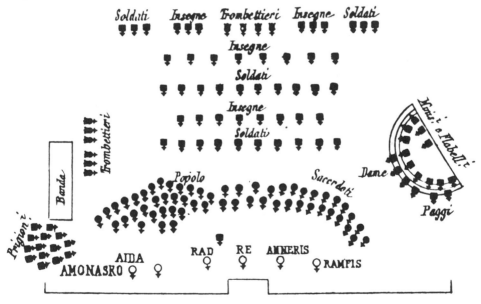

This position is held until the last bar of the finale; then, during the nine bars of the march which end the piece, the following movements rapidly take place:

The King gives his hand to Amneris, and they walk toward the triumphal arch; Radamès and Ramfis follow, then Aida and Amonasro, who gives one last knowing look at the Prisoners; the Officer of the King[9] follows. The Populace backs up to the right, the Priests to the left; the insignia-bearers and the soldiers line up to the right and left, making way for the passing of the King. The Ethiopian prisoners move toward center stage. The insignia and weapons remain raised.

As previously mentioned, this movement should be executed rapidly, since there are only a few bars of music. Everyone should therefore patiently be instructed, in order to avoid noise and confusion, so that the curtain can fall rapidly on the last bar.

This will then be the final position of the masses:[10]

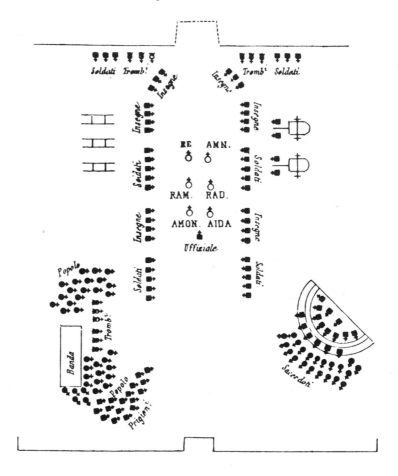

Properties for the Second Act

First Scene

 1 Table for Amneris.
 1 Jewel case.
 1 Silver handmirror for Amneris.
 2 Framed mirrors for the ballerinas.
 1 Cup in which to burn the perfumes.
16 Fans of white feathers for the Moorish slaves (ballerinas).
 4 Harps for the ballet supers.
 1 Diadem for Aida.

Second Scene

 1 Scepter for the King.
 1 Crown of lotus for Amneris.
18 Axes for the first platoon of soldiers.
18 Lances ⎫
18 Shields ⎭ for the second platoon of soldiers.
18 Various insignia.
 8 White feathered fans for the Ministers.
 2 Colorful feathered fans for the flabellum-bearers.
 2 Litters for the ballet supers of the *ballabile*. On the litters, goblets, vases, and various idols of gold and silver.
 1 Litter with idol.
 1 Litter with idol.
 1 Litter with the Ox Apis.
 1 Chariot of war.
 1 Chariot of war.
 1 Throne on a large litter.
 1 Semicircular platform with three steps.
 1 Carpet of red cloth with ornate borders and large fringe.
 2 Thrones.
 2 Footstools.
 3 Straight trumpets, 1.40 meters long.
For the weapons, swords, helmets, etc., etc., see the costume sketches.
The six trumpets for the trumpeters of the band were made according to a special model and are furnished by the firm of Ricordi.

THIRD ACT

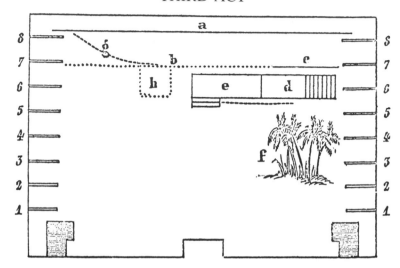

The Shores of the Nile

Palm trees growing among granite rocks. At the top of the rocks, the temple of Isis, half hidden by the branches. It is night. Moonlight.

a. Backdrop, representing the Nile.
b. Low rocks, forming the bank of the river.
c. Temple of Isis.
d. Platform, about 3 meters high.
e. Ramp.
f. Group of palm trees.
g. Tracks on which the boat is brought in.
h. Rocks over which one enters from the river.

The curtain rises at the beginning of the prelude.

The stage is empty. The chorus is placed behind the backdrop to the left. To the right, between the wings, a boat; in it, Amneris, Ramfis, two women covered with thick veils, two oarsmen, four soldiers.

As the backstage chorus begins, the boat slowly starts to move and stops midstage on the tenth bar of the Chorus. Ramfis disembarks first and helps Amneris; then the two women and the four soldiers. The oarsmen row the boat back into the wings.

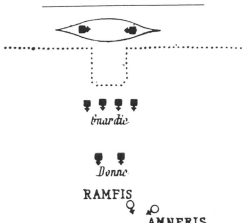

RAMFIS

AMNERIS

After Ramfis's recitative *Andiamo, pregherai fino all'alba*, Amneris, accompanied by the High Priest, goes to the Temple of Isis on the ramp (*e*). The
two women and four guards follow her. For a moment the stage is empty; then
Aida enters from the left. She advances cautiously, in a very agitated mood.
The [dramatic] situation and the artist's talent will provide the stage direction
better than a detailed description. At the third to last bar of Aida's *romanza*
(6/8 in F), Amonasro enters from the right and, passing behind his daughter,
crosses a little to downstage left. Aida, turning in surprise and terror at seeing
Amonasro, exclaims *Ciel! mio padre*.

In this duet the dramatic talent of the artists has the greatest opportunity to
reveal itself. Therefore no musical accent, no detail of mime must be overlooked; the music itself, after all, is the best guide for the actors, so that it will
suffice here simply to indicate movements, etc.

At the beginning of the duet, Amonasro is four or five steps away from his
daughter.

AIDA   AMONASRO

As the CANTABILE in D flat begins, Aida draws nearer to Amonasro.

AMONASRO

AIDA

At the POCO PIÙ ANIMATO in *b flat* minor Amonasro comes even closer;
when Aida asks him *Chi scoprirlo potria?*, he looks about quickly, then,
having backed up two steps, answers her *Tu stessa*. At Aida's *no! giammai*

Amonasro breaks out furiously *Su dunque! sorgete* and takes two steps downstage. Aida approaches him, exclaiming *Ah! padre, padre!*, but he pushes her away.

AIDA   AMONASRO

Suddenly Amonasro seizes Aida by the left arm and, turning slightly to the right, says to her in a dark tone of voice *Una larva orribile*.

AIDA   AMONASRO

At the words *Ti maledice*, Aida, absolutely terrified, frees herself from her father, takes two steps to the right, then turns to him pleadingly; Amonasro withdraws from Aida, but she follows him and throws herself at his knees, which she attempts to embrace.

AIDA   AMONASRO

At the words *Dei Faraoni tu sei la schiava*, Amonasro, at the height of his fury, once more seizes Aida's left arm; she emits a piercing cry, *Ah!* while her father pushes her back so forcefully that she falls to the ground, almost lifeless; she raises herself with her right arm and lifts her left hand pleadingly toward her father. Amonasro withdraws two steps to the left and turns his back on his daughter, remaining in a gloomy and threatening mood.

        AMONASRO
AIDA

Aida crawls on her knees close to her father and attempts to hold his hands and obtain his pardon, promising to obey his wishes.

    AMONASRO

AIDA

At Aida's words *Della mia patria degna sarò*, Amonasro turns to her, lifts her up, and says with grandiose expression *Pensa che un popolo vinto, straziato*. Meanwhile Aida exclaims *o patria . . . quanto mi costi!* Amonasro looks with apprehension to the right and, seeing Radamès arriving from afar, he quickly approaches his daughter and whispers into her ear

Coraggio! ei giunge . . . He runs to hide between the palm trees on the left, turning once more to give Aida a last knowing sign.

As the *tremolo* in D flat begins, Radamès enters on the right and, when he perceives Aida, makes a gesture of satisfaction; crossing diagonally to the left, he comes downstage close to Aida; with the happiest and most amorous enthusiasm he says to her *Pur ti riveggo, mia dolce Aida.*

AIDA◦→   ←◦RADAMÈS

At Aida's words *non t'amerei spergiuro,* Radamès is surprised and sorrowfully replies *Dell'amor mio dubiti, Aida?* Whereupon she draws near to him and tells him expressively *E come speri sottrarti?* Then Radamès backs up two steps slightly to the left and proclaims with majesty *Nel fiero anelito.*

AIDA◦→   ←◦ RADAMÈS

Little by little Radamès becomes excited, his voice more emotional, and approaching Aida by one step, he breaks out once more into the enthusiastic phrase *Sarai tu il serto della mia gloria*; then, more quietly, and with the utmost elegance and sweetness, he says *Vivrem beati d'eterno amor.*

Aida's expression is not yet calm; she is preoccupied with the terrible promise she gave her father, frightened of an uncertain future! Finally she proposes that Radamès flee; Radamès is painfully shocked and, withdrawing somewhat from Aida, exclaims *Fuggire!*

RADAMÈS
◦

AIDA
◦→

Then Aida draws near to him and tells him with intense feeling and an expression of warmest love *Fuggiam gli ardori inospiti*, etc.

After the ANDANTE Radamès, faltering, says *Aida!* She answers him forcefully *Tu non m'ami . . . Va!* and withdraws a little, turning her back on him:

AIDA
◦

RADAMÈS
◦

Radamès draws rather near to her and says with great energy, *Mortal giammai nè dio*. Aida gestures him to withdraw, repeating *va . . . va . . .* At Radamès's words *No! . . . giammai!*, she turns impetuously and, approaching him, exclaims with great force *Allor piombi la scure*.

Radamès can no longer resist and, taking Aida by the hand, begins with passionate determination the ALLEGRO ASSAI VIVO *Sì: fuggiam da queste mura*. The reprise of the motive

must be very decisive. As soon as the ALLEGRO is finished, both of them withdraw rapidly, but Aida suddenly halts on the orchestra's chord

and says to Radamès *Ma, dimmi: per qual via*.

At this point Amonasro advances cautiously from behind the palm trees to hear what Radamès says. At Radamès's words *Le gole di Nàpata . . .* Amonasro suddenly reveals himself and repeats *Di Nàpata le gole!*

At these words, seeing Amonasro, Radamès is terrified and backs up three or four steps to downstage right.

Then, turning toward Amonasro, he tells him with the greatest agitation and surprise *Tu! Amonasro! . . . tu il Re?*

These words must be clearly pronounced, with great dramatic accents, and with a sufficiently sensible pause between each word. While saying *Tu!* the actor should incline a little toward Amonasro, extending his left arm and pointing his finger at him; after these broken phrases, Radamès turns toward the audience and says *a tempo, Numi! che dissi?*, beginning *sotto voce*, very agitated, and becoming more agitated. At the words *no! no!* he takes three more steps forward and pronounces with the greatest power, screaming, *non è ver! . . . no!* Thereafter, trying to delude himself, he says

sogno . . . delìrio è questo . . .

A good actor who studies this most dramatic situation can obtain the greatest effect.

During this time Amonasro has made a sign to his daughter to take heart, and he moves downstage left, while Aida positions herself to the right of Radamès.

AMONASRO

AIDA

RADAMÈS

1st position

RAD

AIDA   AMONASRO

2nd position

Thereafter Aida and Amonasro try to calm Radamès, but he turns to Aida, with an expression of the most piercing sorrow, exclaiming *Io son disonorato . . .* . Amonasro puts his right hand on Radamès's shoulder and says to him *No: tu non sei colpevole*, but Radamès turns again to Aida and cries out in despair, *Io son disonorato . . .*, while the other two actors draw even nearer to him to calm him.

RAD

AIDA   AMON.

This whole sequence must be sung and acted with great fire and with the greatest agitation, which increases as the musical and dramatic action heightens.

In the end Amonasro seizes Radamès by the arm and tells him, while pulling him upstage, *Vieni: oltre il Nil ne attendono*. Aida follows Radamès, pleading with him in gestures to follow her father.

RAD.

AIDA ♂ ⚲⚭ AMON.

Meanwhile Amneris enters from the temple and, arriving on the platform (*d*), sees the group of three persons already on stage; not believing her eyes, she descends to the ramp (*e*). Amonasro has pulled Radamès further upstage and finds himself about center stage; Amneris cries *Traditor!* before leaving the ramp. Radamès, terrified, frees himself from Amonasro; Amonasro runs abruptly to his daughter, who exclaims *La mia rivale!* . . .[11]

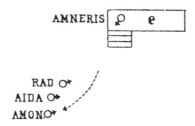

Meanwhile Amneris leaves the ramp, whereupon Amonasro says with the greatest fury *Vieni a strugger l'opra mia!* and is about to hurl himself with a dagger at Amneris; but Radamès intercepts and restrains Amonasro. At this point Ramfis appears on the platform and, turning toward the temple, calls out *Guardie, olà!* Then he descends to stage level. Radamès turns to Aida and Amonasro and, pointing toward the right wings, he pushes them in that direction, saying *Presto!* . . . *fuggite!* . . . Amonasro takes Aida by the arm, and they run desperately into the right wings. At that moment the four guards appear at the top of the platform and quickly descend. As they reach the stage level, Ramfis indicates the right wings to them, saying *Li inseguite!* The guards run precipitously in that direction.

Amneris and Ramfis come forward. Radamès approaches them and, turning to Ramfis, he says proudly to him *Sacerdote, io resto a te*.

The curtain falls immediately.

This action is very difficult to execute, partly because of the fast tempo of the music; therefore the artists must memorize their parts very well to ensure a clear and uninterrupted sequence of all phrases. The baritone must clearly articulate the word *Muori!*, with which the PRESTISSIMO begins, and he must securely set the correct tempo. Since the whole illusion of this scene depends on the timing and coordination of the action, all the movements must be carefully calculated. I therefore indicate in detail the various phases of the scene.

After exclaiming *Traditor!*, Amneris descends to stage level.

1st Position

Amonasro hurls himself at Amneris, crying *Muori!* . . .

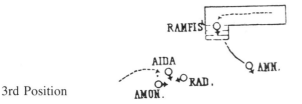

2nd Position

Radamès intercepts Amonasro, saying *Arresta, insano!* . . .

On this bar Ramfis appears at the top of the platform and calls toward the temple *Guardie, olà!* Then he descends to stage level.

3rd Position

Radamès pushes Amonasro and Aida toward the right. Amonasro exclaims *Vieni, o figlia!* and, taking Aida by the arm, pulls her off into the wings on the right. Meanwhile the guards have entered the top of the platform and quickly descend.

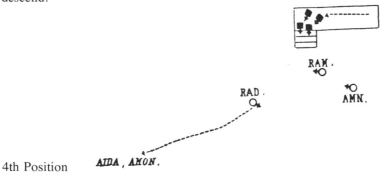

4th Position

At Ramfis's words *Li inseguite!* they run quickly to the side where Aida and Amonasro have fled.

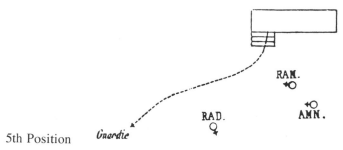

5th Position

Ramfis advances toward center stage. Thus Amneris and Radamès turn toward the Priest.

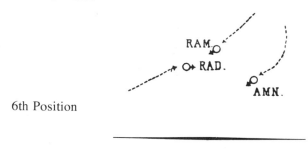

6th Position

Properties for the Third Act[12]

A boat, according to the design furnished with the costume designs.
Two oars, "   "   "   "   "   "   "   "   "

FOURTH ACT
First Scene

Hall in the King's Palace

In the center, but a little toward the left, a large door leading to the subterranean hall of judgments. To the right, a corridor. To the left, a door leading to Radamès's prison.

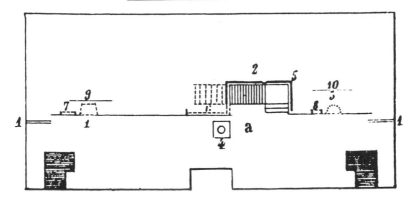

a. Large drop, representing a hall, almost dark, formed by colossal architectural stones, in which reliefs are cut — sphinxes, gods, etc. Reddish light.

1. Door through which the priests enter and exit.

2. Large opening: a wide staircase leads below the stage; this staircase begins with three steps parallel to the proscenium; then there is a landing, then other steps leading to the level of the set below.

3. Small door for Radamès's prison.

The openings 1, 2, and 3 must be capable of being closed with great ease and speed, with sliding doors (marked 6, 7, and 8).

4. Small column, with an idol of porphyry.

5. A movable corner backcloth which closes and forms the wall of the staircase.

6.⎫
7.⎬ Sliding doors (must function held by two small wooden beams
8.⎭ affixed to the backdrop).

9.⎫ Backings for the doors.
10.⎭

This scene must be very narrow, built directly upstage of the curtain, leaving just enough space for the actress (Amneris) to be discovered as the curtain rises.

Immediately upstage of this first set the second set is prepared, which we shall describe later.

The curtain rises quickly. At the sixth bar of the orchestral prelude, Amneris is on stage, posed sadly before the door of the subterranean chamber. The three doors, 1, 2, 3, are open. Upstage of backdrop 9 stand twelve Priests (basses) and Ramfis, ready to enter. Beneath the stage are all the other basses, together with the chorus master, the trumpets of the band, and the player of the bass drum, also of the band, in accordance with the orchestral score. A bass drum of very weighty and resounding quality is needed.

The remainder of the men's Chorus is already in place for the second scene, as will be indicated later, and thus also the women's Chorus, the ballerinas, ballet supers, etc., etc.

Amneris is immersed in deepest sorrow, leaning against the column with the idol, hiding her head between her hands. At the beginning of the recitative, she takes some steps downstage. Because the composer has indicated twice in this recitative PAUSA LUNGA — LUNGO SILENZIO, the artist is requested to observe these indications to the letter, without fear of exaggeration; these pauses create a beautiful dramatic effect and clearly delineate Amneris's terribly perplexed state of mind.

At the word *Guardie* Amneris turns toward the small door on the left; a guard enters immediately and stands on the threshold of that door. The moment Amneris says *Radamès qui venga*, with an imperious gesture of her hand, the guard exits immediately; and on the third bar of the ANDANTE SOSTENUTO 3/4, Radamès appears, accompanied by two guards; the guards stop at the sides of the door, and Radamès advances toward Amneris; the two guards exit. During the entire duet that follows, Radamès must maintain great dignity.

RAD.
AMN.

Amneris begins the duet with all her passion but at the same time tries to hide it from Radamès; he listens to Amneris with calm and serenity, and answers her *Di mie discolpe i giudici* . . . The two artists should stand at least four or five steps from each other; at the words *Salvati dunque e scolpati*, Amneris takes a very small step toward Radamès. He answers her with the utmost resignation, but at the same time with great passion, *d'ogni gaudio la fonte inaridita* . . . At the word *morir* Amneris can no longer control herself; coming still closer to Radamès and turned to him, she exclaims with the most ineffable passion *ah!* . . . *tu dei vivere!* . . . This entire musical section must be sung with the greatest feeling, the accents and words well articulated; Radamès turns a little more toward Amneris, takes a step forward, and says *Per essa anch'io la patria* . . .

AMN.   RAD.

At that answer Amneris scornfully turns away and takes two steps to the right. Radamès approaches her, saying to her *Misero appien mi festi* . . .

AMN.   RAD.

Radamès begins this musical section calmly, *mezza voce*, becoming increasingly agitated, until he exclaims with force and irony *e in dono offri la vita a me?* At those words Amneris turns suddenly to Radamès, answering *Io . . . di sua morte origine!*

During Amneris's account Radamès approaches her, listening with the greatest excitement.

RAD.
AMN

At the words *nè più novella s'ebbe* . . . Radamès turns to the left and, raising his arms toward heaven, says with great calm and tenderness *Gli Dei l'adducano salva alle patrie mura*.

AMN.   RAD.

Amneris, at the height of her excitement, approaches Radamès and tells him *Or, s'io ti salvo* . . . Radamès answers *Nol posso!* . . . taking a small step to the left and turning his back on Amneris, until, with the words *Pronto a morir son già*, he turns once more to her. Thereupon Amneris approaches Radamès with the greatest sorrow, saying to him *Chi ti salva, o sciagurato*.

AMN.   RAD.

As soon as the duet is concluded, Radamès returns quickly to his prison. Amneris takes a step or two toward the door through which he has departed and then crosses down to the left, in the greatest desolation.

In the following *judgment scene* an artist can rise to a sublime performance in her action as well as in her expression of the text. It seems impossible to me to describe the dramatic situation, since the music is so sublime as to be sufficient to inspire the artist. Therefore I shall limit myself to giving tangible stage directions, without discussing the psychological aspects of the scene.

Amneris, who remains alone on the stage, is slightly to the left, in order not to block the door in the center; at the 18th bar of the piece, Ramfis enters from the right door, followed by twelve priests in double file; forming a small arch, they descend through the center door to the subterranean chamber.

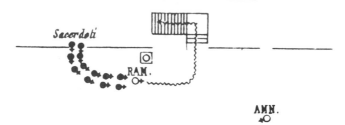

At the word *segnasti!* Amneris turns to the right, sees the Priests, and says *ch'io non vegga quelle bianche larve!* She takes two steps forward, terrified and covering her face with both hands.

When the Priests arrive on the lower level, Ramfis remains closest to the steps so that his voice can be distinctly heard. The conductor must experiment with the positions for Ramfis, as well as for the chorus and the trumpets, to achieve the best musical effect.

Amneris's ALLEGRO, after the invocation, must be sung from the left. At the *fortissimo* attack

Radamès enters immediately from the small door on the right[13] between the two guards, crosses the stage and descends to the subterranean chamber through the center door. At this moment Amneris turns, sees Radamès, and emits a scream *Oh! chi lo salva?*

As soon as he has reached the lower level, the tenor returns to the stage on one of the two escape steps, located at the sides of the stage. At the same time the small door on the left is closed immediately, to make possible whatever preparation is necessary for the following scene.

Amneris, in greatest desolation and sobbing, exclaims *mi sento morir* . . .

A moment of silence . . . then, with a thundering voice, Ramfis begins to interrogate Radamès in the subterranean chamber. Amneris, at the words of the High Priest, staggers to the door that leads to the subterranean chamber, and inclining somewhat toward the staircase, listens with anxiety. At the word *Traditor!* she turns toward the audience and takes a step forward, crying out *Ah! pietà!* . . . Remaining in that position she turns again to the subterranean chamber as Ramfis's second interrogation begins. With the next cry of *Traditor!* Amneris, in ever increasing agony, takes two or three steps toward the footlights and, with even greater forcefulness than before, exclaims *Ah! pietà!* . . .

The third interrogation of the accused takes place, and Amneris returns again to the door leading to the subterranean chamber. Leaning almost senseless against the wall, she awaits Radamès's answer. At the words *Egli tace . . .* Amneris makes a gesture of desolation and after the *Traditor!* exclaims, turning to the audience but without moving, *Ah! pieta!* she remains upset in anticipation of the sentence; when the Priests say *fia schiuso l'avel,* Amneris makes the most marked gesture of despair, of anger and sorrow, and, excitedly crossing toward downstage left, exlaims *A lui vivo . . . la tomba . . .*

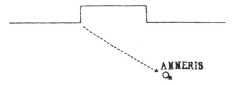

At the FF. COME PRIMA attack, Ramfis, followed by the twelve Priests (basses), returns to the stage from the staircase leading to the subterranean chamber and slowly proceeds toward the right door. Amneris turns, and, perceiving the Priests, runs in front of them and then into their midst, exclaiming with impetus *Sacerdoti!*

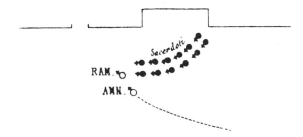

Ramfis stops and turns to Amneris; the other Priests do likewise.

As soon as Ramfis has entered with the twelve Priests, the large door is immediately closed; backdrop 5 is raised, and the open trap descending to the subterranean chamber is closed. At the same time the remainder of the Chorus under the stage will quickly, but in orderly fashion, ascend to the stage and from there to the higher floor of the temple, grouping themselves downstage as will be seen later. Once the door and the trap of the subterranean chamber are closed, whatever is required for the preparation of the subterranean scene will be done immediately.

The stage director should, above all, make certain that everything is organized in a military way. Any confusion, any noise during this operation would destroy the musical effect of the piece that is being played in the scene in front. The same must be said by the director of the chorus; if they ascend to the higher floor in a careless and disorganized manner, they will make excessive noise. ALL should be reminded that the greatest discipline is necessary for performances to function smoothly, and in this case it is absolutely indispensable. Any noise or delay would ruin the whole effect.

At Amneris's words, Ramfis and the Priests reply forcefully *È traditor! morrà*, extending their arms and taking a step forward. Then Amneris turns to Ramfis in particular and, hearing his answer, takes two steps toward the audience, exclaiming *Voi la terra ed i Numi oltraggiate* . . . The Priests and Ramfis then also come slightly forward and say with great force *È traditor! morrà*.

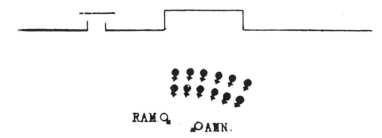

RAM.Q.   ᴏAMN.

During this piece a stagehand enters through door 1 and carries off small column 4.

As soon as they have finished their *forte* phrase and at the commencement of the following bars   Ramfis and the Priests cross

upstage toward door 1, repeating in a low voice and in a dark tone the words *Traditor! Traditor! Traditor!*, the last offstage; Amneris, stupefied with sorrow, turns in the direction of the Priests' exit, in a pose of deepest sorrow.

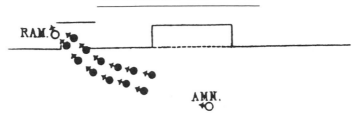

As soon as the Priests have departed, Amneris can no longer restrain herself and, with two or three quick steps to the footlights, cries out in a paroxysm of anger *Empia razza!* Then she runs offstage through door 1.

This door closes immediately, the backdrop is pulled out, and the entire set of the subterranean chamber is ready for the change of scene which must take place immediately after the music of this piece ends.

Radamès prepares to sit on the steps of the staircase that leads from the subterranean chamber to the temple above.

Second Scene

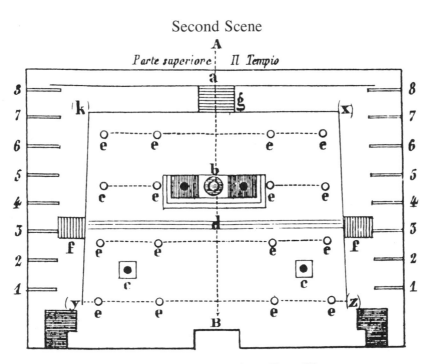

The Scene Is Divided into Two Floors

The upper floor represents the Temple of Vulcan, as in the first act, resplendent with gold and light.

(k), (x), (y), (z) are the upper platform which forms the floor of the temple.

a. Rear backdrop.

b. Altar as in the second scene of the first act.

c. Tripods for the perfumes as in the second scene of the first act.

d. Two steps across the entire upper platform upstage of the second colonnade so that the floor has two levels: the first extends from (y) and (z) to the second lower colonnade; the second, from the same colonnade to (x) and (y),[14] higher above.

e. Columns as in the first act.

f-f. Escape steps for the chorus, ballerinas, and ballet supers.

g. Offstage steps upstage for placing the idol, the altar, etc., etc.

Section of the central line *a.b.*[15]

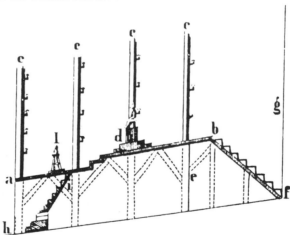

a.b. Upper level forming the floor of the temple.

c.c.c.c. Columns behind which the gas flames are located to brilliantly illuminate the temple.

d. Altar and Idol of Vulcan.

e. Backdrop, representing the subterranean chamber.

b.f. [Upstage] offstage steps.

g. Backdrop, representing the temple.

h.f. Stage floor.

h.i. Staircase on which Radamès supposedly descended into the subterranean chamber.

h.a. Height of the subterranean chamber, about 3 meters.
l. Tripods.

The center arches are larger than those on the sides.

The scenic designer should carefully study the contrast of the two floors: the dark subterranean chamber, with cold colors, illuminated by a grey-green light; the temple in warm colors, resplendent with light; the columns serve quite well to mask the lighting instruments which will preferrably be operated with gas. The imitation of the grandiose *Temple of Vulcan*, as in the *First Act*, is a great challenge to the scenic designer, since here there is less space for the surface and the height. As far as the best construction of the upper floor is concerned, we cannot give precise instructions, because they depend on the resources of the stage and on the ability and talent of the technician who must devise a mechanism to satisfy the following qualifications: *lightness, solidity, ease of construction*.

The subterranean chamber, lighted with colored lenses, is covered on both sides with opaque cloths, which prevent any other light from illuminating the stage.

———————————

At the scene change Radamès is alone in the subterranean chamber, sad and seated on the steps of the staircase by which he supposedly descended.

In the temple above, immediately at the top of this staircase, two Priests are about to put in place with heavy hammers and iron pikes the stone enclosing the subterranean chamber. After seven or eight blows, the two Priests, who are on their knees for this operation, rise and depart. The blows must be simulated, since any noise would disturb the effect of the music. Therefore the two Priests must pantomime the blows; once they have risen and put down the tools, they join the other choristers.

All the other Priests form a circle around the altar of Vulcan, kneeling and with their hands on their chests, as explained in the first act. Be certain that both knees touch the floor, since the Egyptians never knelt on one knee, keeping the other leg folded with the foot on the ground, as is the custom today. In fact, with both knees on the ground, the body must be quite curved and one must sit almost on one's heels. It is necessary that all remain immobile in that position until the moment when they rise, which will be indicated later.

The stage director and the chorus master (I repeat this again) should use all their authority to obtain this perfect immobility, exercising severe discipline and explaining the aesthetic demands of the scene. Even the slightest movement would break the whole mood of the picture before the audience; the smallest distraction would destroy the entire illusion created by this phase of the drama. Once the choristers understand the importance of all those matters, all that is required by the scenic considerations will be obtained without difficulty.

Four or six ballerinas (Priestesses, as in the first act), depending on the size of the set, form groups around the perfume tripods. The ballerinas must also remain immobile until the correct moment.

In the background, on both sides, two or three ballet supers (harp players). Amneris should be ready to enter from behind the left columns.

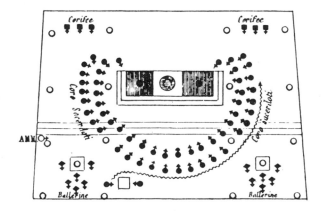

The women's Chorus should be ready on the left,[16] one portion occupying part of the subterranean chamber, one portion in the wings. To mask the Chorus from the audience's view, the opening of the subterranean chamber to the left should be partially closed by a sphinx or some other sculpture. Downstage of the Chorus are two harps and a harmonium.

Subterranean Chamber

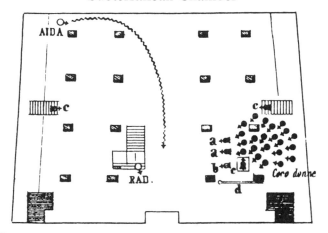

a.a. Harps.

b. Harmonium.

c.c.c. Conductors — the Chorus Master should be near the harmonium, the harps, and the women's Chorus. Another conductor should be on the left escape steps, in a position that will enable him to see the Chorus Master's beat and transmit it to the Chorus of the Priests in the temple (right side). A third conductor should be on the right escape steps; from there he will be able to see the chief conductor's beat, which he can transmit to the Chorus of the Priests (left side). In this manner a good and perfect musical execution is assured, in spite of the difficulty of maintaining an ensemble with so many subdivisions of parts, as long as the people involved are intelligent craftsmen and love their art — this is to be hoped for in our theatres.

d. Ground row to mask the Chorus.

Radamès is seated on the last step of the staircase in a sad pose. He is almost motionless as he declaims his recitative. After the word *ignorar!* and on the notes he rises, surprised, exclaiming, *Qual gemito!* . . .; then, turning toward the background of the subterranean chamber, he speaks the words that follow with great emotion and in a broken voice. Meanwhile Aida staggers forward, wearied, listless, until she is near Radamès, who takes two or three steps toward her and cries out *Cielo!* . . . *Aida!*. She says in a feeble voice *Son io . . .*, to which Radamès replies in greatest despair, as he approaches Aida, *Tu . . . in questa tomba!*

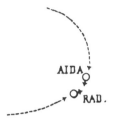

Aida takes a few steps forward and, after the word *morire*, Radamès sings with the greatest passion and tenderness *Morir! sì pura e bella!*

During this entire scene both actors must under no circumstances cross the line formed by the downstage cloth, because they must always remain inside the subterranean chamber.

Then Aida, carried away, takes two steps backward to say *Vedi? . . . di morte l'angelo . . .*

AIDA

RAD.

Two bars before the end of this phrase, the Priests in the temple slowly rise to their feet, so they are standing for the beginning of the funeral prayers, always holding their hands on their chests. At the same time the Priestesses form various groups, moving slowly. On the *ff*

all the Priests raise their hands high. At the bar before this *fortissimo*, Radamès quickly mounts the staircase of the subterranean chamber and, raising his arms against the stone that closes the stairs, makes the greatest effort to remove it, crying out in anger *Nè le mie forti braccia . . .*

After the bars of the *ff* to the *pp* the Priests again bring their hands to their chests, lowering their heads slightly, and remain immobile. The ballerinas form a group around the tripods where, having poured the perfumes, they also remain immobile. At the same time Radamès, crushed, descends the staircase; Aida moves toward him, saying *tutto è finito*, to which he replies with desolate resignation *È vero!*

RAD.

AIDA

Then Aida begins the *O terra, addio . . .*; in this entire section both remain considerably upstage and close to each other.

As the *Immenso Fthà* chorus begins, the Priests once again raise their hands to heaven. Aida and Radamès advance to the limit of the subterranean chamber, exclaiming with enthusiasm:

At the same time Amneris enters the temple, slowly and sadly from the left. A large black veil covers her from head to feet. (While mounting the escape steps, the artist must be careful not to let her veil catch fire, which happened one night in another theatre. It would be a good idea to extinguish the two or three gas flames that might be close to the steps.) She prostrates herself on the stone that closes the subterranean chamber; and while Aida and Radamès in effable bliss exclaim in a close embrace *O terra, addio*, Amneris, her voice suffocated by tears, says *Pace, t'imploro*.

Meanwhile the Priests pray *sottovoce, Noi t'invochiam*, and the Priestesses form one last group. After the last phrase, *si schiude il cielo*, Aida, supported by Radamès, sinks gradually to the ground, dying. Radamès kneels next to her in the most intense sorrow. Amneris, her voice torn by sobs, exclaims in heartrending accents *Pace, pace*. The Priests, inclining almost to the ground (as they did in the invocation of the first act), say *Immenso Fthà*.

In the meantime, and with the *ppp* entrance of the violins, the curtain falls slowly so that it is completely closed on the last bar, but not before.

The stage director is requested to rehearse this closing of the curtain many times so that it is executed with the correct timing and without those major and minor deviations in speed which destroy every effect.

As I arrive at the conclusion of these stage directions, I am unable to refrain from requesting that all persons involved in the production not overlook even the smallest detail, no matter how insignificant it may seem. Because of recent developments in the music-drama, every movement has its *raison d'être* and the old stage conventions are no longer acceptable.

The stage director should distribute the libretto of the opera to the artists in time so they may form a precise concept of the drama. It would be desirable that all the artists even furnish themselves with the *production book*; by studying it, they can save themselves, the stage directors, and the chorus a great many difficulties in rehearsal.

Furthermore the stage director must, before beginning rehearsals, give the choristers a general idea of the opera. In that way they will follow his orders with greater ease and zeal, feeling elevated to great importance and being motivated by self-respect.

The stage director will, under no circumstances and no pretext whatsoever, permit any artist, chorister, dancer, etc., etc., to make even the slightest changes in his or her costumes, wigs, and jewelry, which were scrupulously executed in accordance with the costume designs. These were studied with every possible care and executed by famous artists with scrupulous historical precision.

NOTES TO DOCUMENT XII

1. The numbers to the extreme left and right of the above and subsequent stage plans indicate wing spaces. Consequently this plan shows only the downstage third of the entire stage.

2. Note the beard that Auguste Mariette so firmly objected to in his letters to Draneht of 15 July 1870 and 30 August 1871.

3. The sword that Radames receives from Ramfis is missing from this list.

4. According to the above plan there is only one chair in this scene.

5. The diagram following the list does not correspond to it and differs, in particular, after the entrance of the corps de ballet. (The handwritten additions appear to be those of an unknown stage director.)

6. Apparently Giulio Ricordi refers to the two officers who follow the first three trumpeters, as mentioned in the list and shown in the diagram of the procession.

7. The following diagram does not correspond to the numbers in the list of the procession.

8. This description does not correspond to the following diagram.

9. In the above diagram this officer is not identified but appears upstage of Radames and the King.

10. The three litters and the two chariots of war have, presumably, remained in the positions indicated on p. 588. Note the six nonplaying trumpeters (supers) left and right of the upstage portal. These are not consistent with previous diagrams, or with the prop list given on p. 595, or with the sequence of entrances on pp. 581–82.

11. There are three steps in the following diagram versus the two in the diagram on p. 596.

12. Amonasro's dagger is not mentioned.

13. Giulio Ricordi obviously means the small door to the left, through which Radames exited after the duet with Amneris.

14. Giulio Ricordi apparently means x and k.

15. The letters in the following sectional diagram have nothing in common with those in the previous floor plan.

16. This entire paragraph refers to the lower level of the stage, i.e. the subterranean chamber.

DOCUMENT XIII

Contract for Parma
by
Tito Ricordi

This document, which was drawn up for the production of *Aida* in Parma in 1872, is a typical House of Ricordi contract.

Professor Gustavo Marchesi, who discovered this contract and other documents (see note 2 to Verdi's letter to Giulio Ricordi of 22 November 1871 and *Quaderno n. 1 della stagione lirica 1973–74 del Teatro Regio di Parma*) published a few excerpts from it in *La Gazzetta di Mantova* of 11 May 1975. With his kind permission the entire handwritten document, except for Ricordi's standard printed contract of three and a half pages, is translated and published here for the first time.

Tito di Giovanni Ricordi, music publisher, contract with G. B. Lasina, impresario of the Royal Theatre in Parma:

Milan, 25 January 1872

Additional Articles

a. The above-mentioned rental fee in the amount of *It. Lire 10.000* must be paid in two installments: *L. 4000* before the delivery of the vocal parts and *L. 6000* before the delivery of the orchestral parts.

b. The vocal parts must be distributed as follows:

Aida — Sig.a Stolz

Amneris — Sig.a Waldmann

Radames — Sig. Capponi

Amonasro — Sig. Pantaleoni

Priest — Sig. Vecchi, Luigi

The artist for the role of the *King* must be approved by Sig. Ricordi. If Sig. Ricordi should consider any of the above-mentioned unfit for their assigned roles, he reserves full power, before or after the orchestra rehearsals, to request their substitution with other artists who must also be properly signed by the Management.

c. The opera *Aida* must always be performed in its entirety according to the orchestra score furnished by Sig. Ricordi, and the production can never be interrupted by a *Ballet* not composed for the opera.

d. The dances must be copied from those performed at La *Scala* of Milan and with the number of roles to be indicated by Sig. Ricordi.

e. For the costumes, the sets, the extras, the props, and everything concerning the production, the Management must adhere to the arrangements which will be made by Sig. Ricordi.

f. The orchestra must be composed of 12 first violins, 12 second, 8 violas, 8 cellos, 9 double-basses. For the number of the other instruments, the orchestra score furnished by Sig. Ricordi will be followed. In particular, harps are required. For the orchestra as well as the stage-band the normal diapason (pitch) must be adopted. The choice of the concertmaster and conductor of the orchestra must be subject to the approval of Maestro Cavaliere G. Verdi.

g. The Management pledges itself to have the Commission of the Parma Theatre formally address Maestro Verdi, asking him to supervise the proceedings of the *Aida* rehearsals. Maestro Verdi will therefore have full powers concerning the execution of the present contract in every one of its parts.

h. The chorus must number 82 (eighty-two). The distribution of the voices will be indicated by Sig. Ricordi; and the Management must present a list of the choristers' names as well as the orchestra players' names for Sig. Ricordi's approval and provide for the substitution of those whom he may judge to be unsuitable.

i. If deficiencies should occur in the number or artistic merit of the orchestra or chorus, the Management will have to provide for the filling of the vacancies according to the indications which Sig. Ricordi will give.

j. The Stage-Band will be composed of the best players in the number requested by Sig. Ricordi, in addition to six trumpeters who must play in the Grand March of the second act. Sig. Ricordi will furnish the instruments for the said six trumpeters at a rental fee of *Lire 50.*

k. Sig. Ricordi or his representative will be entitled to assist all piano and orchestra rehearsals, and the Management agrees from this date to comply with his arrangements in regard to everything involving the performance and production.

l. The Management cannot set the date of the first performance without the previous assent of Sig. Ricordi who, in the case of the insufficiency of some artist or of the ensemble or of the musical or the stage direction, even after the dress rehearsal, can forbid the performance of the score. The Management will not be able to oppose [Sig. Ricordi's decision] in any way.

m. The Management is absolutely forbidden to entrust the performance of the leading roles to understudies, to diminish the number of choristers or orchestra musicians, and to substitute in any *Aida* performance during the above-mentioned season other artists for those chosen by Sig. Ricordi.

n. The Management guarantees the custody of the orchestra score and parts, and agrees to accept the precautions to be determined by Sig. Ricordi.

o. The Management will furnish *gratis* to Sig. Ricordi a box in the first or second row for the first two performances of *Aida*.

p. If the Management should fail — which is not expected — in any of the terms of the present contract, it will incur the fine of 6,000 Lire, and Sig. Ricordi will have the right to withdraw the score and not permit the performances even though the Management may cite extenuating circumstances. [. . .]

DOCUMENT XIV

An Anonymous Letter

22 Nov. [19]23

To the Art Critic   [Gaetano Cesari of *Il Corriere della Sera* of Milan]

In your worthy article of yesterday concerning "the premiere of *Aida* at La Scala" I read in regard to the choreographic section of the 2nd scene of the 2nd act the observation that "toward the end of the act, the stage seems to attract to itself the center of gravity which is in the music." Your observation is correct, and it seems appropriate to me to recall an occurrence which I believe to be unpublished; I happen to know about it because at that time (how many years ago, alas!) I too was associated with the arts and witnessed an incident which may interest the readers of the *Corriere*.

When *Aida* was given for the first time at La Scala, Maestro Giovanni Casati was chosen to devise the dances and stage the triumphal march;[1] at that time he was the illustrious Director of the School of Dance at La Scala. This gentleman, who had the true mettle of an artist (as I saw printed also in these columns some months ago in an article that spoke of him), [. . .] made of the great triumphal march a veritable cinematography of movement, achieved grandeur with varied and pictorial groupings of ballerinas, with intertwinings and windings of masses of apprentice dancers and ballet supers in succession, thus forming a marvelous and spectacular apotheosis of glory.

At the first dress rehearsal, Verdi sat in the center of the orchestra stalls, in the midst of a group from the artistic commission, to observe the scenic effect which he saw for the first time in complete action; apparently he thought that such a great movement was excessive and perhaps damaging to his musical requirements. In a sudden outburst he jumped to his feet and shouted, interrupting the rehearsal, "Get rid of those ballerinas! Get rid of those people! There's too much movement!" He climbed quickly on the stage to suggest the desired modifications. But Casati, very proud and sure of his conscientious and efficacious work, felt offended by the Maestro's outburst, in spite of all his friendship and admiration for him. He left the theatre precipitately in the midst of the rehearsal and went home. The moment Verdi learned that Casati was no longer in the theatre, he was terribly upset and sent Giulio Ricordi to Casati's house. [. . .] Ricordi succeeded in persuading Casati to return. Thus between him and Giulio Ricordi the modifications and simplifications requested by the Maestro were worked out, and they were more or less retained in all successive performances of *Aida*. [. . .]

(An anonymous artist)

NOTE TO DOCUMENT XIV

1. Neither Casati nor Monplaisir is mentioned in any of the available reviews or other records concerning the *Aida* premiere at La Scala. Pompeo Cambiasi, *La Scala: note storiche e statistiche 1778–1906* (Milano: G. Ricordi, 1906), p. 174, only lists Ippolito Monplaisir as choreographer for the Carnival and Lent season of 1872.

BIOGRAPHICAL NOTES
ON THE
CORRESPONDENTS

BIOGRAPHICAL NOTES

ARRIVABENE, OPPRANDINO (born 1807, Mantua; died 1 January 1887, Rome). One of Verdi's closest friends, a prominent journalist, art critic, and poet, Arrivabene was the son of Count Ferdinando Arrivabene and his wife Carolina (née Lamberti). He was born into a noble family related to the Byzantine imperial house of Comnenus and to the Mantuan dukes of Gonzaga. All the Arrivabenes were patriots and martyrs who fought the tyranny of the Austrians. As a disciple of Mazzini's *Giovane Italia* movement and an active supporter of Cavour's policies Arrivabene participated in the uprisings against the Austrian occupation in 1831 and 1848.

One of the most illustrious members of Countess Maffei's circle of liberal intellectuals and artists, Arrivabene joined *L'Indicatore Lombardo*, the first weekly review published in Italy. Later this publication became the *Rivista Europea*, whose contributors included some of the most distinguished men in nineteenth-century Italy: Cesare Cantù, Giulio Carcano, Andrea Maffei, Achille Mauri, Count Giulio Pullé, and Carlo Tenca.

Arrivabene's friendship with Verdi lasted over fifty years and even included their respective dogs, in whose names they corresponded for some time. "For one reason or another I think of you every day," Arrivabene once wrote to Verdi, who was also his fellow deputy in the Turin Parliament. In his last letter to his friend, of 31 October 1886, Arrivabene expressed his regret that he might not live to hear *Otello*, "the *great finale* of your artistic career, which will leave a splendor that will have no sunset." *Otello* premiered at La Scala five weeks after Arrivabene's death.

BOTTESINI, GIOVANNI (born 22 December 1821 [the date on Bottesini's birth certificate in Crema], Crema, Italy; died 7 July 1889, Parma). A world-famous virtuoso double bassist, Bottesini was the son of a musician; studied violin, sang in churches, and played timpani as a child. When in 1835 he entered the Milan Conservatory, the only opening was for a double bassist. After a number of appearances in Italy, he accepted the position of first double bass player in Havana, Cuba, in 1846. There he also conducted several operas, including his own first opera, *Cristoforo Colombo*. After touring as a bassist and/or conductor to New Orleans and New York (1848), he appeared in Paris, St. Petersburg, and London.

From 1855 to 1857 Bottesini directed the Italian Theatre in Paris, where he produced his opera *L'Assedio di Firenze* with great success. This was followed by a triumphant concert tour throughout Europe and the acclaim of his opera *Il Diavolo della Notte* in Milan. His opera *Marion Delorme*, with libretto by Antonio Ghislanzoni, was performed at the Teatro Bellini in Palermo while he was its director from 1861 to 1863.

In 1867 Bottesini went on another concert tour through France and Scandinavia. Two years later he was heard in France, with bass or baton, with the violinist Henri Vieuxtemps. Having conducted the first of many performances in London of his most successful comic opera *Ali Baba*, he set out for the *Aida* premiere in Cairo in 1871.

After tours through Spain (1876) and Portugal (1881), "the Paganini of the double bass" lived for some years in London. Under his well-known pen name, Tobia Gorria, Arrigo Boito wrote the libretto of Bottesini's opera *Ero e Leandro*, which premiered in Turin (1879). Altogether Bottesini wrote twelve operas, four of which were never performed, as well as a *Requiem Mass*, the oratorio *The Garden of Olivet* (Norwich Festival, 1887), a great deal of vocal and chamber music, a concerto and a method for the double bass. He also founded the Società del Quartetto in Florence, which played a major role in the development of chamber music in Italy.

Upon Verdi's recommendation, Bottesini was appointed director of the Conservatory in Parma in 1889, where he died in poverty six months later.

CORTICELLI, MAURO. Corticelli was one of Giuseppina Verdi's oldest friends and for decades was intimately associated with both Verdis. Little is known about his life, and the dates of his birth and death cannot be ascertained.

Corticelli was a theatrical agent in Bologna, where, presumably, he was born. From 1859 to 1867, he was secretary for the famous Italian actress Adelaide Ristori, whom he accompanied on her world-wide tours, which included Russia, Egypt, and the United States. He happened to be in St. Petersburg when the Verdis arrived there for *La Forza del Destino* rehearsals in December 1861. "So we shall all meet in the perpetual ice-cream of St. Petersburg," Giuseppina Verdi had written to her friend, advising him that "if la Ristori believes she will hold superiority in the matter of *tagliatelli*, Verdi counts on eclipsing her with *risotto*, which he makes in truly divine fashion" (Walker, *The Man Verdi*, p. 240).

When in 1866 Corticelli experienced financial difficulties and Signora Ristori refused to come to his rescue, Signora Verdi offered to help with her own savings, assuring him that "the gates of Sant'Agata are always open for you." In October 1867, tired of traveling and unemployed, Corticelli gratefully accepted the position as manager of Verdi's estate.

"Of respectable circumference," as Giuseppina Verdi described him, a warmhearted, full-blooded, humorous human being, Corticelli was the cause of much laughter and the frequent object of affectionate jokes. "Don Cappellari," as he was called because he was quick to take offense (*prendere cappello*), was also a woman chaser par excellence, and this led to his downfall. In 1879 "it was found that Corticelli [. . .] had been misusing the savings of the cook and another person of the entourage at Sant'Agata, with whom he had apparently been having a love affair. [. . .] Corticelli was dismissed and six months later tried to drown himself in the canal at Milan. When she read about this in the newspaper, Giuseppina wrote at once to Teresa Stolz:

In view of the catastrophe, which could end in the death of that unfortunate man, any comment or recrimination would be out of place. Compassion is all one can feel in such grave circumstances, and it is compassion that impels me to ask you to go to him in my name [. . .] and ask if I can do anything for him, and what, for I'll do it to the limit of my resources. (Walker, pp. 444–45)

Corticelli survived this tragedy by several years. But we do not know whether he lived long enough to know of his eternal life as Verdi's Falstaff, for whom he, supposedly, was the inspiration.

DE GIOSA, NICOLA (born 3 May 1819 [date on the birth certificate at the Archivio di Stato in Bari], Bari; died 7 July 1885, Bari). De Giosa studied composition with Donizetti at the Conservatory of Naples and wrote several successful comic operas. For some twenty years his *Don Checo* was a favorite of Neapolitan audiences. From 1860 to 1869 he was a conductor at the San Carlo Opera in Naples; in the following year he was called to Cairo for the Italian season. In 1873 De Giosa conducted in Buenos Aires and finally again at the San Carlo, where he ended his career in 1876.

DENNERY, ADOLPHE (also d'Ennery, born 17 June 1811, Paris; died 25 January 1899, Paris). At an early age Dennery left a notary's office to become a journalist and an extremely prolific playwright. A craftsman rather than an artist, he filled the bills of the Paris boulevard theatres with extraordinary success. Almost any subject he encountered — in fiction or nonfiction, in best-sellers or murder stories in the news — served as a pretext for a play; but sometimes he also happened to become involved in culture and art, as with the librettos he wrote for Gounod and Massenet. Accusations that Dennery was guilty of plagiarism prompted the great writer and critic Théophile Gautier to refer to him as "un voleur plein de gout" (a thief full of taste).

Dennery achieved his greatest success in collaboration with Jules Verne when in 1874 they made the latter's *Le Tour du Monde en 80 Jours* (*Around the World in Eighty Days*) into a spectacular play. In spite of his questionable literary taste, Dennery remained one of the most popular authors of the Paris stage for over fifty years.

DE SANCTIS, CESARE (born in Rome; died early March 1881, Naples). Although De Sanctis and his family were among the Verdis' most affectionate friends, very little is known about him, including his birthdate. He was a Neapolitan businessman and music enthusiast of great culture; as Verdi's standard-bearer and unofficial representative in Naples, he was deeply devoted to the Maestro and allied with all of Verdi's Neapolitan admirers, including: the librettist Salvatore Cammarano, who had introduced him to Verdi in 1849; Francesco Florimo, the secretary of the Conservatory; the painter Domenico Morelli; the caricaturist Melchiorre De Filippis-Delfico; the sculptor Vincenzo Gemito; the journalist Vincenzo Torelli; and Baron Giovanni Genovesi, a distinguished musician of the Neapolitan aristocracy.

The limited available correspondence between the Verdis and the De Sanctises seems to indicate that in early August 1864 Cesare De Sanctis's wife Caterina died and that he married again in early 1866. One of the children by his first marriage, Giuseppe, was Verdi's godson and became a painter. Teresa, Cesare De Sanctis's second wife, bore him a son who was named Carlos.

In June 1872 De Sanctis complained about serious economic difficulties, and in the summer of 1873 he asked Verdi for a recommendation to the House of Ricordi in Milan; but in a letter from Paris of 26 August 1873 (Autograph: Accademia dei Lincei, Rome) Verdi advised him against leaving Naples — "trees must be young to be transplanted into foreign soil." In March 1874 De Sanctis asked Verdi for a recommendation to the Mayor of Naples, and Verdi described his old friend as "an honest and spotless character" who "wishes to give up commercial speculation and work for a good and solid company." This did not happen. De Sanctis spent the last years of his life in blindness and poverty. Verdi lent him money, but objected to De Sanctis's inability to repay except by regular shipments of pasta. When Verdi received the news of De Sanctis's death, however, he wrote to Vincenzo Torelli on 10 March 1881: "Poor Cesarino! I knew him for many years — sweet, good, and affectionate. If in these last times there was something irregular, I had forgotten the bad in order to conserve only the memory of the early days of our acquaintance. Poor Cesarino! I know that the last years of his life were very painful. May he find peace in his grave!" (Autograph: Accademia dei Lincei, Rome).

D'ORMEVILLE, CARLO (born 24 April 1840, Rome; died 29 July 1924, Milan). Italian dramatist, librettist, stage director, critic, and theatrical agent. He became a stage director at La Scala in Milan and staged the premiere of *Aida* in Cairo. Even in his early twenties he attracted attention as a playwright in the romantic vein, but he dedicated most of his life to opera. As a theatrical agent in Milan he organized the first great opera companies for Argentina and represented the finest Italian artists abroad. He was a close friend and associate of Katinka Evers, whose obituary he wrote in his *Gazzetta dei Teatri*. Many letters from Emanuele Muzio to D'Ormeville bear witness to D'Ormeville's influence on the world's most prominent opera houses, including Covent Garden and the Metropolitan Opera.

Paul Draneht. A painting by sculptor and painter Prince Paul Troubetskoy (1866–1938), photographed by M. Pierre Honegger at the home of M. Peter Emmanuel Zervudachi in Vevey, Switzerland and reproduced for the first time with the permission of M. Zervudachi.

DRANEHT, PAUL (born Pavlos Pavlidis, 9 March 1815, Nicosia, Cyprus; died 4 February 1894, Rameh near Alexandria, Egypt). As the general manager of the Viceroy's opera house in Cairo, Paul (Pavlos) Draneht, traditionally known as Draneht Bey, played a major role in the history of *Aida*.

In 1827 the Greek Pavlidis family fled Turkish persecution on Cyprus to Egypt where Pavlos was introduced to Egypt's ruler Mohammed Ali, grandfather of Ismail Pasha (see note 2, Muzio's letter to Giulio Ricordi of 7 January 1870). Ali took the youngster into his service and bestowed many favors on him; he was allowed to study chemistry, medicine, pharmacy, and even dentistry in Paris. There Pavlos's professor, the celebrated Baron Louis-Jacques Thénard, became so proud of his student that he offered him his own name spelled backward. When Pavlos Pavlidis returned to Egypt, he took up his post with Mohammed Ali as Paul Draneht.

Mohammed Ali's four successors retained Paul Draneht in their service and also showed him trust, favor, and confidence. Paul Draneht soon became Draneht Bey, a Turkish title of respect, and later he was elevated to Pasha. (*Pasha* is a Turkish honorary title, formerly given to generals, governors of provinces, and other gentlemen of high distinction.) A close friend of Ferdinand de Lesseps, Draneht Bey was involved in the negotiations for the creation of the Suez Canal and also for most of Egypt's foreign loans. Under Viceroy Ismail's reign (see note 2, Muzio's letter to Giulio Ricordi of 7 January 1870) Draneht Bey established the Egyptian railways and was their first superintendent; he had numerous responsibilities, including his post as the first intendant of the Khedivial opera house in Cairo.

A few months before the premiere of *Aida* in 1871, Draneht Bey married Adele Casati, the beautiful nineteen-year-old daughter of a cellist at La Scala who was then playing in the orchestra of the Cairo Opera. In the same year, the newlyweds built the Villa Draneht at Oggebbio on Italy's Lago Maggiore. This estate was in the possession of Draneht Pasha's grandsons until a few years ago. To Monsieur Peter Emmanuel Zervudachi and to the privately printed *Twilight Memories* of his late mother, Madame Despina Zervudachi, the Pasha's only child, we owe the above information about one of Verdi's most powerful associates.

DU LOCLE, CAMILLE (born 16 July 1832, Orange, France; died 9 October 1903, Capri). The son of a sculptor and the son-in-law of Emile Perrin, Camille Du Locle, a librettist and opera producer, represented the avant-garde in the French operatic life of his time. In a letter to Du Locle from Genoa of 1 March 1869 (Autograph: Bibliothèque de l'Opéra, Paris) Verdi, who was not given to flattery, wrote, "You are the personification of amiability and gentility," and invited him "with open arms" to his home. The Verdis were deeply concerned about the fate of the Du Locle family during the Franco-Prussian War. Later Du Locle experienced financial setbacks, causing him to borrow from Verdi. Du Locle's failure to repay Verdi put their friendship to a severe test (see Verdi's letter to Emile Perrin of 23 March 1876 and Günther, "Zur Entstehung von Verdis Aida," p. 39, as well as "Der Briefwechsel Verdi-Nuitter-Du Locle zur Revision des 'Don Carlos' Teil I," pp. 414–44). Years later Charles Nuitter arranged a collaboration for the four-act version of *Don Carlos*, which led to the reconciliation of Verdi and Du Locle.

Having been Perrin's secretary at the Opéra, Du Locle managed the Opéra-Comique, with Adolphe de Leuven (1800–84) from 20 July 1870 until

Camille Du Locle. Du Locle at age sixty-three on the Island of Capri, sketched by Christian Wilhelm Allers (1857–1915). (Note "Chr. Allers 1895 Isola di Capri" in the lower right corner and "Locle" in the upper right.) First published in *The Musical Quarterly*, volume 7, 1921.

20 January 1874, when Du Locle became sole director. As director he promoted contemporary composers — Bizet, among others, whose opera *Carmen* he commissioned and produced in 1875.

A man of great culture and enterprise, Du Locle was the author of several librettos. After Joseph Méry's death in 1865 he completed the text of Verdi's originally French *Don Carlos*, which premiered at the Opéra on 11 March 1867. This period marked the beginning of his close friendship with Verdi. Early in 1868 Du Locle made a trip through Egypt with Auguste Mariette. This association culminated in the creation of Verdi's *Aida*.

With Charles Nuitter, Du Locle translated *La Forza del Destino* and *Aida* into French; in addition he translated *Simon Boccanegra* and the first two acts of *Otello*. Du Locle was also the author of a drama, *André Chénier*.

In the spring of 1875 Du Locle arranged seven performances of Verdi's *Requiem* at the Opéra-Comique, which were conducted by the composer. Economic difficulties — aggravated by the initial fiasco of *Carmen* — and a heart condition forced Du Locle to resign as director of the Opéra-Comique on 5 March 1876. Only forty-four years old at the time, he had lost not only his illusions but also the enthusiasm, vision, and energy that had fathered *Aida* and *Carmen* (see Giuseppina Verdi's letter of 4 April 1876 to Cesare De Sanctis).

ESCUDIER, LÉON (born 17 September 1821, Castelnaudary, France; died 22 June 1881, Paris). A prominent music publisher and opera producer in Paris, Escudier was associated with Verdi for many years.

With his brother Marie (1819–80) Léon Escudier went to school in Toulouse. There they soon dedicated themselves to literature and journalism. When they inherited a printing plant, they edited and published two short-lived literary and political reviews. They then moved to Paris, studied at the Sorbonne, and eventually applied their journalistic and commercial talents to music. In 1838 they founded the weekly *La France Musicale*, which was connected with an agency for the production of opera and the engagement of artists. Marie directed the review, Léon the agency. Thirty years *La France Musicale* fought for the cause of Italian music. Rossini, Donizetti, and Balzac were among the many distinguished contributors to this review, which remains a precious source of information about Europe's musical life in the nineteenth century.

Léon Escudier and his brother also wrote for various other periodicals. The longest and most important chapter in their lives was their battle to have Verdi's work recognized in France. Having acquired the French performance rights for his operas, the Escudiers began with a production of *Ernani* in 1846, followed by a triumphantly successful *Trovatore*, performed simultaneously at the Opéra and the Salle Ventadour.

When in 1860 Léon founded the review *L'Art Musical*, which existed until 1894, the Escudiers' partnership ended. Marie continued as director of *La France Musicale* until its demise in 1870. He then abandoned music and became a foreign correspondent for the Paris newspaper *Le Figaro*. In 1876, against Verdi's advice, Léon took over the management of the Italian Theatre at the Salle Ventadour, where he presented the first *Aida* in France on 22 April 1876 under Verdi's direction. Verdi also conducted several performances of the *Requiem* at the Italian Theatre, and his string quartet was performed for an invited audience.

Léon Escudier's following season at the Italian Theatre, in which he continued to give operas, concerts, and plays with famous and expensive Italian artists, was threatened by financial disaster. On 28 June 1878 the Italian Theatre was closed. Yet Léon Escudier did not give up. With government support he managed to revive the Théâtre-Lyrique at the Salle Ventadour. Having failed with two French operas presented in concert, he tried to save himself with a production of *Aida* in French, but after three performances he was forced to give up. One week before his death he took leave of his readers of *L'Art Musical*, accusing the press and the government of having sabotaged his endeavours.

Léon Escudier's refusal to follow Verdi's advice and his reluctance to pay royalties led to the end of their friendship (see Verdi's letters to Escudier of 19 May 1876 and 21 January 1877, and to Emanuele Muzio of 7 October 1879). Verdi's absence at Escudier's funeral was conspicuous.

EVERS, KATINKA (born 1821, Hamburg; died 16 August 1899, Oggebbio on Lago Maggiore). In his obituary of Katinka Evers, Carlo D'Ormeville describes her as a performer of rare beauty and intelligence who in Italy dedicated herself — presumably as a soprano — exclusively to the repertoire of Donizetti, Bellini, Rossini, and Verdi. In 1848 Katinka Evers left the stage and became the wife of the theatrical agent Giovanni Battista Lampugnani in Milan. After his death in 1873 she took over his office. Judging from many still unpublished letters from Emanuele Muzio to her, and from her friendship with Teresa Stolz, Katinka Evers-Lampugnani must have been a most attractive woman who was successful in business.

FACCIO, FRANCO (born 8 March 1840, Verona; died 21 July 1891, Monza). The son of a modest hotel owner, Franco Faccio became a composer and the conductor of the Italian premiere of *Aida* in 1872. He entered the Conservatory in Milan with his friend Arrigo Boito in 1855. Based on common ideals and artistic activities, this friendship lasted until Faccio's death.

After their graduation from the Conservatory in 1861 the two met Rossini, Verdi, Berlioz, and Gounod in Paris. On his return to Italy, Faccio won acclaim when La Scala premiered his opera *I Profughi Fiamminghi* in 1863. Faccio's opera *Amleto*, to a libretto by Boito, was produced in Genoa in 1865. Verdi thought Faccio one of the most talented Italian composers of that time. On 18 February 1870 Verdi wrote to Du Locle introducing Faccio as one of "our best" young musicians who "would like to set Sardou's *Patrie* to music, but would need the authorization of the author of the drama." (Autograph: Bibliothèque de l'Opéra, Paris)

In 1866 Faccio, with Boito and other friends, joined Garibaldi's forces of liberation. In 1867 he conducted *Il Trovatore*, *Ernani*, *Rigoletto*, *Un Ballo in Maschera*, and other Italian operas in Berlin, where he became acquainted with Wagner's *Lohengrin* and *Tannhäuser*. Later he conducted in Scandinavia. In 1868 he was appointed to the faculty of the Conservatory in Milan; in 1869 became a conductor at La Scala and soon thereafter its artistic director. When *Amleto* failed at La Scala in 1871, Faccio withdrew the work from the repertoire and composed no more operas. After Angelo Mariani's death in 1873 he was considered the most distinguished Italian conductor of his time.

Having conducted the premiere of *Aida* at La Scala in 1872, Faccio became a leading exponent of many Verdi operas in other European countries. In 1887 he conducted the world premiere of *Otello* at La Scala. He was a great admirer of Wagner's works, which he introduced at La Scala, as well as Weber's *Freischütz* in Boito's translation, with recitatives composed by himself. In addition to directing Puccini's early works, Faccio in his rather short life also directed a large variety of prominent French and lesser-known Italian operas at La Scala and promoted symphonic concerts as part of Italy's musical culture.

When cerebral paralysis threatened Faccio's position at La Scala, he followed Verdi's advice to accept the directorship of the Conservatory in Parma. But Faccio was too ill to hold the office, and Boito assumed his duties, leaving the salary to his friend.

Faccio's eminent musicianship and international influence caused George Bernard Shaw to rank him with his great German contemporaries Hans Richter, Felix Mottl, and Hermann Levi.

FILIPPI, FILIPPO (born 13 January 1830, Vicenza; died 24 June 1887, Milan). In all of Europe Filippo Filippi was respected and feared as Italy's most influential music critic. When he graduated in law at Padua in 1853, Filippi, who had had little, if any, formal education in music, became the music editor of a journal in Venice. Therafter Tito Ricordi invited him to write for *La Gazzetta Musicale* in Milan. In 1859 Dr. Filippi became a music and art critic on the editorial staff of *La Perseveranza*, a prominent Milan newspaper, on whose pages he courageously and passionately propounded his often controversial ideas until his death.

During frequent trips abroad, which he described in his book *Musica e Musicisti* (Milan, 1876), he attended the premieres of *Don Carlos* in Paris (1867) and *Aida* in Cairo (1871). As a special correspondent he covered a Tsar's coronation in Moscow and was sent to London, Madrid, Constantinople, Weimar, and Bayreuth, where he was present at the inauguration of the Festival House in 1876.

Filippi's judgments of Wagner's as well as Verdi's works varied between enthusiasm and rejection. In addition to his quest for journalistic sensationalism, Filippi annoyed Verdi with his repeated allusions to Wagner's influence on Verdi's works.

GALLETTI GIANOLI, ISABELLA (born 11 November 1835, Bologna; died 31 August 1901, Milan). Having established a firm reputation throughout Italy in such roles as Norma, Leonora in *Il Trovatore*, and Leonora in *La Favorita*, Isabella Galletti Gianoli was the leading soprano of the Cairo Opera during its first season (1869–70). Rossini considered her "too seductive," and "at Sant'Agata Angelo Mariani was suspected of having designs on her." He wrote to Verdi on 28 July 1870:

> Signora Galletti has written to me from Pesaro to tell me that you are writing an opera for Cairo, and she wants me to recommend you to give her the preference; indeed, she asked me for a couple of lines to you to enclose in a letter she intends to write you about that. [. . .] Imagine! (I tell you this in confidence) she wanted me to thrust her upon you and sing the praises of her . . . *artistic* virtues! (Walker, p. 363)

Signor Gianoli, the prima donna's husband, supported Mariani's recommendation. Verdi suspected an intrigue "which stinks of the theatre at a thousand miles' distance" and wrote to Mariani that "Gianoli would do well to look after his own affairs and not interfere in mine" (Walker, p. 366).

GHISLANZONI, ANTONIO (born 25 November 1824, Lecco; died 16 July 1893, Caprino Bergamasco). As a librettist Antonio Ghislanzoni was in great demand by a number of rather obscure composers. However, he assisted with the first Italian translation of *Don Carlos* in 1867, as well as with the revision of *La Forza del Destino* in 1869. Verdi was so pleased with Ghislanzoni's work and attitude that in 1870 he chose him to versify *Aida*.

A restless, eccentric individual with various talents, Ghislanzoni studied medicine at the University of Pavia while writing stories and poetry; but eventually he became a professional baritone. He appeared in the role of Carlo V in Verdi's *Ernani* in Paris (1851). At that time Ghislanzoni started to write librettos and founded a short-lived opera company which traveled in France. In 1854 he returned to Milan, sick with bronchitis, which ended his singing career the following year. He then turned to journalism and criticism. In 1856 he published his first and most successful novel, *Gli artisti da teatro*; the

Antonio Ghislanzoni. Photograph courtesy of G. Ricordi & C., Milan.

ridiculous plot reflects his own experiences with the theatre and with opera in particular. "The mysteries of the theatre," he writes in his introduction to the novel, "have made me smile many times, but more often filled me with disgust, tore at my heart, made me shudder and cry."

Ghislanzoni was more successful as editor of several reviews, critic of music and literature, and author of several novels. He claimed to have published 2,162 articles. While collaborating with Verdi on *Aida*, he was the editor of Ricordi's *La Gazzetta Musicale* and its by-product, *Rivista Minima* in Milan; but he lived at the little mountain village of Mariaga near Lecco on Lake Como. There, withdrawn from the world like Verdi at St. Agata, he worked on *Aida* and, at the same time, expressed in *Rivista Minima* his very personal, witty, skeptical, and compassionate thoughts about the events of the day, the Franco-Prussian War in particular. And on many pages he also philosophized about a vast range of cultural and sociological matters of worldwide interest. Ghislanzoni's book *Reminiscenze artistiche* contains notes on Verdi and his home at St. Agata.

With approximately eighty-five librettos to his credit, Ghislanzoni emerges from the general mediocrity of Italy's nineteenth-century librettists as a great talent, in company with Donizetti and Bellini's collaborator Felice Romani and, later, Arrigo Boito.

GROSSI, ELEONORA (born ca. 1840, Naples; died January 1879, Naples). Eleonora Grossi, the first Amneris in Cairo, studied as a soprano at the Conservatory in Naples, but its director Saverio Mercadante declared her voice to be mezzo. At eighteen she made her debut as Cenerentola in Messina. From 1860 to 1862 she was on the roster of the San Carlo Opera in Naples, and in 1863 she is supposed to have sung at La Scala. Thereafter she appeared in Turin and Palermo (1862–63), Barcelona (1863–64), Dublin (1863), London (1864, 1865, 1869, 1873), Rome (1864), Madrid (1864–65), Paris (Italian Theatre 1865–68), Lille and Gand (1866), Constantinople and Baden-Baden (1866–67), Berlin, Copenhagen, and Göteborg (1867), Seville, Hamburg, and Bad Homburg (1868), and in Cairo (1869–72, 1875–76). Reviewing her debut in *Martha*, the *London Times* wrote: "A voice of richness almost without parallel since Alboni."

HALANZIER-DUFRENOY, OLIVIER (born 11 December 1819, Paris; died 188–, Paris). The son of a talented comedienne, who had been a provincial theatre director, Halanzier managed the theatres in Strasbourg, Bordeaux, Lille, Marseilles, Brussels, and Lyon before succeeding Émile Perrin as director of the Paris Opéra in 1871. When in 1873 fire destroyed the Opéra in rue Le Peletier, Halanzier moved the company to the small Salle Ventadour. On 5 January 1875 the new Opéra built by Charles Garnier was inaugurated.

Halanzier retired in 1879 and Auguste Emanuel Vaucorbeil became his successor. Even the Bibliothèque de l'Opéra in Paris has not established the date of Halanzier's death.

HILLER, FERDINAND (born 24 October 1811, Frankfurt-on-the-Main; died 11 May 1885, Cologne). Of German birth and cosmopolitan background, Ferdinand Hiller was a total musician who invited Verdi to conduct the *Requiem* in Cologne on 21 May 1877 and became one of Verdi's best friends in the last years of their lives. Hiller was born into a wealthy Jewish family. After his music studies in Frankfurt and Weimar he lived as a pianist and teacher in Paris from 1828 to 1835. From 1843 to 1844 he conducted concerts at the Gewandhaus in Leipzig, replacing his friend Felix Mendelssohn with whom he had much in common. Thereafter he was conductor in Dresden, Düsseldorf, and Cologne, where he won the highest distinction as director of the conservatory which he founded after the pattern of the conservatory in Leipzig.

Hiller was also a prolific composer, writer, and lecturer, but his music has not survived. As a boy he played for Goethe in Weimar and was allowed to visit Beethoven and Schubert in Vienna. In Paris, where the old Cherubini accepted him as a member of the family, he enjoyed the company of Rossini, Bellini, Meyerbeer, and Heinrich Heine, and became a friend of Berlioz and Chopin. In Leipzig he was closely associated not only with Felix Mendelssohn but also with Robert Schumann, who dedicated his only piano concerto, the famous op. 59, to him. In 1884 Hiller asked his young friend Johannes Brahms to become his successor in Cologne but understood when Brahms declined.

Even though he had no sympathy for the man or his music, Hiller held Wagner in high esteem and reacted good-naturedly to Wagner's ridiculing his writings. The Viennese critic Eduard Hanslick describes Hiller as one of the most amiable, urbane, and witty gentlemen of his time.

LAMPUGNANI, GIOVANNI BATTISTA — not the Italian composer (1706–81) of the same name but possibly related to him — (born 30 October 1813, Milan; died 30 April 1873, Milan [dates from the Ufficio Stato Civile of the City of Milan]). An influential theatrical agent, Lampugnani was Draneht's personal representative in Milan and a friend of the conductor Angelo Mariani (1821–73) but apparently not of Verdi's.

In 1848 Lampugnani married Katinka Evers. *La Gazzetta Musicale* of 3 May 1868 reported the death of their daughter Giuditta at the age of ten years.

LUCCARDI, VINCENZO (born 22 February 1811, Gemona near Udine; died 14 November 1876, Genazzano near Rome). He became Verdi's unofficial representative in Rome and one of his most trusted friends. From 1829 to 1832 Luccardi studied sculpture at the Academy of Fine Arts in Venice, where he won many prizes. In 1832 he moved to Florence, and in 1832 he established himself in Rome where he spent the rest of his life. In 1862 Luccardi became a professor at the Roman Academy of San Luca, which provided this information. He was a member of various Italian and other European academies. One of his major works was Metastasio's tomb in Vienna.

MAFFEI, CLARINA (born 13 March 1814, Bergamo; died 13 July 1886, Milan). The daughter of Count G. B. Carrara Spinelli and one of Verdi's earliest friends, Clarina, as Clara was affectionately called, married the writer Andrea Maffei at the age of eighteen. A lady of outstanding charm and intelligence, she attracted the greatest personalities in the arts to her home in Milan. Among them were Giuseppe Verdi and.Opprandino Arrivabene, the writers Giulio Carcano, Antonio Ghislanzoni, Carlo Tenca, who became her life-long companion, and in later years Arrigo Boito, Franco Faccio, and Giacomo Puccini. Verdi expressed his loyalty to both Clarina and Andrea Maffei at the time of their legal separation in 1846 and remained a friend to both throughout their lifetimes. Verdi's wife Giuseppina and Clarina Maffei were devoted to each other as well, and Giuseppina called Clarina a lady "who lives with enthusiasm and has built a temple of friendship."

Countess Maffei's ardent patriotism and political interests were essential elements of her friendship with Verdi. Actively involved in Milan's abortive uprising against the Austrian occupation in 1848, she lived in temporary exile in Switzerland, where she met the Italian patriot and revolutionary Giuseppe Mazzini. Also a friend of Count Camillo Cavour, the father of Italy's unification, she courageously returned to Milan to work in hospitals and in many other ways served the cause of her country's liberation.

In 1868 Countess Maffei arranged Verdi's visit to Italy's poet Alessandro Manzoni, whom Verdi was too shy to approach on his own. This great and noble lady's liberal, generous, and progressive spirit also encouraged the younger generation of her day and helped to further many artists' careers. For fifty years her salon was one of the centers, if not *the* center, of the cultural life in Milan.

When Countess Maffei was stricken with meningitis, Verdi hurried to her bedside and wrote on 22 July 1886 to Antonio Ghislanzoni: "I arrived in Milan in time to see her die! Poor Clarina! So kind, so considerate, and so sensible. Oh, I shall certainly never forget her! We had been friends for forty-four years!!" (Autograph: Istituti Artistici e Culturali, Forlì)

MAGNANI, GIROLAMO (born 25 April 1815, Borgo St. Donnino (Fidenza); died 24 September 1889, Parma). A painter and scenic designer from

Verdi's part of the country, Girolamo Magnani was born into a humble family and went to work for a simple decorator but soon began building sets for strolling players. At fourteen he won a scholarship at the Academy of Fine Arts in Parma, from which he graduated in 1833. Giovanni Boccaccio, a famous landscape painter and scenic designer, was his teacher. Paolo Toschi, the director of the Parma Academy, entrusted Magnani, then only twenty, with painting the rooms in which Correggio's masterpieces were to be hung. In 1848 he became a professor at the Parma Academy.

Magnani was overwhelmed by many kinds of offers and commissions, including the decoration of the Duchess Maria Luisa's bath and library and of a ceiling in the Palazzo Marchi, now the seat of the Institute of Verdi Studies in Parma.

When Maria Luisa died, Duke Carlo III of Bourbon, an enemy of liberals but a patron of the arts, charged Magnani with the restoration of the Teatro Regio in Parma. Before he began this task, Magnani studied the principal opera houses of other European cities such as Vienna, Prague, Dresden, Berlin, Brussels, Paris, and London.

Magnani's phenomenal success with the restoration of the Teatro Regio resulted in invitations to do similar work at the theatres of Reggio Emilia, Piacenza, Genoa, Busseto, Brescia, and, at his hometown, Borgo St. Donnino, which he did without compensation.

Among many other commissions, Magnani decorated the National Bank in Florence in 1869 and in 1873 the dining hall at the Quirinale Palace in Rome. His greatest talent, however, was for scenic design. In 1844 he was engaged to paint the sets for *Ernani* and *I Due Foscari* at the Teatro Regio in Parma. In 1853 he became head of design at that theatre and was invited to work for many other opera houses in Italy and abroad, including those in Cairo, London, Paris, Madrid, Philadelphia, and New York.

After accepting Verdi's invitation to design the Italian premiere of *Aida* at La Scala in 1872, Magnani remained associated with that theatre for a period of over ten years, an immensely successful time, though marred by the jealousies and intrigues of his colleagues.

Despite the small amount of information available about him, Magnani emerges as one of the most active and imaginative operatic designers of his romantic century, a master of perspective and chiaroscuro in the greatest tradition of Italian theatrical painting (see Verdi's letter to Giulio Ricordi of 6 December 1871).

MARIETTE, AUGUSTE, full name François-Auguste-Ferdinande Mariette (born 11 February 1821, Boulogne-sur-Mer, France; died 18 January 1881, Boulaq near Cairo). Generally known as Mariette Bey, Auguste Mariette was

Auguste Mariette. Photograph of drawing, courtesy of the Institut Français d'Archéologie Orientale, Cairo.

an eminent French Egyptologist who wrote the original outline of *Aida*. The son of a modest municipal employee, Auguste Mariette had to overcome extraordinary odds to fulfill his dream of traveling to Egypt, where he was to make some of the greatest archaeological discoveries of the nineteenth century. At eighteen he went to England to teach French and drawing at a school in Stratford. After unsuccessfully attempting to make a living as an industrial designer in Coventry, in 1841 he returned to Boulogne and obtained a bachelor's degree in letters. As a young schoolteacher in his hometown, he became fascinated with an Egyptian sarcophagus covered with figures and hieroglyphic inscriptions at the local museum. His subsequent studies of Egyptian language, history, and mythology led him to Paris where for seven years he worked independently. In 1845 he married and in 1849 he was given a minor post in the Department of Egyptian Antiquities at the Museum of the Louvre.

In 1850 Mariette's dream of seeing Egypt came true. He was sent there to acquire coptic manuscripts. Instead he discovered the Serapis Temple and the Apis Tombs near Memphis. In later excavations he found the Temple of the Sphinx, temples and tombs of the Pharaohs at Giza, Abydos, Sakkara, and Thebes, and an infinity of other treasures, which rewarded him for his perseverance in the face of difficulties of every kind.

In 1857, after a short sojourn in France, Mariette returned to Egypt, where he received the title of Bey in 1858 and of Pasha in 1879. (*Bey* is a Turkish title of respect; *Pasha*, a Turkish honorary title formerly given to generals, governors of provinces, and other gentlemen of high distinction.) Backed by Ferdinand de Lesseps, creator of the Suez Canal, Mariette established the Boulaq Museum of Egyptian Antiquities on the premises of a former post office near Cairo in 1863. As Director of Egyptian Monuments and sometimes assisted by his close friend German Egyptologist Heinrich Brugsch he supervised almost 3,000 workmen at thirty-five different sites from Aswan to the Mediterranean over a period of thirty years. Whole temples such as Luxor and Edfu were discovered and saved, but most of Mariette's innumerable papers were destroyed when his home at Boulaq was flooded three years before his death. Tragedy overshadowed his successes when cholera and other diseases took the lives of five of his eleven children and in 1864 his wife also died.

In 1867 the Paris Exposition enabled him to show Europe some of the results of his work in Egypt. Torn between his allegiance to his native France, which offered him distinction and security, and his duties to the country of his glory, Mariette decided to continue his work in Egypt for the rest of his life. He minded neither his declining health nor the problems of Egypt's rapidly dwindling economy (see note 2, Muzio's letter to Giulio Ricordi of 7 January 1870), which compelled him to borrow money to defray his hotel bills in Paris as late as 1878. Having been trapped in that city during the German siege of 1870–71, he returned there in 1877 to prepare an Egyptian exhibition. A victim of diabetes, he made his last trip to France in 1880, realizing it was his final visit. He wanted to die near the museum he had created at Boulaq, and his wish was fulfilled. When in 1890 the museum — too small to display all its treasures — was moved to Giza, Mariette Pasha's remains were also transferred there. His tomb was guarded by the Four Sphinges of the Serapeum, which he had discovered, but later the sarcophagus in which he was buried was moved to the forecourt of the museum in Cairo, surmounted by a bronze statue unveiled in 1904.

MARIETTE, EDOUARD wrote in his *Lettres et souvenirs personnels* of Auguste Mariette Pasha (see Document I) that he was twenty years younger than his famous brother, that he was very close to him and accompanied him on many of his archaeological trips. Apart from his account of the origin of *Aida*, we know little about him.

MARINI, IGNAZIO (born 28 November 1811, Tagliuno near Bergamo; died 29 April 1873, Milan). Marini was a well-known bass at major opera houses in Italy and abroad. He interpreted several Verdi roles, including the title roles at the premieres of *Oberto*, Verdi's first opera, at La Scala in Milan (1839) and *Attila* at the Teatro Fenice in Venice (1846). In 1843 Verdi addressed Marini as the favorite bass of the Milanese and wrote him that "the roles of the Prophet in *Nabucco* and of Pagano in *I Lombardi* seem as though written for you." (Photocopy of autograph dated 11 June 1843: Istituto di Studi Verdiani, Parma)

MAZZUCATO, ALBERTO (born 28 July 1813, Udine; died 31 December 1877, Milan). When he was a student of mathematics at the University of Padua, Alberto Mazzucato decided to study music and became an admirer of Verdi's. In his younger days he wrote a number of operas which were somewhat successful, including *La Fidanzata di Lammermoor* and *Ernani*. However, Donizetti's *Lucia*, like Verdi's *Ernani*, soon overshadowed Mazzucato's work on the same theme.

In 1839 Mazzucato was appointed to the faculty of the conservatory of Milan. As a teacher of composition, counting Arrigo Boito among his students, he enjoyed great esteem. From 1872 until his death he was the director of the conservatory. Heading the orchestra of La Scala from 1858 to 1868, Mazzucato became the epitome of the modern conductor.

In addition to these pedagogical and professional activities, Mazzucato was an editor of Ricordi's *La Gazzetta Musicale* as well as the author of several books on music theory and music appreciation. Among other writings of importance he translated Berlioz's *Great Treaty of Instrumentation and Orchestration* into Italian.

Having been a member of the committee to organize the *Requiem* for Rossini, which Verdi had suggested and to which he had contributed the *Libera me* — Verdi included parts of this *Libera* in his *Requiem* for Manzoni — Mazzucato wrote to Verdi on 2 February 1871: "You have written the greatest, most beautiful and most immensely poetic pages imaginable." After his death, these lines from Mazzucato's diary were sent to Verdi on the back of a photograph:

Monday, 6 February 1871

I had written to Verdi about the great and profound impression I felt when reading his *Libera me, Domine*. He answered in an expansive letter — unusually expansive when one thinks of his habitual reluctance to speak of his own affairs, or to consider a critic. Verdi surprised me greatly with his *Nabucco* and *I Lombardi*. I saw him descend to popular passions in *Ernani*, *Il Trovatore*, etc. I saw him rise again with *Macbeth*, and increase his stature with *Miller* and *Stiffelio*. He became insuperable with *Rigoletto*, *Boccanegra*, etc.

I adore this composer; and I want him to know this, and thus to know the truth, which interested parties kept from him for over twenty-five years. (Walker, p. 467)

MONALDI, GINO (born 2 December 1847, Perugia; died 5 April 1932, Rome). The descendant of a noble family — mentioned by Dante in *Purgatorio*, VI — the Marquis Gino Monaldi studied music, including composition, with Alberto Mazzucato at the Milan Conservatory, but he did not distinguish himself as a composer. He became a music critic for several Italian papers and later an impresario.

MONPLAISIR, HYPPOLITE-GEORGE, stage name for H.-G. Sornet (born 1821, Bordeaux; died 10 June 1877, Besana, Italy). A dancer and choreographer, the son of Jeanne Sornet and an unknown father, Monplaisir studied dance in Brussels in 1839 and with Carlo Blasis at La Scala in Milan, where he and his wife Adèle — the daughter of the ballet master Victor Bartholomin — were engaged as solo dancers in 1844. The couple also appeared at La Scala in 1845–46 with some of the leading dancers of their time, such as Maria Taglioni and Fanny Elssler, with whom Monplaisir appeared as Albert in *Giselle*. After the 1846–47 season in Trieste, Barcelona, and Lyon, the Monplaisirs made their American debut on 21 October 1847 with Victor Bartholomin's French Ballet Company at the Broadway Theatre in New York. Endowed with excellent dancers as well as beautiful sets and costumes, this company was among the first to visit the United States. It was also extremely successful in the South, particularly in New Orleans. After performances in Boston and Philadelphia, the French Ballet Company returned to the Broadway Theatre in New York in the fall of 1848, and Monplaisir became its director when Bartholomin returned to Europe. The Monplaisirs' successful American tours lasted for several years and brought them as far as California.

Around 1856 Adèle left her husband and became the partner of Léon Espinosa, while, in November 1855, Hyppolite won applause in Meyerbeer's *Prophète* in New York. In 1856 he choreographed Laura Keene's Varieties Theatre in New York. In the fall of that year he was to make his debut as solo dancer in Lisbon, but a foot injury ended his dancing career. He went to Lisbon as a choreographer of *L'Illusion d'un Peintre* by Jules Perrot and seven ballets of his own, and he returned there the following season.

Monplaisir's fame resulted primarily from the ballets he created for La Scala and other Italian theatres from 1861 until his death. Originally influenced by Jules Perrot's romantic style, Monplaisir became attracted to historical, exotic, and spectacular themes such as *Le Figlie di Chèope*, which despite Verdi's protestations took place at La Scala on 31 December 1871.

MUZIO, EMANUELE (born 24 August 1821 [date on his birth certificate at the parish church in Zibello] Zibello near Busseto; died 27 November 1890, Paris). Though intended for the shoemaking craft of his father in Busseto, Emanuele Muzio, a conductor and Verdi's very close friend, studied music at the school of Verdi's teacher Ferdinando Provesi. The child Emanuele was a soloist in several church choirs and eventually studied for the priesthood; however, in need of a modest income, he became an organist and music director in Busseto (1840–43).

In 1844, on the recommendation of Verdi's father-in-law Antonio Barezzi, Muzio went to Milan to study with Verdi, who generously agreed to instruct him in harmony, counterpoint, and composition. Muzio became his apprentice and most devoted companion, writing piano-vocal scores of Rossini, Donizetti, and Verdi operas as well as chamber music and marches. Taking Muzio along for the 1847 productions of *Màcbeth* in Florence and of *I Masnadieri* in London, Verdi introduced his pupil to the stage. In those years Muzio poured all his love and admiration for his Maestro into his letters to Antonio Barezzi, rather naïve travelogues of touching sincerity reflecting the young Verdi's life and work. This happy companionship ended in 1848 when Muzio actively participated in Milan's thwarted uprising against the Austrians. Barezzi and Verdi helped him recuperate from his adventure in the country.

Muzio returned to Milan in 1849 to give private lessons and to compose. In 1850 he conducted at the inauguration of the Italian Theatre in Brussels where his opera *Giovanna la Pazza* was successfully performed the following year. His second opera *Claudia* was given in Milan (1853 and 1855). When in 1858 he became head of the Royal Opera Orchestra in London, Muzio gave up composing.

Extensive concert and opera tours through the United States before and during the years of the Civil War and an unhappy marriage to a young American singer, Lucy Simons, who was born in Transylvania, added to Muzio's experience. The couple was married in New York on 3 April 1865; they had a son, who died when he was one month old and and was buried in his mother's native soil.

In 1867 Muzio returned with his wife to Italy, where he conducted in Venice and in Bologna. In 1869 he conducted a concert for the opening of the Suez Canal at Ismailia, Egypt, and on 1 November 1869, the inaugural performance, *Rigoletto*, of the opera house in Cairo. After his reunion with Verdi in the spring of 1870 in Paris, Muzio assumed the artistic direction of the Italian Theatre in that city. During the 1873–74 season he conducted the first performances of *Aida* in America; (see Muzio's letters to Verdi of 8, 22, and 27 November 1873); but he remained the "prime minister" of the Italian Theatre in Paris until the first (and unsuccessful) performance of *La Forza del*

Destino in France in 1876, which marked the end of his conducting career. Thereafter he taught voice in Paris, and Adelina Patti, whose first New York performances he had conducted in 1859–60, was one of his students. In 1875 Verdi asked his old friend to assist him with the performances of the *Requiem* in Paris, London, and Vienna; in 1877 Muzio helped with the preparation of that work in Cologne.

Talented as he was, Muzio was timid and lacked confidence. Verdi was never sparing with his advice and moral support to his only prominent pupil; he watched over Muzio like an older brother, expressing his opinion and concern to Clarina Maffei: "He is good and has a big heart, his manners are as rough as mine; he is kind of a bear like me, but excellent underneath. [. . .] He has illusions which will never be realized. [. . .] He has not enough of a head to know the world and himself." (Autographs: Collezione Enrico Olmo, Chiari)

Apparently unable to free himself completely from Verdi's influence, Muzio nevertheless had a distinguished career. When death approached in a Paris hospital, he once more wrote of his everlasting devotion to his beloved Maestro and his Maestro's wife. He also appointed Verdi executor of his last will, in which he nobly, but unfortunately, decreed that all of Verdi's letters to him were to be destroyed to prevent their commercial exploitation.

NUITTER, CHARLES-LOUIS-ÉTIENNE, anagram of C.-L.-É. Truinet (born 24 April 1828, Paris; died 24 February 1899, Paris). Having abandoned a brief legal career, Nuitter became the author of numerous librettos of operas, operettas, vaudevilles, and ballets. He frequently collaborated with others, particularly Offenbach, Beaumont, and Delibes. Nuitter also translated several Italian and German operas, including four by Wagner, into French. The Verdi operas he translated were *Macbeth*, with Alfred Beaumont in 1865; *Aida*, with Du Locle in 1872 and with Verdi in 1876; *La Forza del Destino*, with Du Locle in 1882; and *Simon Boccanegra* in 1883.

Nuitter wrote several scholarly books on the origins of French opera and an article on the rehearsals and first performances of *Tannhäuser*. He and his friend Du Locle met Verdi in Paris in December 1865, when they approached the composer concerning a French version of *La Forza del Destino*, which did not come about at that time. In 1866 Nuitter was appointed archivist of the Paris Opéra, whose library he cataloged and enriched with innumerable acquisitions at his own expense. In 1875 Nuitter replaced Du Locle as temporary director of the Opéra-Comique.

At his death Nuitter left one million francs to the artists of Paris and half a million to the library of the Opéra. In the obituary that appeared in *Le Figaro* on 25 February 1899 he was described as a very tall gentleman "of ecclesiastic politeness and extreme courtesy, who lived completely alone and let no one penetrate into the mystery of his private life."

PEDROTTI, CARLO (born 12 November 1817, Verona; died 16 October 1893, Verona). From 1841 to 1845 Pedrotti conducted at the Italian Theatre in Amsterdam. Thereafter he taught and composed in Verona for some twenty years. From 1868 until 1882 he won much acclaim and distinction as conductor of the Teatro Regio in Turin. At the age of sixty-seven Pedrotti was invited to head a music school in Pesaro which had been established in honor of Rossini. In 1893 he resigned from that position and returned to his native town, where some months later his body was recovered from the Adige River, an apparent suicide.

PERRIN, EMILE (born 19 January 1814, Rouen, France; died 8 October 1885, Paris). Perrin began as a successful painter and art critic. His administrative talents came to the fore when in 1848 he became director of the Opéra-Comique. In 1854 the Théâtre-Lyrique was also entrusted to his management. In 1857 he resigned as director of both theatres and in 1862 assumed the management of the Opéra, over which he presided at the time of Verdi's *Don Carlos* premiere on 11 March 1867. Perrin left the Opéra in 1870 and was nominated administrator of the Comédie-Française in 1871.

PIROLI, GIUSEPPE (born 16 February 1815, Busseto; died 14 November 1890, Rome). Born in poverty and a childhood friend of Verdi's, Piroli became a distinguished lawyer and politician. In 1848 he was nominated secretary of the regency of Parma and in that position represented Parma's subsequent provisional government. He taught penal law at the University of Parma and was persecuted by Carlo III, a Bourbon ruler imposed on Parma by the Congress of Vienna. In 1859 Piroli was elected deputy of the Assembly of Parma. In this capacity he proposed the decree that united the province of Parma with the kingdom of Italy. Like Verdi, Piroli belonged to Cavour's liberal party, which opposed the clerical and radical-socialist parties. In 1866 he joined the Council of State in Rome and was nominated vice president of the Chamber. In 1884 he became a senator.

  Mourning the death of his lifelong friend and legal adviser, Verdi described Giuseppe Piroli in a letter to Maria Waldmann on 6 December 1890 as ''a learned, frank, sincere man, of a rectitude not to be equaled. A friend, constant and unchanged during sixty years.'' (Autograph: Conservatorio di Musica ''G. B. Martini,'' Bologna)

RICORDI, GIULIO (born 19 December 1840, Milan; died 6 June 1912, Milan). As Tito Ricordi's oldest son, Giulio became the director of Ricordi & Lucca Publishers at the time of their merger, shortly before his father's death in 1888.

  A gifted writer, musician, painter, and administrator, Giulio Ricordi began his work for the firm at the age of twenty-two. At that time he was interested

Giulio Ricordi. Photograph courtesy of G. Ricordi & C., Milan.

principally in *La Gazzetta Musicale*, whose publisher he became in 1866. Under the pen name of J. Burgmein, he composed a great deal of piano, chamber, and symphonic music, songs, ballets, and operettas, which were performed in his lifetime.

Giulio Ricordi's profound devotion to Verdi did not keep him from supporting the young composers of his time, Puccini in particular. Far beyond his commercial interests, Giulio Ricordi enjoyed the personal friendship of and intense collaboration with many of his composers and librettists. Not only was he their publisher, but for all intents and purposes he was also the producer of their works at La Scala. For many years he acted as Verdi's agent and personal representative, weathering storms that threatened to end their friendship.

With great tact and diplomacy sometimes bordering on outright connivance, Giulio Ricordi managed to introduce his young friends to the aging Verdi. It was he who brought about Verdi's collaboration with Boito. Without Giulio Ricordi's imagination and initiative, *Otello* and *Falstaff* would never have been created.

RICORDI, TITO (born 29 October 1811, Milan; died 7 September 1888, Milan). A son of Giovanni Ricordi, founder of the famous music publishing firm, Tito had been his father's apprentice and collaborator for many years. When he succeeded him as head of the firm, he inherited a securely established business and a wealth of musical material. He also inherited his father's close ties to Verdi.

In addition to being an expert lithographer, Tito Ricordi was an excellent pianist and was personally acquainted with Schumann, Liszt, Meyerbeer, and other famous musicians of his era. In 1842 he founded *La Gazzetta Musicale di Milano*, a prominent review which existed under that name until 1902. He fought and won the battle for the rights of authors in Italy and abroad, was one of the founders of the Società del Quartetto in Milan (1863), enlarged the House of Ricordi's physical plant, and introduced many technical innovations in printing. During Tito Ricordi's reign several other Italian music publishers were absorbed by the House of Ricordi, and branches of the firm opened in other Italian cities as well as in Paris and London. Three months before his death, his achievements were crowned by the merger with the Francesco Lucca music publishers, after years of bitter competition.

Tito Ricordi maintained permanent contacts with the managements of La Scala and other Italian opera houses, and he involved himself in all the production phases of the operas he published. Despite occasional business differences, his personal relationship with Verdi remained constant. Verdi contacted Tito in matters of major policy, and Tito was the only member of the Ricordi family whom he addressed with the personal *tu*.

STOLZ, TERESA (born 5 June 1834, Elbekosteletz, Bohemia; died 23 August 1902, Milan). Teresa Stolz grew up as a soprano among eight brothers and sisters, five of whom became professional musicians; in spite of initial setbacks she became the most famous member of the family. After her studies at the Conservatory in Prague from 1849 to 1851, and later with renowned Italian coaches, she appeared in Bohemian and probably German theatres as well as in Tiflis, Odessa, and Constantinople. Her rise to fame, however, began in 1864 when she sang Leonora in *Il Trovatore* at Spoleto and a number of other roles, including Gilda, Lady Macbeth, and Amelia, in Bologna, Palermo, Florence, and Cesena. Under contract to La Scala in 1865, she won particular acclaim in *Giovanna d'Arco* and *Lucrezia Borgia*. Thereupon Verdi chose her for the first Italian performance of *Don Carlos* in Bologna. Her interpretation of the role of Elisabetta in that opera was a triumph which, in 1867, established her as the greatest Verdi singer of her time. Her success in *Don Carlos* was matched by her appearances in *La Forza del Destino*, *Aida*, and the *Requiem*. Teresa Stolz's vocal power and technique, in the soprano and mezzo-soprano registers, and her noble, sensitive phrasing and diction contributed to her phenomenal success.

The breach of Teresa Stolz's engagement to Verdi's one-time friend, the conductor Angelo Mariani, and her personal relations with Verdi have occasioned much speculation (see Walker, pp. 393–446, and Wechsberg, pp. 139–62). She was close to both the Maestro and his wife, and after Giuseppina Verdi's death in 1897, she remained Verdi's most faithful companion until he died. She survived him by less than two years.

TERZIANI, EUGENIO (born 30 July 1824, Rome; died 30 June 1889, Rome). Son of the conductor and composer Pietro Terziani, Eugenio followed in his father's footsteps. At sixteen, he graduated from the conservatory in Naples. In 1848 he volunteered for combat with Garibaldi's brigades.

Terziani wrote an oratorio, several operas, symphonic and chamber music, but he chose to become a conductor. As such he had served for twenty years at the Teatro Apollo in Rome when in 1868 he was called to La Scala, with Franco Faccio as one of his assistants.

"Terziani is a good conductor, but paralyzed by the war against him," Verdi wrote to Tito Ricordi in 1869, while entrusting to Terziani the Scala premiere of his final version of *La Forza del Destino* (27 February 1869). Filippo Filippi led the war against Terziani who, in 1871, returned to the Apollo in Rome. Judged incapable to lead an orchestra, in 1875 he became a professor of composition at the newly founded music school of Santa Cecilia in Rome.

TORELLI, VINCENZO (born presumably 1806, Bari; died 16 February 1884, Naples). "Don Vincenzo," as he was respectfully called by all of Naples, thrived on his weekly paper *L'Omnibus*, which he founded in 1830 from the sale of a little farm. For thirty years Torelli advanced his ideas on music, theatre, and literature in this journal, which he promoted during his daily rounds of Neopolitan cafés. In 1854 Torelli's unfavorable review of

Verdi's *Alzira* antagonized the composer's friends, but Verdi was probably the first to agree that "no human talent is capable of producing two or three grand operas a year."

As secretary of the San Carlo Opera, the influential journalist became one of Verdi's strongest supporters. But "Torelli, a difficult, rather unscrupulous man, was not popular with some of Verdi's other Neapolitan friends. De Sanctis thought him a heartless and vindictive egotist, and reported various things to his discredit to Sant' Agata" (Walker, p. 230). Giuseppina Strepponi, however, wrote to Torelli in 1858: "Although there are some people who consider you a Big Devil (mind, it's better to be a Big Devil than a big . . . something else!), I am not altogether of their opinion. I think (not to make a comparison, but to express my idea) you're a bittersweet sauce. Well then, unfortunate is he who bumps into you and sets in motion the bitter substances; fortunate, however, he that happens on the sweet ones: you are capable of much good" (Walker, p. 229).

In 1860 Torelli retired from his *L'Omnibus*, dedicating the remaining twenty-four years of his life to his son Achille, a very successful playwright. (A visit to Villa Torelli in the Naples suburb of Capodimonte revealed the original of Vincenzo Torelli's portrait by Domenico Morelli and a few memorabilia. Achille's son, the sculptor Tello Torelli, who at that time — in May 1973 — claimed and appeared to be a hundred years old, could offer no relevant information about his grandfather.)

TORNAGHI, EUGENIO. For over fifty years Tornaghi was the deputy, assistant manager, confidential clerk — and scapegoat — of the House of Ricordi. To date, however, his correspondence with Verdi and Verdi's wife, with Puccini and other prominent personalities is almost the only reliable trace of Tornaghi's inconspicuous existence. According to a death certificate obtained from the Ufficio Stato Civile of the City of Milan, he was the pensioner Eugenio Tornaghi who died in that city on 26 January 1915 at the age of seventy-one. This information was partly confirmed by the discovery of a newspaper clipping in the archives of the House of Ricordi.

USIGLIO, EMILIO (born 8 January 1841, Parma; died 8 July 1910, Milan). Usiglio began studying music as a young child and became a rather successful composer of light opera. As a most talented conductor he was in line to become Angelo Mariani's successor, but Faccio surpassed him.

From 1873 to 1875 Usiglio conducted the first performances of *Aida* in Ancona, Perugia, Florence, Rome, Ferrara, and, in 1881, in Modena. Verdi apparently disliked Usiglio because he lacked discipline and was intemperate. Excessive drinking and gradually increasing deafness accounted for the descent and early end of Usiglio's career.

VAUCORBEIL, AUGUSTE EMANUEL (born 15 December 1821, Rouen, France; died 2 November 1884, Paris). Vaucorbeil was one of the last composition students of Cherubini at the conservatory in Paris. His opera *Bataille d'Amour* to a libretto by Sardou was successfully produced by the Opéra-Comique in 1863. He also wrote sacred music, pieces for piano, and string quartets.

For a considerable time Vaucorbeil was president of the French Society of Composers. In 1872 he became supervisor of all state-subsidized theatres. On 16 July 1879 he followed Halanzier as director of the Opéra and remained in that position, in which he was unsuccessful, until his death.

VERDI, GIUSEPPINA STREPPONI (born 6 September 1815, Lodi; died 14 November 1897, St. Agata). Having studied voice and piano with her father, a composer, Giuseppina Strepponi won a scholarship at the Conservatory in Milan and studied there from 1830 to 1834. Soon thereafter she became one of the leading sopranos of her time. Donizetti wrote the title role of *Adelia* for her. In operas like *L'Elisir d' Amore*, *Lucia di Lammermoor*, and *La Sonnambula* she scored her greatest successes; but the strain of pushing her voice in heavier roles such as Norma shortened her brilliant career. Particularly admired were her crystal-clear timbre, her impeccable musicianship, and her lively personality as an actress.

Giuseppina Strepponi's recommendation of Verdi's first opera, *Oberto*, led to his debut at La Scala on 17 November 1839. While death destroyed Verdi's young family at that time, Giuseppina's life was threatened by a different kind of tragedy. She overexerted herself during pregnancies in order to support her family after her father's death and gave birth to two sons out of wedlock. (According to Walker, pp. 51–95, their father was not the mighty impresario Bartolomeo Merelli, as is commonly assumed, but the tenor Napoleone Moriani, a despicable character.) Giuseppina Strepponi's life seemed ruined. Her star was further eclipsed at the very moment when Verdi's rose through *Nabucco*, in which she appeared as Abigaille at La Scala on 9 March 1842. In subsequent performances of *I Lombardi* and *Ernani* she sang roles beyond her range and withdrew from the stage in 1846.

When in 1847 Giuseppina fled from her past to teach voice in Paris, Verdi wrote her a letter no one else was ever to see. She kept it in a sealed envleope and requested in her last will, "When I am dead, this letter shall be on my heart." In Busseto Verdi and his "Peppina" became the target of small-town gossip and even of Antonio Barezzi's criticism. On 21 January 1852 Verdi replied to his benefactor and former father-in-law in one of his finest letters: "In my house there lives a free and independent lady, who likes seclusion as I do, and who possesses a fortune which puts her out of the reach of care. Neither she nor I owe any account for our action to anyone. On the other

Giuseppina Verdi née Strepponi. Photograph courtesy of G. Ricordi & C., Milan.

hand, who knows what our relations are? Our business? Our connection? Or what claims I have on her and she on me? Who knows whether she is my wife or not? And who knows in this special case, what our thoughts and reasons are for not making it public?'' (*I Copialettere*, pp. 128–31)

The couple's union was finally sanctioned and ecclesiastically legalized on 29 August 1859 at Collonges-sous-Salève, a small Savoyan and then Italian village near Geneva. (A copy of the marriage certificate at the Biblioghèque de l'Opéra in Paris shows this date. The date of 29 April 1859 given by most biographers is wrong. See Walker, p. 223.) Giuseppina Strepponi and Giuseppe Verdi had rescued each other, and ''Peppina'' became his most loving and understanding companion. A great lady of infinite artistic intuition, wit, and sensitivity, she was his collaborator, housekeeper, and secretary. As an avid reader with great linguistic and diplomatic skills, she was especially helpful with Verdi's French correspondence and his dealings in France. She shared all his friendships and weathered the storm of her husband's infatuation with Teresa Stolz, the last of her many ordeals. By every indication, no man and no artist could have been blessed with a more noble, intelligent, and devoted woman than Verdi's "Peppina."

WALDMANN, MARIA (born 1844, Vienna; died 6 November 1920, Ferrara). Dedicating herself to the Italian mezzo-soprano repertoire, Maria Waldmann was heard with Teresa Stolz in September 1869 in a production of *Don Carlos* in Trieste. Thereafter she sang in Moscow and at La Scala in Milan, where, during the 1871–72 season, she appeared in both *La Forza del Destino* and the European premiere of *Aida*.

After Verdi's initial reluctance to engage her for that premiere, she became his favorite Amneris, enjoying his and Giuseppina Verdi's most affectionate friendship. Usually with Teresa Stolz as Aida, and sometimes under Verdi's direction, Maria Waldmann also appeared as Amneris in Parma, Padua, Naples, Cairo, Vienna, Paris (1876), and in various other theatres. Verdi then chose her for the mezzo-soprano part in the *Requiem*, which she sang under his baton in 1874 at the Church of San Marco in Milan and in 1875 at the Opéra-Comique in Paris, at the Albert Hall in London, and at the Imperial Opera in Vienna.

Apart from her extraordinary vocal merits, Verdi was attracted to Maria Waldmann's personality and artistic temperament, qualities similar to those he had found in her compatriots of the Austro-Hungarian Empire, Teresa Stolz, Antonietta Fricci, and Gabrielle Krauss. Verdi regretted, yet most sympathetically understood, Maria Waldmann's decision to end her brilliant career at the age of thirty-four, when she became the Countess, and later the Duchess, Galeazzo Massari of Ferrara.

A BRIEF CHRONOLOGY
OF VERDI'S LIFE
AND WORKS

A BRIEF CHRONOLOGY OF VERDI'S LIFE AND WORKS

10 October 1813	Birth at Le Roncole near Busseto in the Duchy of Parma.
1826–1829	Music studies with Ferdinando Provesi in Busseto.
1832–1835	Music studies with Vincenzo Lavigna in Milan.
4 May 1836	Marriage to Margherita Barezzi in Busseto.
12 August 1838	Death of their daughter, Virginia, born 26 March 1837.
22 October 1839	Death of their son, Icilio, born 11 July 1838.
17 November 1839	Premiere of *Oberto Conte di San Bonifacio* at La Scala in Milan.
18 June 1840	Death of Margherita.
5 September 1840	Premiere of *Un Giorno di Regno* (or *Il Finto Stanislao*) at La Scala in Milan.
9 March 1842	Premiere of *Nabucco* at La Scala in Milan.
11 February 1843	Premiere of *I Lombardi alla Prima Crociata* at La Scala in Milan.
4 April 1843	Verdi conducts the first performance of *Nabucco* at the Kärntnertor Theatre in Vienna.
9 March 1844	Premiere of *Ernani* at the Teatro Fenice in Venice.
3 November 1844	Premiere of *I Due Foscari* at the Teatro Argentina in Rome.
15 February 1845	Premiere of *Giovanna d' Arco* at La Scala in Milan.
12 August 1845	Premiere of *Alzira* at the Teatro San Carlo in Naples.
17 March 1846	Premiere of *Attila* at the Teatro Fenice in Venice.
14 March 1847	Premiere of *Macbeth* at the Teatro della Pergola in Florence.
22 July 1847	Premiere of *I Masnadieri* at Her Majesty's Theatre in London.

659

26 November 1847	Premiere of *Jérusalem*, revised version of *I Lombardi alla Prima Crociata*, at the Opéra in Paris.
25 October 1848	Premiere of *Il Corsaro* at the Teatro Grande in Trieste.
27 January 1849	Premiere of *La Battaglia di Legnano* at the Teatro Argentina in Rome.
8 December 1849	Premiere of *Luisa Miller* at the Teatro San Carlo in Naples.
16 November 1850	Premiere of *Stiffelio* at the Teatro Grande in Trieste.
11 March 1851	Premiere of *Rigoletto* at the Teatro Fenice in Venice.
30 June 1851	Death of Verdi's mother, Luigia.
19 January 1853	Premiere of *Il Trovatore* at the Teatro Apollo in Rome.
6 March 1853	Premiere of *La Traviata* at the Teatro Fenice in Venice.
13 June 1855	Premiere of *Les Vêpres Siciliennes* at the Opéra in Paris.
12 March 1857	Premiere of *Simon Boccanegra* at the Teatro Fenice in Venice.
16 August 1857	Premiere of *Aroldo*, revised version of *Stiffelio*, at the Teatro Nuovo in Rimini.
17 February 1859	Premiere of *Un Ballo in Maschera* at the Teatro Apollo in Rome.
29 August 1859	Marriage to Giuseppina Strepponi in Collonges-sous-Salève.
10 November 1862	Premiere of *La Forza del Destino* at the Imperial Opera in St. Petersburg.
21 April 1865	Premiere of the revised version of *Macbeth* at the Théâtre-Lyrique in Paris.
14 January 1867	Death of Verdi's father, Carlo.
11 March 1867	Premiere of *Don Carlos* at the Opéra in Paris.
21 July 1867	Death of Antonio Barezzi, Verdi's benefactor and his first wife's father.
30 June 1868	Meets Alessandro Manzoni in Milan.
13 November 1868	Death of Gioacchino Rossini.
27 February 1869	Premiere of the revised version of *La Forza del Destino* at La Scala in Milan.
24 December 1871	Premiere of *Aida* in Cairo.
8 February 1872	European premiere of *Aida* at La Scala in Milan.

1 April 1873	First performance of the *String Quartet in E minor* in Naples.
22 May 1873	Death of Alessandro Manzoni.
22 May 1874	Premiere of the *Requiem* under Verdi's direction at the Church of San Marco in Milan.
9–22 June 1874	Conducts seven performances of the *Requiem* at the Opéra-Comique in Paris.
8 December 1874	Nomination as Senator of the Kingdom of Italy.
19 April– 21 June 1875	Conducts performances of the *Requiem* on tour, beginning at the Opéra-Comique in Paris, then at Albert Hall in London, and ending at the Imperial Opera in Vienna, where he also conducts *Aida*.
22–27 April 1876	Conducts three performances of *Aida* at the Italian Theatre in Paris.
30 May– 3 June 1876	Conducts three performances of the *Requiem* at the Italian Theatre in Paris.
21 May 1877	Conducts the *Requiem* in Cologne.
29 June 1879	Conducts the *Requiem* at La Scala in Milan.
22 March– 2 April 1880	Conducts five performances of *Aida* at the Opéra in Paris.
18 April 1880	Premiere of *Pater Noster* and *Ave Maria*, set to texts by Dante, at La Scala in Milan.
24 March 1881	Premiere of the revised version of *Simon Boccanegra* at La Scala in Milan.
10 January 1884	Premiere of the revised version of *Don Carlos* at La Scala in Milan.
5 February 1887	Premiere of *Otello* at La Scala in Milan.
9 February 1893	Premiere of *Falstaff* at La Scala in Milan.
14 November 1897	Death of Giuseppina at St. Agata.
7 April 1898	Premiere of *Stabat Mater*, *Laudi alla Vergine Maria*, and *Te Deum* at the Opéra in Paris.
31 December 1899	Underwrites his endowment of the *Casa di Riposo* in Milan.
27 January 1901	Death in Milan.

A SELECTED BIBLIOGRAPHY

A SELECTED BIBLIOGRAPHY

Abbiati, Franco. *Giuseppe Verdi*. 4 vols. Milano: G. Ricordi, 1959.

Abdoun, Saleh, ed. *Genesi dell'Aida con documentazione inedita*. Parma: Istituto di Studi Verdiani, 1971.

Adami, Giuseppe. *Giulio Ricordi e i suoi musicisti*. Milano: Fratelli Treves, 1933.

Alberti, Annibale, ed. *Verdi intimo: carteggio di Giuseppe Verdi con il Conte Opprandino Arrivabene*. Milano: A. Mondadori, 1931.

Allodi, Ivo, ed. *Teatri di Parma: dal Farnese al Regio*. Milano: Nuove Edizioni Milano, 1969.

Ascoli, Arturo di. *Quartetto milanese ottocentesco*. Roma: Archivi Edizioni, 1974.

Ashbrook, William S., Jr. "Aida's winged words." *Opera News*, 1948, 12, no. 8, 26–27.

Auden, W. H. "A genius and a gentleman." Review of *Letters of Giuseppe Verdi*, ed. by Charles Osborne. *The New York Review of Books*, 1972, 18, no. 4, 17–18.

Barblan, Guglielmo. "Aida." From 1975/76 Teatro alla Scala program.

———. "L'opera." From 1971/72 Teatro alla Scala program.

———. "L'opera di Giuseppe Verdi e il dramma romantico." *Rivista Musicale Italiana*, 1941, 45, 93–107.

———. "Il sentimento dell'onore nella drammaturgia verdiana." *Atti del III⁰ Congresso Internazionale di Studi Verdiani*. Parma: Istituto di Studi Verdiani, 1974, 2–13.

———. *Toscanini e la Scala*, ed. by Eugenio Gara. Milano: Edizioni della Scala, 1972.

Barzun, Jacques. *New Letters of Berlioz 1830–1868*. New York: Columbia University Press, 1954.

Bate, Philip. *The Flute: A Study of Its History, Development and Construction*. New York: W. W. Norton, 1969.

Belforti, Adolfo. *Emanuele Muzio: l'unico allievo di Giuseppe Verdi*. Fabriano: Stabilimento Tipografico Gentile, 1895.

Bellaigue, Camille. *Verdi*. Paris: H. Laurens, 1912.

Bie, Oskar. *Die Oper*. Berlin: S. Fischer, 1923.

———. "Verdi und Wagner." *Die Neue Rundschau*, 1913, 24, 644–55.

Blom, Eric. "Verdi as musician." *Music and Letters*, 1931, 12, no. 4, 329–44.

Boctor, Michel. *Le centenaire de l'opera Aïda: 1871–1971*. Alexandria: Les Cahiers d'Alexandrie, 1972.

Bonavia, Ferruccio. *Verdi*. London: Oxford University Press, 1930.

Botley, Cicely M. "Immenso Phta." *Opera News*, 1954, 18, no. 15, 8–9.

Budden, Julian. *The Operas of Verdi from Oberto to Rigoletto*. New York: Praeger, 1973.

Bülow, Hans von. *Briefe und Schriften*, ed. by Marie von Bülow. 8 vols. Leipzig: Breitkopf und Härtel, 1896–1908. (*Musik in Geschichte und Gegenwart*, vol. II, Kassel und Basel: Bärenreiter, 1952, 451, col. 1.)

Busch, Fritz. *Der Dirigent*, ed. by Grete Busch and Thomas Mayer. Zürich: Atlantis, 1961.

———. *Pages from a Musician's Life*, trans. by Marjorie Strachey. 2nd ed. Westport, Conn.: Greenwood Press, 1971.

Busch, Grete. *Fritz Busch—Dirigent*. Frankfurt-am-Main: S. Fischer, 1970.

Busch, Hans, ed. and trans. "(signed) G. Verdi." *Opera News*, 1972, 36, no. 19, 8–11.

Büthe, Otfried, and Almut Lück-Bochat, eds. and trans. *Giuseppe Verdi Briefe zu seinem Schaffen*. Frankfurt-am-Main: G. Ricordi, 1963.

Cambiasi, Pompeo. *La Scala: note storiche e statistiche, 1778–1906*. Milano: G. Ricordi, 1906.

Carrara Verdi, Gabriella. "Preliminari di Aida." *Biblioteca 70 Busseto*, II, 1971, 9–21.

Cassi, Paolo. "Gerolamo Magnani e il suo carteggio con Verdi." *Vecchie Cronache di Fidenza*. Milano: Stabilimento Tipografico Gazzetta dello Sport, 1941, 129–35.

Cenzato, Giovanni. *Itinerari verdiani*. Milano: Ceschina, 1955.

Cesari, Gaetano, and Alessandro Luzio, eds. *I Copialettere di Giuseppe Verdi*. Milano: Comune di Milano, 1913.

Chop, Max. *Giuseppe Verdi*. 3rd ed. Leipzig: Reclam, 1938.

Chusid, Martin. *A Catalog of Verdi's Operas*. Hackensack, N.J.: Joseph Boonin, 1974.

Ciampelli, Giulio Mario. *Le opere verdiane al Teatro alla Scala (1839–1929)*. Milano: La Scala e il Museo Teatrale e Libreria Editrice Milanese, 1929.

Confalonieri, Giulio. *A Hundred Years of Concerts at "La Società del Quartetto" of Milan*. Milan: La Società del Quartetto, 1964.

Costantini, Teodoro, ed. *Sei lettere inedite di Giuseppe Verdi a Giovanni Bottesini*. Trieste: C. Schmidl, 1908.

Craft, Robert. "The giant of Busseto." *The New York Review of Books*, 1975, 22, no. 4, 3–4.

Dawson, Warren R., and Eric P. Uphill. *Who Was Who in Egyptology*. 2nd ed. London: The Egypt Exploration Society, 1972.

De Angelis, Alberto, ed. "G. Verdi e il Senatore G. Piroli: un epistolario inedito." *Musica d'Oggi*, 1940, 18, no. 3, 59–63.

De Filippis, Felice, ed. *Il Teatro di San Carlo*. Napoli: Città di Napoli, 1951.

――――. "Verdi e gli amici di Napoli." *Bollettino Quadrimestrale dell'Istituto di Studi Verdiani*, 1960, 1, no. 3, 1365–72.

Della Corte, Andrea. *Giuseppe Verdi*. Torino: Edizioni Arione, [1939].

――――. *Le sei più belle opere di Giuseppe Verdi*. Milano: Treccani, 1957.

De Rensis, Rafaello, ed. *Franco Faccio e Verdi: carteggi e documenti inediti*. Milano: Fratelli Treves, 1934.

Destranges, Etienne. *L'évolution musicale chez Verdi: Aïda, Otello, Falstaff*. Paris: Fischbacher, 1895.

Dort, Bernard. "Aïda ou le crépuscule des héros." *l'Avant-Scène Opéra*, 1976, no. 4, 87–88.

Dutronc, Jean-Louis. "Genèse d'Aïda." *l'Avant-Scène Opéra*, 1976, no. 4, 15–19.

Einstein, Alfred. *Greatness in Music*. New York: Oxford University Press, 1941.

――――. *Music in the Romantic Era*. New York: W. W. Norton, 1947.

Fellner, Rudolph. *Opera Themes and Plots*. New York: Simon and Schuster, 1958.

Ferrari, Paolo Emilio. *Spettacoli drammatico-musicali e coreografici in Parma dall'anno 1628 all'anno 1883*. Parma: L. Battei, 1884.

Fétis, François Joseph. *Histoire générale de la musique*. Paris: Librairie de Firmin Didot Frères, 1869.

Filippi, Filippo. *Musica e musicisti*. Milano: Libreria Editrice G. Brigola, 1876.

Fleming, Shirley. "A noisy bantling in old New York." *High Fidelity*, 1963, 13, no. 10, 82–89.

Foerster Loveday, Lilian. "A plan of action." *Opera News*, 1962, 27, no. 6, 9–13.

Friedlaender, Maryla. "*Aida* and the cult of Isis." *Opera News*, 1946, 11, no. 10, 10–12.

――――. "*Aida's* Milan premiere." *Opera News*, 1953, 17, no. 12, 27–28.

――――. "How *Aida* was written." *Opera News*, 1942, 6, no. 18, 20–25.

Gál, Hans. *Drei Meister—Drei Welten: Brahms—Wagner—Verdi*. Frankfurt-am-Main: S. Fischer, 1975.

――――. ed. *The Musician's World: Great Composers in Their Letters*. New York: Arco Publishing, 1966.

Garibaldi, Luigi Agostino. *Giuseppe Verdi nelle lettere di Emanuele Muzio ad Antonio Barezzi*. Milano: Fratelli Treves, 1931.

Gatti, Carlo. *Verdi*. 2 vols. Milano: Alpes, 1931.

――――. *Verdi nelle immagini*. Milano: Garzanti, 1941.

Genest, Émile. *L'Opéra-Comique: connu et inconnu*. Paris: Fischbacher, 1925.

Gerigk, Herbert. *Giuseppe Verdi*. Potsdam: Athenaion, 1932.

Ghislanzoni, Antonio. *Gli artisti da teatro*. 2nd ed. Milano: Ultra, 1944.

Glinski, Matteo. "Forse gli antenati di Aida." *La Scala: Rivista dell'Opera*, 1954, no. 54, 17–21.

Godefroy, Vincent. "Daughter of the Pharaohs." *The Music Review*, 1948, 9, no. 1, 18–28.

———. *The Dramatic Genius of Verdi*. London: V. Gollancz, 1975.

Goldovsky, Boris. *Accents on Opera*. New York: Straus & Young, 1953.

———. "Radames and Aida." *Opera Annual* No. 8. London: John Calder, 1962, 80–92.

Goléa, Antoine. *Gespräche mit Wieland Wagner*. Salzburg: Salzburger Nachrichten Verlags GmbH, 1968.

Gossett, Philip. Review of *Letters of Giuseppe Verdi*, ed. by Charles Osborne. *The Musical Quarterly*, 1973, 59, no. 4, 633–39.

———. "Verdi, Ghislanzoni, and *Aida*: the uses of convention." *Critical Inquiry*, 1974, 1, 291–334.

Graziani, Carlo, ed. *Giuseppe Verdi: autobiografia dalle lettere*. Milano: A. Mondadori, 1941. (2nd ed. Milano: Rizzoli, 1951, published under the pseudonym Aldo Oberdorfer.)

Grébaut, M. "Le transfert du musée de Boulaq à Guizeh" and "Discours." Cairo: *Institut d'Egypte Bullettin*, 1890, 44 and 81–83.

Grout, Donald Jay. *A Short History of Opera*. New York: Columbia University Press, 1954.

Günther, Ursula. "Der Briefwechsel Verdi-Nuitter-Du Locle zur Revision des Don Carlos," Teil I. *Analecta Musicologica: Studien zur Italienisch-Deutschen Musikgeschichte IX*, 14, ed. by Friedrich Lippmann. Köln: Arno Volk Verlag Hans Gerig KG, 1974, 414–44.

———. "Der Briefwechsel Verdi-Nuitter-Du Locle zur Revision des *Don Carlos*," Teil II, ed. by Gabriella Carrara Verdi and Ursula Günther. *Analecta Musicologica: Studien zur Italienisch-Deutschen Musikgeschichte X*, 15, ed. by Friedrich Lippmann. Köln: Arno Volk Verlag Hans Gerig KG, 1975, 334–401.

———. "Documents inconnus concernant les relations de Verdi avec l'Opéra de Paris." *Atti del III° Congresso Internazionale di Studi Verdiani*. Parma: Istituto di Studi Verdiani, 1974, 564–83.

———. "Zur Entstehung von Verdis *Aida*." *Studi Musicali*, Anno II, no. 1. Firenze: Leo S. Olschki, 1973, 15–71.

Hanslick, Eduard. "*Aida* von Verdi im Hofoperntheater." *Die Neue Freie Presse*, Wien, 20 June 1874.

———. *Aus neuer und neuester Zeit. (Der modernen Oper IX. Teil)*, 9. Berlin: Allgemeiner Verein für Deutsche Litteratur, 1900.

———. *Die moderne Oper: Kritiken und Studien*, 1. Berlin: A. Hofmann, 1875.

———. *Suite: Aufsätze über Musik und Musiker*. Wien und Teschen: K. Prochaska, 1884.

Hawks, Francis L. *The Monuments of Egypt*. New York: George S. Putnam, 1850.

Heliodorus of Emesa. *The Adventures of Theagenes and Chariclea*. 2 vols. London: Thomas Payne and Son, 1789.

Henriot, Patrice. "Aïda ou la subjectivité ensevelie." *l' Avant-Scène Opéra*, 1976, no. 4, 4–8.

Herrmann, William Albert. "Religion in the operas of Giuseppe Verdi." Thesis, Columbia University, 1963.

Holl, Karl. *Verdi*. Berlin: Karl Siegismund, 1939.

Honolka, Kurt. "*Aida* — Musikdrama und grosse Oper." From 1969/70 Hamburgische Staatsoper program.

Horgan, Paul. *Encounters with Stravinsky*. New York: Farrar, Straus and Giroux, 1972.

Hughes, Spike. "An afternoon at St. Agata." *Opera News*, 1967, 32, no. 9, 8–13.

———. *Famous Verdi Operas*. Philadelphia: Chilton, 1968.

———. "The look of the thing." *Opera News*, 1968, 33, no. 7, 8–12.

———. *The Toscanini Legacy*. London: Putnam, 1959.

———, and Barbara McFadyean. *Nights at the Opera*. London: Pilot Press, 1948.

Humbert, Jean. "Aïda entre l'egyptologie et l'egyptomanie." *l' Avant-Scène Opéra*, 1976, no. 4, 9–14.

Humphreys, Dena. "Verdi's peak of progress." *Opera News*, 1948, 12, no. 8, 11–15.
Hussey, Dyneley. *Verdi*. London: J. M. Dent, 1940.
Istel, Edgar. "A genetic study of the Aida libretto," trans. by Otto Kinkeldey. *The Musical Quarterly*, 1917, 3, no. 1, 34–52.
Jahnke, Sabine. "La Scala und Verdis *Aida*." From 1972 München Festspiele program.
Kauffmann, Stanley. "Superman and Man." Review of *Collected Letters of Bernard Shaw: 1898–1910*, ed. by Dan H. Laurence. New York: Dodd, Mead, 1972. *World*, October 10, 1972, p. 51.
Kerman, Joseph. *Opera as Drama*. 2nd ed. New York: Vintage Books, 1959.
Klein, Hermann. *The Reign of Patti*. New York: Century, 1920.
Klein, John W. "Verdi's attitude to his contemporaries." *The Music Review*, 1949, 10, no. 4, 264–276.
Kozma, Tibor. "Heroes of wood and brass: the trombone in *Aida*." *Opera News*, 1952, 16, no. 18, 30–31.
Krehbiel, Henry E. *A Book of Operas*. New York: Macmillan, 1909.
———. *Chapters of Opera*. New York: Henry Holt, 1908.
Kühner, Hans. *Giuseppe Verdi in Selbstzeugnissen und Bilddokumenten*. Reinbeck bei Hamburg: Rowohlt, 1961.
———. "Verdi e la Germania." *Atti del I° Congresso Internazionale di Studi Verdiani*. Parma: Istituto di Studi Verdiani, 1969, 364–66.
Lauer, Jean-Philippe. "Mariette à Sakkarah: du Sérapéum à la direction des antiquités." *Mélanges Mariette*. Paris: Institut Français d'Archéologie Orientale, 1961, 3–55.
Lawrence, Robert. "*Aida* — bolt in the blue." *Opera News*, 1948, 12, no. 18, 6–9, 32.
Lee, M. Owen. "Melt Egypt into Nile." *Opera News*, 1976, 40, no. 17, 30–31.
Lingg, Ann M. "All quiet on the Red Sea front." *Opera News*, 1957, 22, no. 4, 28–30.
Lippmann, Friedrich, ed. *Colloquium Verdi-Wagner Rom 1969*. *Analecta Musicologica*, 11. Köln-Wien: Böhlau, 1972.
Luzio, Alessandro, ed. *Carteggi Verdiani*. 2 vols. Roma: Reale Accademia d'Italia, 1935.
———. ed. *Carteggi Verdiani*. 2 vols. Roma: Accademia Nazionale dei Lincei, 1947.
———. *Garibaldi, Cavour, Verdi*. Torino: Fratelli Bocca, 1924.
Mann, Golo. "Der Brief in der Weltliteratur." *Deutsche Akademie für Sprache und Dichtung Darmstadt, Jahrbuch 1975*. Heidelberg: Lambert Schneider, 1976, 77–99.
Marchesi, Gustavo. "Aida, nuova sfinge." *Biblioteca 70 Busseto*, II, 1971, 23–26.
———. *Giuseppe Verdi*. Torino: Unione Tipografico-Editrice Torinese, 1970.
Mariette, Edouard. *Mariette Pacha: lettres et souvenirs personnels*. Paris: H. Jouve, 1904.
Martin, George. *Verdi: His Music, Life and Times*. New York: Dodd, Mead, 1963.
Matz, Mary Jane. "Aida without tears." *Opera News*, 1957, 22, no. 4, 4–8.
———. "An ancestor for Aida." *Opera News*, 1955, 20, no. 8, 4–7, 26–28.
———. "First ladies of the Verdi premieres, VI." *Opera News*, 1954, 18, no. 15, 10–11, 30–31.
———. "Great opera houses: Cairo." *Opera News*, 1962, 27, no. 6, 26–29.
———. "Peppina redeemed." *Opera News*, 1954, 19, no. 8, 4–6, 26.
Merkling, Frank. "Verdi's musical Egypt." *Opera News*, 1950, 14, no. 19, 12–15, 26–28.
Mila, Massimo. *Giuseppe Verdi*. Bari: Laterza, 1958.
———. *Il melodramma di Verdi*. 2nd ed. Bari: Laterza, 1961.
Minervini, Roberto. *Napoletani e Napoli*. Napoli: Edizioni Morano, [1958].
Monaldi, Gino. *Cantanti celebri del secolo XIX*. Roma: Nuova Antologia, [1907].
———. *Idealismo e realismo, ossia il teatro melodrammatico italiano moderno e le sue diverse scuole*. Perugia: Boncompagni, 1877.
———. *Il melodramma in Italia nella critica del secolo XIX*. Campobasso: Molisana, 1927.
———. *La musica melodrammatica in Italia e i suoi progressi dal principio del secolo a oggi*. Perugia: Bartelli, 1875.
———. *Le opere di Giuseppe Verdi al Teatro alla Scala*. Milano: G. Ricordi, 1914.
———. *Le prime rappresentazioni celebri*. Milano: Fratelli Treves, 1910.
———. *Verdi, 1839–1898*. 2nd ed. Torino: Fratelli Bocca, 1926.

Moravia, Alberto. "The anachronism of Verdi," trans. by William Weaver. *High Fidelity*, 1963, 13, no. 10, 79–81.

Morazzoni, Giuseppe. *Verdi: lettere inedite*. Milano: La Scala e il Museo Teatrale e Libreria Editrice Milanese, 1929.

Morenz, Siegfried. *Die Begegnung Europas mit Ägypten*. Zürich: Artemis, 1969.

Munger, Edmund. "Aidas of the past." *Opera News*, 1948, 12, no. 18, 30–31.

Munisteri, Peter P. "Antonio Ghislanzoni, poet of *Aida*." *Opera News*, 1941, 5, no. 22, 25–26.

Newman, Ernest. *Great Operas*. 2 vols. New York: Vintage Books, 1958.

———. *More Opera Nights*. London: Putnam, 1954.

———. *Seventeen Famous Operas*. New York: Alfred A. Knopf, 1955.

Noël, Edouard, and Edmond Stoullig. *Les annales du théatre et de la musique-deuxième année, 1876*. Paris: G. Charpentier, 1877.

Noske, Frits. "Ritual scenes in Verdi's operas." *Music and Literature*, 1973, 54, no. 4, 415–39.

Nugent, Marian. "First American Aida." *Opera News*, 1946, 11, no. 10, 24–25, 32.

Oberdorfer, Aldo. See Graziani, Carlo.

Osborne, Charles. *The Complete Operas of Verdi*. New York: Alfred A. Knopf, 1970.

———, ed. and trans. *Letters of Giuseppe Verdi*. New York: Holt, Rinehart and Winston, 1971.

Osborne, Conrad L. "Narrow triumph." *Opera News*, 1959, 24, no. 4, 4–6.

Pfäfflin, Friedrich. "Der zweite Leser." *Deutsche Akademie für Sprache und Dichtung Darmstadt, Jahrbuch 1975*. Heidelberg: Lambert Schneider, 1976, 134–45.

Pfitzner, Hans. *Werk und Wiedergabe*. Augsburg: Dr. Benno Filser, 1929.

Pfohl, Ferdinand. *Arthur Nikisch: sein Leben, seine Kunst, sein Wirken*. Hamburg: Alster Verlag, 1925.

Pinagli, Palmiro. *Romanticismo di Verdi*. Firenze: Vallecchi, 1967.

Pinzauti, Leonardo. "Aida e Lohengrin." *Atti del III° Congresso Internazionale di Studi Verdiani*. Parma: Istituto di Studi Verdiani, 1974, 401–7.

———. "La solitudine di Aida." From 1972 Arena di Verona program.

Pleasants, Henry. *The Great Singers*. New York: Simon and Schuster, 1966.

Porter, Andrew. "A note on Princess Eboli." *Musical Times*, 1972, 113, no. 1554, 750–54.

———. "Only Verdi." *The New Yorker*, June 21, 1976, pp. 98–103.

Pougin, Arthur. *Verdi: An Anecdotic History of His Life and Works*, trans. by James E. Matthew. New York: Scribner & Welford, 1887.

———. *Verdi: histoire anecdotique de sa vie et ses oeuvres*. Paris: Calman Lévy, 1886.

Prawy, Marcel. *The Vienna Opera*. New York: Praeger, 1970.

Prod'homme, Jacques-Gabriel, ed. "Lettres inédites de G. Verdi à Camille Du Locle (1868–1874)." *La Revue Musicale*, 1929, 10, 98–111; 11, 26–36.

———. "Lettres inédites de G. Verdi à Léon Escudier." *Rivista Musicale Italiana*, 1928, 35, 1–28, 171–97, 519–52.

———. "Unpublished letters from Verdi to Du Locle (1866–1876)," trans. by Theodore Baker. *The Musical Quarterly*, 1921, 7, no. 4, 73–103.

Rachleff, Owen. "Israel and Egypt." *Opera News*, 1962, 27, no. 6, 24–25.

Reich, Willi. "Unbekannte Verdi-Dokumente." *Melos*, 1951, 18, 48–51.

Reyer, Ernest. *Notes de musique*. Paris: G. Charpentier, 1875.

Rinaldi, Mario. *Aida di Giuseppe Verdi*. Firenze: Monsalvato, 1943.

———. *Verdi critico: i suoi giudizi, la sua estetica*. Roma: Ergo, 1951.

Roncaglia, Gino. *L' ascensione creatrice di Giuseppe Verdi*. Firenze: G. C. Sansoni, 1940.

———. *Galleria verdiana: studi e figure*. Milano: Curci, 1959.

———, ed. *Verdi regista*. Modena: Società Tipografica-Editrice Modenense, 1956.

Rosenthal, Harold, ed. *Two Centuries of Opera at Covent Garden*. London: Putnam, 1958.

———, ed. *The Mapleson Memoirs: the Career of an Operatic Impresario, 1858–1888*. London: Putnam, 1966.

Sartori, Claudio. *Casa Ricordi, 1808–1958: profili storici*. [Milano:] G. Ricordi, [1958].

———. "La Strepponi e Verdi a Parigi nella morsa quarantottesca." *Nuova Rivista Musicale Italiana*, 1974, 8, no. 2, 239–53.

Schlitzer, Franco. *Inediti verdiani nell'archivio dell'Accademia Chigiana*. Siena: Ticci, 1953.

Schonberg, Harold C. "Always strictly business." Review of *Letters of Giuseppe Verdi*, ed. by Charles Osborne. *The New York Times Book Review*, 12 March 1972, 6–7, 12.

Schuh, Willi, ed. *Hugo von Hofmannsthal-Richard Strauss: Der Rosenkavalier-Fassungen-Filmszenarium-Briefe*. Frankfurt-am-Main: S. Fischer, 1971.

Seltsam, William H. *Metropolitan Opera Annals. A Chronicle of Artists and Performances: 1883–1947*. New York: H. W. Wilson, 1947.

Sguerzi, Angelo. "O terra addio." *Atti del III° Congresso Internazionale di Studi Verdiani*. Parma: Istituto di Studi Verdiani, 1974, 443–52.

Shaw, Bernard. *London Music in 1888–89 as Heard by Corno di Busseto (Later Known as Bernard Shaw)*. New York: Vienna House, 1973.

———. *Music in London 1890–94*. 3 vols. New York: Vienna House, 1973.

Sheean, Vincent. *Orpheus at Eighty*. New York: Random House, 1958.

Sietz, Reinhold, ed. *Aus Ferdinand Hillers Briefwechsel*. 7 vols. Köln: Arno Volk, 1958–70.

Silvestri, Giuseppe. "Aida dal Nilo all'Adige." From 1971 Arena di Verona program.

———. "Le segrete origini di Aida." From 1968 Arena di Verona program.

Simpson, William Kelly. "At the source." *Opera News*, 1976, 40, no. 17, 32–34.

Stedman, Jane W. "Aida's Ethiopia." *Opera News*, 1949, 13, no. 16, 11–13.

———. "Slaves of love and duty." *Opera News*, 1957, 21, no. 15, 10–13.

Stefani, Giuseppe. *Verdi e Trieste*. Trieste: Comune di Trieste, 1951.

Stevens, David E. "Verdi had a word for it." *Opera News*, 1957, 21, no. 15, 4–7, 33.

Stevenson, Florence. "Ancient places III: Journey to Memphis." *Opera News*, 1976, 40, no. 17, 13–15.

Strauss, Franz and Alice, and Willi Schuh, eds. *A Working Friendship: The Correspondence between Richard Strauss and Hugo von Hofmannsthal*, trans. by Hans Hammelmann and Ewald Osers. New York: Random House, 1961.

Tassoni, Giuseppina Allegri. "Una gloria della scenografia parmense." *Aurea Parma*, 1948, 32, no. 1, 3–13.

Toscanini, Arturo. "La sinfonia dell'Aida." Interview in *Il Teatro Illustrato*, 1913, 9, no. 13.

Toye, Francis. *Verdi: His Life and Works*. New York: Alfred A. Knopf, 1959.

Tubeuf, André. "Discographie." *l'Avant-Scène Opéra*, 1976, no. 4, 102–8.

Vargiu, Adriano. "Il libretto dell'Aida." *Rassegna Musicale Curci*, 1968, 21, no. 3, 148–50.

Verdi, Giuseppe. *Aida, partitura d'orchestra*. Nuova edizione riveduta e corretta. Milano: G. Ricordi, 1953.

Wagner, Wieland. "Aida." From 1961 Deutsche Oper Berlin program.

Walker, Frank. "Four unpublished letters from Verdi." *Music and Letters*, 1948, 29, no. 1, 44–47.

———. *The Man Verdi*. New York: Alfred A. Knopf, 1962.

———. "Verdi and Francesco Florimo: some unpublished letters." *Music and Letters*, 1945, 26, no. 4, 201–8.

———. "Vincenzo Gemito and his bust of Verdi." *Music and Letters*, 1949, 30, no. 1, 44–55.

Weaver, William. "A librettist's novel." *Opera News*, 1955, 20, no. 8, 8–9.

———. "Of poets and poetasters: Verdi and his librettists — from Solera to Boito." *High Fidelity*, 1963, 13, no. 10, 109–13, 171.

———. *Seven Verdi Librettos*. New York: W. W. Norton, 1975.

———. "The making of *Aida*." *Saturday Review*, 25 December 1971, 45–47.

Wechsberg, Joseph. *Verdi*. New York: G. P. Putnam's Sons, 1974.

Weinstock, Herbert. *Rossini*. New York: Alfred A. Knopf, 1968.

Weiss, Piero, ed. *Letters of Composers through Six Centuries*. Philadelphia: Chilton, 1967.

Weissmann, Adolf. *Verdi*. Stuttgart: Deutsche Verlags-Anstalt, 1922.

Weisstein, Ulrich, ed. *The Essence of Opera*. New York: Free Press, 1964.

Werfel, Franz, ed. *Giuseppe Verdi Briefe*, trans. by Paul Stefan. Berlin: Paul Zsolnay, 1926.

——— and Paul Stefan, eds. *Verdi: The Man in His Letters*, trans. by Edward Downes. New York: L. B. Fischer, 1942. 2nd ed., New York: Vienna House, 1970.

Williams, Stephen. *Verdi's Last Operas*. London: Hinrichsen, 1950.

Ybarra, Thomas Russell. *Verdi: Miracle Man of Opera*. New York: Harcourt Brace, 1955.

Zeller, Bernhard. "Die Briefliteratur der letzten 25 Jahre." *Deutsche Akademie für Sprache und Dichtung Darmstadt, Jahrbuch 1975*. Heidelberg: Lambert Schneider, 1976, 113–33.

Zervudachi, Despina Draneht. *Twilight Memories*. Lausanne: Georges Jaccard, 1939.

Zoppi, Umberto. *Angelo Mariani, Giuseppe Verdi e Teresa Stolz in un carteggio inedito*. Milano: Garzanti, 1947.

INDEX

INDEX TO THE LETTERS

Author's note: Inclusive listings do not indicate footnoted information. When text and notes are on the same page or on the facing page, no *n* is indicated; however, when important footnoted data appear on the verso of a page, the *n* is indicated.

Abbiati, Franco, 142*n*, 202*n*, 252*n*, 267*n*, 274*n*, 340*n*, 360*n*, 369*n*, 373*n*, 376*n*, 384*n*, 392–93, 397*n*, 401*n*
Abdoun, Saleh, 234*n*. *See Genesi dell'Aida*
Abul-Soud Effendi, Abdalla, 266*n*
Academy of Music, New York, 352*n*, 354*n*, 410*n*
Adami, Giuseppe, 276*n*
Aida, 333, 402, 412–14: Act I, 32–33, 38–39, 40, 45, 47–48, 55–56, 194, 199, 201, 205, 209–12, 215, 222, 225*n*, 230, 233*n*, 238, 242–43, 246, 250–51, 256, 259–60, 269, 311, 358–59, 375–77, 380; Act II, 12, 33*n*, 38–39, 45, 48–51, 55–56, 61–67, 72, 116, 119, 122, 127, 132, 194–97, 199, 201, 209–12, 222, 225–26, 231–33, 250–51, 258, 260, 262–64, 268–70, 275, 283*n*, 311, 350, 355–56, 358, 380, 382, 394, 405–06, 417, 422; Act III, 32–33, 56, 66–72, 74–79, 82–85, 89, 95, 113, 194–98, 200–03, 205, 210, 212–14, 219–20, 222, 225–28, 250, 254, 269, 274, 292, 295, 299, 350, 358, 371, 380, 382, 394, 409, 410*n*; Act IV, 56, 58, 75, 79–82, 85–95, 97–99, 101–04, 109, 113, 203, 205–06, 209–13, 219, 222–23, 225*n*, 226, 228, 238, 241–42, 246, 255, 263–65, 269, 274–75, 295, 311, 313, 350, 358, 363, 381–82, 390, 393–94, 423; Aida, role of, 45, 51, 53, 64, 69–71, 74–75, 78, 89, 98*n*, 101, 119, 123*n*, 128*n*, 130–31, 141, 149, 153, 156, 161, 164, 168, 170–71, 174, 176, 196–97, 202, 254, 274–75, 327–28, 349–50, 354*n*, 358–59, 371–74, 378, 380, 385, 395*n*, 409, 410*n*, 420–23; Amneris, role of, 45, 48, 80, 85–87, 92–94, 98–99, 101, 123, 128*n*, 131*n*, 152, 156, 158–59, 161–80, 182–83, 185–91, 193, 195, 201, 260, 265–66, 268–69, 326–28, 349*n*, 350, 354*n*, 371–72, 377–81, 385, 418, 420–23; Amonasro, role of, 46, 65, 69–70, 75, 77, 119, 153*n*, 225, 242, 250, 289, 291–93, 327*n*, 354–55, 380, 395*n*, 418, 420–23; beards and moustaches, 34, 208–09, 217, 296*n*; Cairo, first productions in, 11–12, 14–16, 18–20, 22–26, 30, 33–36, 38–44, 46–47, 51, 54, 56–59, 61, 67–68, 90, 100, 111, 151, 154–57, 175, 177–78, 185, 188–90, 207–08, 210, 217, 225, 261, 290, 333–35, 360–61, 367*n*, 372–75, 390–91; Cairo and Milan, first productions in, 37, 45, 49–50, 88, 96–98, 105–06, 108–10, 112–20, 122–26, 133–37, 140–50, 152–53, 158–59, 162, 164, 166, 168–74, 176, 179, 181–82, 184, 186–87, 191–95, 197, 199–202, 204–05, 209, 211–13, 216, 220–24, 228–29, 233–34, 236, 239, 243–48, 255–56, 259–60, 262–64, 266–73, 277, 282, 291, 299, 356–57, 378, 386; contracts with Verdi, 18–19, 22–24, 26–27, 34, 38, 44, 54, 57–59, 98, 100, 105–06, 110–18, 125–26, 135, 137, 162, 174–75, 181, 185–86, 190, 192, 194, 197, 199, 202, 205, 207, 221, 223, 235, 323, 375, 381, 383, 391, 400–01, 405–06, 415, 425; copy, *see* orchestral score; flutes, special, 235–38, 242, 244–46, 250, 255, 259, 265–66; genesis, 3, 6*n*, 10*n*, 11–12, 14–32, 49*n*, 116, 423–25, 428–29; Great

Priestess, role of, 217n, 243n, 268n, 358–59; instrumentation, see orchestral score; Italian libretto, 17, 19, 23, 25, 27, 33, 36, 38, 40–41, 43, 50n, 52n, 70n, 74–75, 82, 90, 101, 109–10, 116n, 158, 168, 171, 173, 175, 179, 181–82, 184–87, 189–90, 192–94, 199, 201, 208–09, 213, 215–17, 219, 221, 234, 249–50, 266, 274–75, 287, 423–24; jewelry, 225, 265, 267, 273, 276–79, 389; King, role of, 119, 127, 163, 165, 208, 351n, 395n; libretto, see Italian libretto and outline; Milan, first productions in, 31, 91, 99, 121, 127–32, 139, 160–61, 163, 165, 167, 180, 183, 203, 206, 214–15, 218–19, 232, 235, 237–38, 240–42, 249–54, 257–58, 265, 274–76, 278–81, 283–87, 289, 292–97, 300, 302, 306–09, 313–16, 318, 320–21, 332, 337, 339–40, 344, 347, 349, 351–55, 358–59, 368–69, 376, 379, 382, 385, 397, 402, 407–10, 413, 417–18, 425; music, see orchestral score and piano-vocal score; Naples, first productions in, 278–81, 284–85, 289–91, 297–300, 302, 308–12, 315–26, 328–33, 335–41, 344–45, 347, 351–52, 358–60, 363–68, 379n, 397, 417; orchestral score, 16, 19, 27–29, 34, 43–44, 88, 100–01, 108–14, 116n, 125, 127, 134, 154, 159, 162, 179, 185–86, 188, 190, 192–95, 199–200, 202–03, 205–07, 209–13, 215, 217, 219–28, 230–33, 241–42, 245n, 250–51, 254–56, 258–60, 262, 264, 270, 277, 295, 319, 359, 367, 386, 400; orchestral seating and distribution, 96, 106, 133, 151, 160–61, 163, 181, 183–84, 212–16, 218–19, 229, 237, 239–41, 262, 323, 356, 427; orchestration, see orchestral score; outline, 11–12, 14–17, 19, 25, 27–28, 31–33, 36, 40, 48–49, 51–52, 54, 69–71, 81n, 89, 116, 158, 209n, 423–24, 428; overture, 250–51, 270, 277, 376–77; Paris, Italian Theatre, first production in, 113n, 364, 386, 390–97, 401–05, 416n; Paris, Opéra, first productions in, 18, 113n, 297–98, 305–06, 317, 319, 415–23, 427; Parma, ırst productions in, 251–52, 254, 282, 286–300, 302–09, 313, 315–16, 318, 320–21, 332, 337–42, 347, 368, 425; Partitura d'orchestra, 206n, 226n, 228n, 233n, 238n, 242n; parts (vocal, choral, orchestral), 27–29, 43, 112, 162, 185, 193–95, 199, 202–03, 205, 207–08, 210–13, 216, 236, 252, 295, 400; piano-vocal

score, 162, 177, 199, 203, 205–06, 212, 245n, 252, 256, 287, 399–400; Prelude, 205, 209, 212, 250n, 270; Priest, role of, see Ramfis; programma, see outline; Radames, role of, 32n, 45, 69, 71, 78, 85, 87, 89, 101, 159, 209, 262, 327n, 354–55, 375–77, 380, 384n, 408n, 420–23; Ramfis, role of, 62, 64, 66; reductions, see piano-vocal score; scenario, 45, 70–71, 79, 81n, 424; synopsis, 69n, 74; Termuthis, role of, see Great Priestess; translations of, 18, 70n, 201, 266, 297–98, 305–06, 312, 317n, 325, 329, 333–34, 368n, 375n, 397–401, 416, 423–24, 426; trumpets, special, 91, 95–97, 99, 106–09, 162, 181, 193–95, 201–02, 220, 235, 237, 246, 250, 255, 259, 265–66, 286, 289, 295, 336, 386, 417, 422; Vienna, first productions in, 309, 316, 325–29, 333–34, 352, 368–69, 375, 377–78, 382–84
Aita, 12
Albergo delle Crocelle, 341n
Alboni, Marietta, 167n, 188
Aldighieri, Gottardo, 380
Alexandria, 18, 25, 28, 35, 68, 90, 208, 222
Allievi, Marietta, 243, 268n
Alseno, 29n
Anastasi, Salvatore, 128n, 143, 146, 168
Ancona, 155n, 328, 333–35, 341
Apel, Willi, 96n, 139n
Aramburo, Antonio, 290
Aroldo, 393n
Augsburg, 318
Augusti, Paolo, 40
Austria, 46, 334
Author's rights, 88, 194, 325, 329, 375, 397–400, 415, 424–26
Ave Maria, 349n
de Ayala, E. Adelardo López, 10, 17

Bagier, 24–25, 144n, 154n
Ballet, 30, 41, 48, 52, 55–56, 61, 200–01, 214, 336, 344, 417–18
Ballo in Maschera, Un, 55, 56n, 120n, 297, 300, 310, 322, 382, 412
Baratti, Gioia, 146
Barbacini, Enrico, 358
Barbiere di Siviglia, Il, 4, 24, 340, 407, 409
Barblan, Guglielmo, 32n, 250n
Baron, 259
Baron, Delphine, 68, 217, 225, 247n
Baron, Hermann, 168n
Barrot, J., 42n, 187n
Bate, Philip, 246n

Battaglia di Legnano, La, 120*n*
Beck, Johannes Nepomuk, 326–27
Beethoven, Ludwig van, 24, 211
Belle Helène, La, 256
Bellincioni, Gemma, 159*n*
Bellini, Vincenzo, 339, 384
Benza, Ida, 166
Berini, Enrichetta, 381
Berlin, 38, 60, 308–09, 316, 328, 352, 368, 375, 384*n*, 386, 388
Bersagliere, Il, 423, 424*n*
Bertani, Prospero, 304–05, 308
Bey. *See* Draneht, Paul. *See also* Mariette, Auguste
Bibliothèque de l'Opéra, 221*n*, 246*n*
Biondi, 190–91
Bismarck, Otto von, 73, 90*n*
Bloch, Rose, 420–23
Boccolini, Cesare, 40, 207–08
Boito, Arrigo, 113*n*, 254–56, 290*n*, 382, 415*n*, 427*n*
Bologna, 29*n*, 91, 120*n*, 124*n*, 229, 252–53, 256, 262–63, 301*n*, 308, 338, 369*n*, 371, 389
Borgo, St. Donnino, 22, 29, 56, 157, 286, 392
Boston, 355*n*
Bottesini, Giovanni, 144, 147, 149, 152–54, 156, 182, 228, 261, 267–69, 356, 362, 426*n*
Boulaq, 208
Brera (Biblioteca Nazionale Braidense), 97
Brescia, 43, 167, 180, 212, 358
Brindisi, 9, 68, 171, 177, 222, 224*n*
Brunello, Anna, 130*n*
Brunello, Giuseppe, 130, 143–44, 148, 150, 160, 166–67, 169
Brussels, 90, 137
Budapest, 169
Bülow, Hans von, 127, 301*n*
Bulterini, Carlo, 298, 300
Busseto, 9, 14, 22, 29*n*, 37, 39, 91, 100, 117, 236, 319*n*, 320, 392, 408, 410*n*, 423–24

Cadenabbia, 27*n*
Cadiz, 179
Cairo and Cairo Opera (Theatre), 3, 5–10, 12, 14–19, 22–24, 34–37, 39–40, 42, 44–45, 47*n*, 49*n*, 51*n*, 53, 57, 68, 88, 90, 96–98, 100, 105–06, 108, 110–17, 119–20, 122–23, 125–26, 134, 137, 140–41, 142*n*, 144–50, 151*n*, 153–56, 159, 162, 166, 168–71, 173–78, 181–82,
185–87, 190, 192–95, 197, 199–200, 202, 205, 207–10, 213, 216, 220–21, 223–24, 226, 229, 234*n*, 236, 246–48, 258–60, 267–68, 272–73, 277, 282, 290, 299, 333, 335, 361, 367*n*, 373*n*, 375*n*, 378, 386, 388, 390–91, 403, 424. *See Aida*: Cairo, first productions in; *Aida*: Cairo and Milan, first productions in
Cambiasi, Pompeo, 96*n*, 254*n*
Cambon, 41
Campanini, Italo, 354–55
Capozzi, Bettina, 40
Capponi, Giuseppe, 120–21, 141, 143–44, 148, 161, 163, 180, 235–36, 238, 241, 249–51, 254, 258, 262, 265, 275–77, 282, 295, 298*n*, 300, 314*n*, 341*n*, 350, 362, 367, 376
Carrara, Maria Verdi, 251*n*
Carteggi Verdiani, 15*n*, 32*n*, 44–45, 79*n*, 139*n*, 250*n*, 286*n*, 343*n*, 360*n*, 371*n*, 376*n*, 393*n*
Cartier, Ernest, 404*n*
Cary, Annie Louise, 354–55
Casamorata, L. F., 151*n*
Cattavi, 52
Cavour, Count Camillo, 390
Cencetti, Giuseppe, 342–43
Cesari, Gaetano, 37*n*, 375*n*, 416*n*. *See Copialettere, I*
Cesarò, Salvatore, 323–24
Chailan Frères, 225, 247
Champollion le Jeune, Jean François, 44
Chaperon, 225*n*
Chicago, 355*n*
Chopin, Frédéric, 387
Choreographers, 41, 52, 56, 146, 200, 214, 321
Chorus, 48, 55, 61, 66–67, 70, 72, 92, 206, 211, 214, 220, 239, 263, 282, 315, 320, 329, 333, 352, 355
Chorus and orchestra, 10*n*, 160–61, 164, 166–67, 180, 183–84, 237, 241, 244, 246, 259, 262, 265–68, 272, 276–77, 279–81, 283, 285–90, 295, 297, 299, 306–08, 310–12, 316–18, 321–22, 324, 337–38, 340, 342–44, 350, 354, 356, 387–88, 390, 394, 402, 407, 420–23
Chusid, Martin, 224*n*, 245*n*, 259*n*
Ciaffei, 353, 358
Clausetti, Pietro, 229, 330–31, 362–66
Clifford, Dale, 90*n*
Colonnese, Luigi, 40–41, 358
Commission for the Reform of the Conservatories, 138–39, 141*n*, 142*n*, 151, 163, 290*n*

Commission of the Theatre, 172, 174, 213, 237, 239
Communal Council, Milan, 148, 162, 172, 174, 181, 218, 239, 241
Commune of Paris, 155n, 394
Conati, Marcello, 341n, 384n
Conductors, 5n, 8n, 13, 14n, 19, 25, 40, 88n, 100, 113n, 118, 124–25, 127–28, 136, 141, 144, 146–50, 152–56, 164–67, 183–84, 188, 206–07, 210, 216, 243, 250–52, 254, 267n, 281n, 282, 288, 290, 293, 298n, 308, 316, 320–21, 326–27n, 333–34, 338, 341n, 347n, 356, 370n, 377–78, 380–81, 383n, 384n, 395n, 396, 416, 421, 423, 428
Conservatories, 96n, 287, 290n, 390
Copialettere, I, 37n, 139n, 202n, 373n, 375n, 416n
Correnti, Cesare, 139n
Corriere della Sera, 416
Corsaro, Il, 120n, 393n
Corticelli, Mauro, 32, 45, 229, 268, 288, 406, 413
Costa, Sir Michael, 166, 177n, 293, 301n
Costa, Tommaso, 176–77, 217, 268n
Costumes, 32, 37, 43, 51, 56, 158, 173, 185, 208, 216, 221, 223, 239, 243, 245–50, 254–58, 260, 264–65, 273, 275, 280, 286, 336, 386–87, 389, 421, 428
Costumes and sets, 11, 16, 18, 22, 24, 26, 33–36, 38–39, 41, 44, 46, 52–53, 90, 97, 100, 106, 108, 110–12, 115–20, 122, 125, 164, 168, 186–87, 192, 195, 199, 209, 214, 224–25, 252–53, 259, 268n, 271, 285, 296, 302, 316–18, 320–22, 326, 340, 342, 394
Cotogni, 146
Covent Garden, Royal Opera, 14n, 141n, 188n, 395n, 404n
Cremona, 29n, 165n

Dall'Argine, Constantino, 254n
Dances. See Ballet
D'Arcais, Francesco, 284, 307n, 338, 349, 372, 382, 387
Darmstadt, 378–79
De Filippis, 243
De Giosa, Nicola, 141, 144, 155
De Giuli, Giuseppina, 128, 130, 132, 148, 152–53, 254
De Rensis, Rafaello, 356n
De Sanctis, Cesare, 7n, 44n, 142n, 281n, 286n, 335n, 338n, 343n, 359, 360n, 371n, 375n, 379n, 393n
Del Puente, Giuseppe, 355n

Del Signore, Carlino, 121n
Designers. See Costumes; Sets
Despléchin, 225n
Destinn-Löwe, Maria, 169–71, 173
Diapason, 96, 126, 183–84, 215, 279–80, 282, 286, 302, 318, 331
Don Carlos, 5, 12n, 48, 98n, 113n, 120n, 139n, 177, 178n, 220n, 251, 252n, 265, 268, 270, 272–73, 278, 282, 284–85, 288, 290, 297, 318, 320–22, 326, 329, 332, 351, 365, 374, 389n, 415n, 421
Don Giovanni, 167, 407, 409
Donizetti, Gaetano, 178
D'Ormeville, Carlo, 217n, 222, 234, 356
Downes, Edward, 13n, 304n
Draneht, Paul, 3n, 8–9, 26, 36n, 52n, 54, 58, 117n, 119n, 124n, 137, 140, 142n, 147n, 149n, 154–56, 159, 164n, 167–69, 173–75, 178n, 187, 193–94, 200, 207, 209n, 211–12, 216–17, 221, 223–25, 234n, 246–48, 269, 277, 314n, 343n, 426n
Droits d'auteur. See Author's rights
Duchesse de Gerolstein, La, 256
Due Foscari, I, 393n
Du Locle, Camille, 3n, 5n, 10n, 12–13, 15n, 16, 18–19, 25–28, 45, 49n, 54n, 59n, 60n, 70n, 81n, 98, 100, 109–13, 118n, 121n, 138–39, 144n, 158, 164n, 175n, 189, 191n, 193n, 209n, 216, 221n, 245, 246n, 254, 256–57, 273n, 286, 296–97, 317n, 321n, 337n, 347n, 359n, 391–92, 398n, 404, 424–26, 429n
Du Locle, Marie, 201, 276, 393n, 404n

Egypt, 3n, 5n, 6n, 10–11, 14–15, 17, 19, 22, 31, 35–36, 39, 42n, 44–45, 54, 57–58, 61, 67, 79, 88, 97, 108, 112, 114, 154–55n, 208–09, 217, 222, 224–25, 233, 247, 253, 261, 268n, 392n
Egyptian ballet, 191, 200, 214, 250–51, 252–54
Egyptian flute, 40, 409
Enciclopedia dello Spettacolo, 142n
England, 14n, 166n, 398, 410n
Ernani, 188, 393n
Escudier, Léon, 9n, 15, 29, 173, 272, 319n, 337n, 364n, 370n, 389, 394, 397–401, 404–05, 415, 425
Ethiopia, 40, 291
Evening Post, The, 410n
Expositions, 3n, 12n, 25, 334, 412

Fabbri, Mario, 142n
Faccio, Franco, 13, 14n, 43, 88n, 118, 127, 131, 149n, 165–67, 169, 180, 184, 191,

202–04, 210, 212, 220n, 242, 249–50,
  255n, 256, 265–66, 281n, 286–87, 289,
  290n, 295, 301–02, 308, 311–13, 320–21,
  325, 328, 332, 334–35, 347n, 356n, 358,
  368, 378, 382, 414n
Falstaff, 153n, 255n, 415n
Fancelli, Giuseppe, 141, 143–46, 148, 161,
  163, 275–77, 281
Fanfulla, 324
Faure, Jean-Baptiste, 387, 388n
Faust, 229, 387
Ferni, Virginia and Carolina, 290
Ferrara, 300, 312, 378n, 405n, 406
Ferrarini, Giulio Cesare, 251, 252n, 254, 282
Ferrario, Carlo, 161
Fétis, François Joseph, 31, 32n, 37, 40, 409
Fiancée du Nil, La, 3n, 10n
Fidenza, 22n, 29n, 286n
Figaro, Le, 24, 43, 45, 59, 60n, 394
Figlie di Cheope, Le. See Egyptian ballet
Filippi, Filippo, 6n, 13n, 79, 127n, 254, 256,
  261–64, 267, 268n, 273, 284, 339, 387,
  402
Fioravanti, 41
Fiorini, 146
Firenzuola, 29, 56
Florence, 40, 128, 141–43, 145–48, 151,
  163, 168, 215, 262, 271n, 301, 343–49,
  351–53, 360–63, 367, 370–71, 384n, 387,
  409
Florimo, Francesco, 138–39, 427n
Forza del Destino, La, 41n, 91n, 103n, 113n,
  128, 150, 164, 180, 237, 241, 250, 255,
  260, 262–63, 265, 268, 270, 272, 276,
  285, 300, 305, 310, 332, 341, 351,
  364–65, 370, 374, 382, 393n, 397, 402,
  406, 413
Fossa, Amalia, 407, 408n
France, 4, 7, 15, 18, 20n, 24, 33, 35, 36n,
  46–47, 49, 52, 54–56, 59, 63, 67–68,
  72–73, 84, 90n, 100, 111, 115n, 125,
  155n, 208, 235, 317n, 386–87, 395n,
  397–98, 400, 424–25
France Musicale, La, 8n
Franco-Prussian War, 6n, 20n, 36–38, 43,
  46–47, 49, 54–58, 60–61, 63, 67–68, 72,
  84, 90n, 97–98, 100, 106, 110–20,
  122–23, 125, 134–36, 138n, 154n, 235,
  271
Franz Josef I, Emperor, 334, 384n
Fraschini, Gaetano, 120–21, 137, 141–42,
  144, 146, 289
Fricci, Antonietta, 98, 112–14, 117, 120-21,
  123–26, 128n, 132–33, 140n, 143, 145,
  165, 179–80, 350, 361, 373–74, 378

Galletti Gianoli, Isabella, 40–42, 47, 51, 53,
  134–35, 137, 144, 146–47, 149, 156, 173,
  177–78, 189, 372
Gallini, Natale, 373n, 397n
Gallo, Antonio, 133
Gatti, Carlo, 250n, 391n, 401n, 416n
Gaulois, Le, 59, 60n
Gazzetta dei Teatri, La, 69, 74
Gazzetta di Torino, La, 374
Gazzetta Musicale di Milano, La, 43, 45, 49,
  60n, 74, 96n, 115, 116n, 142n, 151n,
  254n, 268n, 281n, 304n, 307n, 308, 311,
  368, 374n
Genesi dell'Aida, 142n, 224–25, 234n, 239n,
  246n, 250n, 341n, 373n, 384n
Genoa, 5, 14–15, 27n, 44–45, 54, 101, 103n,
  113–14, 121n, 123n, 125, 127, 133, 142n,
  146–48, 180, 183–84, 187, 197, 199, 201,
  235–36, 238, 249, 251, 252n, 257,
  268–69, 285, 297, 341, 375, 381, 414,
  418, 425
Genovese, Baron Giovanni, 285, 286n
Germany, 46, 55n, 96n, 119n, 172, 174,
  179, 301–03, 306, 308–10, 314, 316–17,
  320, 325, 328, 331, 375, 387–88, 397
Ghislanzoni, Antonio, 13n, 19–20, 22,
  27–31, 33n, 39n, 40, 43, 45, 50–51, 60,
  69n, 70n, 73–75, 79n, 82, 98, 103n, 106,
  109–10, 116n, 194–95, 197, 200, 207,
  216–17, 219, 221–22, 246, 263n, 274n,
  356n, 376n, 423–24
Giovannoni Zacchi, Ginevra, 40, 42, 47, 51,
  53, 141, 143–44, 169, 170n, 172
Gossett, Philip, 7n, 199n
Gounod, Charles, 11–12, 16, 387, 424
Grand Hotel, 383
Grand Hotel et de Milan, 222, 271n
Grande boutique, La. See Opéra
Granger, Leblanc. *See Aida*: jewelry
Grossi, Eleonora (Norina), 40–42, 149, 152,
  172, 175, 178–79, 185, 187–88, 191, 193,
  195, 210, 217, 246, 268n
Gueymard-Lauters, Pauline, 178n, 421n
Guidotti, 40
Guillaume Tell, 4
Günther, Ursula, 3n, 5n, 9n, 12n, 17n, 90n,
  392–93, 404n, 418n, 424–25, 428n
Gye, Ernest, 410n

Halanzier-Dufrenoy, Olivier, 317, 319n, 334,
  416n
Hanslick, Eduard, 384n, 389n
Harvard Dictionary of Music, 96n, 139n
Herbeck, Johann, 326–27, 334
Herodotus, 40, 45

Heugel, Jacques Leopold, 415, 416n
H.H. *See* Viceroy
Hiller, Ferdinand, 301n, 389n
Hôtel de Bâde, 343n, 392
Hyères, 392–93

Isis, 32, 38, 40
Ismail Pasha. *See* Viceroy
Istituto di Studi Verdiani, 246n, 259n
Italian Government Bonds, 57, 59, 391
Italian Stock Certificates, 391, 392n
Italian Theatre, Paris, 24n, 112, 144n, 317n,
    334, 370. *See Aida*: Paris, Italian Theatre,
    first production in
Italian Theatre, Vienna, 390–91
Italy, 4, 6–8, 10n, 22, 39, 41, 43, 46, 49,
    52, 55n, 59, 68, 73, 88, 100, 113n, 120,
    140, 150–54, 158, 173, 208, 246n, 271,
    280–81, 285, 301, 303, 309, 316, 325–26,
    338, 365, 378, 390–91, 397, 402, 410n,
    412, 414–15, 417, 419, 424
Ivanov, Nikolày, 300–01

Jacovacci, Vincenzo, 273, 283, 306–08, 315,
    322, 367n, 370
Jérusalem, 5n
Journal de Débats, Le, 267, 273

Khedive. *See* Viceroy
Klein, Hermann, 410n
Krauss, Gabrielle, 144, 351–52, 359–60,
    401, 420–23
Krehbiel, Henry E., 355n

Labatt, Leonard, 327, 328n
Lamaire, 40
Lampugnani, Giovanni Battista, 39, 51, 137,
    143n, 148–49, 154–56, 171, 177, 178n,
    269n, 396n, 426n
Lasina, G. B., 254n, 288–89, 293
Laurati, Emilia, 146
Lavastre, 225n
Lecco, 33n, 82, 194
Leipzig, 161, 173
Lepsius, Richard, 44
Lewy, Gustav, 326–27
Librettos, 7–10, 13, 14n, 17, 217, 255n,
    393n, 411–12, 415n. *See also Aida*
Lighting system, 407. *See* Sets
Lisbon, 121–22, 127, 133, 139, 140n,
    142–44, 388
Liszt, Franz, 318
Liverani, Domenico, 300–01
Loën, Baron de, 301, 318

Lohengrin, 252–53, 262n, 308n, 389n
Lohengrinianas (*Lohengrinate*), 262, 268
Lombardi alla Prima Crociata, I, 5n, 121n,
    142n. *See Jérusalem*
London, 14n, 141n, 168n, 301n, 369n, 375,
    383, 388, 395n, 403–04, 407–08
Lucca, Francesco, 148
Luccardi, Vincenzo, 88n, 168, 306, 343n
Luzio, Alessandro, 15n, 37n, 44n, 199n,
    286n, 375n, 376n, 393n, 416n. *See
    Carteggi Verdiani*; *Copialettere, I*

Macbeth, 5n, 142n, 310, 344–45, 349, 353,
    368–69, 393n
Madrid, 9, 13n
Maffei, Andrea, 393n
Maffei, Clarina, 9n, 69n, 256, 401n, 419n
Magic Flute, The, 40n
Magnani, Girolamo, 164–67, 169, 172, 174,
    250, 259, 296, 321n
Maini, Ormondo, 121, 148, 161, 163, 180,
    281n, 292, 315, 381n
Malibran, Maria, 388–89
Mallinger, Mathilde, 389n
Mantua, 375
Manzoni, Alessandro, 14n, 342–43
Mapleson, Colonel James H., 14n, 410n
Marcello, Benedetto, 414
Marchesi, Gustavo, 254n
Marchisio, Barbara and Carlotta, 143, 372
Marè, Giovanni, 41, 47, 51, 176
Mariaga, 74
Mariani, Angelo, 113n, 118, 121, 123–24,
    127–28, 131, 139–40, 143–54, 156, 166,
    188, 213, 251, 252n, 308n
Mariani, De Angelis Flora, 335n, 405n, 406
Mariani Masi, Maddalena, 335, 341, 350,
    353–54, 358, 361, 385, 388
Mariette, Alfred, 428
Mariette, Auguste, 3n, 6n, 10n, 12n, 15, 17,
    24, 28, 30, 36n, 38–39, 41, 45–46, 49n,
    52–59, 70n, 81n, 90, 97, 100, 108–09,
    111–15, 117–18, 125, 134–35, 137, 154n,
    164, 168–69, 174–75, 177, 179, 184, 187,
    192–93, 204, 209n, 217n, 221, 223–25,
    234n, 239, 245–48, 255, 257, 268n, 271,
    273, 314n, 343n, 423–25, 428
Mariette, Edouard, 26n
Marini, Ignazio, 151–52, 176
Marseillaise, La, 38, 55
Marseilles, 5n, 9, 25, 58, 90, 186, 190, 225,
    398
Martin, George, 74n, 113n
Masini, Angelo, 384n, 396

Mass. See Requiem
Massari, Count Galeazzo of Ferrara, 378, 401, 421
Massenet, Jules, 414*n*
Materna, Amalie, 327, 328*n*
Matthew, James E., 96*n*, 319*n*
Maurel, Victor, 153, 354*n*, 420–23
Mayor of Milan, 169, 172, 181, 212, 218–19, 222, 229, 235–37, 239, 241*n*, 242, 288, 413
Mayor of Naples, 285, 335
Mayor of Parma, 254*n*
Mayor of Rome, 315
Mazenco, 203
Mazzucato, Alberto, 151*n*, 163, 164*n*
Medini, Paolo, 41, 47, 51, 149, 153, 156, 210, 217, 268*n*, 384*n*, 396
Melzi, Alessandro, 96–97, 172–73, 214
Memphis, 40, 42, 50*n*
Mendelssohn-Bartholdy, Felix, 339, 387
Metropolitan Opera, 14*n*, 153*n*, 159*n*, 352*n*, 355*n*, 396*n*
Meyerbeer, Giacomo, 136, 311*n*, 384
Milan, 6*n*, 9, 12, 14, 20, 26, 28–29, 39*n*, 43, 47, 49, 54, 56, 58, 60*n*, 68, 96–97, 110*n*, 112, 114, 116–17, 119, 121–24, 127*n*, 129, 130*n*, 133, 145–46, 150, 152, 154–55, 157–58, 162–63, 165, 167–68, 171–74, 179, 182–84, 186, 194–95, 201–02, 205–08, 210–13, 216–24, 229, 232, 235, 237–38, 241, 243–44, 246*n*, 249–50, 257–60, 262, 265–67, 270–73, 275, 277, 279–85, 287, 289, 292*n*, 295–97, 299–302, 306–09, 313, 315, 318, 320–21, 323, 328, 330, 332, 334, 337–40, 344–49, 352–53, 358–59, 363, 365, 368, 373*n*, 375–76, 383, 386, 390, 393*n*, 396–97, 400, 402–03, 407–09, 413, 416*n*, 420, 422–23, 425, 427
Milwaukee, 355*n*
Mise-en-scène, 11, 17–20, 24, 33–36, 46, 52, 88, 100, 103, 112, 117–18, 125–26, 136, 161–62, 164, 184, 187, 189, 204, 207–08, 216–18, 220, 222, 233–34, 246, 248–49, 252, 257, 261–62, 266, 270–71, 273–74, 277–81, 283, 287, 292, 294, 296–98, 301–02, 306–07, 313, 317–18, 322, 326, 329, 333–39, 342, 347*n*, 350, 352, 354, 356, 359–60, 364–65, 384*n*, 387–88, 390, 394–96, 402, 407, 411, 413, 417–19, 421–23
Modena, 308
Molinari, Bernardino, 250*n*
Mollien, Countess, 391, 392*n*, 404*n*

Moltke, Count Helmuth von, 212–13
Monaldi, Gino, 276*n*, 408
Mongini, Pietro, 210, 217, 233, 234*n*, 243, 268*n*
Monplaisir, Hyppolite-George, 52, 54, 200, 203, 214, 254*n*
Mont Cenis, 137–38, 347
Monti, Gaetano, 351
Monti, Luigi, 300–01
Morghen, Rafaello, 21
Moro, Angelica, 180, 182
Mourès, 209*n*
Movimento, Il, 268
Mozart, Wolfgang Amadeus, 24, 40*n*
Müller, Georg, 326–27
Musella, Antonio, 279, 284–85, 291, 297, 318, 320, 322–24, 359, 364–66
Mussey, Barrows, 13*n*
Mussolini, Benito, 250*n*
Muzio, Emanuele, 5*n*, 8*n*, 10*n*, 23–25, 28–29, 47, 51, 53, 58, 90, 110*n*, 117, 124–26, 138*n*, 144*n*, 154–56, 208, 210, 281*n*, 343*n*, 352*n*, 359, 395, 399

Naples, 6–7, 9, 126, 136, 139*n*, 157–58, 166–67, 172, 177, 229*n*, 278–80, 284–86, 290, 292*n*, 299–300, 302, 308–10, 315–24, 328–32, 335, 337–41, 344–45, 347, 351–52, 356, 358–59, 360*n*, 362–66, 368, 379*n*, 390, 397, 401, 413, 417
Napoleon III, Emperor, 12*n*, 20, 24, 34, 43, 60*n*, 63, 73*n*
Naudin, Emilio, 34, 40–41, 47, 51
NBC Symphony Orchestra, 250*n*
Nero (*Nerone*), 7, 218
New York, 13*n*, 153*n*, 159*n*, 250*n*, 352*n*, 354*n*, 410*n*
New York Daily Tribune, The, 354–55, 410*n*
New York Herald, The, 359*n*
New York Times, The, 410*n*
Nice, 5*n*, 9
Nicolini, Ernesto, 14*n*, 141, 143–46, 148, 376, 380, 408*n*, 418
Nikisch, Arthur, 384*n*
Nilsson, Christine, 352
Nuitter, Charles, 305, 306*n*, 317*n*, 392*n*, 398–99, 404*n*, 424–25, 428

Oberdorfer, Aldo, 389*n*
Oggebbio, 224*n*
Opéra, 4–5, 7, 10*n*, 12–13, 19–20, 60, 139*n*, 253, 257, 265, 292–93, 296, 337–38, 370, 387, 391, 394, 401, 411, 413. *See Aida*: Paris, Opéra, first productions in

Opéra-Comique, 8, 10, 13, 22, 24, 28, 37, 151, 312, 369n, 383n, 392n
Opinione, L', 284n, 349, 377
Orchestra, 96–97, 106, 113n, 133, 215, 249–50, 260, 264, 269, 296, 313, 328, 336, 368, 376, 386, 396, 408n
Order of Osman, 282, 291
Osborne, Charles, 340n
Otello, 153n, 159n, 255n, 335n, 415n

Padua, 286, 302, 305, 308–21, 332, 334, 350
Palestrina, Giovanni Pierluigi da, 202, 211, 320, 340, 414
Pandolfini, Francesco, 120, 148, 161, 163, 180, 242, 244, 250, 256, 258, 276, 281, 283, 291–93, 314–15, 341, 350, 388, 395n, 396, 418
Pantaleoni, Adriano, 180, 251, 254, 289, 291–93, 295, 298n, 335n, 341n
Pantaleoni, Romilda, 335
Paris, 3–5, 6n, 8–14, 16, 18–20, 22, 24–28, 30, 34–36, 39, 41, 47, 54, 56, 58–61, 67–68, 73, 85, 90, 96–97, 100, 105–06, 108, 110–20, 122–23, 125, 134–37, 139, 144n, 154–55, 158, 174–75, 179, 181, 185–87, 189, 192–93, 195, 200, 202, 204, 207, 210, 216, 221n, 223, 225n, 234n, 236, 243, 246–47, 254, 265, 272–73, 306, 319n, 334, 343, 347–48, 364, 369n, 370n, 375, 383, 386, 389, 390–92, 395, 397n, 398, 401–05, 412–13, 415–16, 418–19, 425n, 428
Parma, 100, 161, 164, 200n, 246n, 251, 252n, 254, 259n, 282, 286–90, 292–95, 298–300, 302–03, 305–08, 313, 315–16, 318, 320–21, 332, 334, 337–41, 347, 356, 368, 372, 425
Patti, Adelina, 13, 130, 141n, 166n, 352n, 357, 381, 403, 407–10
Pedrotti, Carlo, 308, 373–74
Pelitti, Giuseppe, 95, 96n, 193, 195, 202
Peragallo, 329, 399
Pergolesi, Giovanni Battista, 320
Perrin, Emile, 5, 13, 139, 391n, 392n, 404n
Persia, 40
Perugia, 370
Petite boutique, La. See Opéra-Comique
Pfohl, Ferdinand, 384n
Philadelphia, 355n
Piacenza (Plaisance), 29n, 157n, 159, 200, 347
Piave, Francesco Maria, 392–93
Piroli, Giuseppe, 34n, 100n, 112n, 281, 427n
Ponchielli, Amilcare, 255n, 381n, 387

Ponchielli-Brambilla, Teresa, 381
Poniatowski, Joseph Michael Xavier, 11, 12n, 389n
Pope Pius IX, 73
Porter, Andrew, 178n
Pougin, Arthur, 96n, 319n, 342n, 373n, 416n
Povoleri, Paride, 281n
Pozzoni, Antonietta (-Anastasi), 128, 130, 141–43, 145–46, 148, 152–53, 156, 168, 170, 173–74, 204, 210, 217, 246, 251, 260, 268n, 358, 370n, 372, 377, 378n
Pratesi, Ferdinando, 146
Prawy, Marcel, 327n, 384n
Prisse d'Avennes, Achille Constant Théodore Emile, 44
Prod'homme, Jacques-Gabriel, 267n
Property rights, 400–01, 415, 425
Props, 37, 39, 185, 195, 253–55, 257–58, 264, 277, 295–96, 316–17, 320–21, 326, 328–31, 336–38, 340, 342, 359, 407
Prussia, 36n, 46, 63n, 115n
Puccini, Giacomo, 427
Pungolo, Il, 291, 292n, 362, 374

Quartet, E minor, 340, 401
Quattro Pezzi Sacri, 415n
Quintili-Leoni, Vincenzo, 310–12

Raff, Joseph Joachim, 301, 306
Ramses, 40
Reggio Emilia, 303–04, 308
Rental fees, 194, 218, 220, 307, 400
Requiem, 14n, 41n, 121n, 281n, 342–43, 345–46, 348–49, 351, 361–63, 367–69, 371, 375n, 377–78, 381–84, 395, 401, 403, 410, 414
Reszke, Edouard de, 395n
Reszke, Jean de, 395n
Reszke, Josephine de, 395n
Reyer, Ernest, 267, 273, 312
Ricci, Lellá, 145
Ricordi Archives, 139n, 142n, 194n, 202n, 397n
Ricordi, Enrico, 169–70, 172, 174, 248
Ricordi, Giuditta, 325n
Ricordi, Guilio, 3n, 10n, 17n, 26–27, 29, 32, 37n, 43n, 60, 74n, 79, 82n, 91, 96n, 112n, 116n, 118n, 123n, 124n, 127n, 133n, 140n, 142n, 147, 151n, 161n, 168, 171, 174, 179, 184, 191–95, 200, 202–03, 205–06, 208–10, 212n, 219–21, 223n, 232–33, 246n, 250–52, 254–56, 260, 262n, 264–65, 270n, 273n, 274n, 276–77, 284, 294, 298, 306–07, 318, 323, 329n,

332–34, 336n, 338, 347n, 350, 356–57,
369n, 371n, 376–77, 383n, 384n, 406,
408–09, 425, 428–29
Ricordi, House of, 28–29, 33–34, 43n, 60n,
88, 109n, 128, 148n, 166, 171, 192n,
194n, 197n, 199, 205, 211, 213, 217–20,
223, 224n, 229n, 235, 243, 245n, 251n,
272, 285, 297, 301n, 307, 316–17, 322,
324, 330, 334–35, 349, 351, 354, 360,
362–67, 375, 379–81, 384n, 386, 398,
406, 425
Ricordi, Tito, 28, 32, 37, 43, 60, 82n, 91,
163, 169, 173, 184, 194, 200, 212n,
248–49, 251n, 340n, 365–66, 379n, 397n,
398n, 425
Rigoletto, 5n, 28, 182, 297, 393n, 407, 412
Rinaldi, Mario, 376n
Risorgimento, 415n
Roger, 428
Rome, 34n, 73, 88n, 96n, 120, 128, 143,
148, 156n, 250n, 254, 264, 273n, 283,
292n, 306–08, 315–18, 320–21, 324, 338,
341–42, 357–58, 360, 367, 369–70, 372,
377–82, 390, 397, 408n, 423, 424n
Ronzi, Luigi, 346–49, 351, 353, 361–63, 367
Rossi, Giovanni, 251, 254, 282, 286,
288–89, 291, 296, 298n
Rossini, Giacomo, 4, 188n, 263n, 301n
Royalties, 375n, 384n
Rubé, 225n
Ruznamez, 266n

Sadova, 46
St. Agata, 8–10, 13, 22, 25n, 28–29, 31,
37n, 39n, 44–46, 56, 60n, 74, 91n, 96n,
101, 103, 109–10, 118n, 121–22, 139,
142n, 154, 157, 159, 164–65, 168–69,
179, 197n, 200–01, 204n, 206, 212n, 215,
224, 235, 245–46, 248, 251n, 252n, 286,
288, 291, 293, 313n, 319n, 340–41, 347,
354, 369, 384, 389, 401n, 404n, 414, 416,
419, 423, 425n
St. Louis, 349n
St. Onorato, Duke of, 401
St. Petersburg, 113n, 388, 403, 413
Saint-Saëns, Camille, 417
Salle Ventadour, 395n
San Marco, 368n
San Pellegrino, 26–28, 30, 184, 315
Sanz, Elena, 358–60, 378n, 385
Sardou, Victorien, 13, 14n
Sass, Marie-Constance, 139–40, 143, 153,
155–56, 159, 171–72, 175–79, 182,
187–88, 190, 243

Sax, Adolphe, 32–33, 417
Scarlatti, Alessandro, 320
Scenery. *See* Sets
Schubert, Franz, 24, 327n
Schumann, Robert, 339
Sellier, Henri, 420–22
Serrao, Paolo, 290, 338n
Sesostris, 40
Sets, 36n, 54, 58, 161, 165–66, 233–34, 236,
267, 295, 297, 299, 313, 337–38, 356,
359, 390, 393–95, 407
Seville, 292
Shakespeare, William, 294
Sietz, Reinhold, 389n
Simon Boccanegra, 310, 393n, 414–15
Simons, Lucy, 9n, 90, 138n
Singer, Teresina, 349, 353–54, 357–58, 361,
371n ·
Solfeggio (*Solfège*), 139, 340
Sonnambula, La, 188, 407, 409
Spain, 354–55, 385
Stage band, 161, 183–84, 215, 220, 268,
282, 289, 295, 359, 390, 396, 417–18
Stage direction and directors. *See*
Mise-en-scène
Stage lighting. *See* Sets
Stage machinery. *See* Sets
Staging. *See Mise-en-scène*
Stagno, Roberto, 159
Stecchi-Bottardi, Luigi, 268n
Stefan, Paul, 13n
Stefani, Giuseppe, 199n
Steller, Francesco, 153, 207, 210, 217, 225,
268n
Stiffelio, 120n, 393n
Stolz, Teresa, 119n, 121–24, 126, 128,
130–31, 133, 139–40, 142–43, 145–53,
156n, 161, 163–65, 179–80, 197n,
202–04, 206, 212–13, 215, 220n, 224,
238, 252, 254, 258, 260, 265, 276,
278–79, 281, 283–85, 290, 295, 298n,
314n, 316–19, 322, 324, 326, 328,
330–34, 337, 338n, 341n, 344–46,
348–50, 360–61, 367n, 377, 378n,
383–85, 396–97, 401, 403, 410, 415
Strakosch, Maurice, 352n, 355n
Suez, Isthmus of (Canal), 3, 5n, 6n, 424–25

Taide, 379n
Teatro alla Scala, 36n, 40, 130n, 151, 156n,
171n, 217, 288, 329–30, 335n, 345–46,
365, 388–89, 406. *See Aida*: Cairo and
Milan, first productions in; *Aida*: Milan,
first productions in

Teatro Apollo, 273n, 318, 342n, 367n, 370, 372, 378n
Teatro Comunale, 145, 350n
Teatro della Pergola, 142, 145–46, 347n, 351
Teatro di San Carlo, 151, 229, 413. See Aida: Naples, first productions in
Teatro Fenice, 145–46, 413
Teatro Illustrato, Il, 251n
Teatro Malibran. See Venice
Teatro Pagliano, 371n
Teatro Politeama, 425
Technical directors. See Sets
Terziani, Eugenio, 40, 118, 127, 360n
Théâtre-Lyrique, 5n, 10n
Thebes, 3, 40, 42, 50n
Tiberini, Mario, 112–14, 117, 120–21, 125, 173, 193
Torelli, Achille, 386–87
Torelli, Vincenzo, 279–81, 285, 323, 338n, 387n
Tornaghi, Eugenio, 33, 69n, 75n, 82n, 173, 191n, 193n, 197n, 204n, 212n, 229, 310–12, 348, 367n, 371n
Torriani, Ostava, 352, 354n, 359n
Toscanini, Arturo, 250–51, 377n
Toye, Francis, 139n, 142n, 284n
Traviata, La, 28, 49, 141, 142n, 365, 393n, 407, 410n
Tremmel, Wilhelmine, 327
Trieste, 46, 98n, 145, 166–67, 249, 301, 319, 333, 346–47, 350n, 353, 368, 385n
Trovatore, Il, 85, 92, 288, 322, 398
Trovatore, Il, (review), 69n, 92
Turin, 137, 200–03, 206–07, 248, 343, 347, 373–75

Ugolini, Giulio, 143
United States of America, 14n, 90, 138n, 352n, 354–55, 358
Upper Egypt, 3n, 6, 11, 18, 158, 224, 233
Usiglio, Emilio, 250n, 331, 333, 340–41, 370n, 377, 378n, 408n

Van Arnam, Ralph, 14n
Vaucorbeil, Auguste Emanuel, 416n
Venice, 46, 121–22, 124, 129, 133n, 139, 145–46, 150, 375, 403, 413
Vêpres Siciliennes, Les (Vespri Siciliani, I), 5n, 310
Vercolini-Taj, Rosina, 371n
Verdi, Dr. Gabriella Carrara, 96n, 195n, 404n
Verdi, Giuseppe: 3n, 5–13, 10–12, 14, 16–19, 21, 23n, 25n, 28–35, 37n, 39,
41–42, 44–45, 47, 49n, 51–54, 56, 59–60, 67, 69n, 74–75, 82n, 85, 88–91, 96n, 100n, 103n, 109–10, 112–14, 116–19, 122–23, 125n, 127–31, 133n, 138–42, 144n, 147n, 149–50, 153–56, 158–59, 161–62, 164n, 167–69, 171, 175–78, 182, 185–86, 188–95, 197n, 200, 204, 206, 209n, 212n, 215–24, 232–33, 242n, 246n, 250–52, 254–57, 259n, 260n, 262–63, 265n, 269–81, 286–87, 298, 300–01, 305, 307–10, 313–14, 316–17, 319n, 321n, 325–26, 329–30, 335n, 337n, 338n, 340n, 343n, 347n, 349, 351n, 356–57, 359n, 360n, 367–71, 374, 376–77, 379n, 380n, 383n, 384n, 391–98, 404–05, 408–10, 413, 415n, 416n, 419–27, 429n; on authors and composers, 4–5, 7, 10, 13, 17, 24, 40, 138, 252n, 256, 284, 333, 339, 382, 384–87, 397, 408–11, 413, 414n, 417, 426–27; on critics and the press, 4–5, 24, 45, 69, 86, 261–64, 267–68, 284, 291–93, 295, 297, 308, 312, 333, 339, 360, 367–69, 372–74, 382, 387, 396–97, 402, 404, 410–11, 413–16; on cuts and distortions, 302–03, 362–67, 375–77, 379–82, 393–94, 405–06, 409, 410n, 425; on managers and impresarios, 4–5, 111–12, 125, 155–56, 175, 187–88, 254, 259, 278–80, 283–89, 293–94, 297, 302, 306–07, 316–26, 328, 331–35, 337–38, 341–43, 346–47, 351–52, 360–67, 370, 372, 386, 393–94, 397, 402–04, 415–18; on music and other arts, 3–5, 7–8, 10, 17, 86, 126, 136, 150–51, 174, 210–11, 280, 287, 292–93, 296–99, 326, 337, 340, 342–43, 365, 369–71, 384–85, 387, 405–08, 411–12, 414, 426–28; on public and publicity, 4–5, 115–16, 254–56, 261–64, 268, 297, 299, 303–05, 315, 320, 339, 346–47, 373–74, 382, 387–88, 390, 403–04, 407–10, 413–14, 420; on reforms and revivals, 96n, 126, 138–39, 142n, 151, 183, 219, 237, 279–80, 288, 306, 320, 332, 339, 342, 390–91, 402, 405; on war and politics, 37–38, 40, 46, 54–55, 57, 61, 68, 72–73, 84–85, 100, 111–12, 119–20, 125, 135–37, 155, 372
Verdi, Giuseppina (Peppina), 3n, 5n, 9n, 13, 21, 24, 28–30, 32, 37, 44n, 54, 85, 103n, 122n, 136n, 141n, 142n, 170, 173, 201, 204n, 222, 235, 241, 251n, 271, 276, 280–81, 294, 301, 305, 313n, 325n, 336, 343n, 368n, 373n, 375n, 378n, 392–93, 401n, 403, 419–21, 429

Viardot Garcia, Pauline, 167n, 354n, 389n
Vicenza, 167
Viceroy of Egypt, 6, 10–11, 12, 14–20,
    24–27, 30, 33–36, 39n, 41–44, 46, 49n,
    52–54, 57–58, 61, 67, 100, 105, 108,
    110–18, 125, 133, 144, 181–82, 186–89,
    204, 209, 233, 255, 261, 266–70, 282,
    291, 357, 404n, 424–25, 428
Vienna, 96n, 113n, 309, 316, 327–29,
    333–34, 352, 368–69, 375, 377n, 378,
    382–84, 388, 395n, 413
Vitali, Giuseppina, 40, 42, 53
Vittorio Emanuele, II, King, 6n, 73
Viziak, Emma, 156, 163, 166, 171, 319,
    372, 378n
Vogri, Fanny, 319
Vulcan, 38, 328

Wagner, Richard, 7, 12, 16, 183, 218, 296,
    339, 382, 411, 424
Wagnerism, 293, 297, 339, 397
Wagnerites, 327n, 339, 389n
Waldmann, Maria, 158–59, 162–66, 169–72,
    174, 176, 179–80, 182–83, 229, 235, 238,
    249, 251, 254, 258, 260, 262–63, 265–66,
    268–70, 276, 278, 281, 283–85, 290, 298,
    314n, 316–19, 322, 327–28, 330–31,
    333–35, 337–38, 341n, 343–51, 353, 357,
    360–61, 363, 367n, 370–71, 378, 381,
    383, 384n, 396, 401, 403, 405n, 406, 415,
    418
Walker, Frank, 119n, 122–23, 165n, 224n,
    252n
Warsaw, 353, 358
Washburne, Elihu Benjamin, 90,
    138n
Wechsberg, Joseph, 341n
Weimar, 301, 306, 308–09, 316–18
Weinstock, Herbert, 301n
Werfel, Franz, 13n
Wilhelm I, King, 61, 63n, 72
Wilt, Marie, 325–27

Zacchi. See Giovannoni Zacchi, Ginevra
Zamperoni, Luigi, 389
Zocchi, Angelo, 243
Zoppi, Umberto, 121n
Zuccarelli, Giovanni, 35, 36n

ADDENDA AND ERRATA

Page

57   See p. 474*n*. The correct text of Verdi's letter to Camille Du Locle of 26 August 1870 and the pertaining notes should read as follows:

Verdi to Camille Du Locle[1]

St. Agata, 26 August 1870

Dearest Du Locle,

In these very sad times that surround us, I would never have dared to mention the Cairo contract. You have asked me for it, and so I am sending it to you with my signature[2] and with the addition of two articles, which you will find fair and which you will have approved by Sig. Mariette.

You have the kindness, I hope, to collect for me the 50,000 francs, for which I am sending the receipt. From this sum take 2,000 francs and give it as you see fit to aid your courageous and unfortunate wounded. With the other 48,000 buy me Italian Government Bonds. Keep the certificates and give them to me the first time we see each other again; and I hope that will be soon.

I wrote you yesterday.[3] For now I can only take your hand and say that I love you very much. *Addio, addio.*

1. In answer to Du Locle's letter of 21 August 1870.
2. Verdi mailed the contract with this letter.
3. The letter is missing.

71   Line 2: Verdi apparently refers to Du Locle's scenario rather than to Mariette's outline (*programma*). See p. 70*n*.

133   Note 1: Apart from representing Ricordi's interests in Venice, Antonio Gallo's admiration for Verdi's works caused him to become a successful impresario. See Gatti, vol. I, pp. 385, 390–91, 394.

Page

150 In Verdi's letter to Giulio Ricordi, para. 3, line 2, "awkward" should be substituted for "baroque."

178 The second sentence of note 2 on p. 178 should read: See Andrew Porter, "A note on Princess Eboli," *Musical Times*, 1972, 113, no. 1554, p. 751, and Verdi's letters to Lampugnani of 4 May 1871 and to Draneht of 8 June 1871.

197 The first sentence of the first note on p. 197 should read: See Document III and Verdi's letters to Ghislanzoni of 7 and 16 October 1870.

250–51 Claudio Abbado conducted the first·performances in Milan of the overture to *Aida* at La Scala on 2, 3, and 4 November 1977. See Teatro alla Scala program notes by Pietro Spada, who erroneously gives 13 March 1940 rather than 30 March 1940 as the date of Arturo Toscanini's world premiere of this overture with the NBC Symphony Orchestra in New York.

319 Verdi's letter to Giulio Ricordi was obviously written on 26 [or 28] April rather than in August 1872. See Giulio Ricordi's letter to Verdi of 1 May 1872, p. 301, para. 1.

403 In his letter to Maria Waldmann Verdi refers to the first production of *Aida* in Venice on 11 July 1876. It took place at the Teatro Malibran and was conducted by Franco Faccio with Mariani-Masi as Aida, Waldmann as Amneris, Masini as Radames, Pantaleoni as Amonasro, and Medini as Ramfis. The impresario was Antonio Gallo (see addendum to p. 133).

477 Para. 5: Note that Belzoni was Giovanni Battista Belzoni, an Italian archaeologist (1778–1823).
    Para. 6: Cautà is unknown.

558 I am indebted to Professor David Rosen of the University of Wisconsin-Madison for giving July 1873 as the date of publication for Giulio Ricordi's production book (*disposizione scenica*) of *Aida*. The copy of this document which Professor Rosen located in the Ricordi Archives has 8.1873 as its *timbro secco*. See p. 336, note 1, Verdi's letter to Giulio Ricordi of 16 February 1873.

Page

647   Para. 5: Muzio's concert for the opening of the Suez Canal at Ismailia, Egypt, should be mentioned *after* the inaugural performance, *Rigoletto*, of the opera house in Cairo on 1 November 1869. The Suez Canal was opened on 17 November 1869 (and, contrary to popular belief, *Aida* was not written for that occasion). See p. 5, note 1.

H.B.